ALLERGIES A to Z

ALLERGIES A to Z

Myron A. Lipkowitz, R.P., M.D.
Tova Navarra, B.A., R.N.

☑® Facts On File, Inc.

Allergies A to Z

Facts On File, Inc.
11 Penn Plaza
New York NY 10001

Library of Congress Cataloging-in-Publication Data
Navarra, Tova.
    Allergies A–Z / Tova Navarra, Myron Lipkowitz.
        p.   cm.
    Includes bibliographical references and index.
    ISBN 0-8160-3654-3
    1. Allergy—Encyclopedias. I. Lipkowitz, Myron. II. Title.
RC585.N38   1994
616.97'003—dc20   93–33379

Facts On File books are available at special discounts when purchased in bulk quantities for businesses, associations, institutions, or sales promotions. Please call our Special Sales Department in New York at 212/967-8800 or 800/322-8755.

Text design by Grace Ferrara
Cover design by Dorothy Wachtenheim
Printed in the United States of America

RRD IH 10 9 8 7 6 5 4 3 2 1

This book is printed on acid-free paper.

I'll miss
Dr. Merle S. Scherr's (1925–1993)
humor, wisdom, friendship, and love.
He will be missed most of all
by the many patients and camp kids with asthma
to whom he dedicated his life.
Merle S. Scherr was an exemplary, inspiring physician.

To the late Dr. Leonard M. Silber, my comrade
during those first days of medical school in Guadalajara
and whose courage will never be forgotten.

This book is also in memory of Kerry Nail.
—M. A. L.

I wish to dedicate this book
to my aunt and godmother
Dorothy L. Fox, R.N., M.S.N., Ed.S.,
for her outstanding career as a nursing instructor
and her loving encouragement
of all my professional endeavors throughout my life.
—T. N.

CONTENTS

LIST OF TABLES

ACKNOWLEDGMENTS

The authors would like to thank the following individuals for their invaluable inspiration and guidance: brother and associate Dr. Kenneth P. Lipkowitz; members, fellows, and staff of the American College of Allergy and Immunology, especially Dr. Joseph Bellanti, past president, and the American Academy of Allergy and Immunology; friends and fellow allergists Drs. Joseph Raffetto, whose extensive allergy library proved invaluable, the late Merle Scherr, Paul Lipschultz, Bruce De Cotiis, Donald Leibner, Richard Podel, Richard Bukosky, and otolaryngologist Sigmund Sattenspiel; botanist Jim Thompson and Marvin Sattler and Janet Spina of Hollister-Stier; Jeanne Schwoebel; Patricia Cooper and Julie Reynolds of Fisons; and Facts On File, Inc., for their unflagging encouragement and enthusiasm for this volume.

A very special thanks to Jill Lipkowitz and John Navarra, Jr., for their never-ending love, patience, and encouragement and to Christopher Campbell, our computer expert.

—M. A. L. and T. N.

PREFACE

An encyclopedia of allergies provides an overview of the field of allergy and many topics of general interest on an anomaly that emerges in infinite forms all over the world, from an innocent sneeze at the whiff of a minute troublemaker called pollen to a life-threatening swelling of air passages at the mere taste of a peanut. That millions of people have experienced adverse effects of hypersensitivity, which often can be prevented, diminished, or controlled, made an encyclopedia of allergies in plain language a valuable project.

Each entry provides an accessible explanation of a topic; many topics that would otherwise require intricate, scientific discussion have been condensed for the sake of clarity and consistency of style. Terms such as "allergic reaction" and "sensitizer" have been used as general reference to what happens when an allergy occurs; please note that allergic reaction manifests in many forms and in individual forms, making it difficult to elaborate further in the entries on the causes of allergies. Among the typical reactions are hives, rashes, sneezing, wheezing, shortness of breath, and itching. Corresponding to these and countless other manifestations, a sensitizer is any substance capable of causing a hypersensitive, or allergic, reaction; part of the mysterious workings of hypersensitivity in humans relates to the fact that so many substances can elicit an adverse reaction.

Many topics overlap, the result of the fascinating interrelationships of immunology, infectious diseases, and allergy. For example,

AIDS is presented in this book as an inadequacy of immune response, whereas hay fever and other allergic reactions represent the immune system's overreaction to a stimulus, which in some cases can be extreme.

We have included as entries most of the tried-and-true medications that have been in use since ancient times when physicians recognized, albeit embryonically, that certain individuals suffered wheezing, watery eyes, rashes, and other symptoms on contact with what we now call allergens or antigens. To these we have added many of the modern allergy and asthma drugs, as well as alternative treatments, even if they are controversial or unproven despite some people's insistence that they do work.

We have also included some historical background on the field of allergy and biographical information on its major contributors. On a daily basis, the more than 3,500 fellows and members of the American College of Allergy and Immunology and the American Academy of Allergy and Immunology are devoted to scientific research and care and treatment of countless patients with allergic disorders. It is our hope that this volume will serve as a stimulus for inquisitive allergic individuals to better understand the nature of allergy. Moreover, we encourage nonallergic individuals to develop compassion through understanding for those who know how much discomfort a beloved pet cat may cause.

Myron A. Lipkowitz, R.P., M.D.
Tova Navarra, B.A., R.N.

HISTORY OF ALLERGY AND IMMUNOLOGY

- 2640 B.C.: Egyptian pharaoh Menes died from anaphylaxis after a wasp sting.
- Fifth century B.C.: Greek physicians noted that people who had recovered from the plague were immune to recurrences.
- Fifth century B.C.: Hippocrates wrote that some foods were healthy for most people but caused illness in a few. He used cheese as an example.
- First century B.C.: Lucretius noted in a poem, "De rerum natura," that what was good nutrition for one was poisonous for another.
- Second century A.D.: Galen wrote of some reactions to plants.
- Second century A.D.: Aretaeus of Cappadocia described bronchial asthma.
- 11th century: The Chinese inhaled small-pox crusts as a preventive measure against smallpox.
- 1565: Leonardo Botallo described an asthmalike condition that he called the "Rose Cold."
- 1607: J. B. van Helmont wrote of "spasmodic attacks of difficult breathing" with symptom-free periods between attacks.
- 1713: Ramazzini recognized a hypersensitivity-pneumonitis-like lung disease in grain workers.
- 1798: Edward Jenner, after observing that English milkmaids who had contracted cowpox were immune to smallpox, developed the vaccination.
- 1800s: Louis Pasteur's research led to the germ theory of infectious diseases and the development of various vaccines, among his many accomplishments in medicine.
- 1819: John Bostock, an English physician, was one of the first to describe multiple cases suggestive of hay fever, which was called "Bostock's summer catarrh."
- 1831: John Elliotson noted a patient's observation that pollen might be responsible for his symptoms.
- 1855–56: Addison's disease was described, and adrenal glands were found to be essential for life.
- 1872–73: Englishman Charles Blackley and Morrill Wyman at Harvard University published proof of the connection between grass and weed pollens.
- 1880: Robert Koch discovered the tubercle bacillus responsible for tuberculosis as well as the phenomenon of delayed hypersensitivity.
- 1885: Roux and Yersin discovered that the diphtheria bacillus produced a potent bacterial toxin.
- 1890: Von Behring and Kitasato described antitoxins with the ability to neutralize toxins in a process called passive immunization.
- 1893: Pfeiffer and Bordet discovered complement, a bodily substance that aids in the destruction of bacteria.
- 1896: Durham and von Gruber discovered the process of specific agglutination reactions that became the basis for diagnostic tests, such as the Widal test for typhoid fever.
- Late 19th century: Henry Salter concluded a correlation between asthma and hay fever and animal exposure.
- Ca. 1900: Paul Ehrlich proposed the humoral theory of antibody formation, and Elie Metchnikoff proposed the cellular theory of immunity.
- 1900: Landsteiner discovered ABO blood groups.

- 1902: Richet and Portier described anaphylaxis.
- 1903: Arthus described the reaction to which his name has been given (the Arthus reaction).
- 1903: William P. Dunbar, an American physician working in Hamburg, proved that pollen-induced symptoms were caused by a nonirritant mechanism by suspending pollen grains in saline or alcohol. Dunbar, thinking that the pollen was a toxin, tried to produce an antitoxin, called "pollatin," in the form of a nasal spray with a horse-serum base. It seemed to reduce reactions in some patients.
- 1906: Dr. Clemens Pirquet, of Austria, coined the term "allergy."
- 1910: Sir Henry Dale discovered histamine while working on rye poisoning by ergot. He noted the shocklike drop in blood pressure it caused by its effect on smooth muscle.
- 1913: W. P. Dunbar reproduced symptoms of hay fever using pollen extracts.
- 1927: Sir Thomas Lewis demonstrated the production of histamine by cells injured by sun, heat, or cold as a cause of allergies.
- 1900s: Charles F. Cole established a test for histamine.
- 1920s: Kern, Cooke, and Storm van Leeuwen demonstrated that many asthmatics had positive skin tests to house dust.
- 1920s: Storm van Leeuwen removed asthma patients from their homes to demonstrate that changing environment could improve asthma.
- 1924: William Duke described "physical allergy" as skin reactions to heat and cold.
- 1924–39: Sanarelli-Schwartzman described necrotic reactions from endotoxin.
- 1930: Heidelberger reported the quantitative precipitin reaction.
- 1932: Wilhelm S. Feldberg and Carl Draystedt proved that histamine from injured cells was released during anaphylaxis.
- 1934: Marrack introduced the lattice theory.
- 1935–40: Isolation, structural identification, and synthesis of natural glucocorticoids were described.
- Ca. 1937: Bovet and Staub at the Pasteur Institute in Paris noticed that a compound called F 929 blocked some of the actions of histamine in guinea pigs. This discovery stimulated research to find a safe and effective agent for human use.
- 1939: Kabat and Tiselius demonstrated that antibodies are gamma globulins.
- 1940: Pauling described the primary structure of protein.
- 1942: The French produced the first antihistamine safe for human use, phenbenzamine (Antergan), closely followed by pyrilamine maleate (Neo-Antergen). In the United States, researchers developed diphenhydramine (Benadryl) and tripelennamine (Pyribenzamine).
- 1944: Medawar and Burnet described tolerance as "self" versus "nonself."
- 1945: Landsteiner and Chase demonstrated cellular transfer of delayed hypersensitivity.
- 1945: Owen described chimerism, involving diverse genetic constitution of an organ or tissue.
- 1947: Levine and Stetson discovered the Rh blood system.
- 1950: Corticosteroids were first used to treat asthma.
- 1952: Bruton was the first to recognize agammaglobulinemia.
- 1955: Jerne and Burnet described clonal selection.
- 1959 and 1960: Porter and Edelman formulated the structure and formation of gamma globulin.
- 1961: Miller and Good described the role of the thymus gland in the immune system.

- 1964: Voorhorst and Spieksma demonstrated that house dust mites and their fecal waste were allergenic constituents of house dust.
- 1967: Johansson and Ishizaka demonstrated IgE antibodies as the basis for allergic responses.
- 1968: J. T. Connell described the "priming" effect following allergen exposure.
- 1977: Yalow won the Nobel Prize for the development of radioimmunoassay.
- 1980: Dausset and Snell won the Nobel Prize in immunology for discovering histocompatibility antigens.
- 1980: Benacerraf was a Nobel Prize winner in immunology for the genetic control of immune responses.
- 1982: Bergstrom, Samuelsson, and Vane were Nobel Prize winners for discovering leukotrienes as mediators of immediate hypersensitivity reactions and inflammation.

A

ABGs   See ARTERIAL BLOOD GASES.

abietic acid   [sylvic acid]   A pine-rosin ingredient in soaps that improves the texture. It has some irritating properties to skin and mucous membranes and may be allergenic.

abortion, spontaneous   See REPRODUCTIVE IMMUNOLOGY.

acacia   [gum acacia, gum Arabic, catechu] A naturally occurring dried, gummy exudate from the stems and branches of *Acacia senegal* and other species of the woody leguminous plants. The acacia tree is widely distributed in warm climates—the southern United States, the Near East, India, and Africa. In ancient Egypt, acacia was used in paints over 4,000 years ago. Today, acacia gum has wide use in the pharmaceutical industry as a binder for tablets, a suspending agent, and a soothing demulcent for irritated mucous membranes. It is also used in the confectionery industry as a thickener in the manufacture of candy, jellies, and chewing gum to hinder sugar crystallization, and as a food and soft drink stabilizer. Occupational exposure to acacia powder can cause asthma. Acacia can also cause allergic rashes.

acaracides   Chemicals that kill dust mites (see HOUSE DUST MITES). There are two products available to eliminate these allergens from the home: benzyl benzoate (Acarosan) and tannic acid (Allergy Control Solution). Benzyl benzoate, a derivative of Peruvian balsam, listed as a safe food flavoring agent by the Food and Drug Administration (FDA), has been used for many years in medications, perfumes, and cosmetics. In the form of a moist powder, it is applied to the carpet, allowed to dry, and then vacuumed. The product kills dust mites and their larvae and binds house mite fecal waste to allow easy vacuuming. Fecal waste pellets are the most important source of allergen in dust mite allergy. Effectiveness following an application of benzyl benzoate is from six months to a year.

Tannic acid solution also reduces the dust mite allergen population in sprayed carpets. Benzyl benzoate and tannic acid have demonstrated significantly reduced levels of dust mites and symptoms of patients in various studies.

Accolate   Brand of zafirlukast, a leukotriene antagonist used to treat asthma. (See LEUKOTRIENES, ZAFIRLUKAST.)

acetaldehyde   [acetic aldehyde, ethanal] A colorless, volatile, water-soluble organic liquid with a characteristic pungent odor. It is found in coffee, cheese, and many fruits and vegetables, including apples, broccoli, and grapefruit. Used in the manufacture of perfumes, acetaldehyde is irritating to mucous membranes and lungs. Although nonallergenic, inhaled acetaldehyde has anesthetic properties and if ingested in large amounts can cause respiratory arrest. This organic solvent also has wide use in industry for silvering of mirrors and in the manufacture of synthetic rubber.

acetanilid   A coal tar derivative with antipyretic (fever-reducing) and analgesic (pain-killing) properties that has fallen into disuse because of its toxicity. Acetanilid is used as a solvent in nail polishes but may cause allergic skin rashes.

acetarsol   See ACETARSONE.

acetarsone   [acetarsol]   A soluble powder used in mouthwashes, toothpaste, and vaginal suppositories. It has been used for the treatment of amebiasis and trichomonas vaginitis. It may also have limited benefit in the treatment of sarcoidosis and syphilis. Acetarsone has the ability to cause allergic reactions.

acetic aldehyde   See ACETALDEHYDE.

acetic anhydride   [acetic oxide, acetyl oxide] A colorless liquid used in the manufacture of aspirin, dyes, food starch, perfumes, and plastics. Its irritant properties, which may be confused with allergic reactions, may cause burns to the skin and eyes. Acetic anhydride's dehydrated, or acetylated, form can be safely used in hand creams and lotions.

acetone [dimethyl ketone] A colorless liquid, with a characteristic ethereal odor, occurring in small amounts in normal urine but in larger quantities in the urine of diabetics. Acetone is also an industrial solvent obtained by chemical oxidation or fermentation and widely used in nail polish removers, nail finishes, fats, oils, plastics, resins, rubber, and waxes. Inhalation of the fumes may cause lung irritation and trigger asthma. Acetone also can cause skin rashes and peeling and splitting of nails.

acetophenone A coal tar derivative with a characteristic odor of bitter almonds, used in almond, cherry, floral, fruit, strawberry, tonka bean, tobacco, vanilla, and walnut flavorings in baked goods, beverages, candy, chewing gum, and gelatin desserts. Acetophenone, which also occurs naturally in strawberries and tea, may cause allergic reactions.

acetyl cysteine (Mucomist) A mucus-thinning drug. Because it is very irritating to the lungs of asthmatic patients, Mucomist is rarely prescribed. It stimulates cough and has a sulfurlike odor that often causes nausea and vomiting. However, acetyl cysteine is used as an antidote to acetaminophen (Tylenol) poisoning.

acquired immunodeficiency syndrome (AIDS) A life-threatening disease caused by the human immunodeficiency virus (HIV) and characterized by the breakdown of the body's immune defenses. Because a healthy immune system protects the body from potentially harmful foreign invaders, including many species of microbes and other types of material such as pollen, it is important to recognize the function of the immune system as it correlates to the immunoglobulin E and other reactions characteristic of allergy. AIDS is at the opposite end of the spectrum of hay fever and allergic asthma: A typical allergic response is an overreaction of the immune system, and AIDS is the inability of the immune system to protect the host organism (the human body). However, early in the course of AIDS, patients often develop severe hay fever and other allergic manifestations. These individuals are especially prone to drug allergies to the antibiotics needed for treating the difficult infections that they suffer, further complicating this dreadful disease.

AIDS was first recognized in 1981 in a group of homosexual males in California, who were diagnosed as having a rare form of pneumonia, Pneumocystis carinii, seen only in immunosuppressed individuals. Then a rare cancer, Kaposi's sarcoma, which affects the skin and other parts of the body, was reported in alarming numbers in this same population. In 1984, French and American scientists identified HIV as the virus responsible for AIDS.

Prevalence Persons at the highest risk appear to be homosexual or bisexual men and their partners, intravenous drug abusers, persons who received blood transfusions from unscreened donors (before adequate screening was available), and children of infected women. Heterosexuals are becoming increasingly infected.

Risk factors AIDS is not present in all persons who are infected with HIV. Among people who have a positive blood test for HIV but have no symptoms, an uncertain percentage may eventually develop AIDS. Less than 1 percent of those infected with HIV appear to be immune to developing AIDS, and the virus and antibodies to it disappear spontaneously. Once the diagnosis has been confirmed, it is considered a fatal illness.

Outcome Death usually results from an opportunistic infection such as that caused by *Pneumocystis carinii* (a protozoan one-celled organism) or tuberculosis. Opportunistic infections are caused by commonplace organisms that do not usually trouble people whose immune systems are healthy, but take advantage of the opportunity provided by an immunosuppressed, or debilitated, person.

Signs and symptoms Some individuals infected with HIV may remain well. In others, minor illness suggestive of infectious mononucleosis may occur between three weeks and three months following exposure to HIV. Symptoms including fever, sore throat, malaise, muscle and joint aches, swollen glands, fatigue, weight loss, diarrhea, rash, and thrombocytopenia (decreased blood platelet count) appear suddenly and last about two weeks. These symptoms persist in many individuals, and up to 25 percent of those with this persistent condition, known as AIDS-related complex or ARC, may progress to AIDS within one year.

Those with AIDS may have one or more of a variety of disorders, including anomalies of the nervous system; severe and unusual infections, such as Pneumocystis carinii pneumonia, fungal infections, tuberculosis, herpes simplex and zoster (shingles), and oral yeast infections (thrush); and cancerous tumors, such as Kaposi's sarcoma, non-Hodgkin's lymphoma, or primary lymphoma of the brain.

Diagnosis A positive HIV-antibody test result in a person with signs and symptoms of an opportunistic infection or tumor characteristic of the disease must be confirmed by the Western blot blood test.

A negative test result may occur in someone recently exposed to HIV. If that person is at high risk for developing AIDS, a repeat test should be performed in six months or sooner.

Methods of transmission and prevention AIDS is a contagious disease. Any person infected with HIV can transmit the infection, even if that person does not have AIDS or ARC. It is spread by sexual contact, by direct contact of HIV with the bloodstream from reuse of contaminated needles or accidental needle sticks, and from mother to her unborn child through the placenta. Adequate screening at blood banks has made the blood supply for transfusions in the United States virtually free of HIV. The trans-

mission of this disease requires intimate contact, such as sexual intercourse, in which an exchange of infected body fluids takes place. Researchers currently believe that HIV is not transmitted through casual or social contact.

Treatment There is no cure for HIV infection or AIDS, and mutant strains of HIV have already emerged. However, attempts to develop a vaccine are under way. Various antiviral agents, such as zidovudine (Retrovir), formerly called azidothymidine, or AZT, appear to inhibit the progression of the disease. There are serious side effects from these drugs, including anemia, granulocytopenia (an abnormal reduction of granulocytes in the blood), dizziness, and severe headache. It is often difficult to differentiate between adverse drug reactions and effects of the illness. Antibiotics and antifungals have been known to be effective against some of the opportunistic infections. Chemotherapy with interferon has shown promise in early studies, and radiation is used against Kaposi's sarcoma and other malignancies.

KNOWLEDGE AND AWARENESS OF AIDS IN A 1990 U.S. SURVEY

Question	Correct Response	
Have you heard of the AIDS virus HIV?	83.0%	Yes
Are you aware that certain drugs can lengthen the life of persons with HIV?	46.6%	Yes
Are you aware that infected individuals can look normal?	67.7%	Yes
Do you think that persons giving blood can get AIDS?	72.2%	No
Do you think that AIDS can be transmitted by insect bites?	83.9%	No

Courtesy of *Journal of the American Medical Association* 267 (1992): 27–28.

Myths and misconceptions The 1990 Behavioral Risk Factor Surveillance System, or BRFSS, a government-sponsored study, assessed public awareness of HIV/AIDS. In random telephone interviews, 81,556 adults in 44 states and the District of Columbia were surveyed. Results are listed in the table on page 3.

acrivastine (Prolert, Semprex-D)   A nonsedating antihistamine available only in the United States. In clinical trials subjects did not develop tolerance (loss of effectiveness of a drug with continued use) after several weeks of use. Onset of the drug effect starts within one to two hours of the first dose, but the drug must be taken three or four times a day. Acrivastine is expected to be released in the United States in 1993. (See also ANTIHISTAMINE.)

acrylates and acrylics   Chemicals used as plasticlike thickening agents in nail polishes, fake nails, waxy oils, protective coatings, and waterproofing. Inhaled forms can cause allergic or toxic effects.

acrylics   See ACRYLATES AND ACRYLICS.

Actidil   See TRIPROLIDINE.

Actifed   See TRIPROLIDINE.

actinomycetes   Organisms classified as bacteria whose cell structure lacks a nuclear membrane. Infections caused by them respond to antibiotics, and they have cell-wall polysaccharides resembling those of other bacteria. In the past, many scientists considered them to be fungi.

Thermophilic (heat-loving) organisms commonly found in the soil, actinomycetes thrive at 56°–60°C. In the soil, they produce enzymes that help to decompose organic matter and are partially responsible for the typical odor of soil. They are also found in compost, hay, grain, manure, mushroom piles, and sugarcane.

Actinomycetes are also found in silos and as a contaminant in humidifiers and ventilation systems. These microorganisms are probably the most common cause of the allergic pneumo-nialike lung disease called hypersensitivity pneumonitis. Farmers, sugarcane workers, and office and factory workers are most frequently affected.

Among the species of actinomycetes infectious to humans is *Mycobacterium tuberculosis* (the organism causing tuberculosis). Other species are *Micropolyspora faeni, Thermoactinomyces vulgaris, T. viridis, T. saccharii,* and *T. candidus.* Antibiotics, vitamins, and antitumor drugs have been produced from these organisms. (See also AIR-CONDITIONING, ALVEOLITIS, FARMER'S LUNG, HUMIDIFIERS, HYPERSENSITIVITY PNEUMONITIS.)

active immunity   See IMMUNITY, ACTIVE.

Acular   See KETOROLAC TROMETHAMINE.

acupressure   Similar to acupuncture, a technique involving use of the fingers to press on the appropriate body meridians to unblock stagnant energy at painful sites. (See also ACUPUNCTURE.)

acupuncture   An ancient Chinese technique for reducing pain and promoting restoration that calls for the insertion of extremely fine needles into the skin over points related to other parts and functions of the body. (A point near the wrist, for example, is associated with respiration.) Acupuncture is said to be effective in treating sinusitis, asthma, pains, addictions (including depression), and many other digestive, nervous, musculoskeletal, and respiratory conditions. Traditional Chinese medicine refers to the *qi* or *chi* (pronounced chee), the life force or a flow of healthy energy along specific channels or meridians. Disease is thought to be caused by a blockage in one or more of these meridians, and the goal of acupuncture is to relieve the blockages at any of the 14 major "acupuncture points" or meridians. Each meridian contains numerous points and serves as a site for the insertion of the needles.

Studies suggest that acupuncture stimulates the release of the body's natural, opiatelike substances called endorphins. Endorphins act as painkillers, at times as effective as morphine or anesthesia, and are thought also to contribute to the feeling of well-being.

additives   See FOOD ADDITIVES.

adenoids   Lymphatic tissue, the same as the pharyngeal tonsils, named from the Greek word for "glandular." This tissue forms lymph fluid that contains nutrients and lymphocytes (white blood cells that help form antibodies), which fight infections by attacking bacteria. Lymph is found throughout the body.

The adenoids located on the wall of the nasopharyngeal area, often become overactive and swollen, resulting in nasal stuffiness. They can be removed by surgical adenoidectomy, or, when removed with the tonsils, a tonsillectomy. A combined tonsillectomy and adenoidectomy, known as a "T and A" procedure, is no longer as routinely recommended as it was years ago, probably because it may be more advantageous to keep organs serving the immune system intact and also to avoid the risks of anesthesia. (See also TONSILS.)

adenyl cyclase   See CHEMICAL MEDIATORS.

Adrenalin   Trade name for the drug epinephrine. (See EPINEPHRINE.)

adrenergic drugs   Some of the most widely used drugs for the treatment of nasal congestion. Also known as sympathomimetic amines, these drugs control various functions of the autonomic, or involuntary, nervous system. A drug's action depends on its ability to interact with specialized elements on the surface of cells called receptors. Receptors are macromolecules (large molecules) made up of enzymes, lipoproteins, proteins, and nucleic acids.

This interaction between drug and cell receptor triggers a series of biochemical or physiologic events that produce the desired pharmaceutical effect or an undesired adverse effect. There are at least two different receptor systems, alpha and beta. Alpha- adrenergic receptors are associated primarily with excitatory functions, such as constriction of smooth muscle in blood vessels, bronchi, and the urinary bladder. They also cause relaxation of smooth muscle in the intestines. Stimulation of these receptors may raise blood pressure and increase heart rate.

Beta-adrenergic stimulation primarily affects the airways or air passages by allowing smooth-muscle relaxation. There are $beta_1$ and $beta_2$ receptors and drugs that have very broad actions affecting both $beta_1$ and $beta_2$ receptors. More selective drugs react primarily or only with the $beta_2$ receptors. These medicines have fewer side effects and are the most frequently prescribed for the treatment of asthma.

Beta receptors also have inhibitory effects that cause smooth muscle relaxation in the uterus, ciliary (eye) muscles, and blood vessels. However, they stimulate the myocardium, or heart muscle. (See also ALPHA-ADRENERGIC AGONISTS, BETA-ADRENERGIC AGONISTS.)

adverse reactions to foods   See FOOD ALLERGY.

aeroallergens   Substances that, when transported through the air, are capable of causing an allergic reaction when inhaled by an allergic individual. Airborne allergens include pollen grains, fungal spores, and the so-called inhalant allergens such as house dust (which is actually a mixture of many allergens), dead dust mite bodies and pellets of their fecal waste, human and animal danders, and flakes of dead skin. Animal proteins from saliva and urine become aeroallergens as they are absorbed into the environment. Cooking odors of highly allergenic foods and allergenic industrial chemicals behave in a similar manner.

Most airborne allergens range in size from 2 to 60 microns (1 micron = 1/25,000 inch), but some are even smaller. Finer aerosolized particles may pass into the distant terminal bronchioles, but ragweed-sized pollen grains do not usually reach that far.

Since most pollens do not reach the areas where bronchoconstriction is greatest, it is thought that reflex mechanisms occur when the allergen comes in contact with mucosal surfaces within its reach in the upper air passages. For some reason so far undiscovered, this triggers spasm of the bronchial tubes and an asthma attack. (See also ALLERGENS.)

Aerobid, Adrobid-M   Brand of FLUNISOLIDE metered dose corticosteriod inhaler useful for the prevention of asthma symptoms. (See CORTICOSTEROID METERED-DOSE INHALERS.)

aerosols   Tiny droplets of liquid or solid particles suspended in a gas or mist. Aerosol devices include pressurized canisters called metered-dose inhalers, hand-held NEBULIZERS, machine-powered jet or ultrasonic nebulizers, or dry powder inhalers. There are also several types of aerosol nasal sprays. Aerosols are also used in the cosmetic and other industries.

Use of aerosol medications is advantageous because minute effective doses are delivered directly to target areas in the lungs or nasal passages and sinuses with minimal absorption of the drug into the bloodstream. Therefore, side effects are minimal or absent.

Metered-dose inhalers, commonly referred to as MDIs, are miniature spray cans of finely powdered or liquid medication suspended in a gas called Freon. The exact dose delivered is controlled by the size of the valve. A large percentage of the mist released from an MDI is deposited on the mouthpiece and in the mouth and throat, never reaching target lung tissue. Approximately 15% of each spray is deposited on the mouthpiece alone. However, if the MDI is properly used, a sufficient dose reaches the lungs. There are many devices called "spacers" available to assist persons who lack the dexterity for correct use of MDIs (see SPACER).

Dry powder inhalers are marketed under the trade names Spinhalers or Rotohalers. Activating the device involves the rupture of a drug-filled capsule and release of medication into a collecting chamber from which it is inhaled through the mouth. These devices require less dexterity than MDIs, allowing small children or poorly coordinated individuals to use them

easily. Also they do not require hydrocarbons to deliver the medication.

Nasal inhalers deliver a coarser deposition of active drug particles than the asthma inhalers because the particles are released at a lower pressure.

AVAILABILITY OF AEROSOL ASTHMA MEDICATIONS

Type of Aerosol Drug	Nebulizer Solution	MDI	Dry Powder
Albuterol	yes	yes	yes
Corticosteroids	no	yes	no
Cromolyn sodium	yes	yes	yes[1]
Ipratropium	no	yes	no
Isoethrine	yes	yes	no
Metaproterenol	yes	yes	no
Nedocromil sodium	no	yes	no
Pirbuterol	no[3]	yes[2]	no
Terbutaline	yes	yes	no

[1]May be discontinued by the manufacturer.
[2]Approved for use in a device called an Autohaler in 1993.
[3]Available only as ampoules for injection but these may be used as a nebulizer solution.

(See also AEROSOLS, AUTOHALER, NEBULIZER, ROTOCAPS, SPINHALER.)

agar   A dried, gel-like substance extracted from *Gelidium cartilagineum*, *Gracilaria confervoides*, and other species of red algae found in the Pacific and Indian oceans and the Sea of Japan. It is also known as Japanese isinglass. Agar is used as a bulk laxative, emollient, and emulsifier in the pharmaceutical, cosmetic, and food industries. It is also a bacterial culture medium. Agar is mildly allergenic, that is, capable of causing symptoms of allergic reaction in some individuals.

aging   The process of becoming older, exhibiting characteristics of increasing age. Immune function generally declines with age. This decline in immunocompetence may lessen atopy, or allergy, but probably results in higher rates of cancer, infection, and autoimmune disease.

Some studies, but not all, have demonstrated reduced skin sensitivity and lower total immunoglobulin (IgE) antibody levels in allergic persons after age 50. (See IMMUNO-GLOBULIN E.)

agonists   Drugs that react with a cell's receptors, specialized elements of the cell surface with which a drug interacts and triggers a biologic response that increases or decreases cell function. (See ADRENERGIC DRUGS.)

agriculture workers and allergy exposure
See ANIMAL ALLERGY, OCCUPATIONAL ALLERGENS, OCCUPATIONAL ASTHMA, and entries on specific animal allergies.

AIDS   See ACQUIRED IMMUNODEFICIENCY SYNDROME.

airborne antigens   See AEROALLERGENS.

air compressor   See NEBULIZER.

air-conditioning   A system developed to control the temperature, moisture content, purity, and circulation of the air in a room or building. Electric air-conditioning units vary in size from small window units sufficient to cool a small bedroom to huge commercial units that can cool an entire office building.

Benefits to allergy patients   Because many allergens such as house dust mites and molds thrive in warm, moist air, air-conditioning is beneficial to the allergic patient by cooling and drying the air. During days with high pollen and mold spore counts, both of these allergen levels can be reduced by up to 90% compared with outdoor counts by turning on the air-conditioning and closing doors and windows.

Dangers   Serious allergic and infectious lung diseases may be spread by contaminated spray water commercial air-conditioning systems. Actinomycetes are one cause of hypersensitivity pneumonitis, an allergic disease. Legionnaire's disease is an infectious pneumonia also spread by contaminated water in cooling systems.

There are various filtering devices to keep the air clean and pure. It is important to clean these filters regularly to keep them free of contaminants. (See ACTINOMYCETES, HYPERSENSITIVITY PNEUMONITIS.)

air curtain   A method of directing air currents around a patient in order to divert air that might otherwise irritate or contaminate the patient with dust-borne allergens and other undesirable microorganisms.

air ducts, cleaning   The removal of dust, pollen, molds, and other potential environmental contaminants from heating and cooling systems by professional cleaning services for allergy patients with severe reactions.

air-filtration systems   Devices that clean or purify air. Some filters are freestanding, and others are placed on central air heating or cooling (air-conditioning) units.

Their purpose is to remove pollens, mold spores, dust, and irritants such as tobacco smoke or industrial pollutants from the home or work environment. One type, high-efficiency particulate air (HEPA) filters, removes almost all particles of any size. A less effective type, an electrostatic precipitator, places an electrical charge on dust particles as they pass through the filter. The metal plates on which the charged particles are deposited require frequent cleaning.

Any benefit to the allergic patient depends upon the nature of the allergens in the environment. Mold spores, animal dander, and tobacco smoke remain suspended in the air long enough to allow their removal by these devices. Dust mites, whose main source of allergen is fecal pellets, and pollen grains are heavier and fall to the floor, carpeting, or furniture surfaces within a few minutes in the still air of most homes. An air purifier may actually worsen exposure to dust mite allergens because of its air currents, which can lift mite allergens into the air where they can be inhaled.

In 1982, an estimated $150 million was spent in the United States for room air-cleaning devices. In 1987, at the direction of the Food and Drug Administration (FDA), a committee of experts concluded that data available at the time were insufficient to establish standards for room air-cleaning devices. The committee found that use of room air-cleaning devices alone was inadequate, and other forms of environmental control were necessary. Most air-filtering devices are expensive, their long-term effectiveness has not been proven, and they need frequent cleaning. Less expensive, disposable filters placed in a heating system may be as efficient and more convenient.

airflow obstruction   See AIRWAYS, ASTHMA.

air purifiers   See AIR-FILTRATION SYSTEMS.

air sampling   The collection and measurement of allergens or pollutants in an environment by industrial hygienists, who conduct environmental surveys, and allergists, who measure pollens and mold spores in the air. One method uses the earth's gravity to allow solid particles in the air to settle on a microscopic slide coated with soft glycerin jelly. In 24 hours of exposure of this slide to the air, mostly larger particles, such as ragweed pollens, can be collected. Wind, raindrops, and condensation affect the efficiency of this test. Another method involves a device called a Rotorod Sampler. Made with Lucite rods coated with silicone grease, this devise reduces the wind factor and creates more opportunities to study various aspects of the particles collected. (See also POLLEN COLLECTORS, POLLEN COUNT.)

air travel   Changes in an airplane's cabin pressure may cause nasal congestion and ear pain in persons suffering from allergies, sinusitis, or upper respiratory infections (colds). Severe ear pain can be avoided by using a decongestant nasal spray, such as Neo-Synephrine, in each nostril about 20 minutes before takeoff and landing. Such products are not recommended for continuous use because re-

bound congestion may occur. (See RHINITIS MEDICOMENTOSUM.)

airways   Passageways allowing air from the atmosphere to reach the lungs, beginning at the nostrils and mouth and gradually branching into bronchi and bronchioles. They end at the alveolar sacs in the lungs, where oxygen is absorbed into the bloodstream.

During an asthma attack, the airways narrow or become obstructed by either constriction or mucous plugs. At first, muscles in the walls of the bronchioles constrict or go into spasm, called bronchospasm. If this is not relieved immediately, spontaneously or with medication, blood vessels in the airway dilate and fluid leaks into the tissues. Resulting swelling (edema) further narrows the airway. This is followed by an inflammatory response and secretion of mucus, restricting airflow even more.

Wheezing may not be heard until there is at least a 50 percent narrowing of the airways. However, in extremely severe obstruction, there may be no audible wheezing. This can be misleading in a life-threatening situation. In an emergency room or a doctor's office, the degree of narrowing of the airways can be measured by a spirometer or a peak flow meter. Inexpensive peak flow meters are available so patients can measure their peak flow at home, school, or work. Peak flow meters also aid physicians in making treatment decisions. (See also ASTHMA, PEAK FLOW METER, SPIROMETRY.)

albumen, egg   The white, or protein, part of the egg, which is the allergenic in susceptible individuals. (See EGG ALLERGY.)

albuterol (Proventil, Ventolin)   A fast-acting bronchodilating drug used to open up constricted airways in the treatment of asthma. Albuterol is the most widely used of the beta-agonist drugs. Rarely its use is limited by minor tremors or palpitations.

Albuterol is available as a metered-dose aerosol inhaler (MDI), as a solution for use with an aerosol nebulizer, or as a tablet or syrup for oral use. For children or other persons who lack the coordination to use an MDI, the product Ventolin is available in a dried powder form dispensed in Rotocaps and inhaled by using a device known as a Rotohaler. (See BETA-ADREN-ERGIC AGONISTS, ROTOCAPS.)

alcohol   [ethanol]   A chemical used as a solvent, an antiseptic, an astringent, and a component in intoxicating beverages. A common ingredient in cough syrups, alcohol is thought to be a depressant to the cough center and may have some muscle-relaxing effect on the bronchial tubes. It also serves as a vehicle or medium containing other active ingredients. Two common adverse effects of alcohol are sedation and drying of the mucous membranes of the upper respiratory tract.

Most beers contain corn products, although at least one, Michelob, is made with rice, and most rums are corn free. Beers also contain a mix of ingredients, including barley, hops, malt, and yeast. Whiskeys, gin, and vodka are often complex, and an individual sensitive to any of their many ingredients may react when drinking them. Persons sensitive to some beers or other alcoholic beverages may be able to tolerate others. (See also BEER, WINE.)

Alconefrin   See   PHENYLEPHRINE   HYDRO-CHLORIDE.

aldol   A colorless, thick liquid synthesized from acetaldehyde but found in fruits and vegetables, including apples, broccoli, and grapefruit, as well as cheese and coffee. Used in the manufacture of perfumes and rubber, aldol may cause allergic contact rashes. It also has sedative and hypnotic properties.

alizarin   [Turkey red]   A coal tar dye synthetically obtained from anthracene or naturally obtained from the root of the madder plant (*Rubia tinctoria*). Various colors, including black, blue, dark brown, lilac, orange, red, rose, Turkey red, violet, and yellow, can be obtained by mixing the dye with a variety of metals. This

dye is used in the cosmetic industry and to dye wool and can cause allergic contact rashes.

alkyl sodium sulfates and alkyl sulfates   Chemicals that are mild skin irritants widely used in soaps, shampoos, and detergents.

alkyl sulfates   See   ALKYL SODIUM SULFATES AND ALKYL SULFATES.

Allegra   Brand name for the drug fexofenadine, a nonsedating antihistamine that became available in the U.S. in 1996. (See also FEXOFENADINE.)

allergenic extracts   Solutions of allergenically active materials suitable for diagnostic skin testing and immunotherapy treatment (allergy shots).

Since 1913, when W. P. Dunbar first demonstrated that an injection of pollen extract could reproduce hay fever symptoms, extracts of allergens have ranked as the mainstay of allergy testing and immunotherapy.

Collection of materials   Pollens are collected by several methods, including vacuum, water set (a method of pollen collection using unopened buds that are placed in water and whose pollens are collected when the buds bloom), and the drying and grinding of flower heads. The pollens are then washed by passing them through various-sized sieves and, in some cases, floated on perchlorethylene, a chemical solvent. Then they are dried under strict temperature and time controls.

The source for animal allergen extract was once thought to be limited to the epidermis, or skin, and thus the term *epidermals* became widely used. Cat antigen is best extracted from saliva, hair, dander, and pelt, whereas in rats it is mainly found in the saliva and urine. (See entries on specific animal allergies.)

Insect allergy can result from stings, bites, or inhalation of whole bodies of microscopic insects, or insect body parts or waste. The allergen of the stinging insects, bees, vespids (wasps and hornets), and fire ants, is found in their venom. Pure bee venom is obtained by electrically stimulating honeybees. Extracts from vespids contain whole venom sacs.

Whole-body extracts of cockroach are highly allergenic. Extracts of the salivary glands of biting insects are intensely allergenic but not a significant problem in the United States. These extracts would be difficult to produce commercially if they were important.

Dust mites are commercially grown in culture (a nutrient medium in which microorganisms can grow) until they die. The entire culture, including the nutrient, the dead organisms grown in it, and their waste products, is then processed to produce a potent allergenic extract. In a second process, whole mites and their allergenic fecal waste are removed from the culture material.

House dust extracts may contain multiple allergens, including dust mites, depending on their source. They may vary from batch to batch even from the same manufacturer. An endotoxin, or poison, may contaminate the extract or irritate the recipient, and the irritation may be mistaken for an allergic reaction. The Food and Drug Administration (FDA) has proposed removal of these extracts from the market because of manufacturers' inability to standardize them. However, they remain in wide use, and some allergists and their patients feel they are beneficial.

Standardization Standardization ensures accurate and safe diagnosis by skin testing and safe, effective immunotherapy. Because standardization is a complicated process, only a few standardized extracts are commercially available, and some extracts do not significantly differ from the crude ones used 75 years ago.

The source of an allergen is critical to the quality and effectiveness of the final extract. Following a review by an expert panel, the FDA issued a report in the *Federal Register* on January 23, 1985 criticizing more than 1,600 allergenic extracts produced by 21 manufacturers. In the August 9, 1985 issue, a list of products no longer approved included extracts of whole bodies of stinging insects and extracts of chocolate. A subsequent panel of experts recommended that no food extracts be used for immunotherapy.

There are some newer types of extracts not yet commercially available: allergoid, photoinactivated antigen, and polymerized antigen. (See also ALLERGENIC EXTRACTS, POLYMERIZED; ALLERGOIDS; IMMUNOTHERAPY.)

allergenic extracts, polymerized   Extracts chemically modified with gluteraldehyde (an organic substance) to produce an extract for immunotherapy (allergy shots) that can be given for shorter periods of time and with fewer adverse reactions than extracts used currently. Polymerized extracts of ragweed, grass, and tree pollens have been studied with good results, but difficulties with standardization of the process make it unlikely that the Food and Drug Administration will approve their use in the foreseeable future. (See also ALLERGENIC EXTRACTS.)

allergen nomenclature   Names for substances causing allergy (allergens) established by a committee of the International Union of Immunological Societies (IUIS). Allergens are named by using the first three letters of the genus, followed by a single letter for the species and a Roman numeral to indicate the chronological order in which the allergen was identified in each plant or animal. For example, ragweed allergen, formerly called antigen E, is *Ambrosia artemisifolia*, allergen I, or *Amb a* 1. Cat allergen is *Fel d* I. This nomenclature is restricted to highly purified allergens.

allergens   Substances that cause allergy. Allergens are proteins or protein-carbohydrate components with molecular weights of approximately 5,000 to 100,000 daltons (A dalton is a unit of mass, 1/16 of the mass of the oxygen atom. The formula is 1.65×10^{-24} g.) These substances are capable of stimulating the production of antibodies specific to a particular allergen when coming in contact with a susceptible individual. Allergens inhaled from both indoor and outdoor air, called aeroallergens, come in contact with special cells, called mast cells, in the lining of the upper respiratory tract (nose, sinuses, and throat) and lower respiratory tract (bronchial tubes and lungs). (See MAST CELLS.) This contact results in the rupture of mast cells and their release of chemicals that irritate the tissue and cause symptoms of allergy. These symptoms include itching, sneezing, runny nose, coughing, wheezing, and shortness of breath. Similar reactions occur in the eyes, skin, and gastrointestinal tract.

Physician-scientist Thomas E. Platts-Mills, at the University of Virginia Medical School, has demonstrated that at least 40% of acute asthma attacks in adults coming to an emergency room were caused by exposure to indoor allergens. In the United States the three most important sources of indoor allergens are cats, cockroaches, and dust mites (see CAT ALLERGY, COCKROACH ALLERGY, HOUSE DUST ALLERGY, HOUSE DUST MITES).

Other allergens include pollens, molds, epidermals (animal dander, saliva, and urine), foods, food additives, dust mites, insects and insect parts, industrial agents, seeds (cottonseed, kapok, and flaxseed or linseed), oris root (pyrethrum used in insecticides), vegetable gums, and medications, such as aspirin, penicillins, and other antibiotics. Dust may contain a mixture of allergens. Perfumes, tobacco smoke, air pollution, and noxious fumes are irritants, and although they may cause symptoms similar to those of allergies, they are not allergens. (See also AEROALLERGENS.)

allergic angiitis See CHURG-STRAUSS SYNDROME.

allergic bronchopulmonary aspergillosis (ABPA) Pneumonialike disease caused by an allergic reaction to the mold *Aspergillus fumigatus.* It usually occurs in adult asthmatics.

Signs and symptoms This disorder usually involves episodes of fever, shortness of breath and wheezing, and coughing up copious quantities of dark brown, and at times blood-streaked, sputum.

Diagnosis Because the fungus is ubiquitous (found in healthy persons in small quantities that are harmless), the presence of positive sputum cultures is not sufficient to diagnose this disease. The diagnosis is made in persons meeting the following criteria: (1) episodes of asthma; (2) elevated eosinophils (a type of white blood cell) and total immunoglobulin E (IgE) antibodies in the blood; these values are slightly elevated in most allergic individuals but extremely elevated in persons with this disease; (3) pneumonialike X-ray findings, which may be temporary; (4) bronchiectasis (destruction of the muscles in the bronchial walls with chronic cough and large amounts of sputum); (5) positive skin tests to the aspergillus fungus; and (6) positive blood tests for antibodies against the aspergillus allergen.

Treatment Prednisone, a corticosteroid drug, is the treatment of choice. It is used daily, most often for several months, and improvement is usually seen within days. In some cases, recurrences require long-term prednisone use. (See also CORTICOSTEROIDS, PREDNISONE.)

Prognosis If untreated, aspergillosis will damage lung tissues and can be fatal.

allergic conjunctivitis See CONJUNCTIVITIS, ALLERGIC.

allergic contact dermatitis See CONTACT DERMATITIS.

allergic dermatitis See ATOPIC DERMATITIS.

allergic drug reactions See DRUG ALLERGY AND OTHER ADVERSE DRUG REACTIONS.

allergic otitis media See OTITIS MEDIA, SECRETORY.

allergic purpura See HENOCH-SCHONLEIN PURPURA, VASCULITIS.

allergic reactions See HYPERSENSITIVITY, ALLERGY.

allergic rhinitis [pollinosis, hay fever]   An inflammatory condition of the nasal passages, adjoining sinuses, ears, and/or throat that occurs when an allergic person inhales an allergen to which he or she is sensitive. Allergic rhinitis is an immune response that does not occur in a normal or nonallergic individual. Allergic rhinitis may occur periodically (seasonally) or continuously (perennially).

Cause During the allergic reaction of hay fever, mast cells in the lining of the nose rupture when exposed to an allergen in a susceptible person. The mast cells release chemicals, called mediators, that are responsible for allergic symptoms (see CHEMICAL MEDIATORS, MAST CELLS).

Hay fever is an English name given because of symptoms caused by exposure to grass allergens coinciding with the bailing of hay. It usually refers to seasonal allergies, occurring with exposure to the airborne (windblown) pollens of trees, grasses, ragweed, and other weeds and outdoor mold spores. A person may suffer the symptoms during spring, fall, or both seasons.

Perennial, or year-round, allergic rhinitis is usually due to exposure to indoor allergens called "inhalants." Cats, dogs, rodents, house dust, dust mites, and indoor molds are examples of perennial allergens.

Allergic rhinitis is often confused with colds, sinus infections, nasal polyps or other nasal obstructions, and nonallergic, vasomotor rhinitis. Vasomotor rhinitis is nasal congestion that cannot be attributed to another cause, such as allergy. A deviated septum, an abnormality of the cartilage separating the nostrils, is a frequent cause of stuffy noses and can occur in allergic as well as nonallergic individuals. Rarely, more serious conditions such as tumors or nonhealing granulomas may exist. These conditions should be considered in patients who fail to respond promptly to treatment and who have blood-stained nasal mucus. (See also POLYP, NASAL; VASOMOTOR RHINITIS; WEGENER'S GRANULOMATOSIS.)

Overuse or abuse of over-the-counter nasal sprays can result in a common and troublesome disorder called rhinitis medicomentosum (rhinitis means an inflamed nose; medicomentosum means caused by medication). (See RHINITIS MEDICOMENTOSUM.) This condition is often confused with allergy and may occur in both allergic and nonallergic individuals.

Signs and symptoms These vary in severity from person to person. Symptoms include pruritis (itching), sneezing, rhinorrhea (runny and watery discharge from the nose), postnasal drip, and congestion of the nose, ears, and sinuses. A general state of fatigue and malaise (a feeling of being "unwell") may exist during allergy attacks. Loss of smell or taste occurs in severe cases.

Persons with hay fever frequently suffer from allergic conjunctivitis (itchy, watery, and red eyes caused by allergy) and asthma. (See ASTHMA; CONJUNCTIVITIS, ALLERGIC.)

Physical appearance Hay fever sufferers often have a characteristic appearance. A horizontal crease across the lower portion of the nose is called the "allergic crease," caused by the "allergic salute," a constant pushing up on the tip of the nose by the palm of the hand prompted by the discomfort of nasal stuffiness.

Dark circles under the eyes are referred to as "allergic shiners." These are probably caused by blockage of blood flow to the tiny veins in the area because of swelling. Blood trapped in the area under the eyes has a very low oxygen content, resulting in the dark blue-black discoloration. There will often be swelling and puffiness of the eye lids, redness of the eyes, and watery discharge from the eyes and nose. Individuals with persistent nasal obstruction often breathe through their mouth, which causes facial abnormalities, such as long faces, flattened cheekbones, pinched nostrils, and raised upper lips. Orthodontal problems arise more frequently in allergic persons because of narrower retracted jaws, overbites, and high arched palates. (See also HAY FEVER, POLLINOSIS.)

allergic salute See ALLERGIC RHINITIS.

allergic shiners See ALLERGIC RHINITIS.

allergic shock See ANAPHYLAXIS.

allergic skin disorders An umbrella term for rashes, including atopic dermatitis or eczema, allergic contact dermatitis, allergic drug reactions, and urticaria, or hives. Such rashes are among the most common and disabling allergic conditions and are responsible for many lost days at work or school. (See ATOPIC DERMATITIS, CONTACT DERMATITIS, DRUG ALLERGY AND OTHER ADVERSE DRUG REACTIONS, URTICARIA.)

allergic skin reactions See ATOPIC DERMATITIS, CONTACT DERMATITIS.

allergic vasculitis See HENOCH-SCHONLEIN PURPURA, VASCULITIS.

allergist [allergist-immunologist] A physician who diagnoses and treats allergic conditions and related disorders. Asthma, hay fever, eczema, and hives are among the illnesses most frequently treated by allergists. Most allergists complete a two-year fellowship in allergy and immunology following a residency in internal medicine or pediatrics. They are then eligible to become board certified in their specialty by passing a comprehensive examination. (See IMMUNOLOGIST.)

allergist-immunologist See ALLERGIST.

allergoids Allergy extracts modified by treatment with the chemical formalin. This modification results in lower incidence of reactions and shorter courses of immunotherapy (allergy shots). While ragweed allergoid has proven to be excellent, no other allergoids are available in the United States. Because most people need multiple extracts for their treatment, use of the singular allergoid may not be practical.

allergy An overreaction by the immune system to a substance called an allergen that does not cause a similar reaction in nonsensitized persons. An allergen is any protein or proteinlike substance recognized by the body as foreign and capable of provoking an allergic response. (See ALLERGENS.)

Austrian pediatrician Clemens P. Pirquet (1874–1929) first used the term *allergy*, derived from the Greek *allos* ("altered") and *ergia* ("reactivity"), in 1906. He referred both to immunity, which is beneficial, and to harmful hypersensitivity of the immune system as allergy. Today, allergy refers only to the hypersensitivity or injurious effects of the immune system.

Causes Most individuals inherit the tendency to be allergic from one or both parents. It is not known why some persons develop allergies and others do not. It is thought by some that exposure to viral infections, smoking, or hormones influence a person's propensity for allergy. It is also unknown why some individuals will get hay fever and others asthma, or both.

Types of allergy There are four classifications of allergic or hypersensitivity reactions: type I, immediate or immunoglobulin E (IgE) mediated (see IMMUNOGLOBULIN E); type II, in which antibodies are directed against cells; type III, in which toxic effects result from antibody and antigen complexes; and type IV, cell-mediated or delayed reactions.

Pollens, animal proteins (dander, saliva, urine, feathers), house dust mites, molds, drugs, foods, and venoms from insects or reptiles are examples of allergens that can cause immediate, or type I, reactions. After a first exposure, these apparently harmless allergens stimulate the immune system to form IgE antibodies. IgE antibodies are specific to each allergen and attach to the surface of mast cells in the tissues (see MAST CELLS). Upon reexposure, the recognized allergen combines with its antibodies, rupturing mast cells and releasing biochemical mediators that cause the symptoms of allergy. The most severe form of type I allergic reaction is anaphylaxis (see ANAPHYLAXIS).

In type II reactions, also called autoimmune disorders, antibodies attack the body's own tissues. Serum sickness and some allergic lung disorders are type III reactions. Poison ivy is a type IV, or delayed hypersensitivity, reaction (see HYPERSENSITIVITY).

Prevalence The most common allergies include allergic rhinitis (hay fever), asthma, eczema, and urticaria (hives). The National Institute of Allergy and Infectious Diseases estimates that 35 million Americans have allergies and about 10 million have asthma. Approximately 80 to 90% of adult allergies are caused by inhaled allergens from animals, pollens, molds, or house dust. Foods are responsible for about 20% of children's allergies but much less so in adults. A small percentage of allergies are caused by contactants or insect stings. (See also ATOPY.)

allergy control equipment and products
Items designed to prevent, reduce, or eliminate allergic triggers. They include mattress, box spring, and pillow encasings, acaracides (products that kill house dust mites), face masks, and dehumidifiers. (See ACARACIDES, TRIGGERS OF ALLERGIES AND ASTHMA.)

Allergy Control Solution See TANNIC ACID SOLUTION.

allergy diets See DIET, ALLERGY.

allergy injections See IMMUNOTHERAPY.

allergy myths See MYTHS ABOUT ALLERGIES AND ASTHMA.

allergy organizations, lay See Appendix IV.

allergy organizations, professional See Appendix III.

allergy shots Layman's term for immunotherapy. (See IMMUNOTHERAPY.)

allergy to the 20th century See TOTAL IMMUNE DISORDER SYNDROME.

allergy treatment Methods of combating allergic symptoms. Three main phases of treatment are avoidance of allergen exposure, use of drugs, and immunotherapy, or allergy desensitization (allergy shots).

Avoidance of allergy triggers is the management of choice, but it may be difficult or even impossible to achieve. Drugs offer excellent relief from symptoms of allergies and asthma with minimal side effects. Antihistamines, adrenergic agonists or decongestants, beta-agonists and xanthine bronchodilators (theophylline), cromolyn, and corticosteroids (derivatives of cortisone) are available in inhaled, oral, and injectable dosage forms. These drugs are among the most widely prescribed of all medicines. Immunotherapy, successfully used to treat allergic rhinitis (hay fever) for many years, is now also recognized as effective treatment for allergic asthmatic patients. (See ANTIHISTAMINE, AVOIDANCE OF ALLERGENS, BETA-ADRENERGIC AGONISTS, CORTICOSTEROIDS, IMMUNOTHERAPY, THEOPHYLLINE, TRIGGERS OF ALLERGIES AND ASTHMA.)

allergy units (AU) Assigned values given to an allergy extract or serum by the Office of Biological Research and Review (OBRR) following comparative testing to determine its potency. This is done to assure that various batches of allergy serums will be equivalent unit for unit.

OBRR has developed a protocol using inhibition RAST (blood tests that measure immunoglobulin E antibodies for specific allergens) and skin testing to standardize extracts.

allergy vacuum cleaners See VACUUM CLEANERS FOR ALLERGIC PATIENTS.

aloe vera A substance expressed from leaves of the aloe plant and used in various cosmetic preparations. Claims by the cosmetic industry of soothing and healing attributes are disputed by some physicians. Aloe is also used as flavoring for alcoholic drinks. Its cramping properties and kidney toxicity limit its use as a strong laxative. It is also allergenic and cross-reacts in individuals sensitive to balsam Peru and benzoin.

alpha-adrenergic agonists   Drugs that act as nasal decongestants by constricting or shrinking congested blood vessels in the nasal mucosa, or lining of the nose. These medicines are used to provide temporary relief in acute or chronic allergic rhinitis, or hay fever, vasomotor or nonallergic rhinitis, or infections such as colds or sinusitis. Pressure in the eustachian tubes that occurs in otitis media or ear infections may also be alleviated. Decongestants are often combined with antihistamines for the treatment of allergic rhinitis.

Decongestant medications are available as nose drops or sprays, tablets, capsules, or syrups. The topical use is initially more effective, but because of the tendency to develop a rebound worsening congestion, topical use is usually limited to three to five consecutive days. This rebound phenomenon is called rhinitis medicomentosum.

Oral forms of decongestants are preferable for chronic use but are more likely to cause systemic side effects such as insomnia, tremors, dizziness, heart palpitations, and increased blood pressure. Therefore, they must be used with caution in persons with hypertension (high blood pressure), heart disease, diabetes mellitus, and thyroid disease and those on tricyclic antidepressants. They must not be used in persons taking antidepressants called monoamine oxidase (MAO) inhibitors. (See ADRENERGIC DRUGS, NASAL SPRAY, RHINITIS MEDICOMENTOSUM.)

alpha-1-antitrypsin deficiency (AAT deficiency)   An inherited disorder that may lead to serious liver disease during infancy or adolescence or, in early adulthood, severe emphysema that may be confused with asthma.

A typical patient is a smoker between 30 and 45 years of age, who develops shortness of breath, especially with exercise, and usually dies by age 60. Destructive enzymes released in the lungs, if unchecked by alpha-1-antitrypsin, reduce elasticity in the lung tissue and diminish lung capacity. An estimated 20,000 to 30,000 Americans—2 to 3% of Caucasians—have this disease and are at greatest risk if they smoke. The gene for AAT deficiency is located on chromosome 14; carrier screening and prenatal diagnosis can be determined.

Treatment consists of intravenous human AAT (Prolastin) replacement, bronchodilating drugs, oxygen, and reduction of exposure to respiratory system irritants and smoking.

Alternaria   One of a few significant families of airborne mold allergens indigenous to North America. Alternaria is most abundant in the plains, grain-growing states and Canadian provinces, where on an average dry day in late summer or fall, 500 to 1,000 spores float in every cubic meter of air. It is estimated that 10 different allergens produced by Alternaria can cause sinusitis, usually in persons with immunodeficiency conditions such as AIDS, provoking both immediate and late-phase allergic reactions. In asthma, this dual response results in coughing, wheezing, and shortness of breath following a single exposure to Alternaria. Hours after the exposure, the late-phase reaction results in more intense and prolonged symptoms. Wood-pulp worker's disease, an allergic, occupational lung disease, originates in wood pulp contaminated by Alternaria. (See HYPERSENSITIVITY PNEUMONITIS.)

alternative testing and treatment for allergies   Methods for the diagnosis and treatment of allergic disorders developed and practiced by physicians or others that are considered unscientific or unproven by the National Center for Health Care Technology, the American Academy of Allergy and Immunology, and the American College of Allergy and Immunology. (See CONTROVERSIAL APPROACHES TO DIAGNOSIS, EXPLANATION, OR TREATMENT OF ALLERGIES.)

Altounyan, Roger E. C.   Armenian-English physician (1922–1987), born in Aleppo, Syria, who developed disodium cromoglycate, or cromolyn, an anti-inflammatory allergy medication. Altounyan first experimented with khellin, a substance from the dried fruit of an herb, *Ammi visnaga*, indigenous to Egypt and North Africa, because khellin had already been widely used for treating spasms of the intestines, bronchial tubes, uterus, and arterial smooth muscle of the heart. In addition, Altounyan suffered from atopic dermatitis as a child and later on from severe asthma. Using himself as the experimental subject, he investigated 670 synthetic compounds, and in 1967 he recognized the effectiveness of cromolyn.

aluminum acetate   [Burow's solution]   A solution including acetic acid and boric acid whose astringent and antiseptic properties are useful to treat various skin disorders, including the weeping lesions of poison ivy and other contact rashes. This preparation, named for the German surgeon Karl August von Burow (1809–74), is also used in astringent lotions and deodorants and as a disinfectant by embalmers, as a fur dye, and for fabric finishing and waterproofing. Prolonged exposure may cause severe sloughing of the skin, and aluminum acetate may be toxic if ingested.

aluminum chloride   An astringent and antiseptic solution used as an antiperspirant. Aluminum chloride can be irritating and a cause of skin allergy, and it can be toxic if ingested.

Alupent   See METAPROTERENOL.

alveolar sac   See ALVEOLI.

alveoli   Air sacs in the lungs, named from the Latin word meaning "small hollow or cavity." There are about 300 million alveoli in the lungs. Each alveolus comes into direct contact with tiny blood vessels called capillaries. The alveoli and the capillaries are separated by a microscopically thin wall or membrane that allows oxygen and nitrogen to pass into the bloodstream and carbon dioxide and other gases to pass from the blood into the alveoli. Waste gases are exhaled from the alveoli.

Extrinsic allergic alveolitis, or hypersensitivity pneumonitis, is an allergic pneumonialike disorder in which the alveoli become inflamed (see HYPERSENSITIVITY PNEUMONITIS).

In the lung disease emphysema, the air spaces increase beyond normal size, and the alveolar walls are destroyed. The person has difficulty exhaling, and the gas-exchange process is impaired. Severe emphysema with large areas of destroyed alveoli is often referred to as "vanishing lung." There are alveoli in other parts of the body, including the salivary glands, where a component of saliva is produced.

alveolitis   An inflammatory condition of the alveoli, or air sacs of the lungs. Extrinsic allergic alveolitis, or hypersensitivity pneumonitis, is a severe allergic pneumonialike disorder. (See HYPERSENSITIVITY PNEUMONITIS.)

alveolitis, extrinsic allergic   See ALVEOLITIS, HYPERSENSITIVITY PNEUMONITIS.

amantadine   (Symmetrel)   An antiviral drug that is also used in the treatment of Parkinson's disease. During "flu" epidemics, amantadine may lessen the severity, shorten the course, or prevent type A influenza, but it has no effect on influenza B or other viruses. Individuals at risk for severe complications of influenza, including some asthmatics, may benefit from immunization with influenza vaccine and daily doses of amantadine for several weeks until the vaccine becomes effective.

American Academy of Allergy and Immunology   (AAAI)   A professional organization of allergists and immunologists that promotes the advancement of scientific study of allergy and immunology both academically and in the practice of medicine. It was established in 1943 with the merger of the American Association for the Study of Allergy and the Association for the Study of Asthma and Allied Conditions.

The AAAI publishes the *Journal of Allergy and Clinical Immunology*. From time to time the academy issues position statements to clarify confusing issues in the fields of allergy or immunology. An emphasis is placed on aiding the public in seeking competent medical care and avoiding unproven or dangerous techniques for the diagnosis or treatment of these disorders. The majority of fellows and members of the AAAI are board certified in their specialty. (See also CONTROVERSIAL APPROACHES TO DIAGNOSIS, EXPLANATION, OR TREATMENT OF ALLERGIES.)

American Board of Allergy and Immunology

(ABAI) A conjoint board of the American Board of Internal Medicine and the American Board of Pediatrics, established in 1971 as a nonprofit organization. It is sponsored jointly by the American Board of Internal Medicine (ABIM), the American Board of Pediatrics (ABP), the American Academy of Allergy and Immunology (AAAI), the American College of Allergy and Immunology (ACAI), the American Academy of Pediatrics—Section on Allergy, and the American Medical Association—Section on Allergy. The board consists of an even number of directors. The directors are nominated by the Sections on Allergy of the American Academy of Pediatrics and the American Medical Association, the AAAI, ACAI, and the ABAI itself. The nominees are appointed by the ABIM and the ABP. Each board director is appointed for six years.

Purposes of the ABAI The major purposes of this organization are: (1) to establish qualifications and examine physician candidates for certification as specialists in allergy and immunology, (2) to serve the public, physicians, hospitals, and medical schools by providing the names of physicians certified as allergists and immunologists, (3) to improve the quality of care in allergy and immunology to the public and increase the availability of specialists to deliver such care, (4) to establish and improve standards for the teaching and practice of allergy and immunology, (5) to establish standards for training programs in allergy and immunology, and (6) to provide increased opportunities for physicians wishing to specialize in allergy and immunology.

Certification The ABAI is interested in candidates who have embarked voluntarily on a graduate program of study with the express purpose of excelling in the practice of the specialty of allergy and immunology. In outlining its requirements, the ABAI hopes to help the candidates select superior educational programs that will develop their competency in allergy and immunology. The ABAI believes that all allergists and immunologists should have a fundamental knowledge of the biological science basic to this discipline. Such knowledge is essential to the continued professional progress of any qualified allergist and immunologist. The ABAI anticipates that adequate knowledge in basic science, as applied to this discipline, will be acquired by the candidates during a post-medical school training program. The ABAI wishes to emphasize that time and training are but a means to the end of acquiring a broad knowledge of allergy and immunology.

The candidate must demonstrate competency to the ABAI in order to justify certification in this discipline. The responsibility of acquiring the knowledge rests with the candidate. The ABAI is responsible for the establishment and maintenance of the standards of knowledge required for certification. Each candidate for certification must satisfy the general and professional qualifications listed below.

The candidate must qualify for examination by having passed the certification examination of the American Board of Internal Medicine or the American Board of Pediatrics. Certification requires three years of postgraduate general training in programs accredited by the Accreditation Council for Graduate Medical Education (ACGME), by presentation of evidence acceptable to the board of directors of at least two years of full-time residency/fellowship or other acceptable training in allergy and immunology programs accredited by the ACGME upon the recommendation of the Residency Review Committee for Allergy and Immunology. These programs are listed in the *Directory of Graduate Medical Education Programs,* published by the American Medical Association, a copy of which may be found in most medical school libraries.

EXECUTIVE OFFICE
American Board of Allergy and Immunology, A Conjoint Board of the American Board of Internal Medicine and the American Board of Pediatrics
University City Science Center
3624 Market Street
Philadelphia, PA 19104
Telephone: 215–349–9466
Herbert C. Mansmann, Jr., M.D.,
Executive Secretary
Lynn Des Prez, Administrative Director

American College of Allergy and Immunology (ACAI)

A professional organization founded by physicians and scientists to promote and advance the knowledge of allergy and to assure a high quality of care for patients with allergic disorders. Most members and fellows of this organization are board certified in their field.

The college publishes the scientific journal *Annals of Allergy* and from time to time issues position statements promoting the safe and ethical practice of allergy.

American Dietetic Association

An organization based in Chicago from which nutritional and dietary information can be obtained. A list of commonly allergenic foods, including cow's milk, eggs, and wheat, is available.

amines, vasoactive   Potent nitrogen-containing organic compounds found in foods that may cause a wide variety of symptoms especially affecting the central nervous system and gastrointestinal tract. Vasoactive amines, including dopamine, histamine, norepinephrine, phenylethylamine, serotonin, tyramine, and tryptamine, in large quantities may be a cause of headaches, abdominal cramps, and diarrhea. Persons taking antidepressant drugs called monoamine oxidase (MAO) inhibitors may de-

velop severe hypertension when exposed to foods containing vasoactive amines.

The amines are usually formed when bacteria decarboxylate, or break down, amino acids in aged cheeses, contaminated tuna fish, and chocolate. Small amounts of these chemicals are naturally present in avocados, bananas, oranges, pineapples, plums, tomatoes, and red wine. (See HEADACHE.)

amino dyes   See PHENYLENEDIAMINES.

aminophenols   Chemical derivatives of phenol used in orange, red, and medium-brown hair dyes. Adverse reactions range from mild contact rashes to convulsions from severe absorption or asthma from inhalation.

aminophylline   A bronchodilating drug made up of two components, theophylline and ethylenediamine. Available in both tablet and intravenous forms, aminophylline has been a standard treatment for acute asthma attacks for many years. However, recently its use has been related to a backup role with the increased use of the beta-agonist bronchodilators. The action of aminophylline is based on the theophylline portion, which is a methylxanthine derivative and has many adverse effects and drug interactions. (See METHYLXANTHINES, THEOPHYLLINE.)

ammonium carbonate   A neutralizing alkaline chemical used as an expectorant in cough syrups, in permanent wave solutions, and in fire extinguishers. It can cause contact rashes.

ammonium dichromate   Chemical used in red dyes and perfumes. Its irritating properties can be confused with allergic reactions to the eyes and skin.

ammonium iodide   A chemical used as an expectorant in cough syrups. It is also used as a preservative and antiseptic by the cosmetic industry.

amyl acetate   [banana oil, pear oil]   A fruity flavoring agent and cosmetic scent used by the food and cosmetic industries. It can be irritating to skin, and its inhalation in high concentrations can cause irritations of mucous membranes, headache, and chest pain.

anaphylactic shock   See ANAPHYLAXIS.

anaphylactoid reaction   A severe and potentially life-threatening, allergylike reaction characterized by swelling and constriction of airways caused by the direct release of potent biochemical mediators from cells in the body tissues. As opposed to anaphylaxis, anaphylactoid reaction does not involve immunoglobulin E (IgE) antibodies. (See HYPERSENSITIVITY, IMMUNOGLOBULIN E.) Since symptoms of anaphylactoid and true allergic, anaphylactic reactions are indistinguishable, the terms are used synonymously. (See also ANAPHYLAXIS.)

Immediate anaphylactoid reactions can result from poisoning after eating fish containing large amounts of histamine. Tuna, mackerel, and mahimahi are the most common sources. Fish inadequately refrigerated or contaminated by *Proteus morganii* or *Klebsiella pneumoniae* bacteria may also contain dangerously high histamine levels. Allergylike symptoms—flushing, erythema, itchy eyes, nausea, diarrhea, and headache—may last up to 24 hours and are self-limiting (they eventually disappear on their own). Swiss cheese may cause a similar reaction. Tuberculosis patients taking the drug isoniazid (INH) are highly susceptible to these food reactions.

anaphylaxis   [anaphylactic shock]   The most severe or extreme type of allergic reaction, which may be life-threatening, characterized by any or a combination of the following symptoms: itching of the throat or skin, hives, dizziness, tightness and swelling in the throat, difficulty breathing, weakness, sudden drop in blood pressure, or unconsciousness. Anaphylaxis ranges from mild itching to collapse and death and therefore constitutes a medical emergency. True anaphylaxis occurs after exposure to an allergen to which a person has been previously sensitized.

Prevalence   An estimated four deaths per 10 million people from anaphylaxis occur each year. There are insufficient data to determine increased risk for anaphylaxis, such as age, sex, or ethnic criteria. There does not appear to be a predilection to penicillin or insect-sting anaphylaxis in persons known to have other allergies. However, some studies suggest that allergic individuals do have a higher incidence of anaphylaxis.

In the early 20th century, before the availability of antibiotics, horse-serum antitoxin was used to treat the often fatal diseases diphtheria, scarlet fever, tetanus, and tuberculosis. Prior to the penicillin era, horse serum was the most common cause of anaphylaxis.

Penicillin may account for 75% of all fatal allergic reactions: an estimated 500 deaths annually in the United States. One fatality occurs for every 7.5 million injections of penicillin; death may also result from oral, inhaled, or topical contact with the drug.

Hieroglyphics depict death from an insect sting 4,000 years ago. In 2640 B.C. the Egyptian pharaoh Menes reportedly died suddenly after being stung by a wasp. Up to 4% of the population suffers systemic reactions to stings of bees, wasps, hornets, yellow jackets, and fire ants.

Aspirin and the frequently used arthritis drugs called nonsteroidal anti-inflammatory drugs (NSAIDs), such as ibuprofen, may cause anaphylaxis in as many as 1% of individuals. Up to 10% of persons with asthma may exhibit anaphylaxis.

Cause   Despite recognition of fatal allergic reactions dating from biblical times, it was not until 1902 that French professors of medicine Charles Richet (1850–1935) and Paul Portier (1866–1962) linked a case of fatal anaphylaxis to a foreign protein injection that had been previously tolerated by a patient. Anaphylaxis occurs when potent biochemicals such as histamine (also called mediators) are released from mast and other special cells in the body tissues and act in a sequence of events affecting various organs. It is now known that there is more than one mechanism for this reaction.

Type I allergy, also called hypersensitivity or IgE-antibody-mediated allergic reaction, is the most common and best understood cause of anaphylaxis. Following initial exposure of a foreign protein or hapten, antibodies develop during a latent period. Anaphylaxis occurs upon reexposure of this same foreign substance. A hapten, of which penicillin is an example, is a low-molecular-weight and nonallergenic substance until it combines with a larger "carrier" molecule to become allergenic. Hundreds of allergens in drugs (especially antibiotics), foods (the most frequent offenders include eggs, cow's milk, peanuts, fish and shellfish, and tree nuts), food preservatives (especially sulfites), and foreign proteins (including seminal fluid, insulin, and insect and snake venoms) are capable of inducing anaphylaxis in susceptible individuals.

However, other reactions that do not involve antigen-antibody production but stimulate the release of chemical mediators, including histamine, can cause the same symptoms as anaphylaxis. For many years this was referred to as anaphylactoid (anaphylacticlike) reactions. Most allergists feel the term is outdated and refer to all similar reactions as anaphylaxis. Substances capable of inducing these reactions include whole blood, radiocontrast (X-ray) media, aspirin, food dyes, and drugs. Trauma, burns, or infections can also induce anaphylactoid reactions.

Signs and symptoms An initial sensation of warmth, itching, or tingling begins in the axilla or groin and gradually spreads throughout the body. Sneezing, intense itching, and constriction in the throat may progress to generalized hives and angioedema, or swelling of the face and tongue. Wheezing, shortness of breath, abdominal pain, nausea, vomiting, and diarrhea may follow. A drop in blood pressure, described by some as a feeling of "impending doom," may signal collapse (or shock) and death. Any of these signs and symptoms can occur individually or concurrently. The longer the time interval (or latent period) between the initial exposure to an allergen and the onset of symptoms, the less likely it is that death will occur.

Treatment Treatment must be initiated at the first signs or symptoms of impending anaphylaxis, since there is no way of anticipating how severe a reaction may become. Epinephrine (Adrenalin) given subcutaneously (under the skin) is the drug of choice; if it is given immediately, it may be lifesaving. Antihistamines, bronchodilators, corticosteroids, and oxygen are also administered as needed, but they take much longer to become effective and may not be lifesaving.

Arrange transportation of the patient to the nearest emergency room or other medical facility. A delay of even a few moments can be fatal. A person may experience a recurrence of anaphylaxis as long as 24 hours after the initial reaction and should be monitored for at least 24 hours.

Prevention Individuals known to be at risk through a history of a prior severe allergic reaction should carry an adrenaline kit at all times. Identify and avoid a food (rarely more than one) that is thought to be a cause of allergic reaction. Avoidance of a food because another family member has had a serious reaction to it is not necessary. Skin testing for foods can be hazardous and should be avoided if anaphylaxis has occurred; RAST blood food testing is safer but often misleading because of false positive or negative results (see RADIOALLERGOSORBENT TESTS).

Specific preventive measures should be taken by persons with cold-induced urticaria (hives), exercise-induced anaphylaxis, and allergy to seminal fluid, venomous insects, drugs, and radiocontrast (X-ray) dyes. (See also COLD URTICARIA, ESSENTIAL; DRUG ALLERGY AND OTHER ADVERSE DRUG REACTIONS; EXERCISE-INDUCED ANAPHYLAXIS; HYMENOPTERA STING ALLERGY; RADIOCONTRAST MEDIA REACTIONS; SEMEN ALLERGY.)

anaphylaxis, exercise-induced See EXERCISE-INDUCED ANAPHYLAXIS.

Anderson, John F. American physician (1873–1958), born in Fredericksburg, Virginia, who became assistant director of the Hygienic Laboratory under Milton J. Rosenau (see ROSENAU, MILTON J.). He and Rosenau conducted studies on anaphylaxis, especially dealing with severe or fatal reaction to horse serum. After much intense investigation, both Anderson and Rosenau decided that a "strange proteid" was responsible for causing an anaphylactic reaction. (See THEOBALD SMITH PHENOMENON.) Trained in bacteriology, Anderson succeeded Rosenau as director and thereafter worked with Joseph Goldberger to develop an experimental measles model in monkeys. Anderson left the Public Health Service in 1915 to direct the Squibb Research and Biological Laboratories.

anemophilous plants Plants that produce pollen borne by air and cause hay fever.

Not all pollen-producing plants are allergenic. A pollen extract must be skin-tested to determine its allergenic potential. Some plants, like most of the conifers (except juniper and cypress), are great pollen producers but are relatively hypoallergenic. There are thousands of species of anemophilous plants, but only about 100 have significant allergen potential in North America. (See GRASS POLLEN ALLERGY, TREE POLLEN ALLERGY, WEED POLLEN ALLERGY.)

Criteria for classifying an anemophilous plant are: (1) the flowers must be imperfect or unisexual, either pollen producers or recipients; (2) the flowers must be exposed to the wind; (3) petals or sepals are absent or minute, and the flowers are unattractive to both insects and humans; (4) the pollen-producing structures (anthers) and pollen-receiving structures (stigmas) are exposed; (5) there is an absence of odors, nectars, and beautiful colors necessary to attract pollinating insects; (6) the pollen grains are smooth, dry, and small, between 15 to 50 microns (1 micron = 1/25,000 inch) in diameter; (7) the pollen remains attached to the plant, so that a strong wind is required to release it, thus preventing it from falling to the ground in calm air and being unable to reach the plants requiring pollination. (See also POLLEN, POLLEN COUNT, POLLINOSIS.)

anergy The inability of certain individuals to react to a test for hypersensitivity to antigens. Normal individuals almost invariably have positive skin tests to mumps, candida (a common yeast), and tetanus antigens because antibodies to these conditions are present in their blood. However, some skin tests prove negative despite the presence of the antibodies. Several factors influence the possibility of anergy, including the number and type of antigens (bacterial, fungal, or viral) used in the skin test, the characteristics of a positive reaction, and the presence of a mild upper respiratory infection.

Anergy was first noticed when patients with measles lost the ability to react to skin-testing for tuberculosis for a short period of time. Anergy also pertains to one whose skin temporarily does not show a reaction to a tuberculin (e.g., Mantoux) test after receiving a live-attenuated measles, mumps, and rubella (MMR) vaccine. If a tuberculin test is required, it should be administered either before or simultaneously with the MMR vaccine or after three months from the date of the vaccination.

anesthesia, general, for the allergic and asthmatic patient Alternatives to general anesthesia considered for all surgical candidates with allergies or asthma, because any hypersensitivity may be exacerbated by anesthesia drugs with potentially severe results. (The risk of adverse effects of anesthesia, although small, exists even for nonallergic or nonasthmatic normal individuals.) Spinal, epidural, or local anesthesias are excellent choices for many surgical procedures. (See also SURGERY, RELATED TO ALLERGIC AND ASTHMATIC PERSONS.)

anesthetics, local Lotions, creams, ointments, and sprays applied topically in the treatment of local injuries, burns, and insect bites. Other local anesthetics, drugs designed to elim-

LOCAL ANESTHETIC DRUGS

Ester Type (contain para-aminobenzoic esters and may cross-react)

benoxinate (Dorsacaine)

benzocaine[1]

butacaine (Butyn)

butethamine (Monocaine)

butylaminobenzoate (Butesine)

chloroprocaine (Nesacaine)[2]

cocaine

cyclomethycaine (Surfacaine)

hexylcaine (Cyclaine)[4]

procaine (Novocain)[3]

proparacaine (Ophthaine)

tetracaine (Pontocaine)[4]

Amide Type (do not contain para-aminobenzoic esters and do not cross-react)

amethocaine[1]

amydricaine (Alypin)

bupivacaine (Marcaine)

dibucaine (Nupercaine)[3]

dimethisoquin (Quotaine)

diperodan (Diothane)

dyclonine (Dyclone)

etidocaine (Duranest)

lidocaine (Xylocine)[5]

mepivacaine (Carbocaine)

oxethazaine (Oxaine)

phenacaine (Holocaine)

piperocaine (Metycaine)

pramoxine (Tronothane)

prilocaine (Citanest)

pyrrocaine (Endocaine)

[1]More likely to cause contact dermatitis.
[2]May be safest because of its short duration of action.
[3]More likely to cause anaphylaxis or contact dermatitis.
[4]More likely to cause true anaphylaxis.
[5]Most widely used and often combined with epinephrine (Adrenalin), which may be the cause of adverse effects.

inate sensation only in certain areas of the body, may be injected before minor surgery or repair of skin lacerations, or to numb dental tissues before dental surgery.

Snow may have been the first anesthetic agent used and was recognized for its numbing ability by Hippocrates. Cocaine was isolated in 1860 by Niemann from the *Erythroxylon coca* bush. However, the modern era of a local anesthesia was not entered until 1884, when Sigmund Freud and Karl Koller reported the cocaine's ability to numb the eye for surgical procedures.

Although these agents rarely cause true allergic reactions, they often cause vagovagal syncope (fainting spell brought on by a sudden drop in blood pressure), hyperventilation, palpitations, or anxiety reactions. These are non-immune (nonallergic) adverse reactions resulting from excessive doses or other pharmacologic drug reactions easily confused with allergy.

Patients suspected of having a true type I (immediate) allergic reaction to one of these drugs can be tested by injecting them with minute doses, gradually increasing the dose according to standardized protocol. Drugs may cross-react if they belong to the para-aminobenzoic esters group, such as procaine (Novocain) and tetracaine (Pontacaine). Lidocaine (Xylocaine), bupivacaine and others do not cross-react and can usually be substituted for the drug suspected of a reaction without the need for the tedious process of testing and desensitization.

Parabens and other preservatives may be responsible for some adverse reactions rather than the anesthetic drug. Local anesthetics are available in individual, preservative-free dose ampoules. Benzocaine, although commonly used topically for temporary relief of the conditions listed above, may cause a sensitivity reaction of its own and worsen rather than improve the condition for which it is employed. Many allergists and dermatologists warn against their use on the skin; however, drugs like lidocaine offer temporary relief for ulcers of the mouth, rectal lesions, including hemorrhoids, and painful mucous membranes.

Benzocaine, cyclaine, and tetracaine are used to inhibit the cough reflex before invasive diagnostic tests such as bronchoscopy. Another local anesthetic, benzonatate (Tessalon), is available as a prescription cough suppressant.

High-pressure dental equipment can cause air infiltration into local oral tissues, resulting in swelling and wheezing that may be confused with an allergic reaction.

angelica Herbs related to the carrot family whose roots and fruit provide a flavoring oil. The aromatic seeds, leaves, stems, and roots have various medical actions, including the reduction of flatus (intestinal gas), and its bark has emetic and cathartic properties. Angelica is used in inexpensive perfumes and other cosmetic products and may cause a rash upon skin contact and sun exposure. (See PHOTOALLERGIC CONTACT DERMATITIS.)

angioedema, hereditary A rare inherited disorder (genetically known as autosomal dominant) due to the deficiency or malfunction of a substance called C1-esterase inhibitor usually manifesting in late adolescence or early adulthood. Affected persons have less than 15% normal-functioning C1 inhibitor (an inhibitor is a chemical that stops enzyme activity), and family history is positive for this disorder

in 85 to 90% of patients. Lack of C1 inhibitor results in an activation of the complement system (consisting of components related to how antibodies work in the blood) and the release of chemical mediators that produce the symptoms of angioedema (see COMPLEMENT).

The condition is characterized by recurrent episodes of painful swelling of the skin and mucosa of the upper respiratory and gastrointestinal tracts and the extremities. Hereditary angioedema can be triggered by minor trauma, sudden changes in temperature, infections, and emotional upset. An estimated 25% of untreated individuals die of laryngeal edema after dental or throat surgery. Other symptoms include abdominal pain from swelling of intra-abdominal organs, vomiting, diarrhea, and a drop in blood pressure. Unlike idiopathic, or nonhereditary, angioedema, urticaria (hives) and itching do not occur. Diagnosis is made by measuring C1 inhibitor levels, assays that assess functional abnormalities in the presence of normal or near-normal levels of the enzyme, and other complement levels. This life-threatening disease can be treated with synthetic anabolic steroids such as danocrine (Danazol). However, the drug cannot be used in children or adolescents until they have achieved their full growth. Short-term therapy in anticipation of dental or throat surgery includes fresh-frozen plasma given one day prior to surgery. Epsilon-aminocaproic acid and tranexamic acid are drugs sometimes used prior to surgery. Emergency intubation or tracheostomy may be required. (See also ANGIOEDEMA, IDIOPATHIC; ANGIOEDEMA, VIBRATORY; IMMUNE SYSTEM.)

angioedema, idiopathic [nonhereditary angioedemia] Localized swelling of the body involving deeper layers of the skin, subcutaneous and submucosal tissues. The cause is unknown in about 85% of cases. The eyelids, lips, hands, and feet are the areas most commonly involved. Angioedema frequently occurs in association with urticaria, or hives. Hives involve the superficial, or outer, layers of skin. One type of angioedema may be caused by pressure from tight clothing and is referred to as "pressure urticaria and angioedema."

Rarely, angioedema without hives indicates the presence of an underlying malignancy. (See ANGIOEDEMA, HEREDITARY.)

angioedema, nonhereditary   See AN- GIOEDEMA, IDIOPATHIC.

angioedema, vibratory   A rare inherited disorder in which redness and swelling of the skin occur following vibratory stimulation. Usually appearing shortly after birth, it may gradually diminish with age or persist to adult- hood. (See also PHYSICAL URTICARIA.)

angio-neurotic edema   An alternate term for angioedema. (See ANGIOEDEMA, HEREDI- TARY; ANGIOEDEMA, IDIOPATHIC.)

aniline dyes   Indigo pigments derived from coal tar and used to make coal tar coloring agents in the pharmaceutical and cosmetic in- dustries. A synthetic organic dye, aniline in hair-coloring products may cause contact der- matitis.

animal allergy   A reaction occurring from the inhalation of or skin contact with animal proteins in susceptible persons, characterized by typical symptoms of allergy or asthma. Any warm-blooded animal can be a source of aller- gens.

Prevalence   The National Institutes of Health estimates that 43% of American homes have a dog, 28% have cats, and 2% have pet rodents. Although household pets are respon- sible for the greatest number of problems, vet- erinarians, zookeepers, and laboratory and agricultural workers risk significant disability from occupational exposure.

Causes   Although animal allergy is also re- ferred to as "epidermal" (related to the skin) allergy, most important animal allergens are found in the saliva, dander (flaking scales of dead skin similar to dandruff in humans), and urine. Despite widespread belief, animal hair is not highly allergenic. However, saliva from cats and other furry pets who groom them- selves sticks to the hair, and allergens are re- leased into the surrounding air. The airborne allergen (aeroallergen) then becomes part of the house dust inhaled by humans.

Another myth is the "nonallergenic dog." While some allergic persons react more strongly to one breed or another, no warm- blooded animal has been identified not to have caused allergy in a susceptible individual.

Prevention and treatment   Removing the pet for a day or two in order to see if the allergies disappear is not effective. After removal and thorough cleaning of carpets, upholstered fur- niture, ventilation ducts, and heating and air- conditioning filters, it may take as long as six months to rid the home of pet allergens.

Birds and products made from their feathers are also a source of allergen. Feathers remain allergenic years after they have been used to fill down pillows, comforters, or jackets. Although horse-hair mattresses and carpet padding lost a good margin of their popular use in devel- oped countries, these products remain a source of exposure.

If animals cannot be avoided, symptoms from exposure can be prevented or greatly reduced by using preventive or bronchodil- ator and antihistaminic medications. Cromolyn as a metered-dose inhaler (Intal) to prevent asthma, or a nasal spray (Nasalcrom) to prevent nasal allergies, is effective if used prior to exposure.

Special situations may require corticoste- roids (prednisone) to prevent symptoms. For example, if a child known to have severe ani- mal allergies and asthma must spend a few days with a relative who has a cat, the doctor may choose to start prednisone at the first ex- posure rather than risk a severe attack requir- ing hospitalization. This approach might be acceptable management for a brief exposure, but certainly not long term, when the risk of side effects of the prednisone outweighs the benefit.

If continual animal exposure cannot be avoided, immunotherapy (allergy shots) is effective in some cases. Cat allergen is the only standardized animal extract available. (See AEROALLERGENS, FEATHERS, HOUSE DUST ALLERGY, PETS FOR ALLERGIC PERSONS.)

animal models for allergy and immunology research   Armadillos, cattle, cats, dogs, goats, guinea pigs, horses, mice, monkeys, pigs, rats, and sheep used most frequently for study and diagnosis of allergic disorders. Symptoms of allergy experienced by humans can be induced in these animals.

animal products   See ANIMAL ALLERGY, FEATHERS, WOOL.

anise   Fruit and seeds of the umbelliferous plant *Pimpinella anisum* used for food, confectionery, and cosmetic products. Its use in men's fragrances can cause contact dermatitis.

anosmia   The loss of sense of smell. Damage to the olfactory nerve by a brain tumor, injury, or severe allergy may cause permanent loss of smell. Nasal allergy, sinus infections, or colds usually cause a temporary loss. (See also SMELL.)

antagonists   Drugs, such as antihistamines, that block the activity of cells in the immune system by interacting with receptors, structures on the cells' surfaces. For example, antihistamines introduced into the body attach themselves in a lock-and-key fashion to receptors, thus blocking allergens from attaching themselves and triggering allergic symptoms. Other antagonists include the heart drugs beta-blockers and calcium channel blockers and drugs that reverse the actions of narcotics, such as naloxone (Narcan).

anthraquinone   A coal tar dye that may cause allergic contact dermatitis.

antibacterial   See ANTIBIOTIC.

antibiotic   [antibacterial drug, antimicrobial drug]

A substance produced by microorganisms, usually molds or fungi, or produced synthetically, that inhibits the growth of or destroys certain other microorganisms. As early as the 19th century, French chemist Louis Pasteur demonstrated that infections are caused by microorganisms. Robert Koch, a German bacteriologist, isolated and grew some strains of bacteria and identified some as disease-causing bacteria. Paul Ehrlich, a German physician who worked at the Koch Institute for Infectious Diseases in Berlin, introduced the idea that a specific substance could be toxic to some organisms yet harmless to others.

In 1929, Scottish bacteriologist Alexander Fleming accidently discovered that a penicillium mold contaminating a culture plate had killed bacteria. In 1940, the work of Englishman Ernst Chain and Australian Howard W. Florey allowed purified penicillin to be produced. Fleming was later knighted and, with Chain and Florey, received the Nobel Prize for medicine in 1945.

Antibiotics, which literally means "against life," are prescribed as treatments of choice for a wide range of infectious diseases. (See also CEPHALOSPORINS, DRUG ALLERGY AND OTHER ADVERSE DRUG REACTIONS, ERYTHROMYCIN, PENICILLINS, QUINOLONE ANTIBIOTICS, TETRACYCLINES.)

antibody   A substance produced by B cells (lymphocytes derived from the bone marrow) and designed to attack a specific foreign invader called an antigen. For example, a cold virus stimulates a B cell to produce an antibody against that specific virus. The immune process involving antibodies is referred to as humoral immunity.

When a B cell encounters its triggering antigen, T cells and other accessory cells collaborate with it to cause the production of large plasma cells. Each plasma cell becomes a factory for producing antibodies. Antibodies are Y-shaped protein molecules known as immunoglobulins. Transported through the circulation to the site of inflammation or infection, antibodies neutralize or combine with and identify antigens for attack by other cells or chemical mediators. (See ALLERGENS, B CELLS, CHEMICAL MEDIATORS, IMMUNOGLOBULIN A, IMMUNOGLOBULIN E, IMMUNOGLOBULIN G, IMMUNOGLOBULIN M, INFLAMMATION, T CELLS.)

antibody deficiency disorder   Acquired or congenital inability to produce all or selective classes of immunoglobulins. Individuals with this disorder have frequent infections or difficulty overcoming them. Examples are X-linked or Bruton's agammaglobulinemia (lack of gamma globulin antibodies in the blood) and common variable or acquired hypogammaglobulinemia (abnormally low level of gamma globulin in the blood). (See also ACQUIRED IMMUNODEFICIENCY SYNDROME, IMMUNOGLOBULIN A, IMMUNOGLOBULIN D, IMMUNOGLOBULIN G, IMMUNOGLOBULIN M.)

anticholinergics   Bronchodilating drugs that block the action of nerve reflexes that constrict muscles of the bronchial tubes in the lungs. Anticholinergics take 15 to 20 minutes to become effective, as opposed to faster-acting beta-agonists. Atropine and ipratropium (Atrovent) are examples; only Atrovent is available as a metered-dose inhaler (MDI). Adverse effects of anticholinergics, dry mouth and cough, are rarely encountered with ipratropium.

antigen [immunogen]   Any substance that, when introduced into the body, is recognized by the immune system and is capable of triggering an immune response. The term *immune* is derived from the Latin *immunis* (free from taxes or free from burden). An antigen can be a bacterium, fungus, parasite, virus, or a part or substance produced by these organisms. Tissues or cells from another individual, except an identical twin, are recognized by the immune system as foreign and therefore antigenic. (See also ALLERGENS, IMMUNE SYSTEM.)

antigens, cross-reaction among plant families   Allergic reactions that occur from exposure to allergens common to more than one plant family. For example, ragweed, a member of the Ambrosiaceae family, has antigens that cross-react with members of the family Compositae. This cross-reaction explains why ragweed-sensitive persons may react when drinking camomile tea, because camomile is derived from Compositae. Ragweed-sensitive persons also may react to pyrethrum, an insecticide made from chrysanthemums, another member of the Compositae.

Although hay fever sufferers sometimes experience itching and swelling of the palate after eating melons and bananas during the ragweed season, there is no cross-reactivity between ragweed antigen and the botanical families of melon and banana.

antihistamine   Any drug that blocks the effects of histamine, a potent chemical substance produced in the body that is responsible for the body's allergic responses. Also known as H_1 receptor antagonists, antihistamines have been used for nearly 50 years to prevent or relieve the symptoms of immediate, type I hypersensitivity, or anaphylactic allergic reactions. Characteristic symptoms include sneezing, rhinorrhea (watery nasal discharge), congestion, itching, wheezing, and swelling of tissues. During an allergic reaction, allergens bind to histamine type 1 (H_1) receptors on the surface of mast cells and basophils and cause the cells to rupture and release stored histamine and other substances called chemical mediators. Antihistamines bind to these receptors to prevent allergens from binding, which in turn prevents cell rupture and release of the mediators. Histamine blockade of receptors is competitive, and an inadequate dose or a lapse in timing of a dose of antihistamine may result in poor therapeutic response.

Histamine may also be released by other mechanisms during exposures to certain drugs, chemicals, dyes, foods, toxins, alkaloids, venoms, or physical stimuli. Certain foods also contain histamine. Histamine and other released chemical mediators are responsible for the symptoms that occur during anaphylaxis, which may be life-threatening, and antihistamines alone may be inadequate in this situation.

The beneficial effects of antihistamines, as well as any adverse ones, are related to their basic chemical structures. Some antihistamines such as azatadine have a dual action and also prevent the release of the chemical reactors, thus blocking to varying degrees the cascade of events of allergic reaction.

Investigational drugs not yet available in the United States, such as azelestine and ketotifen, have traditional receptor-blocking abilities, but their greatest antiallergic benefits combat inflammatory late-phase reactions (see LATE-PHASE ALLERGIC REACTIONS). Since their primary function is against late-phase reaction, azelestine and ketotifen are not really antihistamines by definition.

Antihistamines are most effective in seasonal allergic rhinitis or hay fever, slightly less effective for perennial or chronic allergic rhinitis, and least likely to improve symptoms of the nonallergic vasomotor and infectious types of rhinitis. Antihistamines are frequently prescribed with nasal decongestants either separately or combined in one tablet, capsule, or liquid preparation (see DECONGESTANTS).

There is no evidence that antihistamines are of any benefit for the treatment of colds, despite their inclusion in many over-the-counter and prescription cold remedies. But an indirect benefit may be attributed to the sedative side effect of most antihistamines, especially when the inducement of drowsiness or sleep is desired. Of the more than 300,000 over-the-counter (OTC) medications available in the United States, excluding the pain relievers aspirin or acetaminophen (Tylenol), six of the 10 largest-selling products in 1990 contained an antihistamine.

The intense pruritus (itching) that accompanies urticaria (hives) and the allergic skin conditions eczema and contact dermatitis are relieved to varying degrees by antihistamines. At night, the added benefit of sedation from the first-generation agents such as hydroxyzine (Atarax) may make them more effective. But the nonsedating astemizole (Hismanal) is effective for suppressing hives and can be given in a single daily dose for convenience. H_1 and H_2 antihistamines (see HISTAMINE H_2 RECEPTOR ANTAGONIST) are sometimes combined in resistant cases of hives.

Minor allergic reactions to insect stings, drugs, foods, and allergy immunotherapy (allergy shots) often respond to antihistamines. When anaphylaxis is impending or has occurred, epinephrine (Adrenalin) should be administered promptly. Diphenhydramine (Benadryl) or other antihistamines are useful only as a secondary treatment.

Prescription and over-the-counter antihistaminic eye drops relieve itching associated with seasonal allergic conjunctivitis (see CONJUNCTIVITIS, ALLERGIC).

Antihistamines are sometimes given prophylactically before a blood transfusion in persons with a history of a prior transfusion reaction. While antihistamine may reduce the itching and flushing that can occur during a transfusion, it does not prevent the serious reactions possible from receiving blood from an incompatible donor.

Many persons experience adverse reactions to radiocontrast (X-ray) dye. Such reactions are complex, and there is a higher incidence in allergic individuals. Antihistamines and corticosteroids should be given to anyone who has had a previous reaction. (See RADIOCONTRAST MEDIA REACTIONS.)

Sedating properties of antihistamines makes them useful as relatively safe, nonhabituating, nonprescription hypnotics. One must be warned, however, that overdoses of these drugs may be fatal. In addition, tolerance develops quickly, limiting their usefulness for chronic insomnia.

Hydroxyzine (Vistaril) and promethazine (Phenergan) are antihistamines often mixed with narcotics such as meperidine (Demerol) to potentiate their effectiveness and also to prevent nausea.

Cyclizine (Marezine), meclizine (Antivert, Bonine), and dimenhydrinate (Dramamine) prevent motion sickness and counteract the disabling vertigo of Meniere's syndrome.

Adverse effects Side effects vary by incidence. Intensity corresponds to the class to which a particular antihistamine belongs. The traditional antihistamines cause drowsiness in many individuals because the drug diffuses into the central nervous system from the general circulating blood, crossing the so-called blood-brain barrier.

Drowsiness varies greatly among individuals, often lessening after several days or disappearing. Great care must be taken when driving or operating dangerous machinery because of impairment of reflexes. Drowsiness intensifies if other sedative drugs or alcohol are used concurrently.

Antihistamines may also disturb coordination and cause dizziness, fatigue, tinnitus (ringing in the ears), diplopia (double vision), and the inability to concentrate.

Instead of sedation from antihistamines, a few individuals, especially infants or toddlers, experience an unexpected excitatory or stimulant effect, at times to the point of insomnia.

Seizures, or convulsions, are a potentially serious adverse effect of antihistamines in some individuals predisposed to them, most often children. Sedation is the most frequent side effect of first-generation antihistamines, also referred to as "classic" or traditional antihistamines, such as chlorpheniramine (Chlor-Trimeton) and dyphenhydramine (Benadryl). Newer antihistamines such as terfenadine (Seldane), astemizole (Hismanal), and the drugs loratadine (Claritin) and cetirizine (Reactin) are generally nonsedating in most persons.

For many years antihistamines were thought to be contraindicated or harmful to persons with asthma. In fact, most over-the-counter and prescription antihistamines come with a warning against their use by these individuals. It was thought that their drying effects would aggravate asthma. Not only has this been disproved, but some antihistamines have mild bronchodilating effects and may actually be beneficial to some asthmatics. Rarely will an antihistamine worsen asthma. The topical use of antihistamines available as over-the-counter remedies for the relief of itching from poison ivy, insect stings, and sunburn should be avoided. These products are skin sensitizers in many persons and frequently cause an allergic contact dermatitis worse than the original condition for which they are recommended.

Anticholinergic, or atropinelike, side effects range from minor dryness of the mucous membranes of the nose, mouth, and throat to constipation, tachycardia (palpitations), excitability, restlessness, nervousness, insomnia, irritability, and tremors. Blurred vision could be a potentially serious problem in a person with untreated or inadequately controlled glaucoma. It is not uncommon for a middle-aged or elderly male to develop a sudden inability to pass urine (acute urinary retention) after taking an antihistamine.

Infrequent gastrointestinal disturbances include anorexia (loss of appetite), nausea, vomiting, abdominal pain, constipation, or diarrhea.

The most important advance since the availability of these important drugs in the 1940s (see "History of Allergy and Immunology") has been the development of the "second-generation" H_1-receptor antihistamines. These newer agents, including terfenadine and astemizole, are nonsedating in up to 99% of users because they do not cross the blood-brain barrier in significant amounts. Some rare side effects of nonsedating antihistamines include increased appetite and weight gain in individuals taking astemizole and hair loss in a few persons taking terfenadine.

A more serious but fortunately an extremely rare problem with both astemizole and terfenadine has been the onset of cardiac arrhythmias (irregularities), including *torsades de pointes*, ventricular tachycardia, and fibrillation, all of which can be life-threatening. Arrhythmias follow doses two or three times the recommended dose. Patients at increased risk have been those also taking the drugs ketoconazole (Nizoral), troleandomycin (TAO), or erythromycin and those with liver diseases such as hepatitis or alcoholic cirrhosis and hypokalemia (a state of low potassium in the blood). (See ASTEMIZOLE, TERFENADINE.)

Rare cases of blood disorders, such as agranulocytosis (a severe depression of the bone marrow's production of granulocytic white blood cells), leukopenia (low leukocytic white blood cell count), thrombocytopenia (destruction or decreased production of platelets), and hemolytic anemia (destruction of the red blood cells), are usually reversible when the offending drug is discontinued.

Considering the millions of doses of these drugs taken every day, the chances of suffering a serious side effect are slim.

Overdose Despite antihistamines' long record of safety, their easy availability makes them popular for suicide attempts. The margin of safety is considerably less for children and thus are more dangerous.

The first signs of overdose usually occur within two hours of ingestion: drowsiness, dizziness, unsteady gait, flushing, dilated pupils, and fever. However, children will often paradoxically appear hyperactive, with hallucinations, toxic psychosis (bizarre behavior), and tremors. In adults, seizures, respiratory failure, cardiac arrest, and death may result.

There is no perfect antidote for antihistamine overdose. Efforts may include eliminating the drug by induced vomiting in a conscious patient or by pumping the stomach in a lethargic or comatose one. Activated charcoal and strong laxatives called cathartics are also given.

The drug physostigmine is sometimes used, but not without risk. It should probably be used only in situations when high temperature or delirium does not respond to cooling by hypothermia blankets, fluids, and cold bathing.

Precautions Antihistamines may mask the early signs of anaphylaxis and should not be used to prevent this reaction when administering immunotherapy (allergy shots).

Use in pregnancy Although the use of drugs during pregnancy, especially during the period of organ development in the first trimester, should be limited, the use of an antihistamine may be unavoidable. Treatment should be based on the same principles for using any drug during pregnancy. Not only must the drug be necessary, but it should have a long record of use during pregnancy without reported adverse outcomes to the pregnancy, and its use must be monitored by a physician experienced in its use during pregnancy. Chlorpheniramine (Chlor-Trimeton) and tripelennamine (Pyribenzamine) are the preferred antihistamines in pregnancy. (See also the table on page 30, PREGNANCY AND RHINITIS, PREGNANCY COMPLICATED BY ASTHMA.)

antihistamine, H$_2$ See HISTAMINE H$_2$ RECEPTOR ANTAGONIST.

anti-inflammatory medications, adverse reactions See ASPIRIN SENSITIVITY.

anti-inflammatory medications, in treatment of allergies and asthma See ASPIRIN THERAPY FOR FOOD INTOLERANCE, CORTICOSTEROIDS, CROMOLYN SODIUM, NONSTEROIDAL ANTI-INFLAMMATORY DRUGS.

antimicrobial See ANTIBIOTIC.

antinuclear antibody tests Laboratory tests for autoantibodies valuable for the diagnosis of autoimmune diseases such as systemic lupus erythematosus (SLE), systemic sclerosis

ANTIHISTAMINES: USES AND SIDE EFFECTS

Chemical Classification	Generic Name (Trade Name)	Anti-allergy Effec-tiveness	Anti-nausea Effects	Sedative Effects	Drying Effects	Gastro-intestinal Effects
Amino alkyl ethers (Ethanolamine)	clemastine fumarate (Tavist), diphenhydramine hydrochloride (Benadryl)	+ to ++[1]	++ to +++	+ to +++	+++	+
Ethylenediamines	pyrilamine maleate (generic), tripelennamine citrate or hydrochloride (PBZ)	+ to ++	0	+ to ++	0 to +	+++
Alkylamines (Propylamines)	brompheniramine maleate (Dimetane), chlorpheniramine maleate (Chlor-Trimeton, Teldrin), dexchlorpheniramine maleate (Polaramine), tripolidine hydrochloride (Actidil) [Other antihistamines of this class usually not used for allergic conditions are not listed.]	++ to +++	0	+ to ++	+	+
Phenothiazines	methdilazine (Tacaryl), promethazine hydrochloride (Phenergan), trimeprazine tartrate (Temaril)	+ to +++	++++	+++	+++	0
Piperidines	azatadine maleate (Optamine), cyproheptadine hydrochloride (Periactin)	++ to +++	0	++ to +++	++ to +++	++ to +++
Piperazines	hydroxyzine (Atarax, Vistaril), phenindamine tartrate (Nolahist)	++ to +++	+++	+ to ++	+ +	0
Nonsedating	acrivastine (Semprex), astemizole (Hismanal), azelestine (Astellin), cetirizine hydrochloride (Zrytec), loratadine (Claritin), terfenadine (Seldane)	++ to +++	0	0 to +	0 to +	0

---

[1] + to ++++ denotes effectiveness of the antihistamine from less effective to very effective.

(scleroderma), rheumatoid arthritis, and others. (See AUTOANTIBODIES, AUTOIMMUNE DISORDER.)

apiol　See PARSLEY OIL.

apnea　A temporary cessation of breathing, usually caused by failure of the respiratory center of the brain to discharge impulses to breathe. Apnea is considered a serious symptom in cardiac, kidney, and arterial disease and in meningitis, and as a result of injury to the brain, including concussion. Healthy children and the elderly may experience apnea during deep stages of sleep.

apple　Fruit borne by the tree of the genus *Malus*, which in persons allergic to birch tree pollen may cause itching of the mouth, palate, and throat.

apple-sorter's disease　Contact dermatitis caused by chemicals used in washing apples.

aquagenic urticaria　A rare type of physical urticaria, or hives. Raised, red, itchy lesions develop on the skin, especially on the upper body, upon exposure of the skin to water of any temperature. The rash appears in two to 30 minutes and lasts for 30 to 60 minutes. Treatment with antihistamines is usually effective. (See PHYSICAL URTICARIA, URTICARIA.)

Aretaeus the Cappadocian　Greek physician (ca. A.D. 120–180) who wrote treatises on causes, symptoms, and treatments of acute and chronic diseases and is credited with the first valid description of asthma. He noted in his writings that exercise or other physical work may induce difficult breathing and that a "sense of suffocation" may occur when a patient reclines. (Aretaeus also refers to orthopnea, which in modern medicine means respiratory discomfort that can be relieved when an individual either stands or sits erect, including the help of props such as pillows. A person may experience relief, for example, by what is called "two-pillow orthopnea.") Also in the writings of Aretaeus are descriptions of

heaviness in the chest, occupational hazards, thickened mucus, coughing and hoarseness, a desire for cold air, expectoration of foamy sputum, and other manifestations of asthma.

Aristacort　See TRIAMCINOLONE.

Arnold's nerve　The auricular branch of the vagus nerve, which, when stimulated, causes coughing. Originating in the medulla oblongata of the brain, the vagus is the 10th cranial (head) nerve, which has the widest distribution in the body of any of the other cranial nerves.

arterial blood gases　(ABGs)　A blood test that determines the body's acid-base balance and the concentrations of the gases oxygen, carbon dioxide, and bicarbonate in the blood. Blood samples are taken from an artery. An ABG test aids in monitoring respiratory failure, because the heart and lungs work to distribute oxygen from inhalation throughout the body via the bloodstream and expel carbon dioxide by exhalation. The normal acid-base balance, also referred to as the pH, or acidity-alkalinity, is 7.39 to 7.41. Asthma, chronic bronchitis, emphysema, diabetes (specifically diabetic ketoacidosis), aspirin poisoning, chronic obstructive lung disease, and symptoms including repeated vomiting may throw ABGs out of the normal range. (See also PREGNANCY COMPLICATED BY ASTHMA.)

Arthus phenomenon　A severe local inflammatory reaction occurring at the site of repeated injection of a nonirritating but antigenic substance, such as egg albumin. It is named after the French physiologist Maurice Arthus (1862–1945).

asbestosis　A lung disease, a variant of pneumoconiosis, resulting from protracted inhalation of asbestos particles (fibrous particles of magnesium and calcium silicate).

aspartame　(Equal, Nutrasweet)　A food additive approved by the Food and Drug Administration (FDA) in 1981 for use as a sweetener in dry foods. Since that time, it has been approved for use in carbonated beverages, fruit juices, iced tea, breath mints, chewing gum, and multivitamins. Aspartame, 180 times sweeter than sugar, is a white, odorless, crystalline powder consisting of two amino acids, L-aspartic acid and L-phenylalanine. The FDA requires the labeling statement "Phenylketonurics: contains phenylalanine" on all products that contain aspartame.

By January 1987, the Centers for Disease Control (CDC) had received about 3,000 reports of adverse effects attributed to aspartame by consumers, their physicians, or other interested parties: 24% were neurologic, 22% headache, 15% gastrointestinal, 10% allergic, 6% behavioral, and 4% seizures. The majority of these reactions were mild, and the CDC reported that there was no conclusive evidence that aspartame was responsible for them. There have been reports of urticaria (hives) caused by aspartame. Generally reactions are thought to be rare, and the FDA has not expressed any reservations to its continued use. (See FOOD ADDITIVES.)

aspergillosis See ALLERGIC BRONCHO-PULMONARY ASPERGILLOSIS.

asphyxia [asphyxiation] Suffocation, a decrease in oxygen and increase in carbon dioxide triggered by an interference with respiration.

aspirin sensitivity Adverse reactions to acetylsalicylic acid (aspirin), namely, two major types of hypersensitivity: respiratory (itching of the eyes, nose, and throat, sneezing, runny nose, coughing, wheezing, and shortness of breath) and skin (hives and angioedema).

Unlike true allergy, a severe adverse reaction may occur with or without prior exposure to aspirin, or related drugs called nonsteroidal anti-inflammatory drugs (NSAIDs), or the related food additive, tartrazine (Yellow Food Dye No. 5). Aspirin sensitivity may be due to the inhibition of the enzyme cyclo-oxygenase in as many as 20% of adults with asthma, who may experience a severe and potentially life-threatening attack after taking aspirin or an NSAID such as ibuprofen. Reactions are more common in severe asthmatics. Therefore it is recommended that all persons with asthma avoid aspirin and NSAIDs unless otherwise directed by a physician.

Some individuals experience hives only after reexposure to aspirin or a single NSAID, whereas others become sensitive after developing chronic hives for another reason.

Analgesics such as acetaminophen (Tylenol) and nonacetylated salicylates (choline magnesium trisalicylate [Trilisate], salsalate [Disalcid], and sodium salicylate [Pabalate]) do not exhibit this mechanism and are usually safe. However, these alternative drugs also trigger asthma in a few individuals. In the event

LIST OF DRUGS TO AVOID IN ASPIRIN-SENSITIVE PERSONS

aspirin
diclofenac sodium (Voltaren)
etodolac (Lodine)
fenoprofen (Nalfon)
ibuprofen (Advil, Medaprin, Motrin, Nuprin)
indomethacin (Indocin)

meclofenamate (Meclomen)
mefenamic acid (Ponstel)
nabumetone (Relafen)
naproxen (Anaprox, Naprosyn)
piroxicam (Feldene)
sulindac (Clinoril)
tolmetin (Tolectin)

Note: Check the labels of any over-the-counter medications for the presence of aspirin or ibuprofen.

aspirin is required for severe arthritis or other conditions, oral desensitization (giving gradually increasing doses of the allergic substance to develop a tolerance) to aspirin and NSAIDs is possible in those with asthma. Because of its high risk, desensitization should only be done by specially trained physicians in an environment where resuscitation equipment is present. There is no evidence that desensitization for aspirin-induced hives is effective. (See ASPIRIN TRIAD.)

aspirin therapy for food intolerance   Aspirin or related nonsteroidal anti-inflammatory drugs (NSAIDS) prescribed to relieve nausea, vomiting, colicky abdominal pain and distention, and diarrhea in a group of persons with food intolerance. In these patients, adverse effects seem to be related to abnormal levels of prostaglandins in the intestines. Caution must be exhibited to assure that patients given this therapy are not sensitive to aspirin or NSAIDS. None of the patients showed evidence of allergy and had normal immunoglobulin E levels and negative skin tests. Researchers do not consider this to be a type I hypersensitivity reaction.

aspirin triad   Asthma complicated by nasal polyps and aspirin sensitivity. However, there are many persons with asthma and nasal polyps who can tolerate aspirin, and others with asthma and aspirin sensitivity who do not have nasal polyps. As a rule, it is usually advisable for any person with asthma to use aspirin and related drugs with caution.

Astelin Nasal Spray   Brand name for azelestine, the only antihistamine approved for topical use in the United States. (See AZELESTINE.)

astemizole (Hismanal)   A nonsedating (second-generation) antihistamine, prescribed for allergic rhinitis and hives, that may take several days to become effective. Astemizole remains in the body for a prolonged period and may suppress hypersensitivity skin-test results for as long as four weeks. It may not be used simultaneously with the antibiotic erythromycin or in persons with severe liver disease because of the possibility of episodes of cardiac arrhythmias. (See ANTIHISTAMINE.)

asthma   A chronic lung disease characterized by recurrent attacks of breathlessness, airways (bronchial tubes) that become hyperactive and constrict when exposed to a variety of stimuli or "triggers," obstruction of the bronchioles that is reversible (but not completely in some patients) either spontaneously or with treatment, and inflammation of the airways. *Asthma* derives from the Greek word for panting.

Cause   The basic cause of asthma is not yet known. The airways of the asthmatic are hyperactive (twitchy) and overly responsive to environmental changes or stimuli called triggers. Triggers result in wheezing and coughing that some researchers think may be set off by an abnormal reaction to sensory nerves in the lungs. As the attack progresses, chemical mediators are released from cells lining the bronchioles, causing inflammation that leads to contraction of airway muscle, production of mucus, and swelling in the airways.

Asthma can be classified as either extrinsic (triggered by outside influences such as allergy) or intrinsic (from within). Each asthmatic reacts to a different set of triggers. Identification of a person's personal triggers is a major step toward learning to control asthma attacks. Although episodes can sometimes be triggered by strong emotions, asthma is not caused by emotional factors, such as a troubled parent-child relationship. However, researchers at the Children's National Medical Center in Washington and the National Jewish Center for Immunology and Respiratory Medicine in Denver have found a relationship between family stress and the onset of asthma by age three in genetically predisposed children. Three factors—marital discord, prolonged maternal depression, and parental problems in day-to-day care of the child—significantly increased asthma predisposition in genetically at-risk children from 17% (if one or none of these stress factors was present) to 42% (if at least two of the risk factors were present). Asthma is a disease, not a psychogenic illness or a sign of emotional instability.

Severity There are great variations in asthma severity from person to person and in the individual asthmatic from time to time. Symptoms range from mild to severe and can become life-threatening. The frequency of episodes ranges from one occurrence in a lifetime to daily attacks. The individual attack may be short-lived, lasting from a few minutes to a few hours, or continuous, with daily symptoms for days or weeks. A severe, continuous state of asthma is referred to as "status asthmaticus."

In one study of more than 300 asthma patients, researchers found that only 54% accurately estimated the severity of their asthma and 27% overestimated the severity. The 20% who underestimated the severity of their asthma were considered to be at a greater risk for suffering a life-threatening attack.

Treatment principles and goals Guidelines for the treatment of asthma have been developed by experts selected to serve on the National Asthma Education Program. The four basic steps in the treatment of asthma are: (1) education of the patient and family; (2) control of the environment; (3) a comprehensive drug regimen that may include immunotherapy (allergy shots); and (4) objectively monitoring progress.

The goals of therapy are to maintain normal or near-normal activity levels including exercise; maintain normal or near-normal lung function test results; prevent coughing, shortness of breath, waking up at night, and loss of time at school or work; prevent the need for emergency room visits or hospitalizations; and avoid medication side effects.

The National Asthma Education Program emphasizes an understanding of asthma by each patient and family members. An educated patient is better able to anticipate and thus avoid situations that might trigger or worsen asthma.

The symptoms of asthma are a major cause of sleep disturbances and time lost from school and work. Although asthma cannot be cured, the symptoms can almost always be controlled with proper treatment. (See also ASTHMA DRUGS.)

Differential diagnosis Asthma may resemble, and can be confused with or might coexist with, other respiratory problems such as emphysema, bronchitis, and lower respiratory tract infection. At times, the only symptom of asthma is a persistent cough, usually at night. In some individuals, coughing and wheezing may occur only with exercise.

In infants and children, symptoms suggestive of asthma must be differentiated from many other conditions that cause wheezing. The sudden onset of unremitting wheezing in an infant or small child may point to an obstruction of the large airways by a foreign body lodged in the trachea, bronchus, or esophagus until proven otherwise. Laryngo-tracheo-bronchomalacia is a congenital disorder involving the softening of cartilage that may be associated with asthma and increased incidence of respiratory infections during a child's first two years.

Croup, caused by a respiratory virus, or acute epiglottitis, a serious bacterial infection that can threaten life (see CROUP; EPIGLOTTITIS, ACUTE), can be confused with asthma because inspiratory wheezing is common to both. Cystic fibrosis (CF) may coexist with asthma and should be suspected in any infant with failure to thrive (poor growth) and recurrent respiratory infections (see CYSTIC FIBROSIS). In older children and adolescents, CF should be suspected in asthmatic patients who have had recurrent pneumonia.

Mitral valve prolapse, which occurs commonly in slender adolescents (females more than males) and causes chest pain during strenuous exercise, may be confused with exercise-induced asthma. It is characterized by a systolic click heard in the mitral area with a stethoscope; diagnosis is confirmed by an

GUIDELINES FOR ESTIMATING THE SEVERITY OF AN ASTHMA ATTACK IN CHILDREN BY NONMEDICAL INDIVIDUALS

Sign/Symptom	Mild	Moderate	Severe
Peak flow[1] % of predicted or personal best	70–90%	50–70%	Less than 50%
Respiratory rate (respirations per minute)[2]	Normal to 30% increase above normal	30–50% above	Increased over 50%
Alertness	Normal	Normal	May be decreased
Degree of breathing difficulty	None or mild; speaks in complete sentences	Moderate; speaks in phrases or partial sentences; infant's cry softer, with difficulty suckling or feeding	Severe; speaks single word or short phrases; infant's cry softer; infant's stop feeding
Accessory muscle use	None to mild	Moderate; chest hyperflated	Severe; chest hyperflated; nasal flaring
Color	Good	Pale	Possibly cyanotic
Chest sounds	Minimal wheeze	Wheezing with inspiration and expiration	May be inaudible

Note: Trained personnel can also assess arterial blood gases and pulsus paradoxus (see PULSUS PARADOXUS and ARTERIAL BLOOD GASES).

[1]Peak flow can be measured with an inexpensive portable meter, which should be made available to any moderate or severe asthma patient (see PEAK FLOW METER).

[2]See RESPIRATORY RATE for normal values.

Source: Adapted from the *Guidelines for the Diagnosis and Management of Asthma*, National Asthma Education Program.

echocardiogram. Hyperventilation syndrome may be misdiagnosed or coexist with asthma, especially in adolescents. The patient typically appears anxious and breathless but without wheezing. A complaint of tingling of the fingers and toes is common. Treatment consists of reassurance and having the patient rebreathe into a paper bag to elevate carbon dioxide levels. Recurrences may require psychological counseling and possibly antianxiety drugs.

In adults, asthma is often confused with the other common lung diseases, emphysema and chronic bronchitis, which to some degree act like asthma. The hallmark of the three lung diseases is airway obstruction. The principal difference in the conditions is the degree of reversibility of the airway obstruction.

A patient with asthma should have normal airflow between attacks. Chronic bronchitis is characterized by obstruction to varying degrees but usually is not completely reversible with treatment. The obstruction found in patients with emphysema is irreversible by definition. However, most patients fall between these strict limits. (See BRONCHITIS, CHRONIC; EMPHYSEMA.)

Asthma may be hard to diagnose and is greatly underdiagnosed. To distinguish asthma from other lung diseases, doctors rely on a combination of the patient's medical history (the patient's recount of his or her symptoms and past disorders), a thorough physical examination, and certain tests: measurement of airflow into and out of the lungs (see PEAK FLOW METER, SPIROMETRY), chest X rays, blood tests, and skin tests. Sometimes challenges with methacholine (a drug that constricts the bronchi in persons with asthma) are indicated (see METHACHOLINE CHALLENGE).

asthma, early warning signs   Symptoms or signals indicating the onset or potential onset of an asthma attack. It is unusual to have a sudden life-threatening attack of asthma without warning signs. Usually signs of an impending asthma attack manifest hours or even days before a full-blown attack develops.

Every asthma patient should have an emergency strategy preplanned with his or her physician. The National Asthma Education Program recommends the use of peak flow meters to follow the progress of an asthma attack. There are inexpensive portable devices to measure the peak flow (airflow in the bronchial tubes). Use of a peak flow meter can be a valuable guide with which to follow a person's progress. Worsening of asthma can usually be detected in time to take corrective measures. (See NATIONAL ASTHMA EDUCATION PROGRAM, PEAK FLOW METER.)

WARNING

Because individuals vary, PATIENTS SHOULD KNOW THEIR OWN SIGNS OF AN IMPENDING ATTACK. The initial sign may be itching of the face or throat, a feeling of tightness in the chest, and mild wheezing. This is the time to act to prevent progressive or sudden worsening of the attack. EARLY INTERVENTION IS THE KEY TO PREVENTING THE NEED FOR EMERGENCY TREATMENT AND ASTHMA FATALITIES.

---

asthma, extrinsic   A form of asthma caused by allergens found in the environment, such as seasonal or perennial allergens such as house-dust mites, but can be triggered by a perennial allergen. A greater percentage of children (up to 85%) than adults (about 50%) suffer from extrinsic asthma. Extrinsic asthmatics usually have positive skin or radioallergosorbent (RAST) tests, but not every asthma patient suffers from allergies.

asthma, food-related   Foods blamed as a cause of asthma. Foods were cited for allergic reactions by patients almost four times as often as allergic rhinitis. However, most experts feel the true incidence of food-induced asthma is much less frequent. In double- blind food challenges (tests in which a suspected allergenic food or placebo is given to a patient and monitored for reaction), symptoms of asthma could only be confirmed in 25 to 33% of the children.

Most cases of food hypersensitivity stem from milk allergy in early infancy. Many adverse food reactions are probably caused by food additives or preservatives such as sulfites, bisulfites, and metabisulfites. (See FOOD ADDITIVES, FOOD ALLERGY, SULFITING AGENTS.)

asthma, intrinsic   Asthma caused by factors other than allergy. Intrinsic asthma occurs in less than 50% of adults and in about 15% of children with asthma. Some children from infancy experience wheezing triggered only by viral respiratory infections. Other children and adults suffer asthma triggered by irritants, emotional factors, and other nonallergenic stimuli. Many of those with intrinsic asthma have nasal polyps and sensitivity to aspirin. Skin tests for allergy are usually negative in these persons, but it is possible to have both intrinsic and extrinsic asthma.

asthma, late-phase reaction   See   LATE-PHASE ALLERGIC REACTIONS.

asthma camps   Recreational facilities that provide a safe, medically supervised, and enjoyable experience for children with asthma who would otherwise be unable to attend camps.

Parameters for the operation of asthma camps have been established by the Consortium on Children's Asthma Camps.

Camp Broncho Junction, formerly in Red House, West Virginia, was a pioneering, 16-year effort. The founders, Dr. Merle S. Scherr and his late wife, Lois, conducted psychological evaluations of the campers in the areas of behavioral and sociopsychological adjustment and provided a sharp profile not only of the individual patients but of the group as a whole. Psychological evaluation was implemented through personal interviews by clinical psychologists and psychiatrists, testing with the California Test of Personality, and counselors' ratings. The results point toward a more realistic and positive integration of the children's physical problems into their total lifestyle. When the children were separated into two groups, those with severe asthma and those with the least severe asthma, improvement was especially striking in the most severe group. Group therapy sessions with children and families and weekend therapy sessions also contributed to patient improvement. The following bar graph demonstrates the benefits that can be derived from a camping experience.

asthma cost Moneys spent on asthma-related health care in the United States. In 1988, the last year for which statistics are available, more than $4 billion was spent on asthma-related health care in the United States, an increase from $2.65 billion in 1985.

asthma death prevention The avoidance of death from asthma by heeding precautionary measures, the principal goal of the National Asthma Education Program. Complacency fosters the highest risk. Education of the patient and the family is paramount.

Other guidelines include identification of triggers at home, school, or work; development of effective and simple drug regimens for the

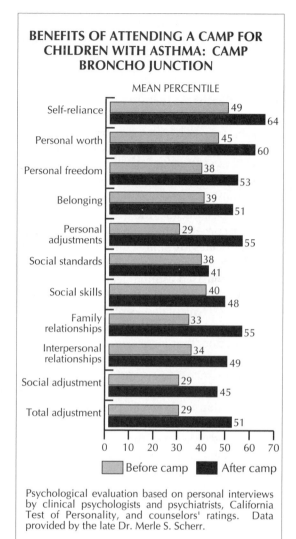

BENEFITS OF ATTENDING A CAMP FOR CHILDREN WITH ASTHMA: CAMP BRONCHO JUNCTION

MEAN PERCENTILE

	Before camp	After camp
Self-reliance	49	64
Personal worth	45	60
Personal freedom	38	53
Belonging	39	51
Personal adjustments	29	55
Social standards	38	41
Social skills	40	48
Family relationships	33	55
Interpersonal relationships	34	49
Social adjustment	29	45
Total adjustment	29	51

Psychological evaluation based on personal interviews by clinical psychologists and psychiatrists, California Test of Personality, and counselors' ratings. Data provided by the late Dr. Merle S. Scherr.

patient to follow; close monitoring of medication dosage adjustments; monitoring effectiveness of advised environmental control measures; monitoring symptoms objectively with doctor's office spirometry and home peak flow meters, devices that accurately measure breathing status; identifying high-risk individuals and providing psychological support utilizing mental health and social services personnel; preparation, frequent review, and revision as necessary of a crisis management plan for the patient and his or her family; aggressive, prompt treatment of acute episodes; and primary care coordinated with a specialist in asthma.

asthma deaths   Mortality as a result of asthma. Minorities from inner-city neighborhoods have a much higher proportion of asthma deaths than whites. In Chicago in a five-year period, 90% of all asthma deaths were persons in minority groups, although minorities accounted for only 40% of the total population.

In the past decade, the greatest increase in deaths occurred in those older than 65 years of age. Nonwhites are almost three times as likely to die from asthma as whites. However, despite recently increased asthma deaths, the number of such deaths in the United States—approximately 4,500 (calculated as of 1988)—is one of the lowest numbers of asthma deaths in the world. Factors that increase risk for a fatal attack of asthma include age over 65, ethnicity (nonwhite race), previous life-threatening asthma attack(s), hospital admission for asthma within the last year, psychological and psychosocial problems, lack of access to medical care, and abuse of asthma drugs.

Age   In the past decade (1980–90), the greatest increase in asthma deaths is seen in older age groups. There has also been a significant trend in deaths among those from five to 34 years of age during the same period.

Ethnicity   African-Americans have almost three times the rate of asthma deaths as Caucasians for all ages. However, in age group 15 to 44, the rate increases to five times the rate for Caucasians.

Previous episodes of life-threatening asthma   Persons who have required intubation and a respirator for respiratory failure, or who have suffered respiratory acidosis (see ARTERIAL BLOOD GASES) in the past, are at increased risk to die from a similar episode.

Hospital admission within the last year   Persons hospitalized within the previous year for asthma were more likely to die from asthma, as well as those with more than two hospitalizations for severe asthma and patients on oral corticosteroid therapy.

Psychological and psychosocial problems   There is an association between children dying suddenly from asthma and prior expressions of hopelessness, despair, and a wish to die. Unemployment, alcohol abuse, recent family loss, recognizable depression, and schizophrenia increase the risk of sudden and unexpected death from asthma for adults.

Lack of access to medical care   Many poor families in urban neighborhoods lack a regular family doctor or asthma specialist. Treatment is often delayed until the patient's diagnosis is status asthmaticus (severe unrelenting asthma). Patients usually seek emergency room medical care only during a crisis. In rural areas, a similar situation can arise because of the great distance to a medical facility or lack of a specialist. Lack of prevention and knowledge of asthma may prevail in any environment.

Overuse of medication   A Canadian study, based on health insurance records of 12,300 asthma patients between 1978 and 1987, demonstrated twice the risk of a fatal or near-fatal asthma attack in patients overusing certain medications. The use of twice the maximum recommended dose of a beta$_2$-agonist metered-dose inhaler was considered the causative factor in this increased risk. (See BETA-ADRENERGIC AGONISTS.)

asthma drugs   Medications prescribed when the symptoms of asthma cannot be prevented by controlling the environment or other triggers such as a viral respiratory infection. The medicines used depend on the frequency and severity of symptoms and may be therapeutic or preventive, or both.

Bronchodilators are chosen for their ability to prevent or reverse airway obstruction. They include beta-adrenergic agonists such as albuterol, metaproterenol, and pirbuterol; methylxanthines such as theophylline; and the anticholinergics atropine and ipratropium.

Anti-inflammatory agents interrupt the development of bronchial inflammation and also act to prevent asthma attacks. These drugs include corticosteroids (cortisonelike drugs), cromolyn, and others that are still investigational.

Beta-agonists alone may be all the therapy necessary for mild, episodic asthma. Metered-dose inhalers (MDIs) on an as-needed, or "PRN," basis are the first line of therapy. These drugs are also taken before exercise or sports to prevent symptoms. Their prolonged use at regular four- to six-hour intervals has been associated with some diminished control of asthma, and the recommended three to four doses a day should rarely be exceeded. Overuse of beta-agonists has been associated with increased risk of death from asthma. (See ASTHMA DEATHS, BETA-ADRENERGIC AGONISTS.)

Oral dosage forms of beta-agonists are also available as short-acting (six to eight hours duration of action) or sustained-release (lasting up to 12 hours) tablets. When both dosage forms of beta-agonists are taken simultaneously, the MDI is reserved for acute episodes or prior to exercise.

Theophylline is the most widely used methylxanthine. It is available in tablet, capsule, and liquid forms, which are short- or long-acting, and for many years was the prime drug for the treatment of asthma. A related drug, aminophylline, is available for intravenous use but is rarely used orally. Theophylline and aminophylline have come under scrutiny because of the frequency of adverse effects, especially in infants.

The 1991 asthma expert panel report from the National Institutes of Health relegates the methylxanthine drugs to a secondary or tertiary role behind beta-agonists and the anti-inflammatory medications. The methylxanthines are thought to inhibit phosphodiesterases, enzymes implicated as a cause of asthma. These drugs dilate constricted bronchioles. Long-acting forms are most useful in preventing nighttime awakening from asthma. In addition, they reduce respiratory muscle fatigue and have a mild degree of anti-inflammatory activity. Close monitoring of blood levels can usually avoid the most serious complications of these drugs. (See THEOPHYLLINE.)

The inhaled anticholinergic ipratropium, an atropinelike drug, is a weak bronchodilator that also blocks reflex bronchoconstriction by inhaled irritants. Although it is less effective than other bronchodilators, ipratropium lacks side effects and is useful in the few individuals who cannot tolerate other drugs. (See IPRATROPIUM.)

Corticosteroids are the most effective anti-inflammatory drugs for the treatment of asthma. They can be given orally as tablets or liquids, by injection, or topically as aerosol metered-dose inhalers.

Despite the fear of adverse effects, systemic corticosteroids, when used appropriately early in an asthma attack, prevent progression and lessen the need for emergency room visits and hospitalizations, and they may be life-saving. In severe asthmatics, they may be required daily or on alternate days.

Inhaled corticosteroids are safe and effective as preventive therapy and are first-line therapy for anyone with frequent symptoms of asthma. In recommended doses, side effects are usually limited to local irritation of the pharynx, though this can be prevented by rinsing the mouth after each use or by using a spacer device. Spacers allow active medication to be inhaled, while irritating larger particles settle in the chamber of the spacer. In addition to reducing adverse effects, they allow poorly coordinated persons, often including young children, to use metered-dose inhalers effectively. (See CORTICOSTEROIDS, SPACER.)

Cromolyn sodium is a preventive, anti-inflammatory drug causing no serious side effects, administered by metered-dose inhaler or nebulizer. It is most effective in children, but not all patients respond to it. (See CROMOLYN SODIUM.)

Asthma Poster Child   See NATIONAL ASTHMA AND ALLERGY POSTER CHILD.

asthma prevalence   An estimated 10 million persons in the United States have asthma. The incidence is higher in children but is equally distributed among males and females. Blacks have a 4.4% rate of asthma, whites 4.0%.

African-Americans are three times as likely to die from asthma as are whites of all ages, but this incidence increases to five times in ages 15 to 44.

Since 1970, the prevalence of asthma has increased from 30.1 per 1,000 persons to 36.6 per 1,000 in 1985. Increases in asthma prevalence have been reported in all ages, races, and both sexes. Individuals with asthma require more than 100 million days of restricted activity per year.

asthma prevention   Methods of staving off asthma attacks, specifically recognizing an individual's "triggers" (see TRIGGERS OF ALLERGIES AND ASTHMA). Taking measures to avoid or limit exposure to the triggers is optimal but may be impractical or impossible to achieve in many situations.

In addition, environmental factors greatly influence severity and the need for hospitalization. In New York City, hospital asthma admissions were strongly associated with premature birth and passive smoking, which was the most important environmental factor, manifesting in 62% of admissions. Carpeting in the bedrooms of 35% of hospitalized children younger than three ranked as the second most significant environmental factor. Simple and inexpensive measures—limiting exposure to tobacco smoke and removing carpeting—are very effective.

When triggers cannot be avoided, use of preventive medications such as cromolyn sodium, corticosteroid metered-dose inhalers, and other antiallergy and antiasthma medications and allergy immunotherapy can limit or prevent symptoms.

The development of asthma as a disease cannot be prevented, but attacks can often be prevented or at least the severity of an attack can be lessened. (See also BETA-ADRENERGIC AGONISTS, CROMOLYN SODIUM, CORTICOSTEROIDS, IMMUNOTHERAPY.)

TRIGGER PREVENTION PLAN

1. If exposures to triggers can be anticipated, start to use cromolyn nasal spray and/or cromolyn metered-dose inhaler and an antihistamine at least one day before an expected exposure and continue throughout the exposure.
2. Use a beta-agonist and/or cromolyn metered-dose inhaler 10 to 15 minutes before exercise orsports for individuals who have exercise-induced asthma (EIA).

PREVENTION OF ASTHMA ATTACKS

1. Identify and avoid personal asthma triggers.
2. If exercise is a trigger, use your medication beforehand (see EXERCISE, EXERCISE-INDUCED ASTHMA).
3. Take prescribed medicines on time, in the correct dose, and in the correct way.
4. Know the early warning signs of asthma.
5. Take peak flow meter readings to monitor lung function.
6. Ask your doctor for a preventive plan to manage or ward off an attack before it gets serious.
7. Stay calm if an attack is coming on, know your plan, and act on it.
8. Do not delay getting to the emergency room if your attack is worsening. Most asthma deaths can be prevented by early intervention. DO NOT WAIT.
9. Stay healthy. Get enough rest, eat properly, drink plenty of liquids, and exercise regularly.
10. Air-conditioning systems in your home and car may help alleviate allergy and asthma symptoms, but be certain that the air that is cooled is not being drawn in from the outside or contaminated with molds.

asthma referral and information hot line
A telephone service sponsored by the American Academy of Allergy and Immunology. For the name of an allergist in your area, call 1-800-822-ASMA.

asthma statistics   Data collected by researchers that give an overview on asthma. For example, it is estimated that about 15 million Americans have asthma. There was a 29% increase in Americans with asthma from 1980 to 1987. During that same period, asthma mortality increased by 31%, from 2,891 deaths in 1980 to 4,360 in 1987 and 4,580 in 1988, according to data from the National Institutes of Health. Asthma is the most frequent cause of hospital admissions for children and the greatest cause of time lost from school for childhood diseases. More than 100 million restricted activity days and six million days of bed-rest confinement annually in the United States are linked with asthma.

Studies also show that asthma patients made 6.5 million office visits to private physicians, five million visits to hospital outpatient clinics, and 1.5 million emergency room visits in 1985. Asthma accounted for almost 1% of all outpatient visits to physicians that year; the visits generated 11.5 million prescriptions. By 1988, physician visits had increased to almost 15 million, 35% of which were for patients younger than 20 years of age. In 1987, asthma ranked as the primary diagnosis in more than 450,000 hospitalizations. Hospitalization among children under the age of 15 has been increasing, and from 1979 to 1987, the rate of asthma admissions rose 43%. Asthma is more prevalent in black children six to 11 years of age than whites (9.4 to 6.2%). Hospitalization rates are greater for Hispanics than white non-Hispanics.

asthmatic breathing   Harsh breathing, often characterized by wheezing and prolonged expiration.

asthma treatment   See ASTHMA DRUGS, AVOIDANCE OF ALLERGENS.

asthma triggers   See TRIGGERS OF ALLERGIES AND ASTHMA.

Atarax See HYDROXYZINE.

atelectasis   A partial or total collapse of the lung that may be caused by mucous plugs, excessive secretions, foreign-body obstruction, or compression of the bronchus by enlarged lymph nodes, tumors, or aneurysms. Atelectasis in varying degrees is often present during asthma attacks, particularly in children. Symptoms range from none to breathlessness. The X-ray appearance of atelectasis may be confused with the markings, or infiltrates, in the lungs associated with pneumonia. (See also PNEUMOTHORAX.)

atmiatrics [atmotherapy]   Therapeutic treatment with medicated vapors.

atmotherapy See ATMIATRICS.

atomizer See NEBULIZER.

atopic dermatitis [allergic dermatitis, eczema, eczematous dermatitis]   A skin condition characterized by intense itching and most common in early childhood. Atopic dermatitis is usually chronic but with varying periods of intensity, depending on the presence of triggering stimuli.

Prevalence and genetics Between 1 and 5% of all infants are affected. If one parent has allergies or has had a history of any allergic disease, there is about a 50% chance their children will have allergies, including eczema. If both parents have allergies, a 75% chance exists for their offspring to develop allergies. Between 50 and 80% of children with atopic dermatitis will eventually develop allergic rhinitis (hay fever) or asthma. If no family member has had eczema or other allergies, the diagnosis of eczema must be questioned. Allergic eczema usually occurs between the sixth week of life and one year. It rarely begins after the fifth year. Eczema accounts for approximately 1% of all office visits to pediatricians.

Cause Although the cause of eczema is unknown, it is known that certain situations trigger episodes of eczema, such as cold air, dry skin, emotional stress, foods, house dust mites, animal dander, skin infection, and irritants. Heat, perspiration, and pollen are less frequently involved.

For many years, it has been an accepted principle that the onset of atopic dermatitis was brought on by contact between the offending allergen and mast cells in the skin, causing an immediate hypersensitivity (allergic) reaction through the release of chemical mediators such as histamine into local tissues. Studies in the 1990s, however, indicate that T cells play an important role in the cause of eczema. Cytokines derived from T cells stimulate mast cell proliferation, which in turn releases histamine that dilates tiny blood vessels. Erythema, or redness, and leaking of fluid from these blood vessels result in intense itching, edema, and swelling. This initial reaction is usually evident within 15 to 60 minutes of exposure to a triggering food or other allergen and subsides in 90 minutes.

Up to four hours later, mild itching usually marks the onset of a second or late-phase reaction. Eosinophils and neutrophilic and other white blood cells are attracted to the inflamed areas of the rash. The delayed response may last up to two days, and the rash may become worse. (See TRIGGERS OF ALLERGIES AND ASTHMA.)

Diagnosis and characteristics Unlike other skin diseases, eczema carries no unique or distinctive rash. Affected areas of the skin range from one or more small, localized patches to a generalized rash. The skin can be erythematous, or reddened, and edematous (swollen with fluid); excoriations (scratch marks) may become crusty with oozing of pus in its acute phase. Itching, scratching, and rubbing often lead to secondary bacterial infections. A chronic state escalates to scaling, lichenification (thickening of the skin), and hyperpigmentation (deepened skin coloration) with fissuring of the involved area.

Since 1892, when the disease was first described, it has been associated with allergic individuals, and food allergies have been strongly implicated as a trigger in infants and young children. Studies by Dr. Hugh Sampson and associates at Duke University in 1985 found that 63 (56%) of a group of children with severe eczema had 101 positive food challenges. Of these 101 reactions, 85 (84%) developed skin rashes. Others developed abdominal pain, nausea, and diarrhea, or rhinitis (runny nose or nasal congestion), cough, and wheezing.

Dr. Sampson demonstrated that the patient recall of foods consumed often failed to correspond with their symptoms. In addition, positive skin and other tests were not accurate in predicting reactions. Despite this, negative skin tests almost certainly exclude food as a cause of food allergy in eczema. It was concluded that a child younger than seven years of age with severe eczema has a greater than 50% chance of having food allergy.

Most of these children react to only one or two foods, even though they will skin-test positive to many others. Egg, peanut, and milk are responsible for nearly 75% of the allergic reactions.

Although positive skin tests to certain foods cross-reacted with other foods of the same plant families, challenges demonstrated that children may be intolerant to one food in a class but tolerant of another in the same category. For example, egg- sensitive individuals may ingest chicken with no adverse effects.

In children four to 10 years of age, the rash of eczema predominantly affects the face, especially around the mouth. In older children and young adults, flexor, or inner, aspects of the elbows and knees, face, neck, upper torso, hands, and feet are most often affected. Eczema is often confused with other rashes, but even though it waxes and wanes, it almost always recurs.

Outcome Food sensitivity disappears over time in about one-third of children with eczema, although the reason for this is not understood, and diet restrictions can then be abandoned. Soy allergy improves in up to 50% of those afflicted within one year, but peanut and fish sensitivity seems to persist for prolonged periods. Despite loss of sensitivity to an offending food, skin tests generally remain positive.

Treatment Treatment for eczema includes avoiding an offending food or foods known to cause a person's symptoms. This is the only proven treatment. Strict dietary adherence may result in total or partial improvement within days. Some persons are susceptible to other triggers, such as extremes of temperature, animal danders, and stress.

Antihistamines, moisturizing lotions, and corticosteroid creams and ointments provide limited relief. Systemic, oral or injectable, corticosteroids should be avoided except in extreme cases. In severe cases, a short hospital stay may allow removal from damaging environmental triggers and allow significant improvement.

Antibiotics are needed when eczema is complicated by infection. Cyclosporin, an immunosuppressant drug (blocks immune response) used to prevent rejection of organ transplantations, has been found to be effective in some resistant patients. Immune- modulating (enhancing) agents such as interferon-μ (IFN-μ) and thymopentin (TP-5) may exert a beneficial effect on T cells and eosinophils. Intravenous immunoglobulin therapy may prove to be effective, but its use is experimental and very expensive.

Grenz rays are safe, highly filtered X rays with penetration limited to the skin. These rays have an anti-inflammatory action that has been used for many years by dermatologists for severe cases of eczema. This treatment is usually given in a course of four to six treatments at two-week intervals. Grenz ray therapy is also useful for the treatment of psoriasis and seborrheic dermatitis.

Prevention Breast-feeding is probably the best way to prevent the onset of eczema. However, the mother must avoid highly allergenic foods, especially eggs, cow's milk, and fish, or the infant may develop classic eczema directly from breast milk exposure or upon the infant's first oral exposure. In one study group, eczema was reduced by more than 50% from the control group when mothers avoided milk, egg, peanut, fish, and beef during pregnancy and lactation, exclusively breast-fed, and delayed introduction of solid food in high-risk infants. Although breast-feeding and delay of introducing solid foods most likely do not prevent the eventual onset of allergy, they may eliminate the most severe phase of infantile eczema.

atopy   The state of hypersensitivity or allergy. The terms *atopy* and *atopic* are derived from the Greek word for "strange." The most common manifestations of atopy are allergic rhinitis, or hay fever, asthma, and eczema. (See also ALLERGY.)

atrophic rhinitis   Deterioration and dryness of the nasal mucous membrane that may be found with advancing age, infections, or trauma. Nasal passages may be excessively patent (unobstructed), or there may be a paradoxical nasal congestion.

atropine sulfate   A drug derived from the plant belladonna with anticholinergic (drying) and bronchodilating (opening of the airways) effects by partially blocking or relaxing the action of the vagus nerve. This cranial nerve controls the normal, but slightly constricted, smooth muscle tone of the bronchioles. Other effects of atropine include tachycardia (rapid heart rate), mydriasis (dilation of the pupils), cycloplegia (paralysis of the ciliary muscle), and relief of abdominal muscle spasms. These effects can be therapeutic, especially by increasing a dangerously low heart rate or aiding in eye examinations and surgery. However, atropine can cause blurred vision, increased pressure in the eye that may precipitate an attack of or worsen glaucoma, and difficulty urinating (usually in older men with enlarged prostate glands). Ipratropium is a derivative of atropine and is an effective drug to treat asthma and chronic bronchitis in selected individuals. (See ANTICHOLINERGICS, IPRATROPIUM.)

Atrovent   See IPRATROPIUM.

attention deficit disorder with hyperactivity

A disorder, also known as childhood hyperkinesis, hyperactive child syndrome, hyperkinetic syndrome, minimal brain damage, minimal brain dysfunction, minor cerebral dysfunction, organic reaction syndrome, and the Strauss syndrome, characterized by hyperactivity, impulsivity, distractibility, and excitability. It was first recognized as early as 1845 by German author H. Hoffman. The term is usually used to describe a child who is difficult to discipline or who receives poor grades in school. This syndrome may represent a true hyperkinetic state, be a temporary state of anxiety, a mild seizure disorder, or a misjudgment by parents or teachers. Prevalence has been estimated to include up to 10% of American school children. Multiple causes may be implicated, including physical factors such as infection, lead intoxication, hypoxia (lack of oxygen), or trauma. It may be genetically inherited or brought on by psychosocial situations such as anxiety, maternal depression, and environmental stresses. The etiology is often unclear.

In 1973, Dr. Benjamin Feingold promoted the theory that hyperactive behavior and learning disability could be attributed to certain foods and food additives. Feingold's book on the subject prompted a Consensus Development Conference on Defined Diets and Childhood Hyperactivity by the National Institutes of Health in January 1982.

Although Feingold stated that 50% of hyperactive children could be helped by his diet, the consensus panel reported that the diet may be helpful, but not consistently, for a small number of children with hyperkinesis. In these few susceptible children the behavioral changes were attributed to pharmacologiclike effects of very high doses of food colors and not due to allergy to these substances.

High sugar content of children's diets has also been implicated as a cause of hyperactivity and antisocial behavior, but the results of controlled studies have disputed these beliefs. (See FEINGOLD DIET, HYPERACTIVITY, SUGAR.)

autoantibodies   Antibodies produced against one's own body tissues. (See ANTINUCLEAR ANTIBODY TESTS, AUTOIMMUNE DISORDER.)

autogenic response testing   See ELECTROACUPUNCTURE.

Autohaler   A device designed to deliver a precise dose of the beta-adrenergic agonist asthma drug pirbuterol (Maxair) by inhalation. It was approved for use in 1993. Inhalation automatically triggers the release of the drug, making the Autohaler generally easier to use than traditional metered-dose inhalers.

autoimmune disorder   A condition resulting from the immune system's mistaken attack on the body's own tissues. Antibodies called "autoantibodies" and T cells join with self antigens, forming immune complexes that accumulate, causing serious damage to various organs.

Examples of autoantibodies are rheumatoid factor found in rheumatoid arthritis and antinuclear antibodies in systemic lupus erythematosus (SLE). (See IMMUNE COMPLEX DISORDERS, IMMUNE SYSTEM.)

autoimmunity   The state of producing antibodies against one's own body tissue. (See AUTOIMMUNE DISORDER.)

autonomic nervous system   The involuntary system that regulates functions of the lungs, heart, blood vessels, visceral smooth muscle of the stomach and intestines, and secretions of exocrine or secretory mucus and salivary glands.

autoprecipitin   See PRECIPITIN.

auto urine injection   See URINE AUTOINJECTION.

avocado   A green or purple fruit of tropical American trees of the genus *Persea*. Sulfites, chemicals that may trigger asthma, may form through chemical interactions when avocado pulp is used in dips.

avoidance of allergens   A fundamental principle in management of any allergic or asthmatic individual. (See INDOOR ALLERGEN CONTROL MEASURES.)

azatadine maleate   (Optimine)   A first-generation antihistamine associated with antiserotonin, anticholinergic, or drying, and sedative effects. Azatadine is combined with the decongestant pseudoephedrine under the trade name Trinalin.

azelastine   (Astelin)   A unique drug with a chemical structure unrelated to any other allergy or asthma medication. Azelastine acts as an antihistamine, blocking the effects of histamine, and as a bronchodilator, reversing constricted bronchial tubes. It also has anti-inflammatory properties similar to those of corticosteroids. It is effective for adults in an oral dose taken twice a day for hay fever or asthma.

In the United States azelastine is available only as a nasal spray for the treatment of allergic rhinitis, or hay fever.

Azmacort   Metered-dose asthma inhaler containing the cortisone-like anti-inflammatory drug triamcinolone. This unique inhaler comes with a white barrel-shaped device called a spacer. Spacers assure that even individuals with less than perfect coordination receive an adequate dose of the drug. (See also CORTICOSTEROID METERED-DOSE INHALERS, SPACER, TRIAMCINOLONE.)

azo dyes   Additives used for coloring foods, drugs, and cosmetics. One azo dye, tartrazine yellow (FD&C No. 5), has been implicated in triggering hives and angioedema and asthma in aspirin-sensitive persons. (See FOOD ADDITIVES.)

B

baby skin products   Creams, lotions, oils, powders, and soaps created to cleanse, protect against irritation, dry or moisturize, and soothe skin, especially in the perianal area. These products may contain lanolin and its derivatives, beeswax, parabens, cornstarch, antiseptics such as chlorobutanol, and other potential allergens. (See CONTACT DERMATITIS.)

bacteria   Living microscopic organisms composed of a single cell and lacking chlorophyll. Structurally, a bacterium bears some resemblance to the human cell. Parts of one bacterium include the nuclear region (or chromosomes), or "central intelligence" in which DNA dictates the characteristics of the cell; ribosomes, which carry RNA and units of protein in the cell's cytoplasm; and the cell membrane and the cell wall, which carry proteins, fats, and sugars. Bacterial infections, especially those affecting the respiratory and integumentary systems, may trigger or intensify conditions of allergy and asthma or be mistaken for them.

The three major categories of bacteria are spherical or ovoid, such as micrococci, diplococci, staphylococci, streptococci, and sarcinae; rod shaped, or bacilli, such as coccobacilli and streptobacilli; and spiral, or spirilla, such as spirocetes and vibrios.

Because bacteria have no chlorophyll and do not photosynthesize the way plants do, they derive their nutrients from organic material, parasites, soil, or nonliving organic matter. Bacteria are considered pathogenic if they are capable of causing disease in their host, but many bacteria are nonpathogenic and perform beneficial functions in the human body and the environment, especially in the nitrogen cycle of the soil. Aerobes are bacteria that thrive on atmospheric oxygen; anaerobes can live without oxygen. Most bacteria reproduce asexually by binary fission, or splitting into two parts.

Certain species of rod-shaped bacteria form spores, which are encapsulated bacterium cells in a resting or dormant stage. While in this stage, spores resist heat, cold, dehydration, disinfectants, and other attempts to destroy them.

Bacteria generally have flagella, or whiplike tails, for motility, and most form colonies that can flourish in soil, water, organic matter, humans, animals, and plants. In humans, undesirable bacteria usually succumb to antibiotic treatment. (See ANTIBIOTIC.)

bagassosis   A form of hypersensitivity pneumonitis. This allergic pneumonialike disease is caused by the inhalation of bagasse dust, the dusty fibrous waste of sugarcane after the sugar-containing sap has been removed. (See HYPERSENSITIVITY PNEUMONITIS.)

baker's asthma   An occupational lung disease caused by repeated exposure to flour, especially wheat, an airborne allergen. There is usually no related allergy to ingested bakery products. In one study, 10% of exposed bakers selected randomly developed asthma. The bakers were exposed an average of 17.4 years before symptoms developed.

Immunotherapy (allergy shots) may be effective treatment for the inhaled food allergen causing baker's asthma. This type of therapy is not recommended when the food allergen exposure is from oral ingestion. (See FOOD ALLERGY.)

baker's eczema   An allergic skin rash caused by the repeated occupational exposure of the skin to wheat and other bakery goods. (See ATOPIC DERMATITIS.)

baker's rhinitis   An allergic condition of the upper respiratory tract caused by repeated exposure to flour, usually airborne wheat allergen.

balm oil   A flavoring agent derived from the fruit and leaves of various plants that may cause allergic or irritant reactions. Balm oil is used in beverages, ice cream, bakery goods, cosmetics, and confections. (See CONTACT DERMATITIS, FOOD ADDITIVES.)

balsam of Peru   A derivative of the Peruvian balsam tree used in perfumes, hair rinses, astringents, other cosmetics, flavoring, rectal suppositories, topical medications, and oil paint. It may cause contact dermatitis, stuffy nose, and skin irritation and have adverse cross-reactive effects with other substances, including benzoin, rosin, orange peel, cinnamon, essential oils, and clove.

bambuterol   An investigational beta-agonist (bronchodilating) drug chemically related to terbutaline. Bambuterol has a direct action in lung tissue; little of the active drug is absorbed into the bloodstream, therefore minimizing the possibility of side effects. It also has the advantage of requiring only one daily dose. (See also BETA-ADRENERGIC AGONISTS.)

banana   A tropical fruit of the herb *Musa sapientum* whose pulp contains natural salicylates that may cause urticaria, or hives, and anaphylaxis (life-threatening allergic shock) in a small number of individuals. Bananas also contain a small amount of chemicals called vasoactive amines. These substances are capable of causing a wide range of symptoms, including abdominal cramps, diarrhea, and severe hypertension, or high blood pressure, if eaten in large quantities. Persons taking antidepressant drugs called monoamine oxidase inhibitors (MAO inhibitors) or the antituberculosis drug INH should avoid eating bananas because of an increased likelihood of a nonallergic but serious reaction. (See FEINGOLD DIET, HYPERACTIVITY, SALICYLATES.)

banana oil   See AMYL ACETATE.

barium sulfate   A powder derived from the salt of the alkaline earth metal barium, used as a white coloring and as a base for some cosmetics including hair removers. Barium sulfate and barium hydroxide, which is also used in cosmetics, may cause skin eruptions.

barium sulfide   A powder used as a base in hair-remover products that is a known skin irritant.

barley   The seed of the cereal grass of the genus *Hordeum.* Allergic reactions include anaphylaxis from exposure to this cereal grain used in breakfast foods and malt beverages. Barley is one of many grains subject to contamination by molds that produce the toxin ergot. This mycotoxin (a toxic or poisonous substance produced by molds) produces a nonallergic food reaction that can result in gangrene of the limbs.

barometric pressure   The pressure of the atmosphere measured by devices called barometers and expressed in terms of milligrams of mercury. A fall in barometric pressure usually predicts the approach of bad weather. Many people who suffer from asthma and "rheumatism," or arthritis, claim that they can predict stormy weather because of their intensified symptoms. Although this has never been proven scientifically, it is speculated that fluids in body cells swell and increase their pressure on surrounding tissues when there is a drop in atmospheric pressure.

barrier agent   Any substance that acts as a protective against potential skin irritants by creating a film on exposed parts. Hand creams and lotions, petrolatum, zinc oxide ointment, zinc stearate, paraffin, silicones, oil, water and insect repellents, and other preparation offer protection against poison ivy, chemical irritations, and other types of contact dermatitis. For example, a cream developed as a barrier for poison ivy and oak contains water, PPG-3 diamine dilinoleate, mineral oil, petrolatum wax, PEG-7 hydrogenated castor oil, glycerin, petrolatum, and aluminum distearate. This product, developed to protect gardeners, campers, hikers, hunters, and fishers, or anyone with known sensitivity, should be applied to all exposed skin prior to possible contact with plant allergens. (See PLANT CONTACT DERMATITIS.)

basophil degranulation and histamine release   An allergy diagnostic technique that measures the release of the potent biochemical substance histamine from basophilic white blood cells exposed to suspected allergens. This procedure is technically difficult and has an 8 to 20% false negative result. Its use is limited to research. (See BASOPHILS.)

basophils [basophilic leukocytes]   White blood cells that contribute to inflammatory and allergic reactions when they and other cells of the immune system release the chemical substance histamine and other potent biochemicals. (See BASOPHIL DEGRANULATION AND HISTAMINE RELEASE.)

bath products   Lotions, oils, soaps, and salts used to freshen, perfume, soften, or moisturize the skin. These products may contain sensitizers known to be the source of allergic reactions including rashes. (See CONTACT DERMATITIS.)

bay oil [oil of Myrcia]   An oil derived from the leaves of the bayberry plant that is used as an astringent and antiseptic in toiletries and Bay Rum. Eugenol in this oil can cause various allergic reactions and toxicity. Bayberry wax, a rosin from the dried root bark of the bayberry shrub, is used in soaps and hair products and may also cause adverse reactions.

B-cell defects   Deficiencies in B cells that result in their failure to produce immunoglobulins, or antibodies. B-cell disorders are known as agammaglobulinemias, if there is a lack of antibodies, or hypogammaglobulinemias if there are too few antibodies. Children with these deficiencies are susceptible to infections and must be given injections of immunoglobulins. (See B CELLS, IMMUNE SYSTEM, IMMUNODEFICIENCY DISEASE.)

B cells [B lymphocytes]   Small white blood cells produced by the bone marrow that are a source of antibodies and are vital to immune defenses. (See B-CELL DEFECTS, IMMUNE SYSTEM.)

bean allergy   Immune response to the seeds of any of a variety of leguminous plants. Beans have been implicated as a cause of Henoch-Schonlein purpura (HSP) or allergic vasculitis (inflammation of the blood vessels), characterized by large areas of bruising and internal bleeding (see HENOCH-SCHONLEIN PURPURA). This condition usually improves when the offending food is removed from the diet.

The common annoying symptoms of burping, flatus (gas), and diarrhea that result from eating large quantities of beans are not related to allergies. (See LEGUMES.)

beclomethasone (Beconase, Beconase AQ, Vancenase, Vancenase AQ, Beclovent, Vanceril)   A corticosteroid drug used as a nasal spray for the prevention of allergic rhinitis and as a metered-dose inhaler for the prevention of asthma. Beclomethasone's anti-inflammatory action, considered safe for use during pregnancy, is also prescribed for the treatment of nonallergic nasal polyps and rhinitis medicomentosum. However, the drug is typically more effective for allergic rather than nonallergic disorders. Some authorities recommend cautious use in persons with active tuberculosis, bacterial, systemic fungal, or viral infections, recent nasal injury or surgery, nasal infection, or ocular herpes simplex. For hay fever, beclomethasone may take a week or more before reaching full effectiveness; in nonallergic conditions, it may take three weeks to prove either effective or noneffective.

Severe asthma should be stabilized by using oral corticosteroids before a beclomethasone inhalant can elicit preventive, anti-inflammatory benefits. Most asthma authorities now advocate the use of this and other anti-inflammatory metered-dose inhalers as first-line maintenance therapy in persons with mild to moderate asthma. (See AEROSOLS, CORTICOSTEROIDS, CORTICOSTEROID NASAL SPRAYS.)

Beclovent   See BECLOMETHASONE.

Beconase   See BECLOMETHASONE.

bedbug   The insect *Cimex lectularius*, whose saliva causes pruritic reaction (itching) or urticarial wheal (hives). Infestation is caused by filth.

beef allergy   Hypersensitivity reactions resulting from the oral ingestion of cattle meat. Beef allergy can occur in infants but is a minor source of hypersensitivity reactions in older children and adults. Persons allergic to milk can usually tolerate beef or inhaled cattle dander. Beef has been used as a protein substitute in some milk-allergic individuals.

Despite its low potential for allergy, beef is probably best avoided along with other foods for the first six to nine months in breast-fed infants.

beer   A fermented alcoholic beverage, made of malt, barley, hops, and brewer's yeast, that may be a cause of asthma from sulfite preservatives. Beer has been implicated by some as a source of "mold sensitivity" and is a test substance included in mold-elimination diets. The validity of this has not been substantiated. (See also ALCOHOL, FOOD ALLERGY, MOLD ALLERGY, SULFITING AGENTS.)

bee sting allergy   See HYMENOPTERA STING ALLERGY.

beeswax   The yellow wax produced by honeybees. Used widely in cosmetics and ointments, it may cause contact dermatitis.

behavioral abnormalities and food allergies   See ATTENTION DEFICIT DISORDER WITH HYPERACTIVITY.

behavioral changes and theophylline   See THEOPHYLLINE.

behavioral therapy   Guidelines or techniques used along with medications and other treatments for allergy and asthma in the event of adverse emotional aspects of either disorder. Sir James Mackensie experimented nearly 100 years ago with the psychological component of hypersensitivity. He placed a paper rose under glass on his desk and then called in a patient with a known diagnosis of rose asthma (an obsolete reference to what may have been hay fever caused by pollen). Upon seeing the rose, the patient started to wheeze and her eyes began to water. Mackensie concluded that a patient could be as sensitive to the idea of a rose as to a rose itself.

Peter H. Knapp, M.D., professor of psychiatry, wrote in 1975 that triggers of allergy and asthma may include negative toilet-training episodes, fear of losing mother, difficulty with give-and-take of affection, a traumatic event (marriage, having a child, etc.), and other childhood behavioral patterns as a response to a contemporary situation. Knapp's eight guidelines for dealing with emotionally induced asthma are: (1) allow the patient to talk about his fears in order to limit his anxiety; (2) allow the patient to ventilate intense feelings; (3) help the patient with basic emotional problems; (4) help the patient overcome feelings of guilt; (5) help the patient express anger; (6) support the patient's need for independence and to be self-assertive; (7) wean the patient slowly off medications upon which she may be physiologically or psychologically dependent; (8) be attuned to the way a patient's emotions or life situation influences his asthma.

Benacerraf, Baruj   Venezuelan physician, born in 1920, who, with immunogeneticists George Snell and Jean Dausset, won the Nobel Prize in physiology or medicine in 1980 for studies in antibody synthesis and types and discovery of genetic control of immune responsiveness through immune response (Ir) genes. An asthmatic during his childhood, Benacerraf was inspired to pursue a career in immunology, with a focus on hypersensitivity.

benzaldehyde   [artificial almond oil]   The fluid extracted from the kernels of bitter almonds (lime is used for synthetic manufacture) included among ingredients in cosmetics, soaps, dyes, and perfumes. Toxicity and allergic reactions are adverse effects.

benzalkonium chloride (Zephiran) An ammonium detergent and germicide added to mouthwashes, eye lotions, after-shave lotions, and topical antiseptics that may cause allergic conjunctivitis and toxicity.

benzocaine [ethyl aminobenzoate] A local anesthetic used in sore-throat lozenges, hemorrhoidal suppositories and ointments, denture adhesives, sunburn preparations, and some toiletries such as after-shave lotion, which may induce contact dermatitis in individuals sensitive to benzocaine. Benzocaine cross-reacts with procaine, tetracaine, butacaine, sulfonamides, and azo dyes.

benzoic acid A substance found in cherry and cassia bark, tea, raspberries, anise, and in gum benzoin that is used as a preservative in various flavorings for beverages, ice cream and other confections, chewing gum, and margarine. It is also used as an antifungal agent. Benzoic acid can be irritating to skin and has been known to cause allergic reactions.

benzophenones A series of 12 organic compounds used in the manufacture of perfumes, soaps, hair sprays, and sunscreens that may cause allergic reactions such as hives and contact dermatitis.

benzoyl peroxide A bleach, chemical hardener, and drying agent used in foods, fiberglass resins, and cosmetics. It is a skin allergen and irritant.

benzyl acetate An aromatic extract of jasmine or other plants used in the manufacture of perfumes and soaps. It can irritate the skin, eyes, and respiratory tract and, when taken internally, causes vomiting and diarrhea.

benzyl alcohol A solvent, preservative, local anesthetic, and topical antiseptic derived from various flowering plants as a pure alcohol. It is irritating to skin and mucous membranes and may cross-react with balsam of Peru in sensitive individuals.

benzylpenicilloyl polylysine (Pre-Pen) Skin test used in determining a patient's allergic potential to penicillin. A negative skin test to this substance is associated with a risk of penicillin reaction of less than 5% in patients subsequently treated with penicillin. A positive reaction suggests a greater than 20% chance of a penicillin reaction with the vast majority of these reactions limited to the skin.

benzyl salicylate A fixing agent and solvent used in perfumes and sunscreens that may cause skin eruptions and photosensitivity.

bergamot, red An oil derived from the rind of *Citrus bergamia*, a pear-shaped orange, used in making perfumes and hairdressings. Upon exposure to sunlight, it can cause brown skin stains, also known as berlock dermatitis.

berlock dermatitis [berloque dermatitis] Abnormal brown skin pigmentation or redness caused by contact with photosensitizers such as eau de cologne and other toiletries containing ethereal and other oils, such as oil of bergamot. The pigmentation usually seen on the face or neck resembles streaks or drops like pendants, hence *berloque*, the French word for a charm hanging from a chain.

beta-adrenergic agonists Drugs, also known as beta-agonists, that act as bronchodilators to relieve spasms of the bronchi during an asthma attack. These potent drugs act by stimulating the beta$_2$ receptors on smooth muscle in the bronchial tree.

Alpha-adrenergic receptor stimulation causes a constriction of blood vessels and may raise blood pressure and heart rate. Beta-adrenergic stimulation primarily affects the airways or air passages. There are two types of receptors, beta$_1$ and beta$_2$. Drugs that act only on beta$_2$ receptors have fewer side effects and are the most frequently used in treating patients with asthma.

More than 5,000 years ago, the ancient Chinese treated asthma with Ma-Huang, an herbal remedy that contains the beta-agonist ephedrine. Epinephrine (adrenaline) is a drug that affects both alpha and beta receptors, and because of its rapid onset of action, it is a useful emergency drug. Within minutes after being injected into the subcutaneous tissues, it induces relief of severe bronchoconstriction and can usually prevent or reverse anaphylaxis if given promptly. Thus, epinephrine can be a truly life-saving drug. Because of its alpha-adrenergic properties, however, it tends to cause

---

ASTHMA MEDICATION SAFE WHEN TAKEN AS DIRECTED
Palatine, Ill., Aug. 9, 1991

Drugs known as beta-2 agonists are safe and effective for the treatment of asthma, and patients taking the medication should continue despite recent reports of potentially fatal side effects associated with overuse of the drugs, according to a national professional organization of physicians specializing in the treatment of asthma.

The American College of Allergy and Immunology said beta-2 agonists are the drugs of choice for the treatment of acute, intermittent and exercise-induced asthma and are safe if taken as prescribed. Beta-2 agonists belong to a class of drugs called bronchodilators and are often administered through an inhaler.

"We have been successfully and safely using beta-2 agonists to treat asthma for more than 10 years," said Dr. Edward O'Connell, president of the college. "As with any drug, there can be side effects if the patient exceeds the prescribed dosage, and we caution patients not to do this."

O'Connell also cautioned against discontinuing medication and said patients should discuss concerns about recent reports with their physicians. About 10 million Americans suffer from asthma, a disease that causes wheezing, coughing and difficulty in breathing, and claims about 4,600 lives each year. Beta-2 agonists relieve the symptoms of asthma attacks by relaxing and expanding the lung airways.

The FDA is considering a review of beta-2 agonists because of reports that taking twice the prescribed dose might be fatal. The danger for asthmatics is that if the prescribed dose of beta-2 agonists does not bring relief, the patient may try taking more of the drug, O'Connell said.

"Patients who are not getting relief from the prescribed dose of medication should never increase the dosage on their own," O'Connell said. "They should talk with their doctors about supplementing with other drugs or switching to a different treatment plan. The essential thing is to develop a treatment plan only under the direction of the doctor."

The 3,600-member American College of Allergy and Immunology is a national organization of physicians who specialize in the treatment of asthma and other allergic diseases. Board-certified allergists complete a three-year residency in either pediatrics or internal medicine and a two-year fellowship study in allergy and immunology.

—Press release from the American College of Allergy and Immunology issued in August 1991.

BETA-AGONISTS AVAILABLE IN THE UNITED STATES

	Dosage Forms Available
albuterol (Proventil, Ventolin)	1, 3, 4
bitolterol (Tornalate)	3
epinephrine (Adrenalin, Primetene)	2, 3, 4
isoetharine (Bronkometer Bronkosol)	3, 4
isoproterenol (Isuprel)[1]	1, 2, 3, 4
metaproterenol (Alupent, Metaprel)	1, 3, 4
pirbuterol (Maxair)	3
terbutaline (Brethair, Brethine, Bricanyl)	1, 2, 3[2]

---

orally=1; injectable=2; metered-dose inhaler (MDI)=3; nebulizer solution=4 (Not all brands are available in all dosage forms.)

Note: The Beta-agonists bambuterol, formoterol, and salmeterol are not yet available in the United States.

[1] Rarely used for the treatment of asthma because of adverse effects.

[2] Terbutaline ampoules for injection may be used as a nebulizer solution.

a jittery feeling and heart palpitations in many individuals.

Albuterol, an example of a selective beta2 drug, with sufficiently rapid onset of action for all but the most extreme situations, has relatively few adverse stimulatory effects and is available in a wide variety of dosage forms.

A Canadian study of more than 12,000 patients over a 10-year period through 1977 raised some questions about the safety of beta-agonists. The Canadian data suggest that merely taking twice the usual dose of beta2 from an inhaler more than doubles the risk of death from an asthma attack.

The drug fenoterol (Berotec) is twice as potent as any beta2 drug available in the United States. In response to media reports concerning the Canadian study, the American College of Allergy and Immunology issued the following news release in August 1991:

beta-adrenergic receptors   See ADRENERGIC DRUGS, BETA-ADRENERGIC AGONISTS.

"beta-blockers"   See BETA-BLOCKING AGENTS.

beta-blocking agents   ["beta-blockers"] Drugs used to treat heart problems, high blood pressure, migraine headaches, and glaucoma. The most serious side effect of beta-blockers is constriction of the bronchial tubes, which can cause or worsen an asthma attack in an allergic or asthmatic person. Epinephrine (Adrenalin), the drug of choice for the treatment of severe allergic reactions or anaphylaxis, may be ineffective in persons taking beta-blocking drugs. Beta-blockers should be avoided by those with asthma or severe allergies.

WARNING

BETA-BLOCKING AGENTS MUST NEVER BE USED IN ANY PATIENT RECEIVING ALLERGY IMMUNOTHERAPY (ALLERGY SHOTS) and must be used very cautiously, if at all, in any allergic or asthmatic patient.

Examples of beta-blocker medications (capsules, tablets, or eye drops) are (brand names in parentheses):

acebutolol (Sectral)
atenolol (Tenormin)
atenolol + chlorthalidone (Tenoretic)
betaxolol hydrochloride (Betopic) eye drops
carteolol (Cartrol)
labatelol (Normodyne or Trandate)
labatelol + hydrochlorthiazide (Normozide or Trandate HCT)
levobunolol (Betagan) eye drops
metopolol (Lopressor)
metoprolol + hydroclorthiazide (Lopressor HCT)
nadolol (Corgard)
nadolol + bendroflumethiazide (Corzide)
penbutolol (Levatol)
pindolol (Visken)
propanalol (Inderal)
propanalol + hydrochlorthiazide (Inderide)
timolol (Blocadren)
timolol (Timoptic eye drops)
timolol + hydrochlorthiazide (Timolide)

N.B.: New beta-blocking drugs may become available following the publication of this book.

beta-naphthol   A preparation from naphthalene, a derivative of coal tar, used in hair dyes and tonics, skin-peeling agents, and perfumes. Besides being poisonous if ingested or applied to skin, beta-naphthol may also cause symptoms of allergy.

Biaxin   Brand of clarithromycin, a macrolide antibiotic similar to erythromycin. (See CLARITHROMYCIN.)

Billingham, Rupert E.   British scientist, born in 1921, educated at Oxford University, who studied under Sir Peter Medawar and later centered his research on immune mechanisms of wound healing.

binder   An agent that absorbs or dispenses water and adds to or enhances the consistency and helps hold together the ingredients of a product or substance. Binders may cause allergic reactions; for example, gum arabic has been implicated in hay fever, dermatitis, and asthma.

bioavailability   The ability of a drug to reach the target organ or tissues in order to act appropriately in the body. For example, one brand of a drug may contain the same active ingredient as another, but one may produce greater or lesser effectiveness because of the variation of binders, solutions, or other nondrug components in the preparation of the drug.

biofeedback   Electrodermal responses recorded on a machine similar to an electrocardiogram. The person is connected to sensors that pick up signals of involuntary bodily activities, including blood pressure, pulse rate, temperature, muscle tension, perspiration, brain waves, gastric acidity, and so on. At a time of stress, these signals are recorded by the machine to inform the person how his body handled that stress. The goal of biofeedback is to help an individual recognize these reactions and learn to alter them through relaxation and similar techniques. Biofeedback is useful in reducing stress as an asthma trigger.

biological response modifiers   (BRMs) Substances that boost, direct, or restore normal immune defenses. They may be natural or synthesized and include interferons, interleukins, thymus hormones, and monoclonal antibodies.

bird allergy   Sensitivity to allergens found in bird feathers. It is estimated that 20% of fanciers of parakeets and canaries suffer from rhinitis and asthma. Persons sensitive to feathers of chicken, goose, duck, and turkey can eat meat or eggs from these foul with no symptoms, unless they are also sensitive to egg protein. Avian hypersensitivity pneumonitis results from exposure to bird droppings. (See FEATHERS, HYPERSENSITIVITY PNEUMONITIS.)

bird breeder's lung   (bird fancier's disease, pigeon breeder's disease)

A pneumonialike disease caused by inhaled allergens in bird droppings. (See BIRD ALLERGY, HYPERSENSITIVITY PNEUMONITIS.)

bird fancier's disease   See BIRD BREEDER'S LUNG.

birth control pills, allergy to   Urticaria, angioedema, and anaphylaxis attributed to oral contraceptive tablets containing the hormone levonorgestrel. Symptoms usually worsen as the dose of the offending hormone increases during the menstrual cycle and improve during menses or resolve upon discontinuation of the medication.

bismuth compounds   Naturally occurring metallic grayish substances. A bismuth-containing powder was originally used to treat syphilis, and later used as an antiseptic and an ingredient in dusting powder, hair dyes, bleaching agents and skin protectives. Bismuth compounds, namely bismuth subgallate, subnitrate, and oxychloride, have been reported to cause allergic skin reactions when applied topically.

biting insects   Insects that bite humans for sustenance, such as mosquitoes requiring blood as food. In the kissing bug, genus *Triatoma*, allergens are present in the saliva, but sufficient quantities are difficult to obtain from the salivary glands of these insects for immunotherapy. Anaphylaxis rarely occurs as a result of a kissing bug bite.

Large localized reactions from the bites of flies, mosquitoes, and fleas are most likely responses to saliva. The allergic nature of such bites is unclear, and there is a minimal potential for anaphylaxis. Therefore, immunotherapy is not employed.

The itching from bites can be treated with oral antihistamines and corticosteroid creams. Topical antihistamines are to be avoided because some persons become sensitized to them. (See ANTIHISTAMINE, INSECT ALLERGY.)

bitter almond oil   Oil extracted from the seed of the small, sweet almond indigenous to

Italy, Spain, and France. Used as an ingredient in perfumes, soaps, emollients, nail polish remover, and eye and hair creams, the pale yellowish oil can cause allergic reactions including rashes and nasal congestion.

bitter orange oil   Oil derived from fresh orange peel. It is used as a flavoring and in perfumes and may cause allergic reactions.

bituminosis   Pneumoconiosis as a result of inhalation of dust from bituminous, or soft, coal.

Blackley, Charles H.   English homeopathic physician (1820–1900) who was inspired to study allergy because of his personal suffering from hay fever. Born in Bolton, England, he performed experiments and published his findings in a book entitled *Experimental Researches on the Causes and Nature of Catarrhus Aestivus (Hay Fever or Hay-Asthma)* in 1873. He developed instruments for making pollen counts. Some of his experiments attempted to determine whether inoculating a part of the skin with pollen would reduce that part of the skin's sensitivity to pollen. His experiments did not show any reduction in sensitivity and also indicated that pollen has no enzymatic ability and that hay fever is not infectious.

bleb   A primary skin lesion, also called blister or bulla.

blemish [blotch]   An imperfection, often referring to a flaw of the skin.

blennoid   Mucoid, or having the characteristics of mucus.

blennorrhea   The flow of mucus from mucosal surfaces.

blennothorax   Accumulation of mucus in the bronchial tubes or alveoli.

blepharitis   Inflammation of the edges of the eyelids involving the hair follicles and glands that open onto the surface of the skin surrounding the eye. Blepharitis may be due to allergy, bacterial infection, parasites, or irritating dust, smoke, or chemicals.

blepharoconjunctivitis   Inflammation of the eyelids and conjunctiva, the mucous membranes that line the eyelids and are reflected onto the eyeball. Vernal conjunctivitis is associated with the onset of spring allergies. (See CONJUNCTIVITIS, ALLERGIC.)

blister   An imperfection in the skin filled with fluid.

blood gases, arterial   See ARTERIAL BLOOD GASES.

Bloom, Barry R.   American scientist, born in 1937 in Philadelphia, Pennsylvania, known for his studies of delayed hypersensitivity reactions and cell-mediated immunity. In 1980, Bloom was appointed chairman of the Microbiology and Immunology Department of the Albert Einstein College of Medicine in New York.

blotch   See BLEMISH.

blueberries   The fruit of various bushes of the genus *Vaccinium* and a source of naturally occurring salicylates that has been implicated as a cause of urticaria (hives). (See SALICYLATES, URTICARIA.)

B lymphocytes   See B CELLS.

bone marrow   Tissue in the center of bones that produces all blood cells.

borax   Sodium borate, primarily used as a detergent, water softener, and weak antiseptic, found in some desert or dry regions, including Death Valley, California. Borax is also used in hair coloring products, cold creams, shaving creams, permanent wave solutions, and as a preventive against skin irritation caused by the antiperspirant aluminum chloride. Borax has been known to cause toxicity when ingested or applied to broken skin.

Bordet, Jules   Belgian physician (1870–1961) who won the Nobel Prize for physiology or medicine in 1919 for his work with complement, a component of the immune system, and other factors related to immunity.

Bostock, John   Belgian physician (1773–1846) credited with coining the term *hay fever*, which he believed was "produced by the effluvium from new hay." In his writings "Case of a Periodical Affection of the Eyes and Chest" and "Of the Catarrhus Aestivus, or Summer Catarrh," Bostock described in accurate detail common symptoms of hay fever as heat, fullness, redness, and itching in the eyes, sneezing with the discharge of mucus, difficulty in breathing, a quickened pulse, restlessness, perspiration, and loss of appetite.

Bouchut's respiration   Exhalation longer than inhalation in children with asthma or bronchopneumonia, named for French physician Jean A. E. Bouchut (1818–91).

Bovet, Daniel   Swiss scientist, born in 1907, who discovered antibacterial sulfonomides and, with Ernest Fourneau in 1933, succeeded in synthesizing the first series of antihistamines. Bovet won the Nobel Prize for physiology or medicine in 1957.

bovine allergy   See BEEF ALLERGY, MILK.

brachypnea   Shortness of breath.

bradykinin   A potent chemical mediator whose vasodilating action plays a role in asthma, pulmonary edema, and anaphylaxis. This slow-moving kinin, a term for a group of polypeptides, influences contraction of smooth muscle, promotes hypotension, increases blood flow in small blood capillaries, and sparks the pain reflex. (See CHEMICAL MEDIATORS.)

bradypnea   Abnormally slow breathing.

brass founder's ague   Tremors resulting from the inhalation of toxic fumes or from zinc or brass poisoning.

breast-feeding and prevention of allergies   Maternal breast-milk allergy is virtually unknown. However, trace amounts of food allergens in a mother's milk are often sufficient to sensitize infants and therefore can be a cause of allergy or colic. Food allergies can possibly be prevented by eliminating common offending foods—milk, eggs, wheat, nuts, citrus, shellfish, and fish—from the breast-feeding mother's diet.

Many advocate breast-feeding as a means of avoiding or delaying the onset of allergy in the infant. Breast milk provides immunoglobulins enhancing allergen resistance in the newborn. (See MILK.)

breast-milk allergy   See BREAST-FEEDING AND PREVENTION OF ALLERGIES, MILK.

Breath Enhancer   A spacer device (see SPACER) to facilitate the use of aerosol metered-dose inhalers for poorly coordinated persons with asthma.

breathing   Normal breathing, or the unhindered process of inhaling and exhaling controlled by the respiratory center in the brain stem. Inhalation causes the diaphragm, a curved muscle between the lungs and the abdomen, to flatten and the rib cage to pull up as lungs expand with air. During exhalation the diaphragm relaxes, the rib cage moves down, and the lungs squeeze out air. The purpose of breathing is to keep the body adequately supplied with oxygen and to dispose of carbon dioxide. The lungs do not fill up or empty completely; new air breathed in (tidal volume) mixes with air that has been retained in the lungs (residual volume). Normal resting breathing replaces only about one-tenth of the air in the lungs with fresh air. Deep breathing, an example of a voluntarily created change in the natural reflex of respiration, may allow one to inhale about three to four liters, of air. (See DYSPNEA, EUPNEA, HYPERCAPNIA, HYPERPNEA, ORTHOPNEA, RESPIRATORY CENTER, STERTOR, STRIDOR, TACHYPNEA.)

breathing exercises   A series of deep breathing techniques to build up lung capacity and to help an individual with respiratory disorders to relax and breathe as normally as possible. The Eastern practice of yoga includes breath control and rhythmic, deep breathing, which are geared to overall physical and mental improvement. Asthmatic children often respond to relaxation breathing techniques when they feel an asthma attack coming on, and in some cases, the full-blown attack can be avoided. Essentially, one is advised to inhale through the nose, filling the belly and then the chest with air, and to exhale through the mouth and contract the muscles in the abdomen. Breathing exercises may also be done with a spirometer, a plastic tube containing plastic balls. As one blows air into the mouthpiece of the tube, the balls rise. This encourages deep breathing, which helps clear the lungs and oxygenate the entire body. Physicians prescribe spirometry for patients with bronchitis, pneumonia, and other, especially chronic, lung diseases.

Brethaire   See TERBUTALINE SULFATE.

Brethine   See TERBUTALINE SULFATE.

Bricanyl   See TERBUTALINE SULFATE.

Bromfed   See BROMPHENIRAMINE.

brompheniramine (Bromfed, Dimetane, Dimetapp)   A mildly sedating, commonly used antihistamine of the alkylamine class. Brompheniramine is available alone or in combination with a decongestant in prescription and over-the-counter allergy preparations. (See ANTIHISTAMINE.)

bronchi   The two large branches extending from the trachea, or windpipe, into the lungs, forming what is commonly known as the "bronchial tree." Because each bronchus is an airway, a buildup of mucus, an infection, physical and chemical irritants, swelling of the bronchial mucosal lining, excess calculi, or a foreign body or obstruction can cause choking, bronchitis, bronchoedema, lung abscess, and pneumonia. A bronchoscope is an instrument through which the bronchi can be examined. Bronchopulmonary disorders are those that involve both bronchi and lungs, such as bronchopneumonia. (See BRONCHIOLES, RALE.)

bronchial asthma   A common term for asthma. (See ASTHMA.)

bronchial breathing   Harsh breathing associated with high-pitched expiration (tubular breathing).

bronchial challenge   See CHALLENGE.

bronchiarctia   A narrowing or constriction of a bronchial tube.

bronchioles   The smaller subdivisions of the bronchial tree in the thorax, so named because the bronchi and bronchioles resemble a tree trunk and its roots. The bronchioles bring air from the trachea, the upper part of the windpipe, to the lungs and participate in the exchange of gases (oxygen and carbon dioxide) in the breathing process. Brionchial glands are mucus-producing organs in the bronchi and bronchioles. (The Greek word for windpipe is *bronchus*.) Among disorders of the bronchioles are bronchitis, bronchiolitis, and bronchopneumonia. (See BRONCHIOLITIS, BRONCHITIS.)

bronchiolitis   An acute inflammatory disease of the bronchioles, or small airways, in infants in which excessive mucus production results in airway obstruction. This obstruction leads to tachypnea (rapid shallow breathing), with a respiratory rate of 50 to as high as 80 breaths per minute, hypoxemia (reduced oxygen content of the blood), and hyperinflation (overinflated lungs).

Bronchiolitis occurs more often in winter and spring months, usually during the first six months of life. It predominantly affects males and may occur in epidemics. During outbreaks, respiratory syncytial virus and parainfluenza are most often the cause. But the bacterium *Mycobacterium pneumoniae* can cause bronchiolitis in older children and may be confused with asthma. X rays, blood gas studies, and physical examination findings are virtually identical. Both illnesses are often caused by viral respiratory infections in infants, although allergy testing in the older child may help to confirm the diagnosis. Congestive heart failure can also be mistaken for both bronchiolitis and asthma in the infant.

Treatment of acute bronchiolitis is based on improving hypoxemia, preventing dehydration, and administering bronchodilating drugs and corticosteroids. Antibiotics are probably of no value unless there is suspicion of a secondary bacterial infection.

Recovery usually occurs within two weeks, but bronchiolitis can be fatal. Some believe that infants with bronchiolitis have a greater chance of developing asthma later on. However, it may be difficult to determine if the original diagnosis of bronchiolitis was correct, or if the infant was actually having an initial attack of asthma. (See RESPIRATORY SYNCYTIAL VIRUS.)

bronchitis   An infection or inflammatory disease in the bronchi and bronchioles caused by viral or bacterial germs, allergy, or irritating dust and fumes. It may be an acute infection or a chronic process. Typical symptoms may include coughing, wheezing, shortness of breath, chills, fever, fatigue, and excessive sputum. (See also BRONCHITIS, CHRONIC.)

bronchitis, chronic   A disorder characterized by excessive mucus production in the bronchial tree with a persistent productive cough. By definition it lasts at least three months of the year for at least two consecutive years.

Chronic bronchitis may or may not be related to asthma. Persons with chronic asthmatic bronchitis have a long history of cough and mucus production and develop wheezing as the disease progresses. Chronic asthma with obstruction is characterized by a prolonged course of wheezing and late onset of a chronic productive cough.

Chronic bronchitis is often confused with emphysema, an expansion of the air spaces in the lungs resulting in destruction of the alveoli, or air sacs. In chronic obstructive lung, or pulmonary, disease (COLD, COPD), the flow of air in and out of the lungs is blocked as a result of chronic bronchitis or emphysema or both. In asthma without chronic obstruction, the blockage is present only during an attack. However, in chronic obstructive lung disease, some obstruction exists at all times.

Approximately 20% of adult males have chronic bronchitis, although only a small number become disabled because of it. Chronic bronchitis is less common in females. Individuals who smoke, have allergies, or are frequently exposed to irritants or pollution in the environment may also suffer the disease. (See also BRONCHITIS, EMPHYSEMA.)

bronchodilating drugs   First-line medications that block the constriction of bronchial tubes during an asthma attack. Bronchodilators include beta-agonists, such as albuterol, and xanthine derivatives, such as theophylline. The exact mechanism by which these drugs exert their beneficial effects is unknown. These drugs are available as metered-dose inhalers, solutions for injection or inhalation, or as oral tablets, capsules, and syrups. (See BETA-ADRENERGIC AGONISTS, THEOPHYLLINE.)

bronchopulmonary aspergillosis   See AL-LERGIC BRONCHOPULMONARY ASPERGILLOSIS.

bronchoscopy   An examination of the bronchi through a device called a bronchoscope. The instrument is inserted into the trachea and down to the bronchi so the physician can diagnose a bronchial abnormality.

bronchospasm   A sudden narrowing or constriction of the bronchial tubes (bronchismus) during an asthma attack or in persons with bronchitis. Bronchospasm is also referred to as bronchoconstriction. (See ASTHMA, BRONCHITIS.)

Bronkodyl   See THEOPHYLLINE.

Bronkometer   See ISOETHARINE.

Bronkosol   See ISOETHARINE.

Bronopol   See 2-BROMO-2-NITROPROPANE-1.

Browning reaction   The heating of lactose-containing milk, which causes an increase in certain carbohydrates, making the milk more allergenic. A similar process occurs in rpiened tomatoes. (See MILK.)

Bryan's cytotoxicity   See CYTOTOXIC TESTING.

budesonide   (Rhinocort, Pulmocort)   Corticosteroid available in the United States as a nasal spray for allergic rhinitis and in other countries as a metered-dose inhaler (expected to be released for use in the U.S. soon) for asthma. Budesonide has a greater potency than many similar drugs. (See also CORTICOSTEROID METERED DOSE INHALERS, CORTICOSTEROID NASAL SPRAYS.)

Burnet, Sir Frank MacFarlane   Australian physician and bacteriologist (1899–1985) who researched viral replication and isolation and embryonic immunology. In 1962, he shared the Nobel Prize in physiology or medicine with Peter Medawar for studies on immunologic tolerance and immune responses of the embryo.

Burow's solution   See ALUMINUM ACETATE.

burrow   The tunnel created in the skin by the itch mite (*Sarcoptes scabei*).

butyl acetate   A colorless liquid used by the cosmetic industry in nail polish, nail polish remover, and for its fruity essence as a perfume fragrance. Its irritant but nonallergic properties can cause conjunctivitis.

butyl alcohol   Solution used in the manufacture of shampoos and as a solvent in waxes, resins, fats, and shellac. Ingestion may cause irritation of mucosal membranes and other symptoms, and inhalation may cause lung irritation or disorder. Butyl alcohol and a similar compound, t-butyl alcohol, cause contact dermatitis.

butylated hydroxyanisole   (BHA)   An insoluble, waxy substance used as a preservative and antioxidant that some, especially allergic individuals, believe causes allergic reactions. BHA is found in beverages, ice cream, candies and desserts, chewing gum, soup stock, dry potato flakes, breakfast cereals, and other foods and has been studied in liver and kidney function experiments in animals. The Food and Drug Administration (FDA) has recommended further studies to determine the possibility of toxicity to humans.

butylated hydroxytoluene   (BHT)   An antioxidant and preservative used in cosmetics and foods (see BUTYLATED HYDROXYANISOLE) that has been implicated as a cause of allergic reactions.

byssinosis   An allergic lung disease caused by occupational exposure to an unknown allergen in the dust from the processing of cotton, flax, hemp, or sisal. Symptoms of shortness of breath and wheezing gradually intensify upon increased exposure and may lead to respiratory failure. Smoking increases the risk of permanent lung damage. Byssinosis is largely preventable by wearing a face mask and treating raw textiles before manufacturing. Because these measures are ignored in developing countries, the incidence of this disease is greater there than in the United States. Government compensation is available in the United States for those afflicted with byssinosis. (See OCCUPATIONAL ASTHMA.)

C

C1 esterase inhibitor See COMPLEMENT IN-ACTIVATOR DEFICIENCY.

caffeine A central nervous system stimulant that triggers migraine-type vascular headaches in some individuals and caffeine-withdrawal, nonvascular headaches in others. Migraine headaches are usually unilateral with an aura or feeling of anticipation of the onset. The withdrawal headaches of heavy caffeine users are usually in the top (vertex) or rear (occipital region) of the head. Caffeine, an alkaloid of coffee and tea, is an ingredient in many headache remedies such as Fiorinal and over-the-counter cold preparations. Caffeine is chemically related to the asthma drug theophylline, and adults with asthma who drink coffee may suffer fewer symptoms. Asthma patients who stop consuming coffee or other caffeine-containing beverages may have a sudden worsening of their condition. In an emergency if an asthmatic does not have access to medication, two strong cups of coffee or tea, which contain about 100 to 150 milligrams of caffeine, hot cocoa, or a couple of chocolate bars may help alleviate symptoms until more effective medication can be obtained. Caffeine is also a diuretic.

calamine lotion A liquid preparation of pink powder containing zinc oxide and a minute amount of ferric oxide used frequently as a soothing, protective dressing for various skin conditions, especially when pruritus is involved.

calcium channel blockers Drugs used to treat heart conditions and hypertension that are generally safe to use in persons with allergies and asthma. Calcium channel blockers available in the United States include verapamil (Calan, Isoptin, Veralan), nifedipine (Adalat, Procardia), nicardipine (Cardene), diltiazem (Cardiazem), isradipine (DynaCirc), felodipine (Plendil), and bepridil (Vascor).

calcium sulfide A powder made by heating gypsum (a mineral often used in making plasterboard) with charcoal at 1,000 °F. A possible cause of allergic reactions, calcium sulfide is used in the manufacture of acne medications, depilatories, and paints and as a food preservative.

camomile See CHAMOMILE.

CAMP See CYCLIC ADENOSINE 3', 5' MONOPHOSPHATE.

camphor oil A crystalline compound derived from the camphor tree, the evergreen *Cinnamomum camphora* of the laurel family. Camphor oil, a possible cause of contact dermatitis, is used as insect repellent and in various skin products and creams. Camphor is toxic if ingested or absorbed through the skin. Camphorated oil was banned in 1980 by the Food and Drug Administration after it was discovered to be toxic when used as a liniment for muscle pain.

cananga oil A natural flavoring obtained from cananga tree flowers, used in the manufacture of cola and ginger ale beverages and desserts. It may cause allergic reactions.

candidiasis An infection, often called "yeast infection," caused by the fungus *Candida albicans*. This fungus is normally found in the vagina and gastrointestinal tract and is balanced by the normal flora (nonpathogenic, or non-disease- causing, bacteria) present in these areas.

Occurrence Candidiasis only becomes infectious when there is a disturbance in this balance, such as that promoted by a course of antibiotics for respiratory, skin, or urinary tract infection common in women. Infants on antibiotics may develop "thrush," a painful oral candida infection. There is an increased incidence of yeast infections in diabetics and in women during pregnancy or during treatment with oral contraceptives (birth control pills).

Significantly, when the body's natural resistance to infection is reduced in conditions such as AIDS or leukemia, candida infections may be life-threatening.

Treatment   Oral, vaginal, and topical antifungal drugs are the treatments of choice.

candidiasis allergy   [candidiasis hypersensitivity syndrome, yeast allergy]   A scientifically unproven theory that attributes many illnesses, including allergy, to the natural yeasts of the gastrointestinal tract. Practitioners of clinical ecology claim that a toxin (micotoxin) produced by excessive growth of yeasts is absorbed into the tissues and causes illness.

Yeasts and molds have been implicated by some investigators as a cause of chronic hives. Ingestion of mold-contaminated foods, or those to which brewer's and baker's yeasts have been added, is reported to be responsible. Allergy to yeasts is rare, and elimination of yeasts from the diet can be helpful in some cases.

Oral antifungal agents can be toxic and should not be used without a proven diagnosis of a fungal disease known to be responsive to that drug. Immunotherapy (allergy shots) with candida antigen for persons with immediate skin-test reactivity has no proven benefit in the treatment of allergies.

In 1986, the Practice Standards Committee of the American Academy of Allergy and Immunology reported in a position statement that, until scientifically designed studies prove otherwise, the candidiasis hypersensitivity syndrome is unsubstantiated.

capacity, vital   The volume of air that can be forcibly exhaled from the lungs after a full inhalation.

capsicum   A genus of tropical herbs and shrubs in the nightshade family whose dried fruit is cultivated for cayenne, African chili, and Tabasco peppers. Capsicum is a known irritant and can cause allergic reactions.

caraway   An herb of the carrot family, *Carum carvi*, used as a seasoning (caraway seed) and in medicinal preparations (caraway oil). Caraway oil, a pale or colorless liquid, is often an ingredient in perfumed soaps and in baked goods, condiments, liquors, beverages, sausage, and other foods. Topical application has been implicated in contact dermatitis.

carbinoxamine   An antihistaminic drug, commonly combined with a decongestant, used to treat allergic rhinitis (hay fever) conditions. It is available in oral formulations as Rondec (Abbott) or as a generic brand. Carbinoxamine may cause drowsiness. (See ANTIHISTAMINE.)

carbohydrate intolerance   Refined sugar intake blamed for behavioral problems in children and antisocial adults. However, in double-blind challenges in children reported by their parents to exhibit disruptive behavior after eating sugary foods, the only significant difference in behavior from the control group given saccharin as a placebo was a *decrease* in activity.

Reactive hypoglycemia, also called "low-blood sugar," "sugar allergy," or the "sugar blues," was once thought to predict the eventuality of diabetes mellitus. Many individuals describe a feeling of restlessness, sweating, increased heart rate, and weakness, all suggestive of anxiety, about two hours after eating some form of sugar. Blood sugar levels are usually normal (although proponents of this theory will label normal levels as "flat or depressed"), and symptoms are attributable to a release of epinephrine (adrenaline) in the bloodstream.

Symptoms of confusion, irritability, listlessness, and coma have been exhibited by persons whose blood glucose (sugar) level drops to dangerous levels below 40 milligrams/decaliters. These individuals are usually diabetics who have taken an overdose of insulin or oral antidiabetic drugs or have a rare, insulin-secreting tumor. Sugar-containing food or liquid must be given to them at once; if a person is unconscious, glucose must be given intravenously.

carbolic acid See PHENOL.

carbon dioxide [CO_2] A colorless, odorless gas exhaled during respiration that is the result of carbon oxidation that takes place in the tissues. Blood levels of CO_2 increase during hyperventilation, characterized by shortness of breath, tingling of extremities, and, at times, vomiting, elevated blood pressure, and disorientation. (See also ARTERIAL BLOOD GASES, HYPERVENTILATION.)

cardiac asthma Severe shortness of breath caused by fluid in the lungs that produces bronchospasm and wheezing. This condition results from an inability of the left chambers of the heart to pump adequately, that is, congestive heart failure. Cardiac asthma is accompanied by hyperventilation, a state of rapid breathing, and the person appears to be having an asthma attack. Primary treatment involves heart drugs such as diuretics, digitalis, and ace inhibitors. Bronchodilators are sometimes helpful.

carmine [carminic acid, Natural Red Dye No. 4] Red dye extracted from the dried bodies of female cochineal insects native to Mexico and Central America. Although carmine is used in the cosmetic industry for eye makeup, it may cause allergic reactions. The Food and Drug Administration has banned its use in foods because of infectious contamination of the dye.

carminic acid See CARMINE.

carotid body resection An unproven surgical technique called glomectomy, in which a carotid body is excised in patients with severe asthma. The carotid bodies, small bilateral collections of nerve tissue at the branch of the

carotid arteries, regulate the respiratory rate by sensing the oxygen and carbon dioxide concentrations in the blood. The carotid bodies then send nerve impulses to the respiratory center in the brain.

Glomectomy was first performed by Japanese physician K. Nakayama in 1942 and became popular in the 1960s. In 1986 the American Thoracic Society published a position statement proclaiming it ineffective for the treatment of asthma.

carpet steam cleaning A process that reduces levels of dust mite allergen, susceptible to heat, for about six weeks. However, it has no effect on levels of heat-resistant cat allergen.

carrot allergy Sensitivity to carrots, the orange root of the plant *Daucus carota*, usually evidenced by itching of the mouth, palate, and throat. Allergic persons may experience crossreaction with parsnips, apples, potatoes, and hazelnuts and from birch tree and grass pollen. Carrot seeds are both diuretic and stimulant. Carrots are also a major source of the yellow crystalline pigment carotene, the precursor of vitamin A. (See VITAMINS.)

casein hydrolysate formulas See HYDROLYSATE FORMULAS.

Casoni, Tomaso Italian physician (1880–1933) whose studies of skin and other diseases led him to develop a demonstration of an intradermal test reaction in individuals with echinococcosis (an infestation of a genus of tapeworms) that established the first diagnostic skin test for infection caused by parasitic worms.

Casoni's reaction A wheal and associated erythema (redness) at the site of an intradermal injection of sterile hydatid fluid to test for the presence of hydatid (watery) cysts after infection by the parasite *Echinococcus granulosus*. The test is named for Italian physician Tomaso Casoni (1880–1933).

cassia oil   Extract from the tropical leguminous plants of the genus Cassia and used as a food and beverage flavoring agent, in perfumes, and as a laxative. It has irritant properties and may cause allergic nasal congestion.

cast, bronchial   Hardened segments of bronchial secretions that accumulate and take on the shape of the bronchial tubes. Bronchial casts may be seen in the sputum of asthma or bronchitis patients. Cast material consists of substances thrown off during the course of pathological conditions (the products of effusion). The substances may also mold themselves to nasal, tracheal, esophageal, renal, urethral, intestinal, and vaginal passages.

castor oil   [palm Christi oil]   A fatty oil extracted from the beans of the tropical, ornamental, Old World castor-oil plant. Castor oil is used in the pharmaceutical industry as a cathartic, the food industry for beverage and baked goods flavoring, and in cosmetic products, especially in lipsticks. The castor bean residue is used as a fertilizer and is such a potent allergen that it may cause asthma in factory workers and in residents of the surrounding area. (See also OCCUPATIONAL ALLERGENS, OCCUPATIONAL ASTHMA.)

cat allergy   Hypersensitivity to carnivorous mammals of the family Felidae caused by exposure to cat allergens. The major allergen from *Felis domestica*, the domestic cat, is produced by the salivary and sebaceous glands and is found in the pelt, dander, saliva, and urine.

Inhalation of the antigen can cause allergic rhinitis (sneezing, runny nose, and itching), allergic conjunctivitis (itching, tearing, and redness of the eyes), or asthma. An estimated 31% of American families own cats, and an estimated six million Americans suffer from cat allergy. As many as 41% of allergic individuals show positive skin tests to cat allergen. Although not everyone who tests positive has symptoms, many of those who are skin-test positive will eventually become allergic upon continuing exposure. Allergic individuals should avoid cats and other furry animals if possible. Unfortunately, cat antigen has been found in shopping centers, hospital corridors, newly constructed homes, and on people's clothing. Dr. Samuel Shamie and associates at the Henry Ford Hospital in Detroit, Michigan demonstrated that a person wearing a new T-shirt and holding a cat for five minutes had a level of cat allergen 100 times the amount needed to produce wheezing in a cat-allergic person.

MEASURES TO REDUCE EXPOSURE TO CAT ALLERGEN

---

1. Keep the cat outdoors or at least limit it to an area of the home away from the bedrooms. (Studies have demonstrated the presence of cat allergen in the ventilation systems even in rooms never entered by a cat. Cat allergen can be measured up to six months following removal of cats from the home.)
2. Remove carpeting and heavily upholstered furniture, and cover pillows and mattresses, because cat allergen is a major component of house dust and collects on the surfaces of household objects.
3. Bathe your cat weekly to remove surface allergen.
4. Wear a mask when handling the litter, and wash your hands and change clothing immediately after this exposure. If possible, have a nonallergic person clean the litter.
5. Use a vacuum with a double filter to trap allergen particles; without an adequate filter, vacuuming will increase the exposure to allergens for hours afterward.

If cats cannot be avoided or the above measures are not effective, a standardized and effective cat allergy extract is available for immunotherapy (allergy shots). (See ANIMAL ALLERGY.)

catarrh   Inflammation of mucous membranes characterized by a dry cough and severe coughing spells with little or no expectoration, especially in the aged with emphysema or asthma.

caterpillar rash   A localized skin eruption caused by the toxin in the hairs of caterpillars.

cat scratch fever   An infection, also known as benign inoculation reticulosis, that develops after a scratch or bite from a cat or other animal. Ninety percent of reported cases occur following a cat scratch. The organism causing this infection has not been well defined but is probably a small gram-negative pleomorphic bacillus (a type of bacterium). These infectious organisms are present in the claws or mouth of the animal, which is not ill and does not need to be destroyed.

Symptoms   Between three and 10 days after the scratch or bite, a painful and tender swollen lymph node appears near the injured site. A fever, headache, rash, and general feeling of ill-being may occur. Within two weeks, unilateral regional lymph nodes in the axilla, epitrochlear, submandibular, cervical, or inguinal area may develop depending on the area of the scratch or bite. There may not be a noticeable break in the skin, but pus may develop if there is an open wound.

Diagnosis   Diagnosis is usually based on the history of a scratch or bite, although the patient is not always aware of its occurrence. A heat-treated suspension of pus aspirated from an involved lymph node can be used as a reliable skin test for delayed hypersensitivity to the responsible antigen to confirm the diagnosis but is not commercially available. One-tenth of a milliliter of test material is injected intradermally (under the skin) and read after 48 hours. A five-millimeter or greater area of induration is considered positive. There is a small percentage of false-positive and false-negative results. A biopsy of the lymph node can also help diagnose this condition.

Outcome and complications   In most cases, the disease resolves completely without treatment. Thrombocytopenia purpura (a condition with reduced platelet counts and large areas of bruising), conjunctivitis, and encephalitis are rare complications.

Treatment   Antibiotics, including tetracycline, ciprofloxacin (Cipro), rifampin (Rifadin or Rimactane), and trimethopri-m-sulfamethoxizole (Bactrim or Septra), are often prescribed and may shorten the course of the illness, but this has not been proven scientifically. At times, surgical excision of an involved area may be necessary.

cavernous rale   Hollow spaces in the respiratory tract that produce a bubbling sound. Cavernous respiration refers to a hollow sound heard when there is a lung cavity.

cedarwood oil   Distilled fluid from the leaves and branches of trees of the genus *Cedrus*. Cedar oil has a strong camphorlike odor and is used as an insect repellent and also in perfumes and soaps. Cedar oil can cause photosensitivity allergic rashes.

celiac disease   See GLUTEN-SENSITIVE EN-TEROPATHY.

celiac sprue   See GLUTEN-SENSITIVE ENTER-OPATHY.

cell assays   Tests in which various circulating cells of the immune system are measured for activity or quantity. These include basophils, eosinophils, lymphocytes, and antibodies. (See BASOPHIL DEGRANULATION AND HISTAMINE RELEASE; EOSINOPHIL COUNT; IMMU-NOFLUORESCENCE, DIRECT; IMMUNOFLUORES-CENCE, INDIRECT; LYMPHOCYTE BLAST TRANSFORMATION.)

cell-mediated immunity   Immune protection provided by the direct action of immune cells such as macrophages. This differs from humoral (bodily fluids) immunity, which chiefly involves B cells and antibodies. The macrophage ingests the antigen, digests it, and then displays antigenic fragments on its own surface. The macrophage then binds to a group of genes called a major histocompatibility complex (MHC). This combined structure attracts a T cell's attention. A T cell whose receptor fits this antigen-MHC complex binds to it and stimulates the macrophage to secrete interleukin-1. Interleukin-1 in turn activates other T cells and starts a series of biochemical processes that may result in certain subsets of T cells becoming cytotoxic, or killer, cells. The T killer cells track down viral-infected body cells. When the infection has been eradicated, suppressor T cells shut down the immune response. (See also B CELLS, HUMORAL IMMUNITY, IMMUNE SYSTEM.)

central vacuum systems   See VACUUM CLEANERS FOR ALLERGIC PERSONS.

cephalosporins   A group of antibiotics derived from the fungus *Cephalosporium acremonium*, effective against a wide range of infections that may be resistant to the penicillins.

Cephalosporins kill bacteria by interfering with the development of the bacterial cell wall and production of proteins by the organism. Older, or first-generation, cephalosporins are sometimes ineffective against some bacteria that produce a defensive enzyme, beta-lactamase, which inactivates the antibiotic before it can kill the bacteria. The newer second- and third-generation drugs in this group are more effective against these infections.

Uses for allergy patients   Cephalosporins are used to treat ear, throat, and respiratory infections, including sinusitis and bronchitis.

Adverse reactions   Allergic reactions include a widespread rash or hives, itching, fever, and, in rare cases, anaphylaxis (a severe life-threatening reaction causing shock). Approximately 10% of persons allergic to penicillins are also allergic to cephalosporins. If one has had a severe allergic reaction to penicillin, cephalosporins should probably be avoided unless the infection does not respond to other antibiotics. Diarrhea is a nonallergenic and potentially serious adverse effect of cephalosporin antibiotics and may require discontinuation. A serious form of colitis (bowel inflammation) may result when a toxin is produced in the colon resulting from the use of antibiotics that disturb the normal balance of nonpathogenic (non–disease-causing) bacteria. This form of diarrhea is caused by *Clostridium difficile* cytotoxin and enterotoxin, which may become life-threatening

if not recognized early. Symptoms may improve without further complications when the offending antibiotic is discontinued or special antibiotics, such as vancomycin or metronidazole, are employed to treat the antibiotic-induced diarrhea.

A less serious complication, candidiasis, or "yeast infection," occurs frequently in women using antibiotics and is treated with vaginal creams or suppositories that do not require stopping the antibiotic. (See CANDIDIASIS.) Milder forms of diarrhea and yeast infections may be prevented in persons requiring antibiotics by taking lactobacillus tablets or granules. Yogurt, a form of curdled milk and a fermentation product of *Lactobacillus*, may be less effective because many persons are lactase deficient and cannot tolerate any dairy products, which themselves cause diarrhea in those persons.

CEPHALOSPORIN PRODUCTS COMMONLY USED IN ALLERGIC PATIENTS

First Generation	Second Generation	Third Generation
cefadroxil[1] (Duricef, Ultracef)	cefaclor (Ceclor)	cefixime (Suprax)
cephalexin[1] (Keflex)	cefuroxime (Ceftin)	
cephradine[1] (Velosef)		

Note: Many other cephalosporins are available for serious infections in injectable forms.
[1] Generic brands available.

cereal allergy   Sensitivity to grains including wheat, barley, oats, corn, and rye. Persons allergic to cereals may also be allergic to birch tree and grass pollens, carrots, parsnips, apples, potatoes, and hazelnuts. Highly allergic infants may tolerate poi, a Hawaiian and Samoan food prepared from the taro root as a substitute for cereals.

ceresin [ozokerite] (Ceresine, Earth Wax) A naturally occurring waxy compound found in Utah, Texas, and the Ukraine, used as a substitute for beeswax and paraffin and in making dental impressions. It may produce allergic symptoms.

cetirizine (Zyrtec) An antihistamine derived from hydroxyzine (Atarax, Vistaril), Zyrtec is less sedating than traditional antihistamines but mildly sedating in up to 14% of patients requiring the full dosage. Significant relief can be seen in as little as one hour and the usual adult dose for symptoms of seasonal and perennial allergic rhinitis or urticaria (hives) is 10 mg once daily. A dosage of 5 mg is recommended for patients with impaired liver or kidney function. Zyrtec does not appear to cause urinary retention in men with enlarged prostates.

cetyl alcohol A waxy substance derived from spermaceti from the sperm whale and used in cosmetics and as a laxative. It may cause hives.

chalicosis A form of pneumoconiosis, or silicosis, a respiratory tract disorder associated with inhalation of dust from stonecutting. See SILICOSIS.

challenge [provocative testing] The administration of a specific substance to determine an individual's reaction to that substance. In conjunctival, nasal, or bronchial challenge, the mucosae of the eyes, nose, or lungs are directly exposed to an allergen to determine that person's sensitivity to a particular allergen. Methacholine is a substance frequently used to determine reactivity of the bronchioles as an aid in the diagnosis of asthma. Oral challenges confirm or reject the diagnosis of food allergy.

Direct provocative testing is the most sensitive test for allergy. Persons whose skin tests are positive often show a negative reaction to the same allergen in a challenge test. Rarely does an individual with a positive challenge test have a negative skin test.

The principal disadvantage of a challenge test is its ability to induce a serious allergic response. Therefore, these tests should be per-formed only if clearly necessary in a carefully monitored setting. Other disadvantages include difficulty in standardizing test materials and measuring responsiveness quantitatively.

chamomile [camomile] A member of the sunflower (composite, aster) family used as an herbal tea that is allergenic in ragweed-sensitive individuals. (See HERB.)

Charcot, Jean Martin French neurologist (1825–93) who first noticed and described colorless, needlelike crystals in the spleen and sputum of a patient with emphysema and bronchitis. Years later, German physician Ernst V. von Leyden (1832–1910) described the significance of these crystals in his studies of patients with asthma. He believed they proved that bronchial asthma is not a nervous disorder but a disease of the airways and their secretions and that identifying the type of secretion leads to diagnosis of bronchial asthma.

Charcot-Leyden crystals (CLC) Six-sided, double-pointed crystals (solid formations made by salts, water, and other substances of the body) found on microscopic examination of sputum from asthma and bronchitis patients. These crystals are also found in the feces of patients with certain inflammatory conditions of the bowels, including amebiasis. Named for French neurologist Jean M. Charcot (1825–93) and German physician Ernst V. von Leyden (1832–1910), these colorless and sometimes needlelike protein crystals are produced by eosinophil cells. (See EOSINOPHIL.)

Chase, Merrill W. American scientist, born in Providence, Rhode Island in 1905, who is known for his immunologic studies, especially one in which he demonstrated that delayed sensitivity reaction can be induced in normal animals by transferring white blood cells of sensitized animals to the normal animals.

cheese A milk product made by compressing casein, or milk protein. Vasoactive amines such as tyramine and histamine present in some cheeses are a significant cause of migraine headaches in susceptible persons. Swiss cheese has been a cause of histamine poisoning.

Any dairy product, including cheese, can cause the gastrointestinal symptoms of bloating, flatulence, cramps, and diarrhea in persons deficient in the enzyme lactase needed to digest lactose (milk sugar). These food reactions do not have an allergic basis. Cheeses of all kinds, including cottage cheese, are eliminated in mold-elimination diets. The significance of molds as a source of allergy symptoms has not been scientifically proven.

cheilitis venerata   Rashes on the lips caused by exposure to chemicals in lipstick or other cosmetics.

chelation therapy   A method of ridding the body of toxic substances by the binding of that substance to metal ions to create a less toxic substance. This resulting compound is subsequently excreted in the body wastes.

Chelation is an effective therapy for lead, arsenic, and mercury poisoning. However, there is no scientific proof that small quantities of chemicals present in our bodies are harmful or that removing them by chelation improves allergies or our health.

chemical mediators   Biochemical substances released by mast cells, basophils, and other cells of the immune system during allergic reactions. Mediators include histamine, heparin, prostaglandins, and leukotrienes. These chemicals cause allergic symptoms such as wheezing, sneezing, runny nose, watery eyes, and itching. Anaphylaxis is its most severe response and is characterized by edema (swelling) of body tissues and a sudden, life-threatening drop in blood pressure. (See ANAPHYLAXIS, BASOPHILS, HISTAMINE, HYPERSENSITIVITY, IMMUNE SYSTEM, LEUKOTRIENES, MAST CELLS.)

chemical sensitivity   A term used by clinical ecologists to describe many ill-defined symptoms, such as irritability, fatigue, and allergylike symptoms, that these practitioners claim are associated with poorly ventilated homes and buildings. Various other names have been given to these complaints, such as "chemical AIDS," "20th-century disease," "multiple chemical sensitivities," or "yeast allergy." Most often there is little or no scientific proof that the environment is responsible for these vague ills.

Serious lung diseases such as hypersensitivity (allergic) pneumonitis can be caused by inhaling organic dusts. Legionnaire's disease results from inhaling bacteria from contaminated air-conditioning systems. However, it is difficult to prove that chemicals in the environment can cause a disease or allergy.

Chemicals of real concern are ozone and nitrous oxide, which can cause temporary or permanent lung disease. A few industrial chemicals are known to cause true allergic reactions, such as the acid anhydrides and isocyanates. Sulfur dioxide as an air pollutant can cause diminished lung function, especially in children or asthmatics.

The most widespread and dangerous indoor pollutant is cigarette smoke. Tobacco smoke increases levels of carbon monoxide, formaldehyde, nitrogen dioxide, acrolein, polycyclic aromatic hydrocarbons, hydrogen cyanide, and many other potential carcinogens.

Gases emanating from furniture and other cleaning products, pesticides, and paints may produce indoor pollutants. Although formaldehyde is an important source of outdoor pollution from gasoline and diesel fuel fumes, it is of minor importance indoors, where smoking is its chief source. Formaldehyde can cause skin sensitivity, but it is not allergenic to the respiratory system.

Wood-burning stoves are found in more than 11 million homes in the United States. Stoves without adequate ventilation give off carbon monoxide, nitrogen and sulfur oxides, benzopyrene, and formaldehyde.

Before symptoms are blamed on home or workplace environment, preexisting medical diseases must be eliminated or a new medical disorder must be ruled out. An industrial hygienist may be necessary to determine the presence of any significant pollutant, review Material Safety Data Sheets available for all chemicals used in the workplace from manufacturers, and use objective measurements of lung function, such as spirometry or peak flow meters to determine the validity of breathing complaints.

Of little or no significant value are expensive RAST testing, tests for Epstein-Barr and autoimmune disorders, and tests for food allergy and airborne molds and bacteria.

chemoreceptor   A sense organ or sensory nerve ending, such as a taste bud, that reacts to chemical stimuli.

chemoreceptor trigger zone   Certain areas of the medulla oblongata of the brain that are sensitive to chemical and pharmacologic stimuli. Responses include vomiting.

Chen, Ko Kuei   Chinese pharmacist and scientist (1898–1988), the first director of pharmacologic research at Eli Lilly Company in Indianapolis, appointed in 1929. Chen researched cyanide poisoning and antidotes, synthetic painkillers, toad poisons, and Chinese herbs, among other subjects. Along with colleague Carl F. Schmidt (1893–1988), Chen conducted studies on Ma-Huang, also known as ephedrine, which were the first investigations of the drug's effect on the cardiovascular system. Chen believed ephedrine relieved the symptoms of asthma and bronchial spasm. (See also EPHEDRINE; SCHMIDT, CARL F.)

chest expansion, normal   The upward movement of the chest as air is taken into the lungs.

chicken   Domestic fowl (*Gallus gallus*), a popular food. Persons allergic to eggs or feathers can usually tolerate chicken meat. Chicken is sometimes avoided in mothers with allergies who are breast-feeding and is a potential allergen in infants but rarely in older individuals.

Elimination diets in children under one year, but older than six months, may contain meat from roosters or capons only.

chicken feathers   See FEATHERS.

chiggers   [redbugs]   Six-legged larvae of mites of the family Trombiculidae, order Acarina, class Arachnida. Chiggers are parasitic on humans and other vertebrates. They lay eggs on the ground that hatch in 12 days, after which they attach themselves to the first possible host (usually a skin surface). They then inject their saliva, which erodes the surrounding skin tissue. A rash results from sensitization to the injected saliva. Treatment preparations include lindane (Kwell) lotion and benzyl benzoate. Diethyltoluamide (Off) repels chiggers.

child crowing   [laryngisimus stridulus]   A spasm that briefly causes closure of the glottis and is followed by a noisy inspiration.

chilblains   [kibe]   Inflamed patches of skin on the hands or feet resulting from exposure to cold.

Chinese restaurant syndrome   A collection of vague symptoms following the consumption of food to which the chemical monosodium glutamate (MSG) has been added to enhance its flavor. MSG is commonly used in Chinese food, hence the name of the syndrome.

Adverse reactions to MSG are not caused by an allergy to it, and there are no confirmed reports of anaphylaxis. However, many experience skin flushing, tightening of muscles in the jaw and chest, nausea, headache, or a combination of these symptoms when eating a meal containing high concentrations of MSG.

Studies by the Food and Drug Administration have failed to confirm any serious ill effects from MSG, and it is considered a safe food ingredient. (See MONOSODIUM GLUTAMATE.)

chiropractic   A widely acclaimed discipline eschewing drugs and surgery and favoring hands-on manipulations (referred to as adjustments) of the spinal cord. Modern chiropractic follows tenets expressed in 1895 by Daniel David Palmer, of Iowa, based on the teachings of Hippocrates, who believed all illnesses had their sources in the spine. According to chiropractic, when vertebrae are subluxated, or dislocated or misaligned, the person experiences any number of ailments, including allergy, headaches, and back and other pain. Although there is a great deal of anecdotal testimony to their effectiveness, chiropractic techniques and theories have not been scientifically proven. Since symptoms of allergy and asthma often wax and wane, improvement following spinal manipulation may be falsely attributed to chiropractic. Because emotional stress triggers asthma (although it is not its cause), a placebo effect may result from chiropractic treatments.

chloramine-T [sulfone chloramide]   See OC-CUPATIONAL ALLERGENS.

chlorhexidine   A topical antiseptic used in cosmetic products, including feminine hygiene sprays, that may cause contact dermatitis.

chloride sweat test for cystic fibrosis   See SWEAT CHLORIDE TEST.

chlorine   An irritating gas that can be destructive to mucous membranes of the respiratory passages. It is also an active bleaching agent and germicide, especially for disinfection of water supplies, swimming pools, and sewage. In the body, natural chlorine is found combined with sodium in the blood and helps maintain osmotic pressure and regulation or stimulation of the muscles. Chlorine is also present in the stomach's hydrochloric acid to aid digestion, activate enzymes, and promote normal gastric secretions.

chloroform   A liquid characterized by a strong etherlike odor, derived from the action of chlorinated lime on methyl alcohol. Chloroform, widely used as an anesthetic before it was banned by the Food and Drug Administration for use in drugs and cosmetics, has been known to cause respiratory and skin allergies when it is an ingredient in cleaning agents.

chlorophenothane   DDT insecticide, which may cause symptoms of allergy, especially respiratory disturbances.

chlorophyll   The green pigment found in plants that undergo photosynthesis used in the manufacture of deodorant and cosmetics. While the light absorbed by chlorophyll provides the earth's major source of energy, chlorophyll may cause light sensitivity in allergic people.

chlorpheniramine (Chlor-Trimeton)   Antihistaminic drug of the alkylamine class, widely used in both over-the-counter and prescription allergy medications for the treatment of symptoms of hay fever and itching. Chlorpheniramine has a low incidence of side effects and is mildly sedating and is considered an antihistamine of choice during pregnancy.

Chlor-Trimeton   See CHLORPHENIRAMINE.

choana   In the posterior nares, a funnel-shaped opening leading from the nasal fossae to the pharynx, thus connecting the nasal passages with the throat. A nasal infection, then, may travel to and affect the throat.

chocolate allergy   Allergic reactions to candies or beverages made of ground roasted cacao or theobroma seeds. True allergic reactions are so rare that there are fewer than 10 documented cases in the allergy literature. At the National Jewish Hospital, in Denver, Colorado, over more than a 10-year period, there was not one unequivocal allergic reaction to chocolate.

Chocolate is a source of phenylethylamine, a vasoactive amine that is often reported to cause migraine. It is also a significant source of the methylxanthine theobromine, which has minimal, if any, behavioral effects but can be associated with central nervous system stimulation, headache, and abdominal pain. Chocolate can also cause reflux esophagitis (heartburn) and has been thought to trigger acne, because excess carbohydrates and fats and gastrointestinal disturbances may be among the factors that cause this chronic inflammatory disease of the sebaceous glands (in the skin) and the hair follicles.

Chocolate has also been implicated as a cause of allergic purpura, a type of vasculitis (an inflammation of blood vessels). There are no adequate double-blind studies to prove these anecdotal reports.

cholinergic urticaria   A type of hives characterized by severe itching of one- to three-millimeter papular skin lesions surrounded by an area of erythema, or redness. Cholinergic urticaria represents about 4% of all cases of hives and may be brought on by hot showers or baths, fever, and by emotional stress in some patients. Treatment is with antihistamines and by avoiding precipitating triggers. (See also URTICARIA, PHYSICAL URTICARIA.)

chromium compounds   Oxides found in the earth's crust that are used in the manufacture of green eyeshadow and green mascara, both of which may cause allergic skin reactions.

chromium sulfate   A potentially allergenic powder used for coloring textiles, paints and varnishes, and cosmetics.

chronic fatigue syndrome (CFS)   A disorder characterized by overwhelming fatigue associated with a prolonged recovery period. Also known as chronic mononucleosis, chronic Epstein-Barr virus infection, postviral fatigue syndrome, and myalgic encephalomyelitis, CFS causes tasks that were formerly routine to become difficult or impossible. The fatigue is accompanied by poor concentration and memory, depression, headaches, sleep disturbances, aches, and pains.

The condition may begin insidiously without apparent cause, or following an acute infection, described as early as 1869 as "neurasthenia . . . a physical not a mental state" by the American neurologist George

Beard in the *Boston Medical and Surgical Journal*. Clusters of cases have been blamed on mass hysteria, since clinical findings are usually nonexistent.

Recently, several viruses have been proposed as causes, but so far this has not been scientifically documented. Epstein-Barr virus, enteroviruses, retroviruses, herpes virus type 6, and the T-cell lymphotropic virus type II have all been implicated as possible causes of CFS.

An Australian study has demonstrated improvements in physical, psychological, and functional symptoms following therapy with intravenous gammaglobulin, suggesting that chronic fatigue syndrome, by whatever name, is an organic disease process and not a psychosomatic disorder. (See also TENSION-FATIGUE SYNDROME.)

chronic obstructive lung disease   See CHRONIC OBSTRUCTIVE PULMONARY DISEASE.

chronic obstructive pulmonary disease (COPD) [chronic obstructive lung disease (COLD)]   A condition in which there is persistent blockage of airflow into or out of the lungs because of chronic bronchitis or emphysema or both. In mild asthma, inflammation that thickens the bronchial walls, constriction of the muscles in the bronchial tubes, or obstruction by excessive mucus is present only during an attack. However, in severe asthma there is usually a degree of chronic obstruction that is reversible with treatment to varying degrees.

Chronic bronchitis is often confused with emphysema, an expansion of the air spaces resulting in destruction of the alveoli, or air sacs in the lungs. Approximately 20% of adult males have chronic bronchitis, although only a small number are disabled because of it. It is less common in females and most common in smokers. But allergies and other irritants, pollution from the environment, and occupational exposure can be causes. Pure emphysema is rare and is not reversible with treatment. The degree of obstruction found in chronic bronchitis is often greater than that found in most asthmatics but less than that in emphysemics. (See BRONCHITIS.)

Churg-Strauss syndrome (CSS) [allergic angiitis and granulomatosis]   A combination of symptoms first reported in 1951 in association with a cluster of 13 cases of severe asthma. Patients have fever, extremely elevated eosinophil counts in their blood, and vasculitis (see VASCULITIS). In addition, they generally have a long history of allergies, usually allergic rhinitis (hay fever) that progresses to asthma. A vasculitis, an inflammatory condition of blood vessels, evolves that may effect almost any organ but most often targets the heart, lungs, skin, central nervous system, muscles and bones, kidneys, or gastrointestinal tract. The person may develop nasal polyps, which cause obstruction of the nasal passages and sinusitis. The most serious complications result from vasculitis.

About one-third of patients have abnormal chest X rays that resemble those seen in cases of pneumonia. If the skin is involved, rashes, hives, bumplike lesions called nodules, or large areas of bruising may occur. Abdominal obstructions and perforations cause pain and diarrhea. Myocardial infarctions (heart attacks) or inflammation of the heart muscle can result in heart failure. Brain and nerve involvement often leads to strokes and is a major cause of serious disability or death. Kidney impairment leads to hypertension (high blood pressure). Symptoms of arthritis and muscle cramping may be present. Churg-Strauss syndrome may begin with a feeling of malaise but may progress quickly with severe weight loss.

The American College of Rheumatology lists six criteria for diagnosing this condition: (1) asthma; (2) eosinophil count increasing to 10% of white blood cells; (3) a mononeuropathy or polyneuropathy (singular or multiple degeneration of nerves resulting in weakness); (4) pneumonialike fluid accumulation seen in chest X rays; (5) abnormality of the sinuses; and (6) characteristic blood vessel biopsy. The presence of four or more of these criteria highly suggests Churg-Strauss.

Cortisone is the treatment of choice, but other immunosuppressive drugs are sometimes used. Five-year survival was greater than 60% in 1977, the last year data are available.

chymopapain   A proteolytic enzyme derived from the plant *Carica papaya* and an ingredient in some meat tenderizers. The enzyme is injected into herniated lumbar disks as an alternative to surgical laminectomy, a fusion of spinal vertebrae. However, chymopapain is estimated to cause sudden anaphylaxis in 1% of patients; 0.15% of reactions are fatal. Because these reactions are true immunoglobulin E–mediated allergic reactions, skin testing can determine who is at risk.

cider   A fermented product of apples that is included in mold elimination diets. The significance of ingested molds as a source of allergen has not been scientifically proven. Cider may contain sulfite-type preservatives to which a subset of asthmatics are sensitive. (See FUNGI AND MOLDS, SULFITING AGENTS.)

cigarette smoke   Fumes from a burning cigarette, which are not in themselves allergenic, although tobacco smoke is an irritant to persons with asthma and nasal or eye allergy. In the past some practitioners have skin-tested and given immunotherapy (allergy shots) to patients believed to be allergic to tobacco smoke, but there is no scientific rationale for this treatment. (See PASSIVE SMOKING; SMOKING, ACTIVE AND PASSIVE.)

cilia   Tiny hairs in the lining of the nasal passages that help the natural movement of mucus, pus, and particles of dust and other foreign bodies.

cimetidine (Tagamet)   A histamine type 2 antagonist (antihistamine) used primarily for the treatment of peptic ulcer disorders. It may also provide some relief for the itching of hives when used in combination with a type 1 antihistamine. (See also HISTAMINE H2 RECEPTOR ANTAGONIST.)

cinnamal A liquid extract from a wood-rotting fungus, natural to cassia and cinnamon bark, used in cosmetics as a scent in various products, including powders, and in mouthwashes. Cinnamal, also called cinnamaldehyde, is an allergen and an irritant to mucous membranes and skin.

cinnamon bark An oil and extract from the dried bark of cinnamon trees, used as an additive in cosmetics and foods and known to cause photosensitivity and other allergic skin rashes.

cinnamon oil [oil of Cassia] Oils composed mostly of cinnamal and used in toothpastes and perfumes. Cinnamon oil can cause allergic dermatitis.

cinnamyl alcohol A potential allergen found in balsam of Peru, cinnamon leaves, and hyacinth oil.

circadian rhythm Approximately the 24-hour cycle in which biologic bodily functions occur; the term *circadian* is a combination of Latin words for "about a day." Biologic rhythms were recognized as early as 1698 when Sir John Floyer observed that asthma attacks occurred frequently during the night. In 1745 botanist Carl von Linne devised a clock of flowers based on the opening and closing of various flowers at different times of day.

Hormones such as cortisol (cortisone) are greatly influenced by this cycle. In an individual on a daytime work or school schedule, who awakens at about 6:30 A.M. and goes to sleep at 11 P.M., the peak production of cortisol occurs between 6 and 8 A.M. Persons afflicted with allergy or asthma often experience exacerbation of symptoms in the middle of the night or very early in the morning because cortisol levels are lowest at these times. Persons on a nighttime work schedule have peak cortisol production in the afternoon. Circadian rhythms also affect the sensitivity of allergy skin-test results, with a peak of testing sensitiv-

ity in late evening and a period of least reactivity in the early morning.

citronella oil A food flavoring derived from an Asian grass that is also used in toiletries and as an insect repellent. Allergic reactions to citronella oil include asthma, hay fever, nasal congestion, and rashes.

citrus fruit Fruit, usually with thick rind and pulpy flesh found in warm regions. Allergic reactions, including anaphylaxis, have been reported. Migraine headaches were triggered by oranges in 39 of 60 (65%) patients studied in one group. However, most investigators attribute only a small percentage of migraines to foods. Orange also is a source of histamine, which can cause headaches. Citrus can be allergenic; it should not be given to infants and should be avoided by mothers who are breast-feeding.

Claman, Henry N. American physician, born in New York in 1930, whose studies of many topics in allergy and immunology led to important findings on the thymus-derived and bone-marrow-derived two-cell system of antibody production.

clarithromycin (Biaxin) Macrolide antibiotic related to erythromycin but with somewhat greater coverage for some mild to moderately severe infections.

Claritin See LORATADINE.

cleaning devices See VACUUM CLEANERS FOR ALLERGIC PERSONS.

clean room A room or environment in which the air—its temperature, pressure, humidity, and purity—is controlled. A filter may be used to remove 99.97% of all particles 0.3 microns (1 micron = 1/25,000 inch) and larger. Clean rooms are used in research and for individuals suffering from severe allergy or chronic infection due to immune system deficiency.

Clear Eyes See NAPHAZOLINE.

clemastine (Tavist) An antihistaminic drug used to treat the symptoms of allergy, including

ing sneezing, runny nose, nasal congestion, itchy eyes, and the itching of hives. It is often combined with a decongestant. (See ANTIHISTA-MINE.)

clinical ecology   An alternative approach to traditional medicine that attributes a wide range of symptoms to exposure to common substances in the environment. Patients are considered to be "allergic" to environmental factors such as food, water, chemicals, and pollutants.

Symptoms attributed to clinical ecology include behavior disorders, depression, chronic fatigue, arthritis, hypertension, learning disabilities, schizophrenia, gastrointestinal and respiratory problems, and urinary complaints.

In a position statement published in 1986, the American Academy of Allergy and Immunology labeled the clinical ecology approach to allergy as unproven and experimental: "The theoretical basis for ecologic illness in the present context has not been established as factual, nor is there satisfactory evidence to support the actual existence of 'immune system dysregulation' or maladaptation. There is no clear evidence that many of the symptoms noted above are related to allergy, sensitivity, toxicity, or any other type of reaction from foods, water, chemicals, pollutants, viruses, and bacteria in the context presented." The statement also included objections to testing methods and therapies, a lack of immunologic data, and the possibility of psychosomatic illness in certain patients.

clove oil   An antiseptic, aromatic, and flavoring derived from the clove tree, *Eugenia Caryophyllus,* known to cause skin irritation and allergic reactions.

clover   A low-lying, flowering herb of the genus *Trifolium* (having three leaves) that, when used as flavoring in foods, can cause photosensitivity.

clubbed fingers   Rounded, swollen fingertips in children with congenital heart disease and adults with long-standing lung disease.

coal tar   A distillate of bituminous coal used in making dyes and drugs. Coal tar derivatives have been reported to be carcinogenic in animals and the cause of allergic skin reactions, including urticaria (hives) and other rashes.

Coca, Arthur Fernandez   American physician (1875–1959), born in Philadelphia, Pennsylvania, who developed "Coca's solution" for allergen extraction and prepared and standardized allergens for skin tests and the treatment of allergy by injections. Coca also founded the *Journal of Immunology* and was its editor for 25 years. He introduced the concept of atopy—from the Greek word meaning "uncommonness," allergy symptoms that appear upon exposure to allergens. In addition, Coca developed the first municipal wide blood donor program in New York City.

coccidiomycosis [San Joaquin or valley fever]   See FUNGAL DISEASES, SYSTEMIC.

cockroach allergy   Hypersensitivity to any members of the order Orthoptera, a common omnivorous insect that infests housing, restaurants, and other buildings and, through its contact with both filth and food, may transmit bacteria, protozoans, and worms to humans. The three species of cockroaches common in the United States are *Blattella germanica* (German), *Periplaneta americana* (American), and *Blatta orientalis* (Oriental), all of which are the most allergenically important because they are a significant cause of allergic rhinitis and asthma.

Cockroaches cause reactions that range from a runny nose to life-threatening asthma or anaphylaxis. There are 5,000 or more species of this 350 million-year-old insect throughout the world. About 55 species infest urban areas. It has been estimated that an average of 13,000 roaches inhabit the average urban apartment building.

Although cockroach allergy was first recognized before 1940, it was not until the 1960s and 1970s that its importance was established. The major antigens are concentrated in the insect's body parts. Fecal waste and egg cases are of lesser importance. Exposure to cockroaches may result in both immediate and delayed allergic reactions.

Experts believe that cockroach allergy depends upon genetic disposition and exposure to large numbers of roaches and their allergens, which adhere to dust particles and become airborne. Sixty-six percent of asthmatics who reside in a cockroach-infested dwelling have positive skin tests to the insects, as opposed to only 43% who live elsewhere.

Americans spend an estimated $1.5 billion annually to exterminate roaches. Retail pesticides are rarely strong enough to eliminate roaches, and only professional exterminators are licensed to use stronger, more effective chemicals. Roaches migrate from place to place to avoid sprayed areas. When the chemicals have dissipated, they return. All rooms of entire buildings must be sprayed simultaneously and regularly. Contents of closets, cabinets, and drawers must be removed so that every crack and crevice can be sprayed. Cockroaches prefer the warm, moist, stagnant air of overheated, airtight buildings. Even dead cockroach particles remain allergenic for long periods of time. Immunotheraphy is effective for asthmatics who cannot avoid exposure to cockroaches. (See also INSECT ALLERGY.)

cocktail headache   A type of vascular headache, sometimes called a "hangover," brought on by the consumption of alcoholic beverages. (See HEADACHE.)

cocoa   A powdery substance derived from the cacao or cocoa tree seed used for the preparation of beverages. Cocoa has been reported to cause various allergic reactions. Cocoa butter, prepared from the fat of the roasted seed of the cocoa tree, is used in the manufacture of lubricants and suppositories. (See also CHOCOLATE ALLERGY.)

coconut oil   The saturated fat derived from coconut kernels used in making soaps, lathers, ointments, creams, and other toiletries. It is a potential allergen, especially to skin.

codeine sensitivity   See DRUG ALLERGY AND OTHER ADVERSE DRUG REACTIONS.

coffee   See CAFFEINE.

cog-wheel breathing   An intermittent respiratory murmur often accompanying bronchitis.

coin test   A diagnostic test for pneumothorax. A coin is placed on the chest over a suspected area of the lung and struck by another coin. If a metallic ringing sound is heard, a cavity containing air is underneath. Physicians now order X rays to confirm the diagnosis.

COLD   Chronic Obstructive Lung Disease. See CHRONIC OBSTRUCTIVE PULMONARY DISEASE.

cold, common   See RESPIRATORY INFECTION, VIRAL.

cold air   An asthma trigger in some persons. Doctors recommend that such persons use scarves, masks, and other protective clothing especially to cover the nose and mouth in cold weather. (See TRIGGERS OF ALLERGIES AND ASTHMA.)

cold cream   A skin cleanser, originally developed by the Greek physician Galen in ancient Greece, that feels cool on the skin. When ingredients include beeswax, rose petals, and other substances, cold cream has been known to cause allergic skin reactions.

cold-dependent dermatographism   The ability to write on skin with a sharp object when the skin is cold, resulting in a raised red line or wheal. (See DERMATOGRAPHIA, WHEAL.)

cold-induced cholinergic urticaria   A form of hives triggered by exercise in a cold environment. In cholinergic urticaria, hives are triggered by excessive body heat. (See COLD URTICARIA, ESSENTIAL.)

cold-induced rhinorrhea [skier's nose]   A runny nose that occurs upon exposure to cold air. It is not an allergy and does not respond to antihistamines, but it may be prevented by using a mixture of atropine sulfate and saline solution as a nasal spray. (See also TRIGGERS OF ALLERGIES AND ASTHMA.)

colds and allergy   See RESPIRATORY INFECTION, VIRAL.

cold urticaria, acquired   See COLD URTICARIA, ESSENTIAL.

cold urticaria, essential [acquired cold urticaria]   The onset of hives two to five minutes after skin contact with cold water or ice, followed by rewarming. The hives last from one to two hours or may develop into angioedema with swelling of the lips and tongue after a cold drink. In its most severe form, total body exposure, such as swimming in cold water, may cause a drop in blood pressure, fainting, anaphylaxis (total collapse), and drowning. The disorder may spontaneously disappear months or years later.

Variations include cold-induced cholinergic urticaria. In this condition, exercise in a cold environment causes hives. In some cases, type I immediate allergic hypersensitivity is involved, which results in the release of histamine and other chemical mediators from mast cells in the skin. In the "ice cube test," an ice cube is placed on the forearm for five minutes. If positive, hives occur in about 10 minutes as the skin warms. In other forms of the disease, proteins called cryoglobulins or cryofibrinogens are found in the blood.

The most effective treatment is avoidance of cold. Cyproheptadine (Periactin) is the antihistamine of choice, but others are often useful. The tricyclic antidepressant drug doxepin (Sinequan) may also be effective. (See also PHYSICAL URTICARIA, URTICARIA.)

cold urticaria, familial   The presence of an erythematous (red), papular, burning rash, associated with headache, joint and muscle pains, fever, and chills. Familial cold urticaria, inherited as an autosomal dominant trait, is not considered to be true hives. The rash, which is rare, is triggered by cold-air exposure for 20 to 30 minutes, although a delayed form may not manifest itself for nine to 18 hours and lasts approximately 24 to 48 hours. If cold-water and ice-test challenges are negative, the condition can be distinguished from essential, or acquired, cold urticaria.

The optimal treatment is avoidance of cold air. There is a poor response to antihistamines. (See COLD URTICARIA, ESSENTIAL; URTICARIA.)

colic, infantile   A sudden acute abdominal pain presumed to originate in an infant's intestinal tract and associated with abrupt and prolonged crying and drawing of the knees to the chest. It frequently occurs in three-month-old or younger infants shortly after feeding. It may be relieved by movement of the bowels or passage of flatus. Milk and other food allergies have been blamed; however, breast-fed infants also suffer from colic. Rarely is dietary manipulation successful in preventing colic.

Adult forms of colic include renal, uterine, menstrual, biliary, and lead colic, which is associated with lead poisoning, especially as an occupational hazard for painters and others exposed to lead-containing substances.

collagen   The protein substance of connective tissue used in the manufacture of cosmetics, especially antiaging preparations, which have not won favor with medical experts as effective. Collagen injections, however, have been used in the cosmetic treatment of acne and other skin conditions (including wrinkles) and may cause allergic reactions in hypersensitive individuals.

collodion   A potentially allergenic liquid made of alcohol, either, and nitrocellulose and used in products such as cement, lacquers, and clear nail polish.

colocynth   A potentially allergenic denaturant, derived from the dried fruit of Mediterranean and Near Eastern regions, used in the cosmetic industry.

cologne   A potentially allergenic liquid fragrance usually made with a citrus or floral base.

colonic enemas   Solutions of various content introduced into the rectum and colon in order to cleanse the lower bowel, to administer medication or anesthesia, or to aid in X-ray procedures. Colonic enemas are often prescribed by alternative practitioners to eliminate "toxins" from the body as part of an allergy-oriented therapy. These enemas may be dangerous, and reports have implicated this treatment in at least two deaths and 30 colectomies (surgical removal of the colon). (See also ALTERNATIVE TESTING AND TREATMENT FOR ALLERGIES; CONTROVERSIAL APPROACHES TO DIAGNOSIS, EXPLANATION, OR TREATMENT OF ALLERGIES.)

colors   See AZO DYES, DYES, FOOD ADDITIVES.

coltsfoot   A wild ginger herb, formerly used in the treatment of asthma because it allegedly opens pores to allow sweating. It has also been used as a soothing ointment.

complement   A complex series of blood proteins whose action "complements" the action of antibodies. (See COMPLEMENT DEFICIENCY DISORDERS, IMMUNE SYSTEM.)

complement deficiency disorders   Diminished or absent level of complement in the immune system (see COMPLEMENT, IMMUNE SYSTEM). Many components and component inactivators of complement have been identified, many of which are deficiencies inherited as an autosomal recessive trait. Some persons with minor complement deficiencies have relatively minor difficulty fending off infections. However, persons with total C1, C4, and C2 deficiencies experience serious recurrent infections and often have autoimmune diseases as well. (See also COMPLEMENT INACTIVATOR DEFICIENCY.)

complement inactivator deficiency   A disorder in which there is a diminished or absent level of the protein C1 esterase inhibitor in the blood, which causes hereditary angioedema. (See ANGIOEDEMA, HEREDITARY; COMPLEMENT.)

Composite family   [Compositae]   Members of a plant family that share a unique floral arrangement. Although most of the 20,000 or more species of composite are entemophilous (insect-pollinating) plants, this family includes the anemophilous (wind-pollinating) *Ambrosia* species (ragweed), whose pollen is the most important weed allergen that causes hay fever. (See ANEMOPHILOUS PLANTS, RAGWEED.)

computerized axial tomography   (CAT scan)   See COMPUTERIZED TOMOGRAPHY.

computerized tomography (CT scan) [computerized axial tomography (CAT scan)] An X-ray scanning technique for picturing internal body structures, especially the brain, chest, abdomen, and pelvis. Images can be limited to the sinuses and are the most accurate diagnostic test for sinus infections and tumors. This procedure is able to visualize the ethmoid sinuses, which are difficult to evaluate with traditional plain sinus X rays.

conenose   See KISSING BUG.

coniosis   Any illness, ailment, or anomaly caused by the inhalation of dust.

conjunctivitis, allergic   Red, itchy, watery eyes in persons with allergy. This eye disorder

INHERITED ERRORS OF THE COMPLEMENT SYSTEM

Inhibitors	Inheritance	Associated Diseases
C1 inactivator	Autosomal dominant	Hereditary angioedema
C3b inactivator	Not known	Recurrent infections

Components	Inheritance	Associated Diseases
C1q	Autosomal recessive	Recurrent bacterial infections
C1r	Autosomal recessive	Lupuslike skin rash, glomerulonephritis
C1s	Autosomal recessive	Systemic lupus[1]
C4	Autosomal recessive	Lupus
C2	Autosomal codominant	Lupus, glomerulonephritis, recurrent bacterial infections[2]
C3	Autosomal recessive	Recurrent bacterial infections
C5	Autosomal recessive	Lupus, recurrent infections
C6	Autosomal recessive	Gonococcal arthritis, nephritis, and meningitis [1]
C7	Autosomal recessive	Scleroderma[1]
C8	Autosomal recessive	Recurrent gonococcal infections[1]
C9		No disease

[1]May have no associated disease.
[2]May be normal in childhood.
Source: Adapted from M. M. Glovsky, "Applications of Complement Determinations in Human Disease," Nichols Institute, 1992.

results when histamine and other chemicals are released from mast cells in the conjunctiva (the mucous membrane lining the eyelids) during an IgE-mediated, or immediate allergic, reaction. It is most common during the fall and spring pollinating seasons and from animal dander exposure.

Cromolyn sodium (Opticrom) is the treatment of choice but has been temporarily discontinued in the United States, although it is available in other countries. Antihistaminic decongestant eyedrops, both by prescription and over the counter, are effective in many cases. Corticosteroid eyedrops are reserved for the most severe cases; they are rarely needed, and their use must be monitored by an ophthalmologist because of the potential for serious adverse effects. Adverse effects of corticosteroid eyedrops include glaucoma, cataract formation, and opportunistic infections (those infec-

tions resulting from suppression of the immune system) including herpes simplex.

Contact sensitivity of the eye is a common disorder causing itching, tearing, and light sensitivity; the eyelids may also swell and become inflamed. It is caused by exposure to sensitizing drugs often used in eye medications, including neomycin, atropine and related drugs, idoxuridine, and contact lens solutions.

Atopic keratoconjunctivitis is related to atopic dermatitis (eczema) and also causes itching, tearing, and light sensitivity. The eyes appear red and inflamed, and the palpebral conjunctivae (the inner lining of the eyelids) also become swollen and inflamed. This disorder is frequently complicated by secondary staphlococcal or herpes simplex infections.

Vernal keratoconjunctivitis is an allergic eye disorder involving IgE antibodies that usually begins before puberty and rarely lasts beyond the second decade. It is more common in warm climates. Patients have severe itching, tearing, stringy mucus discharge from their eyes, and light sensitivity. The upper inner eyelids develop a cobblestone appearance, known as "giant papillae." Plaques may develop on the cornea and impair vision. White opacities called "Trantas' dots" may be seen on the surface of the eye at the corneoscleral border known as the "limbus."

Cromolyn sodium eyedrops (where available) are the best treatment. Decongestant (vasoconstricting) eyedrops may be helpful, but corticosteroids are not safe for long-term treatment. Cold compresses and air-conditioning are helpful.

Phylctenular conjunctivitis is an allergic form of conjuntivitis usually seen in children and characterized by nodules that may ulcerate.

Other immunologic eye diseases often confused with allergic conjunctivitis include cicatrical pemphigoid and Stevens-Johnson syndrome (see STEVENS-JOHNSON SYNDROME).

Consensus Development Conferences
Biomedical investigators, practicing physicians, consumers, and health advocacy groups called upon by the National Institutes of Health to provide a scientific assessment of technologies, including drugs, devices, and procedures, and to seek agreement on their safety and effectiveness. (See Appendix III. See also ATTENTION DEFICIT DISORDER WITH HYPERACTIVITY, FEINGOLD DIET, HYPERACTIVITY.)

contactant A substance causing an allergic response when it touches skin.

contact dermatitis A rash caused by skin contact with a chemical substance that may be allergic or irritant (nonimmune) in nature. Allergic contact dermatitis results from an acquired cell-mediated allergy, or type IV delayed hypersensitivity (see HYPERSENSITIVITY). A chemical allergen binds to a component in the skin and, upon being recognized as "foreign," stimulates macrophages, lymphocytes, and other cells of the

immune system to release chemical mediators, and an inflammatory response occurs. Bloch and Steiner-Wourlisch (ca. 1926) and Landsteiner and Jacobs (ca. 1935) were pioneers in demonstrating mechanisms for this disorder.

Photoallergic contact dermatitis requires a contact allergen in addition to light exposure to produce a rash. Phototoxic contact dermatitis requires skin damaged by an irritant, which is then exposed to sunlight.

It is often difficult to distinguish between irritant and allergic causes of contact dermatitis. Frequent causes of allergic dermatitis include the metal nickel found in jewelry and chromates; latex, or rubber; oily plant substances in poison ivy and oak; various topical drugs; and cosmetics. Some substances act as both irritants and allergens.

The first occurrence of allergic contact dermatitis may be seven to 10 days after initial contact with the sensitizing substance. More often, however, with weaker allergens the reaction occurs only after repeated and prolonged exposure up to years after first contact. After the first reaction, subsequent outbreaks usually occur 24 to 48 hours after contact exposure. Sensitivity usually lasts from many years to a lifetime.

Symptoms The rash appears as erythema (redness), edema (swelling), and a papulovesicular (elevations with and without blisters) on the involved area. The diagnosis of contact dermatitis may be suggested by the distribution of the rash, either sparing clothed areas, involving only covered areas, or areas in contact with jewelry.

Prevalence Contact dermatitis is among the leading causes of workers' disability and compensation cases. There are about 80,000 or more chemical substances in the environment of which approximately 2,800 are known allergens to susceptible individuals. Many of these allergens are found chiefly in the workplace. Contact allergy is no more common in persons with other allergies.

Diagnosis Only 20 of the several thousand causative substances have been approved by the Food and Drug Administration (FDA) for testing in the United States as late as 1991. See the list below.

PATCH TEST ALLERGENS APPROVED FOR TESTING BY THE FDA

Balsam of Peru 25%
Benzocaine 5%
Black rubber mix 0.6%
Carba mix 3%
Cinnamic aldehyde 1%
Colophony 20%
Epoxy resin 1%
Ethylenediamine dihydrochloride 1%
Formaldehyde 1%
Imidazolidinyl urea 2%
Lanolin alcohol 30%
Mercaptobenzothiazole 1%
Mercapto mix 1%
Neomycin sulfate 20%
Nickel sulfate 2.5%
o-Phenylenediamine 1%
Potassium dichromate 0.25%
p-tert-Butylphenol formaldehyde resin 1%
Quarternium 15, 2%
Thiuram mix 1%

There are 92 preservatives listed for use in cosmetics and prescriptions by the FDA; the list below includes the most important and frequently used allergic sensitizers.

MOST FREQUENTLY USED SENSITIZING PRESERVATIVES IN COSMETICS AND PHARMACEUTICALS

(Listed by decreasing frequency of use)
Parabens
Imidazolidinyl urea
Quaternium 15
BHA
Kathon CG-formaldehyde
DMDM hydantoin
Bronopol
Diazolidinyl urea

Unfortunately, many of the most common sensitizers not available for patch testing in the United States are a cause of great disability. For example, glyceryl monothioglycate is found in some "acid" permanent wave solutions. Persistent or recurring rashes on the hands of hairdressers can be of sufficient severity to require a change of occupation. Another example is the preservative chlorhexidine found in many topical medications; it is often responsible for aggravating the condition for which it was prescribed.

Patch test results vary in reliability, and the quality of test materials and expertise of the tester are extremely important. Falsely negative results can be hazardous, because they are unlikely to be repeated. Patches are usually removed 48 hours following application; however, as many as 35% of positive results may be missed by reading results at this time. Some experts advocate reading results at 96 hours. Rarely, sensitization from the patch testing material itself may be a cause of a positive reaction and be confused with the cause of the patient's dermatitis.

Other contact allergens Chemicals found in members of the Compositae family of plants, which includes chrysanthemums, ragweed, calendulas, sagebrush, marsh elder, and feverfew, are known allergens, frequent causes of rashes, but rarely recognized as the cause. Many nursery workers have been sensitized to a potent allergen in the stems and leaves of Peruvian and Inca lilies and tulip bulbs. The common primrose was such a common cause of disability from rashes that its use in the United States was limited for many years because florists refused to handle it. The plant hydrangea is another strong allergen. The stems and leaves of the plants *Heracleaum spondyllium*, *Pastinaca sativa*, and *Dictamnus albus* cause a phototoxic dermatitis when the plant juices come in contact with the skin also exposed to sunlight. This contact occurs from cutting grass or weeds and is best avoided by wearing protective clothing and doing lawn work in the evening.

Many woods are also skin sensitizers, most prominent of which is Australian blackwood. Three potent allergens have been isolated from this wood, with contact rashes often found in forest workers and cabinetmakers.

Epoxy resin compounds used in the manufacture of plastics are common causes of allergic contact, but testing only with the standard available patch kit materials may miss individual sensitivities to other resins in the workplace. A number of patients and dental workers are allergic to various acrylates and dental adhesives. Acrylic artificial nails may cause a persistent burning, tingling, and numbness of the fingertips as well as a contact rash.

Textile dyes should be suspected if a rash appears on areas of the body in direct contact with the materials. The lateral torso, sparing the axilla, the inner thighs, the neck, and the ankles (at the top of socks) are suspect areas. Bed linens can also be a source of contact dermatitis. Excessive perspiration, especially in the obese, may increase leaching out the dye for fabric. A piece of suspected fabric should be soaked in warm water for about 20 minutes before being placed on a clear area of skin for testing.

Allergy to the metal nickel occurs so frequently that the government of Denmark has prohibited its use in jewelry, hair clips, backs of wristwatch cases, watch straps, eyeglass frames, buttons, belts, rivets, and zippers. Denmark also requires the addition of ferrous sulfate to all cement manufactured in that country to reduce the incidence of contact dermatitis to hexavalent chromium in cement workers.

Topical corticosteroid creams and ointments, which are the usual treatment for contact dermatitis, can themselves be a cause of this disorder. The product used to treat these rashes should be suspected if there is a sudden worsening of the condition. The cream or ointment base may also be a source of sensitivity, and this may further confuse the diagnosis.

Although contact rashes from wearing latex gloves have been known for many years, the frequency of this allergy has greatly increased because of the widespread use of gloves and condoms to prevent AIDS. Of greater importance are acute anaphylactic allergic reactions to latex products that may be life-threatening. Catheters, balloons, rubber bands, and elastic products are among other sources of latex exposure. Gloves made of polyvinyl are available to sensitive health care workers and others who must wear protective gloves. (See LATEX ALLERGY.)

Treatment The remedy is primarily to determine and remove the allergen or irritant substance causing the rash. Soothing creams and lotions often containing corticosteroids (avoid products that contain sensitizers) are applied to affected areas. Compresses are applied to weeping lesions, antihistamines are used orally for itching (they may be strong sensitizers when applied to the skin), and antibiotics may be necessary for secondary skin infections.

controversial approaches to diagnosis, explanation, or treatment of allergies

Procedures for diagnosis and treatment or explanations of the causes of allergic and immunologic diseases in which well-designed and controlled studies have not proven their effectiveness or validity scientifically, or such studies have not been done.

In the September 23, 1980 *Federal Register* the National Center for Health Care Technology requested opinions from interested parties concerning unproven techniques for the evaluation of allergy, including cytotoxicity testing (Bryan's test), urine autoinjection (autogenous urine immunization), skin titration (Rinkel method), subcutaneous provocative and neutralization testing, sublingual provocative testing, clinical ecology, candidiasis hypersensitivity syndrome, and carotid body resection.

In 1981 and 1986, statements from the American Academy of Allergy and Immunology or the National Center for Health Care Technology advised that those methods listed above were unproven techniques and should only be used for experimental purposes in well- controlled clinical studies. The United States Health Care Financing Administration excludes these testings from Medicare reimbursement. (See CYTOTOXIC TESTING, PROVOCATIVE AND NEUTRALIZATION SKIN TESTING, PROVOCATIVE SUBLINGUAL TESTING, SKIN TITRATION, URINE AUTOINJECTION.)

Cooke, Robert A.   American physician (1880–1960), born in Holmdel, New Jersey, who in 1918 at New York Hospital established the first structured multistaff allergy clinic in the United States. In 1950, Cooke moved the clinic, which eventually became known as the Robert A. Cooke Institute of Allergy, to Roosevelt Hospital in New York. Cooke served as director until his death. Cooke also introduced the protein nitrogen unit for standardization of extracts and, along with physician Mary Hewitt Loveless, discovered "blocking antibody" (see ANTIBODY). An asthmatic himself, Cooke investigated the concept of hereditary hypersensitivity, concluding that sensitized individuals transmit to their offspring a capacity for allergic reactions to any foreign proteins. Cooke, a breeder of a prizewinning line of Aberdeen-Angus cattle, was the first president of the (Eastern) Society for the Study of Asthma and Allied Conditions and a key developer of standardized training programs in allergy.

cooking odor allergy   Airborne food allergens such as fish or peanuts may be a source of immediate allergic reactions in extremely sensitive individuals. Eating those foods can be highly dangerous for those persons.

Those persons with baker's asthma should avoid airborne exposure; however, ingestion is usually not a problem in these individuals.

Coons, Albert H.   American physician (1912–78), born in Gloversville, New York, who developed techniques for viewing antigens through a microscope and identified globulins through the use of fluorescent labels. His work with immunofluorescence provided a new way to trace antibody production in the body, and

it evolved into the development of the field of immunocytochemistry.

copal   A resin derived from certain tropical plants and used in nail enamels. It may cause allergic symptoms, including skin rash.

COPD   See CHRONIC OBSTRUCTIVE PULMONARY DISEASE.

cord blood and the predictive value for developing allergies   The measurement of immunoglobulin E (IgE antibodies) in blood obtained from the umbilical cord at birth, which may be suggestive of allergic tendency in newborns. Some researchers advise exclusive breast-feeding in children with elevated levels.

coriander oil   An oil of the Old World herb *Coriandrum sativum,* of the carrot family, with aromatic fruit. Both a food and cosmetic additive, coriander oil can cause allergic skin reactions. It is also used as a carminitive, or antigas medication.

corn allergy   Allergic reactions including life-threatening anaphylaxis (allergic shock) to any food product containing or derived from the seeds of the cereal grain. Corn products include oil, syrup, meal, cornstarch, vegetable oil, popcorn, grits, hominy, margarine, and sugars such as dextrose, glucose, dexin, dextrin, and dextrimaltose. Beer, bourbon, Scotch, blended whiskeys, vodka, gin, some wines, and liqueurs are examples of corn alcohols. Malt is often yeast fermented from corn. Corn is often used in the processing of paper containers, including cups, boxes, plates, and milk cartons, and the inner-surface plastic food wrappers may be coated with cornstarch.

There is a wide disparity on the true occurrence of corn allergy. At least one physician, T. G. Randolph, in 1948 reported corn to be the "most significant" food allergen. When F. Speer coined the term "allergic tension-fatigue syndrome" in 1954, he implicated corn among other foods responsible for restlessness, fatigue, and irritability in children. However, in one series of 68 children with suspected food allergies, none proved positive for corn in double-blind food challenges.

corticosteroid metered dose inhalers Various asthma inhalers containing cortisone-derivatives possessing anti-inflammatory properties useful in the prevention of asthma symptoms.

corticosteroid nasal sprays (beclomethasone, budesonide, dexamethasone, flunisolide, fluticasone, mometasone furoate, triamcinolone) Derivatives of the hormone cortisone that relieve symptoms of nasal congestion and excessive discharge from allergic rhinitis (hay fever). They may also give relief for vasomotor rhinitis (nonallergic nasal congestion) and may have a beneficial effect on small nasal polyps.

Also called "steroid" nasal sprays, these medications may take one to two weeks to become effective and may be prematurely discarded by uninformed patients as ineffective. These are considered maintenance medications, and since their effectiveness does not accumulate, they must be used continuously. Because only a minimal quantity of the active drug is absorbed from the nasal passages into the bloodstream, there is little chance for side effects. Use in children, however, must be closely monitored. (See also CORTICOSTEROIDS.)

corticosteroids Naturally occurring (or synthetically manufactured) hormones produced by the adrenal glands, located next to the kidneys. Although corticosteroids do not initiate cellular or enzymatic activity, they are essential for many functions necessary for life, including the regulation of carbohydrate, protein, and fat metabolism and salt and water balance.

Natural and synthetic corticosteroids play a vital role in fighting allergic and inflammatory reactions. Although these drugs can be lifesaving, they also may produce very deleterious effects with large doses or prolonged therapy. Corticosteroids differ from dangerous anabolic steroids, which are often used illegally by athletes to enhance body building.

Antiallergy effects The cortisonelike drugs have the ability to interfere with allergic antigen-antibody reactions. This most likely occurs by blocking the inflammatory tissue injury that results from the release of chemical mediators from mast and basophilic cells. Prostaglandin production is also suppressed by these drugs. In addition, these drugs suppress all types of delayed hypersensitivity or cell-mediated immune reactions. This is especially useful for preventing tissue transplant rejections from occurring.

Metabolic effects Hydrocortisone removes glycogen stores in the liver and raises blood sugar levels. In corticosteroid-treated patients, diabetes mellitus usually develops only in those with a latent diabetic tendency and rarely raises glucose to dangerous levels in normal patients.

Hydrocortisone in physiologic or normal quantities is essential for normal muscle contraction. However, large doses or prolonged therapy causes a negative nitrogen balance by increasing amino acid production from protein, with depletion of body protein. This in turn causes severe muscle wasting, or atrophy, and weakness. A similar effect on bone results in osteoporosis with decreased bone matrix and removal of bone calcium. This process also interferes with normal growth in children. Aseptic necrosis is another serious adverse effect of high-dose corticosteroid therapy.

Hydrocortisone in high doses also causes a redistribution of the body's fat stores with thinning of the extremities and increased disposition in the face and trunk. Thinning of subcutaneous tissue may occur with resulting red or purple striae and ecchymosis, or bruises. Sodium and water retention also occurs, but potassium is lost. Blood pressure elevation may occur with high-dose therapy.

Hormonal changes When used for a prolonged time, corticosteroids may suppress the production of the pituitary hormone corticotropin (ACTH). ACTH secretion stimulates the adrenal glands for the natural production of cortisone. If the adrenal glands atrophy, they may fail to respond adequately to a crisis such as an acute illness, like an asthma attack or the stress of surgery, and if an extra dose of the drug is not administered, the patient may die. Some women develop hirsutism (excessive hair production), and acne is more common as a result of breakdown products of androgens, or male hormones, from prolonged use of corticosteroids, but rarely do these drugs affect menstrual function.

Anti-inflammatory effects   One of the beneficial roles of anti-inflammatory drugs is to assuage reactions in asthma and arthritis; this same ability to suppress inflammation may have a deleterious effect on wounds by interfering with the healing process. The ability to suppress inflammation may be so great that the warning signs and symptoms of a major complication may be missed until there are serious consequences, such as a bleeding peptic ulcer or a severe infection. There may be an increased incidence of gastric or duodenal ulcers in corticosteroid-treated patients.

Central nervous system and behavorial changes   Hydrocortisone stimulates the central nervous system and may cause seizures, especially in children with a seizure disorder. High-dose therapy may induce psychotic behavior, including hallucinations and delusions. Depression or alternately euphoria and insomnia and agitation may result. Effects cannot be predicted by prior personality qualities.

Rarely, increased intracranial pressure develops, resulting in a condition called "pseudotumor cerebri."

Effects on the eyes   Topical corticosteroid eyedrops are frequently prescribed to treat allergic eye conditions, but they can cause a dangerous increase in intraocular pressure and other serious adverse effects that may lead to blindness. They should be prescribed only after evaluation by a physician well trained in their use.

Uses   Corticosteroids are mainstays for allergy and asthma treatment and are often life-saving. In addition, they are effective therapy for arthritis, eye diseases, skin diseases, and many other diseases. Corticosteroids are available by injection, orally, and topically as creams, gels, ointments, lotions, solutions, aerosolized metered-dose inhalers and skin sprays, and nasal sprays.

The potential for adverse effects is great with prolonged systematic use. Use of alternate-day dosing can greatly lessen this potential, but not completely. When allergy patients have been stabilized, they are usually candidates for aerosol corticosteroid therapy to prevent attacks by keeping inflammation under control. Corticosteroid nasal sprays play a similar preventive role for nasal allergies.

Contraindications to the use of corticosteroids   In early 1992 the Food and Drug Administration (FDA) warned about the use of corticosteroids in patients not immune to chicken pox (varicella) or other reduced-immunity illnesses. Several deaths have occurred in otherwise normal, asthmatic children who contracted chicken pox while being treated with corticosteroids. These drugs should be used only if no alternative exists.

Corticosteroids absolutely must be avoided in the presence of herpes simplex infection of the eyes. They must be used cautiously in patients with coexisting diseases, including diabetes mellitus, hypertension, peptic ulcer disease, osteoporosis, diverticulitis, psychotic conditions, renal insufficiency, and congestive heart failure (except in certain inflammatory conditions such as rheumatic heart disease), and following some recent surgical intestinal procedures. Some references recommend against the use of corticosteroids during pregnancy; however, the use of prednisone should not be withheld in patients with asthma and other serious diseases.

Use of these drugs in patients with tuberculosis was once considered an absolute contraindication. However, in life-threatening situations they can be used in combination with antituberculosis drugs.

```
┌─────────────────────────────────────┐
│              WARNING                 │
│  THE RISK OF USING CORTICOSTEROIDS   │
│  MUST ALWAYS BE WEIGHED AGAINST THE  │
│  RISK OF NOT USING THEM.             │
│                                      │
└─────────────────────────────────────┘
```

cortisone   See CORTICOSTEROIDS.

coryza   A head cold of catarrhal inflammation of the mucus membranes of the nose.

coryza spasmodica   Another term for hay fever. See ALLERGIC RHINITIS.

cosmetic allergy   See ATOPIC DERMATITIS, CONTACT DERMATITIS.

cosmetics, hypoallergenic   Various types of makeup and toiletries made with ingredients that are not sensitizing to the vast majority of users.

cost of diagnosing and treating allergic diseases   The economic impact of diagnosis and treatment of all allergic disorders, including allergic rhinitis (hay fever), asthma, autoimmune disorders, and related illnesses, has not been determined. However, costs for asthma alone were estimated to be greater than $4.5 billion in 1985 (see ASTHMA COST), and undoubtedly the total expenditure for all allergic diseases, including time lost from work, constitutes one of the most common and expensive health problems in the United States.

cottonseed   Seed of the cotton plant and one of the most potent allergens for humans. Cottonseed may be a contaminant in inexpensive furniture upholstery, cushions, and mattresses. Most allergic symptoms result from the inhalation of cottonseed dust in animal feed and fertilizers. Cottonseed meal used to grease pans and in baked goods may rarely cause allergic reactions, but processing of cottonseed oil effectively removes allergens. Skin testing with as potent an allergen as cottonseed extract should be done by scratch or prick puncture only, because intradermal injection may cause severe or fatal anaphylaxis.

cottonseed meal   See COTTONSEED.

cottonseed oil   See COTTONSEED.

cough   A reaction, or reflex, of the upper respiratory tract to correct an irritation or blockage of the airways. Dust or other particles, fumes, smoke, gases, and viral and bacterial infections cause the sudden, expulsive rumble characterizing a cough. Some coughs, such as whooping cough, create high-pitched sounds, whereas the inflammation of the upper respiratory tract, especially when children have croup, creates a narrowing of the airways and a barking cough.

When an object becomes lodged in the larynx, or voice box, the cough mechanism is triggered to help expel the object and stop a person from choking. Coughing is also the body's way of expelling mucus, phlegm, or other irritant, in which case it is called a productive cough. A dry, or unproductive, cough, which does not result in expulsion of a substance, may be caused by bronchospasm (a sudden narrowing of the bronchi), featured in asthma, allergic reactions, or infection.

Causes of chronic coughing include smoking and or lung disease, a foreign object trapped in a bronchus, and anxiety or nervousness. Other causes of cough include: upper airway obstruction or irritation; infections; irritation or structural abnormalities; or other disorders of the epiglottis and larynx such as vocal cord paraylsis, polyp, or tumor; tracheomalacia; external compression by lymph nodes, tumor, or vascular ring; intraluminal obstruction by foreign body, mucus plugs, inflammation or tumor; bronchospasm of asthma, chronic bronchitis, or emphysema; cysts; congenital malformation; inflammation from allergic diseases such as hypersensitivity pneumonitis; interstitial lung diseases; congenital heart disease; congestive heart failure; gastroesophageal reflux; hiatus hernia; edema; hysteria; paralysis; adverse effects of drugs such as the ACE inhibitor antihypertensives (benazepril, captopril, enalapril, fosinopril, lisinopril, quinapril, and ramipril) or drug toxicity; smoke from tobacco or fires; noxious fumes or gases; organic dusts containing allergens such as dust mites, animal allergens, industrial allergens, scents in perfumes and household or commercial cleaning agents; aerosol products; cold; humidity; and dryness.

cough, ear   A reflex cough resulting from an ear infection, irritation, or foreign body lodged against the tympanic membrane (eardrum).

counterirritant   A substance applied topically or locally, such as a mustard plaster, to produce an inflammatory reaction for the purpose of affecting some other area near or underlying the irritated region. Rubefacients are counterirritants that cause reddening of the skin. Vesicants produce vesicles (blisters). Escharotics, including acids, alkalies, metallic salts, phenol or carbolic acid, carbon dioxide, and electric cautery, help create tissue necrosis, or sloughing.

cow's milk   See FOOD ALLERGY, MILK.

cracked pot sound   The sound, similar to that of striking a cracked pot, during percussion to diagnose a pulmonary cavity.

crepitation   A crackling sound, such as a rale heard in pneumonia patients, or the grating sound caused when the ends of broken bones rub against another bone or surface.

cromolyn sodium   [disodium cromoglycate] (Intal, Nasalcrom, Opticrom)   A drug that prevents the release of histamine and other chemical substances from mast cells in the eyes, nose, and lungs, therefore preventing allergy symptoms and asthma. This drug is often discarded by patients who underestimate its benefit because it is very slow acting and requires up to two months to exert its full effectiveness. However, cromolyn is a first-line treatment for respiratory allergies and asthma. It also has almost no side effects and is safe to use during pregnancy.

croup   A disease characterized by a metallic cough, often described as a "seal-like" bark, with hoarseness that occurs when breathing in. It is accompanied by thick mucus in the nose and throat, dyspnea (difficult breathing), laryngeal spasm, and, at times, by the formation of a membrane. Catarrhal croup refers to acute catarrhal laryngitis.

Croup is most commonly caused by a viral infection during infancy or early childhood and is generally a benign condition. However, when accompanied by high fever, it may be caused by a dangerous bacteria, *Haemophilus influenza*. Unless antibiotics are started early, the bacterial form of croup may lead to the life-threatening complication known as acute epiglottitis (see EPIGLOTTITIS, ACUTE). The less severe forms of croup can be treated by breathing warm, humid air in a steamed-up shower or small bathroom.

crowing inspiration   A crouplike coughing sound created on inhalation.

cryptococcosis   [torulosis]   See FUNGAL DISEASES, SYSTEMIC.

CT scan   See COMPUTERIZED TOMOGRAPHY.

Curschmann's spirals   Named for German physician Heinrich Curschmann (1846–1910), coiled spirals of mucus seen frequently in the sputum of asthma patients.

cuticle remover   A liquid mixture of water, coconut oil, potassium sulfate, and other chemicals that dissolves the dead skin around the base of the fingernails. Certain ingredients, especially coconut oil, may cause allergic reactions.

cutireaction   Skin reaction.

cyanosis   Purplish, grayish, or bluish discoloration of the skin caused by an oxygen deficiency and an excess of carbon dioxide, during which abnormal amounts of reduced hemoglobin are found in the blood. Cyanosis also results from any interference with air passages, asphyxiation, and overdoses of certain drugs.

cyclic adenosine 3', 5'-monophosphate

(CAMP, cyclic AMP) A substance whose presence is essential for stabilization of mast cells in body tissues, which along with basophils are responsible for the symptoms of allergy. CAMP is deficient in asthmatics. Drugs such as epinephrine (Adrenalin) and theophylline increase CAMP-inhibiting mast cell degranulation and are useful for the treatment of asthma.

cyclosporin

An immunosuppressant drug used to prevent or suppress organ transplant rejection. Researchers at the National Heart and Lung Institute in the United States and the Royal Brompton Hospital in London are investigating cyclosporin as an alternative to dangerously high levels of corticosteroids required by the most severe asthma patients. Although some individuals in one study group had a significant improvement in lung function and less frequent acute episodes of asthma, cyclosporin can cause serious kidney problems and is still considered experimental therapy.

cyproheptadine

(Periactin) An antihistaminic drug useful for its antipruritic properties, especially for cold urticaria (hives). Sedation is its most frequent adverse effect; however, its property of increasing appetite and weight gain is sometimes used therapeutically. This drug should be avoided in infants.

cyst, retention

A cyst, or sac, retaining a gland's secretions, such as a mucous cyst.

cystic fibrosis

(CF) Among the most common fatal inherited diseases, an autosomal recessive genetic disorder. CF affects the exocrine secretory glands of the respiratory and digestive systems.

Excessive production of thick, sticky mucus causes a chronic cough, wheezing, and plugging of the bronchial tubes. Trapped bacteria cause recurrent respiratory infections. Mucus also blocks the pancreatic secretion of digestive enzymes, causing malabsorption of nutrients and foul bulky stools, with failure to gain weight and thrive a common finding in young children.

This disorder is often confused with asthma, pneumonia, or other respiratory diseases when symptoms first appear, usually in infancy. Mild cases may escape recognition until adulthood. Gastrointestinal symptoms may be confused with celiac disease or other disorders. Diagnosis is confirmed by a positive sweat chloride test (see SWEAT CHLORIDE TEST).

Since CF was first recognized as a disease in 1938, it has been estimated to occur in one in 2,000 to one in 1,600 live white births in the United States, but only one in 17,000 blacks. About one in every 20 persons carries the CF recessive gene. Genetic counseling is advisable when a previous pregnancy resulted in CF. Prenatal diagnosis and carrier state of parents can be established by DNA genetic markers.

Until recently the prognosis for CF patients was poor, with very few patients surviving childhood. However, newer antibiotics and aggressive physical therapy to help drain the mucus from the airways by a technique called postural drainage, and the use of pancreatic enzymes and nutritional supplements, can greatly improve the outlook. Males generally outlive female patients, with half of patients living past age 21. Respiratory failure is the leading cause of death. The discovery of the CF gene on the long arm of chromosome 7 gives hope for the possibility of a cure for this disease utilizing gene therapy within a few years.

cytokines

Powerful chemical peptides synthesized during response to foreign antigen exposure that are involved in the regulation of immune responses. Cytokines play an important role in determining the nature of an immune response. They regulate immunoglobulin E (IgE) antibody production and are involved in the activity of eosinophils, mast cells, and the inflammatory process. Cytokines also determine tolerance to the antigen in which there is no apparent immune reaction. While antibodies and T- cell receptors are specific to an antigen, the structure of cytokines is not. In the past, cytokines were called monokines or lymphokines because they were originally thought to be produced by monocytes and lymphocytes. It is now known that any body cell can produce them. They have many biologic functions in addition to their role in allergic responses, ranging from the antiviral activities of the interferons to stimulation of bone marrow components.

Classes of cytokines include interferons, colony-stimulating factors, tumor necrosis factors, lymphocyte chemotaxis factor, histamine-releasing factor, and others. Some of these names may change in the near future because of standardization of nomenclature by scientists. (See EOSINOPHIL, INFLAMMATION, INTERLEUKINS, MAST CELLS.)

cytotoxic testing   An unproven diagnostic technique, also known as cytotoxic leukocyte test, cytotoxicity, or Bryan's cytotoxicity, in which leukocytes (white blood cells) from allergic patients are exposed to suspected food allergens and observed microscopically for changes. Reduced motility, changes in shape, or disintegration of the white blood cells suggests a positive result, that is, existence of allergy.

Controlled studies have not proven these tests to be reliable and reproducible. Therefore, the National Center for Health Care Technology reviewed test data and concluded that cytotoxic testing is unreliable and without scientific basis. The Food and Drug Administration does not allow marketing of this test under provisions of the Federal Food, Drug, and Cosmetic Act. The American Academy of Allergy and Immunology considers the test experimental and its use reserved for well-designed clinical trials only.

In the Sept. 23, 1980, *Federal Register,* the National Center for Health Care Technology requested opinions from interested parties concerning Cytotoxicity Testing (Bryan's Test) and other unproven techniques.

In response to this request, the Executive Committee and the Committee on Unproved Techniques of the American Academy of Allergy and Immunology prepared a position statement which was submitted to the National Center for Health Care Technology. That position statement includes the following conclusions: (1) there is no proof that leukocytotoxic testing is effective for diagnosis of food or inhalant allergy, (2) a number of controlled trials have indicated that leukocytotoxic testing is ineffective for diagnosis of food and inhalant allergy, (3) leukocytotoxic testing should be reserved for experimental use only in well-designed trials.

D

dairy food substitute Imitation milk products, cheese and the like, made from different constituents than are found in real milk products in order to avert adverse reactions experienced from real milk.

dairy products See MILK.

Dale, Sir Henry Hallett English physician (1875–1968), who has been praised as one of the originators of modern physiology and one of the most influential pharmacologists of the 20th century. In addition to his theory of chemical transmission of nerve impulses, which received the Nobel Prize for medicine in 1936 (with German pharmacologist Otto Loewi), he made an enormous contribution to the study of allergy by explaining the physiologic action of histamine. He argued that histamine shock is the basis for anaphylaxis. Dale demonstrated that antibodies had to attach to certain cells before they could react with an antigen or allergen in order for an allergic reaction to occur. This is known as the Dale reaction.

Dale was director of the Wellcome Physiological Research Laboratories in 1904, and in 1920 he became head of the Department of Biochemistry and Pharmacology of the National Institute for Medical Research in Hampstead, England. In 1928, he became director.

dandelion See ENTOMOPHILOUS PLANTS.

dander Scales that flake from the skin or hair of animals or the feathers of birds. Dander may be a cause of allergy in susceptible persons. (See ANIMAL ALLERGY.)

David, John R. British physician, born in 1930, who conducted studies on delayed hypersensitivity and cellular immunity that have augmented studies on parasitic infections as they relate to immunology. David served as assistant professor of medicine at New York University in the 1960s, and in 1973 he became professor of medicine and chairman of the Department of Public Health at Harvard University.

DDT Dichloro-diphenyltrichloroethane, an insecticide effective against fleas, lice, mosquitoes, cockroaches, Japanese beetles, and many other varieties. When ingested by humans, DDT causes vomiting, numbness, partial paralysis of limbs, anorexia, depression, tremors, and death.

Decadron See DEXAMETHASONE.

decongestants A class of drugs referred to as alpha-adrenergic agonists, used topically as nasal spray or drops and orally in capsules, tablets, or syrups for the treatment of nasal congestion. (See ALPHA-ADRENERGIC AGONISTS.)

degranulation technique [mast cell degranulation assay] A controversial procedure in which white blood cells from an animal are mixed with a person's blood serum and a food allergen suspected of causing allergy. Thought to be a diagnostic test for allergy, this assay is technically difficult, and results are unreliable.

degree of asthma severity The ranges or the levels of asthma from asymptomatic to fatal, with the majority of cases described as mild to moderate.

Chronic mild asthma Persons with chronic mild asthma have no abnormalities in baseline pulmonary lung tests, or spirometry, between asthma attacks. During attacks, airflow rates fall 20% below their predicted normal values. Asthma symptoms are usually triggered by exercise; exposure to irritants or allergens such as pollens, animals, or house dust mites; or respiratory infections. Treatment prior to exposure is usually effective in preventing symptoms.

Inhaled beta$_2$-agonists are usually the only therapy necessary to control attacks, and they are used on an as-needed (*prn*) basis only.

Chronic moderate asthma In this category, asthma symptoms are not controlled by the occasional use of a beta$_2$-agonist. There may also be a frequent need for beta$_2$-agonists, possibly more than twice a week. Symptoms in this group may be most apparent at night or, as in mild asthma, may be triggered by the environment or exercise. The lungs function at 60 to 80% of the predicted range for a person's age, sex, and height, indicating a compromise in airway flow.

The National Asthma Education Program's *Guidelines for the Diagnosis and Management of Asthma* recommends the use of an anti-inflammatory agent in any person with moderate or severe asthma. Anti- inflammatory drugs include inhaled cromolyn sodium or inhaled corticosteroids. These safe and effective medications reduce the frequency and severity of asthma attacks and the need for oral corticosteroids.

Nighttime awakening may necessitate the addition of long-acting bronchodilating drugs such as theophylline or albuterol. Occasionally short bursts of oral corticosteroids are needed, but not on a daily or frequent basis. Individuals rarely require urgent emergency room visits.

Chronic severe asthma Individuals whose asthma is not controlled by maximal drug doses and who may be at risk for life-threatening asthma attacks show a pulmonary function less than 60% of baseline. Airflow varies widely during attacks. These persons may require long-term use of daily or every-other-day oral corticosteroids. (See ASTHMA, CORTICOSTEROIDS.)

delayed hypersensitivity See HYPERSENSITIVITY.

delayed pressure urticaria and angioedema See PRESSURE URTICARIA.

depressant, respiratory A drug that lessens the frequency and depth of breathing.

depression A neurotic or psychotic disorder characterized by lethargy, loss of interest in socializing, sex, work, and other activities of daily living, weeping and/or pervasive sadness, insomnia, inability to concentrate, and other symptoms. When asthma and depression occur simultaneously, both conditions can intensify, according to Nancy J. Rubin, PsyD, of the University of Alabama School of Medicine in Tuscaloosa. Rubin reported in the American Medical Association's *Archives of Family Medicine* that people with depressive disorder or depressive symptoms tend to have physical, social, and role-functioning difficulties comparable to the difficulties of those who suffer from one or more of eight major chronic illnesses, including lung disease. One association involves the effect of depression on the respiratory system. A depressed person enters a psychological state of nonaction, associated with decreased energy expenditure, decreased ventilation, low oxygen consumption, and skeletal relaxation. These conditions further complicate asthma, a disorder already characterized by compromised ventilation and borderline blood gas values.

Another theory involves dysfunctional brain mechanisms associated with depression. One group of researchers speculates that neurotransmitter imbalances found in asthma and depression may combine to worsen both conditions. However, the correlation of brain dysfunctions and asthma is not fully understood.

Formal assessment by a mental health professional of the patient with severe asthma is recommended as part of the standard medical assessment.

dermaconiosis Any skin irritation, especially associated with occupational conditions, caused by dust.

dermatitis A term for rash. (See ATOPIC DERMATITIS, CONTACT DERMATITIS.)

dermatitis herpetiformis A chronic skin condition characterized by an itchy, burning, reddened, blistering, symmetrically occurring rash usually found on the elbows, knees, shoulders, scalp, and buttocks. Some afflicted persons may respond to a either a gluten-free or milk-free diet, raising the possibility that this is an allergic disease. (See MILK.)

dermatitis medicomentosum A contact rash caused by the use of a topical medication, often of greater severity than the condition it was prescribed to treat. Frequent sensitizing drug allergens include antihistamines (diphenhydramine), antibiotics (neomycin), and local anesthetic agents (benzocaine). Other ingredients such as preservatives may also be responsible for an adverse reaction. (See CONTACT DERMATITIS.)

dermatitis venerata Any skin inflammation, from simple hyperemia to gangrene, caused by contact with various animal, plant (especially plants such as poison ivy, oak, and sumac), or mineral substances, drugs, acids, and alkalies. Symptoms include erythema, papules, vesicles, itching, and burning. Among the treatments are topical applications of calamine lotion, aluminum acetate (Burow's solution), and corticosteroid creams or, in more severe cases, oral or injected medication.

Desensitization with poison ivy extract injections is unproven and may carry the risk of adverse effects to the kidneys. (See CONTACT DERMATITIS.)

dermatographia [dermographism] The ability to write on skin. A raised white line forms in the pattern of trauma to the skin when the skin is stroked by a sharp object such as a fingernail. A hivelike skin eruption results when tiny blood vessels under the skin constrict, and immediate pruritus (itching), erythema (redness), and linear swelling ensue. This series of events, known as the "triple response of Lewis," appears two to five minutes after skin trauma and lasts from 30 minutes to three hours (see TRIPLE RESPONSE OF LEWIS).

Dermatographia, the most common type of physical urticaria (hives), is thought to occur because histamine or other chemical mediators leak from mast cells in the skin. Although seen more often in persons with chronic urticaria, it is estimated to occur in 2 to 20% of the general population. Itching is troublesome only to a fraction of those afflicted, but a more severe form of this disorder is associated with conditions known as urticaria pigmentosa and systemic mastocytosis. Antihistamines are the primary treatment. (See also ANTIHISTAMINE, MASTOCYTOSIS, PHYSICAL URTICARIA, URTICARIA.)

dermographism See DERMATOGRAPHIA.

desensitization The loss of sensitivity to an allergen or irritating factor, usually accomplished by a series of injections of an antigen over a period of time to build up antibodies and therefore eliminate adverse reactions. (See DRUG ALLERGY AND OTHER ADVERSE DRUG REACTIONS, SERUM SICKNESS.)

dexamethasone (Decadron) An anti-inflammatory derivative of cortisone. (See CORTICOSTEROIDS.)

dexchlorpheniramine maleate (Polaramine) An antihistaminic drug used in the treatment of allergic disorders. This drug is moderately sedating and has few side effects.

dextromethorphan Non-narcotic synthetic derivative of levorphanol similar in structure and effectiveness to codeine as a cough suppressant. Dextromethorphan is found combined with antihistamines, decongestants, and expectorants in many prescription and over-the-counter allergy and cold remedies, including Benylin DM, Delsym, Mediquell, Pertussin, and Robitussin DM.

This antitussive (cough-suppressing) drug is the safest available. It rarely causes minor adverse effects, such as mild nausea or dizziness, and is the cough suppressant of choice during pregnancy.

diabetes mellitus A disease characterized by the body's inability to metabolize glucose, or sugar. The process of metabolic utilization of glucose is controlled by a hormone called insulin, secreted by the pancreas, a gland located in the upper part of the abdomen.

Insulin-dependent diabetes, formerly called juvenile diabetes, is caused by diminished insulin or the absence of insulin secretion. Non-insulin-dependent diabetes, formerly called adult onset diabetes, originates with malfunctioning receptors on the insulin molecule that prevent its utilization.

A joint Finnish and Canadian study found a peptide in the albumin of cow's milk that may trigger insulin-dependent diabetes in susceptible infants who have inherited the tendency. High numbers of bovine serum albumin antibodies were found in children recently diagnosed with diabetes. These antibodies attach themselves to receptors on the surface of beta cells, insulin-producing cells in the pancreas. Researchers hope to be able to prevent this form of diabetes by identifying those infants at risk.

American researchers believe that immunotherapy with glutamate decarboxylase (GAD) may someday prevent insulin-dependent diabetes in persons identified as being in a high-risk group. It has been theorized that GAD, an enzyme produced along with insulin by beta cells in the pancreas, and insulin could be given by mouth to stimulate the immune system to develop a tolerance to these substances and thereby prevent the autoimmune attack thought to cause diabetes mellitus. (See also INSULIN ALLERGY.)

diarrhea   Abnormally frequent and usually watery stools. Cow's milk is the most common allergic cause of diarrhea occurring in infants, but in older children and adults, lactase deficiency is much more common. Lactase deficiency, also termed lactose intolerance, is not an allergic condition but rather a deficiency of the enzyme that digests milk sugar, or lactose. This problem usually develops between age three and puberty. (See LACTOSE INTOLERANCE, MILK.)

Many foods eaten to excess such as cucumbers, beans, and fruits and berries may cause

gastrointestinal upset. Foods contaminated by infectious microorganisms should be suspected when diarrhea is complicated by vomiting and fever. Grain crops that may be infested with toxin-producing mold, including millet, barley, and wheat, can cause headache, vertigo, chills, nausea, vomiting, diarrhea, and visual disturbances.

The immunodeficiency disorder immunoglobulin A (IgA) deficiency, which occurs in approximately one in 800 individuals, may result in mild diarrhea but may be associated with celiac disease, pancreatitis, cirrhosis, inflammatory bowel disorders, and autoimmune diseases that may produce severe debilitating diarrhea. IgA antibodies in the intestinal mucosal lining seem to be involved in protecting against the absorption of allergens. Breast-feeding may provide the infant mucosa with immunoglobulin absent from other sources. However, other reactions involving IgE, IgG, or IgM antibodies may increase the ability of antigens to penetrate the gut.

diary keeping of allergy or asthma symptoms   A chart kept by patients or parents of patients to determine patterns or triggers of the disorder. One example adapted from the National Asthma Education Program is on the following page.

diet, allergen-free   See DIET, ELEMENTAL.

diet, allergy   Food avoidance or manipulation to aid in the diagnosis and subsequent treatment of food allergies.

diet, eczema   Avoidance of foods suspected of causing rashes. The greatest incidence of food allergies occurs during infancy, and more than 80% of those disappear by three years of age; avoidance of foods found to be responsible for eczema may significantly lessen symptoms. Eggs, milk, peanuts, soy, fish, and wheat are the foods that most commonly cause food allergies. Breast-feeding mothers should also avoid these foods. (See ATOPIC DERMATITIS, BREAST-FEEDING AND PREVENTION OF ALLERGIES, FOOD ALLERGY.)

WEEKLY ASTHMA SYMPTOM AND PEAK FLOW DIARY

DATE	Peak Flow	No Symptoms	Mild	Moderate	Severe
A.M.					
P.M.					
A.M.					
P.M.					

Measure your peak flow reading every morning (A.M.) on awakening and every evening (P.M.) at bedtime before taking inhaled medications. Write down the highest reading of three tries in the box for peak flow. Put an X in the box that matches the symptoms you have when you record your peak flow reading. If you are taking asthma medicine, put a circle around the X. If you take more or less medicine than usual, please make a note.

No Symptoms = No symptoms (wheeze, cough, chest tightness, or shortness of breath) even with normal physical activity.

Mild = Symptoms during physical activity, but not at rest.

Moderate = Symptoms while at rest, which may interfere with daily activity.

Severe = Severe symptoms at rest (wheeze may be absent); symptoms cause difficulty walking or talking; retraction of muscles in neck or between ribs when breathing.

diet, elemental [allergen-free diet]   Avoidance of any foodstuffs that contain allergens. There are several commercially available allergen-free or hypoallergenic (low potential to contain an allergen) formulas, including Flexical and Vivonex. These products supply protein in an elemental form with carbohydrate and fat in a single, readily digestible form. (See also HYDROLYSATE FORMULAS.)

diet, elimination   A single- or multiple-food avoidance diet based on the patient's allergy history (observations) is used with the hope of proving the cause of suspected food allergy or allergies. The food or foods are eliminated from the diet for three days to three weeks. The food is then restored to the diet either individually or on a rotating schedule to observe for recurrence of symptoms, and these challenges may be repeated several times.

This method of diagnosis is simple and inexpensive and can be done at home under normal conditions. Disadvantages include the lack of scientific validity, since the findings are based on the patient's or parent's subjective observations and the physician's interpretation and bias. It can also have risk if a food allergy results in a serious reaction such as anaphylaxis.

diet, Feingold   See FEINGOLD DIET.

diet, milk-free   Avoidance of dairy products or by-products that contain lactalbumin or casein (milk proteins) or lactase (milk sugar). (See also FOOD ALLERGY, LACTOSE INTOLERANCE, MILK.)

diet, mold elimination   Avoidance of mold-containing foods in persons suspected of having mold sensitivity. Sensitivity to inhaled molds as a cause of hay fever or asthma rarely correlates with eating mold-containing foods. Although an individual may have both inhaled mold allergy and penicillin drug sensitivity, there is no reason for one allergic to the mold *Penicillium* to refrain from taking penicillin unless that person has had a previous allergic reaction to the drug. Many adverse reactions blamed on molds are actually reactions to other ingredients in the foods.

diet, relactation   Resuming breast-feeding after a period of using cow's milk, other formulas, or solid foods because of the development of food allergies or other adverse effects.

diet, rotary   Diets for persons with food allergies in which groups of foods thought to be allergenic are withheld for a period of time and then reintroduced in smaller quantities than formerly consumed. It is hoped that these foods may be better tolerated in these lesser amounts. There are usually several menus that are rotated so that an individual only consumes one of the implicated allergenic foods once every four days. (See also ROWE'S DIETS.)

diet, wheat-free   See GLUTEN-SENSITIVE ENTEROPATHY.

dietary blind food challenges   Foods and placebo are given in a disguised fashion in order to assess a patient's reactions to foods suspected of causing allergic symptoms. Advantages include the objective, blinded fashion that eliminates subjective bias of patient or physician. Disadvantages are the complicated nature and expense of the testing and the fact that the challenges are not done under "natural" conditions. In addition, late reactions may not be observed by the tester.

diet diary, food allergy   A running record kept by a patient or parent of all foods eaten by the patient over a given period and a description of any symptoms that develop. The physician then reviews and interprets the diary in the expectation that a pattern will indicate a food as a source of allergic symptoms. This method of diagnosis is simple and inexpensive and can be done at home under normal conditions. Disadvantages include the lack of scientific validity, since the findings are based on the patient's or parent's subjective observations and the physician's interpretation and bias. It can also have risk if a food allergy results in a serious reaction such as anaphylaxis. This method is usually used when intermittent symptoms occur and an unknown foodstuff is suspected.

Dilor   See DYPHYLLINE.

Dimetane   See BROMPHENIRAMINE.

Dimetapp   See BROMPHENIRAMINE.

dimethyl ketone   See ACETONE.

diphenhydramine (Benadryl)   An antihistaminic drug used to treat the symptoms of allergic rhinitis (hay fever) and urticaria (hives), including sneezing, runny nose, nasal congestion, itchy eyes, and pruritus (itching). It is given by injection as a secondary treatment for severe allergic anaphylactic reactions (epinephrine, or Adrenalin, must be used as the primary drug in this severe shocklike, life-

threatening condition), such as may occur in persons allergic to bee stings or certain foods.

It also useful as a cough suppressant, for the prevention and treatment of motion sickness, and for parkinsonism. It is widely available topically in creams or lotions for the relief of itching. However, many allergists and dermatologists advise against this use because of frequent adverse effects.

Its principal side effect is sedation, and it is often prescribed as a nonhabituating hypnotic in the treatment of insomnia. (See also ANTIHISTAMINE, DERMATITIS MEDICOMENTOSUM.)

disinfectant   Any chemical that kills bacteria, especially vegetative microorganisms. Examples are chlorine, fluorine, iodine, silver nitrate, sulfurous acids, alkalies, formaldehyde, 70% alcohol, salts of heavy metals, cresols, phenol (carbolic acid), benzoic and salicylic acids and their sodium salts, thymol, potassium permanganate, boric acid, chloride of lime, and iodoform.

disodium cromoglycate   See CROMOLYN SODIUM.

Dittrich's plugs   Small particles, named for German pathologist Franz Dittrich (1815–59), made of pus, detritus, bacteria, and fat globules in fetid sputum.

Dixon, Frank J.   American physician, born in 1920 in St. Paul, Minnesota, who participated in studies on anaphylaxis, including those concerned with ionizing radiation, radiolabeled antigen tracers, serum sickness, and glomerulonephritis; the roles of immune complexes in disease; systemic lupus erythematosus; and molecular genetics in autoimmune mechanisms. Dixon, director emeritus and member of the Research Institute of Scripps Clinic, played an important part in developing the field of immunopathology.

dog allergy   Allergic symptoms, including asthma, from exposure to the domestic mammal *Canis familiaris*. Dogs are found in an estimated 43% of American homes, and up to 30%

of the population skin-tests positive to dogs. However, not all positively diagnosed individuals have symptoms when exposed to dogs. It is a myth that some breeds of dogs are "nonallergenic." Occasionally, however, individuals who seem to tolerate one species or an individual dog will develop symptoms of dog allergy upon continuous exposure. There is also the possibility that an allergic individual will show negative results, known as a "false negative skin test."

Furthermore, persons who are emotionally attached to their dog(s) and constantly exposed to them may not be aware of or be willing to admit the corresponding relationship between their symptoms and the dog. A provocative challenge test with dog allergen may be necessary to prove the relationship. An alternative would be to remove the dog for a period of time, perhaps several weeks, and have the house thoroughly cleaned.

A late-phase reaction (a reaction occurring many hours after exposure to an allergen) may occur, thus creating confusion about the cause of symptoms. For example, an adolescent visits the home of his girlfriend, who has a dog or cat. No apparent symptoms emerge during the brief visit, but later that night the boy is awakened by an asthma attack of wheezing and shortness of breath.

Dog allergen is present in the dander, saliva, and urine of the dog. There is no "nonallergenic" dog. Even short-haired dogs, such as the Chihuahua, can cause allergy.

The treatment of choice is the avoidance of dogs. Allergy shots for dog allergies are usually recommended for only those individuals unable to avoid exposure to the dog. Cromolyn and antihistamines can be taken before known exposure to reduce chances of a severe attack of asthma or allergy. (See also ANIMAL ALLERGY, DANDER, MYTHS ABOUT ALLERGIES AND ASTHMA.)

Donaldson, Virginia H. American physician, born in 1924 in Glen Cove, New York, whose professional focus on hematology led her to discover the genetic absence of a factor in the complement cascade, a function of the immune system. This discovery provided insight into differential diagnosis of allergies. Donaldson has been professor of medicine and pediatrics at the University of Cincinnati since 1967. (See also COMPLEMENT.)

Donnally, Harry H. American physician (1877–1947) who helped establish the United States' first pediatric allergy clinic at the Children's Hospital of Washington. Along with other physicians and scientists, Donnally conducted experiments dealing with the pathogenesis of allergy in utero and in early infancy. From 1923 to 1943, he served as professor and executive officer of the Department of Pediatrics at George Washington University.

doxepin (Sinequan) An antidepressant drug that also has antihistaminic properties that are useful for the treatment of urticaria (hives).

Drinker respirator The apparatus, commonly known as the "iron lung," that presses upon a patient's thoracic area in order to produce alternating positive and negative air, as in the normal breathing process. The device was invented by Philip Drinker, born in 1894, an American engineer in industrial hygiene. The iron lung became widely used for the treatment of poliomyelitis, to which some individuals are predisposed through adverse reaction to routine immunizations and the removal of tonsils and other nose and throat operations. Bronchopneumonia has been known to develop in rare cases of severe poliomyelitis.

drip, postnasal A discharge flowing from the postnasal region (behind the nose) to the throat, caused by allergic or vaso-motor (nonallergic) rhinitis or chronic sinusitis.

drug allergy and other adverse drug reactions An undesired or unexpected allergic or nonimmune result from taking a medication. Allergy accounts for only 5 to 10% of adverse reactions to medications. However, it has been estimated that between one and 15 of every 100 drugs consumed result in an adverse effect. Reactions may be classified as predictable or unpredictable. They may be immunologic (allergic) or nonimmunologic ("pseudoallergic"). At least 75% of adverse reactions are mild and self-limiting with no lasting effects. From one in 1,000 to one in 10,000 drug reactions are fatal.

Predictable reactions are those related to the pharmacologic effect of the drug, such as toxicity from overdose, side effects, and interactions with other drugs. Unpredictable reactions do not occur in most persons and are not related to the pharmacologic effects of the drug. The mechanism for these reactions is often misunderstood. Examples include intolerance to low doses of the drug and idiosyncratic, allergic, and nonallergic reactions.

Allergic reactions Among drugs in which true allergic reactions may occur are penicillin, insulin, and foreign serum. They usually have a pattern in which they do not occur on the first exposure and may occur when taken in very low doses, even below that required for a pharmacologic effect. The four types of allergic reactions are immediate, or anaphylactic; cytotoxic; immune complex; and delayed, or lymphocyte-mediated. More than one of these types may be activated at one time or as time progresses.

Most drugs are small organic molecules with molecular weights of less than 1,000 daltons. (A dalton is a unit of mass, 1/16 of the mass of the oxygen atom, about 1.65×10^{-24} gram.) Therefore, they are too small to initiate an immune response alone. Most drug allergic reactions occur when the drugs combine with tissue or plasma protein to form a complex capable of stimulating the immune system. After initial exposure to a drug, susceptible allergic persons have a latent period of 10 to 20 days, during which the immune system produces effector cells and antibodies that sensitize the person.

Upon reexposure to the drug, type I (IgE-mediated) hypersensitivity, including anaphy-laxis, may occur immediately with a parenteral (injectable intravenous or intramuscular) dose or up to six hours following an oral dose. Penicillin is the most frequent cause of drug-induced anaphylaxis (see below).

FREQUENT CAUSES OF TYPE I ALLERGIC DRUG REACTIONS

Allergen extracts
Asparaginase
Chymopapain
Congo red
Foreign antiserums
Gamma globulin
Hormones (adrenocorticotropic or ACTH; thyroid stimulating hormone or TSH)
Iron dextran
Methylergonovine maleate
Nitrofurantoin
Other antibiotics
Other blood products
Penicillin
Sulfobromophthalein sodium
Vaccines (tetanus toxoid, influenza, measles, other egg-containing vaccines)

When a type II (cytotoxic or antitissue-antibody) reaction occurs, a drug binds to a cell's surface with one or two blood cell components, such as red blood cells, platelets, or granulocytes, becoming involved. The immune hemolytic anemia that occurs from penicillin, quinidine, quinine, cephalosporins, and other drugs is exemplified by this type of reaction. Thrombocytopenia (diminished platelet count) occurs when platelets are destroyed during reactions to quinidine, quinine, acetaminophen (Tylenol), thiouracil, gold salts, and sulfonamides. Granulocytopenia (diminished granular white blood cells) may be caused by taking the drugs aminopyrine, phenylbutazone (Butazolidin), phenothiazines, thiouracils, sulfonamides, anticonvulsants, and tolbutamide. An immune form of anemia sometimes occurs from the drug methyldopa (Aldomet). Treatment is usually successful with the discontinuance of the offending drug, but fatalities may occur.

Serum sickness exemplifies type III (immune complex-antigen-antibody complement) reactions. Complexes of drug antigen and its specific antibody and complement react to cause fever, joint pains, swollen lymph glands, and rashes. The rashes may be particularly severe in the form of urticaria (hives) or purpura (large areas of bruising). Serum sickness may not occur until two to four weeks after the start of drug therapy and does not resolve until the drug or its metabolic breakdown products have all been eliminated from the body (see SERUM SICKNESS). Drugs that can cause type III allergic reactions include penicillins, sulfonamides, thiouracil, and some radiocontrast diagnostic dyes.

Drugs such as hydralazine (Apresoline), procainamide (Procan, Pronestyl), phenytoin (Dilantin), and isoniazid cause a lupuslike syndrome that in many ways, but not all ways, mimics systemic lupus erythematosus. Fortunately, the drug-induced reaction is generally less severe and usually resolves with discontinuance of the causative drug.

Type IV (cell-mediated, or delayed) drug allergy reactions occur usually as contact dermatitis. The topical antibiotic neomycin and parabens, preservatives used in creams and ointments for the treatment of skin disorders, are examples of causes of type IV reactions. The contact dermatitis that results from these drugs is often more severe than the rash they were used to treat (see CONTACT DERMATITIS).

Nonallergic reactions Nonallergic ("pseudoallergic") reactions, drug intolerances, or idiosyncratic reactions simulate an allergic reaction, such as the anaphylacticlike response to radiocontrast media (RCM) during X-ray procedures. Adverse responses to RCM or X-ray dyes were long thought to be allergic in nature, but it is now clear that there is no immunologic basis for these reactions (see RADIOCONTRAST MEDIA REACTIONS). The asthma that results from aspirin is another nonimmune reaction (see ASPIRIN

SENSITIVITY). Nonallergic responses also include nausea, nonallergic rashes, diarrhea, and constipation among others.

Testing for drug allergy Skin tests are the most sensitive, useful, and rapid method of determining type I hypersensitivity (anaphylaxis) to some drugs such as insulin, penicillin, and chymopapain. However, they must be done by an experienced allergist because of risk of a severe reaction to the testing material. In addition, testing materials for penicillin and most drugs are not readily available. The skin test is not useful for low molecular weight chemicals, because an irritant reaction may easily be confused with an allergic response.

In vitro blood tests, such as RAST, theoretically appear to be ideal. But they are not as sensitive as skin tests, and a false-negative response could be misleading, resulting in exposure to a potentially life-threatening anaphylactic reaction. A positive response to a RAST test for a drug is of value, and the identified allergenic drug should be avoided.

Patch tests are useful for detecting delayed reactions to topical medications that may be a cause of contact dermatitis (see CONTACT DERMATITIS, PATCH SKIN TESTS).

Questionable history of drug allergy Many patients are uncertain of a past history of an allergic drug reaction, though they are told they should not take certain drugs, most often penicillin, because of a rash or other possible allergic reaction. Often these possible allergies date from childhood.

If an alternative drug is available, it is simplest to avoid the drug in question. If there is a compelling medical need for that particular medication, a dosing trial can be used cautiously. Minute doses of the questionable drug are given in gradually increasing doses at timed intervals, and health care professionals are prepared to intervene if any reaction occurs. The physician also requests that the patient sign an informed consent form explaining the risks of this procedure.

The goal of the graduated-dose approach is to determine if a person is allergic to a particular drug, and if not, to eventually administer a full therapeutic dose and carry out the treatment.

Desensitization   Similarly, minute doses of a known allergenic drug may be administered to a susceptible individual because no alternative drug is available for a serious medical problem. Because of the hazardous nature of this procedure, it is usually carried out in a hospital setting, possibly in the intensive care unit.

Minute doses are given orally, subcutaneously, intravenously, or as a combination of these and gradually increased so that antibodies directed against the needed drug are removed or reduced.

Most often desensitization, or test dosing, is carried out in patients with a potentially fatal prognosis and whose only chance for survival depends on the offending drugs.

Treatment of drug reactions   When a drug reaction is apparent, the most important principle is to discontinue the suspected drug. Often that is all that is required. In cases in which serious reactions may result, such as with phenytoin (Dilantin) or the sulfonamides (sulfa), the corticosteroid prednisone must be administered soon enough and in sufficiently high dosage in order to prevent the most severe effects of the allergic reaction.

Rarely, a drug must be continued despite an allergic response. Insulin is an example because there is no alternative therapy. The dose is reduced to approximately one-third of the dose that caused the reaction and is slowly increased to required levels. If insulin has been discontinued for several days or longer, a major problem may arise and desensitization may be necessary. (See DESENSITIZATION.)

Dunbar, William P.   American physician (1863–1922) who became director of the State Hygienic Institute in Hamburg, Germany, where he spent his entire career and conducted studies on pollen hypersensitivity that were influential to later researchers.

Dunbar devised a method of collecting pure pollen for the purpose of analysis, originated a technique of titrated conjunctival and nasal challenges to determine individual sensitivity to pollen, and dispelled certain ideas about the cause of hay fever that were popular in his day. Among his many accomplishments, he also confirmed that cat saliva is a source of cat hair allergen, which was not immunologically proven until 1981.

Duo-Medihaler   See ISOPROTERENOL.

dust   Any powder or very fine particles of earth.

dust allergy   See HOUSE DUST ALLERGY, HOUSE DUST MITES.

dust cells   Reticuloendothelial cells in the walls of the alveoli, the air sacs in the lungs, that destroy dust particles.

dusting powder   A fine, usually fragrant powder used as a toiletry and dusted onto the skin. Dusting powder may cause respiratory irritation.

dust mite allergy   See HOUSE DUST MITES.

dyes   Chemicals or natural or synthetic substances used to stain or color another substance. (See AZO DYES, FOOD ADDITIVES.)

dyes, radiocontrast (X-ray), and allergic reactions   See RADIOCONTRAST MEDIA REACTIONS.

dyphylline   (Dilor, Lufyllin)   A bronchodilator drug derived from xanthine and related to theophylline, used for the treatment of asthma.

dyspnea   Difficult or uncomfortable breathing most frequently caused by lung or heart diseases. The patient may express this as being "unable to take a deep breath," being "breathless," "can't get enough air," "heaviness in my chest," or "tightness in my chest."

Dyspnea involves a change in the rate and/or depth of normal breathing. It may be caused by airway blockage, anxiety, pain, obesity, high altitude, damage to the brain stem such as transient ischemic attack (TIA), adverse reaction to a drug, anemia, lung disorders such as pneumonia, pneumothorax (collapsed lung), and emphysema, heart failure and other circulation disorders, and exercise when one is unfit. Breathing difficulty may be accompanied by chest pain, coughing, wheezing, and a feeling of tightness in the chest. Asthmatic persons often experience dyspneic episodes during exacerbation of asthma. Some allergic reactions include dyspnea (see ANAPHYLAXIS). Breathing difficulty may also occur at rest or when the body requires additional oxygen.

VARIATIONS OF DYSPNEA

1. Platypnea is dyspnea that is present in only an upright position.
2. Orthopnea occurs in a supine position.
3. Trepopnea occurs only in right or left lateral positions.
4. Paroxysmal nocturnal dyspnea occurs when a person becomes suddenly very short of breath during the night and must sit up to catch his breath. This usually occurs in persons with congestive heart failure and is at times referred to as "cardiac asthma."
5 *Tachypnea* means very rapid respirations.

E

ear The organ of hearing, consisting of the external, middle, and inner ear. The external ear provides a structure called the external auditory canal, into which sound waves travel to the eardrum, or tympanic membrane. The eardrum vibrates as the sound goes to the middle ear, where structures including the eustachian tubes are located. The eustachian tubes, one in each ear, connect parts of the middle ear to the back of the throat. Because the middle ear is lined with mucous membrane, allergic symptoms or infections from the throat and nose are often carried through the eustachian tube to the middle ear. The purpose of the middle ear is to transmit sound waves from outside to inside the ear to promote hearing. Also in the middle ear are the delicate bones known as the malleus, incus, and stapes. The stapes lies at the end of the chain formed by the two other bones and is between the eardrum and the inner-ear auditory nerves. The stapes' vibrations aid the conduction of sound waves to the auditory nerves, which signal the brain to hear the sound.

The inner ear contains the cochlea and its sensory receptors for hearing, and the vestibule and semicircular canals, which are responsible for a sense of balance and position. The snail-shaped cochlea also houses the organ of Corti, which contains cells including those stimulated by sound waves and is the receptor for hearing. Hearing is mainly governed by the eighth cranial nerve, called the acoustic nerve. This nerve communicates sound to the brain so it may be interpreted by the individual. (See also OTITIS MEDIA, SECRETORY.)

ear infections and allergy See OTITIS MEDIA, SECRETORY.

earlobe skin allergy See CONTACT DERMATITIS.

Earth Wax See CERESIN.

ebastine Antihistamine under investigation. (See ANTIHISTAMINE.)

ecologists, clinical Practitioners and promoters of the belief that human illness stems from influences in our environment. (See CONTROVERSIAL APPROACHES TO THE DIAGNOSIS, EXPLANATION, OR TREATMENT OF ALLERGIES.)

economics of allergy and asthma care See ASTHMA COST.

eczema Atopic or allergic dermatitis, an inflammation of the skin characterized by redness, itching, and vesicles that are crusty or scaly as a result of the secretion of pus or other fluid. The Greek word *ekzema* means "to erupt." (See ATOPIC DERMATITIS.)

eczematous dermatitis Another term for eczema or atopic dermatitis. (See ATOPIC DERMATITIS.)

Edelman, Gerald M. American physician, born in 1929 in New York City, who shared the Nobel Prize for physiology or medicine in 1972 with British scientist Rodney R. Porter. Edelman and Porter each conducted important and revealing studies on the chemical structure of antibodies. Edelman, who also earned a Ph.D., was appointed to the staff of Rockefeller University in 1960.

edema Excessive amount of fluid in body tissues. Edema can be caused by a multitude of diseases and substances. It may result from the release of histamine and other chemicals during an allergic reaction. Other causes include heart and kidney failure, malnutrition, and starvation.

Angioneurotic edema (angioedema) involves large areas of swollen tissues or mucous membranes resulting from allergic sensitivity to foods, drugs, weather conditions such as cold or wind, and unknown causes.

Laryngeal edema, a swelling of the larynx that can be life-threatening when it obstructs airflow to the trachea (windpipe), is caused by anaphylaxis, the most severe form of allergy. (See also ANAPHYLAXIS; ANGIOEDEMA, HEREDITARY; ANGIOEDEMA, IDIOPATHIC; ANGIOEDEMA, NONHEREDITARY.)

edema, laryngeal   See EDEMA.

E.D.T.A.   See ETHYLENEDIAMINE TETRAACETIC ACID.

E.E.S.   See ERYTHROMYCIN.

egg allergy   Immediate reaction directly following the ingestion of egg white (albumen) or the injection of vaccines derived from egg protein. Individuals allergic to eggs can usually eat chicken and do not react to inhaled feather particles. Only 4% of egg-white protein is the heat-stabile ovomucoid type; however, this is the most important of several allergenic proteins.

The vaccines of live measles and mumps are grown in cell cultures of chick embryo, and the manufacturer recommends that persons who have had anaphylaxis (the most severe form of allergic reaction) after eating eggs should not be given the vaccine. Researchers at the Johns Hopkins Children's Center in Baltimore, Maryland gave MMR (measles, mumps, and rubella) to 129 children known to be allergic to eggs. The two adverse reactions that occurred were unrelated to eggs. Other experts report systemic reactions in a similar group of children and recommend that egg-sensitive children be skin-tested with the MMR vaccine and desensitized if they test positive. (See MEASLES, MUMPS, AND RUBELLA (MMR) VACCINE, ALLERGIC REACTIONS.)

Only a minute quantity of egg white is necessary to induce an allergic reaction in susceptible persons. In others, consuming large amounts of egg whites may cause hives and angioedema or headaches by stimulating the release of histamine in an anaphylactoid, or allergiclike, reaction.

Egg allergy may also be a cause of eczema. Egg white contains the antivitamin substance avidin, which results in a rash caused by a biotin deficiency. Individuals highly sensitive to egg must read labels carefully because egg is a hidden ingredient in many foods, especially mayonnaise and salad dressing.

Breast-feeding mothers should avoid eggs so their infants will not become sensitized. (See PRENATAL AND POSTNATAL ALLERGIC SENSITIZATION.)

Ehrlich, Paul   German bacteriologist (1854–1915) who proposed that every living protoplasm consists of a chemical nucleus, or center of activity, accompanied by structures he called "side-chains" that function in a variety of ways. With this concept, which was referred to as the "side-chain theory," Ehrlich attempted to explain antibody production and immune reactions in which the antigen-antibody reaction is compared to a structure of chemical receptors or structures with side- chains.

eicosanoids   Oxygenated derivatives of arachidonic acid (an acid found in most animal fats), including the lipid mediators leukotrienes, prostaglandins, and thromboxane, produced by cells of the immune system. Complex reactions occur between cells and these lipid mediators that are involved in the damaging inflammatory processes in the lungs in asthma. It is thought that future treatments for asthma will involve modifying these processes. (See also CHEMICAL MEDIATORS, LEUKOTRIENES.)

electroacupuncture   A controversial method for the diagnosis of chemical and food allergies in which a patient holds an aluminum plate containing the suspected allergens and an electrode that transmits impulses to a computer. This method is also known as electrodermal response testing, electrodiagnosis, autogenic response testing, or Voll testing. Its proponents claim that adverse reactions can be neutralized by placing drops of identified allergens under the tongue. This technique is used by alternative medical practitioners; traditional allergists advise that this is an unproven technique. (See ALTERNATIVE TESTING AND TREATMENT FOR

ALLERGIES, CONTROVERSIAL APPROACHES TO DIAGNOSIS, EXPLANATION, OR TREATMENT OF ALERGIES.)

electrodiagnosis   See ELECTROACUPUNCTURE.

electrostatic filters   See AIR-FILTRATION SYSTEMS.

electrostatic precipitator   See AIR-FILTRATION SYSTEMS.

elemental diets   See DIET, ELEMENTAL.

elimination diets   See DIET, ELIMINATION.

Elion, Gertrude B.   American scientist, born in 1918 in New York City, who shared the Nobel Prize for physiology or medicine in 1988 with chemist George M. Hitchings for their synthesis of azathioprine, an antimetabolic agent, and for their work in chemotherapeutic and immunosuppressant control of leukemias and autoimmune diseases and prevention of transplant rejection. Elion had served in several academic posts, including those of adjunct professor of pharmacology at the University of North Carolina and research professor of pharmacology and experimental medicine at Duke University.

Elixophyllin   See THEOPHYLLINE.

emedastine   Antihistamine under investigation. (See ANTIHISTAMINE.)

emphysema   A chronic lung disease named from the Greek word *emphysan*, meaning "to inflate," and characterized by difficulty in breathing, especially shortness of breath due to enlarged and damaged air sacs (alveoli) found at the ends of thin-walled air passages called bronchioles. Almost always, emphysema is caused by cigarette smoking; smoke (as well as other pollutants) stimulates the release of alveolar chemicals, which impedes the oxygen and carbon dioxide exchange necessary for normal maintenance of the body's metabolism. The lungs become progressively inefficient, which may result in pulmonary hypertension (increased blood pressure in the pulmonary artery), cor pulmonale (enlargement and/or failure of the heart's right ventricle), edema (swelling due to excess fluid in the tissues), and chronic bronchitis (inflammation of the bronchial tubes). In mild cases this disorder may be confused with asthma.

Symptoms of emphysema may not emerge until the disease is well under way. Initial signs include shortness of breath on exertion, such as climbing stairs, which gradually worsens until a person is short of breath even at rest. The chest may become barrel shaped because air becomes trapped outside the lungs and pushes out the thorax. Coughing and wheezing may be present, too. When cor pulmonale develops, oxygen deficiencies cause edema of the legs, and a person looks blue or purplish. These persons are called "blue bloaters." Individuals who breathe rapidly but retain normal coloring are referred to as "pink puffers." In advanced emphysema, breathing becomes increasingly difficult. Chest X rays and pulmonary function tests determine the extent of the lung damage and breathing capacity.

Treatment includes bronchodilating, diuretic, and corticosteroid drugs, nebulizers, and oxygen administration.

employment opportunities for individuals with allergies and asthma   Occupations or professions in which persons afflicted with allergic disorders or asthma can function in an environment free from occupational allergens or pollutants. An example of an inappropriate choice for an asthmatic person might be a zookeeper, pet shop employee, veterinarian, or farmer. (See OCCUPATIONAL ASTHMA.)

E-Mycin   See ERYTHROMYCIN.

entomophilous plants   Various species of plants whose pollens are transported by insects. Although certain plants have many strong pollen allergens, most are of little clinical significance because the grains are not inhaled. An example is dandelion pollen, which may cause mild hay fever in a child playing in a dandelion patch but will not cause any symptoms to those just a short distance from the flowers.

However, excessive pollen from eucalyptus, willows, some maples, acacia, and a few other species remaining at the end of the fertilization season dries out, becomes airborne, and causes hay fever in susceptible persons.

environmental "allergies"   See CONTROVERSIAL APPROACHES TO DIAGNOSIS, EXPLANATION, OR TREATMENT OF ALLERGIES; SICK BUILDING SYNDROME.

environmental controls to prevent or control allergy symptoms and asthma   Measures taken in the home or workplace to reduce exposure to allergens: prohibiting smoking and eliminating other irritants such as perfumes; use of a dehumidifier and cleaning materials that contain mold retardants; covering pillows and mattresses and removing carpeting; using air-conditioning during pollen seasons; and removing pets.

The ideal home environment is colder and drier, which discourages mite, cockroach and fungal problems. A less effective alternative is to remove carpets and upholstered furniture and to cover mattresses and pillows. By lessening allergic and irritant triggers, symptoms may be so diminished that little or no medication may be required. These measures are considered the backbone of allergy management. (See TRIGGERS OF ALLERGIES AND ASTHMA.)

enzymatic digestion of foods affecting allergenicity   Increases or decreases in allergic symptoms after food proteins are modified by digestive enzymes in the gastrointestinal tract. (See FOOD ALLERGY.)

enzyme   A complex protein produced by body cells that promotes chemical processes and changes without being altered itself. For example, enzymes in digestive juices such as saliva and gastric, or stomach, juices cause the breakdown of foods into simpler compounds so they may be digested and nutrients well

distributed. Hundreds of enzymes have been identified, but researchers suspect that perhaps a thousand actually exist in mammals. Some enzymes are amylolytic enzymes, which change starch to sugar; lipolytic enzymes, which turn fats to fatty acids and glycerol; fermenting enzymes (produced by yeasts or bacteria), which induce the fermentation of substances such as carbohydrates; proteases, a category of enzyme that splits proteins; and respiratory enzymes, which act as catalysts in tissue cells to produce the release of energy. (See also ENZYME ALLERGY, INDUSTRIAL; ENZYME, RESPIRATORY.)

enzyme, respiratory   A system of enzymes, also known as cytochromes of flavoproteins, that speeds up the combination of hexose monophosphoric acid ester with oxygen from the air, thus producing a release of energy in the tissue cells. Cytochrome P-450 is a protein similar to the red blood cells in the liver, ovaries, adrenal glands, testes, and placenta that naturally produce steroids. This cytochrome plays a major role in the body's utilization of steroid hormones and fatty acids and ability to detoxify, or rid the body of, various chemicals and other substances as waste materials. Flavoproteins, or yellow enzymes, are important in cellular respiration, which refers to oxygen combining with other substances within the cells to form carbon dioxide and water and release energy.

enzyme allergy, industrial   Allergic reactions to inhaled proteins used in manufacturing processes. Examples are the enzymes used in detergents. Those found in the pharmaceutical industry, including papain, trypsin, and pancreatic extracts, may also cause allergies, including asthma. See ENZYME, OCCUPATIONAL ALLERGENS, OCCUPATIONAL ASTHMA.)

eosinophil   A cell or similar fundamental structure or element of tissue present in the bloodstream of normal individuals but occurring in greater numbers in many persons with allergic, parasitic, and other diseases. Eosinophils release chemicals damaging to parasites and enzymes that damp down inflammatory reactions. Eosinophils were first identified by bacteriologist Paul Ehrlich in 1879, and soon thereafter elevated levels of eosinophils in the blood were associated with the presence of asthma. A controversy exists as to the role of eosinophils in allergies and asthma: There is conflicting evidence that eosinophils may exacerbate or fight the inflammatory process. Most researchers now believe that eosinophils are striking participants in the inflammatory process. (See EHRLICH, PAUL; EOSINOPHIL COUNT; EOSINOPHILIA.)

eosinophil count   The total number of eosinophilic white blood cells per cubic millimeter of blood, nasal secretions, or sputum. The measure aids in the diagnosis of allergic and parasitic disorders. (See EOSINOPHIL, EOSINOPHILIA.)

NORMAL BLOOD EOSINOPHIL COUNTS

Newborn	20 to 850 cells/cu mm
Children	50 to 700 cells/cu mm
Adults	0 to 450 cells/cu mm

eosinophilia   Elevated levels of eosinophilic leukocytes (white blood cells) in the blood, which suggest the existence of allergic and parasitic disorders. Eosinophils normally number zero to five per 100 white cells when observed in a blood specimen (known as a peripheral blood smear) on a slide under a microscope. An eosinophil count of 5 to 15% points to the presence of allergic disease. Although an eosinophil count of 15 to 40% strongly suggests allergy, parasitic infections, certain medications, immunodeficiency disorders, malignancies, congenital heart disease, cirrhosis, periarteritis nodosa, and dermatitis herpetiformis may all provoke elevated eosinophils. Eosinophil counts above 50% are found in parasitic infections, Hodgkin's disease, and idiopathic hypereosinophilic syndrome. Radiation ther-

apy and peritoneal dialysis also cause a moderate increase in eosinophils Corticosteroids decrease the number of eosinophils, which may be misleading because they are often used to treat disorders with elevated eosinophil counts. (See EOSINOPHIL, EOSINOPHIL COUNT.)

eosinophilia-myalgia syndrome   (EMS) A life-threatening disorder thought to be caused by contaminated batches of the drug L-tryptophan. (See L-TRYPTOPHAN.)

ephedrine   A sympathomimetic drug, similar to adrenaline but somewhat less powerful, that dilates bronchial muscles, contracts nasal mucosae, and elevates blood pressure. In the past, ephedrine was important in the treatment of asthma. An alkaloid originally derived from a species of *Ephedra* (a genus of shrubs), it was used in ancient Chinese medicine as an antipyretic (fever reducer) and diaphoretic (perspiration, or sweat, inducer). Later, its actions were rediscovered, and it was produced synthetically for oral or parenteral administration. (See also SHEN-NUNG.)

epidermis   The cuticle, or outer layer of skin, consisting of four layers or strata: the stratum germinativum (or stratum mucosum or malpighian layer, the innermost layer); stratum granulosum epidermis (immediately above the stratum germinativum); stratum lucidum (the clear layer); and the stratum corneum (the outermost layer). The epidermis serves as a protector of internal body structures. Along with the dermis underneath, it can become inflamed (epidermitis) or irritated by contact with a vast array of substances or agents. (See CONTACT DERMATITIS.)

epiglottis   A slender, leaf-shaped, cartilaginous structure with an outer mucous membrane at the opening of the larynx, or voice box. When a person swallows, the epiglottis covers the larynx to prevent food or liquid from entering the airway.

epiglottitis, acute   Inflammation of the epiglottis, commonly experienced as sore throat, fever, and a barking cough; cyanosis (blue coloration of skin), drooling, and coma may also occur and may be fatal. In extreme cases, a tracheostomy may be necessary to reopen the airway. Treatment includes antibiotic therapy.

epilepsy and food allergies A neurologic disease often characterized by seizures or convulsions caused by exposure to allergens in food. Though findings remain inconsistent, epilepsy is thought to have many causes, including heredity, changes in electric currents in the brain, menstruation, trauma to the brain, sensory stimuli, or lights flashed in the eyes (each situation capable of triggering a seizure), disease or malfunction of the cortex of the brain, or a lesion on the temporal lobe of the brain. Idiopathic epilepsy is a form having no known cause. When seizures do occur, they are either grand mal (frequently preceded by an individual sensation called an aura, followed by unconsciousness, spasms or twitchings, frothing at the mouth, and other symptoms) or petit mal (a brief period of altered or lost consciousness).

In patients with food allergies there has been at least one double-blind challenge with beef in which electroencephalogram (EEG) changes were found only when beef was eaten. Other scattered reports of seizures following the ingestion of specific foods need to be confirmed by scientific studies.

epinastine Antihistamine under investigation. (See ANTIHISTAMINE.)

epinephrine (Adrenalin) One of the two active hormones, along with norepinephrine, produced by the adrenal glands, which sit on top of the kidneys (hence the combination of the Greek words *epi*, meaning "upon," and *nephros*, or "kidney"). Epinephrine has long been used as a vasoconstrictor (especially to prolong the action of local anesthesia), a cardiac stimulant, a topical application for the eye, a bronchiolar relaxant, and as a treatment for asthmatic attacks.

episodic asthma Symptoms of asthma occurring only sporadically, such as during an acute upper respiratory infection, or cold, or upon exposure to a specific trigger. In the interim there is no shortness of breath or wheezing, and lung function studies are normal.

epistaxis A nosebleed, or hemorrhage from the nose, caused by trauma to membranes or structure of the nose or by skull fracture, various diseases, and high altitudes. It may also occur after surgery. Allergy and asthma patients may suffer nosebleeds as a result of violent, repeated sneezing or blowing the nose, or dryness of the mucous membranes.

Equal A brand of artificial sweetener. (See ASPARTAME.)

Erhlander technique Unscientific method reported by some alternative practitioners to aid in the diagnosis of various ailments including allergies. A glass container of a suspected food, chemical, or allergen is placed in a patient's hand, and the opposite arm is tested for muscle weakness by the examiner. The examiner also touches other body parts to assess abnormalities.

ERY-C See ERYTHROMYCIN.

Ery-Ped See ERYTHROMYCIN.

Ery-tab See ERYTHROMYCIN.

erythema Redness of the skin caused by inflammation, a nervous reaction, heat, sunburn, extreme cold, infection, drug reaction, food poisoning, diseases such as rheumatism and tuberculosis, or irritation of the skin by a substance. Erythema, a form of macula, manifests as a diffused redness or rash over a small or large portion of the body. Pain is sometimes associated with certain forms of erythema.

erythromycin (E-Mycin, ERY-C, Ery-tab, PCE, E.E.S., Ilosone) An antibiotic belonging to the macrolide group and produced by a strain of *Streptomyces erythraeus*. Erythromycin is widely used in the treatment of respiratory infections, especially in persons allergic to penicillin. Its principal adverse effects are abdominal pain, nausea, vomiting, diarrhea, and loss of appetite. Erythromycin should be avoided or used cautiously in persons with known liver disorders or those taking the following drugs, which are also metabolized in the liver and frequently prescribed for allergy and asthma patients: terfenadine (Seldane), astemizole (Hismanal), theophylline (multiple brands), and some others used for other disorders.

Essellier, Andre-F.   Swiss physician, born in 1912, who studied and published 31 papers and monographs on eosinophils, or cells in red bone marrow with a cellular structure that can be stained with a red, acid dye called eosin for the purposes of analysis under a microscope. The number of eosinophils in the blood increases in the presence of certain diseases, including asthma.

ethanal   See ACETALDEHYDE.

ethanol   See ALCOHOL.

ethyl aminobenzoate   See BENZOCAINE.

ethylenediamine tetraacetic acid   (E.D.T.A.) A potentially allergenic or irritating ingredient in carbonated beverages and vegetable oils and used in some bandaging materials. E.D.T.A. may trigger asthma.

Euler, Ulf S. von   Swedish physician (1905–83) who shared the Nobel Prize in physiology or medicine in 1970 with Bernhard Katz and Julius Axelrod for studies on various activities of transmitter substances in nerve terminals. Among other scientific and medical accomplishments, von Euler also identified prostaglandin and vesiglandin (active biologic substances that affect the heart, smooth muscle, and uterus), piperidine, and noradrenalin (a vasoconstricting chemical also known as norepinephrine).

eupnea   Normal breathing. (See BREATHING.)

eustachian tube   The tubular structure composed of bone and cartilage linking the nasopharynx, or nose and throat cavity, to the tympanic cavity, or inner ear. Also called the auditory canal, this structure was named for the Italian anatomist Bartolommeo Eustachio, who first described its function in the 1500s. When this organ functions normally, the air pressure in the inner ear is equal to that in the environment. When the eustachian tube becomes blocked by swelling or thick mucus, pain in the ears and sinuses may occur, and bacterial infections may result if drainage is impaired. (See OTITIS MEDIA, SECRETORY; SINUSITIS.)

exanthem   Derived from the Greek word *exanthema*, meaning "eruption," a skin eruption usually associated with an inflammation such as measles, erysipelas, or scarlatina or an acute virus known as exanthem subitum. This virus causes high fever, convulsions, and roseola infantum, a diffuse maculopapular rash that occurs as the fever begins to subside.

excoriation   An epidermal abrasion, or an abrasion of the coating of any organ, caused by chemicals, burns, trauma, and other irritating substances or circumstances.

excretion   Any material expelled in some way from a gland, tissue, or other part of the body, such as sputum expelled from the lungs through coughing and expectoration, or carbon dioxide, water vapor, and other gases through the respiratory process.

exercise   Action of various types intended to promote good health, physical fitness, and improved function of specific body parts. Exercise is also a common trigger of asthma in about 80% of individuals with that diagnosis. In the past, most asthmatics were advised to avoid exercise. However, exercise is now considered an important activity, and medications are taken prior to exercise to allow participation by all but the most severe patients. (See EXERCISE-INDUCED ASTHMA.)

exercise challenge testing   Measurement of lung function using a spirometer before and following exercise on a treadmill or exercise bicycle or by running freely, to determine if an individual has exercise-induced asthma. (See EXERCISE-INDUCED ASTHMA.)

exercise-induced anaphylaxis   A rare disorder in which exercise, or, at times, exercise performed after eating, triggers anaphylaxis (allergic collapse). It may occur from five to 30 minutes after beginning the exercise and lasts one to three hours. Hives and angioedema may also be present. The disorder is more common in young adults, especially joggers, and may run in families.

Celery, shellfish, and wheat are the foods most often suspected of triggering attacks. However, exercise anaphylaxis may occur following the ingestion of any food in some persons or may be unrelated to eating in others. When food is involved, exercise or food alone will not trigger the syndrome. Drugs and other allergens, including fire-ant stings, have also been implicated in triggering exercise anaphylaxis.

Avoidance of exercise for four to six hours after eating is the most effective therapy. Antihistamines and epinephrine (Adrenalin) may also be useful. (See also PHYSICAL URTICARIA.)

exercise-induced asthma (EIA)   The onset of coughing, wheezing, shortness of breath, and a feeling of tightness or pains in the chest following exercise. Exercise endurance is limited and should be anticipated in all asthma patients. Symptoms usually begin after three to eight minutes of strenuous exercise. They may be minimal, occurring only with extremes of effort, or severe enough to require emergency treatment. The presence of cold weather, air pollution, hay fever-causing pollens, or a coexisting cold or sinus infection may lessen the degree of exercise needed to cause symptoms.

Cause   Although the exact cause of exercise-induced asthma is unknown, it is thought by experts to be related to water loss from the bronchial tubes and increased concentration of the remaining fluid in the lining of the bronchi,

provoking smooth muscles in the airways to constrict.

Prevalence   Exercise-induced asthma is possible in about one in 10 student, Olympic, and professional athletes. Well-conditioned athletes may experience symptoms only at the extremes of their abilities; however, even Olympic medal-winning athletes often require asthma drugs to restore their breathing to normal.

1984 U.S. OLYMPIC TEAM—INCIDENCE OF ASTHMA

Athletes	Known to Have Asthma prior to Joining the Team	Found to Have Exercise-induced Asthma (EIA) during Training
597	26 (4%)	67 (11.2%)

Diagnosis   Diagnosis is suggested by a history of the symptoms listed above. The diagnosis of exercise-induced asthma is confirmed by a decrease of at least 15% in lung function after an exercise challenge. Lung function can be documented by using either an inexpensive portable peak flow meter or a more sophisticated computerized spirometer.

Best sports for asthma patients   Swimming, downhill skiing, gymnastics, and karate are sports less likely to trigger asthma. However, well-known professional football and basketball players of superstar stature have asthma.

Treatment   The use of two or three puffs of a beta-agonist bronchodilator metered-dose inhaler (MDI), such as albuterol (Proventil, Ventolin), pirbuterol (Maxair), terbutaline (Brethaire), and metaproterenol, or two to four puffs of the anti-inflammatory drug cromolyn sodium (Intal) 10 to 15 minutes before the start of exercise will prevent exercise-induced asthma in the majority of patients. Alternative drugs include the MDI ipratropium (Atrovent), an anticholinergic (two to three puffs 20 to 30 minutes before exercise), or albuterol (Proventil, Ventolin); metaproterenol (Alupent) syrup or astemizole or terfenadine one hour before exercise may be effective. Albuterol and cromolyn are often combined in resistant individuals.

Do You Have Exercise-induced Asthma? A Yes Response to Any of the Following Questions Indicates a Need to See a Family Physician or a Physician Specializing in the Treatment of Asthma

Yes No
1. Do you cough during or after exercise?
2. Do you wheeze during or after exercise?
3. Do you have chest tightness during or after exercise?
4. Do you have noisy breathing during or after exercise?
5. Do you have chest pain during or after exercise?
6. If you ran a lot of wind sprints or a mile or more at a fast pace, after a rest period of five minutes:
a. Would you feel tightness in your chest?
b. Would you cough or wheeze during the rest period?

Allergy and lung specialists urge the participation of all students and adults in exercise programs. Students should be excused from gym classes only if they are having symptoms on the day of activity and should not be given blanket excuses. (See also EXERCISE-INDUCED ANAPHYLAXIS, EXERCISE CHALLENGE TESTING, OLYMPIC ATHLETES WITH ASTHMA.)

expectorant   A substance or agent that stimulates the ability to remove bronchopulmonary mucus from the lungs, bronchial tubes, and throat. Expectorants may be sedative or stimulating. Ammonium carbonate and ammonium chloride are rarely used today but formerly were frequently found in cough mixtures. Guaifenesin (Robitussin), iodinated glycerol (Organidin), and ipecac may be used alone or in combination with cough suppressants. Proof of their effectiveness has been questioned by some experts.

expectoration   The act of spitting mucus or phlegm from the throat or lungs.

THREE PHASES OF CLINICAL DRUG STUDIES IN THE UNITED STATES

PHASE 1
- The first use in humans, which must be conducted with informed consent
- Investigators must be approved by the Institutional Review Board (IRB) and follow strict guidelines
- A permit known as an investigational new drug exemption (IND) must be granted by the FDA
- Usually only a few healthy volunteers receive the drug in order to determine safe doses

PHASE 2
- Can begin once preliminary safety data have been obtained
- Patients are treated with the new drug under carefully supervised conditions
- Effectiveness of the drug as well as long-term safety is evaluated

PHASE 3
- Widespread use of the drug in clinical trials by as many as 150 practicing physicians with 1,500 to 3,000 patients in most studies
- This phase may last until the FDA determines that the drug is safe and effective for general use

---

experimental drugs   Medications being studied or in various stages of development. Many experimental drugs not available in the United States are available in other countries. Before a drug is approved for general use by the Food and Drug Administration (FDA) in the United States, it must pass through three phases of research (see the chart below). If the three phases have been concluded successfully, a New Drug Application (NDA) is submitted. It usually takes a minimum of four years before a drug reaches this stage, but a much longer period is often required. Postmarketing studies (sometimes called Phase 4) will often result in new uses for drugs in addition to the original officially approved indication. Adverse effects not apparent in the original studies are discovered with more widespread use.

expiration   Breathing out, or expelling air from the lungs. A duration of expiration, or exhalation, longer than inspiration may indicate emphysema, asthma, or other respiratory pathology. In active expiration, one uses muscles including those of the abdominal wall. Passive expiration occurs without muscular effort, but rather with the elasticity of lung and chest tissues and the weight of the chest wall.

exsufflation   The expulsion of air from the lungs that is accomplished by natural force or mechanical exsufflator.

extracts, allergy   See ALLERGENIC EXTRACTS.

eye allergies   See CONJUNCTIVITIS, ALLERGIC.

eyelid allergies   See CONTACT DERMATITIS.

F

falling drop A clinking sound heard during auscultation with a stethoscope over large cavities in which there is air or fluid, such as in hydropneumothorax.

farmer's lung A pneumonialike allergic lung disease from exposure to bacterialike microorganisms called actinomycetes. These organisms thrive in silos when the water content of the hay exceeds 28%. Emptying a silo often causes an attack. (See ACTINOMYCETES; HYPERSENSITIVITY PNEUMONITIS; OCCUPATIONAL ASTHMA; PEPYS, JACOB.)

FAST testing See RADIOALLERGOSORBENT TESTS.

fatigue and allergies See CHRONIC FATIGUE SYNDROME, TENSION-FATIGUE SYNDROME.

FD&C No. 5 See TARTRAZINE.

feathers Light horny growths projecting from the skin of birds and fowl that are a common cause of nasal allergy and asthma. Feathers become more allergenic as they age and become contaminated by dust mites and molds. Usually individuals allergic to the feathers of one bird or fowl react to others as well.

Although pillows are the most common source of exposure, upholstery, mattresses, down comforters, and outerwear may be unexpected sources of allergy symptoms. Feather allergy does not cross-react with egg allergy, although an individual may be sensitive to both of these protein allergens.

Because of the continuous exposure of pillows during sleep, any person with allergies should avoid exposure, regardless of allergy skin or blood test results, since that person may become sensitized at any time. (See also ANIMAL ALLERGY, BIRD ALLERGY.)

Feingold diet A diet, also known as the "Kaiser-Permanente diet," free of natural salicylates, dyes, and preservatives proposed by pediatrician Benjamin Feingold in 1973. Dr. Feingold reported that up to 50% of all hyperactive children could be helped by being placed on his diet. His 1975 book, *Why Your Child Is Hyperactive*, published by Random House, was a best-seller, and Feingold had a great many supporters, both professional and lay. However, a panel of experts concluded that only a very small percentage of children diagnosed as hyperactive were helped significantly by the diet. (See HYPERACTIVITY.)

feminine hygiene sprays See VAGINAL DEODORANTS.

fexofenadine (Allegra) Metabolite, or derivative, of the popular non-sedating antihistamine Seldane. Unlike Seldane, the newer drug bypasses the liver and avoids the drug interactions that can cause potentially life-threatening heart irregularities. Allegra is effective for the treatment of sneezing, itching, runny nose and other allergy symptoms.

fiberglass A fibrous substance made from glass and used in the manufacture of structural materials, textiles, and yarns. Fiberglass disposable filters are used in heating and air-conditioning systems to collect dust and other contaminants. At least one case of an allergic reaction to fiberglass has been confirmed in a 39-year-old female who experienced shortness of breath, facial itching, rash, and swelling when exposed to the substance in a construction area. She had a recurrence of symptoms during patch testing to fiberglass.

fibrosis of lungs Scar tissue that forms in the connective tissue of the lungs after pneumonia, pulmonary tuberculosis, or inflammation.

fire ants Insects whose stings cause allergic reactions in susceptible persons. Reactions range from local pustules at the sting site to fatal anaphylaxis.

Imported from Uruguay or eastern Brazil on produce, the subspecies *Solenopsis richteri* probably entered the United States through the port at Mobile, Alabama in about 1918. The more aggressive ant, *S. invicta*, is native to Brazil and northern Argentina and was first recognized in the United States about 1939.

The fire ant, called the "ant from hell" by *Smithsonian* magazine, measures two to eight millimeters in length, with queens reaching one centimeter. Mounds measuring up to three feet in diameter and one and one-half feet in height may contain as many as 250,000 ants with 300 egg-laying queens.

An attacking fire ant grasps its victim with four teeth and arches its back while stinging with its posterior repeatedly in a circular pattern. There are also reports of anaphylaxis occurring during vigorous exercise following stings.

Range The range of the fire ants has reached as far north as the Tidewater region of Virginia and west to the eastern half of Texas, but they are expected to find their way as far as the Pacific Northwest, possibly reaching Canada by the 21st century. Mounds, up to 200 per acre, cover over 260 million acres of the southern United States, with tunnels extending outward to 130 feet.

Treatment of stings There is no effective treatment for local reactions from stings. More than 50% of those stung develop large local reactions at the sting site. These become reddened, edematous, and intensely itchy.

In severe cases, elevation of an involved extremity and therapy with corticosteroids and antihistamines not only lessens discomfort but may prevent the need for surgical decompression or even amputation. In 1989, the American Academy of Allergy and Immunology reported that 2% of individuals stung develop anaphylaxis; 32 deaths were confirmed.

Immunotherapy for fire-ant allergy Two vaccines have been used to prevent allergic reactions in previously stung individuals: imported fire-ant whole-body extract (IFA-WBE) and venom allergens (IFAV). Theoretically, venom extracts are purer and batches are more consistent, but they are difficult and expensive to produce in large quantities.

Immunotherapy (allergy injections) using an extract made from whole ant bodies seems to be effective in preventing or significantly reducing the severity of subsequent fire-ant stings.

It has been estimated that most patients can tolerate a fire-ant sting without a reaction after two years of immunotherapy. However, it is not clear how long therapy should be continued.

IMPORTED FIRE-ANT DEATHS IN THE UNITED STATES THROUGH 1989

Alabama 4
Florida 10
Georgia 2
Louisiana 2
Texas 12

fish allergy Symptoms of nasal congestion, asthma, or hives caused by eating bony fish; shellfish including mollusks, clams, mussels, and oysters; and the crustaceans shrimp, lobsters, and crabs. Allergy to fish is probably related to a group of allergens in the protein muscle of fish, also found in amphibians. However, these allergens are not present in the muscles of mammals. Especially sensitive persons may experience asthma, angioedema, and anaphylaxis by the inhalation of the steam from cooking fish.

Breast-feeding mothers should avoid eating shellfish and bony fish because their infants may become sensitized. Minute amounts of fish may cause allergy in infants; these babies will usually have positive skin or radioallergosorbent (RAST) blood test results. Although the tests may remain positive for some time, the child may be able to tolerate fish and other allergenic foods in time. Fish and other food allergies are less frequent in older children and adults.

Sixty percent of persons allergic to one bony fish may also react to others. However, those same individuals may or may not be sensitive to shellfish and crustaceans. There is an excellent correlation between positive skin tests for fish and allergy. Fish may be a cause of Henoch-Schonlein purpura (HSP), an allergic vasculitis (a disease of inflamed blood vessels). The condition improved after fish was withdrawn from the diet in some patients with HSP. Fish allergy is especially common in Scandinavia, where cod is a mainstay of the diet. Shrimp has been implicated with other foods as a trigger for exercise-induced anaphylaxis (allergic shock). While fish may trigger acute allergic reactions including anaphylaxis, it also can cause nonallergic reactions called anaphylactoid (like anaphylaxis) in persons who eat large amounts of certain fish that contain great quantities of histamine. By the end of the meal, flushing, erythema (redness), itchy eyes, nausea, diarrhea, and headache occur. This condition can last up to 24 hours and is self-limited. The scombroid fish, tuna and mackerel, mahimahi, and inadequately refrigerated fish most commonly cause these reactions. When fish spoils, bacteria (*Proteus morganii* or *Klebsiella pneumoniae*) cause a buildup and release of histamine. Puffer fish are poisonous, and their effects and the effects of other toxic fish can be confused with allergic reactions. Some fish become toxic because of their consumption of large quantities of algae that contain various toxins. Ciguatera eat other reef fish such as grouper, snapper, and barracuda, which may have fed on toxic algae. These fish are endemic to tropical waters near Hawaii and Florida. Ciguatoxin is not destroyed by cooking; eating the viscera of fish is especially dangerous.

The main toxin in paralytic shellfish is saxitoxin. Muscles, cockles, clams, and scallops can harbor these toxins. By avoiding fishing in areas of "red tides," this problem can be prevented.

Another important cause of asthma in susceptible persons is eating shrimp and other seafood chemically preserved with sulfites.

flaxseed   Seed from any of the herbs of the genus *Linum* of the family Linaceae (flax family), most notably a blue flowering annual, *L. usitatissimum*, cultivated for its fiber. Flaxseed is a source of potent allergens that may be inhaled from cattle and poultry feed, dog food, cosmetic products such as shampoos, depilatories, patent leather, insulating materials, rugs, and materials with some flax in them. Orally ingested products including flaxseed tea, cough remedies, muffins, laxatives, milk from flaxseed-fed cows, Roman meal, and any products containing flaxseed oil may also cause allergic reactions.

flea bites   Punctures in the skin made by fleas, insects of the order Siphonaptera. They siphon, or suck, blood from warm-blooded animals and are capable of carrying and spreading plague bacillus, endemic typhus, brucellosis, tularemia, and other diseases. Bites are erythematous (red) and itchy as a result of the injection of saliva by the fleas.

Flonase   Brand of fluticasone, a corticosteroid for topical use as a nasal spray for the prevention of nasal allergy.

Flovent   Brand of fluticasone, a corticosteroid for topical use as a metered-dose inhaler (MDI) for the prevention of asthma symptoms. Flovent is the only MDI available in three strengths.

flower   The part of plants containing the reproductive organs: stamens, which produce pollen, and a pistil, which produces the ovule. (See ANEMOPHILOUS PLANTS.)

flow meter   A device that measures the flow of a liquid or a gas, including the respiratory gases oxygen and carbon dioxide.

Floyer, Sir John   British physician (1649–1734) who designed a 60-second pulse watch that made it possible to study the pulse and respiratory rates as they are affected by sex, age, emotional state, temperature, climate, diet, drugs, and disease. Floyer also estimated blood volume according to an individual's body weight. An asthmatic, Floyer wrote of his increased difficulty in breathing in the presence of tobacco smoke, dust, and other changes in the air and as a sequel to ingesting certain foods, performing exercise, and experiencing emotional changes. Floyer is credited as the first to observe that asthma and predisposition to asthma are hereditary. In addition, he dissected a "broken winded mare," and his findings provided the first description of a lung physically deteriorated by emphysema.

flunisolide (Aerobid, Nasalide) A corticosteroid for topical use as a nasal spray and metered-dose inhaler for prevention of nasal allergy symptoms and asthma. (See CORTICOSTEROID NASAL SPRAYS, CORTICOSTEROIDS.)

fluticasone (Flonase, Flovent) Corticosteroid for topical use as a nasal spray and metered-dose inhaler for the prevention of nasal allergy and asthma symptoms.

flu vaccine See INFLUENZA VACCINE.

food additives Chemicals or substances added to foods and medications as coloring or flavoring agents, preservatives, sweeteners, or to improve consistency. Adverse reactions are rare from the approximately 2,800 substances approved by the Food and Drug Administration (FDA). But an important and potentially life-threatening reaction can occur in persons susceptible to the preservatives known as sulfiting agents. These additives can cause asthma and anaphylaxis, with symptoms including a flushed feeling, drop in blood pressure, and tingling sensations (see SULFITING AGENTS).

Dyes approved in the Food, Drug, and Cosmetic (FD&C) Act of 1938 are derivatives of coal tar. Tartrazine, or FD&C Yellow Dye No. 5, is frequently implicated as a cause of hyperactivity in children and asthma. However, fewer than 10% of individuals suspected of having adverse reactions to these additives reacted when challenged in a controlled study (see FEINGOLD DIET, HYPERACTIVITY). Aspirin-sensitive asthmatic patients should be aware of the rare possibility of cross-reactivity between tartrazine and aspirin (see ASPIRIN SENSITIVITY).

Parabens, a group of preservatives in creams and ointments, are strong skin sensitizers and can worsen the condition for which they are prescribed. Parabens can cause urticaria (hives) or angioedema (swelling of body tissues) when medications containing them as preservatives are injected. However, oral ingestion of these substances do not seem to cause adverse reactions. Sodium benzoate, a chemically related substance, may cross-react with the parabens and can also cause asthma.

Butylated hydroxanisol (BHA) and butylated hydroxytoluene (BHT) are used in low doses as antioxidants in grain products, including breakfast cereals, and have not been shown to cause any allergic problems. However, since antioxidants are thought by some to prevent cancer and herpes infections and to retard aging, they are often used in megadoses in various health food preparations that may be toxic.

Nitrate and nitrite preservatives commonly used in lunch meats and hot dogs may cause migraine headaches (see HEADACHE). Monosodium glutamate, the cause of "Chinese restaurant syndrome," may rarely cause asthma, hives, or angiodema (see CHINESE RESTAURANT SYNDROME).

The azo dye amaranth (FD&C Red No. 5) was banned by the United States in 1975 because of suspected carcinogenicity. Aspartame (Nutrasweet) is often blamed for adverse effects, but except for a few cases of urticaria (hives), there is no scientific proof of ill effects. Tartrazine is also frequently implicated in causing urticaria and angioedema. However, well-controlled studies such as those at the Scripps Clinic and Research Foundation have rarely confirmed these suspicions. These dyes do play a role as sensitizers in allergic dermatitis. They are often suspected of inducing adverse effects both in the skin and when ingested. Skin reactions are relatively common; when used in foods and medications, they are rarely proven to be the source of the adverse effect.

FDA-APPROVED DYES

Metabisulfite
Monosodium glutamate (MSG)
Nitrates
Nitrites
Parabens (derivatives of parahydroxybenzoic acid)
  butyl paraben
  ethyl paraben
  methyl paraben
  propyl paraben
  sodium benzoate
Potassium sulfite
Sulfites
Sulfur dioxide
Sulfur sulfite
Yellow Dye No. 5 (tartrazine)

food allergy   Adverse reactions to food or food additives caused by exposure to an allergen to which an individual is susceptible. However, many persons refer to any adverse food reaction as an allergy. There are basically two groups of food reactions, allergy-based, or "hypersensitivity," reactions and nonallergic, or food "intolerances."

Incidence   Hippocrates (460–370 B.C.) described stomach distress and hives from cow's milk. Galen (A.D. 131–210) recognized allergic symptoms in a child from goat's milk. Since the early 20th century, medical reports have carried descriptions of many similar reactions. Prevalence of true allergic reactions to food is unknown, but studies estimate the incidence of food allergy at about 1% in the general public. Adverse food reactions of all types, including those with nonallergic causes, may reach as high as 10% among infants if all adverse reactions are included.

Peak sensitivity to foods occurs at about age one in 3 to 4% of infants. Experts believe that 70 to 80% of babies outgrow their food allergies. In double-blind food challenges, it was demon-strated that only one-third of the patients thought to have allergies to a food actually had an adverse effect from a suspected food.

Five hundred consecutive newborns were followed over a three-year period during which 142 (28%) were suspected of having an allergy to at least one food. However, only 27 (5%) reacted when challenged to that food or foods.

True allergy involves an allergen-antibody reaction. A food-allergic reaction sets off a complex series of events when the food allergen (see ALLERGEN) comes in contact with the immune system as it is passing through or being absorbed by the gastrointestinal tract. Once absorbed into the bloodstream, the allergens attach themselves to receptors on mast cells and basophils in other target organs, the skin, respiratory tract, and circulatory system, triggering the release of potent chemicals called mediators. In turn, the mediators bring on the allergic symptoms—sneezing, itching, hives, wheezing, and shortness of breath, or, in the most severe expression of allergy, acute shock, or anaphylaxis.

Anaphylaxis, which may be fatal, seldom occurs and can usually be treated successfully if epinephrine is given immediately. Despite the fact that fatalities are rare, some experts believe that more children and adolescents die from food allergy than bee stings.

Foods that most commonly cause anaphylaxis Only a few foods cause the vast majority of food-allergic reactions. Similar properties among these foods' allergens are their glycoprotein composition, their water solubility, and heat and acid stability. Purified food allergens have been isolated from codfish, soybeans, and peanuts. In most foods, only a small fraction of the available protein is allergenic.

Cooking may alter the allergenic potential of some foods, such as milk. However, heating milk containing lactose (milk sugar) or milk altered by cooking actually increases the allergenic potential.

In children, eggs, cow's milk, and peanuts cause most reactions. In adults, fish, shellfish, tree nuts, and peanuts are the chief source of allergic reactions. Interestingly, various animal products do not always cross-react. Persons may be allergic to milk but usually are not allergic to beef or inhaled cattle dander. Similarly, individuals with egg allergy are rarely allergic to chicken meat or inhaled feather allergens.

Many women in the United States consume large amounts of peanuts, especially in peanut butter, as a source of protein while breast-feeding. Peanut allergen in the breast milk may then sensitize the infant hereditarily prone to peanut or other allergy.

Nuts, peanuts, eggs, or milk were responsible for 13 fatal or near-fatal reactions in one group of allergic children. All children in the group had asthma and most had prior reactions to the same foods.

Outcome and treatment of food allergy Epinephrine (Adrenalin) is available in spring-loaded, self-injecting syringes (Ana-Kit and Epi-Pen are two commercial brands available by prescription). Children weighing less than 30 kilograms (66 pounds) should receive a reduced dose.

Most children who died in the group mentioned above were in school or other public places at the time of the allergic reaction. Those who were immediately given an injection of epinephrine survived. Onset of a severe reaction usually occurs within minutes but may be delayed for 30 minutes or more. In the group of 13 patients mentioned above, none of the individuals who died had received an epinephrine injection before severe respiratory distress developed. An initial reaction may be mild for an hour or more and then suddenly worsen.

In the group of fatalities, half suffered a rapid progression of respiratory difficulty before death. The other half had a two-part response: early oral itching and abdominal distress, with minimal symptoms for one to two hours before the onset of rapid deterioration and death. Therefore, it is imperative that anyone who has symptoms of a food allergy be given epinephrine as soon as possible and transported to an emergency medical facility on an urgent basis and observed for at least several hours.

Prevention of food allergic reactions Adults and children of reading age who have known food allergies should read labels carefully and become familiar with all the alternate names used for some foods. They must ask about ingredients of any foods ordered in a restaurant. Foods are often added unexpectedly; for example, peanut butter may be added to chili for flavoring. The Canadian Restaurant and Foodservice Association has a program in which designated employees of participating members are knowledgeable about all ingredients on their menu.

For persons who have had a prior food reaction and were diagnosed with positive tests for a particular food by a qualified allergist, avoidance of that food is paramount. However, if one showed a positive allergy test but no past reactions to a particular food, it does not have to be avoided.

Immunotherapy (allergy shots) for food allergy Studies are being done to develop a safe method to desensitize food-allergic persons.

WARNING
HOWEVER, AT THE PRESENT TIME, ALLERGY SHOTS FOR FOOD ALLERGIES SHOULD NEVER BE ATTEMPTED IN A PRIVATE PHYSICIAN'S OFFICE. THE RISK OF FATAL ANAPHYLAXIS IS GREAT.

Testing for food allergy Many individuals who have positive tests to foods can eat those same foods without having a reaction. A history of a prior food reaction usually precedes a fatal attack. (See FOOD ALLERGY TESTING, RADIOALLERGOSORBENT TESTS, SKIN TESTS.)

Nonallergic food reactions Various other mechanisms are responsible for an individual's adverse reaction to a food: toxicity from or poisoning by contaminated foods; drug-in-duced effects such as those following ingestion of caffeine; metabolic or enzyme deficiencies, such as the diarrhea induced by the inability to digest lactose (milk sugar) in a person with the lactase enzyme deficiency (see LACTOSE INTOL-ERANCE).

Typical descriptions of adverse reactions to a food include food hypersensitivity, food ana-phylaxis, food intolerance, food toxicity (poi-soning), food idiosyncrasy, anaphylactoid food reaction, pharmacologic food reaction, and metabolic food reaction.

Rashes, diarrhea, colic, and runny nose are often attributed to food allergies but are rarely proven to have origins in allergy.

food allergy testing   Diagnostic tests, in-cluding skin, radioallergosorbent (RAST), and double-blind dietary challenges, for determin-ing an individual's sensitization to a certain food or foods. Diets that eliminate foods and then introduce them one at a time are usually a wasted effort as an allergy test and rarely point to a food-related allergy that could not be found by careful history taking. (See also RADIOALLERGOSORBENT TESTS, SKIN TESTS).

food labeling, ingredients   The listing of all substances used in the production of a food on the package, especially important for persons with serious food allergies.

formaldehyde   A poisonous, foul-smelling, colorless gas that when dissolved in water is used as a preservative for animal tissues. Form-aldehyde is found in abundance in our environ-ment. Also a by-product of the combustion of gasoline and diesel and from cigarette smoke, gas, wood stoves, and kerosene heaters in the home or workplace, this gas is an irritant to the respiratory system. Formaldehyde is also widely used in building materials, especially in mobile homes. Urea formaldehyde foam insu-lation was injected into the walls of homes until 1977, when it was replaced by safer materials. Plywood, molded plastics, and carpeting are additional sources of formaldehyde.

Formaldehyde has been blamed as a cause of the strange symptoms referred to as "mobile home syndrome." Although there is no evi-dence that formaldehyde causes allergy, it is a frequent cause of contact dermatitis and may act as an irritant in respiratory symptoms. (See CONTACT DERMATITIS.)

formoterol   An investigational bronchodi-lating drug of the beta-agonist type used for the treatment of asthma. As a metered-dose in-haler, it has a rapid onset of action whose effec-tiveness peaks in two hours and persists for up to 12 hours. It is approximately 10 times more potent than albuterol.

4-Way Nasal Spray   See NAPHAZOLINE.

Freeman, John   British physician (1877–1962) who investigated tests for immunity and contributed to the development of therapeutic immunization. He served as director of the clin-ics for allergic disorders and bacteriological services at St. Mary's Hospital in London for many years. Freeman also published *Hay Fever, a Key to the Allergic Disorders*, which he dedi-cated to his colleague Leonard Noon, who died of tuberculosis. (See also NOON, LEONARD.)

fumes   Irritating vapors, such as smoke fumes and ammonia gas, that may cause sneez-ing, coughing, choking, tightness in the chest, and shortness of breath or trigger an attack in an asthmatic person. (See TRIGGERS OF ALLER-GIES AND ASTHMA.)

fungal diseases, systemic   [systemic myco-ses]   A group of infectious diseases that affect the lungs, skin, and other organs. Pneu-monialike symptoms may be confused with al-lergic lung disorders. These infections are most often found in immunocompromised persons and are termed "opportunistic." Such infections are most likely to occur in patients following radi-ation, accidental or therapeutic, or during therapy with corticosteroid, immunosuppressive, and antimetabolic drugs. Patients with AIDS, renal fail-ure, diabetes mellitus, bronchiectasis, emphy-sema, Hodgkin's disease, non-Hodgkin's

FUNGAL DISEASES OF THE LUNG OR SKIN THAT MAY BE CONFUSED WITH ALLERGIC DISEASES

Disease	Distribution
Aspergillosis, or allergic broncho pulmonary aspergillosis (see ALLERGY BRONCHOPULMONARY ASPERGILLOSIS)	Worldwide. Incidence is higher in the United Kingdom than in the United States.
Blastomycosis, North American blastomycosis, or Gilchrist's disease	Formerly found predominantly in the southeastern states and the Mississippi valley but recently discovered throughout Africa.
Candidiasis, systemic (see CANDIDIASIS)	Worldwide. Microorganism found in the human gut.
Coccidiodomycosis, San Joaquin Valley fever, or valley fever	Endemic to the southwestern United States.
Cryptococcosis or torulosis	Worldwide distribution but in the United States most often in the southeast.
Histoplasmosis	Endemic in eastern and midwestern United States.
Maduromycosis, Madura foot, or mycetoma	Most prevalent in the tropics and southern United States.
Paracoccidioidomycosis or South American blastomycosis	South and Central America.
Phycomycosis, mucormycosis, or zygomycosis	United States, southeast Asia and Africa.
Sporotrichosis	Temperate and tropical climates.

lymphoma, leukemia, tuberculosis, and serious burns are prone to these fungal infections.

Primary, nonopportunistic fungal diseases are usually found in certain geographic locations (see Table). These are chronic, though rarely acute, infections. Lesions in the lungs develop slowly, and it may take many months or even years before symptoms emerge.

Diagnosis is made by tissue biopsy, with the characteristic fungal identification made by observation through a microscope. Skin tests are available for several of these diseases, but they are often unreliable.

The treatment of choice is antifungal drugs such as ketoconazole (Nizoral), amphotericin B (Fungizone), and fluconazole (Diflucan).

fungi and molds A unique group of organisms similar to tiny plants but different from most plants because they lack chlorophyll, which creates green coloration, and they cannot produce their own food. More than 100,000 species of fungi have been identified, including mildews, molds, and mushrooms. True fungi differ from slime molds and actinomycetes, formerly classified as fungi but now considered bacteria (see ACTINOMYCETES). They have nuclei and cell walls of chitin or cellulose. Except for a few unicellular forms such as yeasts, most fungi are composed of thousands of microscopic threadlike cells called strands, or hyphae. Groups of hyphae form a tangled mass known as a mycelium. The mycelium often grows beneath the surface of its food source. The fruiting body, such as the umbrella of a mushroom, produces reproductive cells called spores. Spores develop into new plants.

Most allergenic fungi can grow on nonliving organic matter, but some types of fungi are parasitic, requiring a viable host. All need moisture, oxygen, and carbohydrates, and some need growth factors to survive. Classification of fungi is based on their structure, growth factors, and method of reproduction. Airborne molds are the most important source of allergens.

Outdoor fungal allergens Alternaria and *Cladosporium* (*Hormodendrum*) are important dry-spore outdoor allergens. Levels of airborne fungal spores, which are high during the growing season in grass and grain-growing areas of the temperate zone, peak in late summer and autumn. *Ascospores* and *basidiospores* are highest at night and on rainy days. In well-ventilated buildings, the outdoor fungal spore levels are high when air sampling is done.

Although it seems likely, it is difficult to prove that outdoor fungal spores cause respiratory symptoms to worsen during humid and rainy weather. Spore levels are higher close to the ground and are stirred up when lawns are mowed or grain is harvested. Sensitive persons often experience symptoms when exposed to hay, compost piles, piles of leaves in the autumn, peat moss, and storage silos.

Indoor fungal allergens Closed buildings during winter or centrally air-conditioned ones in summer show a predominance of *Penicillium*, *Aspergillus*, and *Fusarium* spores. These important indoor allergens are commonly found in damp rooms, especially basements. Other common mold allergens are *Rhizopus nigrican*, or black bread mold; *Saccharomyces cerevisiae*, or baker's yeast; and *Chaetomium, Curvularia, Helminthosporium, Spondylopcladium, Stemphylium, Rhodotorula, Phoma, Pullularia,* and *Trichoderma*. The latter three, in addition to *Fusarium*, are slime molds.

Ingested fungal allergens Many food products rely on fungi for production. *Sacharomyces cerevisiae* are yeasts used to manufacture baked goods, beer, wines, liquors, vinegar, and processed meats. *Penicillium* species are used in the fermentation process of some cheeses, such as Roquefort. Fungi are involved in the preparation of chocolate, steak, and soy sauces.

Rarely will eating massive amounts of yeast-containing foods, such as pizza, cheese, wine, or mushrooms, cause respiratory symptoms. If these foods are suspected as a cause of allergy, they should be withdrawn, and a mold-free diet should be employed. Food allergies should be confirmed by an allergist, who may conduct a test called a diagnostic challenge. (See DIET, MOLD ELIMINATION.)

Fungal diseases Hypersensitivity pneumonitis (extrinsic allergic alveolitis) is a lung disorder associated with intense and often prolonged exposure to inhaled organic dusts and other industrial antigens including fungi.

Allergic bronchopulmonary aspergillosis is a pneumonialike disease caused by hypersensitivity to *Aspergillus fumigatus* antigen. Other fungal allergic disorders include suberosis from moldy cork, malt worker's lung, sequoiosis from contaminated maple logs, wood pulp worker's disease, cheese washer's disease, wood trimmer's disease, thatched roof disease, *Streptomyces*-hypersensitivity pneumonia from contaminated fertilizer, *Cephalosporium* hypersensitivity from contaminated basement sewage, sauna taker's disease from sauna water, and paprika splitter's lung. (See ALLERGIC BRONCHOPULMONARY ASPERGILLOSIS, HYPERSENSITIVITY PNEUMONITIS, OCCUPATIONAL ALLERGENS.)

Mold reduction Home vaporizers and humidifiers connected to central heating furnaces are frequently contaminated and are significant sources of a fungi-containing aerosol mist. Central air-conditioning with closed windows during summer will reduce outdoor dry mold spore levels and indoor molds by reducing humidity.

In areas with dry winters, indoor relative humidity of 20 to 25% is adequate, and the use of humidifiers should be avoided. Meticulous cleaning is essential for enclosed shower stalls and shower curtains, window moldings, refrigerator drip pans, damp basements, and anywhere water condensation collects.

Mold-inhibiting products such as sodium hypochlorite or Clorox, Lysol, X14, Zephiran, or Roccal are only effective for brief periods before regrowth occurs. Small moldy objects can be placed in a plastic container or bag for 12 to 24 hours with a small quantity of paraformaldehyde or propylene oxide. Paraformaldehyde fumes are used to decontaminate closed areas but are toxic, and areas must be well ventilated before human use.

Laboratories attempting to determine significant environmental mold allergens in the workplace or home have analyzed open-culture collecting dishes. The collected molds settling out in the dishes are then microscopically identified. However, small spores often fail to settle, and the larger particles probably do not reflect the causative allergens.

Mold immunotherapy Studies support the use of immunotherapy (allergy shots) for the fungi *Alternaria* and *Cladosporium,* but difficulty in preparing purified extracts of allergens limits the effectiveness for most molds. (See also MOLD ALLERGY.)

G

gamma globulin The collective term for protein that forms in the blood and in concentrated quantities as antibodies, which play a major role in the body's ability to ward off infection. Also known as immune serum globulin (ISG), or immunoglobulin, and abbreviated as Ig, gamma globulin has been identified in five categories: gamma immunoglobulins A (IgA); D (IgD); E (IgE); G (IgG), and M (IgM).

IgA is present in respiratory and intestinal mucin, secretions of exocrine glands such as milk, and other natural lubricants including saliva and tears. IgA protects mucous membranes from bacteria that cause disease. IgD is a myeloma protein found in minute amounts in human blood serum. IgE, an important respiratory and intestinal protein, creates reagin, or antibodies in the blood. IgG, the chief immunoglobulin in human blood serum, is capable of passing through the placenta and therefore responsible for allowing the mother's immunities to reach the bloodstream of her infant shortly before it is born. IgM is responsible for most immune system responses of the body, especially during early stages of the reaction to invading microorganisms or allergens.

The level of immunoglobulins, or antibodies, is known as an antibody titer, that is, the measure of strength per volume of volumetric test solution (such as the blood or serum). (See IMMUNE SYSTEM and entries for individual immunoglobulins [A, D, E, G, M].)

gas, lung irritant Chlorine, phosgene, and other gases that cause burning sensations in the eyes, nose, and throat and may trigger asthma or cause bronchitis and pneumonia.

gastrointestinal reflux and asthma A flow of acidic gastric juices from the stomach into the esophagus (also called heartburn or reflux esophagitis) because the muscle at the junction of the esophagus and stomach does not function well enough to keep the stomach contents from backing up into the esophagus or the throat. The juices may also flow into bronchial tubes and cause asthma symptoms or aggravate preexisting asthma. One of the adverse effects of theophylline, an effective, widely used drug for the treatment of asthma, is reflux esophagitis. Drugs used to treat reflux esophagitis include Tagamet and Zantac. However, Tagamet may increase blood levels of theophylline and therefore should be avoided in patients for whom theophylline products are prescribed. (See HISTAMINE H$_2$ RECEPTOR ANTAGONIST.)

gastrointestinal tract disorders See DIARRHEA, GASTROINTESTINAL REFLUX AND ASTHMA.

Generally Recognized As Safe (GRAS) list See GRAS LIST.

genetics of allergic disorders The probability and possibility of allergic parents producing allergic offspring. If one parent has an allergic disease such as hay fever, eczema, or asthma, there is about a 30 to 40% occurrence of allergy in the offspring. Predisposition increases to 50 to 70% if both parents have allergies.

Maimonides recognized asthma as a familial tendency in ancient Egypt as early as A.D. 1100. In 1916 Robert A. Cooke and his colleagues described the predisposition for allergies to occur in families.

Although allergy is genetic in nature, other factors such as the environment influence its expression. Allergic symptoms can often be prevented by avoiding known allergens. In addition, the expression of allergic disease is rare at birth and diminishes after the age of thirty. It has been determined that the chromosome 11q gene is linked to the inheritance of allergy, but only from the mother. Therefore, since males also influence allergic tendency, other genes must be involved.

Breakthroughs in the study of gene recognition and therapy are anticipated and should produce new therapies to prevent or improve the treatment of allergic disorders, including asthma.

geraniol   A fragrant, unsaturated alcohol found in apples, grapefruit, cherries, bay leaves, ginger, lavender and other sources and used in perfumes and other scented products such as soaps. Geraniol may cause allergic reactions.

geranium oil   A liquid substance derived from flowering plants of the Geraniaceae family, genus *Pelargonium* (of southern African herbs), which may cause allergic reactions in individuals allergic to geraniums. Because of its characteristic rose and geraniol odor, geranium oil is used in the manufacture of perfumes and other toiletries.

Gershon, Richard K.   American physician (1932–83), born in New York City and educated at Harvard and Yale universities, who introduced through his research at Yale the concept of T (thymus) lymphocytes, which are able to suppress immune responses of the body. Gershon's chief interest was the function of lymphocytes, cells of the lymph system that play a key role in immune responses. His studies of them relate to the dynamics of immunoglobulin E (IgE) antibodies during allergic episodes.

Glauber's salt   A crystalline sulfate of sodium named after 17th-century German chemist Johann R. Glauber. Glauber's salt, an ingredient in shampoos and bath salts and used as a laxative, has been reported to cause skin irritations.

Glick, Bruce   American professor of immunology and physiology, born in Pittsburgh, Pennsylvania in 1927, whose research centers on cellular interactions in the immune system of chickens. Educated in poultry science, physiology, and genetics, Glick studied chickens' lymph tissue and found a connection between a chicken's response to an antigenic challenge and human immunodeficiency disorders. After other scientists and investigators learned of Glick's observations, they conducted many studies, including ones that led to the important recognition that the thymus gland and bone marrow play a crucial part in the control of antibody-forming lymphocytes. Glick is also involved in research on the role of nutrition in immunity.

glue ear   A common term for chronic serous otitis media (a persistent buildup of thick fluid in the middle ear). This condition usually occurs in children with frequent ear infections and nasal allergy and may cause hearing loss. If treatment of underlying infection or allergy is not successful, surgical procedures may be necessary. (See OTITIS MEDIA, SECRETORY; TYMPANOMETRY; TYMPANOSTOMY TUBES.)

gluten-sensitive enteropathy [celiac disease, celiac sprue]   An inability to digest and absorb nutrients as a result of an intolerance to gluten, a protein found in grains (wheat, rye, oats, and barley). This malfunction of the small intestine usually manifests in late infancy but may not appear until adulthood.

Cause   This disease may have its roots in either genetic or environmental factors; the precise origin is unknown.

Symptoms   Diarrhea with loose, pale, bulky, greasy, and foul-smelling stools is the cardinal symptom that may cause small stature, malnutrition, a bleeding tendency, hypocalcemia, irritability, and, in infants, a failure to thrive. Common deficiencies include vitamin D, iron, and folic acid, and there may be predisposition to lung diseases, diabetes mellitus, lymphatic and alimentary-tract malignancies, and inflammation of the thyroid and other autoimmune anomalies. The diagnosis of gluten-sensitive enteropathy must be confirmed by biopsy of the intestinal mucosa. The treatment of choice is a permanent gluten-free diet.

glycolic acid   A crystalline compound derived from grapes and sugar beets that can irritate skin and mucous membranes. Glycolic acid is used in the textile and leather industries and in cosmetics to regulate the acid/alkali balance.

goat's milk   See MILK.

gold   A metal element of the earth used for jewelry, as a coloring and in cosmetics, and as an oral or injectable immune-modulating drug used to treat rheumatoid arthritis. Gold salts are capable of causing allergic skin reactions, but according to investigational studies by allergist-immunologists Michael Mullarkey (1988 and 1990 at the University of Washington) and I. Leonard Bernstein (1988 at the University of Cincinnati), low doses of gold salts resulted in a significantly lesser need for steroids in asthma patients. Although the gold salts caused only minimal adverse effects, the possibility of toxicity with long-term use is still in question, and long-term benefits have not been established.

Good, Robert A.   American allergist, immunologist, and researcher known for his studies on the role of the thymus gland in immunology and the lack of and dysfunction of gammaglobulins in the blood. Good was born in 1922 in Crosby, Minnesota and received his M.D. and Ph.D. (in anatomy) from the University of Minnesota in 1947. Currently teaching at the University of South Florida, Good has also published papers on acute-phase reactions, rheumatic fever, and other topics. According to an article he wrote along with three of his colleagues in the professional journal *Surgery* in 1956, the thymus in rabbits does not seem to participate in control of the immune response, but there seems to be some correspondence between the existence of a thymic tumor and the onset of agammaglobulinemia (lack of gamma globulins in the blood).

Grabar, Pierre   French chemical engineer (1898-1986), former chief of the laboratory at the Pasteur Institute in Paris, and considered one of the founders of immunochemistry.

Grabar was also director of the Institut du Cancer at Villejuif in 1960. Grabar developed the technique of immunoelectrophoresis, a test to measure the amount and character of proteins and antibodies in body fluids, and is responsible for the identification of immunoglobulins. He also contributed significantly to studies on the application of diagnostic methods such as ultrasound to disorders of the immune system.

grain allergies   Symptoms of allergy caused by allergens found in flour, often leading to occupational asthma in up to 10% of bakers or those exposed to flour on a regular basis. (See also BAKER'S ASTHMA, GRASS POLLEN ALLERGY, OCCUPATIONAL ASTHMA.)

gram-negative bacilli   In microbiology, microorganisms that lose the first applied stain and take up the color of the counterstain. Identifiable under a microscope, the major pathogenic bacteria are *Pseudomonas mallei* (which causes a contagious infection in horses, donkeys, and mules and is transmissible to humans); *Pseudomonas aeruginosa* (which cause "blue pus"); *Vibrio comma* (the cause of cholera); *Neisseria meningitidis* (the cause of cerebrospinal meningitis); *Neisseria gonorrhoeae* (gonorrhea); *Neisseria catarrhalis* (nasopharyngeal catarrh); *Proteus vulgaris* (suppuration); *Escherichia coli* (which can, but do not always, cause cystitis, pyelitis); *Klebsiella pneumoniae* (sometimes causes pneumonia); *Salmonella typhosa* (typhoid fever) and other *Salmonella* species (which cause paratyphoid fever or food poisoning); *Shigella dysenteriae* (dysentery); *Yersinia pestis* (plague); *Hemophilus influenzae* (meningitis conjunctivitis, influenza); *Bordetella pertussis* (whooping cough); and various species of *Brucella* (undulant fever).

gram-positive bacilli   In microbiology, microorganisms that retain Gram's gentian violet stain as observed through a microscope. The major gram-positive bacteria are *Corynebacterium diphtheriae* (the cause of diphtheria); *Streptococcus pyogenes* (suppuration, scarlet fever, septicemia); *Streptococcus viridans* (subacute bacterial endocarditis); *Staphylococcus* of various species (suppuration, pus in the blood, osteomyelitis); *Sarcina lutea* (sometimes causes suppuration); *Bacillus anthracis* (anthrax); *Clostridium tetani* (tetanus), *botulinum* (botulism), and *perfringens* (gas gangrene); and *Diplococcus pneumoniae* (bronchopneumonia and other infections).

gram stain   A method developed by Danish physician Hans C. J. Gram (1853–1938) to stain bacteria so they could be identified. The method involves the use of a microscope slide on which a specimen containing bacteria is placed, stained with the chemicals gentian violet or ammonium oxylate crystal violet, rinsed in water, and then immersed in Gram's iodine solution. Gram-positive bacteria absorb the violet stain and through the microscope look look purple. Gram-negative bacteria do not absorb the violet stain and appear pink or reddish.

granulomatosis   See CHURG-STRAUSS SYNDROME.

GRAS list   Those food additives "Generally Recognized As Safe" as authorized by Congress in 1958. The additives selected for this list were chosen because of their absence of known adverse or toxic effects rather than scientific proof of their safety. Motivated by the discovery that cyclamate artificial sweeteners caused cancer in laboratory animals, the Nixon administration charged the Food and Drug Administration (FDA) with the responsibility of reevaluating the GRAS list. In 1969 a panel of experts—the Select Committee on GRAS Substances of the Federation of American Societies for Experimental Biology—was assigned this task. By 1980, 305 of 415 substances studied were considered safe enough be given Class I status. Although additional research was recommended for 68 Class II substances, including vitamins A and D, they were approved for use at current levels. Caffeine, BHA, and BHT were listed as Class III ingredients, which required additional studies within a given time frame; however, they were allowed to be used

pending the outcome of those studies. Salt and four starches were placed in Class IV, with limitations on quantities or certain restrictions. Eighteen substances were recommended for removal from the GRAS list because of insufficient evidence for safety. More than 1,700 food additives are currently on the GRAS list.

grass pollen allergy   Hay fever symptoms related to the seasonal exposure of more than 4,500 plant species of the family Gramineae in North America and approximately 9,000 grass species worldwide. Grasses cover roughly 20% of the world's surface. These monocotyledonous, herblike, mostly anemophilous (having wind-borne pollen) plants reach their peak of pollination in temperate climates of North America from mid-May to mid-July. In tropical and subtropical regions, however, pollen may be present throughout the year. The grass flowers are open for only a few hours a day during the pollinating season. The pollen grains are viable for less than one day. A majority of hay fever sufferers experience symptoms when there is a concentration of pollen grains approaching 50 per cubic meter. The weather is largely responsible for pollen counts, with rain washing the air clean and higher winds blowing the pollens away. (See also POLLINOSIS.)

green tobacco sickness   A nonallergenic, toxic disorder occurring in tobacco harvesters from absorption of dissolved nicotine from wet tobacco exposure. (See TABACOSIS.)

grindelia   An American flowering, resinous herb known as a gum weed whose dried leaves and stumps are used in making a remedy for bronchitis as well as a topical preparation for poison ivy rash.

grinder's disease   See SILICOSIS.

grocer's itch   Pruritic (itchy) rash from continuous handling of flour, sugar, and other similar products that resembles eczema or psoriasis of the hands.

GRASSES THAT ARE A CAUSE OF HAY FEVER IN THE UNITED STATES AND CANADA

Common Name	Technical Name	Distribution	Pollination Season
Barley, cultivated	Hordeum vulgare	Cultivated	Jan. (May–June) [1] Dec.
Barley, wall	H. murinum	So. B.C., W. WA	June–July
Barnyard grass	Echinochloa crusgalla	Widespread weed	June–Oct.
[2] Bentgrass	Agrostis maritima	Widespread U.S. and Canada	June–Sept.
[2] Bermuda grass	Cynodon dactylon	Cultivated lawn grass, So. U.S., occ. farther north	Jan. (June–Sept.) [1] Dec.
[2] Bluegrass, annual	Poa annua	Widespread weed	Jan. (Mar.–Aug.) [1] Dec.
[2] Bluegrass, Canada	P. compressa	Nfld. to AK, So. U.S.	June–Aug.
[2] Bluegrass, Kentucky	P. pratensis	Cult. lawn grass, temperate Canada, all but S.E. U.S.	May–Oct.
[2] Bluegrass, pine	P. scabrella	Y.T. to B.C., So. to CA, E. to Alta., MI, MN, WY, CO	Apr.–July
[2] Bluegrass, Sandberg	P. sandbergii	Y.T. to B.C., So. to CA, NV, E. to Sask., ND, SD, CO, NM	Apr.–Aug.
[2] Bluegrass, shady (rough)	P. trivalis	E. Canada and N.E. U.S., AK to CA	May–July
Brome, California	Bromus carinatus	AK to So. CA, E. to Alta., ND, SD, WY, CO, NM, introduced locally farther east	Apr.–Aug.
Brome, mountain	B. marginatus	B.C. to CA, E. to SD, NM	Apr.–July
[2] Brome, smooth	B. inermis	AK to CA, introduced to Lab., VT, OH, NM, Rocky Mts. So. to CO	June–Aug.
Brome, soft (soft cheat)	B. hordeceus (B. molis)	AK to So. CA, E. to ID, MT	May–July
Bunchgrass, northwest	Agropyron spicatum	AK to CA, E. to Atla., ND, SD, NM	June–Aug.
Canary grass, common	Phalaris canariensis	WA to CA, Rocky Mtn. states, E. to Atlantic coast	June–Aug.
Canary grass, little	P. minor	OR to CA, Atlantic coast	Apr.–July
Canary grass, reed	P. arundinacea	So. AK and Canada, all but S.E. U.S.	June–July
Cane, sugar	Saccharum officinarum	Cultivated crop	Rarely allowed to flower

GRASSES THAT ARE A CAUSE OF HAY FEVER IN THE
UNITED STATES AND CANADA (continued)

Common Name	Technical Name	Distribution	Pollination Season
Cheat (chess)	*Bromus secalinus*	Occasional throughout temperate No. America	June–July
Corn	*Zea mays*	Cultivated crop	Jan.–Dec.
Dallis grass	*Paspalun dilatatum*	So. U.S. No. to NJ, TN, AR, OK, OR	Spring–Fall
[2]Darnel	*Lolium temulentum*	From Europe, now naturalized in CA	Apr.–June
Dropseed	*Sporobolus airoides*	WA to So. CA, SD, TX	Apr.–Oct.
Dropseed, sand	*So. cryptandrus*	So. CA to Atlantic coast, LA	May–Aug.
[2]Fescue, meadow	*Festuca elatior*	Cultivated forage and lawn grass	May–Aug.
[2]Fescue, red	*F. rubra*	AK to Nfld., So. to So. CA, NM, TX, and SC	June–Aug.
[2]Fescue, sheep	*F. ovina*	AK to Nfld., So. to CA, NM, and NY	May–Aug.
Gama grass	*Tripsacum dactyloides*	S.E. U.S.	Summer–Fall
Grama grass	*Bouteloua species*	So. Canada to So. Mexico, E. to WI, IL, OK, W. to MT, NV, So. CA	Summer–Fall
Johnson grass	*Sorghum halepense*	Widespread weed over much of central and Southern U.S.	July–Oct.
June grass	(see Koeler grass)		
Knotgrass	*Paspalum distichum*	Common E. and So. U.S., occ. elsewhere	Aug.–Oct.
Koeler grass (June grass)	*Koeleria cristata*	B.C. to CA, E. to Ont. and ME, DE, LA, TX	May–July
Melic, California	*Melica imperfecta*	C. and So. CA	Apr.–May
Oat grass, tall	*Arrhenatherum elatius*	S.W. B.C. to CA, E. across Canada to ID and MT	May–July
Oats, common wild	*Avena fatua*	Common throughout W. No. America	Mar.–Sept.
Oats, cultivated	*A. sativa*	Cultivated crop	May–Aug.
Oats, slender wild	*A. barbata*	S.W. U.S.	May–June

GRASSES THAT ARE A CAUSE OF HAY FEVER IN THE
UNITED STATES AND CANADA (continued)

Common Name	Technical Name	Distribution	Pollination Season
[2]Orchard grass	*Dactylis glomerata*	Common throughout most of No. America	June–Aug.
Pampas grass	*Cortaderia selloana*	Cultivated ornamental	June–Sept.
Quack grass	*Agropyron repens*	Widespread in much of temperate and subarctic No. America, except deserts	June–Aug.
[2]Redtop	*Agrostis alba*	Widespread in Canada and U.S.	June–Sept.
Rescue grass (south. chess)	*Bromus uniloides (cathariticus)*	Cultivated for forage in southern states	Summer
Ripgut	*B. rigidus*	B.C. to So. CA, E. to ID, Rocky Mts. in CO and NM	Apr.–June
Rye, cultivated	*Secale cerale*	Cultivated crop	May–July
Ryegrass, alkali	*Elymus triticoides*	C. WA to So. CA, E. to MT, WY, CO, NM	June–Aug.
Ryegrass, giant	*E. condensatus*	CA	June–Aug.
[2]Ryegrass, Italian (annual)	*Lolium multiflorum*	Cultivated lawn grass and widespread weed	May–July
[2]Ryegrass, perennial	*L. perenne*	Cultivated forage crop and lawn grass	May–July
Ryegrass, western	*Elymus glacus*	So. AK to So. CA, E. to Ont., MI, IN, IA, CO, NM	June–Aug.
Salt grass, coastal	*Distichlis spicata*	Vancouver Is. to So. CA, Canada to FL, LA, TX	June–Sept.
Salt grass, desert	*D. stricta*	So. B.C. to So. CA, E. to Sask., MO, OK, TX	May–July
Sudan grass	*Sorghum sudanense*	Cultivated crop	Jan.–Dec.
[2]Timothy	*Phleum pratense*	Cultivated hay crop	June–Aug.
[2]Velvet grass	*Holcus lanatus*	AK to CA, E. to Nfld., So. to GA, TN, MO, AZ, except Rocky Mts.	July–Sept.

GRASSES THAT ARE A CAUSE OF HAY FEVER IN THE
UNITED STATES AND CANADA (continued)

Common Name	Technical Name	Distribution	Pollination Season
[2]Vernal, grass, sweet	*Anthoxanthum odoratum*	AK, B.C. to CA, E. Canada, central and eastern U.S.	Apr.–July
Wheat, cultivated	*Triticum aestivum*	Cultivated crop	Apr.–June
[2]Wheatgrass, crested	*Agropyron cristatum*	Arid W. U.S.	June–Aug.
[2]Wheatgrass, slender	*A. tenerum*	AK to So. CA, Pacific to Atlantic coast	June–Aug.
[2]Wheatgrass, western	*A. smithii*	B.C. So. to E. WA, OR, NV, AZ, E. to Ont., NY, TN, TX	June–Aug.

[1]Months in parentheses are prime pollen months.

[2]Pollen is a major source of hay fever.

Adapted from *Pollen Guide to Allergy,* Hollister-Stier.

ground itch Skin inflammation and itching caused by larval hookworms, Ancylostoma or Nectator, at their point of entry to the body. Ground itch is also called anclyostomiasis cutis.

growing out of allergies and asthma Disappearance of childhood allergic symptoms and asthma upon reaching puberty. Generally the more severe the symptoms in childhood, the more likely the continuance during adolescence and adulthood. Usually the tendency for hyperreactivity of the airways remains for a lifetime, although often there are no symptoms. The tiny bronchioles of infancy widen profoundly with age, and therefore a greater triggering stimulus is required to cause wheezing or shortness of breath.

British studies have established that most asthma begins during childhood. As many as 11% of all children experience asthma symptoms at least once. Eighty-five percent, or the vast majority, have mild asthma, and 50% stop wheezing once they achieve adulthood and almost all have milder attacks. Children whose asthma develops after the age of six months and who do not have allergies have the best chance to outgrow their asthma tendency by adulthood.

guaifenasin (Robitussin) An expectorant drug used singly to loosen thick mucus or to help expel mucus and in conjunction with cough suppressants. (See EXPECTORANT.)

guided imagery See VISUALIZATION.

Guidelines for the Diagnosis and Management of Asthma See NATIONAL ASTHMA EDUCATION PROGRAM.

gum arabic See ACACIA.

gum benzoin A potentially allergenic resin from trees (genus *Styrax,* native to Southeast Asia) used as a topical skin protector and as a preservative in ointments.

gum karaya   The dried fluid of an Asian Indian tree that may be an ingredient in various cosmetics, toothpaste, hair sprays and other preparations, denture adhesives, and shaving cream. Because of its potential to cause asthma, dermatitis, and allergic rhinitis, gum karaya is not used in hypoallergenic products.

gum tragacanth   A highly allergenic, gummy exudate from various plants of Asia or eastern Europe (genus *Astragalus*, e.g., *A. gummifer*) used in the manufacture of a wide range of cosmetics, toothpastes, hand lotions, and hair removers. Like karaya, tragacanth swells in water and creates a gel, which makes it a desirable ingredient to enhance a product's consistency. But tragacanth has been reported to have caused hay fever, asthma, and other allergic reactions.

gustatory rhinitis   The nasal congestion and inflamed mucous membranes that follows smelling or tasting a substance to which an individual may or may not be allergic.

H

Habitrol   See NICOTINE PATCHES.

hair analysis   An unproven technique for the diagnosis of diseases including allergy. Investigators studying the technique have found results to be inconsistent and of no value in the diagnosis of allergic disorders. For example, two or more specimens from the same individual submitted to the same or different laboratories under different names were reported to have received different results. Even when results are similar, it is rare that they are of medical significance.

hair dye   Any type of coloring agent, whether permanent, semipermanent, or temporary, used on the hair for cosmetic purposes, which can cause severe contact dermatitis or conjunctivitis in hypersensitive persons. The silver nitrate or aniline dyes may be the most offensive chemical components of the coloring agent. (See CONTACT DERMATITIS.)

hay fever   A common name for allergic rhinitis or nasal allergy. The term originated in England when symptoms were observed as they occurred simultaneously with the harvesting of hay. However, exposure to hay does not usually produce the characteristic sneezing, runny and stuffy nose, or itchy, watery eyes and does not cause fever. Seasonal hay fever occurs in the spring and fall with exposure to pollinating trees, grasses, and weeds in susceptible persons. Perennial hay fever affects some allergic individuals and occurs year-round from exposure to animal danders, house dust mites, and molds.

An estimated 22 million Americans suffer from seasonal allergies and spend approximately $225 million for 8.4 million doctor visits and testing, $300 million on prescriptions drugs, and $2 billion on over-the-counter medications. These individuals suffer six million days of bed rest, 28 million days of restricted activity, 3.5 million days out of work, and two million lost school days. (See also ALLERGIC RHINITIS, GRASS POLLEN ALLERGY, PERENNIAL ALLERGIES, POLLINOSIS, RAGWEED, SEASONAL ALLERGY.)

headache   A general term for pain in the head, which may be classified as vascular or migraine, muscle contraction or tension, cluster, sinus, and mixed.

Allergies, especially to foods, have been associated with headaches since about 1927. Many persons with allergies suffer from headaches, but allergies are not always to blame. Controlled studies have failed to confirm type I, or immediate-onset, allergic reactions as a direct cause of headaches. Allergy can indirectly lead to headaches by causing sinus congestion and a painful buildup of pressure in the sinus cavities. Chemicals such as tyramine occurring naturally in foods and drugs are frequent causes of nonallergic headaches.

Vascular, or migraine, headaches "Classical migraine" occurs in only about 20% of headache sufferers. Characteristically, it is three times more common in females in approximately 10% of the population. Often hereditary, migraines can start in childhood or begin at puberty and subside at menopause. They often coincide with menstruation.

Migraines begin with an aura, or signal, that the patient comes to recognize. Blood vessels constrict (the vasoconstrictive phase). Neurologic disturbances may follow: scotoma (partial visual field loss), flashes of light, slight speech difficulty, transient partial blindness, and hemiparesis (weakness of one side of the body). The vasodilation phase, in which blood vessels dilate, triggers an intense throbbing, disabling headache limited to one side or alternating sides of the head, accompanied by nausea and vomiting. This theory has recently been questioned and it is now thought by researchers that the pain of migraine may not be due to vaso-constriction followed by vasodilation, but by other reactions occurring in the hypothalamic and cortical regions of the brain.

Many persons experience variations of migraine known as atypical or variant migraine. These headaches may follow a different sequence of events, or various phases may be absent from the classical migraine pattern.

Muscle contraction or tension headaches These headaches are very common, characterized by a dull, constant pain often relieved by sleep. They are more common in adults, three times more common in women, and affect up to 80% of the population.

Cluster headaches Cluster headaches occur as often as two or three times a day over a period of weeks or months. They are characterized by stabbing pain on one side of the head with watering of the eye and nose and the reddening of the eye and skin over the painful area. Onset is sudden and lasts approximately 90 minutes. Cluster headaches may be brought on by stress or emotional trauma, but no singular cause has been established. They may cease and return without warning. Not a hereditary disorder, they affect men almost exclusively and affect 0.5 to 1% of the population.

Sinus headache Because sinuses are located in various parts of the front of the skull, especially around the eyes and nose, a sinus headache occurs across the forehead or under the eyes over the maxillary sinuses on one or both sides of the face. Sinus headaches are associated with any condition that blocks the drainage of mucus from the sinuses, such as allergy or infection.

Foods as causes of headaches Foods containing chemicals known as vasoactive amines frequently trigger migraine. These include tyramine, dopamine, phenylethylamine, norepinephrine, serotonin, and histamine. These chemicals exert a druglike rather than an allergic affect to cause headaches.

Fermentation greatly raises tyramine levels especially in aged cheeses and red wines. Choc-olate contains phenylethylamine. Many foods and drinks cause the release of histamine: wine, particularly red varieties, egg whites, strawberries, shellfish, tomatoes, citrus fruits, and alcohol. Foods containing stimulants such as methyl xanthines, caffeine, and theobromine—for example, coffee, tea, cola drinks, chocolate, and cocoa—may also cause headaches.

Caffeine may trigger a migraine-type headache. Discontinuing the regular use of caffeine may induce a headache that differs from migraine in that pain occurs at the top and back of the head.

Excessive doses of vitamin A or D can cause headaches as well as other serious toxic effects. Synthetic diets containing excessive amino acids such as methionine, isoleucine, or threonine can cause headaches and nausea. Mycotoxins, such as aflatoxins, trichothecenes, and ergot, are important products of molds whose poisonous effects include intense headaches. (See also FUNGI AND MOLDS.)

hearing loss Blockage of the eustachian tube caused by nasal and sinus allergic conditions and disorders. (See EUSTACHIAN TUBE; OTITIS MEDIA, SECRETORY.)

heating fuels and heating systems Kerosene, wood, coal, and other substances used in stoves and heating units. Forced hot-air heating systems may encourage airborne dust to accumulate. Persons with allergies and asthma may be susceptible to symptoms caused by heating. Air that is excessively dry may irritate bronchial tubes, and air that is overly humid may induce mold allergens and an increase in dust mites. (See also WOOD- AND COAL-BURNING STOVES.)

heat urticaria See CHOLINERGIC URTICARIA.

HEFA filters See AIR-FILTRATION SYSTEMS.

Heiner's syndrome A chronic lung disease associated with iron deficiency anemia, characterized by coldlike symptoms and caused by allergy to cow's milk. (See MILK.)

Henoch-Schonlein purpura (HSP) An allergic reaction causing vasculitis, an inflammation of blood vessels. This disorder was first recognized by Heberden in the late 1700s, and in 1808 by English physician Robert Willan, but was named for the two German physicians Johann Schonlein and Edward Henoch, who termed the condition "peliosis rheumatica." HSP has also been called anaphylactoid purpura, allergic purpura, rheumatoid purpura, leukocytoclastic vasculitis, and allergic vasculitis.

The cause is unknown, but food allergy and streptococcal and viral infections have been suspected in some cases. HSP most often occurs in children; symptoms include bruises on the lower abdomen, buttocks, and legs accompanied by joint pains, and internal bleeding in the stomach, intestines, and kidneys (indicated by blood found in the urine). The condition is usually self-limiting and improves in about six weeks, unless kidney involvement is severe. In cases involving the kidneys, long-term follow-up is necessary. (See also VASCULITIS.)

herb A seed-producing, soft-stemmed plant of the annual, biennial, or perennial variety that is used in medicine, fragrances, or as flavoring in foods. (See HERBALISM.)

herbalism The medical discipline of treating diseases with natural herb preparations and other substances obtained from plants. Many conventional drugs are derived from plants, and the same precautions that apply to the traditional drugs must be exercised with the natural substances. For example, herb robert extract, from the plant *Geranium robertianum*, used as a flavoring agent in beverages, ice cream, candy, chewing gum, baked goods, jellies, and gelatin desserts, may cause allergic reactions in individuals sensitive to geraniums.

Asthmador cigarettes, which contained stramonium, a plant-derived, atropinelike drug, were promoted in the past as a treatment for asthma. However, any benefits were far outweighed by the inhalation of smoke and other contaminating substances.

Chamomile is allergenic, ginseng has hormonelike effects, and sassafras has been shown to be carcinogenic. Alfalfa seeds contain an amino acid, L-canavanine, that has been shown to induce a lupuslike autoimmune disease.

Great care must be exercised when choosing herbal drugs because lack of adequate controls can lead to contaminated products, toxic doses, or even mistaken identity of the substance. In the latter situation, a toxic substance could be mistakenly substituted for a nontoxic one.

The Chinese herb Bi Yan Pian, Cyperus 18 (Seven Forests), is used for generalized hay fever and sinusitis. Lopanthus Anti-Febrile Pills (Hou Hsiang Cheng Chi Pien) are used for treatment of food sensitivities. (See also HERB.)

heredity or hereditary allergy See GENETICS OF ALLERGIC DISORDERS.

Hippocrates Greek physician of the fifth century, considered by many "the father of modern medicine." Among his major tenets are that physicians should observe all, evaluate honestly, assist nature, work for the good of the patient, treat the whole person and not simply the illness, and, above all, do no harm. Modern chiropractic also employs Hippocrates' idea that all illness stems from panomalies of the spine. In Hippocrates' writings, he described the symptoms of pulmonary edema: "Water accumulates; patient has fever and cough; the respiration is fast; the feet become edematous; the nails appear curved and the patient suffers as if he had pus inside, only less severe and more protracted. One can recognize that it is not pus but water. . . . If you put your ear against the chest you can hear it seethe inside like sour wine."

Hippocrates also wrote that some foods known to be safe and healthful for most people caused illness in some, possibly, he speculated, because of a "poison" in the food, such as cheese, to which some people were particularly sensitive.

Hismanal   See ASTEMIZOLE.

histaminase   An enzyme found throughout the body that counteracts histamine. See HISTAMINE.

histamine   A natural substance liberally distributed throughout the body (especially in the skin, heart, lungs, gastrointestinal mucosa, and the brain and other organs) and a major substance released by mast cells of the tissues to initiate an allergic reaction. Inflammation, excess acid production in the stomach, constriction of the bronchi in the lungs, red flushing of the skin (as occurs with a burn), red rashes, decrease in blood pressure, and headache are among the symptoms characteristic of histamine release. Antihistamines are substances that counteract histamine. (See ANTIHISTAMINE.)

histamine H$_1$ receptor antagonist   An alternate term for antihistamine. (See ANTIHISTAMINE.)

histamine H$_2$ receptor antagonist   A drug that blocks the effects of the chemical histamine by competing for receptor sites on the surface of cells in the stomach, thus preventing the secretion of gastric acid in the treatment of peptic ulcers. H$_2$ blocking drugs available in the United States include cimetidine (Tagamet), ranitidine (Zantac), nizatidine (Axid), and famotidine (Pepcid). Traditional antihistaminic drugs, called H$_1$ receptor antagonists, differ from H$_2$ agents by blocking the allergic symptoms caused by histamine primarily in the respiratory system and skin. H$_1$ and H$_2$ antihistamines are sometimes combined for the treatment of hives.

H$_2$ antagonist drugs rarely have adverse effects; however, cimetidine causes a rise in theophylline levels and should be used with caution in asthmatic patients taking both drugs. The other drugs in this class are probably free of this problem. (See also ANTIHISTAMINE, CIMETIDINE, RANITIDINE.)

histamine headache   Headache that appears to be a direct result of histamine given by injection or ingested through certain wines containing histamine. (See HEADACHE.)

histoplasmosis   A fungal respiratory infection characterized by acute shortness of breath, coughing, fever, pains in the joints, potential adrenal gland failure, and other symptoms if the disease goes untreated or becomes chronic. Infection may be caused in susceptible or immunocompromised individuals who inhale the spores of the fungus *Histoplasma capsulatum*, found in soil (especially when contaminated by fecal material of birds or bats) in the southern and central United States, regions of South America, Africa, and Asia. In severe cases ulcers may appear in the gastrointestinal tract, and the spleen and liver may become enlarged. Other aspects of the disease may include weight loss, leukopenia, anemia, and adrenal necrosis. Histoplasmosis may be fatal. Treatment with antifungal medications is usually effective. Histoplasmosis is not an allergic disorder, but it may easily be mistaken for symptoms of allergy or asthma.

history of asthma   See "History of Allergy and Immunology" p. xiv.

history taking in the diagnosis of allergy The questionnaires and discussions between the physician and patient that help determine diagnoses, treatments, care planning, and other related aspects of health care. Health care professionals need to know an individual's statistics (age, sex, ethnicity, and other personal traits), past and existing medical problems, allergies (especially to drugs), and the medical problems in the patient's family. The patient's history evolves with each encounter with the physician, who keeps a chart, or running documented account, of the patient's condition, treatments administered, and hospitalizations. When a person suffers from allergies or asthma, precise documentation of the person's condition is as important for an optimal result as precise administration of immunotherapy and medications. In addition, good history taking helps professionals caring for a patient to understand his or her emotional state as it relates to the diagnosis.

hives The common name for urticaria. (See URTICARIA.)

hoarseness A raspy or rough-sounding voice caused by an inflammation of the throat and vocal cords. Among the causes are allergy to certain foods, chemical irritants, tobacco, and alcohol. Persistent hoarseness may be a sign of benign or malignant polyps in the throat.

holistic medicine A newly recognized discipline of Western medicine that incorporates some theories of Eastern medicine and the recognition of the patient as both a physiological and psychological being. Holistic practitioners believe that psychological factors affect well-being and disease processes. They employ various techniques, including relaxation, guided imagery and visualization, and hypnosis, along with conventional methods of treatment appropriate to the ailment, and they advocate the patient's participation in his or her own healing. (See also HIPPOCRATES.)

homeopathy An alternative treatment system based on the theory that "like cures like," that is, if a substance causes a symptom, it can conversely cure it when taken in a highly diluted form or in minute quantity. Remedies are made from plant, animal, and mineral sources and are available at health food stores. Homeopathy relates to desensitization techniques used to treat allergic patients. Depending upon the patient's complaints, homeopathic remedies are reported to have had positive effects against allergies, sore throats, arthritis, indigestion, colds and flu, chronic pain, and infections.

homeostasis The body's innate ability to balance its metabolic substances, including blood, lymph, and tissue fluid, and to regulate its functions.

home remedies Actions that individuals can take on their own to help combat allergies and asthma and augment treatments prescribed by the physician. According to some experts, one can seal bedding in plastic liners to keep mattresses free of dust and dust mites, get rid of carpeting, use fungicides in damp areas of the house, avoid fireplace fires, install air-conditioning, maintain a sensible diet and avoid foods that may be allergenic, and other such measures. However, home remedies may not substitute for professional care.

honeybee sting allergy The reaction to honeybee stings, which usually occur only when these insects are disturbed by accidently brushing against a flower in which the bee is at work or by interrupting its direct flight from the flower to its hive. Bees are attracted by bright and fragrant flowers, smooth water surfaces, perfumes, aftershave lotions, and colognes. Some house paints have a fragrance that excites bees to act aggressively.

Unlike other stinging insects, honeybees leave their stinger behind and die, thereby helping to identify the source of a sting. (See HYMENOPTERA STING ALLERGY.)

hormone A natural substance produced in an organ or gland that, when conveyed by the bloodstream, stimulates either increased or decreased functioning in various parts of the body. Among the most commonly known hormones are thyroid hormone, parathormone, cortisone, estrogen, progesterone, testosterone, human growth hormone, insulin and glucagon, adrenocortical hormone, ACTH (adrenocorticotropic hormone), and gastric hormone. Cortisonelike synthetic hormones, known as corticosteroids, are often used in the treatment of asthma because they act against inflammation.

hornet sting allergy The adverse reaction to the sting of an insect of the Vespidae family, or wasps. Hornets' nests are made of paper and may be close to the ground or high above it.

Reactions range from hives to anaphylaxis. (See HYMENOPTERA STING ALLERGY.)

horse and horse serum allergy   See ANAPHYLAXIS, SERUM SICKNESS.

hot dog headaches   See FOOD ALLERGY, HEADACHE.

house dust allergy
Reactions attributed to dust exposure in the home. Vacuum-cleaner-collected dust may include animal and human hair and dander, dead insect parts and their fecal waste, bacteria, cotton, wool, synthetic fibers, mold spores, cellulose, detergents and house cleaning chemicals, pesticides, and food particles. Traditionally the various house dust extracts prepared by several companies for testing and immunotherapy differed even from batch to batch by the same manufacturer. The Food and Drug Administration has recommended withdrawal of these unstandardized products. However, they are still available. It is suspected that most individuals testing positive to house dust extracts are really sensitive to house dust mites or animal dander, and many allergists have abandoned the use of house dust mixtures. (See also HOUSE DUST MITES, IMMUNOTHERAPY.)

house dust mites
Microscopic members of the class Arachnida, subclass Acari. Species known to be important as allergens are *Dermatophagoides pteronyssinus* (skin-eating, feather-loving), *D. farinae*, *D. microceras*, *Euroglyphus maynei*, and *Blomia tropicalis*.

Many asthma experts consider dust mites to be the single most important allergen associated with asthma. Two principal groups of allergens of considerable importance are digestive enzymes, one group of them found in high concentrations in the fecal pellets, and a second group found in both fecal pellets and mite bodies.

Two micrograms of Der p I (mite allergen) per gram of dust is considered a risk factor for sensitization and the development of asthma in susceptible individuals. A concentration of 10 micrograms of allergen per gram of dust is a risk factor for triggering acute asthma in these persons.

Prevalence House dust mite exposure is especially great in the Gulf coast region and Pacific Northwest of the United States, the United Kingdom, northern Europe, Australia, New Zealand, Brazil, and Japan. Dust mites require high humidity, moderate temperatures, and a food source that includes human skin scales.

In the United Kingdom, an estimated 80% of asthmatic children are sensitive to house dust mites. When placed in a dust-mite–low environment, such as a hospital ward or a high-elevation, mountainous region, sensitive individuals invariably improve. Unfortunately, it takes several months for the condition to improve; as soon as allergic individuals were placed in their former environment, the asthma returned.

Prevention Dr. Thomas A. E. Platts-Mills and colleagues at the University of Virginia in Charlottesville have proposed that asthma might be prevented or delayed in some infants by avoidance of dust mites and other environmental allergens.

Dust mite control Removal of the dust mite from the environment by either killing them with the acaricides benzyl benzoate or tannic acid (see ACARACIDES) or changing the environment is an effective measure.

The relative humidity in bedrooms should be kept below 60%. Uncarpeted floors are best, but treatment of carpets with acaracides is recommended. Vacuum cleaners with double bags may be beneficial, but most often vacuuming increases airborne levels of mites. HEPA filters on vacuum cleaners are of little or no value. Covering mattresses, box springs, and pillows and hot washing of bedding can reduce mite allergen levels significantly.

Dust mites were discovered in 1964. House dust mites are microscopic (approximately one-third of a millimeter in length), sightless, eight-legged arthropods that are natural inhabitants of our indoor environment. These mites are not an indicator of uncleanliness and do not transmit human diseases. However, they are a major cause of asthma, allergic rhinitis (hay fever), and atopic dermatitis (eczema).

The most important house dust mite allergens result from proteins in the mite's digestive tract excreted in the fecal waste rather than the mite itself. The tiny fecal particles break down to an extremely fine powder that sticks to surrounding absorbent materials. The allergen-containing powder becomes airborne when carpets are walked upon, upholstery is disturbed by sitting or rising, shaking out blankets and quilts, or airing out rooms.

The growth and reproduction of house dust mites is dependent on a food supply, relative humidity, and temperature. They feed on human and animal dander (flakes, scales, or dandruff) and other materials such as fiber and feathers. The average human sheds up to 1.5 grams of skin particles per day. The mites thrive at temperatures between 68° and 84°F and a relative humidity of 65 to 80%.

Distribution Moist areas such as the South, the Gulf coast region, and the Pacific Northwest present excellent breeding grounds for these microscopic organisms. House dust mites mature and breed from May to October and may be responsible for triggering as many as 44% of acute asthma attacks in these areas. Since the dust mites do not thrive where relative humidity is above 90% or below 33%, they are rarely found at dry climates over 3,600 feet above sea level.

In England and many other parts of the world, up to 85% of asthmatics are sensitive to dust mites.

There are 47 recognized species in 17 genera of the family Pyroglyphidae. Species common in temperate and tropical regions are *Dermatophagoides, Euroglyphus, Hirstia, Malayoglyphus, Pyroglyphus,* and *Sturnophagoides. Dermatophagoides* or *Euroglyphus* species can be found in most homes in North America, western Europe, Japan, New Zealand, and Australia.

House dust mite control The highest number of dust mites are found in bedding, upholstered

furniture, and carpeting. They also inhabit pillows, quilts, children's stuffed animals, and areas where pets sleep. They are rarely found in hospitals.

It has been established that a level of 100 dust mites per gram of dust is a risk factor for sensitization and the development of asthma in susceptible persons. A level of 500 mites per gram of dust is considered a major risk factor for the development of acute asthma in a sensitized individual.

Bedrooms are usually the chief target of avoidance measures for dust mites because of the allergic individual's continuous exposure. Asthma has been demonstrated to improve in mite-free environments. The following measures have been found to reduce dust mite exposure by tenfold or more: (1) covering mattresses, (2) hot washing of all bedding at least every 10 days, (3) removal of carpets and upholstered furniture, (4) reduction of humidity, (5) use of acaracides (see ACARACIDES).

Test kits are available to measure the quantity of dust mites in a particular room. After treatment to reduce the mite population, tests can be repeated to determine the success or failure of the measures taken.

Immunotherapy When avoidance measures are unsuccessful or impossible to achieve, standardized allergen extracts for *Dermatophagoides* subspecies *farinae* and *pteronyssinus* are available in the United States for immunotherapy.

housefly bites Bites by common houseflies often thought to cause allergic reaction, but any adverse effects are considered nonallergic reactions.

Huang-Ti Legendary ruler of China in the 25th century B.C., according to Chinese historians, known as the "Yellow Emperor" because he reigned under the influence of the earth, whose elemental color was believed to be yellow. Huang-Ti is considered the author of the oldest recorded canon of internal medicine called the *Nei ching su wen.* In this work, Huang-Ti conducts a discussion between himself and his physician-minister Ch'i Po on the physical and mental aspects of health and disease. The *Nei ching* is valued today by many for its observations on "noisy breathing," serving as the original description of asthma.

"huffing"   Slang term used by youths to describe the inhalation of airplane glue, aerosol gas, solvents, gasoline fumes, and other noxious substances in order to achieve euphoria, or a "high." Because the exact contents of these substances may be unknown by the user, they have the potential of causing a life-threatening allergic reaction or of masking symptoms of asthma.

humectant   A substance used as a moisturizer, especially helpful to individuals with eczema.

humidifiers   Devices that increase the humidity in a building or room by blowing moisture into the air, including ultrasonics, cool-mist impeller types, evaporative units, and steam vaporizers. Humidifiers may be part of a centralized or portable heating/air-conditioning unit. These units have the potential to cause harm because they may promote the growth of molds and distribute them as an aerosol into the local environment. Even if the units are kept mold free, increasing the relative humidity of a room may stimulate growth of molds and dust mites. Steam vaporizers are considered by some experts to have the lowest potential of contamination of the humidifying units in light of the fact that the steam kills many offending microorganisms. (However, the danger of burns exists if this type of unit is knocked over or the steam comes into direct contact with skin.)

The Environmental Protection Agency discovered that ultrasonic units, which claim to kill microorganisms by ultra-high-frequency sound waves, can nonetheless send out particles of dead bacteria and molds into the room air. Evaporative units on central heating systems, some with tanks in which water stays warm, have also been criticized as potential breeding harbors for bacteria.

Commercial units may be sources of microorganisms, such as actinomycetes and fungi, that may cause the allergic lung disease hypersensitivity pneumonitis. Severe sinusitis has also been linked to contaminated humidifiers. One report describes "humidifier fever," a syndrome characterized by flulike symptoms including fever, chills, cough, headache, and malaise. It was first recognized when large numbers of office and factory employees became ill and the origin of their illness was central humidifying systems contaminated by microorganisms. After the systems were cleaned, affected individuals recovered. According to research scientists at the University of Michigan, all humidifiers are contaminated, leading to warnings of possible health hazards issued by the federal Consumer Products Safety Commission (CPSC). Some research indicates that humidifying dry air is of little or no health benefit because oral and nasal passages are designed to stay moist under all environmental conditions. (See ACTINOMYCETES, AIR-CONDITIONING, HOUSE DUST ALLERGY, FUNGI AND MOLDS.)

humidity   The amount of moisture, or water vapor, in the air, ranging from 100% humidity (air completely saturated with moisture) to small percentages. An extremely humid atmosphere may seem oppressive to some individuals; those with allergies or asthma may experience discomfort in cold, dry air, often an asthma trigger. In addition, dust mites and molds thrive in humidity greater than 60%. The ideal humidity for persons with allergies is 25 to 40%; higher relative humidity may be irritating to the respiratory system. Humidification of the air from swimming pool water is excellent for moisturizing bronchial tubes, and the slow, deep breathing during swimming can be beneficial to asthmatics.

humoral immunity   The component of the immune system regulated by immunoglobulins, or antibodies. (See ANTIBODY, IMMUNE SYSTEM.)

hunger, air   Shortness of breath, breathlessness, dyspnea. (See BREATHING.)

hydroconion   An atomizer that emits a fine spray. (See AEROSOLS.)

hydrocortisone   See CORTICOSTEROIDS.

hydrolysate formulas   Milk proteins processed to render them nonallergenic. They are also lactose and sucrose free; any other ingredients, such as fats and vitamins, are of low potential for allergy.

Infants allergic to milk protein or who have multiple food allergies may suffer from colic or persistent diarrhea. The hydrolysate formulas, used for infants who cannot tolerate less expensive milk or soy formulas, are easy to digest and help maintain adequate nutrition until the infant's gastrointestinal tract has recovered.

Casein hydrolysate formulas are usually used until the infant is four to six months, at which time gradual introduction of solid foods begins. If necessary, it can remain the major source of nutrition for much longer or as a milk substitute in conjunction with other nutrition. However, measures must be taken to ensure adequate protein, calcium, and vitamins during prolonged use of these formulas. Despite the term non- or hypoallergenic, a small number of children with milk sensitivity will react to even these products.

Examples of casein hydrolysate formulas are Nutramigen, which contains corn oil as its fat and sucrose as its carbohydrate; Pregestimil, with medium-chain and long-chain triglycerides and dextrose; Alimentum, with medium-chain triglycerides, safflower and soy oils, and sucrose and tapioca starch; and Flexical, with soy oil, medium-chain triglycerides, and glucose.

hydropneumothorax   A collapse of a lung or lungs in which gas and fluids have accumulated in the space surrounding the lungs (pleural cavity). (See PNEUMOTHORAX.)

hydropneumotosis   Liquid and gases found in body tissues that cause edema and emphysema.

hydrorrhea   Excessive watery discharge from the nose, eyes, or other body parts. This symptom may be suggestive of allergic rhinitis (hay fever). (See RHINORRHEA.)

hydroxyzine (Atarax, Vistaril)   An antihistaminic drug prescribed for pruritus (itching) as a result of allergic reactions such as urticaria (hives), atopic dermatitis (eczema), and contact dermatitis. Hydroxyzine's chief side effect is drowsiness; because of this property, it is also used as a nonaddicting sedative to treat anxiety.

Hymenoptera sting allergy   Allergic reactions to stings from an order of insects including bees, wasps, ants, sawflies, ichneumon flies, and others that maintain complex social colonies and are characterized by four membranous wings and a pedicel under the abdomen. Hymenopterons' stings resemble a hypodermic injection, and the venom deposited in the victim's skin may result in reactions that range from an irritant, nonallergic, local pain and swelling at the sting site to potentially life-threatening anaphylaxis (allergic collapse) in susceptible allergic persons. An estimated 5% of individuals have experienced a significant insect sting reaction. The American Academy of Allergy and Immunology reports that at least 40 deaths occur each year from insect stings.

Venom-producing Hymenoptera also include species of honeybees, yellow jackets, and hornets. The venom of imported fire ants cause a toxic, rather than allergic, reaction.

Severe local sting reactions must be differentiated from more serious systemic reactions. Children often have less severe reactions, but those who have had systemic allergic reactions involving respiratory distress or hypotension (drop in blood pressure) and adults with any degree of systemic reaction should be considered candidates for venom immunotherapy (allergy shots). Dr. Martin D. Valentine and his colleagues at the Johns Hopkins Asthma and Allergy Center have data that support withholding immunotherapy in children who have had only skin reactions such as hives; however, they lack sufficient data for adults with these type of reactions and therefore do treat adults with these injections.

Despite the myth that successive allergic sting reactions inevitably become more severe, this finding has not been confirmed. Evidence indicates similar reactions on restinging. There is an estimated 60% chance for a systemic reaction in an allergic adult who is restung. Children with a history of only a skin reaction have an estimated 10 to 20% risk of a systemic reaction.

Skin testing using venom extracted from the insects is the most accurate method of determining sting allergy. The five venoms commercially available are honeybee, yellow jacket, yellow hornet, white-faced hornet, and *Polistes*, or paper wasps. Positive RAST blood tests are significant but are less sensitive than skin tests; therefore a negative test result may be unreliable. Positive test results indicate prior sensitization to venom allergen, but future reactions cannot be predicted based on test results alone.

Treatment Ana-kit, Epi-Pen, and EpiPen Jr. epinephrine kits are available by prescription for insect-sting-allergic persons. An epinephrine (Adrenalin) injection given or self-administered immediately following a venomous sting is the best treatment for a severe reaction and may be lifesaving. If anaphylaxis occurs with a sudden decrease in blood pressure, intravenous fluids are essential. The stung individual with anaphylaxis must be transported immediately to the nearest emergency room for observation or further treatment. Persons known to be sensitive to insect stings should carry a wallet card or wear a medical alert bracelet advising of this allergy.

Less severe reactions, such as local swelling and itching or mild hives, may respond to an antihistamine. More severe local reactions may require treatment with the corticosteroid prednisone for a few days.

Prevention of stings Insects sting in defense of themselves or their nest, whereas biting insects seek humans for nourishment. When a stinging insect approaches, DO NOT MOVE. DO NOT BRUSH OFF OR SLAP AT IT: It will not sting unless frightened. Carefully shake out clothing left on the ground before putting it on. Avoid wearing dark clothing, perfumes, aftershave lotion, and hair sprays in orchards, flower gardens, or clover fields in bloom. Avoid gardening, lawn mowing, and hedging. Trap insects in a car with a thick "bee cloth," or keep an insecticide spray handy. Avoid throwing things at or poking at insect nests.

Use professional exterminators, firefighters, or beekeepers to remove nests. Yellow jacket nests should be destroyed at night, when the insects are in them, by dousing them with gasoline, kerosene, or lye at least twice. Do not ignite the liquids; the fumes alone will kill the insects. Have a professional perform this task or wear protective beekeepers' clothing. Spray wasp nests with insecticide and then knock them down with a broom handle.

Prevention of anaphylaxis from stings Immunotherapy (allergy shots) with venom extracts is safe and effective in protecting allergic persons. Studies demonstrate that reactions are rare in persons having completed a course of immunotherapy lasting at least five years. (See also HONEYBEE STING ALLERGY, HORNET STING ALLERGY, WASP, YELLOW JACKETS.)

hyocine See SCOPOLAMINE.

hyoscyamine A drug with the ability to decrease mucus production and an ingredient used in some allergy medications.

hyperactive child syndrome See ATTENTION DEFICIT DISORDER WITH HYPERACTIVITY, HYPERACTIVITY.

hyperactivity A pattern of behavior in some children described as continual fidgeting, irritability, recklessness, impulsiveness, and aggressiveness that frequently leads to poor concentration and learning and antisocial acts.

Possibly affecting about 4 to 10% of children (more boys than girls) in the United States, hyperactivity has also been referred to as attention deficit disorder, hyperkinetic syndrome, minimal brain damage or dysfunction, and minimal or minor cerebral dysfunction. Children older than four who are overactive and whose behavior can be differentiated from normal behavior are considered hyperactive.

The cause of hyperactivity has not been established, though some experts have suggested that it stems from slight brain damage, that it may be inheritable, especially from hyperactive fathers, or that children with cerebral palsy, mental retardation, or temporal lobe epilepsy may be likely candidates. The treatment of choice is stimulant drugs such as amphetamine and methylphenidate, which create a paradoxical effect by stimulating the underaroused midbrain, thereby quieting the excessive activity. Professional psychological and educational counseling and remedial basic skills are also helpful. Special diets that eliminate certain food colorings and other additives or sweeteners are often prescribed, but they may not be effective.

Because of differing opinions among physicians, parents, teachers, and professional and lay groups about the validity of the Feingold diet for hyperactive children, the National Institutes of Health held a Consensus Development Conference on Defined Diets and Childhood Hyperactivity on January 13 through January 15, 1982.

The Consensus Development Panel (see CONSENSUS DEVELOPMENT CONFERENCES) was asked to answer the following questions:

1. What constitutes the hyperactivity syndrome in children? Is it a single disease or a cluster of diseases? Can it be graded or scaled in quantifiable variables such as attention span, learning ability, and social adjustment and by whom (teachers, parents, medical personnel)?
2. What are the defined diets?
3. Is there empirical evidence for an effect of these diets on hyperactivity?
4. Is there any biologic explanation to support an effect of defined diets on hyperactivity?
5. If defined diets are effective, how and under what circumstances should they be employed?
6. What are the directions for research?

The panel's conclusions were that a minimal number of young children may be helped by the Feingold diet, certainly not nearly the 50% of such children reported by Feingold. Even in those children whose hyperkinetic activity was felt to be possibly related to diet, the findings were inconsistent in well-controlled studies.

The panel of experts also recognized that further studies were needed before all the questions could be answered. (See ATTENTION DEFICIT DISORDER WITH HYPERACTIVITY, FEINGOLD DIET, FOOD ALLERGY.)

hypercapnia Increased level of carbon dioxide in the blood.

hyper-IgE syndrome A series of symptoms that may represent a number of conditions, including Job's syndrome. A combination of rashes that may become infected with staphylococcal bacteria and candidiasis and extremely high levels of immunoglobulin E (IgE) characterize the syndrome, perhaps an immune system defect.

hyperpnea Abnormally rapid breathing. (See BREATHING.)

hyperreactivity An alternate term for hypersensitivity, hyperresponsiveness, or allergy. (See HYPERSENSITIVITY.)

hypersensitivity An exaggerated response of the immune system upon exposure to a foreign substance; it is usually called "allergy." This reaction may range in intensity from barely noticeable to life-threatening. Hypersensitivity reactions have been classified by Gell and Coombs according to the mechanism of action and time of onset following exposure to the inciting allergen, types I through IV.

Three factors appear to be necessary for an allergic response to occur: (1) an individual must be susceptible; (2) the offending substance must be capable of evoking an allergenic response; and (3) there must be exposure to that specific allergen.

Hypersensitivity Type I: IgE-mediated, anaphylactic, or immediate hypersensitivity Pollens, animal proteins in dander, saliva, urine, feathers, house dust mites, molds, drugs, foods, and venoms from insects or reptiles are examples of allergens that can cause immediate, or type I, reactions. After a first exposure, these apparently harmless allergens stimulate the immune system to form immunoglobulin E, or IgE, antibodies.

IgE antibodies are specific to each allergen and attach to the surface of mast cells in the tissues. Upon reexposure, the recognized allergen combines with its antibodies, rupturing mast cells and releasing biochemical mediators that cause the symptoms of allergy. Reactions range from mild sneezing in a hay fever sufferer to allergic asthma or life-threatening anaphylaxis from a bee sting or penicillin injection. Anaphylaxis, a medical emergency, is a state of collapse that may proceed to death. However, most often anaphylaxis is reversible with prompt treatment and may improve spontaneously.

Type I allergic reactions usually occur within minutes of exposure, as exemplified by injected drug reactions. However, type I oral drug reactions may occur up to six hours later. (See DRUG ALLERGY AND OTHER ADVERSE DRUG REACTIONS.)

Hypersensitivity Type II: cytotoxic or antitissue-antibody reaction This is an immediate reaction involving an interaction between an IgE antibody and an antigen on a cell membrane and also involves the complement system of specialized proteins. Type II reactions, also called autoimmune disorders, occur when antibodies attack the body's own tissues. Systemic lupus erythematosus (SLE) is an example of type II allergy and may occur as a disease or as an adverse drug reaction.

Serious blood disorders, such as Coomb's positive hemolytic anemia, may be caused by type II allergic drug reactions to penicillin, quinine, quinadine, and others. Thrombocytopenia, a decrease in the platelet count that may cause serious internal bleeding, is another example of drug allergy. (See ANAPHYLAXIS.)

Hypersensitivity Type III: immune complex–antigen-antibody complement reactions This type of reaction occurs several hours to days after antigen exposure. Large molecules of antigen-antibody complexes interact with the complement system and are deposited in the walls of blood vessels.

Serum sickness is a result of this process and is caused by some drug reactions, such as a delayed response to penicillin or cephalosporin antibiotics or injections of a serum derived from an animal source such as horses. Allergic pneumonialike lung disorders are another example of type III reactions.

Hypersensitivity Type IV: cell-mediated or delayed allergic reactions This type usually peaks two or three days after exposure. T cells react with an antigen and induce cell production and the release of chemical mediators, which start a cascade of other cell involvement. Poison ivy and other types of contact dermatitis, as well as certain phases of transplantation ejection reactions, are included in this category of allergic reactions. (See also ALLERGY.)

hypersensitivity angiitis   See VASCULITIS.

hypersensitivity pneumonitis   (HSP) [extrinsic allergic alveolitis] An allergic lung disease caused by repeated exposure to organic dusts or other offending agents. In an acute case, flulike symptoms may include cough, shortness of breath, fever, chills, sweating, headaches or generalized pains, malaise, and nausea with onset from two to nine hours after exposure. Symptoms peak between six and 24

CAUSES OF HYPERSENSITIVITY PNEUMONITIS

Disorder	Source
Aspergillosis	*Aspergillus* spores
Bagassosis	Moldy sugarcane
Bible-printer's lung	Moldy typesetting water
Bird-breeder's lung	Avian droppings or serum
Budgerigar-fancier's lung	Parakeets
Chicken-handler's lung	Chickens
Pigeon-breeder's lung	Pigeons
Turkey-handler's lung	Turkeys
Cephalosporium hypersensitivity	Contaminated sewage
Cheese-washer's lung	Cheese mold
Coffee-worker's lung	Coffee dust
Corn-farmer's lung	Corn dust
Detergent lung	Detergents (*Bacillis subtilis* enzyme)
Drug-induced	Amidarone, gold, procarbazine
Duck fever	Duck feathers and proteins
Epoxy resin lung	Heated epoxy resin
Familial hypersensitivity pneumonitis	Contaminated wood dust in walls
Farmer's lung	Moldy hay or grain
Furrier's lung	Hair dust
Humidifier–air-conditioner lung	Thermophilic actinomycetes, amoebae
Laboratory-technician's lung	Rat urinary proteins
Malt-worker's lung	Moldy malt, malt dust
Maple bark-stripper's lung	Moldy maple bark
Miller's lung	Grain contaminated by wheat weevils

Disorder	Source
Mummy-handler's lung	Cloth wrappings of mummies
Mushroom-worker's lung	Mushroom compost
Paint refinisher's disease	Automobile spray painting (diisocyanate)
Paper-mill worker's lung	Moldy wood pulp
Paprika-slicer's lung	Moldy paprika
Pituitary snuff syndrome (snuff-taker's lung)	Bovine and porcine proteins
Plastic worker's lung	Plastics, varnish (diisocyanates)
Rat lung	See Laboratory-technician's lung
Sauna-taker's disease	*Pullularia* in sauna water
Sequoiosis	Moldy wood from maple logs and moldy redwood dust
Small pox-handler's lung	Smallpox scabs
Streptomyces hypersensitivity pneumonia	Contaminated fertilizer
Suberosis	Moldy cork dust
Summer type	House dust contaminated with *Trichosporon cutaneum*
Tea-grower's lung	Tea plants
Thatched-roof disease	Dried grasses and leaves
Wheat weevil's disease	Infested wheat flour
Wood-joiner's lung	Sawdust
Wood pulp-worker's lung	Moldy logs
Wood-trimmer's disease	Moldy wood trimmings

hours and last from several hours to several days.

A subacute form that may gradually worsen over a period of days to several weeks may be much more severe, with shortness of breath progressing to the point of cyanosis and requiring hospitalization.

The chronic form has an even more gradual onset with increasing cough, shortness of breath, fatigue, and weight loss over several months.

Diagnosis is based on a history of exposure to a recognized allergen and confirmed by positive skin tests, finding antibodies in the blood to that allergen, and biopsy. Chest X-ray findings range from normal to severely abnormal.

The diagnosis may be confused with other types of pneumonia, immune deficiency diseases, pulmonary mycotoxicosis (atypical farmer's lung), toxic organic dust syndrome (grain fever), idiopathic interstitial fibrosis (cryptogenic fibrosing alveolitis), cystic fibrosis, silo-filler's lung, psittacosis, eosinophilic pneumonias, allergic bronchopulmonary aspergillosis, collagen vascular diseases, granuloma-vasculitis syndromes, or sarcoidosis.

hypersusceptibility   Increased ability to develop allergy or infection when exposed to allergens or infectious microorganisms. (See also HYPERSENSITIVITY.)

hyperventilation   Rapid breathing resulting in diminished carbon dioxide levels in the bloodstream. Tingling or numbness in the extremities, muscle spasms, and a feeling of anxiety may simulate, or in some cases trigger, an asthma attack.

hypnosis   See HYPNOTHERAPY.

hypnotherapy [hypnosis]   A technique used by psychiatrists and other psychotherapists to guide the patient into a state of altered awareness, deep relaxation, or trance in order to help treat anxiety, panic attacks (which sometimes simulate asthma attacks or coexist with or are confused with asthma attacks), addictions (including to nicotine), and numerous other psychological problems.

hypoallergenic diets   See DIET, ELEMENTAL.

hypocapnia   Abnormally low level of carbon dioxide in the blood.

hypochondriac   One who constantly fears, worries about, or blows out of proportion the possibility of contracting diseases to the point of seeing a physician for even the most minor, or in some cases imaginary, ailments. (See also HYPOCHONDRIASIS.)

hypochondriasis   The morbid fear of, or abnormal concern about, contracting diseases, accompanied by the projection of symptoms and often the delusion of having a serious illness. Allergic disorders, especially food allergies, are often imagined.

hypoepinephria   A decrease in epinephrine secretion in the body.

hypoergy   A lower-than-normal sensitivity to allergens.

hypomyxia   A decrease in mucus secretion.

hyposensitization   See IMMUNOTHERAPY.

hypotension   A state of abnormally low blood pressure. A sudden drop in blood pressure may occur during anaphylaxis, the most severe form of allergic reaction, which may be life-threatening.

hypothyroidism   A disorder of the endocrine system in which there is a deficiency of thyroid hormone. This hormone controls many vital functions, including metabolism. Nasal congestion may be a troublesome symptom often confused with or coexisting with and aggravating allergic rhinitis (hay fever).

hypoventilation syndrome   Abnormally diminished respiration with reduced depth of inspiration and rate. It is characterized by cyanosis (skin or nail beds that appear blue), clubbing of the fingers, decreased oxygen content with a subsequent increase in red blood cells and blood hemoglobin (in the body's attempt to improve the oxygen supply to the tissues), and an increase in carbon dioxide (level builds up because of the inability to exhale adequately).

Hypoventilation occurs with the severe chronic obstructive lung diseases such as chronic bronchitis and emphysema and from massive obesity (also called "Pickwickian syndrome"). Severe obstruction of the upper respiratory tract, which may occur in cases of extremely enlarged tonsils or adenoids, may result in diminished breathing during sleep; it usually improves with adenoidectomy. Less severe blockage may occur in cow's milk allergy (also called Heiner's syndrome), and this usually improves with elimination of cow's milk protein from the diet. (See CHRONIC OB-STRUCTIVE PULMONARY DISEASE, HEINER'S SYNDROME, MILK, PICKWICKIAN SYNDROME.)

hypoxemia   Lack of sufficient oxygen in the blood.

hypoxia   Lack of sufficient oxygen circulating to body tissues.

hysteria   A state of severe anxiety that can involve emotional and physical symptoms, uncontrollable laughter, crying, or fear reactions. Individuals who experience severe shortness of breath may become so stressed as to be hysterical. The term, derived from the Greek word *hystera*, or "womb," was once applied to a women's disorder; contemporary terms for such anxiety include conversion, disassociative, or somatization, disorders and psychoneurosis.

I

ice cube test   A test using ice cubes to diagnose cold-induced urticaria, or hives: When positive, the hives occur two to five minutes after skin contact with cold water or ice followed by rewarming of the area. The hives appear only at the site of contact. (See COLD-INDUCED CHOLINERGIC URTICARIA, URTICARIA.)

ichthyosis vulgaris   A skin condition, caused by an inherited autosomal dominant gene, characterized by dry, scaly skin resembling that of a fish and appearing between the ages of one and four. Both males and females may be affected, but one type of ichthyosis (also called ichthyosis migricans) is found only in males who have inherited the recessive gene from their mother. This condition is also called "porcupine disease."

idiosyncrasy   An individual's unexpected abnormal response to a food, drug, or other usually nonallergenic substance. (See DRUG ALLERGY AND OTHER ADVERSE DRUG REACTIONS.)

"id" reaction   [dermatophytid eruptions] An itchy, vesicular (blisterlike) rash secondary to a fungus occurring elsewhere on the body. The "id" rash usually appears on the hands and is free of the fungal elements present on another part of the body. (See also ATOPIC DERMATITIS.)

ID tags   See MEDICAL ALERT BRACELETS AND NECKLACES.

IgE-mediated reactions   An alternate term for immediate allergic reactions. (See HYPERSENSITIVITY, IMMUNOGLOBULIN E.)

Ilosone   See ERYTHROMYCIN.

immediate hypersensitivity   An alternate term for immediate allergic reactions.
  (See HYPERSENSITIVITY.)

immotile colia syndrome   See KARTAGENER'S SYNDROME.

immune complex   A cluster of interlocking antigens and antibodies found in the bloodstream and usually cleared away by cells known as phagocytes, which "consume" and destroy other cells recognized as invaders. When this process fails, immune complexes may be deposited in, injure, and cause inflammation in tissues, such as kidney, lung, skin, joints, and walls of blood vessels. Diseases in which these complexes are involved include those in the category of type III hypersensitivity (antigen-antibody complement reactions): drug-induced systemic lupus erythematosus, serum sickness, nephritis, bacterial endocarditis, and others. (See COMPLEMENT, IMMUNE COMPLEX ASSAY, IMMUNE COMPLEX DISORDERS.)

immune complex assay   Methods of detection of circulating clusters of antigens and antibodies, or immune complexes, that are used to measure disease activity in patients with vasculitis, systemic lupus erythematosus, some malignancies, and other diseases. Immune complex assay is of doubtful importance in allergy diagnosis. (See IMMUNE COMPLEX DISORDERS.)

immune complex disorders   A group of diseases associated with failure of the complement system and other components of the immune system. Immune complexes are aggregations or clusters of interlocking antigens and antibodies. Usually, these complexes are removed from the circulation by large phagocytic cells (macrophages) in the spleen and Kupffer cells in the liver. Research suggests that deficiencies of certain components of the complement system or complement receptors disrupt this process, allowing circulating immune complexes to accumulate inappropriately in certain organs such as the kidneys, lungs, skin, joints, or blood vessels and interfering with their function. An example is systemic lupus erythematosus ("lupus"). In this autoimmune disease, a continuous supply of autoantibodies overloads the immune system's ability to remove the immune complexes. Immune complexes also play an important destructive role in many other diseases, including infections such as viral hepatitis, malaria, and allergic lung disorders such as farmer's lung.

immune system   A complex network of specialized cells and organs that protect the body against attacks by foreign invaders such as infections. When the immune system is intact, it fights off pathogenic, or disease-causing, bacteria, viruses, fungi, and parasites. When it is weakened or fails, the results can range from a minor allergy such as hay fever to the usually fatal acquired immunodeficiency syndrome, or AIDS.

The immune system protects by barring the entry of, or destroying, dangerous foreign organisms while fostering peaceful coexistence of protective or beneficial organisms. The immune response requires a complex but cooperative interplay between the various cells of the system, including effector lymphocytes (killer T cells, antibody-producing B cells, mast cells), regulating lymphocytes (T-helper and T-suppressor cells), and phagocytes. Many other factors, some not yet understood by scientists, are involved in the control of and response to immune stimuli. The immune system is further influenced by genes that determine the body's ability to respond to an antigen. Mutation, congenital or acquired, of certain genes may impair our response not only to allergens and infectious microorganisms but to cancerous cells as well.

Tissues and organs of the immune system   Immune system components are scattered throughout the body. Bone marrow, thymus, spleen, tonsils, adenoids, lymph nodes, the appendix, and Peyer's patches in the small intestine are known as lymphoid organs, named for their ability to produce, develop, or control white blood cells, or lymphocytes.

There are two major types of lymphocytes: B cells and T cells. Bone marrow is soft tissue in the hollow shafts of long bones. The marrow produces all blood cells, including mature B cells. T cells migrate to the thymus, a gland located behind the breastbone, where they multiply and mature. In a process called "T-cell education," these cells become immunocompetent—that is, they develop the ability to evoke an immune response—and learn to distinguish self from nonself cells. B and T cells circulate throughout the blood vessels and lymphatics, a network similar to blood vessels.

Clusters of lymph nodes, located in the neck, armpits, abdomen, and groin, contain collections of B and T lymphocytes and other cells capable of engaging antigens and causing an immune response.

The spleen is a scavenger of the immune system. An encapsulated, highly vascular, fist-sized organ in the left upper portion of the abdomen, the spleen contains two distinct regions of tissues, the red and white pulp. Red pulp disposes of worn-out blood cells. Red pulp also contains immune cells called macrophages, which trap and destroy microorganisms in blood passing through the spleen during the circulatory process. White pulp contains lymphoid tissue similar to that of the lymph nodes and is similarly subdivided into compartments specializing in different types of immune cells. Patients with a nonfunctioning spleen or who have had the spleen surgically removed are highly susceptible to infections. The tonsils and adenoids in the respiratory tract and the appendix and Peyer's patches in the digestive tract are nonencapsulated clusters of lymphoid tissue in the body's main ports of entry—the mouth, nose, and anus.

Lymph is a clear fluid that travels through the lymphatic vessels, bathing the body tissues. Lymph, along with lymphocytes, macrophages, other cells, and foreign antigens, drains out of tissues and seeps across the thin walls of lymphatic vessels to be transported to lymph nodes, where antigens can be filtered out and attacked by immune cells. Other lymphocytes enter and exit the nodes from the bloodstream. Tiny lymphatics feed into larger and larger channels, like small creeks joining larger streams and rivers. At the base of the neck, large lymphatic vessels merge into the thoracic duct, where its contents are emptied into the bloodstream to begin the cycle again.

Self and nonself The ability of the immune system to distinguish between self and nonself is vital to its function. All body cells have distinctive molecules that allow them to be recognized as "self." When the immune system malfunctions, it may attack its own body. This occurs in diseases such as rheumatoid arthritis and systemic lupus erythematosus, which are referred to as autoimmune disorders.

Antigens, allergens, or immunogens Any substance capable of triggering an immune response is called an antigen, allergen, or immunogen. An antigen can be a bacterium, fungus, parasite, virus, or a part of a substance produced by those organisms. However, not all antigens are capable of causing an antibody response, and some may provoke a cellular, or delayed hypersensitivity, response or even tolerance. Tissues or cells from another individual, except an identical twin, are also antigenic, that is, recognized as foreign.

The structure of antigenic molecules varies from proteins, polysaccharides, lipids, or nucleic acids. The molecular weight of antigens ranges from less than a thousand to several million daltons (a unit of mass = approximately 1.65×10^{-24}) but must reach a threshold size in order to stimulate an immune response. Although the exact size required for allergenicity is unknown, the larger the size of a molecule, the better the chance that it will invoke a reaction. From the human organism to the smallest and simplest microbes, all cells have structures called epitopes on their surfaces that are characteristic and unique to that cell. Epitopes enable the immune system to recognize

foreign cells and are the smallest antigenic structure capable of recognition by an antibody. Most cells carry different kinds of epitopes, which may number up to several hundred, on their surface. However, these epitopes differ in their immune-stimulating capabilities.

Haptens are molecules too small to elicit an immune response in themselves. However, when haptens are coupled to a carrier immungenic molecule, usually a protein or synthetic polypeptide, they can cause a very strong allergic response. Penicillin is one of many drugs that are haptens that bind with serum protein. This complex molecule then stimulates an allergic reaction to the penicillin or other drug. Other examples are the allergic responses to plant substances or metals that cause rashes upon contact with skin. The sensitizing allergens in poison ivy, oak, and sumac are haptens that combine with proteins in the skin. Upon subsequent exposure to these substances, antibodies in the skin react, causing the often debilitating contact dermatitis. Antigens such as pollen grains or cat dander are categorized as allergens because of their ability to provoke an allergic response in susceptible individuals. The first time an allergic individual is exposed to an allergen, the immune system responds by making a corresponding antibody. The antibody molecules are called immunoglobulin E (IgE). IgE molecules attach to the surfaces of mast cells in tissues or basophils in the circulatory system.

Multiple factors determine the potential for an immune response. Among these are foreignness and chemical structure of the antigen. The genetic disposition of the exposed individual and the method of exposure—by injection, orally, skin or mucous membrane contact, or inhalation—affect the strength of immune response.

Cells of the immune system The immune system maintains a huge array of cells, some always present and others manufactured upon demand. Some cell types control general body defenses, while others target specific, highly selective targets. A competent immune system relies on the interactions of many of these cells by direct contact or by the release of chemical messengers by some.

When mast cells or basophils with IgE antibodies on their surface encounter specific allergens, they release biochemical substances called mediators. Mediators include histamine, heparin, prostaglandins, and leukotrienes. These chemicals cause allergic symptoms—wheezing, sneezing, runny nose, watery eyes, and itching. The most serious response of the immune system is anaphylaxis, characterized by edema or swelling of body tissues and a sudden, dangerous decrease in blood pressure that can be life-threatening.

Antibodies Immunoglobulins, commonly called antibodies, are protein molecules produced and secreted by B cells (lymphocytes manufactured in the bone marrow) designed to attack a specific foreign invader called an antigen. The resulting antibody is capable of binding, or attaching, to that specific antigen. For example, a cold virus stimulates a B cell to produce an antibody against that specific virus. When a B cell encounters its triggering antigen, T cells and other accessory cells collaborate with it to cause the production of large plasma cells. Each plasma cell becomes a factory for producing antibodies. Transported through the circulation to the site of inflammation or infection, antibodies neutralize or combine with and identify antigens for attack by other cells or chemical mediators.

All antibodies have a common Y-shaped molecular structure consisting of two light (L) and two heavy (H) polypeptide chains bound together by two disulfide linkages or bridges. The resulting light and heavy chain section is called the fragment antigen binding, or Fab. A third portion of the immunoglobulin, Fc fragment, does not combine with antigen. The Fc portion of the antibody binds to cells, fixes complement (see COMPLEMENT), and allows for placental transfer. The five classes of immunoglobulins (Ig) identified in humans are IgG, IgA, IgM, IgD, and IgE. These immunoglobulins are distinguished by the structure of heavy chains called, respectively, τ, ∝, μ, ς, and Σ. The two types of light chains are kappa (k) or lambda (L). IgG is the predominant human antibody and along with the other immunoglobulins has special roles in maintaining body defenses (see IMMUNOGLOBULIN A, IMMUNOGLOBULIN D, IMMUNOGLOBULIN E, IMMUNOGLOBULIN G, IMMUNOGLOBULIN M).

Genes direct the manufacture of all body protein molecules including antibodies. (Insulin is another example.) Although there is a limited number of genes, the immune system apparently can produce an unlimited number of antibodies. The DNA segment of most genes is fixed; however, antibody genes are constructed from fragments of DNA scattered throughout the genetic material. A B cell sorts through the available material, arranging and rearranging these fragments and piecing them together to form a new gene that with the antibody it encodes is unique. Each B cell proliferates, or clones, identical antibody-producing cells. As the cells continue to multiply, mutants arise that allow for the selection of antibodies that target specific antigens. This process enables antibodies to respond to an enormous range of antigens. T cells, or T lymphocytes, are processed by the thymus gland, act directly by attacking viruses and fungi, and are involved in transplantation rejection reactions. T cells react with specific antigens similar to antibodies. There are three types of T lymphocytes: "killer" T cells, which directly attack antigens; "helper" T cells, which help the killer cells; and "suppressor" T cells, which regulate the killer cells' activity and stop their action when an infection has been controlled.

Phagocytic white blood cells destroy invading foreign microbes by

directly engulfing them. Most phagocytes are macrophages, large mononucleated cells derived from monocytes, which are produced and mature in the bone marrow. After a few days, they leave the general circulation and enter various tissues. Other phagocytic cells include Langerhans cells of the skin, dendritic cells, keratinocytes, and brain astrocytes. These cells affect chemotaxis (cell movement) by engulfing foreign antigens, ridding the body of dead tissues and cells. In the process of phagocytosis, these cells process the antigen and present an immunologically active antigen to the T lymphocytes. The macrophages are not antigen-specific like lymphocytes. Microphages consume bacteria.

Complement is a complex series of blood proteins whose action "complements" the action of antibodies. The complement system comprises about 25 proteins that coat bacteria or immune complexes. This coating facilitates their ingestion and destruction by phagocytes. Complement also destroys bacteria by puncturing their cell membranes.

When the complement system is activated by either the "classic" or an "alternative pathway" (also called the "proteolytic" or "properdin" pathway), an inflammatory response occurs. Immune complexes, consisting of IgG or IgM classes of immunoglobulin antibodies combined with antigen, activate a pathway targeting an invading substance. During this process, the enzyme C1 esterase sets off a cascading-type reaction against the invader. The "proteolytic" alternative, or "properdin" pathway, can be activated without the presence of antibodies.

The complement system not only aids in the body's defense against infection but also helps protect against immune-complex diseases. However, if there is a deficiency of certain components of the system or cell receptors are deficient, the complement can actually induce immune-complex disorders such as serum lupus erythematosus.

Serum complement levels are often measured to help diagnose hereditary angioedema, bacterial endocarditis, acute glomerulonephritis, serum sickness, systemic lupus erythematosus, and other autoimmune diseases.

A deficiency in any component of the immune system may result in an immune deficiency disorder. In some cases there are no clinical manifestations, but in others recurrent minor or life-threatening infections may occur.

(See ANTIGEN, B CELLS, CHEMICAL MEDIATORS, COMPLEMENT DEFICIENCY DISORDERS, IMMUNE COMPLEX DISORDERS, entries on individual immunoglobulins [A, D, E, G, and M], INFLAMMATION, T CELLS.)

WHAT CAN OCCUR WHEN A FOREIGN SUBSTANCE INVADES THE BODY

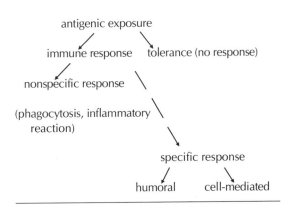

immunity   The quality of being protected from, or resistant to, infection, disease, and any "invasion" imposed on the body. Being immune involves the ability of the immune system—consisting of white blood cells manufactured by the bone marrow, thymus, lymph, and other structures—to prevent or fight an infectious disease. Natural resistance or immunity refers to the human body's rejection of certain cells, such as those causing Texas cattle fever, which cannot live in human tissues. Immunity is described in various ways: natural, passive, humoral, and cell-mediated (cellular). (See IMMUNITY, ACTIVE; IMMUNITY, PASSIVE.)

immunity, active   Protection from disease via the body's production of antibodies in response to a foreign, potentially pathogenic, organism. In the fifth century B.C., Greek physicians observed that persons who had recovered from the plague were immune to subsequent attacks of plague. This acquired natural, or "active," immunity results when T cells and B cells of the immune system are "programmed" at the time of first exposure to an invading microorganism. In response to a foreign antigen, B and T cells manufacture antibodies that remember and attack the invader if it is encountered in the future. Mounting an immune response depends on one's inherited disposition to do so to a particular antigen.

Vaccination (immunizations), as well as invading infections, can stimulate acquired active immunity. Vaccines contain killed or modified microorganisms or parts of them in sufficient amounts to trigger an antibody response without causing the actual disease. (In rare cases, a subclinical infection, a weakened manifestation of a disease, is produced by vaccine.) Some live-virus vaccines have been sufficiently diluted to render them safe for immunization. The medical breakthrough of genetic engineering has allowed the manufacture of safer vaccines.

The duration of immunity depends on the type of antigen, quantity encountered, and its means of entering the body, but active immunity generally lasts from many months to a lifetime. Active immunity requires an inductive (latent) period between immunization and the development of protective antibodies. This process could take from several days to several months and may require "booster" doses of the vaccine. (See entries on individual vaccines; IMMUNITY, PASSIVE; VACCINE.)

immunity, passive The protection from disease afforded by way of antibodies received by an infant from its mother through the placenta or breast milk, or antibodies conveyed by injecting immune serum globulin (gamma globulin) from an individual known to be immune to a certain disease into a susceptible individual. Passive immunity is short-lived, but immediate protection against an infection.

Serum from immune individuals or animals is pooled to achieve a highly concentrated suspension of antibodies against a specific infection such as hepatitis or tetanus. Immediate tetanus protection can be administered to a non-immunized person by injecting human tetanus immunoglobulin. Horse-derived equine tetanus antitoxin is rarely used because of the frequent occurrence of severe adverse reactions. (See ANTIBODY; GAMMA GLOBULIN; IMMUNITY, ACTIVE.)

immunizations, allergic reactions See entries on individual vaccines.

immunodeficiency disease A defect or insufficiency of one or more components of the immune system resulting in an inability to fight off infections. A variety of immunodeficiency disorders can be inherited, acquired through infection or other illness, or caused by an adverse reaction to certain drugs.

Some children are born with abnormal B-cell components and lack the ability to produce immunoglobulins, or antibodies. These defects may be absolute, as in agammaglobulinemias, or partial, as in hypogammaglobulinemias. Injections of immunoglobulins can protect these children against infections. Children who lack T cells as a result of abnormal or missing thymus glands can be treated by thymus transplantation. Rarely, an infant lacks all immune defenses, which is referred to as severe combined immunodeficiency disease (SCID). These are the so-called bubble children who often live for years in germ-free rooms. Bone marrow transplants have cured a few of these children.

Acquired immunodeficiency syndrome, or AIDS, is caused by the human immunodeficiency virus, or HIV. In AIDS, a virus destroys helper T cells, allowing microorganisms that are normally harmless to cause life-threatening infections. These are referred to as "opportunistic infections." (See ACQUIRED IMMUNODEFICIENCY SYNDROME.)

immunofluorescence, direct A test to detect antibodies in tissue specimens used to aid in the diagnosis of glomerulonephritis, systemic lupus erythematosus, Goodpasture's syndrome, pemphigoid, pemphigus, and dermatitis herpetiformis, and herpes simplex infections.

immunofluorescence, indirect   A test to measure the presence and quantity of antibodies in body fluids. It is especially useful in detecting autoantibodies in diseases including diabetes mellitus, thyroiditis, myasthenia gravis, chronic active hepatitis, systemic lupus erythematosus, systemic sclerosis, pernicious anemia, pemphigus, and bullous pemphigoid.

immunogen   Any substance capable of triggering an immune response.   Immunogens may also be called antigens or allergens. An antigen can be a bacterium, fungus, parasite, virus, or a part of a substance produced by those organisms. (See ANTIGEN, IMMUNE SYSTEM.)

immunoglobulin A   (IgA) [secretory antibody] The primary immunoglobulin in body orifices, or entrances.   IgAs are concentrated in body fluids such as the bronchial and intestinal secretions, especially tears and saliva. IgA recognizes invading microorganisms in the mucous membranes as foreign protein. It combines with these invaders in antigen-antibody reactions to prevent viral and bacterial infections such as brucella, diphtheria, and poliomyelitis. IgA deficiency is the most common primary immunodeficiency, occurring in about one in 400 to 800 individuals, and more frequently in those with allergy. Most persons with low IgA levels produce sufficient IgM antibodies to provide an adequate defense against infections. However, IgA deficiencies are commonly associated with chronic lung infections, autoimmune diseases, especially rheumatoid arthritis and systemic lupus erythematosus, gastrointestinal disorders, hepatitis, and some malignant tumors.   There are no known cures, and treatment is directed at the underlying disease or infection. Human immune globulin contains only minimal levels of IgA (see IMMUNOGLOBULIN G) and is of no value in treating IgA deficiency disorders. In addition, IgA may cause anaphylaxis in persons with this deficiency. (See also MILK.)

immunoglobulin D   (IgD)   A class of antibodies found in very small concentrations in human serum. IgD antibodies, first discovered in the 1960s, are found on the surface of lymphocytes. Although the IgD antibody's exact role has yet to be defined, it seems to play a role as a specific surface receptor in the immune response.

immunoglobulin E   (IgE)   Antibodies manufactured by the immune system that play an important role in primary type I hypersensitivity, or immediate allergic, responses. Once called "reaginic antibodies," these antibodies are normally present in very small quantities. Allergic individuals generally have higher total IgE levels in their blood.   However, other diseases can also be associated with very high levels of IgE antibodies.

DISORDERS ASSOCIATED WITH ELEVATED SERUM IgE LEVELS

Acral dermatitis
Allergic diseases (severely elevated levels in allergic
bronchopulmonary aspergillosis)
Bone marrow transplantation (immediately post-transplantation)
Bullous pemphigoid
Celiac disease (gluten-sensitive enteropathy)
Drug-induced interstitial nephritis
IgE myeloma
Infectious mononucleosis
Job-Buckley syndrome
Kawasaki disease
Laennec's cirrhosis
Minimal change nephritis
Parasitic infections
Polyarteritis nodosa
Pulmonary hemosiderosis
Selective IgA deficiency
T-cell deficiency (DiGeorge syndrome, Wiskott-Aldrich
syndrome, Nezelof syndrome)
Wegener's granulomatosus

Skin-sensitizing, anaphylactic antibodies are of this type. IgE antibodies' unique biologic properties are based on their ability to bind with special receptors on mast cells and basophils in body tissues. People differ in their ability to develop an IgE response to common allergens in the environment. The tendency to produce IgE antibodies is genetic.

When IgE antibodies specific to a previously sensitized allergen are reexposed to that allergen, cells degranulate and chemical mediators of anaphylaxis and type I reactions are released.

Serum levels of IgE antibodies can be measured as "total IgE" or to identify specific allergens. This measurement is performed by a method called radioallergosorbent tests, or RAST (see RADIOALLERGOSORBENT TESTS).

Testing for allergen-specific IgE by RAST is useful when skin testing is unreliable because of generalized skin disease or dermatographia (see DERMATOGRAPHIA) or if the patient is unable to discontinue antihistamines. (See IMMUNOGLOBULIN E [IgE] ASSAY.)

immunoglobulin E (IgE) assay [total IgE, PRIST, RIST]   A quantitative test measuring immunoglobulin E antibodies in the blood serum to assess an individual's tendency to have allergies. An elevated level of IgE antibody in blood obtained from the umbilical cord at birth correlates with an increased risk of the development of allergy in later life. Persons with high total IgE levels are usually sensitive to many allergens, but an individual can be sensitive to specific IgE allergens and have a low total IgE level. Furthermore, allergic bronchopulmonary aspergillosis, parasitic infections, and other rare diseases can cause extreme elevations in total IgE. (See the Table on page 148.)

There may be elevations of circulating IgE antibodies in some persons with food allergies, but the Allergy Council on Scientific Affairs of the American Medical Association considers this test investigational and experimental.

PRIST and RIST are methods of measuring total IgE. In 1981, the Immunology Unit, a committee of the World Health Organization, recommended against the measurement of total IgE as a screening test for allergy.

RELATIONSHIP OF IgE LEVELS TO DIAGNOSIS OF ALLERGY

Total IgE U/ml	Predictability of Allergic Tendency
>100	Multiple allergens highly likely
25–100	Intermediate
<25	Low probability of allergy

RADIOALLERGOSORBANT (MST) LEVELS (Traditional method)

RAST Class	Level of Antigen-Specific IgE
4	Very high
3	High
2	Moderate
1	Low
1/0	Very low
0	Below detection

immunoglobulin E (IgE) immune complexes   The percentage (up to 50%) of immunoglobulin E (IgE) circulating in the bloodstream in immune-complex form. The relevance of these complexes to allergy is unknown.

immunoglobulin G (IgG)   The most common antibody in human serum, found throughout the circulatory system and other body tissues. IgG immunoglobulins enjoy a relatively long half-life (the time required for half the amount of a specific substance to be eliminated or to disintegrate in the body) of 23 days and readily cross the placenta.

Antibodies of this class are involved in the immune system's defense against bacterial, viral, parasitic, and some fungal infections. Receptors for IgG are found on the surface of monocytes, on polymorphonuclear leukocytes, or polys, on reticuloendothelial cells in the spleen and liver, and some lymphocytes. IgG antibodies also activate complement. (See COMPLEMENT, IMMUNE SYSTEM.)

immunoglobulin G (IgG) subclasses Minor differences in molecular structure among a specific class of antibodies. Two IgA and IgD and four IgG immunoglobulin subclasses have been discovered. The minor variations, however, may result in significant differences in the function of these subclasses. Repeated infections may occur in individuals who have normal levels of total IgG levels but absent or reduced levels of one or more of the subclasses. Such persons fail to develop antibody responses to naturally occurring infections or to vaccines.

immunoglobulin M (IgM)   The largest antibody molecules of the immune system, found almost exclusively in the circulation. IgM is the major antibody of the early humoral response to foreign invaders, particularly to nonprotein bacterial antigens. Although its large molecular size prohibits transfer through the human placenta, its structure allows for IgM's ability to agglutinate, or clump, particles of bacteria and red blood cells and fix, or attach, to complement.

immunoglobulins   Another term for antibodies. (See ANTIBODY, IMMUNE SYSTEM, IMMUNOGLOBULIN A, IMMUNOGLOBULIN D, IMMUNOGLOBULIN E, IMMUNOGLOBULIN G, IMMUNOGLOBULIN M.)

immunologist   A physician who diagnoses and treats disorders of the immune system, such as acquired immunodeficiency syndrome, or AIDS. Many immunologists are also allergists, but some are nonphysician scientists who do not care for patients. Upon completion of medical school, a two- or three-year residency in pediatrics or internal medicine, and a two-year fellowship in allergy and immunology, these doctors are then eligible for a board-

certification examination in their specialty. (See also ALLERGIST, IMMUNOLOGY.)

immunology   The study of immunity and immune responses, which are the bodily processes whose main function is to maintain a constant internal environment and to protect the body from, and/or help the body fight, the invasion of disease-causing microorganisms. The field of immunology evolved from the ancient Chinese practice of variolation as early as the eleventh century, in which intradermal applications of powdered smallpox scabs were used to prevent smallpox. (See also IMMUNOLOGIST.)

immunopathology   The study or science of the body's immune reactions to disease-causing, or pathogenic, microorganisms.

immunopolysaccharide   Antigenic substances obtained from the bodies of specific infectious bacteria that have the ability to stimulate the production of antibodies to protect against that particular infection. Immunizations against pneumococcal pneumonia and hemophillus influenza (cause of meningitis in infants) are examples of polysaccharide vaccines.

immunostimulant   Any foreign agent, including allergens, microbes, or vaccines, that will cause the production of antibodies.

immunosuppressant   Any agent, such as cancer-fighting drugs, that inhibits the immune response.

immunotherapy   [allergy shots]   A series of injections of solutions of allergenic extracts administered to a person suffering from allergies (see ALLERGENIC EXTRACTS). By injecting in gradually increasing doses specific allergens to which that individual has been shown to be sensitive, the individual is expected to develop a tolerance to those allergens and experience few or no symptoms upon environmental exposure.

Mechanism of action Researchers believe a positive response to allergy immunotherapy requires an increase in immunoglobulin G (IgG)–blocking antibody, which is capable of blocking allergic reactions mediated by IgE antibodies. Five changes in the immune response have been recognized in persons receiving immunotherapy: (1) a rise in blood levels of IgG-blocking antibodies; (2) a suppression of the usual seasonal rise in IgE antibodies followed by a slow decline in the level of specific IgE antibodies during continued immunotherapy; (3) an increase in levels blocking IgA and IgG antibodies in body secretions; (4) a diminished ability of basophilic cells to react to allergens; and (5) a tempering of the reactivity of lymphocytic cells in contact with allergens in vitro (tests performed in a test tube or an artificial environment). An individual may be sufficiently protected from allergy without demonstrating all five postulates.

Treatment course Treatment usually begins once or twice weekly until a maintenance dose is achieved. Therapy is usually continued at monthly intervals for three to five years. In most persons, however, symptoms eventually recur, and treatment is sometimes repeated. Immunotherapy usually requires six to 12 months of regular injections; if there is no beneficial response within two years, it is generally recommended that treatment be discontinued.

Allergens included in immunotherapy are based on skin or blood tests and a detailed medical history of the patient to determine a person's sensitivity to a particular allergen or multiple allergens. Many individuals show positive tests to substances that are not the cause of their allergy symptoms. Allergens not directly responsible for triggering an individual's symptoms should not be included in the solution. Allergy immunotherapy is a consideration when avoidance of offending allergens and medications are ineffective. Immunotherapy has been shown to be effective for allergy symptoms associated with grass, tree, and weed pollens, house dust mites, cat dan-

der, and certain molds. Stinging insect venom immunotherapy is also highly effective (see HYMENOPTERA STING ALLERGY).

House dust mixture is prepared from dust collected by beating carpets or vacuuming. Responsiveness is related to the presence of cat and dog dander, house dust mite, cockroach, and other allergens in the preparation. But variation in potency and effectiveness of batches of extract does not permit standardization, and the availability of house dust extract may eventually be withdrawn by the Food and Drug Administration.

immunotherapy, oral The administration of an allergen extract liquid by mouth, a method of immunotherapy now being investigated by researchers at the Johns Hopkins Asthma and Allergy Center. Administering an allergen dose 100 times that of a typical injected dose of ragweed antigen to patients resulted in clinically significant improvement of hay fever symptoms, such as sneezing, nasal congestion, and itchy eyes. Side effects have been minimal; a few patients show a mild worsening of symptoms, abdominal cramps, or a tightness in the throat. These adverse effects cleared up with slight reduction in dosage of the allergen.

Oral immunotherapy has been shown to be effective against allergy through the body's increased ability to promote an IgG-blocking antibody response. It is anticipated that oral immunotherapy may be available to the average patient before the year 2000.

immunotransfusion Transfusion of blood from a donor who has antibodies against a specific infection from having been inoculated with bacteria from the recipient patient, or from the specific infection, or who has recently recovered from that infection.

impetigo Crusty-looking pustules on the skin caused by bacteria found in common dirt. This condition, treatable with antibiotics, is most often seen in children and is highly contagious. (Some people have erroneously called it "infantigo.") Impetigo may be a complication

INDOOR ALLERGY CONTROL MEASURES

Allergen	Measures
Cats and dogs	Remove pets if allergies are severe. Do not groom pets indoors. Wash pets monthly. Remove carpets, or use area rugs that can be cleaned outdoors frequently.
Cockroaches	Obtain services of a professional exterminator to kill them. Orthoboric acid may be useful, but keep children away during its use.
House dust mites	Keep temperature below 70°F with relative humidity below 45%. Use air-conditioning or a dehumidifier when necessary. Avoid humidifiers. Encase mattresses and box springs in hypoallergenic covers. Avoid feather or foam-rubber pillows and encase synthetic pillows with hypoallergenic coverings. Remove upholstered furniture from bedrooms and other living areas. Leather, vinyl, or wood furniture are good substitutes. Remove carpets, or if not possible, treat them with benzyl benzoate powder (Acarasan) or tannic acid 3% spray. Wash bed clothing every seven to 10 days in hot water (130°F). Vacuum weekly, using a mask; remain out of the room for 20 minutes. Use a double vacuum cleaner bag.
Molds	Control moisture with air-conditioning or dehumidifier. Avoid humidifiers and vaporizers. Treat susceptible surfaces for mold growth monthly with mold retardants. Remove or fill water collectors.
Pollens	Keep windows and doors closed and use air-conditioning during pollen seasons.

of allergic skin conditions such as eczema and poison ivy.

incrustation The formation of crusts or scabs on the skin seen in cases of contact dermatitis and allergic and infectious skin conditions.

indoor allergen control measures Adjustments made in the home, workplace, or other enclosed environment to reduce exposure to allergens.

infection Invasion of the body by pathogenic, or disease- producing, microbes and the symptoms that occur from the presence of these bacteria, viruses, parasites, or fungi, or from toxins produced by these organisms. An infection may also be present without detectable symptoms.

infertility See REPRODUCTIVE IMMUNOLOGY.

inflammation Redness, heat, and pain associated with cellular injury upon the exposure to allergens or pathogens and occurring when white blood cells migrate to a traumatized or hypersensitive area of the body. Inflammation is a major contributing factor to chronic asthma. After each exposure to an allergen that results in inflammation in lung tissues, the tissues attempt to repair themselves. This leads to subepithelial fibrosis, thickened noncellular (basement) membranes that may be permanent and occur very early in the course of asthma. Anti-inflammatory therapy is a mainstay of asthma treatment. Cromolyn sodium (Intal), nedocromil sodium (Tilade), and corticosteroids by metered dose are used to prevent inflammatory changes in the lungs. However, systemic corticosteroids, by injection or orally, are often required in moderate to severe cases. The inflammatory changes that occur with allergic skin disorders such as contact dermatitis result in the itching, burning, and rashes characteristic of these conditions. The rashes are frequently treated with topical corticosteroid creams, ointments, lotions, and aerosol sprays. In severe cases, systemic forms of corticosteroids may be necessary. (See ASTHMA, ATOPIC DERMATITIS, CONTACT DERMATITIS.)

influenza ("flu") vaccine   An immunization derived from fluid of fertilized chicken egg culture inoculated with a particular strain or strains of an influenza virus. After the culture has been purified and chemically inactivated, the vaccine is used to prevent the viral respiratory infection that occurs throughout most of the world annually, with severe strains appearing every few years. An individual who has been infected by a specific strain of influenza usually acquires a lifelong immunity to that strain. Strains of influenza include types A and B, swine, Hong Kong, Taiwan, and others named for the place or source of initial appearance of the virus.

Groups at increased risk for serious illness or death from complications of flu are those over 65 years of age and children and adults with chronic heart and lung diseases. Influenza vaccine should not be given, or given cautiously, to persons allergic to eggs. Persons unsure of their status should be skin-tested for egg allergy prior to receiving this vaccine. Hives, angioedema, and asthma following immunization are rarely encountered.

In 1976, a swine flu vaccine caused an increased incidence of the paralyzing neurologic disorder Guillain-Barre syndrome (GBS). GBS and other adverse effects of flu vaccine are now unusual because of improved purification of the vaccine. Other minor symptoms, including fever, muscle tenderness at the site of injection, and generalized aches, are minimal and infrequent.

PERSONS FOR WHOM INFLUENZA VACCINE IS GENERALLY RECOMMENDED

- Persons 65 years of age and older
- Children and adults with chronic heart or lung diseases or other chronic diseases, including asthma, diabetes mellitus, and kidney failure
- Nursing home residents and any patient in chronic-care facilities
- Children and teenagers taking aspirin therapy and who therefore may be at risk for Reye's syndrome if they become ill with the flu
- Persons who are immunosuppressed, such as those with acquired immunodeficiency syndrome (HIV or AIDS) and leukemia
- Health care workers, employees of health care facilities, and household members of any of the above high-risk persons

inhalation challenges   See   CHALLENGE, METHACHOLINE CHALLENGE.

inhalation therapy   The act of breathing in medicines dissolved in water vapors or gases through devices such as nebulizers and aerosolized metered-dose inhalers. Inhalation therapy is a mainstay of treatment for patients with asthma and other lung disorders. (See also AEROSOLS, NEBULIZER.)

inhaled medications   Drugs dissolved in water vapors or gases and administered by metered-dose inhalers or nebulizers for the treatment of asthma and other lung disorders. Inhaled drugs include albuterol (Proventil, Ventolin), metaproteranol (Alupent), pirbuterol (Maxair), terbutaline (Brethaire), and cromolyn sodium (Intal). (See also AEROSOLS, BETA-ADRENERGIC AGONISTS, INHALATION THERAPY.)

inhalant allergies   Symptoms of hay fever and asthma triggered by contact of the respiratory system with allergens, including pollens, house dust mites, fungi, and animal dander, that have been inhaled through the nose or mouth. (See ALLERGIC RHINITIS, TRIGGERS OF ALLERGIES AND ASTHMA.)

inherited allergies See GENETICS OF ALLERGIC DISORDERS.

injection Administration of any drug dissolved in a liquid through a needle under the skin (subcutaneous), into a muscle (intramuscular), or into a vein (intravenous). In allergic patients, examples of subcutaneous injections include immunotherapy (allergy shots) and the administration of epinephrine (Adrenalin). Corticosteroids are given intramuscularly or intravenously. (See also IMMUNOTHERAPY, INOCULATION.)

injections, allergy See CORTICOSTEROIDS, EPINEPHRINE, IMMUNOTHERAPY.

ink poisoning Redness and sometimes tiny pustules or cracked skin caused by contact with ink or substances used to remove ink stains.

This is not a true poisoning but rather an irritation or contact dermatitis. (See CONTACT DERMATITIS.)

inoculation The process of introducing a substance into the body to develop immunity to an allergy or infection by placing a drop of the substance on the skin and scratching or puncturing the surface or by injection under the skin. (See IMMUNOTHERAPY, TUBERCULIN TEST, VACCINE.)

Insecta A class of the phylum Arthropoda. Commonly called insects, some members of Insecta are parasites, some are carriers of disease-causing organisms, and some are pests that can cause allergic reactions from their bites or stings. (See HYMENOPTERA STING ALLERGY, INSECT ALLERGY.)

insect allergy Adverse reaction to exposure to venoms, body parts, and waste materials of insects. Symptoms range from itching and hives to shortness of breath, wheezing, tightness in the chest, constriction in the throat, and a drop in blood pressure that may be life-threatening (anaphylaxis), usually resulting from stinging by a member of the order Hymenoptera. Symptoms of hay fever and asthma may result from the inhalation of insect parts of other types, including cockroaches.

Nonallergic symptoms resulting from stinging insects include local swelling, redness, and pain. Toxic effects, including headaches, nausea, dizziness, fainting, convulsions, or fever, may occur with the injection of large amounts of venom from multiple stings. Biting insects including mosquitoes and flies generally do not cause allergic symptoms. However, at least one biting insect, the kissing bug, or conenose, genus *Triatoma*, injects allergens present in its saliva to the victim. Anaphylaxis rarely occurs as a result of a kissing bug bite. (See BITING INSECTS, COCKROACH ALLERGY, HOUSE DUST MITES, HYMENOPTERA STING ALLERGY.)

insects, biting See BITING INSECTS, INSECT ALLERGY, KISSING BUG.

inspiration See BREATHING.

insufflation The inspiration of a powder or vapor into the lungs or other body cavity. Examples of insufflation drugs for the treatment of asthma include cromolyn sodium (Intal) and albuterol (Ventolin) powders. (See SPINHALER.)

insulin allergy Redness, swelling, and itching at the injection site used by an insulin-dependent diabetic. This local allergic reaction occurs occasionally and usually clears without treatment in a few days or weeks. Less frequently, but of greater importance, a generalized rash (which may be hives), shortness of breath, wheezing, drop in blood pressure, rapid pulse, or sweating may occur. The most severe form of allergic reaction—anaphylaxis, which may be fatal—is extremely rare from insulin.

Insulin is a hormone produced by the pancreas, a gland that lies in the upper abdomen near the liver and stomach. A complex protein, insulin is secreted by beta cells in the gland in response to the presence of glucose and other nutrients. The pancreatic process enables the body to properly store and utilize food for energy. Diabetes mellitus is a disease caused by a deficiency of insulin. Until recently, commercially produced insulin was extracted from the glands of pigs and cattle. Therefore, when pork or beef insulin was injected into human patients, it was at times recognized by the immune system as foreign, thus causing allergy symptoms. Scientists discovered that nondisease-producing *Escherichia coli* bacteria can be programmed to produce insulin identical to that produced by normal humans. This process, called recombinant DNA, is accomplished by genetically altering the bacteria with the addition of the human gene that causes insulin production.

Patients allergic to pork insulin may be able to tolerate beef insulin, or vice versa, or the DNA recombinant form. In the unlikely event that there is allergy to all forms of insulin, skin-testing can be done to detect the least allergenic type of insulin for that individual. The individual can subsequently be desensitized by injecting that type of insulin starting with minute doses, such as .001 of a unit given subcutaneously (under the skin), and doubling the dose every 20 to 30 minutes until therapeutic levels are reached. An alternative method is administered over a few days. Once desensitization has been completed, regular therapeutic doses of insulin can be given. As many as 15% of insulin-allergic patients still experience allergic symptoms during or following desensitization and may require an antihistamine, corticosteroids, or both to suppress reactions. Fortunately, most insulin allergy improves after a few weeks. (See also DIABETES MELLITUS.)

Intal   See CROMOLYN SODIUM.

integumentary system, or skin   The body system and immune organ composed of the external body protective covering, namely skin, and its appendages of hair and nails. There are two main layers of skin, the epidermis (outer layer) and dermis (inner layer). The competent integumentary system protects the body against invaders, such as antigens and parasites, and injury. It also helps regulate body temperature, elimination, and hydration and serves as a source of vitamin D. The skin contains sensory nerves that help one distinguish between hot and cold, pressure and pain, and various textures.

In allergy, disorders of the skin include urticaria and numerous other rashes (atopic dermatitis, contact dermatitis, drug reactions), lesions, erythema, and abnormal textures. (See also IMMUNE SYSTEM.)

interleukins   A major group of proteins, called lymphokines and monokines, that mediate the interactions between immune and inflammatory cells. Seven interleukins (IL 1 through 7) that promote growth, differentiation, and function of cells have been discovered to date. Each of the interleukins has both unique and overlapping biologic activities.

Macrophages produce IL 1 and 6, which are involved in both immune and inflammatory processes and induce fever. T cells produce IL 2 to 6. IL 7–producing cells have been found in the bone marrow, thymus, and spleen and are primarily involved in the growth of B-cell precursors. While IL 7–producing cells have no effect on mature B cells, they do have some effect on T-cell growth. IL 5 promotes the growth of eosinophils (white blood cells prominent in allergic reactions). IL 2 acts as a potent signal for T cells; IL 4, 5, and 6 stimulate the multiplication of B cells and the production of immunoglobulins (antibodies). (See IMMUNE SYSTEM.)

intermittent positive pressure breathing apparatus   (IPPB)   Device that forces air into the lungs during inspiration but allows normal exhalation. This type of breathing assistance, formerly used to treat chronic bronchitics or patients with emphysema, should generally be avoided in these as well as asthmatic patients because lung tissues may be seriously injured by excessive pressure from the device.

international unit   The amount of a substance, especially vitamins, enzymes, and certain vaccines, that is internationally accepted as the standard amount. Determined by the International Conference for Unification of Formulae, the measure is abbreviated as I.U.

intertrigo   A form of dermatitis characterized by chafing and redness that affects the folds of the skin or areas of skin that rub against each other. The usually damp area is often conducive to yeast or fungal infections. Often accompanied by a softening and abrasion of the skin, intertrigo is also referred to as erythema intertrigo.

intradermal reaction   [intracutaneous reaction]   See SKIN TESTS.

intrinsic asthma   See ASTHMA, INTRINSIC.

in vitro test   Tests done in a test tube or other artificial environment. An example of an in vitro test for allergies is the radioallergosorbent, or RAST, test. (See RADIOALLERGOSORBENT TESTS. See also IN VIVO TEST.)

in vivo test   Tests done in the living body. Examples are skin tests to detect allergies. (See SKIN TESTS. See also IN VITRO TEST.)

iodinated glycerol   (Iodur, Iotuss, Organidin, Par-Glycerol, Tussi-Organidin)   Mucolytic expectorant containing a mixture of several iodinated compounds formed by the reaction of iodine and glycerin.

This prescription drug is frequently combined with the cough suppressants dextromethorphan or codeine.

Iodine-containing preparations should be avoided during pregnancy, in nursing mothers, or in the newborn. These products should be avoided or used with caution in those individuals with thyroid disorders or who have experienced an adverse reaction to these or other iodine-containing foods or drugs in the past. Allergic or other adverse reactions include rashes, enlarged thyroid glands, and swelling of the parotid glands (acute parotitis).

iodine and iodide salts sensitivity   Allergic or other adverse reactions to the nonmetallic element iodine or its many salts. Complex iodides are used as radiocontrast, or X-ray, dyes, and their iodine content has been blamed for many adverse reactions to these dyes. However, the iodine is probably not responsible for these reactions (see RADIOCONTRAST MEDIA REACTIONS). Rashes and other allergic manifestations of iodides do occur in susceptible persons upon exposure to the multiple prescription and over-the-counter products available.

Iodur   See IODINATED GLYCEROL.

Iotuss   See IODINATED GLYCEROL.

ipratropium   (Atrovent)   Atropine-like drug with bronchodilating properties useful for treating bronchospasm in patients with chronic obstructing lung disorders, such as chronic bronchitis, and occasionally asthma. The drug is especially effective in smokers or former smokers. Atrovent is available as both a metered-dose inhaler and solution. The latter is suitable for addition to nebulizers, where it can be combined with albuterol. The drug has virtually no adverse effects. There is also an Atrovent nasal spray effective against the runny noses of common colds and allergies.

iridology   An unproven technique in which unorthodox practitioners claim to identify certain body areas and disease processes and relate them to locations on the iris of the eye.

irrespirable   Term used to describe any vapor, gas, or atmospheric condition unfavorable to breathing or incapable of being inhaled.

irritant   Any substance or agent that causes inflammation or adverse reaction either topically, such as skin reactions, or systemically, affecting internal body systems. Irritants trigger allergies and asthma even though they may not be considered allergens. Examples are dust, perfumes, insecticides, cleaning chemicals, cold air, paints and varnishes, smoke (especially tobacco smoke) or fumes, pollutants, and ozone.

Ishizaka, Kimishige and Teruko   Japanese-born husband and wife (Kimishige born in 1925, Teruko in 1926) physicians and scientists whose research in the fields of allergy and immunology led to the discovery that ragweed allergy (hay fever) and other immediate allergic reactions were linked to immunoglobulin E (IgE) antibodies. (See IMMUNOGLOBULIN E.)

Ishizaka, Teruko   See ISHIZAKA, KIMISHIGE AND TERUKO.

isoetharine (Bronkometer, Bronkosol)   A selective, beta-adrenergic agonist bronchodilating drug used for the treatment of asthma by inhalation. (See BETA-ADRENERGIC AGONISTS.)

isoproterenol (Duo-Medihaler,   Isuprel, Medihaler-Iso)   A beta-adrenergic agonist bronchodilating drug formerly in wide use for the treatment of asthma by inhalation. However, isoproterenol has a greater potential for causing tremors and a feeling of nervousness than newer beta-agonist drugs such as albuterol or pirbuterol. (See BETA-ADRENERGIC AGONISTS.)

Isuprel   See ISOPROTERENOL.

itching   See PRURITUS.

ivy poisoning [poison ivy]   See   CONTACT DERMATITIS, PLANT CONTACT DERMATITIS.

ixodiasis   Skin lesions caused by tick bites found in Lyme disease, Rocky Mountain spotted fever, relapsing fever, and tularemia (rabbit, squirrel, or muskrat fever). Ixodidae, a family of ticks in the order Acarina, class Arachnida, are parasitic and transmit diseases in domestic animals and humans.

J

Jadassohn, Josef German physician (1863–1936) considered a preeminent dermatologist of his time. He studied many diseases, including leprosy and syphilis, and contributed to the field of allergy with his clinical research on eczema, drug reactions, and positive anergy (inability to react to specific antigens) in sarcoidosis, a skin disease characterized by tuberclelike lesions in the skin, lymph nodes, lungs, and bone marrow. Jadassohn also recognized the different reactions to drugs administered systemically and drugs directly applied to the skin. This observation led to his design of the patch test for mercury sensitivity.

Jamaica ginger See POLYNEURITIS, JAMAICA GINGER.

jellyfish A species of marine life with a transparent, gel-like flat, circular body and tentacles with stinging cells, which can cause a skin eruption in humans. Larvae of the thimble jellyfish may be the cause of an intensely itchy seabather's eruption (SE), also called sea lice. It is believed by some physicians that the larvae of a jellyfish, *Linuche unguiculata*, causes seabather's eruption, but studies are pending. After a 25-year hiatus, cases of seabather's eruption began to appear in southern Florida in 1981, an increasing number of cases since 1988. According to the *Journal of the American Medical Association*, more than 10,000 cases of SE were reported in 1992.

SE is found primarily on skin covered by bathing suits or other clothing worn while swimming. Symptoms including itchiness, and small lesions usually appear within 24 hours of ocean exposure and last three to five days before clearing up spontaneously and without treatment. Physicians believe the thimble jellyfish larvae (about 0.5 millimeters in length) pass through bathing suit fabric and sting the skin. Recommendations for avoiding jellyfish sting include changing swimwear as soon as possible after getting out of the water; showering without the bathing suit, since wearing a suit while showering may make SE worse; wearing a wet suit with restrictive cuffs if you are a surfer, snorkeler, or diver; taking off T-shirts before swimming; wearing a two- piece instead of a one-piece bathing suit; and avoiding the ocean altogether in the case of children as well as people with allergies, autoimmune disease, or other immune-mediated condition.

Jenner, Edward British physician (1749–1823) whose ideas on acquired immunity led to the technique of vaccination. Jenner observed that milkmaids who had recovered from cow pox were immune to smallpox. He conducted experiments and published his view that one may be inoculated with fluid obtained from cow pox vesicular lesions in order to build immunity to smallpox. Jenner was widely honored for his accomplishments, including the first description of local inflammation at the vaccination site, a hypersensitivity reaction that corresponds to the function of the immune system.

jimsonweed Another name for stramonium, an atropine derivative formerly used in the treatment of asthma, the active ingredient in Asthmador Cigarettes. (See STRAMONIUM.)

Job's syndrome See HYPER-IgE SYNDROME.

K

Kabat, Elvin A. See TISELIUS, ARNE W. K., AND KABAT, ELVIN A.

kapok Fibrous substance derived from the seed hair of kapok trees native to Indonesia. Kapok at one time was commonly used as a filling material for inexpensive pillows, upholstered furniture, mattresses, stuffed toys, and, because of its buoyant properties, life jackets and boat seat cushions. Kapok, like feathers, becomes a potent allergen with aging. It is often a component of house dust allergy extract. Kapok should be removed from an allergic individual's environment.

Kartagener's syndrome [immotile colia syndrome] A congenital disorder inherited as an autosomal recessive trait that is characterized by a structural abnormality of the cilia, hairlike projections from the surface of epithelial cells that line the respiratory system. Normal cilia propel mucus, dust, and other debris, preventing excessive accumulation in the nasal passages, sinuses, and bronchi. The defective cilia do not move normally or at all, and the thick mucus that builds up obstructs the sinuses, eustachian tubes, and lungs, causing chronic sinusitis and bronchitis. Nasal polyps are also common.

Kartagener's syndrome may also be complicated by incomplete or total sitis inversus (reversal of body organs including the heart) and fertility problems in both sexes—especially immotile sperm in males. The syndrome occurs in an estimated one in 50,000 births. Symptoms usually occur within the first year of birth and require frequent antibiotics as well as bronchodilator and decongestant medications.

Kellaway, Charles H. See TRETHEWIE, EVERTON R., AND KELLAWAY, CHARLES H.

Kenacort See TRIAMCINOLONE.

ketorolac tromethamine (Acular)

A nonsteroidal anti-inflammatory drug, commonly referred to as an NSAID, available as an eyedrop to relieve the itching of seasonal allergic conjunctivitis, or hay fever.

ketotifen An oral drug with antihistaminic properties used prophylactically to prevent symptoms of asthma. Although investigational in the United States, it is available in Europe and Japan. Ketotifen appears to be only mildly effective and may take as long as one to three months to demonstrate an effect. Ketotifen is sedative but otherwise has few adverse effects.

kibe See CHILBLAINS.

Kisselbach's plexus A concentration of tiny blood vessels near the tip of the nostrils that often bleed when inflamed. Individuals with allergic rhinitis or hay fever frequently experience inflammation of the nasal passages and bleeding.

kissing bug [conenose] A biting insect of the genus *Triatoma* that injects allergens present in its saliva to the victims. Immunotherapy is impractical because of the difficulty of obtaining sufficient quantities of allergenic extracts from the salivary glands of the insect. Furthermore, anaphylaxis rarely occurs as a result of a kissing bug bite. (See BITING INSECTS.)

Kitasato, Shibasaburo Japanese physician (1856–1931) who discovered the tetanus bacillus and later, with Prussian surgeon Emil von Behring, discovered the tetanus antitoxin.

Klebsiella pneumonia A cause of pneumonia, bronchitis, and sinusitis and other respiratory infections. (See GRAM-NEGATIVE BACILLI.)

Klieg eye Inflammation of the eye (conjunctivitis), excessive tears, and photophobia (light sensitivity) caused by bright lights used in theatrical productions and filmmaking. This condition intensifies an existing allergy or infection that causes watery eyes and light sensitivity. (See CONJUNCTIVITIS, ALLERGIC.)

Koch, Robert   German physician (1843–1910) who won the Nobel Prize for his study of anthrax. Educated in Gottingen, he also did basic research that showed the reduced reaction of previously infected animals to being reinfected by the same infectious agent. He based his study on the inoculation of guinea pigs with tuberculosis and was startled to find that the reduced reaction also occurred if the original exposure had been to bacilli killed by exposure to extreme temperatures or certain chemicals.

Koch's *Grundversuch*   [Koch's phenomenon] A scientific finding by physician Robert Koch that demonstrated that animals previously exposed to certain infections, such as anthrax and tuberculosis, had a modified response when reexposed to the same infection. (See KOCH, ROBERT.)

Koch's phenomenon   See KOCH'S *GRUNDVERSUCH.*

koniology   The study of dust and its effects.

koniometer   An instrument to measure the amount of dust in the air.

Kupffer's cells   A type of phagocytic cell (one that "eats" foreign particles or invading microorganisms) in the liver.

L

laboratory tests   Various diagnostic tests for allergy, which, if a diagnosis of allergy is to be reliable, must be reproducible and cost-effective. Some tests may be useful but lack proof of effectiveness. Other tests are unreliable, nonreproducible, questionable, or even fraudulent.

Testing may be in vitro (observable outside the body, such as in a test tube) or in vivo (in a living body, such as skin tests). The Panel on Allergy of the Council on Scientific Affairs assesses in vitro tests for reliability and establishes guidelines for the appropriate use. (See also CONTROVERSIAL APPROACHES TO DIAGNOSIS, EXPLANATION, OR TREATMENT OF ALLERGIES; IN VITRO TEST; IN VIVO TEST.)

labyrinthitis   Inflammation, usually accompanied by an acute or chronic infection, of the labyrinth of the inner ear, an intricate bone consisting of the vestibule, three semicircular canals, and the cochlea. Important for maintaining balance, the labyrinth, in the event of infection, may be implicated in Meniere's disease, otitis media, meningitis, vertigo, vomiting, nystagmus, and other anomalies. The labyrinth may become also inflamed or purulent in the course of chronic allergic rhinitis.

lactase deficiency   See LACTOSE INTOLERANCE.

lactose intolerance   A common adverse reaction to any food containing lactose, or milk sugar. Although many people call it "milk allergy," it is not an allergy but rather an enzyme deficiency. The lack of the enzyme lactase prevents lactose in the small intestine from being digested. In its milder form, this results in a bloated feeling from excessive gas production; at its worst, patients often experience explosive diarrhea and severe abdominal cramps.

The condition of lactose intolerance may be temporary, following a viral infection causing diarrhea, or become lifelong following its onset. However, it is rarely, if ever, present at birth and is not the cause of milk-induced diarrhea of infancy. Most individuals develop the intestinal lactase deficiency between age three and puberty.

In some population groups, such as blacks, Asians, Greenland Eskimos, and Israeli Arabs, up to 80% of the population suffers from lactose intolerance, whereas only 3% of Danes are afflicted.

Diagnosis of lactose deficiency can be confirmed by either an oral lactose tolerance test or a lactose breath hydrogen test.

Lactase tablets (or powder) are available so that all but the most severely deficient individuals can consume some dairy products. Since dairy products are an important source of calcium, most patients on a milk-free diet should be given a calcium supplement. (See also MILK.)

Laennec's pearls   Round, gelatinlike mucous particles or "pearls" found in the sputum of patients with asthma. These particles were first described by Rene T. Laennec, French physician and inventor of the stethoscope (1781–1826).

Landsteiner, Karl   Viennese physician and scientist (1868–1943) whose discovery of human blood groups earned him the Nobel Prize in 1930. His other achievements at the Rockefeller Institute for Medical Research, where he worked from 1922 until his death, have helped advance our knowledge of immunology.

lanolin   [wool fat, wool wax]   A substance produced by the oil glands of sheep that is used in the pharmaceutical and cosmetics industries. Claims that lanolin in ointment bases or emollients increases the product's ability to penetrate the skin are unsubstantiated. Furthermore, lanolin is itself a common allergen and often worsens a skin rash for which it may have been prescribed as treatment. Lanolin alcohols derived from pure lanolin are somewhat less likely to cause allergic reactions and are widely used in cosmetics. (See also CONTACT DERMATITIS.)

laryngismus   Spasm of the larynx such as that which occurs during a severe allergic reaction.

laryngismus stridulus   See CHILD CROWING.

laryngitis   Inflammation of the larnyx, or voice box, the musculocartilaginous upper end of the windpipe (trachea) lined with mucous membrane. Characterized by a sore throat and hoarseness or temporary inability to speak (aphonia), laryngitis may be caused by improper use or overuse of the voice, exposure to wet and cold, extension of a nose or throat infection, or inhalation of irritating vapors or dust. Although the larynx is part of the respiratory system, which is often affected by allergic symptoms, allergies themselves are not generally a cause of laryngitis. Patients with persistent hoarseness should be evaluated for polyps or other disorders of the vocal cords.

laryngorrhea   Excessive mucus discharge from the larnyx.

laryngospasm   Sudden muscular contractions, or spasms, of the larynx. (See ANAPHYLAXIS; ANGIOEDEMA, HEREDITARY; ANGIOEDEMA, IDIOPATHIC; ANGIOEDEMA, NONHEREDITARY.)

larynx   The vocal cords, or voice box, located at the upper end of the trachea below the root of the tongue. The larynx, a Greek word meaning the "upper part of the windpipe," is made of nine cartilages bound by an elastic membrane and lined with mucous membrane. When moved by muscles and aided by air pressure, the mouth, and the tongue, the larynx produces sounds, including speech.

late-phase allergic reactions   Symptoms of allergy or asthma that occur hours after initial exposure to an allergen. Inhalation of an allergen first triggers immediate symptoms, such as itching, sneezing, wheezing, and shortness of breath. Bronchospasm occurs promptly in the lungs; this constriction is often reversible with bronchodilating drugs.

In about half of individuals with asthma, however, a delayed, or late-phase, reaction occurs four to eight hours after exposure to an allergen. In this stage, bronchi (airways) become hyperactive and likely to constrict, but more important, they become inflamed with increased mucus production and obstruction. During this process, increased numbers of inflammatory cells—eosinophils, lymphocytes, and macrophages, which bring about a release of chemical mediators—are present. Administration of anti-inflammatory medications exemplified by corticosteroids tempers the inflammatory changes. Late-phase reaction is often preventable by pretreatment with cromolyn and corticosteroid metered-dose inhalers. Bronchodilator drugs probably provide no protection against the late-phase response.

Similar late-phase reactions may occur in allergic skin disorders (eczema), allergic rhinitis, and conjunctivitis. (See ASTHMA, INFLAMMATION.)

latex allergy   Anaphylaxis, or immediate allergic reaction in susceptible individuals, that manifests upon exposure to raw and processed latex, a substance derived from *Hevea brasiliensis*, the rubber tree. Latex, also derived from various plants including milkweed, spurge, and poppy, is frequently used in the manufacture of adhesives, paints, and other coatings. In addition, latex is the source of rubber, guttapercha, chicle, and balata.

Although European physicians have recognized this problem since 1979, the recently increased use of protective gloves by health care workers, especially in light of the AIDS epidemic, has amplified the problem. It has been speculated that the increased demand for latex gloves led to improper purification in the manufacturing process of latex products, particularly those imported from Southeast Asia. A survey of surgical nurses in one hospital showed that 13% had a positive skin reaction to latex extract. According to the Diagnostic Products Corporation (DPC) in Los Angeles, California, at least 275 latex-associated anaphylactic reactions and more than 12 deaths have been reported. And in one hospital, there were six anaphylactic reactions to latex in four months in preoperative surgical preparation.

The DPC added that a person's medical history may help determine his or her susceptibility to latex allergy. Patients, especially those with spina bifida, who have had many surgeries are at higher risk of adverse reactions.

Symptoms range from hives and severe rash from skin contact to fatal anaphylactic shock with mucosal contact or injection. Latex-free surgical suites are now available in many centers for patients known to have latex sensitivity. Hives seem to be a more accurate predictor of latex allergy than itching and redness on contact. However, individuals testing positive to latex may not react to it when exposed.

High-risk individuals Children with spina bifida or severe urogenital birth defects and health care and rubber industry workers appear to be at greater risk for latex allergy than others. The increased incidence in the pediatric population seems to be associated with more frequent rectal and bladder exposure to latex products. Injectable medications may be contaminated by the presence of a rubber stopper on multiple-dose vials of drugs. There are also persons known to have cross-reactivity to banana, chestnut, avocado, and latex.

Testing for latex allergy In vitro tests, such as radioallergosorbent, or RAST, testing for latex allergy, do not correlate well with either history, skin testing, or severity of allergy. Unfortunately, there are no approved skin-testing preparations available in the United States. Furthermore, there are reports of severe allergic reactions occurring in extremely sensitive persons being skin-tested to latex.

Prevention of latex reactions Every attempt must be made by persons known to be sensitive to latex to avoid its contact. Individuals whose reactions are less severe may tolerate contact with some latex products.

lavender oil   Colorless liquid extracted from the fresh flowery tops of a Mediterranean mint plant (*Lavendula officinalis*). Its characteristic aromatic fragrance is widely used in the cosmetic industry, and its dried flowers are used in sachets. Lavender is used as a flavoring in beverages, including ginger ale, ice cream, candy, baked goods, and mouthwashes. It may cause photoallergic dermatitis.

learning disabilities and allergy   Poor school performance attributed to allergy symptoms. For example, temporary hearing loss because of fluid buildup in the middle ear (otitis media) in children with respiratory allergies may interrupt the child's learning processes. In addition, constant nasal congestion, sneezing, and itchy or watery eyes may distress and distract school children. However, there is no proof that children with allergies are more likely to suffer from other disabilities such as dyslexia. (See also FEINGOLD DIET, HYPERACTIVITY.)

learning disabilities and theophylline   Behavioral changes and inattentiveness resulting in poor performance in school that are attributed to the use of theophylline as treatment of childhood asthma. (See THEOPHYLLINE.)

legumes   The edible fruit, seed, or pod of high-protein vegetables such as peas, beans, and lentils. The nitrogen content in legumes nearly equals that in meat. They are also high in B vitamins.

Although some persons allergic to peanuts may also be sensitive to peas, soybeans, and other legumes, anaphylaxis is most common with peanut allergy. (See also PEANUT.)

leiodermia   A form of dermatitis in which the skin atrophies, or shrinks, and takes on an abnormal glossiness and smoothness.

lentigo   Freckles or yellow-brown colored areas of the skin that may be caused by exposure to the sun.

lepidosis, pityriasis   Any scaly or flaky skin eruption. An example of lepidosis, pityriasis refers to a group of skin diseases characterized by scale formations of various types. The causes of pityriasis include parasitic infestation and exacerbations of eczema and seborrhea of the scalp and face. In the case of pityriasis rosea, a noncontagious rash affecting mostly children and young adults, the cause is unknown.

Leptus autumnalis   Parasitic mite larvae causing itchiness and wheals that may be confused with hives or other allergic skin condition. (See CHIGGERS.)

lesion   An abnormal change, including ulceration, abscess, chancre, boil, wheal, tumor, wound, excoriation, crusts, scales, scars, pustules, rash, pimple, fissure, or cancer, in a bodily structure. In the case of a skin lesion, the diseased tissue is found in a circumscribed area, or a single patch of infected skin. A lesion that emerges early in a disease process is called a primary, or initial, lesion, such as the appearance of a chancre in syphilis. A structural lesion refers to a change in tissue, whereas a systemic lesion may occur in organs that function similarly. Among other lesions are degenerative, those that cause a deterioration of the affected area, and diffuse, which spread over a large area.

Certain types of lesions indicate allergic reaction, especially raised red wheals (hives). Other lesions may easily be confused with non-allergic reactions.

leukocyte histamine release assay   Another name for basophil degranulation and histamine release. (See BASOPHIL DEGRANULATION AND HISTAMINE RELEASE.)

leukocytes   White blood cells produced in bone marrow, lymph nodes, and cells lining capillaries in organs such as the spleen. There are two types of leukocytes: granulocytes, which have granules in their cytoplasm, and agranulocytes, which do not have granules. Granulocytes include juvenile neutrophils, segmented neutrophils, basophils, and eosinophils, and agranulocytes include lymphocytes (produced in the lymph nodes) and monocytes, all of which participate in helping the body fight infection and in the inflammatory processes that occur during allergic reactions. Leukocytes of all types circulate throughout the body, especially to troubleshoot in areas where there are injured tissues or infections. The normal adult white blood cell count is approximately 4,000 to 10,000 leukocytes per cubic millimeter of blood. Leukopenia refers to fewer than 4,000 white blood cells; leukocytosis is indicated by a count greater than 10,000.

A white blood cell differential count, which examines the various types of leukocytes in the circulating blood and other body secretions, helps diagnosis many medical disorders, including allergies and infections. For example, bacterial infections usually cause an increased number of total white blood cells, whereas viruses may slightly increase, decrease, or maintain a normal count. Bacterial infections most often result in an increase in polymorphonuclear cells (also called neutrophils, polys, or segs) relative to the increase in total white cells. Viral infections may cause an increase in the number of lymphocytes. The presence of more than 5% eosinophils in the white blood count frequently suggests an allergic or parasitic disorder. (See EOSINOPHIL, IMMUNE SYSTEM.)

leukotrienes C and D   See LEUKOTRIENES, SLOW-RELEASING SUBSTANCE.

leukotrienes   Potent biochemicals produced and secreted by various types of immune cells such as macrophages, mast cells, eosinophils, basophils and monocytes along with other chemical mediators (natural substances in the body that act like drugs), including histamine. Leukotrienes and other substances including proglandins, collectively called eicosanoids, are fatty acids derived during the metabolism of arachidonic acid, an essential component of the cell membrane. Certain leukotrienes may be held partly accountable for effects of asthma such as bronchospasm or constriction, increased airway hyperresponsiveness to triggers, increased microvascular permeability (the ability to pass substances through the walls of tiny blood vessels) and excessive production of mucus. These chemicals may be 100 to 1,000 times more potent and exert a more prolonged effect than histamine in contracting the smooth muscle of airways. The presence of leukotrienes may also be a reason that antihistaminic drugs, which block the action of histamine, do not fully alleviate allergic reactions.

Zafirlukast (Accolate) is the first of a class of drugs effective for the treatment of leukotriene-mediated reactions to be approved for use in the U.S., which also includes experimental drugs pranlukast (Ultair), montelukast (Singulair) and cinalukast. Accolate antagonizes or blocks the effects of LTD4 and is useful to prevent inflammatory changes that occur in mild to moderate asthma. It is not known if the effects of these agents will be additive to other inflammatory drugs such as corticosteroids. Accolate is approved for the treatment of mild to moderate asthma. There do not appear to be any serious adverse effects.

Zileuton (Zileutrol) inhibits, or prevents, the action of 5-lipoxygenase, and is expected to be released in the U.S. in 1997. Zileutrol may have additive effects to inhaled corticosteroids. Other drugs that inhibit the formation or actions of leukotrienes are in various stages of investigation and will probably become available in the late 1990s.

levocabastine   An experimental antihistamine effective for the treatment of allergic disorders of the eye. This drug works quickly, and its action lasts up to 12 hours.

lichen planus   One of the self-limiting, but often persistent, inflammatory skin disorders associated with lichenification, a thickening and hardening of skin caused by chronic irritation. The intensely itchy rash may consist of reddish or violet-colored papules and scaly patches. The cause is unknown.

lidocaine   (Xylocaine) A local anesthetic used to relieve itching, burning, and pain from rashes, to alleviate the pain in oral and rectal lesions, and to provide local anesthesia during suturing of lacerations and dental surgery. It is also used as an antiarrhythmic drug for certain heart disorders. When used on intact skin, it may cause allergic reactions and worsen the rash for which it was prescribed. (See ANESTHETICS, LOCAL.)

linalool   A fragrance and flavoring obtained from the tree *Lignum aloes* that may cause allergic reactions.

linseed oil   A yellowish oil derived from the seed of the flax plant (of the genus *Linum*, especially *L. usitatissimum*, a kind of herb) that gradually thickens when exposed to air and has a strange odor and bland taste. Linseed oil, a known allergen, is used in shaving cream, demulcents, medicinal soaps, and emollients and in the manufacture of paint, varnish, and linoleum.

local anesthetics   See ANESTHETICS, LOCAL.

locations ideal for asthma and allergy patients   Geographic areas considered to provide improved living conditions, depending upon the specific allergens to which an individual is sensitive. Some people feel the need to move from their present homes to avoid allergens indigenous to that area, but climates and geographic characteristics can change in time, causing previously favorable areas to become havens for new allergens and pollutants. For example, Arizona was once thought to be an ideal climate for asthmatics. However, pollutants (including the introduction of pollinating plants and grasses by the incoming new residents) and environmental changes such as urbanization and irrigation have turned populated areas of this state into high-risk zones. In addition, the stress of moving and new environmental exposures may intensify asthma and allergy symptoms.

loratadine (Claritin) An antihistamine with a lower potential for sedation than traditional allergy drugs. Introduced in the United States in 1993, loratadine is taken once daily on an empty stomach.

lotion A liquid applied to the skin for moisturizing, softening, soothing, or medicating purposes. Some lotions may contain allergenic ingredients.

L-tryptophan One of nine amino acids essential in the human diet. A three-ounce serving of fish or meat will satisfy the 200-milligram minimum daily adult requirement. L-tryptophan has questionable therapeutic value as a supplement for the relief of insomnia, depression, and premenstrual tension (PMS).

Eosinophilia-myalgia syndrome (EMS) is a serious and life-threatening adverse effect caused by L-tryptophan. In 1989, physicians in New Mexico reported three cases of severe muscle pain and very high blood eosinophil counts (see EOSINOPHIL) linked to L-tryptophan. When many other cases were reported, the Food and Drug Administration (FDA) recalled on November 17, 1989 most products containing this substance. On March 22, 1990 an additional recall was ordered.

The Centers for Disease Control (CDC) defines EMS in terms of a patient who has an eosinophil count of at least 1,000 cells per cubic millimeter, generalized myalgia (muscle pain) severe enough to interfere with an individual's daily activities, and absence of any infection or tumor that could account for the first two factors.

By September 1, 1991, 1,507 cases of EMS, including 31 fatalities, had been reported to the CDC. It has been estimated that as many as 5,000 persons probably have been afflicted, although most cases might not have been reported and there have been many milder cases

with "flulike" symptoms that would not satisfy all three requirements for a diagnosis of EMS.

The real cause of EMS is thought to be a contaminant of the L-tryptophan, but until that substance can be identified and eliminated from the manufacturing process, all brands of this drug should be avoided. Most cases respond favorably to discontinuing use of the drug. Some require corticosteroid therapy.

Lucas-Championniere's disease Pseudomembranous bronchitis (related to croupous bronchitis, inflammation of the bronchi including some of the symptoms of croup: difficult breathing and spasm of the larynx), named for French surgeon J. M. M. Lucas-Championniere, (1843–1913). This condition may be confused with asthma. (See BRONCHITIS.)

Lucretius The Latin philosopher and poet Titus Lucretius Carus (98–55 B.C.), who is best known for his Epicurean ideas, especially that "food to one is poison to another," a popular quotation in allergy literature.

Lufyllin See DYPHYLLINE.

lung function assessment See PULMONARY FUNCTION TESTS.

lungs The main organs of the respiratory system. The lungs are two spongelike structures located in the chest within the rib cage that provide life-sustaining oxygen to the body. Lungs contain air sacs, called alveoli, that accommodate air taken into the lungs by inhalation and exhalation, during which oxygen is transmitted to the bloodstream and carbon dioxide is expelled.

In the process of breathing, air from the atmosphere enters the trachea, or windpipe, and passes into the two large bronchi, each branching into a lung on either side, then to the smaller bronchi and the bronchioles. The entire structure resembles a tree. The lungs, which move upon inhalation and exhalation, are encased by pleurae, protective membranes that allow each lung to expand and contract. (In the event of pleurisy, these membranes swell and rub against each other, causing pain during respiration.) The right lung is divided into three lobes, or sections, and the left lung is divided into two lobes. Pulmonary circulation describes blood traveling from the heart to the lungs and back to the heart. Diseases of the lung include bronchial asthma, pneumonia, bronchitis, emphysema, tumors, and anomalies caused by injury to the lungs. Many diagnostic procedures include chest X ray (X rays of the lungs), pulmonary function tests, bronchoscopy, biopsy of lung tissue, blood tests, and sputum analysis. (See BREATHING.)

lupus   See LUPUS ERYTHEMATOSUS, SYSTEMIC.

lupus erythematosus, discoid (DLE)   A skin condition, or dermatitis, characterized by reddish, circular, scaly patches that leave scars after healing. Usually worsened by exposure to sunlight, this form of lupus is a chronic but benign disorder, more common than the related autoimmune disease, systemic lupus erythematosus (SLE). Treatment for DLE calls for antimalarial drugs such as hydroxychloroquine (Plaquenil).

lupus erythematosus, systemic (SLE) [lupus] A chronic multisystem disease characterized by the presence of autoantibodies (antibodies or allergic reaction directed against one's own body), which are the cause of many of SLE's manifestations. The finding of various autoantibodies in the serum is also helpful in the diagnosis of lupus. Lupus occurs in about one in 2,000 in the general population. One in 700 women between the ages of 20 and 64 years is afflicted; the disease is most frequent in females of childbearing age. However, black women have a higher incidence, estimated to be one in 245.

Although the cause of lupus is unknown, the ability of those afflicted to produce autoantibodies against many of their own tissues is paramount to its development. Lupus is an immune disease that may involve the skin, heart, lungs, brain, blood, and joints. Symptoms affecting all

or some of these structures may be present simultaneously or at various intervals in the course of the disease. Diagnosis of lupus is based on the finding of four or more criteria present in a patient (see the accompanying chart).

SLE may remain dormant for many years or become progressive and fatal. With treatment, 90% of patients survive at least 10 years. Corticosteroids, antimalarial drugs such as chloroquine and hydroxychloroquine, and nonsteroidal anti-inflammatory agents such as aspirin and ibuprofen are the mainstay of therapy. In severe cases, however, immune-modulating drugs such as cyclophosphamide (Cytoxan) may be necessary.

A number of drugs, including procainamide, hydralazine, anticonvulsants, and chlorpromazine, produce a lupuslike illness, which is milder than non-drug-induced disease and responds to discontinuation of the offending drug. (See AUTOIMMUNE DISORDER.)

ELEVEN CRITERIA ON WHICH THE DIAGNOSIS OF SYSTEMIC LUPUS ERYTHEMATOSUS IS BASED

Criterion
1. Malar ("butterfly") rash: red rash, flat or raised, over nose and cheeks
2. Discoid rash: red, raised patches with thick scaling, blockage of pores, atrophy and scarring of skin
3. Photosensitivity: rash upon exposure to sunlight
4. Oral ulcers: usually painless
5. Arthritis: nondestructive joint swelling and tenderness
6. Serositis: pleuritis or pericarditis (inflammation of the tissue covering the lungs or heart) with chest pain and the presence of a characteristic rub heard with a stethoscope
7. Kidney disorder: excessive proteins, and casts in the urine
8. Neurologic disorder: seizures, psychosis
9. Blood disorder: anemia, leukopenia (reduced white blood cell count), thrombocytopenia (reduced platelet count)

10. Immunologic disorder: confirmed by special blood tests
11. Antinuclear antibody: confirmed by special blood tests

Source: Adapted from J. J. Condemi, "The Autoimmune Diseases," *Journal of the American Medical Association* 258 (1987): 2920–29. Copyright 1987, American Medical Association.

lycoperdonosis   A respiratory disease caused by inhaling significant quantities of *Lycoperdon* spores from the mature mushroom commonly known as "puffball." Most puffballs belong to this genus of fungi.

lymph   The clear, colorless fluid of the lymphatic system. Formed in tissue spaces throughout the body, lymph contains white blood cells and proteins (including serum albumin, serum globulin, and serum fibrinogen), water, urea, creatinine, glucose, organic fats, and salts. Chyle, or lymph formed in the intestine, also contains substances derived from the intestine. Lymph vessels carry the fluid around the body and eventually to the thoracic duct or the right lymph duct. The ducts end at the point of connection with the internal jugular and subclavian veins; here lymph reenters the bloodstream.

lymphocyte blast transformation   An in vitro blood test that measures DNA synthesis after a patient suspected of allergy is exposed to antigen. It can be useful to evaluate drug sensitivity. However, this application is still experimental.

Other uses include evaluating immunocompetence (ability to mount an immune response) and assessing the compatibility of donor and recipient prior to human organ transplantation.

lymphocytes   Small leukocytes, or white blood cells, produced in the bone marrow that are of prime importance to the immune system. There are two major types or classes of lymphocytes: agranular, small B cells (5 to 15% of lymphocytes) and T cells (approximately 65% of the total). The remainder are non-B and non-T large, granular lymphocytes. The marrow produces all blood cells, including mature B cells. T cells migrate to the thymus, located behind the breastbone, to multiply and mature. In the maturing process these cells become immunocompetent, that is, developing the ability to evoke an immune response and learning to distinguish self from nonself cells. B and T cells circulate through the blood and lymph systems to supply the body tissues with immune cells. (See B CELLS, IMMUNE SYSTEM, T CELLS, THYMUS GLAND.)

lymphokines   Cytokines secreted by B cells and T cells that are potent chemical messengers of the immune system. Lymphokines bind to specific receptors on target cells, attracting other cells and substances of the inflammatory response. They stimulate cell growth and activation, direct cellular traffic, destroy target cells, and activate macrophages. (See IMMUNE SYSTEM, INTERLEUKINS.)

lysozyme   An allergenic substance accounting for 11% of egg-white proteins. (See EGG ALLERGY.)

M

macule   A flat spot or discolored patch of skin.

macrophages   Important monocytic white blood cells involved in the immune response. (See IMMUNE SYSTEM, LYMPHOCYTES, PHAGOCYTES.)

Maimonides, Moses   Jewish physician (1135–1204) who wrote *Treatise on Asthma*, among other scientific and philosophical works, which was the first of his medical books currently available in English translation. In the treatise, Maimonides recommends that attacks of various illnesses, including asthma (which he also called shortness of breath), can be made less frequent and less severe if the air is kept clean; if diet, excretions, and spiritual emotions are regulated; and if proper rest and exercise are maintained.

Educated by his father, who was a judge, and by Rabbi ibn Migas, Cordova-born Maimonides also wrote about religion and religious law, logic, astronomy, preventive medicine, drugs, toxins, Galen's teachings, sex, and other topics. He became known as the greatest Jew after Moses and one of the preeminent figures of modern medical ethics along with Hippocrates. Because of religious persecution, Maimonides' family fled to Cairo, where he became a physician. His holistic practice included advocating bathing and massage.

manchineel   (*Hippomane mancinella*)   A tropical tree whose milky sap produces skin blisters on contact. The fruit of this tree is poisonous. (See CONTACT DERMATITIS.)

Mantoux test   See TUBERCULIN TEST.

massage   An expanded form of the traditional back rub. Various methods of massage are popular, including the Japanese shiatsu, which concentrates on pressure points of the body, and massaging the hands and feet. Essentially, any type of massage induces relaxation and may be useful when stress acts as a trigger for asthma. (See also ACUPRESSURE, REFLEXOLOGY.)

mast cell degranulation assay   See DEGRANULATION TECHNIQUE.

mast cells   One of the major cells in body tissues responsible for the onset of allergic symptoms. Mast cells contain histamine and other chemically active substances. During a type I, or immediate, allergic reaction, mast cells are activated. There are two types of mast cells, connective tissue mast cells and mucosal mast cells. Each are coated with immunoglobulin E (IgE) antibodies, which bind to receptors on the mast cell's surface. The receptors correlate to individual allergens (substances capable of causing an allergy).

One mast cell may have from 5,000 to 500,000 individual IgE antibody receptors on its surface. After exposure to an allergen, the surface antibodies "recognize" their specific allergens, causing the mast cell to release chemical mediators. Chemical mediators are potent biochemicals, including histamine, prostaglandins, and leukotrienes, among others. In an asthmatic patient, the release of the mediators causes a sudden constriction and inflammation of the bronchioles, which results in wheezing and shortness of breath.

The mast cells also produce proteases and cytokines, substances involved in the process of tissue inflammation, growth, and repair. (See also CHEMICAL MEDIATORS, MASTOCYTOSIS.)

mastocytosis   A disorder caused by the presence of an excess of mast cells. Mast cells are located in the skin, lining of the gastrointestinal tract (stomach and intestine), and connective tissues, including the cartilage and tendons.

Mast cells are important in the immune response defending the body against foreign invaders, such as allergens or infectious microorganisms, by releasing chemical mediators or alarms such as histamine. Mast cells also signal other cells of the immune system to respond to the crisis.

There are two types of mastocytosis—cutaneous or skin form and systemic. Urticaria pigmentosa, another name for cutaneous mastocytosis, was first described in 1869 and is characterized by an abnormally high concentration of mast cells in the skin. The diagnosis is made by a skin biopsy.

Diagnosis Systemic mastocytosis, first reported in 1933, is marked by an increased number of tissue mast cells in organs, including the liver, spleen, and small intestine, and in bone marrow. Diagnosis is suggested by sustained elevated blood levels of histamine or mast cell protease and high levels of the metabolic breakdown products of histamine, such as prostaglandin D_2, in the urine. A bone marrow test may aid in confirming the diagnosis.

Symptoms Symptoms of mastocytosis include hives, itching, abdominal cramps, anorexia, nausea, vomiting, diarrhea, ulcers, palpitations, headaches, fatigue, irritability, inability to concentrate, bone pain, and skin lesions. This disorder's most severe manifestations are hypotension (very low blood pressure) and anaphylactic shock. Individuals who develop the cutaneous form during childhood often have their symptoms resolve spontaneously. However, adult onset of this disorder more frequently leads to the more severe systemic form.

Treatment Cromolyn sodium (Gastrocrom) is the only specific therapy for mastocytosis. Given orally, this drug reduces or improves many of the symptoms. Antihistamines are frequently used to relieve itching, and anticholinergic (atropinelike) drugs may reduce abdominal cramps and diarrhea. In severe cases corticosteroids are needed. (See also MAST CELLS.)

MAST test See   RADIOALLERGOSORBENT TESTS.

Maxair See PIRBUTEROL.

measles, mumps, and rubella (MMR) virus vaccine, live, allergic reactions   Adverse responses rarely occur from immunizations administered to infants and older children for protection against measles (rubeola), mumps, and German measles (rubella). Because vaccines of live measles and mumps are grown in cell cultures of chick embryo, the manufacturer recommends that persons who have experienced anaphylaxis (the most severe form of allergic reaction) after eating eggs not be given this vaccine. Researchers at the Johns Hopkins Children's Center in Baltimore, Maryland gave MMR to 129 children known to be allergic to eggs, and no adverse reactions were reported. However, two children who did not have egg allergy had severe reactions from the vaccine. Nevertheless, other experts report systemic reactions in a similar group of children and recommend that egg-sensitive children be skin-tested with the MMR vaccine and desensitized if they test positive.

Anaphylactoid (allergylike) reactions may occur in some individuals from neomycin present in the vaccine. MMR vaccine should not be given to pregnant women; women anticipating pregnancy should avoid becoming pregnant for three months after immunization, because its effects are unknown at the present time. It should also be withheld during any febrile illness, untreated tuberculosis, or in any person suspected of being immunocompromised, including those with HIV, leukemia, lymphoma, and similar diseases. Although the MMR vaccine can be given to individuals receiving corticosteroids for replacement therapy in Addison's disease, it should generally be avoided by those taking these drugs.

The *Physician's Desk Reference* or company literature should be consulted for other nonallergic adverse reactions. Serious adverse effects from live viral vaccines are extremely rare, and the risks are far greater from the diseases the vaccines prevent than from the vaccine itself.

mediators   See CHEMICAL MEDIATORS.

medical alert bracelets and necklaces   Engraved metal plates worn like jewelry to identify a chronic medical condition or allergy in the event that an individual becomes unable to communicate.

medication allergy   See DRUG ALLERGY AND OTHER ADVERSE DRUG REACTIONS.

medications for the treatment of allergic disorders   See ANTIHISTAMINE, BETA-ADRENERGIC AGONISTS, BRONCHODILATING DRUGS, CORTICOSTEROIDS, entries on individual drugs.

Medihaler-Iso   See ISOPROTERENOL.

Medrol   See METHYLPREDNISOLONE.

melons   Various fruits in the form of gourds, such as cantaloupe and watermelon, known to be a rare cause of anaphylaxis (allergic shock). Although there have been reports of itching and swelling of the palate in patients allergic to ragweed who eat melons and bananas, these plants are not botanically related.

Meltzer, Samuel J.   German physician (1851–1920) who immigrated to the United States in 1883 and worked at Belleview Hospital and Columbia University. In 1907 Meltzer became head of the Division of Physiology and Pharmacology at the Rockefeller Institute. He published his studies on the mechanics of swallowing, shock, hemolysis, and the effect of adrenaline. He theorized that asthma was an anaphylactic phenomenon, which means asthmatics have been sensitized to a substance and suffer an attack whenever they are "intoxicated" by that substance. He described a functional disease, not a neurosis, and eliminated the previously accepted concept of "nervous asthma."

membrane, mucous   The soft, pink lining of certain body structures, including the mouth, nose, throat, eyelids, bladder, vagina, and intestinal tract, that secretes mucus, a sticky fluid that keeps the surfaces of these and other organs moist.

Menes   King of the first Egyptian dynasty, also known as Manis the Warrior, Sumerian emperor of Mesopotamia around 2655 B.C., according to some scholars such as L. A. Waddell, author of *Egyptian Civilization, Its Sumerian Origin and Real Chronology* (1930). Waddell believed Menes died after suffering anaphylaxis as the result of a wasp or hornet sting. Others have refuted Waddell's interpretation of Menes' death as the first documentation, appearing in the Babylonian Talmud in the second century B.C. to the third century A.D., of a fatal anaphylactic reaction to the venom of an insect. (See ANAPHYLAXIS.)

menstrual cycle and allergy   The correlation of allergic symptoms and menstruation. An estimated 33 to 40% of asthmatic women experience intensified allergy symptoms a few days prior to or during their periods. In several groups of women, hives may occur seven to 10 days before the period and disappear on the third day of the period. The hormones estrogen and progesterone have some beneficial and some adverse effects on asthma, but no clear explanation of these effects has been established.

meperidine   (Demerol)   See DRUG ALLERGY AND OTHER ADVERSE DRUG REACTIONS.

mercurial rash   A nonallergic skin irritation induced by the topical application of or contact with mercury or mercurial preparations.

metabisulfite challenge   A professional study in which a sulfite-containing drink is given to individuals suspected of having sensitivity to this food additive. Carefully measured amounts of potassium metabisulfite are added to Hi-C brand of lemonade. The patient swishes the cold solution for 10 to 15 seconds before swallowing, thus warming the solution. The release of sulfur dioxide gas is then inhaled.

The challenged subject subsequently undergoes pulmonary function studies (spirometry) to detect a drop in airflow rates. A significant decrease in spirometric values indicates a positive test for sulfite-induced asthma. (See SULFITING AGENTS.)

metabolic food reaction   Adverse reaction to a food or food additive resulting in some effect on the metabolism, which involves all the mechanical and chemical energy and material changes that take place in the living body.

metal fume fever   See POLYMER FUME FEVER.

metallic tinkling   A ringing, like the sound of metal being tapped, heard through a stethoscope over the chest area in which the lung has collapsed. (See PNEUMOTHORAX.)

metals and metallic salts   Common causes of contact dermatitis (skin rash) especially from wearing jewelry made of metal, or from industrial contact with metals and metallic salts. Nickel is the most common sensitizer, found in jewelry (necklaces, bracelets, earrings, and wristwatches), stainless steel wire, and some dyes. Potassium dichromate, a metallic salt, is found in photographic supplies, leather goods, tanning agents, yellow paint, and bleaches. Mercury bichloride is used in thermometers, batteries, silk, disinfectants, and skin lighteners. Cobolt sulfate and chloride are found in tattoo and hair dyes, adhesives, and clays. Ferric chloride, a component of Monsel's solution and styptic pencils, rarely sensitizes. Gold chloride is used in photographic materials. Copper sulfate is a component in insecticides, dyes, coins, and food processing. Hair dyes and caustic pencils contain silver nitrate. Aluminum chloride is used as an antiperspirant in deodorants and as an astringent in antiseptics. Sodium arsenate is a sensitizer used in hair tonics and insecticides. The manufacture of most types of cement involves the use of chromates; chromates are also important to the tanning, dying,

and printing industries. (See also CONTACT DERMATITIS.)

Metaprel   See METAPROTERENOL.

metaproterenol (Alupent, Metaprel)   A beta-adrenergic agonist, or bronchodilator, drug widely used in the treatment of asthma. Metaproterenol is available as a metered-dose inhaler, tablet, liquid, and solution for nebulizer use. (See BETA-ADRENERGIC AGONISTS.)

Metchnikoff's theory   The concept now known as phagocytosis, named for the Russian zoologist Elie Metchnikoff (1845–1916). Phagocytosis is a bodily process in which cells called phagocytes and leukocytes protect the body against infection by destroying harmful invading microbes. (See PHAGOCYTES.)

metered-dose inhalers   See AEROSOLS.

methacholine challenge   A test to diagnose asthma in individuals with confusing or minimal symptoms by the inhalation of the drug methacholine in gradually increasing quantities. An asthmatic person will have a diminished flow rate during spirometry (pulmonary function study), whereas a normal individual will maintain normal flow rates.

methotrexate   A chemotherapeutic agent used in the treatment of cancer, psoriasis, and rheumatoid arthritis. Its effectiveness is now being studied as a steroid-sparing, anti-inflammatory drug for severe asthma. Although reports indicate conflicting results, methotrexate is thought to be especially beneficial to corticosteroid-dependent asthmatics. One report recommends that methotrexate be discontinued after 36 months because of the possibility of inducing bronchial hyperreactivity (BHR) or exacerbation of asthma. Prolonged use and higher doses than those used for the treatment of asthma have been known to cause hepatotoxicity, fibrosis, and cirrhosis; in addition, methotrexate may be lethal to a fetus or cause congenital abnormalities and therefore should not be administered to pregnant women with rheumatoid arthritis, psoriasis, or asthma. Other adverse effects of methotrexate include lung disease, bone marrow depression, and gastrointestinal disturbances.

methscopolamine nitrate   The generic name for an ingredient in the drugs Dura-Vent/DA, Extendryl, Histaspan, Histor-D, Rhinolar, and Dallergy. Methscopolamine nitrate, in conjunction with other agents in these preparations, acts as an antihistaminic decongestant prescribed for relief of respiratory congestion, allergic rhinitis, and allergic skin reactions, including angioedema and hives.

methyl methacrylate monomer   A chemical used as nail lengtheners or extenders that was banned in 1974 by the Food and Drug Administration because of severe reactions that could destroy the nail bed. (See also NAIL-MENDING KITS.)

methylprednisolone   The generic name for the drugs Depo-Medrol and Medrol. An anti-inflammatory glucocorticoid agent, methylprednisolone aids the body in modifying immune responses to various stimuli. It is prescribed for treatment of endocrine, rheumatic, ophthalmic, hematologic, neoplastic, respiratory, gastrointestinal, and other disorders. In addition, methylprednisolone can control severe allergies, including seasonal allergic rhinitis, contact dermatitis, atopic dermatitis, drug hypersensitivity reactions, serum sickness, pemphigus, bullous dermatitis herpetiformis, and bronchial asthma. (See CORTICOSTEROIDS, TROLEANDOMYCIN.)

methylxanthines   A class of stimulants related to caffeine and theobromine (components in coffee, tea, cola, chocolate, and cocoa), including the bronchodilating drugs theophylline and aminophylline. Adverse effects may include central nervous system stimulation, headache, nausea, and abdominal pain. A cup of coffee (150 milligrams of caffeine) contains a significant amount of methylxanthines. (See AMINOPHYLLINE, THEOPHYLLINE.)

mice allergens   Hair, feces, urine, and other physical aspects of mice, especially in infested buildings or areas, that cause adverse effects, or allergic reactions, in some individuals. Research laboratory workers may experience allergic symptoms and asthma in conjunction with exposure to the urine, skin, and saliva of mice and rats. (See ANIMAL ALLERGY.)

middle ear infection   See OTITIS MEDIA, SECRETORY.

midge   A small-winged fly of the order Diptera. The larvae of nonbiting midges (chironomids) may cause occupational asthma in those who handle fish foods. (See OCCUPATIONAL ASTHMA.)

migraine   See HEADACHE.

mildew   Fungal growth that coats any material susceptible to dampness. (See FUNGI AND MOLDS.)

military service and asthma   The correlation of armed forces' policies and candidates with asthma. Anyone who has had symptoms of asthma over the age of 12, whether symptoms still occur or not, may be excluded from the military academies. During Operations Desert Shield and Desert Storm, nearly 10% of admissions to a fleet hospital in Saudi Arabia were for asthma. Although 12 of the 94 patients did not have asthma, 51 needed to be evacuated from the country. Nearly half of the asthmatics displayed a gas-mask intolerance or phobia. The nerve-gas antidote pyridostigmine increased asthma symptoms in more than 25% of asthmatic patients. Desert sand storms triggered asthma in 34% of the patients.

milk   The nourishing fluid secreted by the mammary glands, or breasts, of female mammals. Although human milk is nonallergenic, allergens in the maternal diet may cause sensitization of the newborn. In these cases, mothers should avoid the suspect foods in their own diet.

Cow's milk is frequently substituted for human milk, and many infants develop allergies to one or more of its proteins. Seventy percent of babies with milk allergy have a positive family history of allergy. Beta-lactoglobulin is the most highly allergenic component of cow's milk. This sensitivity may be worsened by a secondary disaccharide intolerance, resulting in severe diarrhea. Vomiting may also occur. Damage to the tissues lining the intestines may result in malabsorption of lactose (milk sugar) and fat, resulting in malnutrition.

Milk-induced syndrome with pulmonary disease, also called Heiner's syndrome, is a lung disease associated with iron-deficiency anemia that is caused by allergy to cow's milk (see HEINER'S SYNDROME). The colic of infancy has often been blamed on milk, but this has not been proven. However, gastrointestinal bleeding from cow's milk occurs most frequently in infants as bloody diarrhea. Fortunately the condition improves within days with the withdrawal of milk from the diet, and most babies are able to tolerate milk within a few months. In older children, bleeding may not be readily apparent and, if prolonged, may result in considerable loss of blood. Subsequently, the children develop iron-deficiency anemia. This condition is thought to be related to the heat-labile cow's milk proteins. After avoidance of homogenized milk for a few years, individuals are usually able to resume milk consumption.

Hippocrates (460–370 B.C.) was among the first to report the adverse effects of cow's milk, including hives and gastrointestinal disorders. Galen (A.D. 131–210) described allergic reactions to goat's milk. Since 1905 there have been reports in the modern literature recognizing allergic responses to cow's milk. The true incidence of cow's milk allergy is unknown, but estimates range from one in 1,000 in the exposed population at any age to 10% of infants. However, these estimates include any adverse reaction—rashes, diarrhea, colic, rhinitis (runny nose), or wheezing. Many of these are attributed to allergy because no other mechanism has been found. As many as 25% of infants who also suffer from infantile eczema (see ATOPIC DERMATITIS) may have cow's milk allergy. As with most food allergy, the manifestations of cow's milk allergy diminish with age, and only the rare child will exhibit true milk allergy after age two.

Even persons highly allergic to cow's milk can usually eat beef or inhale cattle dander with no adverse effects. Although heat may denature some milk protein allergens, the opposite effect may occur in a process known as the "Browning reaction": the mild heating of milk in the presence of lactose (milk sugar) causes a modification of beta-lactoglobin, which increases the milk's allergenicity.

A chronic skin disorder, dermatitis herpetiformis, may respond to a milk-free diet in a small number of patients. In various studies, up to 30% of children with nasal congestion improved upon the withdrawal of milk from the diet. Symptoms recurred with a challenge test for milk allergy. Because of the high incidence of otitis media (middle ear infections) in children with nasal congestion, milk may be a factor.

Only trace amounts of milk-protein exposure may be needed to cause diarrhea. As with other food allergies, radioallergosorbent tests, or RAST, and prick skin tests (see RADIOALLERGOSORBENT TESTS, SKIN TESTS) may result in a positive reaction to milk. However, positive skin tests commonly occur in individuals who do not exhibit symptoms of allergy and therefore may be considered "false positives." False positive tests should be ignored if they do not correlate with symptoms.

In 1942, A. F. R. Andresen proposed food allergy, and especially milk, as a cause of ulcerative colitis. But this cause-and-effect relationship has not been proven. By far, the most common cause of milk-induced diarrhea in older children and adults is a deficiency in the intestinal enzyme lactase. Lactase aids in the digestion of lactose, or milk sugar, and lactose deficiency is not an allergic disorder (see LACTOSE INTOLERANCE). The colic of infancy is rarely improved by the elimination of milk from the diet, and food allergy is of doubtful importance in its treatment (see COLIC, INFANTILE).

Milk allergy may be associated with a deficiency in antibodies known as immunoglobulin A (IgA). Many persons with mild immunodeficiency disorder have antibodies to cow's milk in their circulation (see IMMUNOGLOBULIN A). The aspiration of cow's milk into the lungs during sleep has been proposed as a cause of sudden infant death syndrome (SIDS) because of higher-than-expected levels of antibodies to milk in studies with guinea pigs. However, the autopsy findings in the infant lungs did not suggest anaphylaxis as a cause of death. Milk may also be a cause of thrombocytopenia (low platelet count) in some infants.

Other conditions attributed to ingestion of milk that are not related to allergy may be caused by unpasteurized or spoiled milk. Cows may also graze on toxic weeds, although in the United States that possibility is remote. Persons who are extremely sensitive to penicillin or other antibiotics may react when exposed to milk from treated animals.

The protein in goat's milk is so similar to that of cows that it is not a good substitute. Soy-based infant formulas may also be allergenic. For the majority of milk-sensitive babies, hypoallergenic amino acid products prepared by enzymatic digestion of casein, known as protein hydrolysate formulas, are well tolerated. Nutramigen, Pregestimil, and Alimentum are such products, fortified with corn oil, sugar, starch, vitamins, and minerals (see HYDROLYSATE FORMULAS).

Milk-sensitive individuals, or their parents, must be aware of all products containing milk or milk by-products. Flexical and Vivonex are a source of elemental protein, carbohydrate, and fat in a totally allergy-free and easily digestible product. This formula is used for only the most highly allergic persons. Human breast milk ranks as the best alternative to cow's milk in the event of allergy to cow's milk. (See also BREAST-FEEDING AND PREVENTION OF ALLERGIES, FOOD ALLERGY.)

mites See HOUSE DUST MITES.

Mithradates VI Eupator Born in 132 B.C. in Greece, the son of Mithradates V, king of Pontus in Asia Minor (modern Turkey). Known as Eupator, or the Good Father, Mithradates VI succeeded his father to the throne. In addition to the great acclaim he enjoyed in his lifetime for his skills as hunter, warrior, strategist, ruler, and linguist, Mithradates VI is recognized for his study of poisons and his experimentation with acquiring immunity to poisons by ingesting minute amounts of them on a daily basis, and by so doing, rendering them harmless. In one unsuccessful experiment, Mithradates prepared a drink containing the blood of ducks who fed without consequence on plants known to be poisonous to humans. Mithradates did not understand the concept of oral tolerance, however, and this also foiled his attempted suicide by drinking poison.

mizolastine Antihistamine under investigation. (See ANTIHISTAMINE.)

mold allergy Symptoms of allergic rhinitis (hay fever) and asthma caused by the inhalation of indoor and outdoor fungal spores commonly called molds. Wind-borne pollen allergens and dry fungal spores are usually removed from the environmental air during rain. Therefore, allergy symptoms during periods of high humidity are most likely due to high mold spore counts found in clouds and mist. Few individuals are sensitive to fungal allergens alone, but fungal sensitivity is common. (See also FUNGI AND MOLDS.)

mometasone furoate An investigational topical nasal corticosteroid nasal spray that when used once a day has equal effectiveness of older twice-a-day products. It may prevent allergic nasal syptoms if begun prior to the onset of pollen seasons. The drug has a safety profile that did not differ from that of a placebo. (See also CORTICOSTEROID NASAL SPRAYS.)

monoclonal antibodies   Artificially produced antibodies that react with only one specific antigen. Each antibody-forming cell and its clones (a group of genetically identical cells) are created when a normal antibody-secreting lymphoid, or B cell, is fused with a myeloma cell of human or animal origin. The cells produced by this process are called hybridomas and can be reproduced indefinitely, whereas normal plasma cells die after a few cell divisions. Monoclonal antibodies are used in the diagnosis of various infectious diseases and the diagnosis and treatment of some types of cancer.

monosodium glutamate (MSG)   A flavor enhancer used frequently in the preparation of food. Many individuals report adverse effects from this food additive. Because of its wide use in Chinese food, reactions are often referred to as the "Chinese restaurant syndrome."

Studies by the Food and Drug Administration (FDA) have failed to confirm any serious ill effects from MSG, and it is considered a safe food ingredient.

Adverse reactions to MSG are not caused by an allergy to it. There are no confirmed reports of anaphylaxis (see ANAPHYLAXIS). However, some people experience skin flushing, tightening of muscles in the jaw and chest, nausea, or headache or a combination of these symptoms when eating a meal containing high concentrations of MSG.

A group known as "NO MSG" and some doctors have reported life-threatening reactions and brain injuries, but the FDA claims the reports are anecdotal and have not been scientifically substantiated.

In the form of a broth derived from the seaweed called "sea tangle," MSG has been used in Asia for at least 2,000 years. MSG is the sodium salt of glutamic acid, a naturally occurring amino acid. Glutamate, or glutamic acid, is a constituent of many food proteins, including cheese, meat, peas, mushrooms, and milk.

To enhance the taste of food, glutamate must be in a free form, that is, unbound to other amino acids. MSG can be purchased as a fine, white crystal substance in food markets and has no taste of its own. It is thought that MSG stimulates taste buds on the tongue to enhance the flavor of foods. The Japanese attribute the powers of MSG to a fifth basic taste, different from salty, sweet, sour, and bitter, which they call *umami*, from their word for "deliciousness."

The FDA plans labeling requirements to include the phrase "contains glutamate" for food containing MSG.

morphine   See DRUG ALLERGY AND OTHER ADVERSE DRUG REACTIONS.

moth   An insect of the order Lepidoptera, typically recognizable by its antennae, wings, and dull coloring (as opposed to butterflies), whose larvae are plant-eating caterpillars. Silkworm moths and Douglas fir tussock moths may be implicated in occupational allergies for silk industry workers, individuals who raise moth larvae for fish bait, and others.

mucormycosis   See ZYGOMYCOSIS.

mucosal tests   Diagnostic tests for bacteria and other harmful microorganisms in mucus.

mucus   See MEMBRANE, MUCOUS.

mumps vaccine   See MEASLES, MUMPS, AND RUBELLA (MMR) VIRUS VACCINE, LIVE, ALLERGIC REACTIONS.

mushroom   A fungus of the class Basidiomycetes, some of which are edible and some poisonous. The poisonous varieties are commonly called toadstools. Mushrooms grow in woods and damp areas. They are rarely a source of ingested allergy, but when their reproductive spores are inhaled, they can cause respiratory symptoms. (See FUNGI AND MOLDS.)

mushroom worker's lung disease   See HYPERSENSITIVITY PNEUMONITIS.

mycoderma   Mucous membrane. (See MEM-BRANE, MUCOUS.)

mycoses, systemic   See FUNGAL DISEASES, SYSTEMIC.

myths about allergies and asthma   Old wives' tales and ill-founded theories concerning individuals who have allergies or asthma. For example:

- **Myth**: Some think of asthma as strictly an emotional disorder, or asthma is "all in your head."
  Truth: While emotional stress can certainly trigger an asthma attack, it is not the cause of asthma (see ASTHMA).
- **Myth**: Children outgrow asthma.
  Truth: Some children do seem to lose their allergic and asthma symptoms upon reaching puberty. However, usually the more severely afflicted the children, the more likely they will continue to suffer symptoms during adolescence and adulthood (see GROWING OUT OF ALLERGIES AND ASTHMA).
- **Myth**: People with asthma should move to another part of the country, especially to Arizona.
  Truth: Some individuals do find relief by moving to a different climate, but unfortunately the immune response to allergens does not change. Arizona, once thought to be a safe haven for asthmatics, has severe pollen exposures both from unique native allergens and those imported by persons immigrating to the area. Moves by individuals whose symptoms are triggered by high humidity and molds or cold air may benefit from a move to a warm, dry climate. There is no way to predict if exposure to new environmental allergens will result in symptoms in allergic individuals.
- **Myth**: Petting a Chihuahua does not trigger asthma.
  Truth: No species of dog is truly nonallergenic, because allergens are present in the skin, saliva, and urine, something all dogs have in common. There are some persons who seem to tolerate one species or an individual dog, but upon continuing exposure, they will more than likely develop symptoms of dog allergy (see DOG ALLERGY).
- **Myth**: Asthma is not fatal.
  Truth: Asthma deaths have actually increased in the past decade. In 1980 there were 2,891 asthma deaths, and in 1988 there were 4,580, according to data from the National Institutes of Health (see ASTHMA DEATHS).
- **Myth**: Asthma does not require medical treatment.
  Truth: Even the mildest cases of asthma require close monitoring and regular follow-up because many persons with asthma require drugs to prevent inflammation and damage to the lungs. Unfortunately, asthma is often undertreated because of the misguided and unrealistic fear of ingesting "foreign" substances (drugs, medications). The best time to treat an asthma attack is before it happens. Medications can sometimes be avoided in the mildest cases of asthma, largely by avoiding asthma triggers such as furry pets, pollens, or cold air (see TRIGGERS OF ALLERGIES AND ASTHMA), but such measures are either too restrictive or impossible. Drugs commonly used to treat asthma are much safer than having an asthma attack. (See BETA-ADRENERGIC AGONISTS.)
- **Myth**: More left-handed people have asthma than right-handed people.
  Truth: Unproven. Limited studies have shown that incidences of asthma in both left-handed and ambidextrous individuals are not statistically different from right-handedness.
- **Myth**: Theophylline (a bronchodilating drug) causes learning disabilities.
  Truth: Theophylline is generally well tolerated in children, although there may be

minor irritability and other minor adverse effects in some adults and children. Studies have demonstrated normal school performance in students with asthma taking theophylline on a daily basis when compared with nonasthmatic children. (See THEOPHYLLINE.)

- **Myth**: Antihistamines should not be taken by people with asthma.

  Truth: Antihistamines are recognized as safe and effective for the treatment of allergies associated with asthma by asthma experts despite warning labels on the packages of many of these drugs against their use in asthmatic patients. (See ANTIHISTAMINE.)

[Authors' note: Questions suggested by the above myths are often raised by well-meaning but uneducated friends and relatives. It is essential for persons with allergies and asthma to get the scientifically proven or disproven facts. Physicians who are members of the American College of Allergy and Immunology, the American Academy of Allergy and Immunology, or the American Thoracic Society or lay support groups such as the Asthma and Allergy Foundation or Mothers of Asthmatics (see Appendix IV for a more complete list of organizations) can be helpful in providing information that is both factual and accessible.]

myxasthenia   Insufficient production of mucus, which may aggravate respiratory disorders such as asthma.

myxiosis   A secretion of mucus.

N

nail-mending kits Cosmetic products used to repair broken fingernails that may contain acrylic adhesives, known to cause allergic rashes and eye irritation. Nail extenders containing methyl methacrylate monomer were banned in 1974 by the Food and Drug Administration because of severe reactions that in rare cases destroyed the nail bed, prohibiting regrowth of the nails. (See CONTACT DERMATITIS.)

nail polish Nail polish contains many dyes and chemicals, some of which may cause allergic skin rashes, especially to the eyelids and neck, and local irritation of the nail area. Nail-polish remover, usually acetone and other chemicals, including lanolin (an allergenic substance), has been reported to cause tightness in the chest upon inhalation of nail-polish remover fumes. Fake nails are composed of resins and acrylic glues that may also cause allergic rashes.

naphazoline A decongestant drug used in eyedrops and nose drops and sprays including the over-the-counter products Clear Eyes, Naphcon-A, 4-Way Nasal Spray, and Privine.

Naphcon-A See NAPHAZOLINE.

naphthalene A derivative of coal tar used in the manufacture of antiseptics, dyes, lubricants, and solvents and as a moth repellent (mothballs) that can cause allergic skin reactions.

naphthol A coal tar derivative found in antiseptics, hair dyes, and products used to treat eczema, psoriasis, and ringworm that is known to be a cause of allergic skin reactions and may worsen symptoms it is supposed to alleviate.

narcotics See DRUG ALLERGY AND OTHER ADVERSE DRUG REACTIONS.

Nasacort, Nasacort AQ Nasal Spray Brand of the cortisone-like anti-inflammatory drug triamcinolone.

nasal challenge [nasal provocation tests] Diagnostic allergy tests involving either inhalation or direct mucosal contact with a suspected allergenic substance. The tests are occasionally helpful when allergy skin-test results do not correlate with a person's medical and allergy history. When performing a nasal challenge, the physician must carefully observe the patient for signs of a systemic reaction. The patient should be relatively free of allergic symptoms and must not have taken antihistaminic drugs for the past several days. Positive challenge results are indicated by itching, sneezing, watery discharge from the nose, and swelling of the nasal mucosa. In some cases, the tests fall short because they are time-consuming and because only one allergen at a time can be tested; in addition, if nasal symptoms are already present, the test may not be valid.

nasal congestion Swelling of the nasal passages, which is a symptom of allergic rhinitis (hay fever), vasomotor (nonallergic) rhinitis, upper respiratory infections (colds), and rhinitis medicomentosum (rebound congestion caused by abuse of nasal sprays). Complications of nasal congestion include sinus and ear infections and worsening of asthma. Decongestants are the main treatment of nasal congestions; however, antihistamines and the preventive nasal sprays cromolyn and corticosteroids are useful for allergic patients.

Nasalcrom See CROMOLYN SODIUM.

nasal endoscopy See RHINOSCOPY.

Nasalide See FLUNISOLIDE.

nasal irrigation A procedure that helps rid the nasal passages of excess mucus and bacteria. Saline (salt water) is available from local pharmacies or can be made fresh daily at home with one teaspoonful of table salt and a pinch of baking soda in one pint of warm water. Many proprietary brands (Ocean Spray and Salinex are examples) are available as nasal sprays.

Saline irrigations should be done before using other medications in the nose. One may inhale or "snuff" the saline solution from the palm of the hand or squirt it into the nose with a rubber ear syringe.

nasal obstruction   Blockage of the nasal passages either uni- or bilaterally. The most common cause of unilateral stuffiness is a deviated septum, which may be a congenital deformity or a result of trauma to the nose. It can be surgically corrected by rhinoplasty ("nose job") if the obstruction is severe. In babies, a frequent cause of obstruction is a foreign body, a tiny object such as a button or a piece of a toy. Unilateral nasal obstruction may also indicate benign or malignant tumors, which should be discovered by the physician.

nasal polyp   See POLYP, NASAL.

nasal provocation tests   See NASAL CHALLENGE.

nasal secretions   Mucus discharge from the nose that is characterized by quantity (none, minimal, moderate, or profuse), consistency (none, thin, mucoid, or crusted), and color (colorless, clear, white, or colored). The description aids the diagnosis of allergy, infection, or other anomaly.

nasal smear   A screening test used to diagnose nasal symptoms. Nasal secretions are obtained by blowing the nose into waxed paper and transferring the collected material to a glass slide. Hansel's or Wright's stain is applied to the slide, which is examined microscopically for leukocytes, or white blood cells, such as eosinophils and polymorphonuclear leukocytes, or polys. Allergic diseases may be present if eosinophils account for 10% or greater of the total white cells observed on a nasal smear. A predominance of polys suggests an infection, and absence of a significant number of cells suggests vasomotor, or nonallergic, rhinitis.

nasal spray   Nebulizer or aerosol used to treat excessive nasal discharge and congestion characteristic of hay fever, colds, or other nasal disorders. Nasal sprays include over-the-counter decongestants. However, many individuals quickly develop tolerance, or loss of effectiveness, to these sprays, which leads to a worsening of congestion referred to as rebound. The rebound phenomenon is called rhinitis medicomentosum.

Saline solution is used to irrigate dry, inflamed nasal passages but has no therapeutic effect to prevent discharge or congestion. The prescription drugs cromolyn sodium and corticosteroids (cortisone derivatives) are effective for the long-term prevention of allergy symptoms. (See CORTICOSTEROID NASAL SPRAYS, CROMOLYN SODIUM, RHINITIS MEDICOMENT-OSUM.)

nasal spray habituation   See RHINITIS MEDICOMENTOSUM.

nasal turbinates   Four bony structures arising from the nasal septum. The two most important ones are the inferior and middle turbinates. The turbinates are lined with cells similar to those in the tracheobronchial tube and regulate airflow into the upper respiratory system. (See also NOSE.)

nasopharynx   Part of the nose that extends to the portion of the throat located above the soft palate, or postnasal space. Nasopharyngitis, an inflammation of this passage, may occur in conjunction with postnasal drip and allergic rhinitis.

nasopulmonary reflex   The occurrence of wheezing when only the nasal passages are exposed to triggers such as allergens or irritants. Scientists have debated this reaction and attempted to prove its presence for many years without success.

nasosinusitis   See SINUSITIS.

National Asthma and Allergy Poster Child
A contest sponsored annually since 1983 by the Asthma and Allergy Foundation of America

(AAFA). The foundation selects a child who has a documented history of asthma and allergies as well as certain qualities, such as an outgoing personality. This child represents the hopes of millions of others who find ways to overcome their illness.

National Asthma Education Program A series of guidelines on asthma diagnosis and management, asthma in pregnancy, and others developed by the National Heart, Lung, and Blood Institute (NHLBI) of the National Institutes of Health, under director Claude Lenfant, M.D. The purpose of the program is to reduce morbidity and mortality from asthma through awareness. In 1991, the NHLBI released a document entitled *Expert Panel Report: Guidelines for the Diagnosis and Management of Asthma.*

Physicians are instructed to encourage patients by raising their expectations and goals. The National Asthma Education Program published a second document in the fall of 1992 entitled *Management of Asthma during Pregnancy.*

National Cooperative Inter-City Asthma Study A five-year project begun in February 1991 by the National Institute of Allergy and Infectious Diseases of the National Institutes of Health. The study is being conducted at eight institutions in seven U.S. cities. It is known that the seriousness of asthma is related to many factors, but it is not yet known to what degree access to and quality of care are responsible for the differences in severity of asthma in children residing in urban environments.

Initially those involved in the study will attempt to identify factors related to increased symptoms and death from asthma in urban populations.

The second phase of the study focuses on a comprehensive approach to reduce the events thought to be responsible for a poor prognosis. This segment encompasses therapeutic measures, education, and environmental in-

NATIONAL ASTHMA AND ALLERGY POSTER CHILD CONTEST RULES

- Candidates may be of either gender, between the ages of nine and 14 years, with documented histories of asthma and allergies.
- Candidates should be outgoing, articulate, and personable. It is helpful if they have appeared before groups of people, but this is not mandatory.
- The candidate to be selected and his or her parent(s) must be able and willing to travel to participate in AAFA-sponsored events.

For more information and an application, contact your nearest AAFA chapter, or call the AAFA national information line at 1-800-7ASTHMA.

PAST NATIONAL POSTER CHILDREN

1993	Amanda Johnston, Portland, Oregon
1991–92	Chris Dulman, Michigan
1990	Jennifer Carol Price, Midland, Texas
1989	Chele Williams, Newport News, Virginia
1987–88	Scott Halverson, Omaha, Nebraska
1986	Jamie Noland, Ft. Collins, Colorado
1985	Ann Cordrey, Cincinnati, Ohio
1984	Reggie Smith, Baltimore, Maryland
1983	Lanny Bert Powell, Greenville, South Carolina

GOALS OF THE NATIONAL ASTHMA EDUCATION PROGRAM

1. Maintain normal (or near to normal) lung function tests.
2. Maintain normal activity levels, including exercise.
3. Prevent chronic and troublesome symptoms.
4. Prevent frequent acute attacks.
5. Avoid adverse effects from asthma medi ations.

tervention to improve factors identified as major contributors to the problem.

National Jewish Center for Immunology and Respiratory Medicine   A nonprofit, nonsectarian institution founded in 1899 for the treatment of patients of all ages with severe lung ailments, allergic conditions, and other immune system disorders. Formerly the National Jewish Hospital/National Asthma Center, the facility is also a training center for physicians and medical researchers.

Natural Red Dye No. 4   See CARMINE.

"natural way" to control asthma   The option of home remedies to treat asthma, or the myth that asthma does not require drugs for treatment. (See MYTHS ABOUT ALLERGIES AND ASTHMA.)

neat's-foot oil   A fat derived from boiling the feet and shinbones of cattle and used as a lubricant in cream and lotion preparations and as a waterproofing agent and dressing for leather. Neat's-foot oil may cause allergic reactions.

nebulizer [atomizer]   A device that produces a fine spray used to deliver allergy and asthma drugs to the nasal passages or lungs.

nedocromil sodium (Tilade)   A preventive allergy and asthma anti-inflammatory drug approved for use in the United States in 1993. Although nedocromil has properties similar to those of cromolyn (see CROMOLYN SODIUM), its effectiveness may be apparent within hours; however, it may take two weeks of regular dosage to realize its full potential. Cromolyn may require several months to realize benefits. Nedocromil may also be needed only twice a day, whereas cromolyn requires use three to four times a day.

Similar to cromolyn, nedocromil does not interact with other asthma drugs, such as theophylline, and will be available as a metered-dose inhaler. This drug works for children and adults. A solution for aerosol nebulizers, a nasal spray, and eyedrops may also become available. There are no significant adverse effects to the product, although slightly more than 10% of patients complain of an unpleasant taste.

neomycin sensitivity   Allergic reaction to the antibiotic neomycin, which is used in deodorants and topical creams and ointments to treat minor skin infections. Approximately one out of 100 persons will develop a swollen, red rash that disappears when the drug is discontinued or the rash is treated with corticosteroids. (See CONTACT DERMATITIS.)

Neo-Synephrine   See PHENYLEPHRINE HYDROCHLORIDE.

nervous system disorders and their relationship to allergies   Psychiatric disorders (including schizophrenia, neurosis, and depression), headaches, attention deficit disorders, hyperactivity, and tension-fatigue syndrome frequently blamed on food sensitivities. Most of these claims have been disproved by well-controlled, double-blind scientific studies. However, some migraine headaches are triggered by certain foods, and other headaches are caused by caffeine and other potent chemicals. (See HEADACHE.)

nettle rash   An itchy skin rash resulting from contact with nettles, stinging or prickly plants.

neurodermatitis   An itchy skin inflammation that may be caused by emotional disturbance. Disseminated neurodermatitis, a chronic form of neurodermatitis, can be inherited, usually in families with a history of allergy. It may be confused with eczema and other skin conditions.

neutrophils [polymorphonuclear leukocytes (PMNs), polys, segs]   White blood cells, classified as granulocytes, that normally account for 60 to 70% of the total white cell count in the circulating blood of adults. Neutrophils are produced by the bone marrow, which increases their production in response to an infection.

These circulating cells travel to infected tissues where they act as phagocytes, engulfing bacteria. After destroying the bacteria, these cells disintegrate and form pus, a collection of dead neutrophils, bacteria, and tissue.

nickel allergy A rash from contact with the metal nickel, frequently used as an alloy in jewelry. Nickel sulfate is also used in astringents, hair dyes, and nickel plating. (See CONTACT DERMATITIS.)

Nicoderm See NICOTINE PATCHES.

Nicorette See NICOTINE GUM.

nicotine gum (Nicorette) Chewing product containing nicotine that allows smokers to gradually reduce their dependency on the addicting substance in tobacco while avoiding withdrawal symptoms such as irritability and chest pains. (See also NICOTINE PATCHES.)

nicotine patches (Habitrol, Nicoderm, Nicotrol, Pro Step) Band-Aid–like adhesive delivery system containing the drug nicotine. The patch is placed on the skin of smokers as a means to stop smoking. Nicotine is the addicting substance in tobacco. The patches contain varying amounts of nicotine, and doses are gradually tapered, usually in two or three steps, to avoid the withdrawal symptoms of nicotine. The adhesive in the patch frequently causes an allergic contact rash. Some individuals are not sensitive to all brands of nicotine patches; if one brand causes a rash, another brand may be tried. (See also NICOTINE GUM.)

Nicotrol See NICOTINE PATCHES.

nitric acid An oxidizing agent in hair coloring products and other cosmetics whose fumes may cause choking and, with prolonged exposure, bronchitis. Nitric acid also may irritate skin.

nitrogen dioxide An environmental pollutant present in the atmosphere that has been associated with an increased incidence of lung disease following prolonged exposure in homes and workplaces.

nitrous oxide [laughing gas] A colorless, sweet-tasting, pleasantly aromatic gas used as a light general anesthetic, especially by dentists. In high doses, nitrous oxide may cause asphyxiation. Use of a local anesthetic agent such as lidocaine is probably safer in patients with asthma. (See ANESTHESIA, GENERAL, FOR THE ALLERGIC AND ASTHMATIC PATIENT.)

N.K.A. An abbreviation for "no known allergies" in medical charts.

nocturnal asthma The occurrence of symptoms of asthma during the night. Nearly 40% of asthmatics experience nightly symptoms; approximately 64% have episodes three nights a week, and about 75% at least one night per week. Asthma attacks seem to occur most often between 10 P.M. and 7 A.M., peaking at about 4 A.M. When several things simultaneously trigger asthma, results can be severe. The most devastating asthma attacks that lead to respiratory arrest and possibly death most often occur between midnight and 6 A.M.

During sleep, mucus secretions accumulate in the bronchial tubes, and the backup, or reflux, of stomach acid (see GASTROINTESTINAL REFLUX AND ASTHMA) may spill over into the lungs, causing irritation and inflammation of lung tissue.

The circadian fall (see CIRCADIAN RHYTHM) in the body's production of cortisone and adrenaline and the rise of other chemicals, such as histamine, further worsen the situation during the night. In addition, the cell counts of neutrophils and eosinophils (cells that release mediators of inflammation) are higher in patients with nocturnal asthma symptoms. Timing medications to coincide with peak effectiveness and times of greatest need can greatly reduce symptoms and allow patients to sleep through the night. (See ASTHMA.)

nonallergenic pollinating plants See ENTOMOPHILOUS PLANTS.

nonallergic food adverse reactions   See FOOD ADDITIVES, FOOD ALLERGY.

nonoxynol-9 spermacide (Semicid, Today Vaginal Sponge)   A sperm-killing agent used intravaginally that is generally safe, but local irritation affecting either partner may be the result of an inactive perfume ingredient. Choosing a similar product with different ingredients may alleviate the reaction. The spermacidal sponge product may cause toxic shock syndrome if not removed within 24 hours.

nonsteroidal anti-inflammatory drugs (NSAIDs)   Arthritis and painkilling medications closely related to aspirin in effectiveness and adverse effects. (See ASPIRIN SENSITIVITY.)

Noon, Leonard   British physiologist and immunologist (1877–1913) whose research on immunity, the nature of toxins and antitoxins of tetanus, and pollen extracts has had an enduring impact on modern treatment of hay fever. Noon believed that injections of pollen extracts resulted in an individual's ability to develop pollen antitoxin in his or her system and therefore an immunity to adverse reactions to pollen.

Noon graduated from Cambridge University and later worked as assistant in the Innoculation (*sic*) Department of St. Mary's Hospital (now the Wright-Fleming Institute) in London. Noon erroneously attributed the effects of hay fever from pollens to toxins, but he died before he could finish his experimentation. His colleague John Freeman carried on his work on hay fever. (See FREEMAN, JOHN.)

nose   One of the chief organs of the respiratory system through which air flows into and out of the body. The external portion of the nose is made of a triangle of cartilage (the top of which constitutes the bridge of the nose, where the two nasal bones are joined) and skin-covered bone lined with mucous membrane. The internal portion contains two chambers divided by a septum. The chambers lead to various sinuses.

The nose is also an olfactory organ that facilitates the sense of smell and warms, moistens, and filters air breathed in. Physicians may observe a patient's nose for its size, shape, color, evidence of injury, discharge, tenderness over sinuses, and interferences with breathing. For example, a chronically red nose caused by dilated blood vessels may be a result of alcoholism, acne, boils, or digestive disorders. An offensive discharge may indicate local infection, cavities in the teeth, a cold, or an impacted foreign body. A chronic, clear, watery discharge usually suggests the presence of allergy. Rhinitis refers to inflammation of the nasal mucous membrane; allergic rhinitis refers to seasonal allergy such as hay fever.

Nostril   See PHENYLEPHRINE HYDROCHLORIDE.

NSAIDS   See NONSTEROIDAL ANTI-INFLAMMATORY DRUGS.

nut   Hard-shelled dry fruit or seed of plant origin, including almond, Brazil nut, cashew, chestnut, hazelnut, hickory, macadamia, pecan, pistachio, and walnut. Peanuts are legumes and not true nuts (see PEANUT). The kernel, or meaty portion, of most edible nuts is rich in protein and fat; a few are high in starch. In many parts of the world, nuts and nut-containing foods make up a substantial part of the diet.

However, nuts are highly allergenic to some individuals and are among the most common causes of severe, at times fatal, anaphylactic reactions. (See also FOOD ALLERGY.)

nutmeg   An aromatic spice derived from the seed of the nutmeg, the fruit of the tree *Myristica fragrans*. Used as a flavoring in cola beverages, vermouth, eggnog, baked goods, ice cream, pickles, condiments, icings, candies, and meats, nutmeg has been known to cause contact dermatitis and other symptoms.

Nutrasweet   Brand of the artificial sweetener aspartame. (See ASPARTAME.)

nutrition   The study of the foods, vitamins, and minerals necessary to assure growth, maintenance, and repair of body tissues. As early as the 12th century, the physician Maimonides counseled the importance of good diet for individuals with asthma, but he recognized that diet alone was not a cure for this disorder (see MAIMONIDES). Experiments with various dietary substances such as fish oil have not clinically improved the course of asthma.

Ascorbic acid (vitamin C) has been demonstrated to be a very mild bronchodilator, though insufficient to control asthma. Some researches believe individuals with asthma may be deficient in pyridoxine (vitamin B_6); this has not been confirmed, and excessive doses of the vitamin may have serious adverse effects.

Asthmatic patients dependent on corticosteroids should acquire a sufficient dietary supply of calcium and vitamin D, which may help prevent osteoporosis. (See also CORTICOSTEROIDS.)

nylon   A tough, elastic synthetic fiber widely used in textiles, plastics, stockings, and mascara and other cosmetics that may cause allergic reactions in hypersensitive individuals.

O

obesity   See HYPOVENTILATION SYN-
DROME, PICKWICKIAN SYNDROME.

obstructive lung disease, chronic   See
CHRONIC OBSTRUCTIVE PULMONARY DISEASE.

occupational allergens   Substances capable of eliciting a type I, or immediate, hypersensitivity reaction in allergic individuals
whose exposure is in the workplace.

(See also ALLERGENS, CONTACT DERMATITIS,
OCCUPATIONAL ASTHMA.)

occupational asthma   Shortness of breath,
coughing, wheezing, and other symptoms of
asthma from exposure to sensitizing substances found in the workplace. These substances may be allergens (see OCCUPATIONAL

ALLERGENS), or they may be nonallergic or toxic
substances, such as ammonia, chlorine, smoke,
or other noxious fumes that inflame the lungs
of workers accidentally exposed to them.

History   As early as the second century A.D.,
miners covered themselves with clothing as
protection from dust. In 1713, Bernardino
Ramazzini, considered to be the father of industrial or occupational medicine, recommended in his book, *De Morbis Artificum
Diatriba*, inquiry into a patient's occupation
when he discovered attacks of shortness of
breath in sifters and millers exposed to grain
dust. Ramazzini described asthma as an occupational hazard in individuals who "are short
of breath and cachectic and rarely reach old
age." In 1877, the term *byssinosis* was coined for

OCCUPATIONAL EXPOSURES TO ALLERGENS IN THE WORKPLACE

Occupation	Substance
animal handlers in laboratories, farms, pet shops, zoos, and veterinary practices	animal dander, pelts, saliva, urine, feathers (proteins from rats, mice, cats, dogs, horses, birds, etc.)
automobile painters	dimethyl ethanolamine toluene diisocyanate
bakers	wheat protein
beauticians	persulfate (henna)
bookbinders, postal workers	glue (fish)
entomologists	insects
farmers, dairy	storage mites
farmers, soy	soy bean dust
farmers, poultry, and poultry workers	poultry mites, droppings, feathers, and amprolium
florists, gardeners, botanists	pollens or plants
food and beverage workers	castor bean, egg, green coffee bean mushroom, pepsin
pharmaceutical industry workers	penicillin and other antibiotics, methyl dopa, ipecac, piperazine, salbutamol, psyllium, cimetidine, sulfonechloramides
plastics industry workers	hog trypsin
printers	acacia, arabic, tragacanth gums
rubber-processing workers	formaldehyde, ethylene diamine phthalic anhydride
seafood processors, bait handlers	crustaceans, mealworm, mollusks
sewage treatment workers	sewer fly, crustaceans, mealworm, mollusks
welders	stainless steel fumes

ALLERGENS KNOWN TO CAUSE OCCUPATIONAL ASTHMA

Allergen	Classification
abirukana	plant
acacia	gum (printing)
adipic acid	chemical
African maple	plant
African zebra wood	plant
Alternaria	fungi
aluminum fluoride	metal
aminoethyl ethanolamine	soldering fluxes
aminophylline	drug
ammonium persulfate	chemical
amprolium hydrochloride	drug (poultry food additive)
animals, laboratory	animal proteins (dander, saliva, urine)
apple tree mite	arthropod
arabic	gum (printing)
aspergillus	fungi
azobisformamide	dye
azodicarbonamide	dye
Baby's breath	plant (florist industry)
Bacillus subtilis enzymes	biologic enzymes (used in the manufacture of detergents)
bee moth	arthropod
bromelain	plant enzyme (used in the food industry)
buckwheat	food
butterflies	arthropod
California redwood	plant
carmine	dye
carmine beetle	arthropod
castor beans	food (manufacture of castor oil)
cats	mammal
cattle	mammal
cedar of Lebanon	plant
Central American walnut	plant
cephalosporins	drugs
chromates	metal
chrysanthemum	plant
cibachrome brilliant scarlet	dye
cimetidine	drug
cinnamon	food
cobalt	metal
cocabolla	plant
cockroaches	arthropod
coffee beans	food
colophony (pine resin, or abietic acid)	soldering fluxes
cotton[1]	plant

ALLERGENS KNOWN TO CAUSE OCCUPATIONAL ASTHMA (continued)

Allergen	Classification
crickets	arthropod
crop storage mites	arthropod
cyanoacrylate	chemical
Daphnia	arthropod
diastase	plant enzyme (used in the pharmaceutical industry)
dichloramine	drug
diisocyanates	catalyst hardener
dimethyl ethanolamine	catalyst hardener
dioazonium salt	chemical
dogs	mammal
Douglas fir tussock moth	arthropod
Drimaren brilliant blue and yellow	dyes
eastern white cedar	plant
electrocardiography ink	chemical
endofluorane anesthetic	drug
ethylenediamine	chemical
feathers	bird
flaviastase	biologic enzyme
flax	drug
fluoride, fluorine	chemical
formaldehyde	chemical
Freon	chemical
fungal amylase	fungi
fungal food products	fungi
furan base resin	chemical
garlic	food
gentian powder	drug
glue	fish
gluteraldehyde	chemical
grain dust[1]	food
grain dust mite	arthropod
grain field fungi	fungi
grain weevil	arthropod
guinea pigs	mammal
hemp[1]	plant
hexachlorophene	drug
hexahydrophthalic anhydride	catalyst hardener
hog trypsin	manufacture of plastics
hops	food
horses	mammal
housefly maggots	arthropod
hoya (sea squirt)	invertebrates
humidifiers	water (contaminated)
ipecac	drug

ALLERGENS KNOWN TO CAUSE OCCUPATIONAL ASTHMA (continued)

Allergen	Classification
iroko	plant
ispaghula	drug
karaya	gum (food)
kejaat	plant
lanau	plant
Levafix brilliant yellow	dye
locusts	arthropod
lycopodium	drug
magnolia	plant
mahogany	plant
maiko	food
mayfly	arthropod
mealworm	arthropod
methyldopa	drug
methyl methcrylate	chemical
Mexican bean weevil	arthropod
mice	mammal
midges	arthropod (fish food)
mother of pearl	invertebrates
mulberry	plant
mushroom spores	fungi
nickel salts	metal
oak	plant
organophosphate	chemical (insecticide)
oyster shells	invertebrates
pancreatic (extract) enzyme	biologic enzyme/drug
papain	biologic enzyme/drug/food (meal tenderizer)
parakeets	birds
paraphenylenediamine	dye
pectinase	plant enzyme (used in the food industry)
penicillins	drug
pepsin	biologic enzyme
persulfate and henna	dye
phenylene glycine acid chloride	drug
phthalic anhydride	catalyst hardener
pigeons	birds
piperazine dihydrochloride	drug
platinum salts	metal
Plexiglas dust	chemical
polyetheralcohol	soldering fluxes
polypropylene glycol	soldering fluxes
polyvinyl chloride	chemical
poultry mites	arthropod
prawns	arthropod

ALLERGENS KNOWN TO CAUSE OCCUPATIONAL ASTHMA (continued)

Allergen	Classification
protease bromelain	biologic enzyme
psyllium	drug
quillaja ramin	plant (gum), manufacture of saponin
rabbits	mammal
rats	mammal
salbutamol intermediate	drug
screwworm fly	arthropod
sheep	mammal
silkworm moths and larvae	arthropod
sky blue	dye
snow crab	arthropod
South African boxwood	plant
soya bean	food
spiramycin	drug
sponge	invertebrates
stainless steel	metal
strawberry pollen	food
styrene	chemical
sugar beet	food
sulfathiazole	drug
sulfone chloramide (Chloramine-T and halazone)	drug (used to purify water)
sunflower	plant
tamarind	food
Tanganyika aningre	plant
tannic acid	chemical
tea dust	food
tetrachlorophthalic	catalyst hardener
tetracycline	drug
tobacco	plant
toluene diisocyanate	catalyst hardener
tragacanth	gum (printing)
triethyl tetramine	chemical
trimellitic anhydride	catalyst hardener
tungsten carbide	metal
urea formaldehyde	chemical
vanadium zinc	metal
welding fumes	metal
western red cedar dust (plicatic acid)	plant/chemical
wheat flour	food

[1]Cotton, hemp, and grain dust are irritants and not true allergens.

asthma in cotton workers, and in 1911 platinum salt exposure was recognized as a cause of asthma in photographic workers. More recently British physician Jack Peppys stimulated interest in this problem in the 1960s.

Prevalence It is estimated that 2 to 15% of all asthma cases are caused by occupational or workplace exposure. Up to 44% of bakery workers and up to 10% of persons exposed to laboratory animals have symptoms. In Japan, an estimated 15% of asthma cases in males may be from industrial exposure. In some industries, very few workers develop symptoms, but in others, large numbers are affected. For example, nearly 100% of workers exposed to platinum salts for at least five years develop at least some symptoms.

Cause of occupational asthma More than 200 substances have been reported to cause occupational asthma, and the list continues to grow. To cause an immediate immune response, a substance must have a molecular weight exceeding 1,000 daltons, with most weighing more than 20,000. These allergens are proteins or glycoproteins, including animal proteins, biologic enzymes, grain dust, or irritants such as dusts, gases, or fumes, that cause early or immediate onset of symptoms and are relatively easy to correlate with exposure.

Lower-molecular-weight allergens (irritants of less than 1,000 daltons), such as andrides, diisocyanates, formalin, Freon, metals, pharmaceuticals such as penicillin dust, solder fluxes, urea formaldehyde, and wood dust, usually cause late-phase responses; symptoms may not be evident for many hours after exposure.

High-molecular-weight compounds cause a true allergic reaction. The worker inhales the allergen, which stimulates the immune system to produce immunoglobulin E (IgE) antibodies (see IMMUNOGLOBULIN E). The antibodies then become attached to structures called receptors on immune cells (mast cells and basophils) in the body tissues. After a person has been sensitized in this manner, subsequent exposures to the same allergen cause a reaction between the allergen and its corresponding antibody, which results in the rupturing of these cells and the release of chemicals such as histamine. The released chemicals cause the allergic response or symptoms. Most of the lower-molecular-weight substances fail to elicit such a response, although they do cause similar symptoms to occur via other mechanisms.

Many of the substances responsible for occupational asthma can also be encountered outside the workplace, and materials can be transported outside the original areas of contact on clothing or in the hair or on the skin of workers. They can also pollute the surrounding environment.

Common fungal and bacterial species may contaminate air-conditioning units and water-cooled machinery, causing an infectious pneumonia such as Legionnaire's disease, or the allergic-type hypersensitivity pneumonitis (see HYPERSENSITIVITY PNEUMONITIS).

Other occupational exposures include the inhalation of iron particles in dust or fumes, resulting in siderosis, also called arc-welder's disease, or hemosiderosis, a pneumonialike lung disease. Tributyl tin oxide (TBTO) is an organic compound contained in a carpet deodorizer that is a suspected cause of asthma. TBTO is also used in the manufacture of plastics, silicone, and paint products and is an antifungal agent in paper. This substance can also cause an irritant dermatitis.

Talc triggers occupational asthma by acting as an irritant. In the 1970s and 1980s, the *Bacillus subtilis* enzyme added to detergents became an important cause of allergic symptoms in workers as well as consumers. Hog trypsin used in the plastics industry is another industrial allergen. Castor bean allergy not only may affect factory workers, but neighboring inhabitants may become sensitized by exposure to smoke from castor oil factories. Smoking is a complicating factor because of its influence on increasing airway reactivity.

Symptoms Accompanying the asthma resulting from allergen exposure in the workplace is a latent, or waiting, period between the initial exposure and the onset of symptoms. Often symptoms do not appear for several weeks or take several years to appear. Only about 20% of those exposed to occupational allergens develop allergy. Once symptoms occur, they usually become progressively more severe with continued exposure. If exposure is stopped soon enough, symptoms will usually cease unless a person is reexposed. However, if exposure is prolonged, symptoms of asthma may become persistent even after exposure is terminated. Conjunctivitis, or inflammation of the eyes (commonly called "pink eye"), may be the earliest symptom of allergen or irritant exposure in the workplace. Rhinitis, or runny nose, may also be an early sign. Wheezing, coughing, and shortness of breath can occur within minutes of exposure or not until later in the day or even 24 to 48 hours afterward. The later onset of symptoms often makes diagnosis or proof of cause difficult (see LATE-PHASE ALLERGIC REACTIONS). A valuable clue to the existence of workplace allergy is that symptoms often improve over the weekend or on holidays; however, it may take weeks, months, or years to improve depending on the length of previous exposure. The asthma caused by a single heavy exposure to toxic fumes may last for years.

Medical-legal issues Documentation of occupational cause of symptoms is often difficult because individuals may have preexisting asthma. This issue may be clarified if other employees have similar symptoms. A survey may be necessary to uncover this. Federal or state public health agencies may be called upon to help affected employees. Patients' symptoms of asthma can be monitored by using objective measuring devices such as a Wright's Peak Flow Meter or much less expensive meters made by various manufacturers such as Access, Mini-Wright, and Vitalograph. These devices can measure the patient's airflow rates both at home and in the workplace every one

to two hours for a period of one or two weeks or until a pattern develops.

Individual peak flow should not vary beyond 10% of the flow predicted for a normal person throughout the day. A 20% or greater decrease in flow rate is considered significant.

If peak flow results are inadequate for legal documentation, an inhalation challenge may be necessary to identify the suspected allergen. The challenge carries a risk of a severe attack of asthma and should only be performed by specially trained medical personnel with resuscitation equipment available.

Although it may be difficult, it may be necessary to determine if the patient's symptoms are solely a result of an occupational exposure. The individual with preexisting asthma may have a worsening of symptoms when he or she experiences some trigger such as a dusty environment in a new job or change in working conditions in an existing job. Or a patient with preexisting but dormant asthma may be exposed to an occupational allergen and then finds it difficult to prove that this is a new occupationally caused asthma. The best objective criterion for diagnosing occupational asthma is the specific bronchoprovocation test (SBPT), in which the suspected worker is challenged with the implicated substance. In this test, the worker is given the suspected substance by inhalation under carefully controlled conditions. The patient's lung function is studied before and after this challenge. Unfortunately, this is very difficult to arrange, and less accurate methods of assessment are used instead for practical reasons, including expense and nonavailability of experienced specialists, equipment, or standardized testing materials. The incriminated agent must be standardized so that repeated testing will give the same results (reproducibility) and be specific for the involved materials. An example is the chemical toluene diisocyanate (TDI) used in plastics and varnishes. When this substance was administered to a control group of known asthmatic patients with no prior exposure to this substance, they did not react to a challenge. However, when previously exposed workers suspected of being sensitized to this substance were given the challenge, they showed a decrease in their lung function tests.

Two main questions must be addressed in these situations: First, is there a disability? Second, can the work environment be improved to allow continued employment? About 70% of patients with workplace-induced asthma will continue to have symptoms even years after exposure has stopped. Disability from occupational asthma is often lumped together with that from exposure to silicon and asbestos, which are a cause of serious lung disease (see ASBESTOSIS, SILICOSIS).

ocular allergy   See CONJUNCTIVITIS, ALLERGIC.

odors, as cause of allergy   Inhalation of strong fumes from cooking foods that may cause asthma, angioedema, and anaphylaxis in highly sensitive persons. Allergic reactions, although rare, occur most often from the inhalation of cooking fish. (See FISH ALLERGY.)

oil of Cassia   See CASSIA OIL.

oil of Myrcia   See BAY OIL.

olfactory nerves   The first pair of the 12 pairs of cranial nerves, which facilitates the sense of smell by enervating the mucous membranes of the nose.

Olympic athletes with asthma   An average of approximately 10% of all athletes in competitive sports have asthma. Sixty-seven of the 597 United States participants in the 1984 summer Olympiad in Los Angeles tested positive for exercise-induced asthma (EIA). A total of 41 medals were won by those 67 asthmatics.

The following drugs for the treatment of asthma and allergy are approved for international athletic competition: inhaled beta₂ agonists, albuterol (Proventil, Ventolin), bitolterol (Tornalate), metaproterenol (Alupent), pirbuterol (Maxair), and terbutaline (Brethaire);

cromolyn sodium (Intal); theophylline; antihistamines; non-narcotic cough suppressants, dextromethorphan and pholcodine; and inhaled corticosteroids. Banned legal drugs include oral forms of the beta₂ agonists; sympathomimetic amines (stimulants), ephedrine, pseudoephedrine, phenylephrine, isoproterenol, isoetharine; narcotic cough suppressants, codeine, hydrocodone, oxycodone, and dihydrocodeine; and oral and injectable forms of corticosteroids.

(See also EXERCISE-INDUCED ASTHMA.)

OLYMPIC MEDALS WON BY ATHLETES WITH EXERCISE-INDUCED ASTHMA

Event	Gold	Silver	Bronze
Basketball	4		
Cycling	3	3	2
Equestrian		1	
Field hockey			2
Pentathlon		2	
Rowing	1	4	
Shooting		1	
Swimming	5	1	
Track and field	1	1	
Volleyball		3	
Water polo		4	
Weight lifting			1
Wrestling	1		
Yachting		1	
Total	15	21	5

opportunistic infections   Invasions of bacteria, parasites, fungi, or other microbes that literally take the opportunity to flourish in persons who are immunocompromised; their immune systems lack the ability to fight infections that normally would not take hold. These infections frequently occur with acquired immunodeficiency syndrome (AIDS), leukemia, and congenital immune diseases. Persons taking large or prolonged courses of antibiotics or corticosteroids (cortisone derivatives) also risk secondary, or opportunistic, infections. (See also ACQUIRED IMMUNODEFICIENCY SYNDROME.)

Opticrom   A brand name for cromolyn sodium eyedrops effective against allergic eye disorders. This product is not currently available in the United States because of production problems, which the manufacturer is attempting to correct. (See CROMOLYN SODIUM.)

Optimine   See AZATADINE MALEATE.

oral desensitization   See IMMUNOTHERAPY, ORAL.

orange   A tropical citrus fruit containing cellulose, citric acid, sugar, and small quantities of vasoactive amines (potent nitrogen-containing organic compounds) that in large quantities may be a cause of migraine headaches. (See also AMINES, VASOACTIVE; FOOD ALLERGY; HEADACHE.)

Organidin   See IODINATED GLYCEROL.

organ transplantation rejection reaction   See REJECTION REACTION.

orrhoreaction   See SERUM SICKNESS.

orthopnea   A condition of shortness of breath when in a recumbent or supine position, commonly seen in patients with congestive heart failure but which also may occur in some patients with asthma or other lung conditions. Patients usually prop themselves up with several pillows or sit in a chair to sleep in order to avoid feeling as though they are suffocating. A patient may be referred to as having "two-pillow" or "three-pillow" orthopnea, depending on the number of pillows needed to allow him or her to breath more comfortably.

Osler, Sir William B.   Canadian physician (1849–1919) who at age 25 was appointed professor of medicine at McGill University and pathologist at the Montreal General Hospital. After serving as professor of clinical medicine at the University of Pennsylvania, Osler ac-

cepted the original post of physician in chief and professor of principles and practice of medicine at the new Johns Hopkins University Medical School in 1889. Osler's book, *The Principles and Practice of Medicine,* published in 1872, established the authoritative reference on the subject as it is known today. Osler's career also included the Regius Professorship of Medicine at Oxford University and an appointment to the Radcliffe Infirmary. Although Osler was honored for his humanitarianism, many modern allergists refute his idea that bronchial asthma includes "a strong neurotic element."

otitis media, secretory   [serous otitis media, glue ear]   A persistent buildup of thick fluid in the middle ear. Normally, the middle ear is ventilated three to four times per minute when the act of swallowing opens the eustachian tube. This tube allows drainage of fluid from the middle ear to the oropharynx (mouth and throat).

Secretory otitis media frequently occurs in children under the age of seven but may occur in any older child or adult with an obstruction to adequate drainage of the eustachian tube. It may be unilateral or bilateral.

Diagnosis Since thick fluid interferes with the normal movement of the eardrum, diagnosis can be made when there is a retraction of the tympanic membrane (eardrum) visualized through an otoscope (an instrument that combines a bright light with magnification). This can be confirmed by tympanometry. A tympanometer is an electronic device that emits a fixed tone combined with varying external pressure against the eardrum and measures its compliance. It can then be determined from a graph the instrument provides if there is fluid present behind the eardrum or if the drum is perforated. This can also be detected by attaching a rubber bulb and tubing to an otoscope, through which the observer can blow air against the eardrum. In the presence of fluid, the normal light reflex (see EAR) is distorted or absent, and the eardrum has reduced mobility, thus the term "glue ear."

Causes Frequent ear infections, nasal allergy, and enlarged adenoids may interfere with the normal drainage from the middle ear into the eustachian tube and pharynx (throat). The normal angle for drainage of the eustachian tube is 40°, and about 10° in infants. In addition to pain or a feeling of pressure in the ear, the condition may cause hearing loss. Many experts feel that a persistence of this condition for more than four months can affect children's behavior and language development, resulting in poor school performance.

Children under age three who were exposed to tobacco smoke had a 38% higher rate of middle ear infections than children living in smoke-free homes. Exposure to smoke was confirmed by measuring blood levels of cotinine (a metabolate of nicotine) in a study by the University of North Carolina.

Treatment Treatment of underlying infection or allergy is the initial therapy, but if unsuccessful, surgery may be necessary. Surgical procedures include a simple incision in the tympanic membrane (eardrum) called a myringotomy, to drain the thick fluid; the placement of ventilating tubes in the membrane to prevent recurrence; and an adenoidectomy. (See ADENOIDS; EUSTACHIAN TUBE; OTITIS MEDIA, SECRETORY; TYMPANOMETRY; TYMPANOSTOMY TUBES.)

otitis media, serous See OTITIS MEDIA, SECRETORY.

otoblennorrhea Discharge of mucus from the ear.

otolaryngologist Physician who treats diseases of the ears, nose, and throat medically and surgically. Otolaryngologists also may perform surgery of the head and neck and plastic surgery of the face.

otolaryngology Medical specialty concentrating on diagnoses and treatments of disorders of the ears, nose, and throat.

otorhinolaryngologists   See OTOLARYNGOLOGIST.

otoscope Instrument that combines a bright light with magnification and is used to view the external (outer) ear canal, the tympanic membrane (eardrum), and the ossicles (tiny bones in the middle ear).

The presence of fluid in the middle ear can be detected by attaching a rubber bulb and tubing to the otoscope and blowing air against the eardrum. (See EAR; OTITIS MEDIA, SECRETORY.)

Oudin, Jacques French physician and scientist (1908–85) who contributed to the study of immunochemistry through his development of replicable techniques, including gel immunodiffusion for analyzing antibodies and antibody-antigen systems, and his discoveries of various characteristics of immunoglobulins and antibody molecules. Oudin served as professor and chief of the Service of Analytical Immunochemistry and as director of research at the National Center of Scientific Research. He retired from the Institut Pasteur in Paris in 1978.

outgrowing allergies See GROWING OUT OF ALLERGIES AND ASTHMA.

Ovary, Zoltan Hungarian-Romanian physician and scientist, born in 1907, who developed the passive cutaneous anaphylaxis (PCA) technique, which led to important insights into IgE (immunoglobulin E)–mediated cellular reactions, subclasses of IgG (immunoglobulin G), and various immune hypersensitivity reactions. (See also IMMUNOGLOBULIN E.)

Owen, Ray D. American scientist, born in Genesee, Wisconsin in 1915, whose research on the inheritance of blood groups in dairy cattle led to extensive studies of immune mechanisms and genetic factors in tissue transplantation. Since 1983, Owen has been professor emeritus at the California Institute of Technology.

oxidation dyes See PHENYLENEDIAMINES.

oximeter   Photoelectric device for measuring the amount of oxygen in the blood.

oxitriphylline (Choledyl)   A derivative of theophylline, a bronchodilating drug used in the treatment of asthma. (See THEOPHYLLINE.)

oxygen   An odorless, tasteless, and colorless gas that is essential to life. It is used therapeutically for patients with respiratory distress in diseases such as asthma, emphysema, severe pneumonia, and congestive heart failure. Oxygen content in the body can be determined by measuring arterial blood gases or oximetry. (See also ARTERIAL BLOOD GASES, OXIMETER.)

oxygen therapy   Treatment of oxygen deficiency by administering oxygen via oxygen mask, tent, or nasal catheter.

oxymetazoline   Generic name for the alpha-agonist drug or decongestant nasal sprays or solutions available under the trade names Afrin, Dristan, 4-Way Nasal Spray, NTZ, and Neo-Synephrine. These drugs are noted for their rapid facilitation of nasal decongestion; however, tolerance may develop after only a few days of continuous use. This phenomenon, called "rebound," or rhinitis medicomentosum, results in addiction to their use for many persons. (See ALPHA-ADRENERGIC AGONIST, RHINITIS MEDICOMENTOSUM.)

oyster   A shellfish that may be the source of the infectious hepatitis virus or cause allergic reactions including anaphylaxis. (See FISH ALLERGY.)

ozone   A type of oxygen with a pungent odor and a bluish color, formed by three oxygen atoms, known as the molecule O_3. An environmental pollutant, ozone causes asthmalike hyperreactivity of the bronchioles similar to that in a viral respiratory infection. Inhalation of ozone and other environmental pollutants (including tobacco smoke, nitrogen dioxide, and sulfur dioxide) produces inflammation in the airways. Adverse response to ozone can also be seen in nonasthmatic, or normal, persons.

P

PABA See PARA-AMINOBENZOIC ACID.

pachydermia laryngis An abnormal thickening and growth of the mucous membrane of the larynx, or voice box, usually seen in patients with chronic inflammation of the larynx (laryngitis).

palm Christi oil See CASTOR OIL.

palpitation, heart An abnormal awareness of the heartbeat that is often described as fluttering. This may be associated with a slow, normal, or rapid heart rate.

***p*-aminobenzoic acid** See PARA-AMINO-BENZOIC ACID.

pansinusitis Infection involving all of the sinuses. (See SINUSITIS.)

panting Labored breathing or breathing hard as in overexertion.

papain A proteolytic enzyme (capable of breaking down proteins) derived from the papaya fruit. It is used as a meat tenderizer and as a local injection into a herniated lumbar disk as an alternative to surgery. Papain causes anaphylaxis (a potentially lethal allergic shock) in approximately one out of every 100 persons injected. About one in 1,500 deaths results from papain injection. Patients are skin-tested for papain sensitivity before undergoing procedures for spinal disk problems.

papaya A tropical fruit of the *Carica papaya* tree. Papain is a proteolytic enzyme (capable of breaking down proteins) derived from the fruit. (See PAPAIN.)

paper radioimmunosorbent test (PRIST) A blood test for the total amount of immunoglobulin E (IgE). This test is often used as an aid in determining if an individual is an atopic, or allergic, person. Elevated levels are suggestive but not conclusive of the presence of allergies,
since several other disorders such as parasitic infections can also cause high levels of IgE. (See also IMMUNOGLOBULIN EASSAY.)

papule Red, raised patch of skin commonly called a pimple. Papules occur in many conditions that cause rashes, including eczema and other allergic disorders.

para-aminobenzoic acid [*p*-aminobenzoic acid, PABA] A B-complex vitamin dissolved in a lightly scented solution and used as a sunscreen and as a local anesthetic in sunburn products. It may cause allergic contact rashes with or without sun exposure in susceptible persons. (See CONTACT DERMATITIS, PHOTOALLERGIC CONTACT DERMATITIS.)

parabens A group of chemical derivatives of phenol (short alkyl esters of *p*-hydroxybenzoic acid), including methylparaben, propylparaben, and butylparaben. The parabens are the most widely used preservatives in the cosmetic industry and are present in approximately 30% of all cosmetic products. They are also widely used in pharmaceuticals such as topical creams, ointments, and lotions and in some injectable medications.

The parabens are effective and safe antibacterial agents but in rare cases may cause allergic contact dermatitis. (See CONTACT DERMATITIS.)

para dyes See PHENYLENEDIAMINES.

paraffin A waxlike distillate of wood, coal, petroleum, or shale oil used in many cosmetic products. Although pure paraffin has no adverse effects, if it is contaminated with irritants, it may cause an eczematous rash.

paraffin jelly See PETROLATUM.

paranasal sinuses See SINUSES, PARANASAL.

parasites Organisms that depend upon another organism, or host, for survival. Some parasites are responsible for diseases, and they cause an elevation in blood eosinophils (a type of white blood cell) that can be confused with the elevated levels that occur in allergic disorders. Some parasitic infections are prevalent in immunosuppressed hosts, such as persons with AIDS. (See also OPPORTUNISTIC INFECTIONS.)

Par-Glycerol   See IODINATED GLYCEROL.

Parker, Charles W.   American physician and scientist, born in St. Louis, Missouri in 1930, whose research on several immunochemistry and immediate hypersensitivity topics, including lymphocytes, drug reactions, chemical mediators of allergic inflammation, and antigen-antibody reactions, served as models for studies of allergy to drugs and biologic substances. From 1979 to 1989, Parker served as director of the Howard Hughes Laboratory for the Study of Clinical Immunology and Allergy.

parrot fever   See PSITTACOSIS.

parsley oil [apiol]   A distillate of ripe seeds of the parsley plant (*Petroselium crispum*) and a member of the carrot family. Sensitive persons may break out in a rash when areas of the skin come in contact with parsley oil and are exposed to light. (See PHOTOSENSITIVITY.)

passive smoking   The potentially dangerous situation created when tobacco or other smoke is inhaled by nonsmoking persons who are in the company of one who smokes or who are exposed in some way to harmful smoke over a prolonged period of time. Adverse effects on the nonsmoking persons may become as serious as in smokers. Passive smoking may also trigger asthma. (See TRIGGERS OF ALLERGIES AND ASTHMA.)

passive transfer skin tests   Diagnostic procedures rarely used and limited to scientific allergy and disease research studies. There is a risk of transferring diseases such as hepatitis and acquired immunodeficiency syndrome (AIDS) with tests of this type.

Pasteur, Louis   French chemist and biologist (1822–95) whose studies of fermentation for the wine and vinegar industries led to his development of "pasteurization," a partial heat sterilization process to prevent perishable foods from spoiling. Pasteur, who also discovered the cause of silkworm disease, began to study veterinary diseases such as anthrax, cholera, erysipelas, and rabies (for which he discovered the cause). So astounding and influential were his findings that the Institut Pasteur was founded, with Pasteur as its internationally acclaimed director. As Pasteur experimented with rudimentary rabies "vaccines" in attempts to prevent the disease in humans, immunology was established as an important field in medicine.

patchouli oil   An essential oil derived from the leaves of *Pogostemon cablin*, an East Indian shrubby mint. The oil is used for its Oriental fragrance in cosmetics and soaps. It may cause allergic skin reactions.

patch skin test   A technique in which a chemical suspected of causing an allergic contact dermatitis, a skin disorder characterized by a severe pruritic (itchy) rash, is placed on an unaffected area of skin and covered by an impermeable bandage material (similar to a Band-Aid). The skin around and under the patch is observed at 48, 72, and 96 hours.

A positive reaction results in an inflamed and indurated red rash at the test site. An irritating chemical may also cause a nonallergic rash; therefore, quality control of the testing materials is essential. The patch skin test has been an important diagnostic test for skin allergy because the origin of many skin eruptions can be confused with other disorders. (See also CONTACT DERMATITIS.)

pathergy   Abnormal response to an allergen or many allergens. (See ALLERGY.)

Paul, William E.   American physician and scientist, born in Brooklyn, New York in 1936, who succeeded Baruj Benacerraf as chief of the

National Institute of Allergy and Infectious Diseases (NIAID) Laboratory of Immunology in 1970. Paul's research on lymphokine interleukin 4 (B-Cell Stimulatory Factor) has been influential in the study of allergic reactions.

Pauling, Linus C.   American scientist, born in Portland, Oregon in 1901, who won the Nobel Prize twice, for chemistry in 1954 for his discovery of the molecular abnormality that causes sickle-cell anemia, and the Peace Prize in 1963 for his work toward a nuclear testing ban. After Pauling retired from the faculties of Stanford University and the University of California at San Diego in 1974, he established the Linus Pauling Institute of Science and Medicine in Palo Alto, California, where he is chairman of the board and research professor. The institute is known for its studies of vitamin C in the prevention and treatment of viruses, including cancer. Pauling's work in immunochemistry helped clarify the structure of crystals and proteins (especially hemoglobin, a protein in red blood cells). Pauling performed experiments involving the molecular complementariness of antibodies and antigens and the successful conversion of normal globulin into antibody.

PBZ   Abbreviation for the antihistamine tripelnnamine (Pyribenzamine). (See TRIPELEN-NAMINE.)

p-cymene   A hydrocarbon solvent used as a flavoring and fragrance that has been reported to cause skin eruptions and inflammation of mucous membranes.

PDR   Abbreviation for *Physician's Desk Reference*, a major source book on prescription and over-the-counter drugs.

pea   Edible seeds found in pods of a climbing vine grown in temperate zones. The high protein value of peas places them in the category of legumes. An individual allergic to peas may also be allergic to other legumes, such as soybeans and peanuts. (See also LEGUMES.)

peak flow   The maximum flow rate that can be generated with the most forcible expiration a person can manage. One of the important indicators of asthma, the peak flow of expired air is measured by a peak flow meter in liters per second. The best of three readings is considered the peak expiratory flow rate (PEFR). The PEFR determines if there is an obstruction in one's airway. This objective measurement is similar to taking a person's blood pressure with a sphygmomanometer. The PEFR provides an accurate way to monitor the response to asthma therapy and exacerbations of asthma, detect asymptomatic deterioration in lung function before it becomes critical, determine the degree of airflow obstruction and detect early stages of obstruction, and indicate when emergency care is required. Because the peak flow measurement tests patency only of the large airways, an individual with mild asthma relating to small airways may be undiagnosed unless spirometry, which measures flow rates at low lung volumes, is employed. An objective measurement of airflow obstruction, such as PEFR, in persons with asthma is desirable because subjective measurements (dyspnea and wheezing, for example) by physicians and patients may be inaccurate. One study demonstrated that only 44% of physicians could estimate PEFR within 20% of the actual measured PEFR of patients. By the time wheezing can be detected with a stethoscope, the PEFR has already decreased by 25% or more. Patients' symptoms are also an unreliable indicator of airway obstruction. One of the major factors causing delay in treatment of severe asthma and asthma exacerbations is poor perception of the severity on the part of the doctor and the patient.

The accuracy of the PEFR measurement depends on the person's willingness and ability to exhale as hard as he or she can into the peak flow meter.

peak flow meter   A portable device that measures patency of the airways, especially useful in the management of asthma. Various types of peak flow meters are available. The patient takes a deep breath and blows forcibly into the device, after which the flow of air from the lungs can be compared with the normal values predicted for the patient's age, height, and sex. The peak flow meter aids in the diagnosis of asthma and exercise-induced asthma and the detection of an impending asthma attack. It also indicates the severity of an attack and helps to optimize medication dosage.

peanut   A legume, the oily seed of the *Arachnis hypogaea* vine, which is a popular food, ingredient in food manufacturing (known often as a "hidden" allergen), and the source of peanut oil. Peanut is among the most common foods responsible for serious and at times fatal allergic reactions. Although parents of children with a strong family history of allergy are advised to avoid peanut for the first two years of life, most children have been exposed by age two. Peanut allergy usually is not outgrown. Properly distilled peanut oil is probably safe for peanut-sensitive persons. However, if the exact source and quality is unknown, this product should be avoided, since the oil may be contaminated by peanut protein. (See also FOOD ALLERGY, LEGUMES.)

pear oil   See AMYL ACETATE.

pecans   Tree nuts (from the *Carya illinoensis* tree) that can cause allergic reactions including anaphylaxis (life-threatening allergic shock) and can be affected by toxin-producing molds (mycotoxins). (See also FUNGI AND MOLDS.)

pectin   A carbohydrate derived from the roots, stems, and fruits of plants, or any variation of water-soluble substances, that, when added to foods such as fruits and vegetables, binds adjacent cell walls in the food's tissues and causes them to thicken and jell. Pectin, a polysaccharide most abundant in lemon and orange rind, is commonly used to make jellies, fruit preserves, candies, salad dressings, ice cream, and gelatin desserts. It may also be among the ingredients in toothpaste, hair- set-

ting preparations, cosmetic creams, and anti-diarrheal medications. Pectin has not been known to be toxic or allergenic.

PEG   Abbreviation for polyethylene glycol. (See POLYETHYLENE GLYCOLS.)

pemphigus   A chronic, blisterlike rash of unknown origin that can be confused with allergic contact dermatitis. A condition usually afflicting adults, pemphigus causes itching, burning, and general malaise. Crops of bullae, or lesions, appear suddenly on skin and leave discolored spots when they disappear. Corticosteroids, immunosuppressants, antibiotics, and fastidious skin care typically constitute treatment. Certain types of pemphigus, such as pemphigus acutus and pemphigus vulgaris, may be life- threatening. Pemphigoid and dermatitis herpetiformis are related skin diseases also characterized by bullous lesions.

Pemphigoid, considered to be an autoimmune disorder affecting mostly elderly people, is not as serious a condition as pemphigus.

penicillinase   An enzymelike substance found in some bacteria that prevents penicillin from killing the infection. A purified strain of *Bacillus cereus* has been used to treat allergic reaction to penicillin.

penicillins   A group of antibiotics derived from cultures of the mold *Penicillium* or made synthetically and used to kill bacteria, especially cocci, which cause infections. The many derivatives of penicillin include penicillin G, V, ampicillin, amoxicillin, cloxicillin, dicloxicillin, carbenicillin, and nafcillin. Penicillins' bacteriocidal (bacteria-killing) action depends on their ability to interfere with cell-wall synthesis of actively multiplying bacteria.

Hypersensitivity reactions, which are common, to the antibacterial drugs of the penicillin family may be of any of the Gell and Coombs allergy types I through IV. The penicillin molecule, called a hapten, is too small to cause an allergic response, but it is highly chemically reactive: When it combines with a large carrier molecule, usually a protein, it becomes allergenic.

Individuals allergic to one form of penicillin should be considered allergic to all penicillins because they are so chemically similar. The cephalosporin antibiotics are also structurally related to the penicillins. An estimated 5 to 15% of penicillin- allergic persons will also react to cephalosporins.

An estimated 13% of penicillin-allergic reactions are type I (anaphylactic, immediate, or IgE mediated), and as many as 9%, or from 400 to 800, of these prove fatal each year in the United States. Most severe reactions occur when penicillin is administered by injection. Other allergic reactions may result in rashes or serum sickness. Unfortunately, a history of penicillin allergy is often unreliable. In a study by the American Academy of Allergy, only 19% of about 3,000 persons with a history of penicillin allergy were positive when skin-tested. Seven percent of a group of 1,229 patients with no prior history of penicillin allergy proved positive by skin-test.

Furthermore, penicillin can often be detected in individuals who have no knowledge of ever having received it. Exposure is possible from contaminated meat prepared from animals who have been treated with penicillin.

Skin tests may be useful; however, fatal reactions have occurred during testing. Radioallergosorbent tests (RAST) are free of adverse effects but less sensitive than skin tests, so negative tests may be unreliable.

In the rare instance in which there is no acceptable alternative to penicillin, such as in the treatment of life-threatening infective endocarditis, desensitization may be carried out according to one of several protocols, orally or by injection. (See ANTIBIOTIC, BENZYLPENICILLOYL, POLYLYSINE, DESENSITIZATION.)

Penicillium   A genus of broomlike molds belonging to the Ascomycetes (sac fungi). *Penicillium* forms the blue molds that grow on fruits, cheese, bread, and other substances. A number of *Penicillium* species are the source of the antibiotic drug penicillin. More than a dozen common types of *Penicillium* are common indoor and outdoor allergens that produce respiratory, external ear, skin, and certain occupational allergies, such as suberosis, caused by the inhalation of *Penicillium frequentans* (a cork-dust mold). Individuals allergic to *Penicillium* mold are not necessarily also allergic to penicillin. (See FUNGI AND MOLDS.)

peppermint oil   An oil derived from the leaves and tops of the plant *Mentha piperita* and used as an additive in candies, beverages, desserts, chewing gum, toothpaste, and cosmetic products. It can cause an allergic reaction similar to hay fever and skin rashes. A few individuals have developed cardiac irregularities caused by excessive ingestion of foods containing peppermint oil.

Pepys, Jacob (Jack)   South African physician and scientist, born in 1914, who researched pulmonary infections, asthma, and allergic disorders. His work, which includes explanations of various allergic responses to airborne fungal, microbial, and animal antigens, has been important to the understanding of farmer's lung and other occupational allergies and diseases. (See also FARMER'S LUNG.)

perennial allergies   Allergic rhinitis and asthma that are present throughout the year, as opposed to seasonal allergies such as hay fever. Perennial allergens include exposure to animal danders (especially cat and dog), housedust mites, feathers, and molds.

perfume   Alcohol-based liquid (named perfume from the Latin-based French words literally meaning "to smoke thoroughly") made fragrant by adding floral essences or synthetic substances and used cosmetically. It can cause contact skin allergy or trigger asthma by its irritant properties (fumes). Incense was one of the first perfumes in history. Perfumes are eliminated from many products designed to be hypoallergenic.

Periactin   See CYPROHEPTADINE.

permanent wave lotions   Preparations used to set the hair in various styling patterns. Chemicals in permanent wave lotions, including thioglycolic acid and sodium lauryl sulfate, may cause skin contact rashes, chemical burns, and swelling of affected tissues of the scalp, face, neck, eyelids, and ears. (See also CONTACT DERMATITIS.)

pernio   A chilblain or an adverse reaction to cold, also called perniosis.

peroxide dyes   See PHENYLENEDIAMINES.

Pertussis vaccine   This vaccine was developed in the 1930s and is usually combined with diphtheria and tetanus vaccines for the immunization of infants and children. Pertussis vaccine is not routinely advised after age seven because the infection is rarely serious after this age. Unfortunately, serious adverse effects occur in a small number of infants, and the use of this vaccine was severely limited for a few years during the 1980s until a government fund was established to deal with liability issues related to this product. Newer vaccine production measures promise to lessen the frequency and severity of reactions.

pertussis   [whooping cough]   Highly contagious bacterial infection transmitted by droplets containing *Bordetella pertussis*. Pertussis starts like a common cold but worsens until by the third or fourth week a characteristic paroxysmal "whooping" is heard. This debilitating cough may persist for several months and may be fatal.

pesticide   Any chemical agent used to kill insects. Many fruits and vegetables are sprayed before harvest time. Pesticides may be irritants, and food should be washed before eating, but pesticides are not known to be allergenic substances.

petechiae   Tiny reddish or purplish spots containing blood that appear on the skin or on mucous membranes during the course of some infectious diseases, often indicating a defi-

ciency or dysfunction of platelets. Petechiae may also occur in conjunction with bleeding and immune disorders. (See HENOCH-SCHONLEIN PURPURA, PLATELETS, VASCULITIS.)

petitgrain oil   A volatile oil obtained from the leaves, twigs, and unripe fruit of the bitter orange tree. When used in perfumes, it may cause allergic skin rashes, especially in conjunction with skin exposure to sunlight. It is also used as a food flavoring agent.

petrolatum   [petroleum jelly, paraffin jelly] (Vaseline)   Purified, water-insoluble, semi-solid mixture of hydrocarbons obtained from petroleum. Widely used in the cosmetic and pharmaceutical industries, petrolatum rarely causes allergic skin rashes.

petroleum jelly (Vaseline)   See PETROLATUM.

pets for allergic persons   Domestic animals considered the only "safe" pets for allergic or asthmatic patients. Among them are fish, amphibians (frogs and salamanders), and reptiles (turtles and snakes). However, some of the "cold-blooded" species may carry salmonella or other infections that can be transmitted to humans. (See ANIMAL ALLERGY.)

Peyer's patches   Part of the immune system, groups of lymphoid nodules mainly found in the ileum. Their function is unknown, but the patches in mammals resemble the avian bursa of Fabricius, an organ in birds that seems to be responsible for producing B lymphocytes. Peyer's patches are named after Johann Conrad Peyer, a Swiss anatomist (1653–1712). (See also IMMUNE SYSTEM.)

phacoanaphylaxis   Hypersensitivity to the protein of the crytalline lens of the eye.

phagocytes   Cells of the immune system that attack, ingest, and destroy infectious microorganisms and debris in a process called phagocytosis. (See IMMUNE SYSTEM, LYMPHOCYTES, MACROPHAGES.)

pharynx The musculomembranous airway from the nasal cavity to the larynx that also provides a route for food to go from the mouth to the esophagus, and for sound to be carried from the larynx to outside the body. The pharynx is a tube commonly called the throat. Pharyngitis refers to an inflamed condition of the throat often included in symptoms of upper respiratory allergy.

Phenergan See PROMETHAZINE.

phenethyl alcohol Naturally occurring chemical derived from oranges, raspberries, and tea used as a cosmetic preservative, as a floral scent in perfumes, and a fruit flavoring agent. It can cause allergic skin rashes.

pheniramine An antihistamine used in the treatment of allergic eye disorders. Pheniramine is an ingredient in AK-Con-A, Opcon-A, and Naphcon-A, in which it is combined with the decongestant drug naphazoline.

phenol [carbolic acid] Coal tar derivative used in the cosmetic and pharmaceutical industries as an antiseptic and anesthetic agent. Phenol can cause hives and other skin rashes and may be highly toxic. Fatalities resulting from skin absorption of phenol have been reported, and phenol must be avoided during infancy and pregnancy.

phenylenediamines [PPD, amino dyes, oxidation dyes, para dyes, peroxide dyes] A group of chemical substances in hair dyes that can cause allergic contact rashes and toxicity if ingested and can trigger asthma. Phenylenediamine compounds are banned in Europe because of their ability to cause cancer in animals. The safety of the compounds has been questioned in the United States in recent years.

phenylephrine hydrochloride (Alconefrin, Neo-Synephrine, Nostril) Alpha-adrenergic, decongestant drug in over-the-counter nasal drops and sprays and eyedrops. Phenylephrine hydrochloride is also used in combination with antihistamines for the treatment of hay fever and colds. Tolerance to phenylephrine nasal products often causes a dependency known as rhinitis medicomentosum, which may require treatment with corticosteroids in order to break the cycle and symptoms of dependency. (See ALPHA-ADRENERGIC AGONISTS, RHINITIS MEDICOMENTOSUM.)

phenylpropanolamine A derivative of the stimulant drug amphetamine used as a decongestant drug for the treatment of nasal allergies and colds. The safety of phenylpropanolamine has been questioned, but in normal decongestant doses it probably does not significantly increase blood pressure. However, the drug is available in higher doses as an over-the-counter appetite suppressant and may be a risk for hypertensive persons. (See ALPHA-ADRENERGIC AGONISTS.)

phenyltoloxamine An antihistamine usually combined with decongestant drugs for the treatment of hay fever. (See ANTIHISTAMINE.)

phlegm Mucus, also called sputum, secreted by the cells lining the respiratory tract and capable of causing congestion in upper respiratory passages including the nose and sinuses. (See SPUTUM.)

phlycyenosis The formation of blisters, vesicles, or pustules.

phosphodiesterase An enzyme that may be involved in causing asthma. Asthma drugs such as theophylline may block this enzyme's action.

photoallergic contact dermatitis Skin rash or other allergic reaction to ultraviolet light, especially from the sun, in combination with an allergen, such as sulfonamides in antibiotic creams and ointments; certain sunscreens containing para-aminobenzoic acid (PABA) and digalloyl trioleate; salicylanilides, bithionol, dichlorophen, and hexachlorophene in cosmetics and antiseptic soaps; lipstick and other chemical dyes containing acridine, eosin, fluorescein, methylene blue, and rose bengal;

hair preparations containing quinine; and the fungicide chlorsalicylamide.

Individuals allergic to one of the aforementioned substances may also be allergic to others. Photoallergic contact dermatitis is diagnosed by photopatch testing, in which a suspected allergen is placed on two different skin sites. After 48 hours, one of the test areas is exposed to sunlight or other source of ultraviolet rays. A day or two days later, both areas are examined for rash. (See also PARA-AMINOBENZOIC ACID.)

photography chemicals   See CONTACT DERMATITIS.

photosensitivity   An adverse reaction to sunlight, frequently caused by both topical allergens (see also PHOTOALLERGIC CONTACT DERMATITIS) and ingested allergens, such as tetracycline antibiotics, parsnips, mustard, artificial sweeteners (cyclamate), coal tar derivatives in hair dyes, estrogen, the antihistamine promethazine (Phenergan), sulfonylureas (oral antidiabetic drugs), tranquilizers such as chlorpromazine (Thorazine), antifungal agents such as griseofulvin, and diuretics such as thiazides. Photosensitive reactions essentially imitate sunburn. The rash may be hives or a more generalized skin eruption that may be mistaken for many other allergic and nonallergic causes.

pH probe monitor   A device used to determine the presence of acid in the esophagus and to confirm the diagnosis of reflux esophagitis. Esophagitis often triggers or worsens asthma. (See GASTROINTESTINAL REFLUX AND ASTHMA.)

phthalic acid   A derivative of the chemical benzene or derived from the fungus *Gibberella fujikuroi,* used in the manufacture of cosmetics, especially nail polish. Phthalic acid is a skin and mucous membrane irritant.

phthalic anhydride   A derivative of naphthalene used in cosmetic dyes and artificial resins that is a skin and mucous membrane irritant.

phthisic   From the Greek word *phthisikos,* another term for asthma or asthma sufferer.

phthisis   Pulmonary tuberculosis, black lung, and other wasting or atrophic disease of the lung.   (See   OCCUPATIONAL ASTHMA, STONECUTTER'S PHTHISIS.)

phylaxis   The body's innate self-protection against infection. The opposite is anaphylaxis. (See ANAPHYLAXIS.)

physical appearance of allergic patients The revealing characteristics of hypersensitive persons, including longer faces, narrower jawbones with flattened cheeks, pinched nostrils, raised upper lips, protruding teeth resulting in overbite and high arched palate, and retracted chin. Individuals with hay fever often have a horizontal crease across the lower portion of the nose, called the "allergic crease," and dark circles under the eyes, or "allergic shiners." There may be swelling and puffiness of the eyelids, redness of the eyes, and watery discharge from the eyes and nose. (See also ALLERGIC RHINITIS.)

physical education, physical fitness   See EXERCISE-INDUCED ASTHMA.

physical urticaria   A group of disorders characterized by the presence of hives precipitated by physical means. Hives appear in the upper layer of skin as circumscribed, raised areas of erythema (redness) and edema (swelling caused by a collection of fluid). They are usually associated with intense pruritus (itching).

Cold, exercise, heat, light, pressure, or vibration to the skin may provoke hives in susceptible persons. As estimated 17% of all chronic cases of hives are associated with physical causes. The physical hives are often limited to areas of direct contact with or exposure to the physical stimuli. More than one physical trigger may be involved in some individuals.

The characteristic raised urticarial lesions are most likely a result of the release of histamine and other chemical mediators from mast cells in the skin. (See ANGIOEDEMA, VIBRATORY; AQUAGENIC URTICARIA; CHOLINERGIC URTICARIA; COLD URTICARIA, ACQUIRED; COLD URTICARIA, ESSENTIAL; COLD URTICARIA, FAMILIAL; DERMATOGRAPHIA; EXERCISE-INDUCED ANAPHYLAXIS; PRESSURE URTICARIA; SOLAR URTICARIA; URTICARIA.)

Pickwickian syndrome   A state of diminished respiration because of obesity, named for the massively obese character Pickwick, created by Charles Dickens. (See also HYPOVENTILATION SYNDROME.)

pigeon breeder's disease   A pneumonia-like lung disease caused by allergy to pigeon droppings. (See BIRD ALLERGY, BIRD BREEDER'S LUNG, HYPERSENSITIVITY PNEUMONITIS.)

pigeon droppings and feathers   Natural materials containing allergens that may cause a form of the allergic lung disease hypersensitivity pneumonitis, or pigeon breeder's disease. (See HYPERSENSITIVITY PNEUMONITIS.)

pillows, allergenic and hypoallergenic A soft sac filled with material that holds shape and is used to support the head or other parts of the body, especially during sleep. The average individual spends one-third of his or her life in direct contact with a pillow. Certain natural materials, such as goose down, feathers, or kapok, may be allergenic; synthetic fillers such as polyester are considered hypoallergenic, or nonallergenic. House dust mites contaminating the filling material may also be a significant trigger for allergic symptoms or asthma. (See also FEATHERS, HOUSE DUST MITES, KAPOK, TRIGGERS OF ALLERGIES AND ASTHMA.)

pillows, hypoallergenic   See PILLOWS, ALLERGENIC AND HYPOALLERGENIC.

pineapple   Tropical fruit (*Ananas comosus,* of the family Bromeliaceae) that contains small amounts of chemicals called vasoactive amines, which, in large quantities, may cause headaches, abdominal, cramps and diarrhea. (See FOOD ALLERGY, VASOACTIVE AMINES.)

pine tar   A distillate of pine wood used as an antiseptic in skin disorders that can be a skin irritant.

pine tar oil   A food flavoring agent and cosmetic solvent derived from pine wood. It is irritating to skin and mucous membranes.

pink eye   See CONJUNCTIVITIS, ALLERGIC.

piperonal   A crystalline alkaloid found in vanilla and black pepper with the fragrance of heliotrope used in perfumes and lipstick. Piperonal causes skin rashes.

pirbuterol (Maxair)   A beta-adrenergic agonist, or bronchodilating drug, available as a metered-dose inhaler for the treatment of asthma. (See BETA-ADRENERGIC AGONISTS, AEROSOLS.)

Pirquet's test   A skin test for tuberculosis, especially for children, named after the Austrian pediatrician Clemens P. Pirquet (1874–1929).

pityriasis alba   A transient loss of skin pigmentation seen in some patients with eczema.

pityriasis rosae   A common rash of unknown cause but thought to be a viral infection, since it seems to occur in epidemics. The typical rash is signaled by a large oval plaque suggestive of "ringworm" and referred to as a "herald patch." A generalized rash consisting of red, slightly raised lesions on the trunk appears in one to four weeks following the herald patch. The rash usually runs its course in six to eight weeks without treatment. However, antihistaminic drugs are often used for itching.

plant contact dermatitis   [*Rhus* dermatitis] An inflammation or eruption of the skin caused by contact with leaves, stem, or other parts or secretions of various plants. In North America, members of the *Rhus* genus, poison ivy, poison sumac, and poison oak, are the most common offenders. Other plants, such as members of the Compositae family, which includes chrysanthemums (of greater significance in Europe) and ragweed, are also sensitizers but rarely cause the disability associated with the *Rhus* plants. Many woods are also skin sensitizers, most prominent of which is Australian blackwood. This and other woods may be associated with contact rashes found in forest workers and cabinetmakers.

Allergic rashes caused by plant contact are a significant occupational hazard and frequently result in time lost from work. For this reason it is important to distinguish the source of the rash so appropriate treatment can be given but also so avoidance measures can be taken to avoid recurrences. Direct contact with the plant oleoresins is responsible for the rashes of poison ivy and the other *Rhus* plants. Although the allergenic resins in the sap of these plants are more plentiful in the spring and summer, they can cause reactions throughout the year even in dry plants. Contact can occur by touching clothing or the fur of pets to which the resin has clung. The oleoresins must be washed off within 15 minutes after exposure to prevent or minimize the rash.

Complicating the diagnosis can be the contact rash resulting from chronic airborne exposure to ragweed species and feverfew. Allergic contact rashes can also be confused with those of eczema or photosensitivity reactions (see PHOTOSENSITIVITY). Patch testing for diagnosic purposes is difficult to perform because of the irritant properties of the testing materials and cross-reactivity between some plant species.

Although desensitization against poison ivy has been attempted for many years by injections and oral ingestion of the active allergen, there is no scientific basis for these measures. Immunotherapy (allergy desensitization) is based on the principles of an antigen (allergen)–antibody reaction, referred to as type I, or immediate, hypersensitivity. *Rhus* plants, however, cause delayed (cell-mediated, or type IV) allergy, and there is no proven benefit of desensitization to prevent these rashes. Furthermore, oral ingestion of the *Rhus* material often causes inflammation and itching of the mouth and anus or a more serious condition involving the kidneys (nephritis). Persons sensitive to *Rhus* often have delayed allergic reactions when eating the inedible rind of mangoes and ginkgo tree fruit.

Treatment of plant-allergic reactions includes topical, oral, or injectable corticosteroids, soothing lotions such as calamine, and oral antihistamines (used for sedation and probably do not relieve itching). Topical over-the-counter products containing antihistamines or local anesthetic agents should be avoided because they may cause a contact dermatitis that worsens the condition. At least one product, Stokogard, contains a linoleic acid derivative that forms a barrier on the skin. The product is applied to exposed skin surfaces and traps oleoresin particles on the skin surface so they can be washed off up to eight hours after exposure. (See also CONTACT DERMATITIS.)

plant protein allergies   Sensitivities occurring from contact with proteinaceous materials from plants. Allergens may be present in flowers, leaves, stems, roots, wood, and pollens. Allergen-containing dusts from cereal grains, wheat flour, legumes, and seeds are frequent causes of occupational asthma. Plant materials may also cause contact dermatitis. (See OCCUPATIONAL ALLERGENS, OCCUPATIONAL ASTHMA, PLANT CONTACT DERMATITIS.)

platelets   Disklike components in the blood that contain no hemoglobin. Platelets contribute to the processes of blood coagulation and hemostasis and the formation of blood thrombi. During anaphylactic shock, the number of platelets decreases (thrombocytopenia). (See also ANAPHYLAXIS, PETECHIAE, THROMBOCYTOPENIA.)

platinum   Salts of this heavy precious metal are highly allergenic, sensitizing virtually all workers exposed to it for at least five years. Platinum salts are among those allergens capable of causing late-phase asthmatic symptoms. (See also LATE-PHASE ALLERGIC REACTIONS, METALS AND METALLIC SALTS, OCCUPATIONAL ALLERGENS.)

pleura The moist membrane lining the lungs and the walls of other structures of the thorax and the diaphragm. Because of their serous secretion, both the right and left pleurae help reduce friction between the lungs and other structures during the movements of breathing.

Pleurisy refers to inflammation of a pleura, which often results in painful respiration, coughing, and fever. Pleural fibrosis is a complication of pulmonary tuberculosis in which the pleura thickens and causes crowding in the pleural cavity (space between the layers of the pleurae).

pleurisy See PLEURA.

PMN See NEUTROPHILS.

pneodynamics [pneumodynamics] The mechanism or mechanics of breathing.

pneopneic reflex A change in respiratory rate and depth that occurs as a result of inhalation of an irritating vapor. Coughing, shortness of breath, and pulmonary edema may result.

pneumatic otoscope A device used to determine the presence of fluid behind the tympanic membrane, or eardrum. A rubber bulb and tubing are attached to an otoscope (an instrument used to view the external ear canal and eardrum), and the bulb is squeezed to blow air against the membrane. In the presence of fluid, the eardrum has reduced mobility. (See OTITIS MEDIA, SECRETORY; OTOSCOPE.)

pneumococcal vaccine polyvalent (Pneumovax, Pnu-Imune) Immunization for protection against 23 strains of bacteria that cause approximately 90% of pneumococcal pneumonia. This type of pneumonia occurs in all age groups but is especially prominent in the elderly. Despite antibiotic therapy, there are still many deaths attributed to this type of pneumonia. Immunization with pneumococcal polysaccharide vaccine is advised for any individual at higher-than-normal risk for serious complications from pneumonia. High-risk persons include anyone older than 65, children older than two, and adults who are immunocompromised, such as those without a spleen or whose spleen is nonfunctional; persons with Hodgkin's disease, lymphoma, multiple myeloma, chronic renal failure, and nephrotic syndrome; persons who have had organ transplantation; and anyone who is HIV positive. Other high-risk patients are those with chronic medical conditions such as heart or lung disease, diabetes mellitus, alcoholism, cirrhosis, and leakage of cerebrospinal fluid.

Protective antibody levels from the pneumococcal vaccine are usually present five years following immunization but then may fall. Revaccination is recommended only for children at extremely high risk of pneumococcal pneumonia: those without a spleen or with nephrotic syndrome.

Adverse effects from pneumococcal vaccine are rare. Most common reactions are local swelling and redness at the injection site or slight fever. The vaccine should be avoided during an active infection and in children younger than two, and it should not be given during pregnancy unless there is a clear need.

pneumoconiosis Lung disorder caused by chronic inhalation of dust and other irritating particles. See SILICOSIS.

pneumonia Inflammation of the lungs characterized by chest pain, fever, cough (often producing bloody or purulent sputum), and other symptoms. The causes of various types of pneumonia include bacteria, viruses, and irritating fumes from chemicals. Pneumonia symptoms may be confused with those of hypersensitivity pneumonitis, which is sometimes an allergic reaction to drugs, chemical irritants, plant and animal material, and dust. In addition, allergic alveolitis, or inflammation of the alveoli (air sacs) in the lungs, may produce similar symptoms; the most common causes are inhalation of mold spores and animal and plant material. Occupational allergies (such as farmer's lung) can simulate pneumonia symptoms. (See also HYPERSENSITIVITY PNEUMONITIS.)

pneumonitis, hypersensitivity   See HYPERSENSITIVITY PNEUMONITIS.

pneumothorax   Collapse of the lung. (See CHRONIC OBSTRUCTIVE PULMONARY DISEASE, LUNGS.)

Pneumovax   See PNEUMOCOCCAL VACCINE POLYVALENT.

Pnu-Imune   See PNEUMOCOCCAL VACCINE POLYVALENT.

poikiloderma   A skin rash characterized by discoloration, itching, bruising, atrophy, and spiderlike skin lesions called telangiectasia.

poison ivy   See PLANT CONTACT DERMATITIS.

poison oak   See PLANT CONTACT DERMATITIS.

poison sumac   See PLANT CONTACT DERMATITIS.

Polaramine   See DEXCHLORPHENIRAMINE MALEATE.

poliomyelitis vaccine   An oral or injectable combination of polioviruses administered to prevent poliomyelitis, an infectious disease that may lead to paralysis of limbs and other parts of the body, such as respiratory muscles necessary for adequate breathing and sections of the brain necessary for swallowing reflexes. Widespread utilization of the oral live viral vaccine, developed by Dr. Albert Sabin, has almost eliminated the threat of polio throughout most of the world. Immunization is extremely important, because there is no drug that cures polio.

Inactivated poliovirus vaccine, developed in 1955 by a team led by Dr. Jonas Salk, is produced in monkey kidney cells and made noninfectious by treatment with formalin. The injectable form was replaced in the early 1960s by the oral vaccine. The oral vaccine is the immunization of choice, being more potent, although there is a slight chance of developing paralytic polio (about one incidence in 2.6 million doses administered) that does not occur with the Salk vaccine. Nonimmunized persons in contact with someone given the oral vaccine are also at risk.

The Sabin oral vaccine should not be given to a person with severe diarrhea; individuals whose immune systems are compromised, such as those with HIV infection, lymphoma, or other widespread malignancies; patients on corticosteroids (including asthmatics); or persons undergoing cancer chemotherapy or radiation therapy. It should also be avoided by members of a household in which there is an immunocompromised person.

The Salk vaccine can be given safely to these patients, but protection might be inadequate.

pollen   The microspores, which resemble dust or powder, giving rise to the male gametophyte of seed plants, including trees, grasses, and weeds. A pollen grain is similar to the male spermatozoon and contains half the genetic material necessary to reproduce. Virtually all seed plants depend on pollen grains to reproduce.

Pollen is the major cause of allergic disorders throughout the world; grass is the most important source. The allergic symptoms of pollinosis, another name for hay fever, are caused by the seasonal exposure to large quantities of windborne pollen from anemophilous plants. However, only about 10% of seed plants are anemophilous and capable of inducing hay fever. Allergenic extracts containing pollen are used in diagnostic allergy tests in order to determine the pollen to which an individual is hypersensitive. (See also ANEMOPHILOUS PLANT, GRASS POLLEN ALLERGY, POLLINOSIS, SKIN TESTS, TREE POLLEN ALLERGY, WEED POLLEN ALLERGY.)

pollen collectors   Instruments used to accumulate pollen grains and mold spores in order to enable a count of pollen grains and mold spores in a given area on a particular day in the hay fever season. These measurements are called the pollen and mold spore counts. The two basic methods of collection for aeroallergen sampling are gravitational and volumetric. In the gravitational method, microscope slides are coated with glycerin jelly and exposed to air for 24 hours. Then they are examined for the quantity of pollen grains and mold spores that have settled on the slide. Accuracy of this method is limited by wind currents, rainfall, and moisture from condensation. Collected sample counts are usually very law, and small particles often do not settle on the slides. The other methods are the volumetric techniques. They are recognized for their improved accuracy for pollen counts and include the rotating air impactor and inertial suction samplers such as the Hirst spore trap. Mold spores in the air are trapped on an adhesive-coated surface in the device as air is drawn past it at a controlled speed of two millimeters per hour. After they are collected, the amount of mold spores can be measured in various ways.

pollen count   The number of pollen grains, grass in the spring and ragweed in the fall in North America, present in one cubic meter of air. The quantity of pollen present in the environment at any time is dependent on many factors, including the number of pollen grains produced by the plant, the number of plants, and the efficiency of aerial transport.

pollinosis [hay fever]   Seasonal allergic rhinitis requiring the presence of pollen and capable of eliciting an allergic response in an atopic or allergic subject. The term *hay fever* is now used regardless of season (see HAY FEVER). Under most circumstances, only anemophilous, or windborne, pollen present in sufficient quantity can cause hay fever.

Huge quantities of pollens are generally required to produce the symptoms of hay fever. Once the symptoms are evident, much smaller amounts of pollen will continue to elicit them. The source of the pollinating plants may be up to hundreds of miles away, being transported by seasonal winds. However, high-pollen-producing trees such as elms, oaks, and others (see the table below) can provoke intense symptoms with exposure to only a single tree.

Pollen release is generally promoted by warm, dry conditions. Ragweed pollen shedding ceases or falls sharply at 10°C (approximately 50 °F) or when the relative humidity is above 70%. Many flowers store pollen until optimal conditions exist, favoring release during the daytime. Exceptions abound however, with ragweed and some grasses also releasing pollen at night.

In order to cause hay fever, a plant must meet Thommen's five postulates: (1) The plant must be seed bearing (spermatophyte); only seed-bearing plants produce pollen. (2) The plant must have wide distribution, or the plant must be close to the human environment. (3) The plant must produce large quantities of pollen. (4) The pollen must be light enough to be airborne, between 15 and 50 microns (1 micron=1/25,000 inch) diameter. (5) The pollen must be allergenic.

A plant species meeting all five rules is considered a primary or index species. Species meeting fewer than five are of little or no significance. Occasionally an individual will seem to have symptoms related to a plant not meet-

RAGWEED POLLEN COUNTS AND THEIR RELATIONSHIP TO HAY FEVER SYMPTOMS

Quantitative Count (ragweed pollen grains/ cubic meter)	Qualitative Count	Symptoms of Hay Fever Will Appear in Individuals Allergic to Ragweed
None	Absent	No symptoms
1 to 20	Low	Only the extremely sensitive will have symptoms
20 to 200	Moderate	Many will have symp toms
Over 200	High/very high	Almost all individuals will have symptoms

---

TREES CAPABLE OF PRODUCING
SIGNIFICANT HAY FEVER SYMPTOMS

Single Trees Capable of Producing Significant Hay Fever Symptoms	**Small Groups of Trees Producing Significant Hay Fever Symptoms**
Elm	Black cherry[1]
Hackberry	Brazilian pepper tree[1]
Mulberry	Elderberry[1]
Oak	Eucalyptus[1]
	Tree of heaven[1]
	Wild grape[1]

---

[1] Although these trees are amphiphilous (partially wind pollinated) or entemophilous (insect pollinated), under the proper conditions of exposure they may provoke symptoms.

---

ing the criteria, but this is rare, and often the wrong plant is blamed (such as goldenrod, which is blamed for symptoms probably caused by ragweed).

Pollinating plants are limited to the temperate climates, and evergreen conifers and flowering plants, algae, fungi, mosses, and ferns are not pollen producers. In Arctic regions there is an absence of significant pollinating plants. The subarctic regions are largely populated by the conifers (evergreens), which produce a nonallergenic pollen.

Since pollen is hygroscopic, or able to absorb water vapor from the atmosphere, it becomes too heavy to be wind-borne. Therefore, hay-fever–causing plants are rare in humid tropical climates. In these areas, pollination depends upon insects, birds, and bats. (See also ANEMOPHILOUS PLANTS, POLLEN.)

pollutant   Any particle, chemical, irritant, or other substance that contributes to or creates bad air, that is, impure air capable of causing adverse reactions when it flows in and out of the body.

pollution   The condition of being polluted, or defiled, by impurities. (See POLLUTANT.)

polyblennia   An abnormal secretion of mucus.

polyethylene glycols   Polymerized resins of ethylene used as water-soluble ointment bases. Only lower-molecular-weight polyethylene glycols, such as p. glycol 400, may cause hives or allergic contact dermatitis.

polymer   A natural or synthetic chemical created by combining molecules of the same substance, such as the formation of paraformaldehyde from three molecules of formaldehyde.

polymer fume fever   [metal fume fever] Tightness in the chest, fever and chills, weakness, and sore throat associated with inhaling fumes of certain polymers when heated to 300° to 700° C or higher.

polymorphonuclear leukocytes   See NEUTROPHILS.

polyneuritis, Jamaica ginger   An inflammation, also known as ginger paralysis, of the nerves of the extremities as a result of eating Jamaica ginger.

polyp, mucous   A soft polyp exhibiting mucoid degeneration.

polyp, nasal   Soft tissue normally found lining the ethmoid sinuses that protrudes into the nasal cavity. Most often nasal polyps occur bilaterally, are usually benign, and cause nasal obstruction.

Prevalence   An estimated one to 20 adults per 1,000 population, males by a ratio of from two to four to one, have nasal polyps at some time during their lives. Allergic individuals are no more likely than others to develop polyps. Benign simple polyps are rarely found before age 20, and if present in children before the age of two, a serious defect in the base of the skull may be present. Nasal polyps occur in 8% of cystic fibrosis patients, and when seen in children over the age of two, they may be a manifestation of this serious inherited disorder. They are also found in two other rare diseases,

Kartagener's syndrome and Young's syndrome. Polyps arising from the maxillary sinuses are called antrocoanal polyps and grow into the postnasal space.

Complications Approximately one-third of patients with nasal polyps are asthmatics, and about 8% also have aspirin sensitivity (referred to as a triad, or three linked disorders). Patients with the triad may develop problems with foods containing the yellow dye tartrazine. Polyps may worsen asthma because the nose's normal warming of the inspired air before it reaches the lungs is blocked, forcing bronchoconstricting cold air to reach the lungs through the mouth because of nasal obstruction.

Treatment About half of all cases of nasal polyps respond to corticosteroid nasal sprays. Those not responding will most likely need surgery. Endoscopic resection of polyps is the procedure of choice. Many patient have recurrences. (See ASPIRIN SENSITIVITY, CYSTIC FIBROSIS.)

polypnea   Extremely rapid breathing or panting.

polys See NEUTROPHILS.

polysinusitus Infection involving more than one of the sinuses. (See SINUSITIS.)

pompholyx The Greek word meaning "bubble," referring to warm, itchy bullae (large blisters) developing only on the hands and feet. This condition is seen in long-term smokers, coffee drinkers, and debilitated individuals. It usually lasts four to six weeks. Good hygiene and lotions and other topical preparations are the usual treatments. X-ray therapy may be required in resistant cases.

porcupine disease   See ICHTHYOSIS VULGARIS.

pork insulin A protein hormone of the pancreas of a pig used in the treatment of diabetes mellitus. Insulin promotes proper metabolism of carbohydrates essential to human life. Insulin-dependent individuals who are allergic to beef insulin may be able to tolerate pork insulin. Because of the availability of biologically engineered human insulin, animal insulin is now rarely used. (See DIABETES MELLITUS, INSULIN ALLERGY.)

Porter, Rodney R.   British scientist (1917–85) who made important contributions to the study of protein chemistry, including protein fractionation, genetic markers of immunoglobulins, complement components, the structure of antibodies, and complement genes. In 1972, Porter shared the Nobel Prize for physiology or medicine with Gerald M. Edelman, American physician and scientist, born in 1929 in New York City. The two men worked independently to elucidate the chemical structure of antibodies.

Portier, Paul   French scientist (1866–1962) who served as professor of comparative physiology at the Sorbonne in Paris. He became a close friend of Prince Albert I of Monaco, who was well known for his oceanographic studies. On a cruise in the Mediterranean arranged by the prince, Portier met Dr. Charles Richet, with whom he was to discover anaphylaxis and share the Nobel Prize in 1913.

Succeeding Richet in the Academy of Sciences, Portier wrote papers on insects, parasitism, symbiosis, and the physiology and evolution of aquatic animals. (See also RICHET, CHARLES.)

post nasal drip Sensation of mucus in the back of the throat commonly occurring in persons with nasal allergy, sinusitis, colds, and other upper respiratory infections.

postural drainage A series of techniques that take advantage of gravity to encourage mucus to move out of the lungs or bronchi. For example, one technique requires the patient to be placed on an incline or over the edge of the bed face down, with his or her head lower than the rest of the body. The health care professional or caregiver then cups his or her hands and gently claps the patient's back (over the lung area). The clapping causes productive coughing, that is, expectoration of sputum. Other techniques based on the gravity principle depend upon which part of the lung is affected. Because postural drainage may aggravate a person's asthma or other respiratory disorder, a trained professional should perform the initial therapy and evaluate the patient's tolerance.

potassium iodide   The crystals of the mineral potassium (a salt), having a slight iodine odor, that have been prepared as an expectorant. When used as a mucolytic drug, a potassium iodide solution may help alleviate mucus buildup in the lungs and bronchial passages, but it may also cause acnelike skin lesions and hypothyroidism. (See also EXPECTORANT.)

potato   A popular vegetable, the edible part of a tuber containing starch. Potato may cause allergic symptoms in persons also allergic to birch tree pollen, but this is rare. Potato chips, however, contain the preservative sodium metabisulfite, which may cause asthma.

Prausnitz-Kustner reaction   A passive transfer of hypersensitivity from an allergic person to a nonallergic person, as demonstrated in a classic experiment by two German physicians, Otto Carl W. Prausnitz and Heinz Kustner, in 1921. Kustner was highly allergic to fish and skin-tested positive to fish extract. The nonallergic Prausnitz injected some serum taken from Kustner into his own skin, and a wheal and redness resulted 24 hours after an injection of fish extract at the same injection site. The PK passive transfer reaction, as it is called, has been modified for many allergy tests, including pollens, animal danders, and drugs.

precipitin   [autoprecipitin, precipitinogen] Antibody formed in the blood when exposed to a soluble allergen, usually a foreign protein. When added to a solution of the allergen, precipitation occurs. Precipitation of a substance refers to that substance separating from the solution in which it is suspended and floating at the top or falling to the bottom. The injected protein is called the antigen or allergen, and the antibody produced is the precipitin.

precipitinogen   See PRECIPITIN.

prednisolone   See CORTICOSTEROIDS.

prednisone   The most commonly prescribed corticosteroid drug for the treatment of allergies and asthma. (See CORTICOSTEROIDS.)

pregnancy, Food and Drug Administration (FDA) drug risk categories   Five categories of prescription drugs for use in pregnant women included in the precautions section of the package insert (the literature that accompanies every prescription drug). Drugs are categorized according to their potential for risk to the developing fetus as follows:

FDA Pregnancy Category A: Controlled studies in women fail to demonstrate a risk to the fetus in the first trimester (and there is no evidence of a risk in later trimesters), and the possibility of fetal harm appears remote.
FDA Pregnancy Category B: Either animal reproduction studies have not demonstrated a fetal risk, but there are no controlled studies in pregnant women, or animal reproduction studies have shown an adverse effect (other than decreased fertility) that was not confirmed in controlled studies on women in the first trimester (and there is no evidence of a risk in later trimesters).
FDA Pregnancy Category C: Either studies in animals have revealed adverse effects on the fetus (teratogenic, embryocidal, or other effects) and there are no controlled studies in women, or studies in women and animals are not available. Drugs in this category should be given only if the potential benefit justifies the risk to the fetus.
FDA Pregnancy Category D: There is positive evidence of human fetal risk, but the benefits for pregnant women may be acceptable despite the risk, as in life-threatening or serious diseases for which safer drugs cannot be used or are ineffective. An appropriate statement must appear in the "warnings" section of the labeling of drugs in this category.

FDA Pregnancy Category X: Studies in animals or humans have demonstrated fetal abnormalities, or there is evidence of fetal risk based on human experience, or both, and the risk of using the drug in pregnant women clearly outweighs any possible benefit. The drug is contraindicated in women who are or may become pregnant. An appropriate statement must appear in the "contraindications" section of the labeling of drugs in this category. (See also TERATOGENS.)

[Author's note: The FDA Pregnancy Categories can be misleading and may unduly cause fear for the entire pregnancy when a drug classified as a "C" or "D" is prescribed. Most of the drugs used to treat allergies and asthma during pregnancy have a "C" rating, yet they have been used safely for many years. Many physicians believe the letter designations should be eliminated or modified with a more in-depth written statement relating the known experience of each particular drug in the pregnancy section of the package insert.]

pregnancy and rhinitis Rhinitis, or nasal congestion, that occurs in approximately 35% of pregnant women. In one study, during pregnancy the congestion worsened in 34% of the women, improved in 15%, and was unchanged in the rest. Severe rhinitis can interfere with sleep and aggravate asthma.

As in nonpregnant individuals, runny and stuffy noses can be caused by allergies, or hay fever; or by vasomotor, or nonallergic, rhinitis, or infections, such as colds and sinusitis.

Treatment should be based on the same principles for using any drug during pregnancy. The drug must be necessary and have a long record of use during pregnancy without reported adverse outcomes to the pregnancy, and its use must be monitored by a physician experienced in its use during pregnancy.

pregnancy complicated by asthma Asthma is present in at least 4% of all pregnancies and may occur in as many as 10%. Asthma may occur for the first time during pregnancy. Preexisting

asthma may worsen or improve during pregnancy. About one-third of pregnant women with asthma worsen during pregnancy, one-third continue unchanged, and one-third improve.

GENERAL TREATMENT PRINCIPLES OF ASTHMA DURING PREGNANCY

- Asthma is a chronic condition with acute exacerbations or attacks; close monitoring by both patient and doctor is necessary to detect subtle changes throughout pregnancy.
- Prevention of attacks is of upmost importance. Identify and avoid triggers, and optimize measures to reduce the presence of indoor allergens, such as furry pets, dust mites, and molds. ESPECIALLY AVOID TOBACCO SMOKE. Use air-conditioning in pollen seasons to reduce exposure. Use preventive drugs daily exactly as prescribed.
- Anticipate or intervene early during an attack. Use a peak flow meter to detect subtle changes in breathing and have a plan to act before attacks become severe or catastrophic.
- Although using as few medications as possible is generally desirable during pregnancy, normal breathing and oxygen levels must be maintained in the mother to assure normal oxygen supply to the fetus. Inhaled drugs are preferred, but if they are not totally effective, systemic drugs should be used to achieve normal lung function.
- Disorders that aggravate asthma, such as sinus infections, nasal allergies, and heartburn, should be treated promptly so they will not trigger asthma.

Asthma's potential adverse effects on pregnancy Whether a pregnant woman's asthma worsens, remains the same, or improves, uncontrolled asthma can produce serious complications for mother and fetus. Maternal complications from asthma include preeclampsia (a toxemia of pregnancy), gestational hypertension, hyperemesis gravidarum (severe nausea and vomiting during pregnancy), vaginal hemorrhage, toxemia, and induced and compli-

---

PREFERRED DRUGS FOR THE TREATMENT OF ASTHMA DURING PREGNANCY

Drug Type	Specific Drug
Anti-inflammatory	beclomethasone (Beclovent, Vanceril)
	cromolyn sodium (Intal)
	prednisone
Bronchodilator	inhaled beta$_2$ agonist: albuterol (Proventil, Ventolin), metaproterenol (Alupent), pirbuterol (Maxair), terbutaline (Brethaire)
	theophylline (Constant-T, Quibron, SloBid, Slo-Phyllin, Theo-Dur, Theo-24, Theolair, Theovent, Uniphyl) [serum levels must be monitored to avoid toxicity]

---

cated labor. Fetal complications include increased risk of fetal death, diminished growth, prematurity, low birth weight, and neonatal hypoxia. The more severe the asthma, the greater the risk, but even mildly uncontrolled asthma is a risk. When asthma is well controlled, even if medications are required, the outcome of pregnancy should be the same as in a nonasthmatic mother.

Effect of mother's breathing on fetal oxygen supply During pregnancy, there are changes that occur in the mother's body, unrelated to asthma, that cause a mild sensation of shortness of breath in many normal women. However, these "normal" changes affect neither the supply of oxygen to the fetus nor the results of breathing tests that are used to measure the severity of asthma in the mother.

However, during an asthma attack, the mother's body utilizes available oxygen, reducing the amount supplied through the placenta to the fetus. A small fall in oxygen concentration that would result in only minimal to moderate distress to the mother can be catastrophic to the baby.

Goals of therapy and general treatment principles Traditionally, asthma was viewed as an intermittent acute illness whose symptoms were due to constriction of the bronchioles, and the goal of drugs was to reverse this spasm. Since scientists have determined the importance of lung inflammation in asthma, the goal of treatment is not only to improve symptoms during an attack but also to prevent symptoms from recurring. Treatment of asthma during pregnancy follows the same principles as for the nonpregnant individual. Avoidance of asthma triggers may reduce the need for drugs. When drugs are needed, the preventive anti-inflammatory cromolyn and corticosteroid inhalers are especially useful, safe, and effective.

Monitoring mother's breathing status For pregnant patients with asthma, objective measurement of lung function is essential. This can be done in the doctor's office with spirometry (see SPIROMETRY) or a peak flow meter (see PEAK FLOW, PEAK FLOW METER). Inexpensive handheld peak flow monitors can be used at home or in the workplace to detect changes that may indicate the onset of an asthma attack. The peak flow meter may detect changes before symptoms are apparent.

Fetal monitoring For pregnant women with asthma, fetal evaluation is based on objective measurements such as sonography (ultrasound), electronic fetal heart rate monitoring, and by subjective means, such as the mother's assessment of fetal kicks ("kick count"). Sonography from 12 to 20 weeks provides a guide to fetal growth and should be followed frequently in cases in which asthma is moderate or severe to detect growth retardation.

Effects of asthma drugs in pregnancy In considering the possible effects of drugs and disease on pregnancy, it is important to keep in mind the incidence of adverse pregnancy outcomes in the general population. Congenital anomalies (birth defects) occur in 3 to 8% of all newborns, and of these only 1% or fewer are attributable to drug exposures.

Both animal and human data are studied to evaluate the safety of drugs. If studies in animals, where huge doses are used during testing, are reassuring, the potential for effects in humans is low. However, animal data do not always give complete information. It may not be possible to know whether the effects of a drug on the newborn were caused by the use of excessive doses by the mother, the disease process itself, or multiple other factors. Human studies rarely include large numbers of patients exposed to a particular drug. Therefore, drugs that have been used for many years without a significant number of reported adverse effects are considered most reliable.

Immunotherapy Immunotherapy (allergy shots) may prevent asthma symptoms triggered by allergy, therefore reducing the need for drugs. Desensitization by injecting minute amounts of allergy extracts for cat dander, dust mites, molds, and pollens is generally safe and effective. The principal concern for giving immunotherapy during pregnancy is the same as in nonpregnant individuals, to avoid anaphylaxis (the most severe form of allergic reactions). Because a severe reaction may threaten the lives of both mother and fetus, injections of allergy extracts must be given cautiously and doses are usually not increased or slightly decreased during pregnancy. It is generally recommended that allergy immunotherapy not be initiated during pregnancy, because it takes several months for any benefit to be evident and doses must be given in increasing amounts during the early stages of treatment.

Influenza ("flu") vaccine Annual flu vaccine is recommended for all patients with moderate or severe asthma. Influenza vaccine is based on a killed virus, and there is no evidence of risk to mother or fetus.

Physical activity Physical activity should be encouraged and no different from that of a non-asthmatic pregnant woman. If necessary, pretreatment with a beta-agonist metered-dose inhaler such as albuterol or cromolyn five to 60 minutes before exercise should be used (see EXERCISE-INDUCED ASTHMA).

Summary Pregnant women with asthma need asthma treatment. Nondrug measures are preferred such as improving the environment to avoid known triggers—allergens or irritants such as tobacco smoke. Drugs with many years of safe use are those of choice. A panel of experts from the National Institutes of Health strongly recommends that asthma be as aggressively treated in pregnant women as in nonpregnant women. [Author's note: The section on pregnancy and asthma is adapted from the National Asthma Education Program's report *Management of Asthma During Pregnancy* (NIH Publication No. 93-3279A, October 1992).]

PREFERRED DRUGS FOR THE TREATMENT OF ALLERGY OR RESPIRATORY INFECTIONS COMPLICATING ASTHMA DURING PREGNANCY

Drug Type	Specific Drug
Antibiotics	amoxicillin
Antihistamine	chlorpheniramine (Chlor-Trimeton)
	tripelennamine (Pyribenzamine)
Anti-inflammatory	cromolyn sodium (Nasalcrom nasal spray)
	beclomethasone (Beconase, Vancenase)
Cough	dextromethorphan, guaifenesin (Robitussin)
Decongestant	oxymetazoline (Afrin) nasal spray or drops [must be used sparingly to avoid rebound worsening of nasal congestion (see RHINITIS MEDICOMENTO-SUM)],
	pseudoephedrine (Sudafed)

prenatal and postnatal allergic sensitization
Immunoglobulin E (IgE) antibodies and other immunities developed in the fetus whether the mother has produced them or not. A well-controlled Swedish study of 212 pregnant women indicated that the occurrence of allergies in babies is not influenced by the mother's diet. Smoking does affect the outcome of pregnancy, however: Babies of smokers had a greater than threefold higher risk of developing allergies before 18 months of age, which indicates that the infants' immune systems became compromised while in the uterus. Breastfeeding can delay the potential onset of allergy if the mother avoids the major known allergenic foods (eggs, cow's milk, and fish) during the first six months of breast-feeding.

Pre-Pen   Brand of benzylpenicilloyl, a substance useful for the testing of penicillin allergy.

preservatives   See FOOD ADDITIVES.

pressure urticaria   A form of hives occurring four to six hours after the application of sustained pressure to a specific area of the body, such as foot swelling after prolonged walking, hand swelling after clapping or hammering, shoulder swelling after carrying heavy objects, swelling of the buttocks after sitting, and swelling under areas of tight clothing, belts, or girdles. In some individuals, hives may occur with or without swelling. Fever, malaise, joint pain, and other symptoms accompany the hives in certain cases. Treatment includes antihistamines, aspirin, nonsteroidal anti-inflammatory drugs such as ibuprofen, and occasionally prednisone. (See also PHYSICAL URTICARIA, URTICARIA.)

prevalence of allergies and asthma   See ALLERGY, ASTHMA STATISTICS.

prevention of allergies   See PRENATAL AND POSTNATAL ALLERGIC SENSITIZATION.

prickly heat   Red, itchy, and tingling nonallergic rash occurring during hot weather, especially in babies. It is caused by obstruction or inflammation of the sweat glands and may be confused with eczema. (See ATOPIC DERMATITIS.)

prick test   See SKIN TESTS.

priming effect   The heightened response to allergen exposure following repeated exposure to the same dose of allergen, or the added effect of multiple allergen exposure. An example is an exposure to the same dose of ragweed pollen each day for several days, during which the patient gradually experiences increasing hay fever symptoms. Or a patient sensitive to both ragweed and grass pollen becomes more sensitive to ragweed after exposure to grass pollen. Immunotherapy has been shown to reduce the priming effect.

PRIST   See PAPER RADIOIMMUNOSORBENT TEST.

Privine   See NAPHAZOLINE.

procaine hydrochloride   (Novocain)   White or colorless crystalline compound, less toxic than cocaine, used as a local anesthetic. Allergic reactions are rare. (See ANESTHETICS, LOCAL.)

Prolert   See ACRIVASTINE.

promethazine   (Phenergan)   An antihistaminic, sedative, anti-motion-sickness, antinausea, and anticholinergic drug, used in the treatment of cough and allergic reactions.

prostaglandins   A group of fatty acids that act like hormones and are found throughout the body but exert important functions in the brain, lungs, gastrointestinal tract, kidneys, uterus, semen, and blood. During allergic reactions, mast cells release histamine and other chemical mediators, which in turn generates secondary mediator products by cells of the immune system, producing prostaglandins and leukotrienes. Prostaglandins cause the pain of arthritis, stimulate uterine contractions during labor, lower blood pressure, and protect the stomach and duodenum against peptic ulcers. Various prostaglandins have opposite effects in the lungs; prostaglandins known as PGE_1 and PGE_2 dilate the airways in the lungs, whereas prostaglandins known as PG_A and PGF_2 cause the constriction seen in asthma. Aspirin may cause an imbalance in the prostaglandins, causing asthma in some individuals. Several of them cause inflammation in body tissues. PGE_2 and PGF_2 may be responsible for the adverse reactions to foods that cause nausea, vomiting, colicky abdominal pain, bloating, and diarrhea.

Synthetic prostaglandins are used to induce labor or an elective abortion. Nonsteroidal antiinflammatory drugs (NSAIDS), aspirin, and corticosteroids are used to counteract the effects of pain and inflammation caused by prostaglandins. NSAIDS have been shown to protect some individuals from nonallergic adverse food reactions in the gastrointestinal tract if doses of the drugs were taken 30 to 60 minutes before eating the offending foods.

ProStep   See NICOTINE PATCHES.

protein   Complex compounds of amino acids containing nitrogen, hydrogen, oxygen, carbon, sugars, fats, and other elements necessary to maintain life, growth, and healing of animal tissue. A source of bodily heat and energy, protein may be obtained from meat, fish, eggs, milk and dairy products, legumes including various beans, and other sources. Excess protein increases the nitrogen content in the body, which is detectable in the urine and may indicate a disease process. Animal and plant proteins are often a source of occupational allergens (see OCCUPATIONAL ALLERGENS).

Proventil   See ALBUTEROL.

provocation and neutralization skin testing
A controversial method of diagnosis and treatment of allergies in which a quantity of an allergen of sufficient strength to provoke symptoms is injected into the subcutaneous tissues of the arm. This is immediately followed by a second injection of a weaker or a stronger

quantity of allergen in the expectation that the patient's symptoms will be relieved.

In the September 23, 1980 *Federal Register*, the National Center for Health Care Technology requested opinions from interested parties concerning this method and other unproven techniques. The American Academy of Allergy and Immunology published a position statement in response to the request in which the following conclusions were stated:

1. Subcutaneous provocation and neutralization as a method for the treatment and diagnosis of allergic disease has no plausible rationale or immunologic basis.
2. Four controlled clinical studies have shown this method of diagnosis and treatment to be ineffective.
3. Subcutaneous provocation and neutralization treatment should at present be reserved for use in controlled experiments only.

provocative sublingual testing   Method for the diagnosis and treatment of food allergies in which drops of an allergenic extract are placed under the tongue of the patient, who is then observed for the onset of allergy symptoms for 10 minutes. When the physician is satisfied that he or she has found the cause of respiratory, gastrointestional, or other systemic symptoms, a "neutralizing dose" (a very dilute solution of the same extract) is given again under the tongue. Proponents of this testing method claim that a neutralizing dose given prior to eating a meal containing the offending food will prevent symptoms.

In the September 23, 1980 *Federal Register*, the National Center for Health Care Technology requested opinions from interested parties concerning this method and other unproven techniques. The American Academy of Allergy and Immunology published a position statement in response to this request in which the following conclusions were stated:

After careful consideration of the available data, the opinion of the Executive Committee of the American Academy of Allergy and

Immunology is at this time:

1. No controlled clinical studies indicating a diagnostic or therapeutic effect of sublingual antigen administration on human atopic diseases are known to the Committee. Moreover, there are no known immunologic mechanisms that can account for the "neutralizing effects" of dilute solutions of allergenic extracts.

2. Since the results of other controlled studies indicate that the method is ineffective, demonstration of the effectiveness of this method for diagnosis and therapy should be the responsibility of the proponents of the method. Until such studies are performed, the method should be considered unproven.

3. Sublingual provocative testing and desensitization should be reserved for experimental use only in well-designed trials.

(See also CONTROVERSIAL APPROACHES TO DIAGNOSIS, EXPLANATION, OR TREATMENT OF ALLERGIES.)

provocative testing   See CHALLENGE.

prurigo   A term used by some dermatologists to refer to a chronic eruption of extremely itchy papules or pimples on the arms and legs. The cause is unknown, but prurigo usually begins in childhood and may be lifelong. Prurigo estivalis is a form of this condition associated with exposure to the sun in hot weather. Prurigo nodularis, characterized by severe itching of firm nodules beneath the skin, occurs most frequently in middle-aged women. Simple acute prurigo may be caused by hypersensitivity to insect bites. During the second or third trimester of pregnancy, prurigo may appear on the arms, legs, and upper torso. These lesions eventually disappear.

pruritus   Itching. Essential pruritus is itching that occurs without any known cause or the presence of any discernible anomaly. Degeneration of the skin in the aged may cause pruritus senilis but may be a sign of a serious underlying disease, including malignancy.

Itching associated with a specific disease is called symptomatic pruritus. Duhring's pruri-

tus, also called pruritus hiemalis, is itching caused by cold weather.

pruritus, oral   Itching of the palate is a common symptom of food and upper respiratory allergies.

pseudoallergic reaction   Symptoms suggestive of an allergic reaction but which are not a true allergic reaction. (See ALLERGY.)

pseudoephedrine   The generic name for Sudafed, Afrinol, and other drugs, including many over-the-counter preparations, used alone or combined with antihistamines in the treatment of nasal congestion caused by allergies and colds. (See ALPHA-ADRENERGIC AGONISTS.)

pseudoreaction   A false response to an injected substance used to determine the presence of an allergen. However, this response is due to the presence of an unexpected allergen and not the one the skin test was intended to find.

psittacosis [parrot fever]   A *Chlamydia psittaci* infection characterized by headache, nausea, chills, and sometimes pulmonary problems. The disease, rarely fatal, can be transmitted to humans from birds—parrots, pigeons, and fowl are the main carriers—by inhalation of dust contaminated with bird droppings. Approximately 100 cases of psittacosis are reported annually in the United States, though some professionals believe many cases go unreported. Bird or poultry handlers are at the greatest risk of infection. Antibodies specific to the *Chlamydia* species found in human blood confirm the diagnosis. Tetracycline is the treatment of choice. Psittacosis may be confused with asthma or allergy to birds.

psora   The Greek word meaning "itch," referring to scabies or an itching disease of the skin.

psoriasis   A chronic, itchy rash characterized by thick, scaly, red to silvery skin lesions. Lesions most commonly occur on the elbows and knees and are often confused with allergic rashes such as eczema. (See ATOPIC DERMATI-TIS.)

psyllium seed The dried ripe seed of a flea-wort plant, *Plantago psyllium*, that swells when moist to form a gelatinous mass and is used to treat bowel dysfunction. Psyllium is a natural therapeutic fiber and acts as a bulk-forming agent. It is the active ingredient in the proprietary product Metamucil and is useful for both constipation and diarrhea characteristic of irritable bowel syndrome. Psyllium is classified as an occupational allergen, since exposure can cause severe reactions including anaphylaxis. Therefore, health care professionals and pharmaceutical industry workers who handle large amounts of the psyllium-containing products should take precautions to avoid inhaling the dust.

ptarmus Sneezing spasms.

pulmonary fibrosis Thickening and scarring of alveolar lung tissue resulting from inflammatory lung diseases such as hypersensitivity pneumonitis (an allergic lung disease), pneumonia, tuberculosis, some drugs, and many other lung disorders. In over 50% of cases the cause is unknown. The major symptom is progressive breathlessness. Diagnosis is based on abnormal chest X-ray and pulmonary function test results. Corticosteroids may be effective in some cases of this sometimes fatal disease.

pulmonary function tests Procedures used to diagnose and evaluate the severity of asthma and some other lung disorders. (See PEAK FLOW, SPIROMETRY.)

pulmonologist Physician who specializes in the diagnosis and treatment of lung diseases, including asthma.

pulsus paradoxus A mercury fall of greater than 10 millimeters in the systolic blood pressure during inspiration that occurs during a severe life-threatening asthma attack.

punctate rash Skin eruption characterized by tiny red pointed dots.

purpura, allergic See HENOCHSCHONLEIN PURPURA, VASCULITIS.

pustules Skin lesions containing infected fluid known as pus.

pyodermatitis An infected rash that causes inflammation of the skin.

pyrethrum An insecticide made from dried flowering heads of the chrysanthemum plant, a member of the Compositae family, which includes ragweed. Persons with ragweed-sensitive hay fever may have allergic symptoms when exposed to the insecticide.

Pyribenzamine See TRIPELENNAMINE.

pyrilamine An antihistaminic drug of the ethylenediamine class used for the treatment of allergic disorders. (See ANTIHISTAMINE.)

Q

quackery   Misrepresentation by an individual or individuals who pretend to have knowledge of medical diagnosis or treatment but whose knowledge and methods are inaccurate or unproven. (See CONTROVERSIAL APPROACHES TO DIAGNOSIS, EXPLANATION, OR TREATMENT OF ALLERGIES.)

questionnaire for screening asthma   A set of questions patients are requested to answer in order for the physician to determine if they are at risk for having asthma. For example:

	Yes	No
1. Is asthma worse in certain months?	—	—
2 If the answer to number 1 was yes, are there hay fever symptoms—sneezing, itching, runny nose, nasal congestion—at the same time?	—	—
3. Do symptoms occur when visiting a house where there are indoor pets?	—	—
4. If there are pets in your home, do symptoms improve when the patient is away from home for a week or longer?	—	—
5. Do symptoms of hay fever (see above) improve when away from home?	—	—
6. Do symptoms become worse the first 24 hours after returning home?	—	—
7. Do eyes itch and become red after handling a pet?	—	—
8. If a pet licks you, does a red, itchy welt develop?	—	—
9. Do symptoms appear in a room where carpets are being vacuumed?	—	—

10.

	Yes	No
Does making a bed cause symptoms?	—	—
11. Do symptoms occur when you are around hay or in a barn or stable?	—	—
12. Do symptoms develop when you go into a damp basement or a vacation cottage that has been closed up for a period of time?	—	—
13. Do symptoms develop related to certain job activities, either at work or after leaving work?	—	—
14. If symptoms develop at work, do they improve when away from work for a few days?	—	—

One or more yes answers to any of the above questions strongly suggests the presence of allergic rhinitis (hay fever) or asthma.

Allergens are very likely to be a cause of symptoms if answers are "yes" to questions indicated as follows:

1. and 2. pollens and outdoor molds
3. and 4. animal dander
5. and 6. house dust mites, indoor molds, animal dander
7. and 8. animal dander (and other allergens found in saliva and urine)
9. animal dander or dust mites
10. dust mites
11. molds and mites (or farm animal dander and other animal allergens)
12. molds
13. and 14. Refer to the list of occupational allergens (see OCCUPATIONAL ALLERGENS).

Adapted from the *Guidelines for the Diagnosis and Management of Asthma*, National Asthma

Education Program, National Institutes of Health.

Quibron   See THEOPHYLLINE.

Quidel test   A visual "dipstick" for an in vitro screening test to detect the presence of IgE antibodies against common allergens. At least one study suggests this test to be approximately the equivalent of radioallergosorbent testing, or RAST. (See also RADIOALLERGOSORBENT TESTS.)

Quincke's disease   Huge hives also known as angioneurotic edema of the skin, named after German physician Heinrich I. Quincke (1842–1922). (See ANGIOEDEMA, HEREDITARY; ANGIOEDEMA, IDIOPATHIC; URTICARIA.)

quinolone antibiotics   A unique group of broad-spectrum antibiotics that attack an enzyme, DNA gyrase, essential for the reproduction of infection-causing bacteria. Nalidixic acid, an earlier quinolone drug, had limited usefulness, but derivatives of this drug became available for use in the early 1990s; there are now four different clinically important quinolone derivatives available in the United States: ciprofloxacin (Cipro) and norfloxacin [(Norloxin), (Floxin), and (Maxaquin)]. Another antibiotic in this category, ofloxacin, was recalled shortly after it was introduced following reports of deaths related to its use.

With the exception of norfloxacin (used primarily for urinary tract infections), these antibiotics are frequently prescribed for patients with respiratory infections. However, since some of the quinolone antibiotics raise theophylline levels, which possibly causes toxicity, they must be used cautiously or avoided in patients who are also taking this asthma drug.

Quintest   A device used for allergy skin tests allowing a uniform dose spaced at regular intervals and at a constant depth for multiple allergens.

R

rabbits   Furry animals of the family Leporidae with long ears and long hind legs. Rabbits are valuable laboratory animals used for medical research including studies of the immune response (allergic reactions). They are frequent home pets, and rabbit dander, an allergen similar to that found in cats and other animals, is a source of allergic rhinitis, fever, and asthma symptoms in allergic persons. (See also ANIMAL ALLERGY.)

rabies immune globulin (human)   A sterile solution of antirabies immunoglobulin (antibodies) prepared from human plasma. Plasma is pooled from human donors who have been immunized with rabies vaccine, and the resulting product provides immediate but short-lasting protection against the rabies virus. Since the immune globulin gives only passive immunity to rabies, it is used only for individuals not previously immunized with rabies vaccine who have proven adequate serum levels of rabies antibodies. The immune globulin should be given immediately after a bite by a suspicious animal in addition to the rabies vaccine.

Since the availability of human immunoglobulin, adverse effects are rare. However, epinephrine (Adrenalin) should be available in case of anaphylactic reactions to the product. Persons with immunoglobulin A (IgA) deficiency are at greater risk for developing severe allergic reactions when exposed to blood products containing IgA upon reexposure to these products after immunization with rabies immune globulin.

racial factors in the incidence of asthma and allergy   Differences characteristic of various races that are difficult to determine because environmental influences seem to play an important role in the development of allergies. American Indians, Eskimos, and a few scattered island peoples seem to have a lower rate of asthma, but incidence in other races seems to differ by location. (See also ASTHMA DEATHS.)

Rackemann, Francis E.   American physician (1887–1973), born in Milton, Massachusetts, considered the first to believe that asthma may not always be proven to be an allergic disorder. Rackemann conducted a study of 150 asthmatics and concluded that: (1) bronchial asthma is a symptom that may be caused by various "extrinsic" or "intrinsic" factors; (2) a history of asthma, hay fever, or food poisoning occurs in the immediate family of 58.7% of extrinsic asthmatics, and in 10.5% of intrinsic asthmatics; (3) skin tests help confirm the diagnosis of allergy; and (4) the "nervous" element is important in asthma but does not explain why certain individuals have asthma. Rackemann served as the second president, succeeding Robert Cooke, of the (Eastern) Society for the Study of Asthma and Allied Conditions in New York City.

radioallergosorbent tests (RAST)   Quantitative measurements of immunoglobulin E molecules (IgE class of antibodies) in the serum specific for particular allergens. RAST is the most widely available in vitro laboratory method (see IN VITRO TEST) for the diagnosis of allergy. If performed in a state-of-the-art laboratory facility, it is roughly equivalent to the prick-puncture method of skin testing in sensitivity. However, RAST is less sensitive than intradermal skin tests and may fail to diagnose many patients with low yet significant sensitivities.

RAST tests available from various laboratories include those for pollens, molds, animals, foods, industrial allergens, drugs, and insects. Advantages of this method include the ability to measure many allergens with a single blood sample; in addition, antihistamines (drugs used to treat allergies) that interfere with skin testing do not have to be stopped prior to testing, and patients can be tested even if acutely ill with asthma or other allergic disorders. Persons with severe skin disorders such as eczema or dermatographia can also be tested.

Disadvantages of RAST include lesser sensitivity, increased expense, and results that are not immediately available when compared with skin testing. A positive RAST test result can be present in an individual who does not exhibit symptoms when exposed to a certain allergen. This is called a "false-positive" result. Therefore, a careful history and physical examination must be done in conjunction with test results to determine the significance of results.

"Modified" RAST is a more sensitive RAST test available from a number of laboratories. Many allergists feel that the increased sensitivity sacrifices specificity, and that low positive results are of questionable significance. MAST and FAST are similar blood allergy tests. (See Appendix II for a list of RAST tests available. See also IMMUNOGLOBULIN E, SKIN TESTS.)

radiocontrast media reactions Adverse reactions upon exposure to radiopaque dyes used in diagnostic radiology studies. Most dye reactions occur because the osmolarity (osmolarity of a solution is determined by the concentration of dissolved ions) of the solution injected is greater than the concentration of blood (hyperosmolar). These adverse reactions are usually idiosyncratic, or allergylike, but not true immunologic responses (see DRUG ALLERGY AND OTHER ADVERSE DRUG REACTIONS). When these hyperosmolar agents are introduced into the bloodstream, they can cause damage to the blood vessels, constrict the blood vessels in the kidneys, have a depressant effect on heart muscle, or damage brain tissues. They probably rupture basophilic cells of the immune system, resulting in the release of anaphylactic chemical mediators such as histamine. In severe cases, there is a sudden drop in blood pressure, nausea, vomiting, and shock. Hives or wheezing may also occur.

Approximately two out of 100 persons receiving these agents experience adverse reactions. About one in 50,000 patients undergoing an intravenous pyelogram (IVP) to detect abnormalities in the kidneys and urinary tract have a fatal reaction.

The hyperosmolar triiodinated benzoates, such as diatrizote, iothalamate, or metrizoate, are the most common radiocontrast materials used. However, newly developed low-osmolarity agents such as iopamidol are available and may lessen the chance of a reaction, but they are very expensive. It is impossible to predict the chance of recurrence of an adverse reaction to X-ray dye.

Patients with a history of a prior adverse reaction to these agents or a history of asthma can be pretreated with prednisone and antihistamines. Where available, a newer, safer medium is used for high-risk procedures.

radiodermatitis Rash caused by exposure to X rays or radioactive elements.

ragweed Species of the anemophilous (wind-pollinating) genus *Ambrosia* in the plant family Compositae (see COMPOSITAE FAMILY), whose pollen is the most important weed allergen that causes hay fever. Ragweed pollen can be detected as early as late July and usually peaks by early September, when thousands of grains per cubic meter of air afflict an estimated five million Americans. The season ends with the first frost about mid-October.

Although ragweed is most abundant in the central plains and eastern rural areas of the United States, approximately 40 species are distributed throughout the warmer regions of the Western Hemisphere. About a dozen species of ragweed are present in sufficient quantity to be important sources of pollen, but the two most prolific are short, common, or dwarf (*Ambrosia artemisifolia*) and giant (*A. trifida*). Short ragweed flourishes in northern Mexico, the Midwest, Ozark plateau, and Gulf states to the Atlantic coast. It is also present to some extent in the Pacific Northwest. Giant ragweed, whose growth may exceed 15 feet in height, is most abundant along the flood plains of southeastern rivers and the Mississippi delta, as well as over the range of short ragweed (sparing northern Mexico and the Pacific Northwest).

Another important species of ragweed is perennial (*A. psilostachya*), which despite a wide range is only significant in the Great Plains and Great Basin areas, where it grows in dry, sandy soil. Southern, or slender, ragweed (*A. bidentata*) is found from southern Indiana to western Tennessee, Louisiana, Texas, and Nebraska. Perennial slender ragweed (*A. confertiflora*), annual bur ragweed (*A. acanthicarpa*), canyon ragweed (*A. ambrosioides*), rabbit bush (*A. deltoidea*), and burroweed (*A. dumosa*) are found in dry soils of the West, especially the arid southwestern states. The latter three species are exceptional in that they pollinate in the early spring. Several of these species were formerly called "false ragweed" and classified in the genus *Franseria*. However, they are now recognized as meeting the criteria to be considered true pollinating plants. In the arid Southwest, western, slender, and false ragweed proliferate.

A few species are distributed throughout South America and in the Caribbean, but ragweed-caused hay fever is uncommon in those areas. European ragweed (*A. maritima*) and an African species (*A. senegalensis*) have a limited range. Short ragweed has appeared in some European countries, with significant hay fever seasons recognized in eastern France, the Balkans, and in the Krasnodar region of the former Soviet Union. Most of Europe including Great Britain, Asia, Australia, and Africa are mainly free from ragweed.

Antigen E, although only 6% of the total protein in ragweed extract, is the most reactive allergen, 200 times more potent than the whole extract. Immunotherapy (allergy shots) with standardized ragweed extract is effective for reducing symptoms and medication requirements in most individuals with hay fever sensitive to this pollen. (See also WEED POLLEN ALLERGY.)

rale   Any abnormal sound heard through a stethoscope placed on the chest. Produced upon inhalation or exhalation, rales occur when air passes through the bronchi during a spasm, thickening of their walls, or constriction caused by the presence of excess mucus. Moist rales, frequently associated with congestive heart failure, may often be described as crackling sounds in various degrees of severity. Consonating rales are loud and sharp. Dry rales associated with asthma, bronchitis, and early pulmonary tuberculosis may also be described as snoring, whistling, tinkling, low-pitched or high-pitched. A narrowing of the bronchial tubes caused by muscular spasm or a thickening of the tubes' mucous lining is responsible for dry rales. The existence of a rale, a French word meaning "rattle," often indicates a pulmonary disease process.

Ramazzini, Bernardino   Italian physician (1633–1714) who suffered from malaria, studied malaria and other epidemiologic problems, and wrote a treatise, "Diseases of Tradesmen," which addresses 53 trades and illnesses related to them. Ramazzini included graphic descriptions of "pulmonary passages lined with crust" caused by particles of flour in bakers and millers, and intense itching, inflamed and watery eyes, and the obstinate cough of sifters and measurers of grain.

ranitidine (Zantac)   A histamine H_2 receptor antagonist, used in the treatment of peptic ulcers and reflux esophagitis (heartburn), that is a frequent trigger of asthma. Ranitidine causes fewer drug interactions, especially when used in conjunction with the asthma drug theophylline. Because cimetidine (Tagamet) raises theophylline levels, which can become dangerously high, ranitidine may be safer for asthmatics. H_2 antagonist drugs such as ranitidine are sometimes used in combination with antihistamines of the H_1 receptor type to treat hives. (See HISTAMINE H₂ RECEPTOR ANTAGONIST.)

rash A skin eruption or inflammation having various origins. Rashes can be localized to a small area of skin or cover large areas of the body. Some rashes accompany infections and in the case of fever are called exanthums. Other rashes occur in allergic or other immune disorders.

The lesions of rashes include papules, macules, blisters or vesicles, and bullae (large blisters). Rashes can be dry or weeping (moist). Some rashes characterize the disease, like chicken pox or measles. They may or may not be pruritic, or itchy.

Examples of allergic rashes include atopic dermatitis (eczema), contact dermatitis, drug reaction, and vaccine rash. Caterpillar rash is a localized eruption caused by the toxin in the hairs of caterpillars. (See also ATOPIC DERMATITIS, CONTACT DERMATITIS, URTICARIA.)

RAST See RADIOALLERGOSORBENT TESTS.

rat allergy See ANIMAL ALLERGY, MICE ALLERGENS.

rat-bite fever [sodokosis] An infectious disease that may be mistaken for rat allergy caused by the bite of the rat, a rodent also known as rattus. It is characterized by fever, vomiting, skin inflammation, and joint pains. The infestation of rats is usually associated with the potential of spreading disease, especially in densely populated and poverty-stricken areas.

reaction, allergic See ALLERGY, HYPERSENSITIVITY.

reagin Another term for immunoglobulin E (IgE) antibody. (See IMMUNOGLOBULIN E.)

reapers' keratitis A nonallergenic eye disorder, characterized by inflammation of the cornea of the eye caused by irritation by grain dust, that may be confused with allergic conjunctivitis.

Rebuck skin windows See SKIN WINDOWS, REBUCK.

receptors See ADRENERGIC DRUGS, ALPHA-ADRENERGIC AGONISTS, BETA-ADRENERGIC AGONISTS, HISTAMINE.

red bugs See CHIGGERS.

red eyes See CONJUNCTIVITIS, ALLERGIC.

Reduvius personatus A bug belonging to the family Reduviidae, also called the kissing bug or masked hunter, that sometimes bites humans, especially about the face, and causes severe allergic reaction. (See BITING INSECTS.)

reflex The body's or a body part's involuntary reaction to a certain stimulus. For example, a sneeze is a reflex designed to push air out of the nose or mouth with some force when some particle, agent, change of temperature, light, or other irritation interferes with the respiratory process. In allergic individuals, sneezing is often a response to pollen in the air, which irritates the mucous membranes lining the nose.

reflexology A technique of foot massage based on the theory that the feet reflect the entire body and organs, especially the soles, which are massaged in various ways at "reflex" points. This is said to promote relaxation and is used to help alleviate headaches, sinusitis, allergic symptoms (such as stuffy nose) and related anxiety, and stress-related gastrointestinal problems.

Registry for Allergic and/or Asthmatic Pregnant Patients Study of drugs used to treat allergic disorders and asthma during pregnancy by the American College of Allergy. It is thought that pregnant patients with asthma and other allergic disorders should usually be treated in a manner similar to those patients who are not pregnant. It is further thought that to do so will assure a normal outcome for both mother and offspring. It is also recognized that there is a baseline incidence of birth defects, spontaneous miscarriages, low birth-weight and stillborn babies unrelated to therapies used in the management of pregnancies complicated by illness or disease. There are very little data on the safety of most drugs for use during pregnancy. It is anticipated that RAAPP will provide reassuring data on the drugs used to treat allergies and asthma, allowing physicians to prescribe for pregnant patients with confidence. See also PREGNANCY COMPLICATED BY ASTHMA. [Editor's note: Dr. Myron A. Lipkowitz is a co-coordinator of RAAPP, which began in 1996 and is expected to run for many years.]

rejection reaction The body's nonacceptance of a transplanted organ or tissue graft attributed to allergic sensitization, or incompatibility of tissue cells between the organ or graft donor and the recipient. Nearly all cells except red blood cells have transplantation or histocompatibility antigens (antibodies), which may be identified genetically in each individual. Some surgical procedures, such as cornea transplantation in order to restore sight in some patients, have high rates of success overall, whereas other, more complicated procedures involving vital organs, such as heart, liver, or kidney transplantations, seem rife with difficulty. Researchers have found that the closer in genetic makeup the donor is to the recipient, the more likely the transplantation will endure. For example, an autograft, which refers to transplanting one's own tissue from one area of his or her body to another area, is not in danger of causing an allergic rejection reaction. If an identical twin donates tissue or an organ to his or her twin—the transplantation known as an isograft—there is little if any chance of rejection reaction, because identical twins possess the same genetic constitution. In homografts, or allografts, and heterografts, however, the risk of rejection is high. An allograft is a transplant from one person to another who is not genetically identical. A heterograft refers to a transplant from one species to another, such as a baboon heart transplanted into a human body.

Allografts and heterografts may initially develop blood vessels and seem to work well, but frequently an acute inflammation occurs about 10 days after the operation, and the tissue or organ is rejected by the recipient's body. If a second graft is made using the same donor, the rejection-reaction time may be much shorter and the transplant rejected in less than a week. This process originates with histocompatibility, or specific transplantation, antigens formed in the recipient's blood and probably distributed further by lymph fluid to the site of the transplant. Among the most successful allografts are those performed in the anterior chamber of the eye and in the brain coverings because of the lack of lymphatic fluid at these sites.

In addition, the presence of a fetus in the mother's womb is considered an allograft (mother and fetus are not genetically identical), but the separation of the mother's circulatory system from that of the fetus by the placenta appears to eliminate an allergic rejection reaction.

In rare cases, fetal red blood cells pass into the maternal blood through the placenta. If these cells act as foreign antigens and trigger an immune reaction in the mother, an antibody produced by the mother then crosses the placenta to the fetus and destroys the fetus's red blood cells. The antibody reacts to an isoantigen known as the Rhesus, or Rh, factor in the red blood cells of the fetus. Erythroblastosis fetalis, which occurs in the newborn as a result of the hemolysis (destruction of red blood cells), causes jaundice, bruising, edema, and heart failure. The infant may require a total transfusion of blood in order to survive. By administering antibody to Rh isoantigens to a pregnant woman who possesses the Rh isoantigen (Rh+), the development of erythroblastosis in her infant can be prevented.

About 80% of humans are Rh+ (Rh positive), and about 20% are Rh- (Rh negative). If the father is Rh+ and the mother Rh-, their children may be either Rh+ or Rh-; fetal blood that is Rh+

indicates the possibility of erythroblastosis fetalis. When an Rh+ baby's mother is Rh-, the risk of destruction of the baby's red blood cells is slim.

relaxation techniques Deep relaxation taught or administered to patients in order to help promote positive changes in physiology, including reducing stress, blood pressure, and heart rate. These techniques can be used in the treatment of everything from the side effects of chemotherapy to premenstrual syndrome, pre-operative preparation, some forms of infertil-ity, asthma, and other problems. Guided imagery and visualization work together with relaxation techniques. (See VISUALIZATION.)

remote allergy practice The diagnosis and prescribing of allergy immunotherapy (allergy shots) based on the patient's filling out a questionnaire and a physician's determining the patient's diagnosis without seeing or examining the patient. The method is considered inadequate and inappropriate by the American Academy of Allergy and Immunology and the American College of Allergy and Immunology.

rennet Fluid from calf's stomach lining used to make cheese or junket. The main constituent of rennet is rennin, an enzyme that coagulates milk and may be allergenic or mistaken with an allergic reaction to milk.

reproductive immunology The study of immune mechanisms as they relate to the bio-logic process of human reproduction.

Infertility or spontaneous abortion The inability to conceive or to carry a viable fetus to term may have an immunologic basis. Antibodies against sperm may prevent fertilization at any of several stages of the process. The antibodies present may interact with isolated gametes, or the zygote, and this may occur before, during, or following implantation.

A lack of immune response in the female may result in repeated spontaneous abortions owing to a lack of, or deficiency in, protective blocking antibody and/or suppressor T cells.

The lack of response to the foreign sperm may allow formation of an immune response against the gestational tissues. This may occur in cases where paternal/maternal tissues are too close a match.

reserve air Additional quantity of air that can be expelled from the lungs after a normal expiration.

residency training in allergy and immunology A two-year postgraduate fellowship training program in allergy and immunology that adheres to rigid standards established by the Board of Medical Specialties. Each participating fellow must have completed at least two years of residency training in pediatrics or internal medicine. Completion of the fellowship qualifies the physician to take the board of certification examination in allergy and immunology. Thus he or she becomes "board eligible." (See AMERICAN BOARD OF ALLERGY AND IMMUNOLOGY.)

residual air [residual volume] The quantity of air remaining in the lungs after an individual has exhaled as forcibly as possible.

residual volume See RESIDUAL AIR.

resonance Sound generated by vibrations. In medicine, resonance of various types is heard through a stethoscope or by percussion over a hollow part of the body, such as the chest. For example, "cracked-pot" resonance, a strange clinking sound, may be heard on percussion of the chest in patients with advanced tuberculosis. Other types of resonance are characteristic of pneumothorax (collapsed lung) and some pulmonary diseases. The lungs also have a normal resonance, that is, a resonance not associated with any abnormality.

Respid See THEOPHYLLINE.

respiration See BREATHING.

respirator A machine or mechanism that produces artificial breathing or supports breathing in patients who cannot breathe normally because of severe lung incapacity. A respirator, or ventilator, promotes pressure into the lungs, which causes the lungs to function without the help of the patient's own breathing reflexes.

respiratory center   The area in the medulla oblongata of the brain that regulates the movements—inhalation and exhalation—of breathing. Part of the pons, a fibrous part of the brain, is also responsible for respiratory movements. (See also BREATHING.)

respiratory infection, viral   [common cold] A syndrome caused by a virus including sneezing, nasal discharge and congestion, sore throat, and coughing, all of which are often confused with or coexist with allergy symptoms. Viral colds can also trigger asthma (see TRIGGERS OF ALLERGIES AND ASTHMA); shortness of breath and wheezing may persist for a prolonged period following resolution of the viral infection. Some patients have asthma symptoms only when they "catch" a cold.

respiratory rate   The number of inhalations per minute. The normal respiratory rate is highest in infancy. At six months, the respiratory rate ranges from 22 to 31 breaths per minute while asleep to 58 to 75 breaths per minutes while awake. By age six, rates have diminished to 13 to 23 breaths per minute asleep and 15 to 30 awake. Adults inhale at a rate 15 to 20 breaths per minute.

respiratory syncttial virus   (RSV)   A virus that commonly causes a respiratory infection called bronchiolitis in infants. An estimated 35 to 50% of children who develop RSV infections will later have bronchial asthma. (See BRONCHIOLITIS.)

restaurant asthma   See CHINESE RESTAURANT SYNDROME, SULFITING AGENTS.

reticuloendothelial system   Cells throughout the body that are capable of ingesting bacteria or any microscopic particles. The system helps to defend the body against disease, rid the body of debris, and repair injured tissue.

rheum   Any watery discharge.

rhinalgia   Painful nose.

rhinitis   Inflammation of the mucous membrane lining the nasal passages. Rhinitis caused by allergies is called allergic rhinitis, or hay fever. Rhinitis can also be caused by respiratory infections; and if the cause is unknown, it is referred to as vasomotor rhinitis. (See ALLERGIC RHINITIS, RHINITIS MEDICOMENTOSUM, VASOMOTOR RHINITIS.)

rhinitis, allergic   See ALLERGIC RHINITIS.

rhinitis, vasomotor   See VASOMOTOR RHINITIS.

rhinitis medicomentosum   Severe nasal congestion with swelling of the mucous lining of the nasal passages from overuse of over-the-counter decongestant nasal sprays. Abuse of these nasal sprays results in a rebound phenomenon, in which nasal congestion initially improves but the spray loses its effectiveness and is required with increasing frequency until the individual is using the spray or drops constantly. Use of these products should be limited to three to five days. Corticosteroids are frequently needed to improve this condition. Oral drugs, such as the reserpine used to treat high blood pressure, can also cause rhinitis medicomentosum. Symptoms of rhinitis medicomentosum are frequently confused with allergies, and this condition should be considered before a person is evaluated for allergy.

Rhinocort Nasal Spray   Brand of cortisone-like anti-inflammatory drug budesonide. See BUDESONIDE, CORTICOSTEROID NASAL SPRAYS.

rhinolaryngitis   Inflammation of the nasal passages and larynx, or voice box. Rhinopharyngitis is an inflammation of the nasal passages and the pharynx, or throat.

rhinorrhea   A thin watery discharge from the nose. Conditions causing rhinorrhea include allergies, the common cold, and cluster headaches. A watery discharge following a serious head injury may indicate the leakage of cerebrospinal fluid.

rhinoscopy A diagnostic procedure in which an instrument, a rhinoscope (rigid or flexible fiberoptic), is introduced into the nostrils to view the nasal passages. With the fiberoptic rhinoscope, the observer can also see openings to the sinuses and eustachian tube, and the oropharynx and trachea. The procedure is useful for determining the cause of nasal symptoms such as allergic rhinitis, sinus infections, or obstructions such as a deviated septum or tumor.

rhonchus Snoring, or any rattling in the windpipe or chest.

Rhus A genus of trees and shrubs including poison ivy, poison sumac, and poison oak that cause allergic rashes (Rhus dermatitis). (See PLANT CONTACT DERMATITIS.)

rice A cereal grass (*Oryza sativa*) raised for its seed or grain. In rare cases rice has been a cause of allergic symptoms including anaphylaxis (allergic shock). Because of its low potential for allergic reactions, it is used in elemental allergy elimination diets.

Richet, Charles French physician (1850–1935) and professor of physiology at the Faculty of Medicine in Paris. He received the Nobel Prize with Paul Portier, a French scientist, in 1913 for the discovery and study of anaphylaxis following their famous cruise in the Mediterranean in 1901. They identified two essential conditions for anaphylaxis: (1) increased sensitivity to a poison after previous injection of that same substance, and (2) development of increased sensitivity only after an incubation period. The discovery was made while they were attempting to determine the toxic dose of a poison found in the tentacles of sea anemones. A number of dogs had been given a dose of the poison insufficient to kill them. They recovered and appeared healthy. When they were given a second dose in the same amount several weeks after the first, they died, gasping for breath and vomiting blood, within 25 minutes. This indicated that an accumulation of the toxin was not the cause of their deaths. (See also PORTIER, PAUL.)

Riley, James F., and West, Geoffrey B. British scientists who described the mast cell granule as a fundamental source of histamine in tissues, which contributed to the study of inflammatory and allergic disorders. Riley (1912–85) worked as a surgeon until he developed dermatitis of the hands. West, born in 1916, studied pharmacology, particularly adrenaline and noradrenaline, and is coeditor of the professional journal *Progress in Medicinal Chemistry*.

Rinkel method See SKIN TITRATION.

RIST See PAPER RADIOIMMUNOSORBENT TEST.

Robitussin See GUAIFENASIN.

roentgen ray See X RAY.

Rondec See CARBINOXAMINE.

rose cold See ROSE FEVER.

rose fever [rose cold] Another name for hay fever occurring in the spring pollen season. Rose pollen is transferred by insects and is not an important allergen. Persons who have hay fever symptoms in the spring are allergic to tree or grass pollens or both. (See ALLERGIC RHINITIS, HAY FEVER.)

Rosenau, Milton J. American physician (1869–1946), born in Philadelphia, and director of the Hygienic Laboratory, the forerunner of the National Institutes of Health. Rosenau also became the first full-time professor and chairman of the Department of Preventive Medicine and Hygiene at Harvard Medical School in 1909. Four years later, he assumed the directorship of Harvard's School of Public Health, the first American school of this discipline. In 1936, after he had retired from Harvard, Rosenau became dean and director at the University of

North Carolina's School of Public Health. Along with Virginia-born physician John F. Anderson, Rosenau conducted significant experiments on the nature and causes of anaphylaxis. (See ANAPHYLAXIS; ANDERSON, JOHN F.)

rotary diets   See DIET, ROTARY.

Rotocaps   Capsules containing the dry, powdered bronchodilating asthma drug albuterol (Ventolin). The capsules are placed in a device called a Rotohaler, which is activated by puncturing the capsule and releasing the powder into a small chamber. The powder is then inhaled through the mouth into the airways. This Rotohaler method of inhalation is useful for patients lacking the coordination necessary to activate a metered-dose inhaler. (See ALBUTEROL.)

Rowe's diets   Food elimination diets first recommended by A. H. Rowe in the *Journal of Allergy* in 1931 for detecting food hypersensitivities. Rowe diet 1 is very restrictive and is gradually liberalized in subsequent diets 2 and 3. These diets and modified versions are given for two to three weeks, and if the suspected symptoms are not improved, a normal diet is resumed. If symptoms have improved, however, foods are reintroduced into the diet at three- to five-day intervals in an attempt to identify a specific food that produces an adverse reaction. A controlled study of asthma patients showed that Rowe's cereal-free diet did not benefit them. (See also DIET, ROTARY.)

rubella vaccine   See MEASLES, MUMPS, AND RUBELLA (MMR) VIRUS VACCINE, LIVE, ALLERGIC REACTIONS.

rusts   Fungi belonging to the class Basidiomycetes, order Uredinales, whose members are parasitic on plants, producing reddish brown pustular lesions. Many of these fungi are important allergens in grass and grain fields of agricultural areas. (See also FUNGI AND MOLDS.)

rye   A cereal grass, *Secale cereale*, of the Gramineae family whose grain is commercially important for food (bread and cereals) and beverage (rye whiskey) production. It is also an important cover crop and of moderate importance as a source of pollen. Rye produces the toxin ergot when infected by a fungus.

ryegrass   A group of grasses of the genera *Elymus* and *Lolium* used as crop grasses in the southern United States and in New Zealand. Species important as a source of seasonal pollen are alkali (*Elymus triticoides*), giant (*E. condonsatus*), western (*E. glaucus*), and Italian annual (*Lolium multiflorum*), and perennial (*L. perenne*). (See also GRASS POLLEN ALLERGY.)

S

salicylates   Natural substances, similar in structure to aspirin, that occur in varying but usually small amounts in many foods, including bananas, blueberries, peas, and licorice. The presence of natural salicylates in foods is the basis for the Feingold theory of food and food additives as a cause of hyperactivity in children. The validity of this theory has not been determined.

Salicylates have also been implicated as a cause of urticaria, or hives. Individuals known to be sensitive to aspirin (acetylsalicylic acid) have been challenged with foods containing salicylates. In controlled studies, most experts dismiss them as a significant cause of hives. (See ASPIRIN SENSITIVITY, FEINGOLD DIET, FOOD ADDITIVES, URTICARIA.)

saline nasal spray   Saltwater solution with the salt concentration of tears (.09%), used as a spray to irrigate the nasal passages.

salmeterol   An investigational bronchodilating drug of the beta-adrenergic agonist type for the treatment of asthma. Salmeterol is available as a metered-dose inhaler in the United Kingdom.

Its effect lasts for 12 hours or longer without tolerance or loss of effectiveness. Studies also indicate that continued use does not result in worsening asthma symptoms. (See BETA-ADRENERGIC AGONISTS.)

salt   The chemical sodium chloride (the same as table salt), an inorganic, mineral constituent of the body that is vital to cell function and life. The main body salts include chlorides, carbonates, bicarbonates, sulfates, and phosphates. These are compounds of sodium, potassium, calcium, magnesium, and iron along with chlorine, sulfur, phosphorus and carbon dioxide. Salts help maintain and regulate water balance and blood volume, facilitate the roles of enzymes and hormones, and maintain capability for blood coagulation, normal muscle and nerve activity, acid-base balance, and cell membrane permeability.

English researchers have reported that excessive intake of dietary salt may increase asthma mortality.

Salter, Henry H.   British physician (1823–71) who practiced in London and was associated with R. B. Todd at King's College. Salter, an asthmatic, published a respected work entitled *On Asthma: Its Pathology and Treatment*, in which he pointed out the dangers and questioned the effectiveness of the use of opium in treating asthma. He saw in opium a tendency to cause involuntary muscular action and induce spasms. He attributed its prescription by physicians of his day to their unthinking acceptance of its routine use and their failure to monitor closely their own patients' response.

Salter also wrote articles on the pancreas and tongue for Todd's *Cyclopedia*. In 1854, he became a lecturer in physiology and in medicine at Charing Cross Hospital in London.

salt rheum   An alternate term for eczema. (See ATOPIC DERMATITIS.)

saltwater sprays   See SALINE NASAL SPRAY.

Samuelsson, Bengt I.   Swedish physician and scientist, born in 1934, who shared the Nobel Prize for physiology or medicine in 1982 with Sune Bergstrom and John Vane. Samuelsson identified and described leukotrienes and their role in asthma, allergy, and inflammation. At the Karolinska Institute in Stockholm, Sweden since 1972, he has served as professor of medical and physiologic chemistry, chairman of the Department of Chemistry, dean of the medical faculty, and rector.

San Joaquin fever   See FUNGAL DISEASES, SYSTEMIC.

Sarcoptidae   A family of mites including those that cause the intensely itchy rash called scabies, which can be confused with allergic skin eruptions such as eczema.

scabies   See SARCOPTIDAE.

Scherr, Merle S.   American allergist (1925–93) internationally known for his research and teaching in his field and who pioneered overnight camps for children with asthma. A graduate of the University of Maryland School of Medicine in 1948 and of the Johns Hopkins Hospital Allergy Program in 1951, Scherr founded Camp Broncho Junction in 1965, in a remote wilderness area of West Virginia. Railroad cars were transported on flatbed trucks to a mountainous site near Red House, miles from the closest railway, and converted into bunkhouses.

Children throughout the United States, and visiting camp doctors including medical school faculty and fellows training to be allergists, were referred to the camp. Campers had daily interaction with physicians, nurses, and other personnel and developed a thorough understanding of asthma and its treatment. Therefore, despite the rigors of camp life in an environment rife with asthma triggers, most of the children had an improvement in their symptoms and required less medication by the end of their stay at Broncho Junction. Although Bronco Junction is no longer active, it still serves as a model for asthma camps.

Schick, Bela   Hungarian pediatrician (1877–1967) and associate of Clemens von Pirquet, with whom Schick published a study of serum sickness in 1905. Schick developed a skin test—known as the Schick test—to determine a child's susceptibility to diphtheria. In 1923, Schick came to the United States as chairman of the Department of Pediatrics of Mount Sinai Hospital in New York. In a tribute to Schick on his 80th birthday, pediatric allergist John McGovern quoted Schick as having said: "First, the patient, second, the patient, third, the patient, fourth, the patient, fifth, the patient, and then maybe comes science."

schistosome dermatitis   Rash resulting from penetration of blood flukes, a species of parasitic worm, common around lakes of the northern United States. Other terms for the rash are seabather's eruption and swimmer's itch.

Schloss, Oscar M.   American physician (1882–1952) born in Cincinnati, Ohio, educated at the Johns Hopkins University and professor of pediatrics at Harvard and Cornell universities. Schloss was known for his teaching skills, his compassionate personality, and his research, which in 1912 established von Pirquet's scratch test for tuberculosis as a practical diagnostic procedure for hypersensitivity in humans. Schloss's interest in the scratch test and the intracutaneous Schick test with diphtheria toxin eventually led to R. A. Cooke's development of the intracutaneous test for hypersensitivity in 1915. Schloss wrote in "A Case for Allergy to Common Foods" (*American Journal of the Diseases of Children,* 1912): "At the very outset it was necessary to devise some test other than actual feeding by which the toxic substances could be identified. Owing to the decided and at times alarming symptoms produced by the ingestion of the toxic foods, this method of investigation was considered unjustifiable."

Schmidt, Carl F.   American physician (1893–1988), born in Lebanon, Pennsylvania, who conducted research with Chinese physician and scientist Ko Kuei Chen on the cardiovascular effects of ephedrine (see also SHEN-NUNG) and originated studies on sympathomimetic amines, substances that produce similar effects to those elicited when the sympathetic nervous system is stimulated.

scholarships for students with asthma   Financial aid for college provided to outstanding students with asthma. Scholarships are awarded annually by the Fisons and Schering pharmaceutical companies and are based on scholastic, leadership, and athletic abilities. Applications can be obtained through allergists or other physicians who treat asthma or through the drug companies.

Schonlein-Henoch purpura   See HENOCH-SCHONLEIN PURPURA.

school attendance of allergic students   The tendency of allergic and/or asthmatic children of school age to stay home from school because of exacerbation of allergic or asthmatic symptoms, often a serious problem in children and adolescents with asthma or severe nasal allergy. Attendance can be greatly improved with proper planning, however. Since allergies and asthma are among the most common medical problems, school officials have an obligation to provide for the use of regular medications during school hours. Such a plan must not be disruptive to classes and other activities. School nurses, teachers, and coaches should receive training in dealing with allergy and asthma emergencies. Teachers must be informed of food allergies and the need to avoid even a taste of foods that may contain any allergen.

Before school starts, parents should make an appointment with the school principal, teachers, or nurse to discuss their child's condition. Find out if there is an emergency protocol and how an asthma emergency is best managed. Have the physician complete medication forms to assure that children can participate in all activities or note specific limitations. Every school should have a peak flow meter available; the nurse should be aware of each child's red, yellow, and green peak flow zones (see PEAK FLOW METER), and a written plan should be supplied for each student. This includes emergency phone numbers and which medication to use for attacks based on the peak flow reading.

The school should facilitate treatment of minor attacks and allow the child to return to class if he or she improves. However, the student may need to refrain from gym class or sports for the balance of any day in which he or she is short of breath. Federal law prohibits discrimination against individuals with asthma as well as other disabilities. Parents who feel there are unsafe conditions at a school can seek aid from local, state, or federal officials to improve a school environment.

Schultz, William H.   American professor of pharmacology (1873–1953), born in Canal Fulton, Ohio. Schultz earned a Ph.D. from the Johns Hopkins University in 1907, and a year later he accepted the position of associate pharmacologist at the Hygienic Laboratory of the Public Health and Marine Hospital Service. He also served as professor and chairman of the Department of Pharmacology at West Virginia University and the University of Maryland. Schultz, who earlier had been associated with the studies of Rosenau and Anderson (see ANDERSON, JOHN F.; ROSENAU, MILTON J.) at the Hygienic Laboratory, became involved in experiments with histamine conducted by Sir Henry H. Dale. In accordance with the results of these experiments, Schultz and Dale documented that, when exposed to a certain antigen, a strip of presensitized guinea-pig ileum (part of the intestine) would contract. This discovery became known as the Schultz-Dale phenomenon, which led to further study of anaphylaxis, mediators of sensitization, and various antiallergic and antihistaminic drugs. (See ANAPHYLAXIS, HISTAMINE.)

scopolamine   Derivative of atropine or anticholinergic drug used to treat nausea and vomiting and as a Band-Aid–like patch (Transcope) to prevent motion sickness. This drug should be avoided in patients with glaucoma and intestinal obstruction. Frequent side effects include blurred vision, sedation, rapid heartbeat, dry mouth, and decreased sweating.

scorpion sting   The injection of venom composed of neurotoxin, hemolysins, cardiac toxins, and agglutinins from any member of the class Arachnida, order Scorpionida. Scorpions are common in tropical and subtropical climates but may be found as far north as the Canadian province of Alberta. A stinger is located at the tip of the tail and is supplied with a poisonous venom that flows from two glands at the base. Although toxic reactions have long been feared, they are rarely fatal. But scorpion stings may also cause severe allergic reactions similar to bee stings.

scratching   The act of scraping, clawing, digging, or abrading the skin in response to itching. (See PRURITUS.)

scratch testing   See SKIN TESTS.

seabather's eruption   See SCHISTOSOME DERMATITIS.

seafood allergy   See FISH ALLERGY.

seasonal allergy   [seasonal hay fever]   Nasal and eye allergies and asthma that occur in the spring and fall upon exposure to pollinating trees, grasses, and weeds in susceptible persons. Many who suffer from perennial, or year-round, allergies also have seasonal allergies and tend to suffer more in the spring and fall. (See ALLERGIC RHINITIS, ASTHMA, HAY FEVER, POLLINOSIS.)

secretory antibody   See IMMUNOGLOBULIN A.

seeds   Grains or ripened ovules of plants. Peanuts, sesame, sunflower, and other seeds are common allergens, and reactions to them may include anaphylaxis (life-threatening allergic shock). Cottonseed, flaxseed, or linseed, and kapok are highly allergenic plant fibers. The manufacturing processes render most fabrics made from these fibers nonallergenic, but unrefined materials used to stuff upholstery or toys may contain significant quantities of seeds and flower-part allergens. (See also FOOD ALLERGY.)

segs   See NEUTROPHILS.

Sela, Michael   Polish biologist, born in 1924, who made numerous contributions to the study of immune response and the chemical structure of enzymes and immune reactants, and the development of synthetic vaccines, protein molecules, and antigens. Sela joined the Weizmann Institute in 1950 and has served as its president, dean of the faculty of biology,

head of the Department of Chemical Immunology, and professor of immunology.

Seldane   See TERFENADINE.

self-help groups and information   See SUPPORT GROUPS.

self-treatment risks   The danger of underestimating the severity of asthma or allergic reactions until they become more difficult to treat, cause serious irreparable damage to the lungs, or provoke a life-threatening situation. A person with asthma may have gradually become accustomed to his or her shortness of breath and have an unrealistic perception of its severity. (See ASTHMA.)

semen allergy   Reactions to the male ejaculate including urticaria, or hives, and asthma. In rare cases, life-threatening anaphylaxis has been reported. Most often the allergens were proteins in the prostatic fluid. Other possible causes include drugs taken by the male secreted with the semen or contaminants in lubricating gels. Nonallergic reactions may include inflammation of the vulva or vagina with pain or itching and swelling.

Although the use of condoms are usually successful in preventing this problem, some individuals also have latex allergy (see LATEX ALLERGY). Allergy immunotherapy (allergy shots) with seminal components has been used. Artificial insemination with washed spermatozoa has been successful. (See also REPRODUCTIVE IMMUNOLOGY.)

Semicid   See NONOXYNOL-9 SPERMACIDE.

Semprex-D   See ACRAVASTINE.

sense of smell, loss   [anosmia]   Inability to detect odors, either permanently by destruction of the olfactory (or first) cranial nerve, or temporarily by nasal obstruction or allergies.

sensibilin   An antibody that forms in the tissues when a foreign protein is initially injected. This procedure relates to sensibilization, which is also called sensitization, or producing intensified susceptibility to a particular substance. Sensibilization is synonymous with anaphylaxis. (See ANAPHYLAXIS, ANTIBODY.)

sensitinogen   All the allergens of the body that can possibly produce an allergic reaction. Sensitinogens include anaphylactogen and sensibilisinogen. (See also SENSIBILIN.)

sensitivity   A person's level of susceptibility to allergens, also known as antigens, which may produce a varied number of symptoms. (See ALLERGY, HYPERSENSITIVITY.)

septum, nasal   The bone and cartilaginous, membranous wall that divide the nasal cavity into two chambers whose openings are the right and left nostrils. The chambers lead to various sinuses. A deviated septum can cause blockage and congestion, which may accelerate the congestion caused by allergies and asthma.

seroreaction   Any rash, fever, pain, or other symptom that occurs as a result of an injection of serum (the watery portion of blood after clotting). (See SERUM, SERUM SICKNESS.)

serous otitis media   See OTITIS MEDIA, SECRETORY.

serum   The Latin word for whey, any fluid that lubricates membranes, especially the watery fluid of blood after the clotting process. Serum contains plasma: white blood cells, platelets, water, salts, glucose, proteins, fats, bile pigment, and gases. Serum is colorless or slightly yellow because of the absence of red blood cells. Animal serum from an animal immune to certain disease-causing organisms may be used for vaccines for humans against those diseases.

serum rash   See SEROREACTION.

serum sickness   An allergic reaction characterized by skin rash, fever, enlarged lymph nodes and spleen, and painful joints, resulting one to three weeks following the injection of a foreign serum or the introduction of an antibiotic. However, if an individual has been pre-

viously exposed to the serum or drug, he or she may exhibit symptoms sooner, usually with hives.

Health professionals administering a serum, vaccine, or any drug, should determine a person's history of allergy to that substance or related compounds. A prick test with a minute amount of any horse or other foreign serum (see SKIN TESTS) should be given to all persons who are about to receive it to determine sensitivity prior to receiving the product. An individual with a negative skin test will rarely develop anaphylaxis, although a negative reaction will not predict sensitivity to subsequent injections.

Persons with allergy to a foreign serum can be desensitized, but the procedure carries the risk of a serious allergic reaction and should only be done where oxygen, epinephrine (Adrenalin), and resuscitation equipment are available. (See DESENSITIZATION, DRUG ALLERGY AND OTHER ADVERSE DRUG REACTIONS.)

seven-year itch   A colloquial name for scabies. (See SARCOPTIDAE.)

sexual activity and allergy   Rashes or anaphylactic reactions resulting from contact with semen or latex in women or latex condoms in men. (See LATEX ALLERGY, SEMEN ALLERGY.)

sexual activity and asthma   The physical exertion of intercourse that in asthmatic persons may result in wheezing or shortness of breath and should be treated as exercise-induced asthma. (See EXERCISE-INDUCED ASTHMA.)

shellfish allergy   Symptoms of allergy caused by eating the meat of aquatic invertebrate animals with a shell, including mollusks, clams, mussels, and oysters, or crustaceans such as shrimp, lobsters, and crabs. (See FISH ALLERGY, FOOD ALLERGY.)

Shen-Nung   The legendary founder of Chinese medicine and agriculture and the "Fire Emperor" of China from 2838 to 2698 B.C. who devised the *Pen-Ts'ao*, or the Divine

Husbandman's Materia Medica. This reference described how drugs and plants could be used to treat diseases. Shen-Nung's work was continued by other investigators long after his death. His original reference to Ma-Huang, the plant source of the drug ephedrine, has been studied pharmacologically up through the 20th century. According to Shen-Nung, Ma-Huang, or ephedra, redirects a reversed flow of *ch'i* (in Eastern medicine, *ch'i* refers to the air, or essential spirit, of the human body), which causes coughing and difficulty in breathing. Today, ephedrine is an effective drug in the treatment of hay fever and asthma. (See EPHEDRINE.)

shock, allergic   See ANAPHYLAXIS.

shrimp   An edible crustacean that frequently causes allergic reactions. (See FISH ALLERGY.)

sick building syndrome   [tight building syndrome]   Symptoms suggestive of allergy occurring in groups of office workers. Since the energy crisis of the 1970s, changes in building construction were designed to improve heating and air-conditioning efficiency. These changes frequently resulted in poor ventilation, which leads to respiratory irritation and the possible retention of allergens in the air.

Symptoms range from itching and burning of the mucous membranes of the respiratory system to rashes and central nervous system complaints (see list below). In more than 450 evaluations made by the National Institute of Occupational Safety and Health (NIOSH), there have rarely been severe or permanent illnesses as a result of these symptoms. The exceptions have been cases of hypersensitivity pneumonitis, an allergic lung disease caused by repeated exposure to organic dusts or other offending agents, or infectious pneumonias such as Legionnaire's disease. (See HYPERSENSITIVITY PNEUMONITIS.)

side effect   Any undesirable result of a drug or other substance. (See DRUG ALLERGY AND OTHER ADVERSE DRUG REACTIONS.)

TWO TYPES OF BUILDING-ASSOCIATED ILLNESS

I. Similar symptoms with an identifiable cause:
- indoor chemical agents such as cleaning materials, pesticides, gases from building materials
- outside chrmical pollutants such as auto exhaust fumes
- infectious agents such as Legionnaire's disease
- allergy sensitizing agents (hypersensitivity pneumonitis, humidifier fever)

II. Symptoms are vague and nonspecific; despite expert evaluation, no causative agent can be found. Symptoms include:
- itching or burning eyes
- dry or sore throat
- runny or stuffy nose or sneezing
- coughing, wheezing, or tightness in the chest
- itching and rashes
- headaches, dizziness, fatigue, malaise, anxiety, confusion, and difficulty concentrating

---

siderosis   A chronic, pneumonialike lung disease, also known as arc-welder's disease or hemosiderosis, caused by the inhalation of iron particles in dust or fumes. (See OCCUPATIONAL ASTHMA.)

silicosis   A chronic, pneumonialike lung disease caused by the chronic occupational inhalation of quartz dust, or silica, stone dust, sand dust, or flint dust that contains silicon dioxide. Silicosis is also called grinder's disease, or pneumoconiosis. (See OCCUPATIONAL ASTHMA.)

Similasan   Eye drop for allergic conjunctivitis that does not sting or discolor contact lenses.

Sinequan   See DOXEPIN.

sinopulmonary infections and immunoglobulin A (IgA) deficiency   A higher incidence of respiratory infections in the sinuses and lungs in persons with a deficiency in antibodies of the IgA class. (See IMMUNODEFICIENCY DISEASE, IMMUNOGLOBULIN A.)

sinus CT scan   See COMPUTERIZED TOMOGRAPHY.

sinus drainage   See SINUSITIS.

sinuses, paranasal   Hollow air-filled cavities in the bones of the skull located over the eyes (frontal), behind the eyes (ethmoidal), behind the nose (sphenoid), and behind the cheeks (maxillary). The frontal sinus is not present at birth and usually develops fully by the late teens (or it may never develop in some persons). The function of the sinuses is unknown; however, infection in one or more of the sinus cavities is a source of frequent disability that can be severe. (See SINUSITIS.)

sinus infections   See SINUSITIS.

sinusitis   An inflammation of the mucous membrane lining one or more of the sinus cavities in the head, caused by inadequate drainage characteristic of allergy, infection, or physical obstruction. Sinusitis may be acute, lasting for a few days to weeks, or chronic, lasting for many months to years. It has a tendency to recur.

During an attack of sinusitis, tiny hairs that keep the sinuses clear lose their effectiveness, and the sinus cavities become blocked. The blockage results in the symptoms of pressure or pain characteristic of sinusitis. Headache and facial pain caused by migraine, trigeminal neuralgia, or from a dental problem are often erroneously called "sinus headache" but must be distinguished from sinusitis. Fever and a thick yellow-green mucus discharge are often associated with sinus infection.

Diagnosis   The diagnosis of a sinus condition is usually suggested by a history of the typical symptoms described above. However, the diagnosis may be unclear at times. As many as 10% of sinus infections are related to dental problems.

Diagnostic procedures to confirm the presence of sinusitis include transillumination of the frontal and maxillary sinuses in a completely darkened room. A bright light source is placed over the orbital area of the face, and the hard palate is observed for the absence of transmission of light indicative of sinusitis. The light source is then placed against the hard palate to observe light transmission over the cheek bones behind which the maxillary sinuses are located. Transillumination is of lesser value for the frontal sinuses and of no use to diagnose disease in the ethmoid and sphenoid sinuses.

Ultrasound is a technique in which inaudible sound waves in the frequency of approximately 20,000 to 10 billion cycles/second are passed through body tissues. Differences in the velocity with which sound passes through various tissues are used to outline their shape and aid in the diagnosis of disorders. Despite early promises of being a safe, noninvasive means to diagnosis sinus conditions, unfortunately it lacks the sensitivity to be a reliable diagnostic method.

X rays are the mainstay for accurate diagnosis of sinus disease. Plain films are useful for detecting thickness suggestive of chronic sinus disease or air-fluid levels correlating with acute infection. However, X rays have limited ability to view the deeper ethmoid and sphenoid sinuses. Computerized tomography (CT or CAT scan) is the most sensitive means for the diagnosis of sinus disorders. Magnetic resonance imaging (MRI) is capable of detecting minute changes in tissues, but it is two or three times more expensive than a CT scan (see COMPUTERIZED TOMOGRAPHY).

Allergies are probably the most common cause of sinus symptoms, and skin or blood tests are helpful in making that diagnosis (see ALLERGIC RHINITIS, RADIOALLERGOSORBENT TESTS, SKIN TESTS). Although bacterial infections frequently complicate sinusitis, cultures of material obtained from nasal secretions are unreliable in determining the cause. *Streptococcus pneumoniae* and *Hemophilus influenzae* are responsible for approximately 50% of proven sinus infections, but *Staphylococcus aureus* and *Branhamella catarrhalis* (formerly called *Neisserias catarrhalis*) and other bacteria are important causes of infected sinuses. Less frequently, fungal infections occur in the sinuses. Many sinus infections are preceded by viral upper respiratory infections or colds.

Treatment Most sinus conditions respond to decongestant drugs, antihistamines for allergic individuals, and antibiotics. Antibiotics should be taken for a minimum of 10 to 14 days but may be needed for up to six weeks in persistent cases. Anti-inflammatory, corticosteroid nasal sprays may be helpful in controlling sinus symptoms and preventing recurrences (see ANTIHISTAMINE, ALPHA-ADRENERGIC AGONISTS, NASAL SPRAY).

Sinus irrigation, the mainstay of treatment prior to the introduction of antibiotics, is still useful in stubborn cases. If adequate antibiotic therapy and sinus drainage are unsuccessful, surgical procedures by otolaryngologists ("ENT" doctors) skilled in various procedures may be necessary. Unfortunately, sinus surgery has a high rate of failure in preventing recurrences of sinusitis.

sinus surgery   See SINUSITIS.

sinus X rays   See SINUSITIS.

skier's nose   See COLD-INDUCED RHINORRHEA.

skin   The external, protective covering of the body and its internal structures. Known as the integumentary system, skin consists mainly of the epidermis and the dermis, or the outer and inner layers of tissue containing many types of cells, pigment, lymphatics, nerves and nerve endings, blood vessels, elastic fibers, and oil and sweat glands. Hair and nails (or feathers or fur if one is referring to a different species) are appendages of the skin. Skin provides protection from injury and parasites. It prevents dehydration and helps the body eliminate salts and urea (waste products) through perspiration. Skin also helps regulate body temperature and acts as a sense organ for temperature, touch, and pain.

Abnormal dryness or moistness, discolorations, swelling, rashes, wrinkling, and eruptions of the skin may indicate a disorder or allergy. In addition, skin may be grafted, or removed in small sections, from a healthy part of the body and implanted in an injured part.

skin test antigens or allergens   See ALLERGENIC EXTRACTS.

skin tests   A method for determining an individual's reactivity to various substances by injecting the substance into or beneath the surface or by placing it on the surface of the skin. Injected skin tests are used to detect allergies that cause allergic rhinitis (hay fever), asthma, or some infectious diseases. Allergenic extracts are useful in the diagnosis of IgE-mediated, type I (immediate) hypersensitivity allergic diseases such as allergic rhinitis (hay fever), asthma, urticaria (hives), atopic dermatitis (eczema), and Hymenoptera sting (bee sting) allergy. There are also skin tests for delayed type IV allergy. These intradermal (under the surface of the skin) injections determine the competence of cell-mediated immunity (see HYPERSENSITIVITY). Patch skin tests are used for the diagnosis of allergic contact dermatitis (see PATCH SKIN TEST).

Skin tests identify antibodies in the skin that are present in that individual. In a positive response to a skin test, the antigen attaches to the antibody on the mast cell, causing the release of chemicals called mediators, the most prominent of which is histamine. In positive tests, within 15 minutes a "wheal and flare," which is a reddened, raised welt, will appear.

The size of a skin-test response is critical and may be affected by the patient's age: Reactions are usually weaker in infants, very young children, and the elderly. Skin sensitivity is greater on the upper back, but it is safer to perform skin tests on the forearms.

Extracts for testing are available for pollens, molds, animal danders, house dust mites, cockroaches, fire ants, bees, other venomous insects, and foods. Allergens chosen for testing are based on a carefully documented patient history and physical examination. Positive skin tests are used to confirm suspected causes of allergy. Antibodies on mast cells of the skin usually correlate with those of the respiratory and gastrointestinal tracts.

There are four methods of skin testing. For a scratch testing, a small scratch is made on the skin of the upper back or arm without breaking the surface of the skin. A drop of allergen is then placed on the abraded area. With the puncture method, a dull- pointed needle is dipped into the allergen and applied to the skin, or a drop of allergen is first placed on the skin and the needle is then applied to the skin through the material. The prick method is similar to the puncture technique except that a slight lifting motion is used. The intradermal skin test is the most sensitive. A tiny quantity (about .02 millimeters) of allergen is injected under the skin's surface.

Both false-positive and false-negative skin tests may occur. The tester's technique is very important for accuracy; positive and negative controls are essential in determining the significance of the results. Scratch tests are no longer recommended because they are less reproducible than prick or puncture tests. The sensitivity of prick and puncture is approximately equal to radioallergosorbent blood tests (RAST). Intradermal tests are the most sensitive but are somewhat more likely to provide false-positive results (a positive result where there are no symptoms attributable to that allergen).

Skin-test results are graded by measuring the diameter of the resulting raised wheal and surrounding erythema (redness) and comparing it with the negative control. The control consists of the diluent in which the allergens being tested are dissolved.

Inaccurate skin-test results can be due to the use of outdated or improperly stored, prepared, or preserved materials or incorrectly diluted allergenic extracts. Testing too many allergens at one time or failing to allow adequate spacing of individual tests can cause difficulty in interpreting results.

Antihistaminic medications can inhibit skin-test results for a period of time ranging from approximately 12 hours with short-acting chlorpheniramine (Chlor-Trimeton) to as long as 40 days with astemizole (Hismanal). Most over-the-counter allergy drugs suppress skin reactivity for up to three days; hydryzine (Atarax or Vistaril) up to ten days; cyproheptadine (Periactin) up to three days; terfenadine (Seldane) and loratadine (Claritin) up to seven days. Clemastine (Tavist) and ketotifen, an investigational antiallergic drug, may block responsiveness for as long as ten days.

Phenothiazine tranquilizers, tricyclic antidepressants such as imipramine (Tofranil), and antinausea drugs with antihistamine properties may also suppress skin-test results for prolonged periods, up to several weeks.

Cimetidine (Tagamet), ranitidine (Zantac), and other H2 antihistamines used for the treatment of peptic ulcer disorders may suppress skin reactivity for an uncertain amount of time, and it is recommended that they be discontinued prior to skin testing for at least a few days. Most allergists do not feel that theophylline must be stopped prior to skin testing, and short-acting corticosteroids such as prednisone do not interfere with results. Oral and injectable beta-adrenergic agonists, such as terbutaline, may depress reactivity somewhat and are best avoided. However, inhaled forms of the drugs need not be discontinued. Cromolyn drug products do not interfere with skin-test results.

WARNING

ACUTE LIFE-THREATENING ANAPHYLAXIS (A STATE OF ALLERGIC COLLAPSE) CAN OCCUR IF SKIN TESTING IS ATTEMPTED WHILE A PATIENT IS TAKING A BETA-BLOCKING DRUG SUCH AS PROPANOLOL (INDERAL). (See BETA-BLOCKING AGENTS for a complete list of the drugs.)

Skin-test results of seasonal allergens such as ragweed are probably not influenced by time of year. However, in highly allergic persons, it may be wise to wait until the pollen season has passed because of the likelihood of an exaggerated systemic reaction during testing.

In the following instances, allergy RAST or similar blood tests (see RADIOALLERGOSORBENT TESTS) may be used in place of skin tests: (1) if skin fails to react positively to the histamine control; (2) if there is severe skin disease; (3) if there is dermatographia (see DERMATOGRAPHIA). In most other circumstances, skin testing is less expensive and more sensitive than blood allergy tests and is the method of choice by the Panel on Allergy of the American Medical Association (AMA) Council on Scientific Affairs. Testing multiple antigens with no clinical bearing in an individual is not only considered abusive, but false-positive test results may be misleading. False-positive reactions occur frequently from food antigens and often result in the mistaken belief that a person must avoid those particular foods (see FOOD ALLERGY). The Allergy Panel also advises that rarely are more than 50 skin tests required.

skin tests, patch   See PATCH SKIN TEST.

skin titration   [Rinkel method]   A method of skin testing for allergies using gradually increasing strengths of allergenic extract. This method is also called end-point titration. In this technique, the weakest dilution that produces a positive skin reaction is called the end point.

Physician H. J. Rinkel claimed the method is useful for determination of a safe starting dose and the optimal therapeutic dose in the treatment of allergies by immunotherapy. Rinkel also claimed that the specified optimal therapeutic dose rarely, if ever, causes adverse reactions and in many cases promptly relieves symptoms.

In the September 23, 1980 *Federal Register,* the National Center for Health Care Technology requested opinions from interested parties concerning skin titration (Rinkel method) of al-

lergy treatment and other unproven techniques. In response to this request, the Executive Committee and the Committee on Unproved Techniques of the American Academy of Allergy and Immunology submitted a position statement to the National Center for Health Care Technology with the following conclusions:

1. The Rinkel method of skin titration has been shown to be effective for quantifying patient sensitivity to ragweed pollen and for providing a rough guide to safe starting dose for immunotherapy.
2. The Rinkel method of skin titration has not been shown to be an effective guide to therapeutic dose.
3. Several controlled studies have shown that immunotherapy of the patient highly sensitive to ragweed pollen with 0.5 milliliter of end-point dilution is no more effective than immunotherapy with placebo for reducing symptom-medication scores or for producing changes in serum levels of anti-ragweed IgG and IgE.
4. Use of skin-test end-point titrations to determine therapeutic dose for immunotherapy should be reserved for experimental use only in well-designed therapeutic trials.

(See also CONTROVERSIAL APPROACHES TO DIAGNOSIS, EXPLANATION, OR TREATMENT OF ALLERGIES.)

skin windows, Rebuck   A method for testing the effectiveness of leukocytes, white blood cells that fight foreign invaders in the body, in which small areas of skin are abraded with a scalpel blade and covered by coverslips (a tiny piece of thin glass that is placed over a specimen on a microscopic slide). The coverslips are changed every half hour to two hours over a 24-hour period and then stained and observed microscopically for leukocytes, which adhere to the surface of the glass. A normal response reveals the migration of polymorphonuclear granulocytes (polys or PMNs) to the inflamed abrasion sites within two hours. By 12 hours the polys are replaced by mononuclear cells.

Skoda's rales Named for Austrian physician Josef Skoda (1805–81), crackling noises heard in the bronchial tubes of the lungs of pneumonia patients upon auscultation, or the act of listening to body sounds through a stethoscope.

Slo-Bid See THEOPHYLLINE.

Slo-Phyllin See THEOPHYLLINE.

slow-releasing substance (SRS) [leukotriene C and D] Potent biochemical substance produced and released by mast cells of the immune system during anaphylaxis (severe allergic reaction). SRS causes smooth-muscle contraction especially in the bronchial tubes and increased permeability of blood vessels. (See CHEMICAL MEDIATORS, LEUKOTRIENES.)

smell The ability to detect and distinguish odors, aromas, fragrances, or scents. The process of smelling originates with a stimulus to the olfactory nerves (the first set of cranial nerves), which triggers perception of an odor or scent in the brain. (See also ANOSMIA.)

Smith, Theobald An American physician (1859–1934) born in Albany, New York, whose scientific contributions are recognized in pathology, immunology, physiology, bacteriology, and protozoology. The "Theobald Smith phenomenon" described in Smith's own writings refers to an experimental anaphylaxis he observed in guinea pigs after they had been given serum as part of an attempt to standardize the potency of diphtheria toxin and antitoxin. Smith wrote in 1934, "Anaphylaxis is probably related to the reactions appearing in hay fever, asthma, and food idiosyncrasies." (See THEOBALD SMITH PHENOMENON.)

smog A combination of smoke and fog, or generalized air pollution.

smoke allergy See CIGARETTE SMOKE.

smoking, active and passive The act of inhaling the gaseous products of burning tobacco or other substance. Smoking causes approximately 365,000 deaths and is the number one cause of preventable deaths each year in the United States. The U.S. surgeon general first reported the hazards of smoking in 1984. Despite the reduction in number of smokers in the past 27 years, almost 30% of the general population—about 50 million Americans—still smokes. The estimated cost of health care and related business losses is more than $40 billion.

Pregnant asthmatic mothers and smoking During pregnancy, since carbon monoxide, nicotine, and cyanide cross the placenta from a smoker's blood and enter the fetal circulation, there is even a greater risk to the fetus when the mother also has asthma. The levels of these dangerous substances are usually higher in the fetal than maternal circulating blood.

The average birth weight in these newborns is 200 grams less than in nonsmoking mothers. Mothers who quit smoking by the beginning of the second trimester (third or fourth month) can prevent lower-birth-weight offspring.

There is strong evidence of increased instances of spontaneous abortion, the placental abnormalities placenta previa and abruptio placentae, premature birth, and perinatal death. There may also be abnormal fetal lung development.

There is some evidence that newborn infants of smokers may have a greater risk of developing minimal brain dysfunction and hyperactivity, although the reason for these has not been determined. A far greater perinatal risk for mortality, which may approach 35% may be due to heavy smoking.

Passive smoking This refers to the exposure of nonsmokers to the same gases and particulate matter as smokers except to a somewhat lesser degree. Cigarette smoke contains slightly different compositions from each end of the cigarette. Smoke from the lighted end produces "sidestream" smoke; the smoker's end is called "mainstream" smoke.

TYPES OF CIGARETTE SMOKE

Composition	Sidestream Ratio to Mainstream
Carbon monoxide	2.5:1
Nicotine	2.7:1
Ammonia	73:1
Tar	1.7:1
Naphthalene	16:1
Benzo (a) pyrene	3.4:1
Aniline	30:1

Sidestream smoke constitutes about 85% of the smoke in a smoke-filled room and contains a much greater concentration of potential carcinogens. Therefore, a great risk to nonsmokers is present in any smoking environment.

Healthy children exposed to passive smoke, especially during the first year of life, suffer from an increased number of upper respiratory infections, including ear infections and tonsillitis and lower respiratory infections, such as bronchitis, bronchiolitis, and pneumonia. There is also a diminished resistance to viral infections and a small but statistically significant decrease in lung function studies or breathing capacity (See SPIROMETRY) in otherwise healthy children. In allergic and asthmatic children and adults, there is also a worsening of their usual symptoms. However, there is no evidence that exposure to passive smoking increases allergic tendencies in newborn or older children.

Passive smoking was the most important environmental factor occurring in 62% of children younger than three hospitalized for asthma in a New York inner-city hospital.

snake bite, poisonous   The bite of a venomous, scaly reptile, or serpent, which causes a toxic rather than an allergic reaction.

sneezing   The involuntary and usually forcible expulsion of air, and sometimes mucus, from the nose and mouth. The sneeze reflex is triggered by any irritation of the mucous membranes of the nose or when allergens are present in the air and a person is hypersensitive to them, such as in hay fever. Repeated sneezing may indicate an allergic reaction.

snoring   See STERTOR.

sodium metabisulfites   See SULFITING AGENTS.

sodokosis   See RAT-BITE FEVER.

soft drinks   See ASPARTAME, FOOD ADDITIVES.

solar urticaria   Hives that occur on exposed areas of the skin of susceptible persons from one to 30 minutes after exposure to the sun. Within 15 minutes to three hours, tolerance develops and the skin becomes resistant to new lesions for 12 to 24 hours. There are no other symptoms, unless the person also has the diseases systemic lupus erythematosus, an autoimmune disorder (see LUPUS ERYTHEMATOSUS, SYSTEMIC), or erythropoietic protoporphyria, a disorder of the red blood cells. Either condition may trigger hivelike markings on the skin.

Solar urticaria occurs most often in the fourth of fifth decades, but when it occurs in

EFFECTS OF SMOKING ON THE FETUS

Substance	Effect on Fetus	Fetal Result
Carbon monoxide	Reduces oxygen supply	Slows growth of fetus with lower birth weight
Nicotine	Constricts blood vessels reducing blood supply to the fetus	
Cyanide	Reduces oxygen supply	Slows growth of fetus with lower birth weight

children, the diagnosis of erythropoietic protoporphyria must be considered. Sunblocking agents, antimalarial drugs, or beta-carotene may be effective. Antihistamines taken one hour before exposure may be protective in some cases. (See PHYSICAL URTICARIA, URTICARIA.)

Solis-Cohen, Solomon   American physician (1857–1948), born in Philadelphia, Pennsylvania, who was professor of clinical medicine at the Jefferson Medical College in Philadelphia for his entire career. He recognized that vasomotor disturbance (involuntary spasms of blood vessels) is often associated with common allergic disorders. He initiated the use of adrenal substance in the treatment of hay fever and asthma in those cases in which vasomotor disturbance is present. According to his article, "The Use of Adrenal Substance in the Treatment of Asthma," published in the *Journal of the American Medical Association* in 1900, some patients were often sensitive to even slight changes in the weather. Others showed peculiar reactions to drugs or had their cardiovascular systems disturbed by emotional or dietary stress.

sonorous rale   Occurring in a bronchial tube in which there is an excess of mucus secretion, a noise that vibrates, causing a low-pitched, dry crackling heard through a stethoscope. (See also RALE.)

soybean   From the Hindu term *soya*, the bean of the leguminous plant *soja hispida (Glycine soja)*, which is high in protein. Soybeans may cross-react with other legumes, such as peanuts and peas, and can cause anaphylaxis. Soybeans may be goitrogenic (cause enlarged thyroid glands) if eaten in excessive amounts, but this effect can be countered by sufficient dietary iodine. Soy appears less desirable as a source of nutrition for infants than breast milk. Soy milk substitutes are used for individuals who are allergic to cow's milk. (See also LEGUMES, MILK.)

spacer   A drug-delivery device in various shapes and sizes for metered-dose inhalers that affords the user, including small children or poorly coordinated individuals, the full benefits of an aerosol asthma medication. Spacers allow small particles of active medication to enter the airways, and trap large inactive particles that could irritate the mouth and throat. The spacer is especially helpful with the corticosteroid metered-dose inhalers and lessens the likelihood of oral yeast infections.

sperm allergy   An adverse reaction to contact with human semen. (See REPRODUCTIVE IMMUNOLOGY, SEMEN ALLERGY.)

spermatozoa allergy   See SEMEN ALLERGY.

spider bite   An attack on human skin by an insect belonging to the phylum Arthropoda, subclass Arachnida. Bites can cause simple, localized reactions such as redness and slight swelling as well as dangerous reactions such as pain, necrosis (the death of body tissues), and even death from toxins. These reactions are nonallergic, but they may be mistaken for other bites or stings that can cause allergic symptoms.

Spieksma, Frederick (Frits) Th. M.   Dutch biologist and zoologist, born in 1936, who, with Dutch physician Reindert Voorhorst (born in 1915), identified house dust mites as allergens. The studies of Spieksma and Voorhorst led to studies on the immunochemical characterization of house dust mites, namely *Dermatophagoides pteronyssinus*.

spiloplania   Red patches of skin that move from one area to another.

spinach   A plant belonging to the goosefoot family, Chenopodiaceae, with dark green edible leaves known essentially for their calcium and vitamins A and C. Only 50% of the iron content can be utilized by the body. Once used by the Persians as medicine, spinach has been known to cause anaphylaxis (life-threatening allergic shock).

Spinhaler   A drug-delivery device formerly used with cromolyn sodium (Intal) capsules. The powder-containing capsules were placed inside a whistlelike plastic tube and activated by twisting the device and inhaling the released drug. The Spinhaler has been replaced by the metered-dose inhaler. (See AEROSOLS.)

spirit of glyceryl trinitrate   An alcoholic liquid once used as a relaxant for the treatment of asthma and angina pectoris (chest pain related to heart disease).

spirogram   A printout made by a spirometer that records breathing function. (See SPIROMETER, SPIROMETRY.)

spirometer   An instrument that measures the air capacity of the lungs. It is used to make treatment decisions for patients with asthma and other lung disorders. It is also used to determine the severity of lung disease and to help determine disability or determine if a specific job should be precluded.

Spirometry equipment must meet rigid specifications as recommended by the American Thoracic Society (ATS) in an official policy statement published in the *American Review of Respiratory Diseases* in 1987. (See also PULMONARY FUNCTION TESTS, SPIROMETRY.)

spirometry   An objective measurement of lung function. A patient's measured values of airflow are compared with predicted normals based on age, height, and sex. Resulting values assist in diagnosis of lung diseases such as asthma and emphysema. Degrees of severity of lung disease can objectively be measured by spirometry. (See also SPIROMETER.)

spleen   An encapsulated, fist-sized organ in the left upper portion of the abdomen that contains two distinct regions of tissues, the red and white pulp. Red pulp functions to dispose of worn-out blood cells. The red pulp also contains immune cells called macrophages. Macrophages trap and destroy microorganisms in blood passing through the spleen during the circulatory process. The white pulp contains lymphoid tissue similar to that of the lymph nodes and is similarly subdivided into compartments that specialize in different types of immune cells. Patients who have a nonfunctioning or surgically removed spleen are more susceptible to infections. (See IMMUNE SYSTEM.)

spontaneous abortion   See REPRODUCTIVE IMMUNOLOGY.

spore   Derived from the Greek word meaning "seed," a reproductive cell of certain plants, especially fungi and protozoans (the simplest, mostly unicellular, animal form). Spores are usually asexual (able to reproduce by fission), but certain sexual forms are associated with molds, such as ospores, zygospores, and asgospores. Fungal or mold spores are a significant source of allergic symptoms. (See FUNGI AND MOLDS.)

sports and asthma   See EXERCISE-INDUCED ASTHMA, OLYMPIC ATHLETES WITH ASTHMA.

spring conjunctivitis   See CONJUNCTIVITIS, ALLERGIC.

sputum   A combination of mucus, pus, blood, cellular debris, infectious microorganisms, and caseous material expelled by individuals with pneumonia and other pulmonary diseases when they cough or clear their throats. Types of sputum vary according to the diagnosis. In bronchial asthma, sputum is often purulent (containing pus), grayish, and possibly frothy and contains Charcot-Leyden crystals (hard formations formed from salts and other substances). In bronchitis it contains thick mucus and pus that is greenish yellow. In bronchopneumonia, mucus may look like prune juice in color and can be frothy, thin, mucoid, purulent, and bloody. (See ASTHMA, BRONCHITIS, CHARCOT-LEYDEN CRYSTALS, PNEUMONIA.)

squash   One of many plants with seeds, hard rind, and edible flesh, such as acorn squash, pumpkin, and zucchini, that may or may not cause adverse reaction. It is often used in elimination diets to determine food allergies. (See DIET, ELIMINATION; FOOD ALLERGY.)

squatting in asthmatic children   The crouching position assumed by some children with asthma, heart disease, or other disorders affecting normal breathing during play or physically strenuous activity. This characteristic squatting helps relieve chronic oxygen deprivation, especially after exertion, by facilitating use of accessory muscles of respiration and thus making breathing easier.

stain, gram   See GRAM STAIN.

starch   A complex carbohydrate in food and food by-products, also used in pharmaceuticals, adhesives, and laundering. Vegetable starches are derived from potatoes, arrowroot, and legumes such as peas, lentils, and beans. Grain starches are derived from corn, wheat, oats, barley, rye, and rice.

In the process of digestion, all starches are reduced to simple sugars before the body can absorb and utilize them. Starches that can cause allergic reactions, especially wheat flour and cornstarch, should be replaced by other less allergenic flours, including rice, potato, and soy flours and tapioca. Corn and other starches may also be considered hidden allergens; for example, cornmeal may be spread onto the bottom of bread ovens and thus become cooked into the bread.

Cornstarch is also a popular home remedy to soothe skin rashes and other irritations. (See CORN ALLERGY, FOOD ALLERGY, WHEAT.)

status asthmaticus   The condition of intractable asthma, a diagnosis that indicates that a patient is so debilitated that emergency management in a hospital is required. (See ASTHMA.)

sterility   See REPRODUCTIVE IMMUNOLOGY.

sternutation   The medical term for sneezing. (See SNEEZING.)

steroid therapy   See CORTICOSTEROIDS.

stertor   The medical term for snoring. Stertorous breathing also refers to loud breathing that sometimes sounds like a hen's clucking. Hencluck stertor is often found in patients with postpharyngeal abscess. Stertorous breathing may also occur in persons with asthma or respiratory allergy symptoms.

stethoscope   An instrument consisting of two rubber tubes connected to a bell at one end and ear pieces at the other. It is used to listen to respiratory, cardiac, pleural, arterial, venous, uterine, fetal, intestinal, and other body sounds for diagnostic purposes.

Stevens-Johnson syndrome   The alternate name for ectodermosis erosiva pluriorificialis, named after American pediatricians Albert Mason Stevens (1884–1945) and Frank Chambliss Johnson (1894–1934). Stevens-Johnson syndrome is an allergic reaction to various drugs, especially sulfonamides and some anticonvulsants, to which no desensitization is possible. The potentially lethal syndrome is characterized by fever, eruptions of the skin, and conjunctiva and mucosal lesions of the mouth, anus, penis, and other areas. Corneal ulcerations may lead to scarring and blindness. This condition is among the most severe reactions and fatal in 2% of the cases. (See also DRUG ALLERGY AND OTHER ADVERSE DRUG REACTIONS.)

stillicidium lacrimarum   The medical term for watery eyes.

stillicidium narium   The medical term for watery mucus discharged from the nose associated with allergies or the common cold.

stimulant, respiratory   Any substance that increases breathing function.

stonecutter's phthisis   Wasting form of bronchopneumonia as a result of irritation of the lung by inhaled stone dust. (See PHTHISIS.)

stoves   See WOOD- AND COAL-BURNING STOVES.

stramonium   An antispasmodic drug derived from the dried leaves of *Datura stramonium* and related to the drug atropine. Atropine blocks the constricting action of the vagus nerve on the bronchial tubes. Stramonium was the active ingredient in Asthmador cigarettes, inhaled by asthma patients to relax smooth muscle in the bronchial tubes in a now-obsolete treatment of asthma. Adverse effects of this treatment, including irritation from the cigarette smoke, eventually outweighed any possible benefit. Atropinelike drugs, however, are now prescribed mainly for the treatment of chronic bronchitis and occasionally asthma. (See ATROPINE SULFATE.)

strawberries   The red, juicy fruit of various low-growing plants containing a salicylic element that can cause a skin rash.

straw itch   A skin irritation and itching caused by contact with straw.

stress   Physical or emotional tension that may be well tolerated by the body for efficient function or ill tolerated, which often results in some form of debilitation. Negative stress, or distress, is considered a trigger for asthma. (See TRIGGERS OF ALLERGIES AND ASTHMA.)

stridor   A shrill or harsh sound, like wind whistling through pipes, created during respiration by individuals with severe asthma or acute obstruction of the larynx.

strophulus   Formerly a medical term for many types of skin rash including prickly heat and some types of hives.

stuffed animals   Soft toys resembling animals that may be made with allergenic fibers and materials such as kapok. (See KAPOK.)

subcutaneous/sublingual provocation testing   See CONTROVERSIAL APPROACHES TO DIAGNOSIS, EXPLANATION, OR TREATMENT OF ALLERGIES.

sugar   A sweet-tasting, water-soluble carbohydrate derived from sugarcane, sugar beets, sorghum, and maple and palm trees. Sugar, an important nutrient and preservative, is commonly thought to cause hyperactivity in children, but there are no known allergies to sugar or its many forms. (See HYPERACTIVITY.)

sulfa drugs   Drugs of the sulfonamide group, used as antibacterial agents. They are a common cause of allergic reactions. (See also DRUG ALLERGY AND OTHER ADVERSE DRUG REACTIONS.)

sulfiting agents   Food additives used to prevent discoloration of food and to inhibit growth of certain microorganisms in the fermentation process during the manufacture of wine. Sulfur dioxide gas, or powdered or liquid potassium metabisulfite, and other sulfiting agents have been used for hundreds of years and are the most important additives that can cause serious adverse reactions. Ingestion of sulfites have no apparent effects on normal persons, but approximately 5% of asthmatic individuals are sulfite-sensitive, with symptoms ranging from mild wheezing to death. The average diet in the United States contains about 2 to 3 milligrams of sulfites daily. Each ounce of beer or wine contains 5 to 10 milligrams. Prior to a Food and Drug Administration ban in 1986 on their use in restaurants, a meal contained from 25 to 200 milligrams of sulfites. As little as 5 milligrams of ingested sulfite can provoke an asthmatic response in susceptible persons, and there are at least 12 documented asthma deaths from sulfiting agents. Allergic symptoms including urticaria (hives), angioedema (tissue swelling), and anaphylaxis (allergic shock) may be caused by sulfites, but only a few individuals who react to these additives have positive skin tests to them. The cause of sulfite reactions may be related to a deficiency of the enzyme sulfite oxidase, which is required to inactivite sulfite in the body.

Highest levels of sulfites are found in dried fruits, potatoes, seafoods, and wine. Sulfite use is prohibited in any food served fresh in restaurants. Since January 1988, packaged foods and bottled wines must be labeled if they contain more than 10 parts per million of sulfur dioxide (SO_2).

THE MOST COMMON FOODS THAT MAY CONTAIN SULFITES

Processed potatoes (chips, fries, dehydrated)
Dried and packaged fruits and beverages
Shrimp and other seafood
Beer and wine
   Salads and all ingredients in salad bars in countries outside the United States (sulfite use is banned in restaurant salad bars in the United States)
Precut fruit outside the United States
Avocado, guacamole, and other dips
Cider and wine vinegars
Pickled vegetables
White grapes
Maraschino cherries
Fresh mushrooms
Beet sugar
Wet-milled corn
Conditioned dough

Some medications used as solutions in the emergency treatment of asthma contain sulfites. Isoetharine (Bronkosol) solution contains sodium bisulfite as a preservative, and isoproterenol (Isuprel) contains sodium metabisulfite, also as a preservative. Although these medications are rarely used since the introduction of albuterol and metaproterenol, asthma patients and their physicians should be aware that these solutions for aerososl treatment of asthma may actually worsen asthma in some individuals.

WARNING

ASTHMA MEDICATIONS USED TO TREAT ACUTE ATTACKS MAY CONTAIN SULFITES AS ANTIOXIDANT PRESERVATIVES AND ACTUALLY WORSEN ASTHMA IN A SMALL NUMBER OF PATIENTS.

---

sulfone chloride See CHLORAMINE-T.

sulfur dioxide A gas used in the manufacture of acids and electrical refrigerators and as a bactericide and disinfectant. Sulfur dioxide poisoning from the inhalation of the chemical's fumes may result in suffocation. Any air pollutant, including sulfur dioxide, may exacerbate allergies and asthma. (See also SULFITING AGENTS.)

supplemental air See RESIDUAL AIR.

support groups Lay and professional organizations, such as the American Lung Association, the Asthma and Allergy Foundation, and Mothers of Asthmatics, that have been established to bring asthma patients and their families together with others in similar circumstances in order to assuage some of the physical management problems and emotional difficulties encountered by asthmatics. (See Appendix IV.)

suppuration The medical term for the formation of pus, or infected body fluid.

surfactant, pulmonary The natural substance that lubricates the lungs and prevents them from collapsing during exhalation.

surgery, related to allergic and asthmatic persons Individuals with asthma and/or allergies to drugs including anesthesia need to consider certain factors when they require an elective surgical procedure: (1) Do not schedule surgery when a viral infection or exacerbation of asthma is present. (2) Have the physician evaluate breathing status, blood oxygenation and lung function one or two days before the surgery. (3) Review all medications and blood levels of medications with the physician and surgical team before the surgery. (4) Use local anesthesia, which does not interfere with breathing mechanisms, if possible. (5) Avoid nitrous oxide (laughing gas) as dental anesthesia; a local anesthetic and a mild tranquilizer are recommended. (6) Ensure that the patient will be assisted in bringing up mucus and secretions after the surgery, if necessary.

In the event of emergency surgery and the use of general anesthesia, most often there is minimal increased risk for the allergic or asthmatic patient in light of available medications and adequate monitoring. (See also ANESTHESIA, GENERAL, FOR THE ALLERGIC AND ASTHMATIC PATIENT.)

sweat chloride test   A diagnostic test used to determine the presence of cystic fibrosis. The test, which measures the salt content in the sweat, is performed on children who are wheezing or who have a family history of cystic fibrosis, failure to thrive, recurrent pneumonia, or other pulmonary disorder that involves gastrointestinal disturbances.

swimmer's itch   See SCHISTOSOME DERMATITIS.

swimming and asthma   See EXERCISE-INDUCED ASTHMA.

Symmetrel   See AMANTADINE.

sympathicomimetic drugs   See ALPHA-ADRENERGIC AGONISTS.

sympathomimetic drugs   [sympathicomimetic drugs] See ALPHA-ADRENERGIC AGONISTS.

symptoms of allergy   From the Greek word meaning "occurrence," a symptom is a change or ill effect experienced by an individual and potentially indicating a disease process. Specific symptoms of allergy include sneezing, itching, wheezing, runny nose, nasal congestion, shortness of breath, tightness in the chest, rashes, swelling of body tissues, discharge from the eyes, and other discomforts. (See also ALLERGIC RHINITIS, ASTHMA, URTICARIA.)

system, integumentary   See SKIN.

system, respiratory   The lungs, bronchi, pleura, throat, larynx, nose, and other structures responsible for the body's intake of oxygen from the air and expulsion of waste products (carbon dioxide) out of the body. Oxygen enters the nose and mouth, where it is moistened and warmed, and proceeds down the trachea, or windpipe, to the lungs. Through millions of alveoli, the lungs' tiny air sacs, oxygen goes into the bloodstream, which transports it to all parts of the body. Carbon dioxide is filtered back to the alveoli so it may be exhaled.

The respiratory system may be irritated by pollutants, pollen, and other substances in the air, especially in allergic or asthmatic individuals, and breathing may become difficult. (See BREATHING.)

T

tabacosis   Tobacco poisoning, especially from the inhalation of tobacco dust by tobacco handlers. Exposure to tobacco dust is a cause of occupational asthma. (See also GREEN TOBACCO SICKNESS, OCCUPATIONAL ASTHMA.)

tachyphylaxis   The injection of small, consecutive doses of a toxic substance in order to induce a rapid immunization to that substance. (See also TOLERANCE.)

tachypnea   Abnormally rapid breathing.

Tagamet   See CIMETIDINE.

talc   A powder made from soapstone or hydrous magnesium silicate and used as a dusting powder or counterirritant for prickly heat, diaper rash, and other skin eruptions. Talc is an irritant that can trigger asthma. (See OCCUPATIONAL ASTHMA.)

Talmadge, David W.   American physician, born in Korea in 1919 of missionary parents, who wrote a paper in 1957 on antibody production and specificity that first provided the concept that cell selection is the basis of antibody production. Talmadge's subsequent studies and papers led to the development of cellular immunology. He is Distinguished Professor of the University of Colorado.

Tan, Eng M., and Tomasi, Thomas B., Jr. Physicians and scientists who discovered and defined the structure, locations, and function of immunoglobulin A (IgA). Tomasi, born in Barre, Vermont in 1927, became chairman of the Department of Immunology at the Mayo Medical School in 1973 and Distinguished University Professor and chairman of the Department of Cell Biology and director of the Cancer Center at the University of New Mexico in 1980. Tomasi is director of the Roswell Park Cancer Institute in Buffalo, New York and head of the Molecular Medical and Immunology division

in the Department of Medicine at the State University of New York (SUNY).

Tan, a Malaysian physician born in 1926, served for 10 years as head of the Division of Allergy and Immunology at the Scripps Clinic and Research Foundation in California. Tan also was professor of medicine and head of the Division of Rheumatic Diseases at the University of Colorado. In 1982 he became director of the William Keck Autoimmune Disease Center and head of the Division of Rheumatology at Scripps.

tannic acid solution (Allergy Control Solution)   A product derived from certain plants and trees (found in coffee and tea) that, when sprayed on carpets, kills house dust mites. (See ACARACIDES.)

TAO   See TROLEANDOMYCIN.

tartrazine   [tartrazine yellow, Yellow Dye No. 5, FD&C No. 5]   A yellow azo dye derived from coal tar (see AZO DYES). Yellow Dye No. 5 is the color additive most widely used by the food, cosmetic, and drug industries. It is also used to dye wool and silk. Diets in the United States contain significant amounts of tartrazine. This food and drug additive is frequently blamed for causing urticaria (hives) and asthma. Persons who also have nasal polyps, and in whom asthma is triggered by exposure to aspirin, are more likely to develop hives when exposed to tartrazine. However, true tartrazine sensitivity is rare, especially in children. (See also ASPIRIN SENSITIVITY, FOOD ADDITIVES.)

Tavist   See CLEMASTINE.

T cells   Lymphocytes (white blood cells) that develop in the bone marrow but mature in the thymus gland and secrete chemical substances called lymphokines. These chemicals have important functions in controlling the immune system, especially in graft rejection and delayed, or type IV, hypersensitivity reactions. There are two types of T cells. The first, T helper cells, stimulate the production of antibodies by B cells. The second, suppressor T cells, inhibit B-cell activity. (See ANTIBODY, B CELLS, IMMUNE SYSTEM, THYMUS GLAND.)

tension-fatigue syndrome   A term coined by physicians, patients, or families of patients who associate periods of anxiety and listlessness or fatigue with allergies to foods.

In his 1922 article entitled "Neuropathic Manifestations in Infants and Children as a Result of Anaphylactic Reaction to Foods Contained in Their Dietary," W. R. Shannon associates food-allergic children with irritability and constant crying. A. H. Rowe in 1930 reported a syndrome including fatigue and impaired concentration, not improved by sleep, and headaches, gastrointestinal upset, and joint and muscle aches and pains. Rowe claimed relief of symptoms when food and inhalant allergies were treated.

However, controlled studies have failed to prove a relationship between allergy and central nervous system symptoms. (See also CHRONIC FATIGUE SYNDROME.)

teratogens   From the Greek word *teras*, meaning "monster," any environmental agent (drug, chemical, infection, or pollutant) whose exposure during pregnancy has the potential to harm the developing fetus. Drugs, either prescribed or over the counter, immunizations, vitamins, alcohol, illicit drugs, smoking, diseases (maternal diabetes mellitus or phenylketonuria) and infections (rubella, or German measles) occurring before or during pregnancy, and chemicals, pesticides, and radiation exposure in the home or workplace may be potential teratogens. To determine the possibility of a drug causing a birth defect, the drug must be ingested during the time the organ or organs involved are developing in the fetus. Many drugs commonly used to treat allergic disorders and asthma during pregnancy are safe, but some drugs are preferable because of their

many years of safe use. (See PREGNANCY, FOOD AND DRUG ADMINISTRATION (FDA) DRUG RISK CATEGORIES; PREGNANCY AND RHINITIS; PREGNANCY COMPLICATED BY ASTHMA.)

terbutaline sulfate   (Brethaire, Brethine, Bricanyl)   A selective beta$_2$ bronchodilating drug used to treat asthma. As an oral or inhaled medication, its effectiveness and safety are similar to those of albuterol. It can be used by subcutaneous injection for asthma emergencies and has an action similar to that of epinephrine, but it takes up to 15 minutes to become effective (epinephrine usually works within one minute). (See also BETA-ADRENERGIC AGONISTS.)

terfenadine   (Seldane)   A second-generation or nonsedating antihistaminic drug used to treat allergic rhinitis (hay fever) and urticaria (hives). There have been rare but life-threatening cardiac arrhythmias (irregular heartbeat) associated with the use of terfenadine given simultaneously with certain other drugs, including the antibiotic erythromycin, the antifungal drug ketoconazole and with grapefruit juice. A risk also is associated with the use of this drug in persons with liver disorders.

tetanus, tetanus antitoxin, tetanus immune globulin, and vaccine   A bacterial infection caused by the organism *Clostrium tetani*, which enters the body through a contaminated wound or burn. Symptoms of tetanus, which are fatal in about one-third of all persons contracting it, include severe muscle spasms and inability to open one's mouth or swallow. Tetanus toxoid is a vaccine that induces the body to manufacture tetanus antitoxin, or antibodies against the bacteria that block the disease. This reaction is called active immunity (see IMMUNITY, ACTIVE). A series of injections is given beginning in infancy and is usually combined with vaccines against pertussis and diphtheria until age seven, and with only diphtheria after that age. These vaccines are referred to as "DPT" and "DT," respectively.

If an individual has been injured and has not received full immunization, human tetanus immune globulin is given at once and with a tetanus toxoid injection. The human immune globulin has been prepared from donors who have been immunized with tetanus toxoid to produce protective antibodies to the tetanus organism, *Clostrium tetani*. The resulting product provides passive immunity (see IMMUNITY, PASSIVE) and should be given to anyone whose immunization against tetanus is questionable.

Before the introduction of human immune globulin, horse serum was used and was effective, but it caused many severe allergic reactions. Since its introduction in 1938, tetanus toxoid has also been a cause of anaphylactic reactions, but they are less common than those occurring from horse serum. Despite improved purity of the vaccine, reactions still occur infrequently. More commonly reported adverse reactions are mild fever, or soreness, swelling, and redness where the shot was given. Patients who are severely allergic can be desensitized and successfully immunized (see DESENSITIZATION).

tetanus antitoxin See TETANUS.

tetanus immune globulin [antitoxin] See TETANUS.

tetanus vaccine See TETANUS.

tetracyclines A group of broad-spectrum antibiotics first discovered as a result of systematic screening of soil samples collected from around the world in a search for microorganisms that could produce antibiotics. The first of these drugs produced was chlortetracycline in 1948. Since then three other naturally occurring antibiotics have been produced from species of the bacteria *Streptomyces*, tetracycline (Achromycin, Sumycin, Panmycin, Robitet), oxytetracycline (Terramycin), and demeclocycline (Declomycin). Methacycline (Rondomycin), doxycycline (Vibramycin, Doryx), and minocycline (Minocin) are semisynthetically derived by manipulation of the natural tetracyclines.

The antibiotic effect of the tetracyclines is due to their ability to interfere with protein synthesis in bacteria. However, by some other mechanism, the drugs are effective against rickettsia and chlamydia infections. Although tetracyclines are frequently used for the treatment of respiratory infections such as sinusitis, bronchitis, and pneumonia in patients with asthma or allergic rhinitis, many microorganisms have developed a resistance to them. Adverse effects of the tetracyclines include rare cases of anaphylaxis, and all drugs in this class should be avoided in persons with a history of serious allergic reaction to any of them. More commonly, rashes occur, especially with sun exposure. Demeclocycline causes the most severe and frequent photosensitivity reactions; doxycycline reactions are less severe. Most of the photosensitivity rashes resemble severe sunburn and occur on exposed skin areas. Paresthesias (tingling of the hands, feet, and nose) may be the first sign of adverse reactions to tetracyclines and the sun.

Tetracyclines also cause numerous other adverse effects, most often gastrointestinal upset, which are usually mild and self-limiting. Rarely, neurologic disturbances are exhibited, such as pseudotumor cerebri (increased pressure in the brain that gives symptoms suggestive of a brain tumor).

Tetracyclines are absorbed by bones and teeth and depress bone growth and tooth development. Therefore they should probably not be given to pregnant women or children before the age of eight or nine. In rare instances with life-threatening infections such as Rocky Mountain spotted fever, their use may be necessary.

"Theobald Smith phenomenon" The anaphylactic reaction of guinea pigs to diphtheria toxin and antitoxin as observed by German-American physician and microbiologist Theobald Smith in 1903–4. Smith, who held many distinguished posts, including director of the Department of Animal Pathology at the Rockefeller Institute for Medical Research at

Princeton and professor of comparative pathology at Harvard University, had been working on standardizing the potency of diphtheria toxin and antitoxin when he noticed that some of the guinea pigs died. When other scientists such as Paul Lewis and Paul Ehrlich read Smith's report, they asked Professor Richard Otto to replicate the experiments. Smith had determined that anaphylaxis, a severe hypersensitivity reaction, was indeed related to the administration of the diphtheria toxins and antitoxins to some guinea pigs who had not received any previous dose of the substances; but there were also guinea pigs who received incremental doses, starting with a relatively large initial dose, who became immune to the substances. Otto dubbed this reaction "Das Theobald Smithsche Phanomen der Serum Uberemphindlichkeit" ("the Theobald Smith phenomenon of serum hypersensitivity").

Theoclear   See THEOPHYLLINE.

Theocron   See THEOPHYLLINE.

Theo-Dur   See THEOPHYLLINE.

Theolair   See THEOPHYLLINE.

theophylline (Bronkodyl, Elixophyllin, Quibron, Respid, Slo-bid, Slo-Phyllin, Theo-24, Theoclear, Theocron, Theo-Dur, Theolair, Theo-Sav, Theostat, TheoX, Uniphyl)   A commonly used bronchodilating drug belonging to the xanthine class. Theophylline was isolated from tea leaves in 1888. At first, it was used as a diuretic for cases of congestive heart failure, and for a brief period in the 1950s it was used to treat angina. A modified version of the drug, aminophylline, became popular in the 1940s to treat asthma, but it was not until the late 1970s and 1980s that its popularity peaked with the introduction of long-acting formulas.

The basis of theophylline's activity has not been well defined but is thought to be complex. Theophylline is known to block the action of adenosine, which causes constriction of the bronchioles in asthma. The drug strengthens the contractibility of the diaphragmatic muscle

and diminishes fatigue. Theophylline seems to stimulate the respiratory center; in patients with both chronic bronchitis or emphysema and heart failure (cor pulmonale), theophylline strengthens the cardiac output. The drug also may inhibit the release of inflammatory mediators.

There is considerable disagreement among physicians about theophylline's role in the treatment of asthma. Some researchers feel theophylline is more effective than beta$_2$ agonists and should be a primary drug, whereas others have relegated theophylline to a backup role to be added to a regimen of other asthma drugs.

Despite its reputation for causing many side effects, the only major drawback of theophylline is overdose, which can be avoided by monitoring serum levels. Tachyphylaxis (tolerance) does not occur, and it is the only bronchodilator drug for which there is a fixed dose that is independent of the severity of the disease.

The use of theophylline in children is also controversial. The drug has been blamed for causing both learning disabilities and hyperactivity. Studies have demonstrated normal school performance in students with asthma taking theophylline on a daily basis when compared with nonasthmatic children.

GUIDELINES FOR SAFE USE OF THEOPHYLLINE

---

1. Serum levels from 15 to 20 micrograms/ml were considered optimal until recently. Now levels from 5 to 15 are considered adequate and safer for most patients.
2. During pregnancy, and in chronic bronchitis or emphysema, levels from 8 to 12 are advised.
3. Doses should be taken at regular intervals and in the same relationship to meals.
4. Various brand-name products and generic formulations are not interchangeable, and

levels may vary greatly when switching from one formulation to another.

5. If another illness occurs while on theophylline, especially heart failure, liver disease, or viral upper respiratory infections (including the common cold), theophylline doses may need to be adjusted downward. If unable to reach your doctor, you should skip a dose and lower subsequent doses until the physician can be consulted.

6. Many drugs affect the theophylline level by diminishing its excretion from the body, thus raising levels to a possible toxic degree. Cimetidine (Tagamet), mexiletine, ciprofloxacin and other quinalone antibiotics, erythromycin, allopurinol, propanolol, and oral contraceptives may increase levels. Influenza vaccine also raises theophylline levels for a short time. The anticonvulsant medications phenytoin, phenobarbital, and carbamazepine, the antibiotic rifampin, and cigarette smoking may lower theophylline levels.

7. The following patient types should probably avoid theophylline except in very carefully monitored settings:

   a. elderly frail patients with multiple medical problems
   b. patients susceptible to nausea and vomiting
   c. premature babies and infants under one year
   d. patients known to have sudden changes in their heart rhythm (arryhthmias)
   e. any patient who might misuse medications

Theo-Sav See THEOPHYLLINE.

Theostat See THEOPHYLLINE.

Theo-24 See THEOPHYLLINE.

Theo X See THEOPHYLLINE.

therapeutic touch Contact with an individual by the laying on of hands in order to soothe and in many cases relieve pain or disease. Many health professionals who practice therapeutic touch believe that even simple contact such as holding hands can have a calming, reassuring effect upon a patient. Therapeutic touch also refers not to touch per se but to a technique that is performed by holding the hands a few inches away from the patient's body and searching the energy field for places that feel congested, hot, cold, tingly, painful, or uncomfortable. Once they are located, the caregiver uses smooth, long strokes to adjust the adverse condition back to optimal balance and order. According to Dolores Krieger, Ph.D, R.N., author of *The Therapeutic Touch*, this technique has brought positive results in reducing stress, decreasing high blood pressure, relieving headaches, reducing edema, increasing circulation, and, in some cases, decreasing the average amount of healing time of fractures. Therapeutic touch may reduce the stress that triggers asthma attacks.

thrombocytopenia A reduction in the blood platelet count that may be caused by many factors, including immune disorders, which may suppress platelet synthesis by the bone marrow, cause the spleen to store an excessive number of platelets, or destroy existing platelets. Platelet counts below 20,000 are considered severe, with normal count ranging from 150,000 to 350,000 platelets per cubic millimeter.

Thrombocytopenia may be a sign of allergic vasculitis (see HENOCH-SCHONLEIN PURPURA) or drug allergy (see DRUG ALLERGY AND OTHER ADVERSE DRUG REACTIONS). Infant allergy to cow's milk may cause this platelet disorder; however, food allergies account for only about one in 1,000 cases of this blood disorder. The most common symptoms of thrombocytopenia are petechiae (small, purple or red spots on the skin or mucous membranes) and ecchymosis (large purplish bruises) that indicate bleeding into the subcutaneous tissues. (See also PLATE-LETS.)

thrush [oral candidiasis]   A fungal (yeast) infection of the mouth and throat characterized by a whitish coating of the mucous membranes and painful ulcers in the mouth. *Candida albicans*, a normal inhabitant of the gastrointestinal tract, is usually kept in balance by the normal bacterial flora, but antibiotics often kill the beneficial as well as harmful bacteria, and the yeast bacteria become prominent.

Thrush occurs more frequently in diabetics and individuals with immune deficiency disorders such as AIDS. It may also occur as a side effect from the use of orally inhaled corticosteroids for the treatment of asthma. This adverse effect can usually be prevented by rinsing the mouth after each use of the corticosteroid metered-dose inhalers and by using a spacer device. Thrush is treated with antifungal drugs such as nystatin, or clotrimazole lozenges (Mycilex Troches). (See also ACQUIRED IMMUNODEFICIENCY SYNDROME, CANDIDIASIS.)

thymus gland   A lymphoid organ of the immune system located behind the breastbone. T cells migrate from the bone marrow to the thymus, where they multiply and mature. In a process called "T-cell education," these cells become immunocompetent, developing the ability to evoke an immune response and learning to distinguish self from nonself cells. (See T CELLS.)

tickle   An irritation usually felt in the nose and throat attributable to reflex muscular movements. This irritation is a common complaint of hay fever sufferers. It may also occur during laughter.

tidal air   The air inhaled and exhaled in normal breathing.

tight building syndrome   See SICK BUILDING SYNDROME.

Tilade   See NEDOCROMIL SODIUM.

time reaction   [late-phase reaction]

The period between the onset of a stimulus and response to it, especially concerning the exposure to an allergen and the time it takes to cause an individual to experience symptoms or have some recognition of the exposure. (See LATE- PHASE ALLERGIC REACTIONS.)

tine test   A skin test for tuberculosis widely replaced by the more accurate Mantoux test. (See TUBERCULIN TEST.)

tinnitis   A ringing or buzzing in the ear characteristic of certain diseases or adverse effects from drugs prescribed for disorders of the external, middle, or inner ear, such as otitis media (ear infection) and aspirin toxicity.

Tiselius, Arne W. K., and Kabat, Elvin A. Scientists who established the identity of antibodies as serum gamma globulins and the chemical character of hereditary antibodies. Tiselius, born in Sweden (1902–71), won the Nobel Prize for chemistry in 1948 for his development of electrophoretic techniques to study antibodies. Kabat, born in New York in 1914, joined Columbia University-Presbyterian Hospital Medical Center as professor of microbiology in 1941. He has published books entitled *Experimental Immunochemistry* (Manfred Mayer is coauthor) and *Blood Group Substances, Their Chemistry and Immunochemistry*. Kabat has served as expert consultant at the National Institutes of Health since 1976 and has continued his research on immunologic proteins and immunoglobulin chains.

titer, serum   The level of an allergen-specific antibody present in the blood.

titration, skin   See SKIN TESTS, SKIN TITRATION.

tobacco smoke   See CIGARETTE SMOKE.

Today Vaginal Sponge   See NONOXYNOL-9 SPERMACIDE.

tolerance   The ability to withstand a drug, toxin, or food without adverse effect that would usually cause an adverse effect in most persons. This condition explains why an individual may require higher and higher doses of a drug in order to experience its effect. Tolerance also refers to the ability to live with an allergen without allergic reaction.

tolerance level   The maximum amount of an additive substance allowed in food. Levels are determined by the United States Food and Drug Administration and are usually below the amount considered dangerous. (See FOOD ADDITIVES.)

tolerogen   A substance that does not produce the expected allergic response when an individual is exposed to an allergen.

Tomasi, Thomas B., Jr.   See TAN, ENG M., AND TOMASI, THOMAS B., JR.

tomato   An herb of the nightshade family, genus *Lycoperscon*, that is cultivated for its edible fruit. Tomatoes can cause severe allergy including anaphylaxis (allergic shock). They can also cause a perioral (in the area of the mouth) rash. The red fruit contains histamine and can cause headaches.

Tonegawa, Susumu   Japanese biologist, born in 1939, who won the Nobel Prize for physiology or medicine in 1987 for his discovery of how certain inherited genes split and rearrange themselves within developing antibody-producing cells. In 1981, Tonegawa became professor of biology at the Center for Cancer Research of the Massachusetts Institute of Technology in Cambridge.

tonsillitis   Tonsillitis is an inflammation of the tonsils at the back of the throat, treatable by antibiotics or surgical removal.

tonsils   Oval-shaped masses of lymphatic tissue whose lymph contains nutrients and lymphocytes (cells that help form antibodies) found throughout the body. They are named from the Latin word *tonsilla*, meaning "almond." The palatine tonsils are located on either side of the uvula, the tiny structure that hangs from the back of the palate. Nasal tonsils are on the septum, which divides the nose into two chambers; lingual tonsils are found at the root of the tongue. Cerebellar tonsils are in the cerebellum of the brain. Pharyngeal and tubal tonsils are in the auditory tube near its opening into the throat. Tonsils help form white blood cells, which fight bacteria in the body.

torulosis   See FUNGAL DISEASES, SYSTEMIC.

total immune disorder syndrome   Multiple somatic complaints attributed to allergy to multiple foods and the environment. Also referred to as being "allergic to the 20th century," these severely distressed persons often have underlying psychiatric problems that may include multiple personality disorder. The syndrome must not be confused with severe immune deficiency disorders that may be life-threatening (see IMMUNODEFICIENCY DISEASE).

Persons with total immune disorder syndrome are often found in communes set up by clinical ecologists in rural areas and may live a miserable existence, possibly becoming severely malnourished by avoiding most foods. If they are agreeable, they may be helped by being placed in an environmental care unit, or ECU, such as the Presbyterian/St. Luke's Medical Center in Denver. These units are carefully constructed to eliminate all suspected materials known to give off gases or other irritants, and patients are given a very elemental diet. They are gradually introduced to more normal surroundings and a less restricted diet while they undergo extensive psychotherapy.

toxin   A poison or dangerous substance derived from an animal or plant. Ingestion of, inhalation of, or contact with a toxin may induce various symptoms or illness, deterioration of body tissues, or skin eruptions.

toxoid   An injectable liquid made from a toxin that has been stripped of its destructive characteristics but still is able to stimulate the production of protective antibodies. Examples are tetanus toxoid, administered to prevent tetanus, or lockjaw, and diphtheria and pertussis (whooping cough) toxoids. These immunizations stimulate the immune system to produce antibodies against infections and therefore create active immunity. (See IMMUNITY, ACTIVE; TETANUS.)

trachea   A cartilaginous, membranous tube known commonly as the windpipe, the main airway between the mouth and the lungs. The inside of the trachea looks like about 20 horseshoes piled up flat against each other. These cartilage "horseshoes" maintain the tube's shape, thus keeping it open for airflow. The trachea, part of the throat, extends from the larynx (vocal cords) to the bronchi branching into the lungs. An inflammation of the trachea, or tracheitis, may be associated with bronchitis and laryngitis. (See also TRACHEITIS.)

tracheitis   An inflammation of the trachea, or windpipe, which may be acute or chronic. Tracheitis is usually caused by a viral respiratory infection and may also involve the larynx and bronchioles. When the trachea becomes obstructed, a surgical procedure called a tracheostomy, or tracheotomy, may be necessary: An incision is made into the skin over the throat, and a hollow tube is inserted so that patient can breathe through it. (See also TRACHEA.)

tract, respiratory   See LUNGS.

Transcope patch   See SCOPOLAMINE.

Transderm Scop   Transdermal therapeutic system (patch).

transfer factor   See PRAUSNITZ-KUSTNER REACTION.

transplant, rejection   Transplanted organs or tissue recognized by the recipient's body as "foreign" and resulting in an immune, or allergic, response. The acceptance or rejection by the recipient's body of a transplanted organ or tissue is based on his or her immune response.

transplantation   The surgical procedure to install a live organ or tissue from a newly deceased donor (usually) into the body of an individual in whom that organ has become diseased and nonfunctional.

travel   Traveling may trigger allergy or asthma attacks because of exposure to allergens usually avoided at home, increased stress level, and other factors, including change of climate and quality of air. Persons with allergies and/or asthma should be prepared for a possible attack while away from home:

• Take extra medication with you; don't forget your inhaler or any other equipment you normally use at home.
• If you are severely allergic to bee stings, a food, or other substance and you have experienced anaphylactic shock because of this, wear a medical alert bracelet engraved with important information about your allergy and the treatment. This will help a doctor in an emergency room offer you more immediate treatment. You may even need to carry a syringe and adrenaline for emergency use.
• Travel with a companion who is aware of your condition and knows what to do in case you have an attack.
• Carry a copy of your asthma chart listing episodes and treatments; carry a letter from your doctor explaining your condition and how he or she has treated it so far.
• When children are traveling on their own, they should have a doctor's letter, including clear instructions for medications and other treatment.
• Avoid smoking sections on airplanes or trains, in restaurants, and other places if smoke irritates your respiratory system.
• Avoid traveling to places notorious for air pollution, certain species of weeds, grasses, or trees, or other characteristics that could exacerbate your condition, such as going to the home of a relative who has cats.
• Know the difference between hyperventilation and an asthma attack. Learn relaxation deep-breathing techniques before

TREES THAT ARE A CAUSE OF HAY FEVER IN THE UNITED STATES AND CANADA

Common Name	Technical Name	Plant Family	Distribution	Pollination Season
Acacia	*Acacia decurrens*	Leguminosae	Cultivated ornamental (subtropical)	Mar.–May
Acacia, Bailey's	*A. baileyana*	Leguminosae	Cultivated ornamental (subtropical)	Mar.–May
Acacia, longleaf,	*A. longifolia*	Leguminosae	Cultivated ornamental (subtropical)	Mar.–May
Alder, red (Oregon)[1]	*Alnus rubra*	Betulaceae	Pacific coast from S.W. Y.T. to So. CA, rarely more than 50 mi. from salt or over 2,500 A. elev.	Mar.–Apr
Alder, Sitka[1]	*A. sinuata (A. sitchensis)*	Betulaceae	AK So. to Olympic Mts., Cascade Mts., No. CA, E. WA, N. E. OR, Rocky Mts.	May–July
Alder, slender[1]	*A. tenuifolia*	Betulaceae	N.E. MN, ND to B.C., So. to NM	Mar.–May
Alder, tag (speckled)[1]	*A. incana (A. rugosa)*	Betulaceae	Nfld. to N.W.T. and B.C. So. to MD., No. to IN and MN, MT, ID, WA	Mar.–May
Alder, white	*A. rhombifolia*	Betulaceae	No. ID to E. slope Cascades, to So. OR, W. slope of Sierra Nevada, So. to Coast Range in CA	Jan.–Apr.
Arborvitae, Chinese	*Thuja orientalis*	Cupressaceae	Cultivated ornamental	Apr.–May
Arborvitae, western (white cedar)	*T. occidentalis*	Cupressaceae	P.Q. and N.S. to Hudson Bay, So. to NJ, OH, No. IN and IL, WI, MN, Mts. NC and TN	Apr.–May
Ash (Arizona velvet)	*Fraxinus velutina*	Oleaceae	CA, AZ, So. NM, E. TX. Cultivated in these areas	Mar.–Apr.
Ash, black	*F. nigra*	Oleaceae	Nfld. and P.Q. to Man., So. to DE, KY, IA	Spring
Ash, green (ash, red)	*F. pennsylvanica*	Oleaceae	P. Q. to Man., So. to FL and TX	Spring

TREES THAT ARE A CAUSE OF HAY FEVER IN THE
UNITED STATES AND CANADA (continued)

Common Name	Technical Name	Plant Family	Distribution	Pollination Season
Ash, Mexican	F. uhdei	Oleaceae	Cultivated ornamental	Winter
Ash, Oregon	F. oregona	Oleaceae	C. CA, No. to B.C.	Mar.–May
Ash, white	F. americana	Oleaceae	N.S. to MN, So. to FL and TX	Spring
Aspen	Populus tremuloides	Salicaeae	Lab. to AK, So. to NJ, VA, TN, MO, Rocky Mts., Sierra Nevada, Cascades	Spring
Beech, American	Fagus grandifolia	Fagaceae	N.S. to MN, So. to FL and TX	Spring
Beefwood (Austral. pine)	Casuarina equisetifolia	Casuarinaceae	Cultivated ornamental (subtropical)	Jan.–Mar.
Birch, cherry (black)	Bettila lenta	Betulaceae	IA, So. ME and So.W. P.Q. to DE and KY, along Appalachians to GA	Mar.–May
Birch, European (white)	B. pendula alba	Betulaceae	Cultivated ornamental	Mar.–May
Birch, paperbark	B. papyrifera	Betulaceae	Lab. to AK, So. to NJ, WV, No. IN, N. E. IA, W. to MT, WA	Mar.–May
Birch, river (red)	B. nigra	Betulaceae	NH to FL, W. to So. OH, So. MI, S.E. MN, E. KS, and TX	Feb.–June
Birch, spring	B. fontinalis	Betulaceae	AK to CA, E. to Sask., ND, SD, Rocky Mt. States	Feb.–June
Birch, yellow	B. lutea	Betulaceae	Nfld. to Man., So. to DE, PA, No. OH	Spring
Bottlebrush	Calistemon species	Myrtaceae	Cultivated ornamental (subtropical)	All seasons
Box elder, ash–leaved (maple)	Acer negundo	Aceraceae	So. Canada, VT to FL, W. nearly to Pacific coast Man.	Mar.–May
Butternut (white walnut)	Juglans cinerea	Juglandaceae	Cultivated ornamental and native tree, N.B. to Ont., No. MI, ND, So. to VA, CA, AR, KS	Apr.–May

TREES THAT ARE A CAUSE OF HAY FEVER IN THE
UNITED STATES AND CANADA (continued)

Common Name	Technical Name	Plant Family	Distribution	Pollination Season
Carob	*Ceratonia silitlua*	Leguminoseae	Cultivated ornamental	Late winter, early spring
Cedar, Atlantic	*Cedrus atlantica*	Pinaceae	Cultivated ornamental	Winter
Cedar, deodar	*C. deodara*	Pinaceae	Cultivated ornamental	Winter
Cedar, giant (canoe)	*Thuja plicata*	Cupressaceae	AK to C. CA, W. MT	Apr.–May
Cedar, incense	*Libocedrus decurrens*	Cupressaceae	CA to No. OR, W. to NV	Apr.–May
Cedar, Japanese	*Cryptomeria japonica*	Taxodiaceae	Cultivated ornamental	Spring
Cedar, Salt	*Tamarix gallica*	Tamaricaceae	Introduced, common in alkali western soils, along watercourses	Mar.–Aug.
Cherry	*Prunus cerasus*	Rosaceae	Cultivated crop and ornamental	Mar.–May
Chestnut, American	*Castanea dentata*	Fagaceae	Appalacia. Rare; nearly exterminated by blight	Spring
Chestnut, horse	*Aesctilus hippocastanum*	Hippocastanaceae	Cultivated ornamental	May–June
Cottonwood, black	*Populus trichocarpa*	Salicaceae	So. CA to AK, IN, NV	Feb.–Apr.
Cottonwood (Carolina poplar)	*P. deltoides (includes P. sargentii)*	Salicaceae	P.Q. and New England to So. Man., MN, to eastern Rocky Mts., So. to FL and TX	Mar.–Apr.
Cottonwood, Fremont	*P. fremontii*	Salicaceae	C. and So. CA to NV, AZ	Mar.–Apr.
Cypress, Arizona	*Cupressus arizonica*	Cuppressaceae	Native to AZ and E. NM; cultivated in CO and S.W.	Mar.–Apr.
Cypress, bald	*Taxodium distichum*	Taxodiaceae	DE to FL, W. to IL, MO, AR, and TX	Spring

TREES THAT ARE A CAUSE OF HAY FEVER IN THE UNITED STATES AND CANADA (continued)

Common Name	Technical Name	Plant Family	Distribution	Pollination Season
Cypress, Italian	*Cupressus sempervirens*	Cupressaceae	Cultivated ornamental	Feb.–Mar.
Cypress, Monterey	*C. macrocapa*	Cupressaceae	Monterey peninsula	Spring
Elderberry	*Sambuctis glauca*	Sambucaceae	So. CA. to B.C., Alta., ID	June–Sept.
Elm, American (white elm)	*Ulnitis americana*	Ulmaceae	Nfld. to Man., So. to FL and TX, also cultivated	Feb.–Apr.
Elm, Chinese	*U. irvifolia*	Ulmaceae	Cultivated ornamental	Aug.–Sept.
Elm, fall-blooming (cedar elm)	*U. crassifolia*	Ulmaceae	MS to AR and TX	July–Oct.
Elm, Siberian (Chinese)	*Ulmus pumila*	Ulmaceae	Cultivated ornamental	Mar.–Apr.
Elm, slippery (red elm)	*U. fulva*	Ulmaceae	P.Q. and ME to ND, So. to FL and TX	Mar.–Apr.
Fir, Douglas	*Pseudotsuga menziesii*	Pinaceae	S.W. B.C. to C. CA, E. to S.W., Alta., MT, WY, CO, W. TX	Apr.–May
Fir, noble (red)	*Ables nobilis*	Pinaceae	Cascade Mts., WA, OR, CA	June–July
Fir, white	*A. concolor*	Pinaceae	W. WY, So. ID to NM, AZ, CA	May–June
Gum, blue	*Eucalyptus globulus*	Myrtaceae	Cultivated ornamental	Dec.–May
Gum, sweet	*Liquidambar styraciflua*	Altingiaceae	CT to So. OH, So. IL, OK, So. to FL, TX, cultivated ornamental	May
Hackberry	*Ceitis occidentalis*	Ulmaceae	P.Q. to Man., So. to NC, TN, AR	Spring
Hazelnut, America	*Corylus americana*	Corylaceaeto	ME to Sask., So. CA and OK	Jan.–Apr.
Hazelnut, beaked	*C. cornuta*	Corylaceae	Nfld. to B.C., So. to No. NJ, PA, OH, MO, No. CA, W. to No. CA, OR, WA	Jan.–Apr.

TREES THAT ARE A CAUSE OF HAY FEVER IN THE UNITED STATES AND CANADA (continued)

Common Name	Technical Name	Plant Family	Distribution	Pollination Season
Hemlock, Canada (eastern)	*Tsuga canadensis*	Pinaccae	N.B. to Ont. and No. MN, So. to DE, WV, E. OH, C. MI, WI	May–June
Hemlock, western	*T. heterophylla*	Pinaccae	AK, to No. CA, to S.E. B.C., No. ID, to N.W. MT	May–June
Hickory, shagbark	*Carya ovata*	Jugulandaceae	P.Q. and ME to MI and S.E. MN, S. FL and TX	May–June
Hickory, shellbark	*C. laciniosa*	Jugulandaceae	NY. to So. Ont. to IA, So. to NC, MS, OK	May–June
Hickory, white (mockernut)	*C. tomentosa*	Jugulandaceae	MA. to Ont., MI, IA, So. to FL and TX	May–June
Hornbeam, American	*Carpinus carolineana*	Carpinaceae	N.S. to MN, So. to FL and TX	Mar.–May
Hornbeam, hop, (ironwood)	*Ostrya virginiana*	Carpinaceae	N.S. to Man., So. to FL and TX	Mar.–Apr.
Juniper, California	*Juniperus californica*	Cupressaceae	C. and So. CA	Jan.–Mar.
Juniper, Chinese	*J. chinensis*	Cupressaceae	Cultivated ornamental	Winter–spring
Juniper, mountain	*J. sabinoides*	Cupressaceae	W. and So. TX into Mexico	Winter
Juniper, one-seed	*J. monosperma*	Cupressaceae	N.W. OK, W. TX to UT, NV, S.E. AZ, and NM	Spring
Juniper, Pinchot	*J. pinchotii*	Cupressaceae	C. TX. to S.E. NM, W. OK	Spring
Juniper, Rocky Mountain	*J. scopulorum*	Cupressaceae	So. B.C. to MT, ND, SD, Rocky Mt. states	May–June
Juniper, Utah	*J. utahensis*	Cupressaceae	CA. to S.W. ID, S.W. WY, W. NM	Spring
Juniper, Virginia (red cedar)	*J. virginiana*	Cupressaceae	So. P.Q. and ME to ND, So. to AL, TX	Mar.–Apr.

TREES THAT ARE A CAUSE OF HAY FEVER IN THE
UNITED STATES AND CANADA (continued)

Common Name	Technical Name	Plant Family	Distribution	Pollination Season
Juniper, western	*J. occidentalis*	Cupressaceae	Mountain slopes and higher. Prairies of E. WA, W. ID, So. in mt. ranges to So. CA	May–June
Larch (tamarack)	*Larix occidentalis*	Pinaceae	So. B.C., So. to E. Cascades to OR, E. to N.W. MT, N. ID	May–June
Linden, American	*Tilia americana*	Tiliaceae	P.Q. to ND, So. to VA, NC, KY, MO	June–July
Locust, black	*Robinia pseudoacacia*	Leguminosae	PA to So. IN and OK, So. to GA, LA, cultivated ornamental	June
Maple, bigleaf (canyon, coast)	*Acer macrophyllum*	Aceraceae	CA to AK	Apr.–May
Maple, red	*A. rubrum*	Aceraceae	P.Q. to MN, So. to FL and TX	Mar.–Apr.
Maple, silver (soft map)	*A. saccharinum*	Aceraceae	N.B., P.Q. to MN, SD, So. to FL, TN, OK, cultivated ornamental	Mar.–Apr.
Maple, sugar	*A. saccharum*	Aceraceae	P.Q. and NJ to Man., ND, So. to NJ, GA, AL, TX	Apr.–May
Mesquite	*Prosopis juliflora*	Leguminosae	C. and So. CA to Gulf of Mexico	Apr.–June
Mock orange (syringa)	*Philadelphus* species	Philadelphaceae	Cultivated ornamentals and widespread native shrubs	May–June
Mulberry, black	*Morus tatarica*	Moraceae	Cultivated ornamental	Spring
Mulberry, paper	*Broussonetia papyrifera*	Moraceae	Cultivated ornamental	Winter–spring
Mulberry, red	*Morus rubra*	Moraceae	Cultivated ornamental	Spring
Mulberry, white	*M. alba*	Moraceae	Cultivated ornamental	Spring

TREES THAT ARE A CAUSE OF HAY FEVER IN THE
UNITED STATES AND CANADA (continued)

Common Name	Technical Name	Plant Family	Distribution	Pollination Season
Oak, Ariz. Scrub (canyon oak)	*Quercus chrysolepis*	Fagaceae	So. CA to OR, NM	Apr.–May
Oak, Arizona (white)	*Q. arizonica*	Fagaceae	W. TX to AZ	Apr.–May
Oak, black	*Q. velutina*	Fagaceae	So. ME. to MI, MN, So. to FL and TX	Spring
Oak, black jack	*Q. marilandica*	Fagaceae	So. NY. to So. MI, IA, So. to FL and TX	Spring
Oak, Blue	*Q. douglasii*	Fagaceae	CA	Apr.–May
Oak, Bur	*Q. macrocarpa*	Fagaceae	N.B., P.Q. to Ont. and So. Man., So. to VA, AL, AR, TX. Shrub in W. MN and IA to Canada	Spring
Oak, California (Black)	*Q. kelloggii*	Fagaceae	So. CA to OR	Apr.–May
Oak, California scrub	*Q. dumosa*	Fagaceae	CA	Mar.–May
Oak, chesnut	*Q. prinus*	Fagaceae	Appalachian Mts., ME to No. CA to Atlantic coast as far as So. VA, W. to So. IN	Spring
Oak, coast live (Encina)[1]	*Q. agrifolia*	Fagaceae	C. and So. CA	Mar.–Apr.
Oak, Emory	*Q. emoryi*	Fagaceae	TX to AZ	Spring
Oak, Engelmann	*Q. engelmannii*	Fagaceae	So. CA	Apr.–May

TREES THAT ARE A CAUSE OF HAY FEVER IN THE
UNITED STATES AND CANADA (continued)

Common Name	Technical Name	Plant Family	Distribution	Pollination Season
Oak, Gambel	Q. gambelii	Fagaceae	So.W. TX to CO, WY, So. to AZ, abundant on dry slopes of Rockies	Spring
Oak, Garry[1]	Q. garryana	Fagaceae	No. CA, W. OR, WA	Spring
Oak, holly	Q. ilex	Fagaceae	Cultivated ornamental	Spring
Oak, interior live	Q. wislizenii	Fagaceae	C. and No. CA	Mar.–May
Oak, Palmer	Q. palmeri	Fagaceae	So. CA, AZ	Apr.–May
Oak, pin	Q. palustris	Fagaceae	MA to MI, IA, E. KS, So. to NC, TN, OK	Spring
Oak, post	Q. stellata	Fagaceae	S.E. MA, So. NY to IN, IA, So. to FL and TX	Spring
Oak, red (northern red oak)	Q. rubra (Q. borealis)	Fagaceae	N.S. to No. MI and MN, So. to VA, AL, MS, AR	Spring
Oak, Spanish (southern red oak)	Q. falcata	Fagaceae	NJ, PA to FL and TX, along coastal plain and No. in interior to OH, IN, MD	Spring
Oak, valley (Roble)	Q. lobata	Fagaceae	C. and So. CA	Mar.–Apr.
Oak, Virginia live	Q. virginiana	Fagaceae	Coastal plain, S.E. VA to FL and TX	Spring
Oak, water	Q. nigra	Fagaceae	Coastal plain, DE to FL and S.E. TX, No. in interior to S.E. MO	Spring

TREES THAT ARE A CAUSE OF HAY FEVER IN THE UNITED STATES AND CANADA (continued)

Common Name	Technical Name	Plant Family	Distribution	Pollination Season
Oak, white	Q. alba	Fagaceae	ME to MI and MN, So. to FL and TX	Spring
Olive	Olea europaea	Oleaceae	Cultivated crop and ornamental	
Orange, Osage	Maclura pomifera	Moraceae	Cultivated hedge and native tree, AR, OK, TX	Apr.–May
Palm, Canary Island date	Phoenix canariensis	Palmae	Cultivated ornamental	Spring
Palm, date	P. dactylifera	Palmae	Cultivated crop and ornamental	Spring
Palm, dwarf	Chamaerops humilus	Palmae	Cultivated ornamental	Spring
Palm, queen	Cocos plumosa	Palmae	Cultivated ornamental	Spring
Palo Verde	Cercidium torreyana	Leguminosae	So. CA, AZ	Mar.–May
Peach	Prunus persica	Rosaceae	Cultivated crop and ornamental	Mar.–May
Pear	Pyrus communis	Rosaceae	Cultivated crop	Mar.–May
Pecan	Carya pecan	Juglandaceae	Cultivated crop and ornamental, S.W. OH to IA, So. to AL, TX	Spring
Peppertree, Brazilian	Schinus terebinthifolius	Anacardiaceae	Cultivated ornamental naturalized in So. FL	Jan.–Dec.
Peppertree, Peruvian	So. molle	Anacardiaceae	Cultivated ornamental	Winter
Pine, Australian (beefwood)	Casuarina equisetifolia	Causuarinaceae	Cultivated ornamental	Spring

TREES THAT ARE A CAUSE OF HAY FEVER IN THE
UNITED STATES AND CANADA (continued)

Common Name	Technical Name	Plant Family	Distribution	Pollination Season
Pine, bull (digger)	Pinus sabiniana	Pinaceae	C. and So. CA	Apr.–May
Pine, Canary Island	P. canariensis	Pinaceae	Cultivated ornamental	Spring
Pine, eastern white	P. strobus	Pinaceae	Nfld. to Man., So. to DE, GA, KY, IA	Spring
Pine, Japanese (black)	P. thunbergii	Pinaceae	Cultivated ornamental	Spring
Pine, loblolly	P. taeda	Pinaceae	NJ to FL, TX, No. in interior to AR and TN	Spring
Pine, lodgepole	P. contorta	Pinaceae	CA, AK, Rocky Mts.	June–July
Pine, longleaf	P. palustris (P. australis)	Pinaceae	Coastal plain, S.E. VA to FL and TX	Spring
Pine, Monterey	P. radiata	Pinaceae	Monterey peninsula and adjacent coastal counties	April
Pine, Pinyon	P. edulis	Pinaceae	So. CA to WY, TX, AZ	Spring
Pine, ponderosa (west. yellow)	P. ponderosa	Pinaceae	So. CA to B.C., Rocky Mts.	May–June
Pine, red (Norway)	P. resinosa	Pinaceae	NS. to Man., So. MA, PA, MI, MN, in mts. to WV	Spring
Pine, short-leaf (yellow)	P. echinata	Pinaceae	So. NY to WV, So. IL, S.E. KS, So. to FL and TX	Spring
Pine, single-leaf (one-leaved)	P. monophylla	Pinaceae	C. and E. CA to UT, AZ	May
Pine, Virginia scrub (Jersey)	P. virginiana	Pinaceae	So. NY to So. IN, So. to GA, AL	Spring

TREES THAT ARE A CAUSE OF HAY FEVER IN THE UNITED STATES AND CANADA (continued)

Common Name	Technical Name	Plant Family	Distribution	Pollination Season
Pine, western white	*P. monticola*	Pinaceae	So. B.C. to CA, W. NV, E. to ID, S.W. AK, W. MT	May–June
Plum	*Prunus domestica*	Rosaceae	Cultivated crop and ornamental	Mar.–May
Poplar, balsam	*Populus balsamifera*	Saliaceae	Lab. to AK, So. to CT, No. PA, No. IN, IA, N.B., OR	Mar.–Apr.
Poplar, black	*P. nigra*	Saliaceae	Cultivated ornamental	Mar.–Apr.
Poplar, Lombardy	*P. nigra italica*	Saliaceae	Cultivated ornamental	Mar.–Apr.
Poplar, white (silver)	*P. alba*	Saliaceae	Cultivated ornamental	Mar.–Apr.
Privet, California	*Ligustrum ovalifolium*	Oleaceae	Cultivated ornamental	Spring
Privet, common	*L. vulgare*	Oleaceae	Cultivated ornamental	Spring–summer
Privet, southern	*L. lucidum*	Oleaceae	Cultivated ornamental	Spring
Redwood	*Sequoia sempervirens*	Taxodiaceae	C. CA. to S.W. to OR	Mar.
Silk tassel bush	*Garrya eliptica*	Garryaceae	C. CA to OR	Jan.–Mar.
Spiraea (bridal wreath)	*Spiraea species*	Rosaceae	Cultivated ornamentals and widespread native shrubs	Spring–summer
Spruce, Colorado blue	*Picea pungens*	Pinaceae	Cultivated ornamentals, native to C. CO	June–July
Spruce, red	*P. rubens*	Pinaceae	P.Q. and Ont. to PA, NJ, So. in mts. to NC and TN	Spring–summer
Spruce, Sitka	*P. sitchensis*	Pinaceae	AK to C. CA in coastal mts.	May

TREES THAT ARE A CAUSE OF HAY FEVER IN THE UNITED STATES AND CANADA (continued)

Common Name	Technical Name	Plant Family	Distribution	Pollination Season
Sweet gale	*Myrica gale*	Myricaceae	Circumboreal, in North America, So. to NY, PA, NC, MI, MN, WA	Apr.–June
Sycamore (London Plane)	*Platanus orientalis*	Platanaceae	Cultivated ornamental	Spring
Sycamore, eastern (buttonwood)	*P. occidentalis*	Platanaceae	S.W. ME to So. MI and S.E. MN, So. to FL, TX	Spring
Sycamore, mapleleaf	*P. acerifolia*	Platanaceae	Cultivated ornamental	Spring
Sycamore, western	*P. racemosa*	Platanaceae	C. and So. CA	Feb.–Apr.
Tree of heaven	*Ailanthus altissima*	Simaroubaceae	Cultivated ornamentals and urban weed	June
Viburnum	*Viburnum*	Caprifoliaceae	Cultivated ornamental, widespread native shrubs	May–July
Walnut, Arizona	*Juglans rupestris*	Juglanaceae	W. OK, TX to S.E. NM, AZ	Spring
Walnut, black	*J. nigra*	Juglanaceae	Cultivated crop, ornamental native W. New England to MI, MN, N.B., So. to FL, TX	Apr.–May
Walnut, California	*J. californica*	Juglanaceae	So. CA	Apr.–May
Walnut, English	*J. regia*	Juglanaceae	Cultivated crop	Apr.–May
Walnut, Hinds black	*J. hindsii*	Juglanaceae	C. and No. CA	Apr.–May
Walnut, Japanese	*J. sieboldiana*	Juglanaceae	Cultivated ornamental	Apr.–May
Willow, Arroyo	*Salix lasiolepis*	Salicaeae	CA to WA, ID, NM	Feb.–Apr.

TREES THAT ARE A CAUSE OF HAY FEVER IN THE UNITED STATES AND CANADA (continued)

Common Name	Technical Name	Plant Family	Distribution	Pollination Season
Willow, black	*So. nigra*	Salicaeae	So. N.B. to C. MN, So. to FL, TX	Spring
Willow, pussy	*So. discolor*	Salicaeae	Cultivated ornamental, native shrub, Nfld. to B.C., So. to DE, KY, MO, SD, MT	Spring
Willow, red	*So. laevigata*	Salicaeae	CA, UT, AZ	Mar.–May
Willow, yellow	*So. lasiandra*	Salicaeae	CA to AK, ID	Mar.–May

[1]Pollen is a major source of hay fever.
Adopted from *Pollen Guide for Allergy*, Hollister-Stier.

you travel. They can help ward off an asthma attack or possibly relieve one.

• Get in shape before you travel; regular and appropriate exercise facilitates optimal body functioning. Losing excess weight makes it easier for you to breathe and your body to function well. If you may find yourself in a strenuous situation while traveling, make sure you take your medication before exertion, if your doctor advises it.

• Understand that as long as you can manage your condition, you can travel successfully. Ask your allergist for advice specific to your symptoms.

tree, bronchial   See BRONCHI.

tree pollen allergy   Seasonal hay fever and/or asthma caused by inhalation of the pollen of wind-pollinating, or anemophilous, trees. Insect-pollinating, or entemophilous, trees and wind-pollinating conifers, whose pollen has a thick outer covering, have a very low potential for causing allergic symptoms.

Each tree genus has pollen that is distinct from any other. An individual may exhibit allergy to one or many of the trees in his or her region. Pollinating seasons are brief, often intense, and usually occur before, during, or shortly after leaves develop in deciduous trees, especially in the spring.

Trethewie, Everton R., and Kellaway, Charles H.   Australian physicians and scientists who explained that smooth-muscle contractions that occur during anaphylaxis are caused by histamine and a slow-reacting substance (SRS-A). Trethewie (1913–84) and Kellaway (1889–1952) also researched venoms, toxins, pharmacologic aspects of cell and tissue injury, and other topics, and Kellaway's studies included the advancement of electrocardiogrpic techniques.

triamcinolone   (Aristacort, Azmacort, Kenacort)

A corticosteroid drug frequently used in the treatment of allergies and asthma. (See CORTI-COSTEROIDS.)

triggers of allergies and asthma   Stimuli, including pollens in hay fever season, a viral respiratory infection such as a cold, cold air, and dust, that can trigger an asthma attack by irritating the bronchial tubes, inducing them to release chemicals that cause inflammation or spasm of the muscles in the walls of the bronchial tubes.

tripelennamine   (Pyribenzamine or PBZ) An antihistaminic drug of the ethylenediamine class. This drug is especially useful for the treatment of allergic disorders during pregnancy because of its long history of safe use. It has a mild sedative effect, but it may cause some gastrointestinal distress that can be minimized by taking the drug with food. Tripelennamine is available as topical cream for the relief of itching, but it can be a cause of allergic rashes in some individuals, worsening the skin condition for which it is prescribed. Because of this adverse effect, it is rarely prescribed. (See CONTACT DERMATITIS, DERMATITIS MEDICOMENTOSIUM.)

triple response of Lewis   A reaction seen on the skin through dermatographia, when a blunt instrument is applied to the skin as though writing on the skin. The triple response of Lewis involves: (1) vasodilation of blood vessels in a localized area, causing redness; (2) further vasodilation beyond the original area, which causes a flare of increased redness; and (3) edema in the area of redness. (See DERMATOGRAPHIA.)

triprolidine   (Actidil)   An antihistamine of the alkylamine class with mildly sedating properties. It is usually combined with pseudoephedrine in the proprietary product Actifed. This combination drug is widely used for the treatment of the nasal congestion of colds and hay fever.

troleandomycin   (TAO)

TRIGGERS CAPABLE OF CAUSING SYMPTONS IN SUSCEPTIBLE INDIVIDUALS

Trigger	Allergic Disorder That Is Triggered		
	Allergic Rhinitis	Asthma	Atopic Dermatitis (Eczema)
Anger		+	
Animal exposure	+	+	
Barometric pressure drop		+	
Cigarette smoke		+	
Cockroaches	+	+	
Cold air		+	+
Crying		+	
Dry skin			+
Dust/dust mites	+	+	
Emotional stress		+	+
Exercise or exertion		+	
Feathers	+	+	
Foods	+	+	+
Heat			$+\backslash-^3$
Humidity increase		+	
Infections (colds, flu, sore throats and bronchitis)		+	
Infections, skin			+
Irritants		+	+
Medications aspirin NSAIDS[1] beta-blockers[2]	+	+	
Molds, inhalant	+	+	
Mouse urine	+	+	
Odors	+	+	
Pollens	+	+	
Sweating			$+\backslash-$
Windy weather		+	

[1]NSAIDS are nonsteroidal anti-inflammatory agents used to treat arthritis and pain.
[2]Beta-blockers are used to treat glaucoma, heart problems, and high blood pressure.
[3]+\- may or may not trigger this allergy.

A rarely used macrolide antibiotic whose use as a corticosteroid sparing agent is controversial. In patients requiring high-dose corticosteroids to control their asthma, the combination of methylprednisolne and TAO may allow a lowering of the dose of the corticosteroid. The TAO slows the metabolism of the steroid; however, the adverse effects of steroids may not be lessened. Because both drugs are metabolized by the liver, severe liver toxicity can occur, and liver function tests must be followed carefully. There is a report that TAO may be helpful in eczema resistant to corticosteroid therapy. (See also CORTICOSTEROIDS, METHYLPREDNISOLONE.)

tropin   An agent in the blood that triggers phagocytosis, which refers to the process of cells called phagocytes that destroy or "eat" foreign, potentially harmful cells.

tryptophan   See L-TRYPTOPHAN.

tuberculin test, Mantoux   A screening test that determines if one has been exposed to tuberculosis. A purified protein (called PPD) derived from the tubercle bacillus (the bacteria that causes tuberculosis, or TB) is injected under the skin and observed in 48 to 72 hours. If a raised, red wheal at the point of injection measures more than 10 millimeters in diameter, the test is considered positive. This test is an example of a type IV delayed allergic or hypersensitivity reaction (see HYPERSENSITIVITY). A positive or negative Mantoux result may not be conclusive, and chest X Rays and sputum or other body cultures are necessary to confirm the diagnosis of tuberculosis.

Tungra penetrans   A tropical flea whose bite can cause skin inflammation and infections. (See CHIGGERS.)

turkey feathers   See FEATHERS.

turkey-raiser's disease   Continuous exposure to an allergen in turkey droppings that may cause hypersensitivity pneumonia (an allergic pneumonialike lung disorder). (See HYPERSENSITIVITY PNEUMONITIS.)

turkey red   See ALIZARIN.

turnip   An herb belonging to the mustard family whose thick roots are eaten as a vegetable. Consuming abnormally large quantities of turnips may cause formation of a goiter (enlarged thyroid glands), an immune response.

Tussi-Organidin   See IODINATED GLYCEROL.

tussis   The medical term for a cough.

2-bromo-2-nitropropane-1   (Bronopol) A solvent and preservative used in the cosmetic industry, especially for nail polishes. This substance is the fifth leading cause of preservative-caused contact dermatitis, according to the American College of Dermatology. When combined with certain other organic chemicals (amines or amides), it is suspected of being a carcinogen.

tympanometry   A method for determining functional status of the tympanic membrane (eardrum) and the middle ear. A small probe is placed into the ear canal, and a tone is transmitted that electronically measures the competence of the membrane. The procedure is useful to determine the presence of fluid in the middle ear. (See OTITIS MEDIA, SECRETORY.)

tympanoplasty   A surgical procedure involving the tympanic membrane (eardrum) in order to restore normal function or relieve the symptoms of chronic otitis (inflammation of the ear).

tympanostomy tubes   Tiny tubes, also called ventilating tubes, inserted into the tympanic membrane (eardrum) to allow drainage in cases of persistent otitis media. (See OTITIS MEDIA, SECRETORY.)

tyramine   A naturally occurring vasoactive amine, found in aged cheese, beer, broad-bean pods, yeast, wine, and chicken liver, that may trigger vascular headaches. A potentially dangerous reaction may occur when foods containing tyramine are consumed by individuals taking medications called monoamine oxidase inhibitors. The so-called cheese reaction can involve severe hypertension (high blood pressure), headaches, and palpitations, and there is the possibility of intracranial hemorrhage (stroke). (See HEADACHE.)

U

ultrasound   A technique using high-frequency sound waves to form images of internal body structures on a monitor similar to a television screen that can be photographed. It has the advantage of not requiring X-radiation. Ultrasound is useful for diagnosing gallstones, heart defects, and prebirth fetal abnormalities. However, for the evaluation of sinus abnormalities, ultrasound is limited. Computerized tomography (CT scan) is the most effective procedure for obtaining images of the sinuses. (See also COMPUTERIZED TOMOGRAPHY, SINUSITIS.)

undulation, respiratory   Changes in blood pressure corresponding to the movements created by breathing. (See also PULSUS PARADOXUS.)

unguent   A synonym for ointment, derived from the Latin word *unguentum.* Unguents may be used to soothe skin irritation caused by contact with an allergenic substance.

Uniphyl   See THEOPHYLLINE.

unit, antigen   See ALLERGY UNITS.

upper respiratory infection   Another term for the common cold or any infection, viral, bacterial, or fungal, affecting the nose, sinuses, and oropharynx.

urine autoinjection   A process in which an allergic patient's urine is collected using sterile technique and then injected into that patient. It was first proposed in 1947, on the premise that, because urine contains body wastes including allergens, the injections would stimulate the immune system to develop protection as it would through immunotherapy (allergy injections).

The effectiveness of urine injections has never been scientifically proven. They also carry the risk of inducing serious kidney disease. Therefore, the American Academy of Allergy and Immunology (AAAI) and the National Center for Health Care Technology have condemned the method as unproven and unsafe.

In the Sept. 23, 1980, Federal Register, the National Center for Health Care Technology requested opinions from interested parties concerning Urine Autoinjection (autogenous urine immunization) and other unproven techniques. The California Society of Allergy and Clinical Immunology and the California Blue Shield came forth with the following opinion with the help of the Blue Shield Advisory Panels on Allergy, Internal Medicine, and Dermatology: It is the unanimous opinion of members of the Advisory Panels on Allergy, Internal Medicine, and Dermatology that urine injections are not acceptable medical practice in the treatment of allergic diseases. Advisory Panel members agreed with the position paper on this subject prepared by the California Society of Allergy and Clinical Immunology. They also emphasized that this treatment modality must be considered experimental until controlled studies are done proving its benefit or harm and further, that physicians using urine injection therapy should be encouraged strongly to do such studies.

The AAAI has concluded:

1. Urine autoinjection is not standard medical practice.
2. The treatment has not been proved effective by published studies.
3. The treatment has not been proved safe by published studies. It is potentially dangerous in that injections of kidney protein (glomerular basement membrane, in particular) might induce nephritis.
4. The advertised procedure for obtaining the treatment is dangerous in that the patient is advised to expose himself to the known

allergen before coming for his first treatment.

5. There is no rationale or immunologic basis for this treatment.

6. The treatment should be reserved for experimental use only in well-designed trials.

urtica   A wheal, or round, red, raised patch of skin, derived from the Latin word for a stinging nettle.

urticaria [hives]   A disorder in which circumscribed, raised areas of erythema (redness) and edema (swelling caused by a collection of fluid) appear in the outer layer of the skin. The lesions vary in size from 1 millimeter to many centimeters in diameter and are usually multiple. An individual lesion lasts up to 48 hours but may disappear and be replaced by others. Hives are almost always pruritic (itchy). Episodes of hives lasting up to six weeks in duration are called acute; cases lasting more than six weeks are considered chronic.

Prevalence   An estimated 20% of the population has had hives at some time.

Causes   Many cases of acute urticaria are caused by type I (immediate or IgE-mediated) hypersensitivity. However, chronic hives are rarely of this type. Foods or drugs, and rarely other substances, trigger mast cells in the skin to release histamine and other chemical mediators when they combine with antibodies of the immunoglobulin E (IgE) class on the mast cell's surface. Physical agents such as cold, heat, light, and pressure can also cause a similar response. Penicillin and sulfonamide drugs cause hives most frequently. Aspirin may aggravate hives, but individuals may continue to experience the hives if aspirin is no longer taken. Aspirin and NSAIDS (nonsteroidal anti-inflammatory drugs) such as ibuprofen rarely cause immediate type I allergy, but they can cause adverse reactions by some other mechanism (see ASPIRIN SENSITIVITY). Morphine and other narcotics also cause hives by a nonallergic mechanism. Chemicals such as parabens, used as preservatives in topical creams and ointments, can cause hives.

Seafood, fish, nuts, peanuts, and eggs are the leading foods that cause acute urticaria. Food additives such as tartrazine yellow dye and salicylates are often blamed, though they rarely cause hives.

Inhaled allergens such as pollens during hay fever season infrequently cause hives; they are more commonly caused by exposure to animal dander or saliva. Insect stings and bites (especially Hymenoptera or bee stings) can cause hives. Skin penetration by toxins from the Portuguese man-of-war, moth scales, sea nettles, and tarantula hairs are among other offenders.

Blood transfusion reactions, cryoglobulinemia, hepatitis B, serum sickness, systemic lupus erythematosus (SLE), and certain types of vasculitis cause hives by activation of the complement cascade. Complement is a series of proteins in the blood that trigger various immune responses including the release of histamine from mast cells (see COMPLEMENT).

Alcoholic beverages, emotional stress, exertion, fever, heat, and the disorder hyperthyroidism (Grave's disease) may cause hives by dilatation of the blood vessels in the skin. Premenstrual hives are caused by the hormone progesterone in a similar way.

Some rare forms of hives, such as cold urticaria, hives associated with deafness and amyloidosis, and a form of solar urticaria associated with erythropoietic protoporphyria, are often inherited.

Viral infections often cause transient hives in children but seldom in adults. Parasitic infections may cause hives in areas of the world where they are endemic. Chronic bacterial infections of the sinuses, gums, teeth, and gallbladder have been implicated as causes of hives, but this remains unproven.

Cholinergic urticaria may be associated with emotional stress in some patients; generally stress is not a cause of most cases of hives. Dermatographia, or "writing on skin," occurs when the skin is stroked and a linear wheal or hive (a red, raised line) appears on the skin. (See also CHOLINERGIC URTICARIA; COLD-INDUCED CHOLINERGIC URTICARIA; COLD URTICARIA, ESSENTIAL; DERMATOGRAPHIA; PHYSICAL URTICARIA; PRESSURE URTICARIA; SOLAR URTICARIA.)

Diagnosis The history obtained from the patient or a child's family is most important in determining the cause or trigger of acute hives. However, in cases of chronic hives (those that last more than six weeks) the cause cannot be determined in up to 85% of cases. When a food, drug, or other easily recognized cause cannot be determined, only a limited laboratory workup is indicated because extensive work will not reveal different results. When a serious but uncommon underlying disease is suspected, a more extensive evaluation is then warranted.

Treatment Avoidance of food or drug or other cause is best if the offending agent can be determined. Antihistamines, singly or in combinations, are the mainstay of therapy to relieve the itching. If they are not effective, an H2 blocking agent such as cimetidine (Tagamet) or the tricyclic antidepressant drug doxipin may be added to a traditional antihistamine (H1) drug. Epinephrine (Adrenalin) may give transient but immediate relief for severe swelling and itching of hives. In resistant cases it may be necessary to use corticosteroids. One cause of hives is the hormone estrogen, in which case the addition of progesterone may improve the hives. (See also ANTIHISTAMINE, CIMETIDINE, CORTICOSTEROIDS, EPINEPHRINE.)

urticaria, physical   See PHYSICAL URTICARIA.

urticaria, solar [light urticaria]   See SOLAR URTICARIA.

urticaria pigmentosum   A rash characterized by brown papular (raised) skin lesions that form hives when stroked (Darier's sign).

V

vaccine   Inoculation with bacteria or bacterial products in order to immunize, or protect, an individual against a certain disease. (See IMMUNITY, ACTIVE; entries on individual vaccines.)

vaccines, adverse reactions   See entries on individual vaccines.

vaccines, for use in allergic patients   See entries on individual vaccines.

vacuum cleaners for allergic patients   Dust- and dirt-collecting devices with double bags, which offer protection to allergic persons. The ordinary-type vacuum cleaners allow small suspended particles containing most collected allergens to pass through the collection bag back into the surrounding air. An allergic person should avoid a recently vacuumed room for an hour or two following vacuuming. If possible, have a nonallergic person do the vacuuming. An alternative is for the allergic individual to wear a mask capable of trapping small particles.

Vacuum cleaners with elaborate special HEPA, or water-filtering, devices may not be more efficient than ordinary vacuums. However, vacuums with double bags may be the most effective. When possible, such as when planning a new home, install a central vacuum system with motor and collection bag in the garage.

vaginal deodorants   [feminine hygiene sprays]   Aerosolized cosmetic products used to mask the natural odor of the vaginal area that may be unpleasant to some. Many individuals, including men exposed during sexual relations, may be sensitive and get allergic rashes from ingredients in these products, including antibacterial agents such as benzalkonium chloride, perfumes, and propellants. (See CONTACT DERMATITIS.)

vaginitis, yeast   See CANDIDIASIS.

valley fever   See COCCIDIOMYCOSIS.

Vancenase   See BECLOMETHASONE

Vanceril   See BECLOMETHASONE.

vanillism   Irritation of the skin and mucous membranes and conjunctiva of the eye caused by a mite that sometimes invades those who work with or handle the flavoring vanilla.

vaporizers   See HUMIDIFIERS.

vasculitis   Inflammation of blood vessels that occurs in some allergic and other diseases. Vasculitis caused by allergic reactions to drugs such as penicillin and sulfonamides and is characterized by fever, pruritic (itchy) rashes, or skin ulcerations. The following lung diseases have vasculitis as a prominent feature: Wegener's granulomatosis, Churg-Strauss syndrome, and polyangiitis overlap syndrome. Takayasu's arteritis, polyarteritis nodosa, Henoch-Schonlein purpura, hypersensitivity vasculitis, and the collagen vascular diseases, rheumatoid arthritis, systemic lupus erythematosus, and progressive systemic sclerosis, are among widespread systemic diseases that may involve the lungs. These serious diseases are often difficult to diagnose and may be confused with less serious allergic rhinitis (hay fever), sinusitis, and asthma. (See CHURG-STRAUSS SYNDROME, HENOCH-SCHONLEIN PURPURA, WEGENER'S GRANULOMATOSIS.)

Vaseline   See PETROLATUM.

vasoactive amines   Chemical substances including histamine, tyramine, tryptamine, phenylethylamine, dopamine, norepinephrine, and serotonin that are contained in a variety of foods. These chemicals are capable of causing a multitude of symptoms, especially headaches and gastrointestinal and central nervous system disturbances.

Aged cheeses, chocolate, and contaminated fish contain large quantities of vasoactive amines; smaller amounts are found in avocados, bananas, oranges, pineapples, plums, tomatoes, and red wine.

Patients taking the antidepressant drugs called monoamine oxidase inhibitors or the antituberculosis drug INH can develop severe hypertension (high blood pressure) if they eat foods containing vasoactive amines. (See FOOD ALLERGY, HEADACHE.)

vasoconstrictor   Any substance that can cause constriction, or narrowing, of blood vessels.

vasodilator   Any substance that dilates or increases the circumference of blood vessels.

vasomotor rhinitis   Nasal congestion that cannot be attributed to any other cause, such as allergic rhinitis (hay fever) or upper respiratory infections (colds, sinusitis). Vasomotor rhinitis is thought to be caused by excessive stimulation of certain nerve endings in the nose for unknown reasons.

Nasal congestion, often accompanied by large amounts of clear watery mucus, does not respond to antihistamines or allergy nasal sprays containing the drugs cromolyn or corticosteroids. Alpha-agonist (decongestant) drugs, such as pseudoephedrine (Sudafed) orally or topical nasal sprays, are sometimes helpful. Abuse of over-the-counter nasal sprays may cause a rebound effect. This worsening of nasal congestion caused by the overuse of drugs is called rhinitis medicomentosum. Treatment with oral or topical (nasal sprays or drops) decongestant drugs and anticholinergic drugs such as atropine and ipratropium may be effective. However, antihistamines are not effective, and anti-inflammatory corticosteroid nasal sprays are occasionally helpful. (See also ALPHA-ADRENERGIC AGONISTS, RHINITIS MEDICOMENTOSUM.)

vegetable gums   Food additives, including acacia gum or gum arabic, cellulose, karaya or Indian gum, and tragacanth, are known to trigger asthma, urticaria (hives), angioedema (swelling of body tissues), and anaphylaxis (allergic shock) in susceptible individuals. Avoidance of these additives is the most effective treatment. (See also ACACIA, GUM BENZOIN, GUM KARAYA, GUM TRAGACANTH.)

vegetables   Any of a group of herbs whose edible portions may include leaves, stems, seeds, seed pods, flowers, roots, tubers, and fruits. Vegetables are an important source of nutrition and are especially valuable for essential vitamins and minerals. In the form of dehydrated products they may contain chemical preservatives, including sulfites, that may cause asthma in susceptible individuals. (See SULFITING AGENTS.)

venom   A poisonous substance of complex chemical composition injected by Hymenoptera insect stings or snake bites and by some other animals. Potency varies; in extreme cases, venomous stings or bites may be fatal. Reactions may be anaphylactic, as in bee or other insect stings, or toxic, as in most snake reactions. Scorpion stings are usually toxic, but recently there has also been evidence of anaphylaxis. Some sea animals' stings are also capable of causing venomous reactions. (See HYMENOPTERA STING ALLERGY; SCORPION STING; SNAKE BITE, POISONOUS.)

ventilation   The act of drawing air into and expressing air out of the body through the respiratory system in order to oxygenate the blood. Ventilation also refers to a system of providing air circulation, heating, or cooling in a building. Artificial ventilation is another term for respirator. (See RESPIRATOR.)

Ventolin   See ALBUTEROL.

vesicant   A chemical, gas, or other agent that produces blisters on the skin.

vesicle   A blister, or any small elevation on the skin that contains fluid—for example, the dermatitis venerata characterizing poison ivy or oak, or, vesicular eczema. Fluid may sometimes contain pus or blood and possibly be associated with burning pain or severe itching.

vibratory angioedema   See ANGIOEDEMA, VIBRATORY.

vinegar   An acidic liquid (also known as acetic acid, or a solution containing about 4 to 6% acetic acid) resulting from weak, fermented alcoholic beverages such as wine or beer. Vinegar is also a condiment and food additive that may contain chemical preservatives, including sulfites that may cause asthma in susceptible individuals, and it may cross-react in those allergic to corn. Acetic acid occurs naturally in many foods, including apples, cheese, grapes, and milk. (See SULFITING AGENTS.)

virus   An organism that requires electron microscopy to be seen. Viruses are parasitic: They depend on nutrients in living cells for their metabolic and reproductive processes. Size ranges from the 20 nanometers (nm) of the poliovirus to 250 x 300 nm for the poxviruses. A viral particle (viron) is composed of a central core of either a strand of deoxyribonucleic acid (DNA) or ribonucleic acid (RNA) and enclosed in a protein covering called the capsid. In some viruses the capsid is surrounded by a lipoprotein membrane resembling an envelope.

More than 300 viruses have been isolated from animals. Although many are harmless, they are an important cause of diseases, including measles, mumps, chicken pox and other herpetic infections, the common cold, influenza, yellow fever, smallpox, poliomyelitis, and acquired immunodeficiency syndrome (AIDS). RNA viruses most commonly are disease producers in humans.

Various methods are used to classify viruses. Size and shape are important characteristics. Viruses are often classified according to their DNA or RNA content. They may be shaped like spheres, rods, bricks, bullets, or tadpoles. The geographic site of initial discovery of a particular virus may also be involved in the naming of it, such as coxsackievirus, isolated from two children in Coxsackie, New York in 1948.

Adenoviruses, picornaviruses, rhinoviruses, coronaviruses, orthomyxoviridae   (include the influenza viruses), and paramyxoviruses are among viruses that cause respiratory infections that can complicate asthma or allergic rhinitis. There are very few antiviral drugs and they suppress rather than kill viruses, whereas antibiotics usually cure bacterial infections by destroying the micoorganisms. Acyclovir (Zovirax) is an example of an antiviral agent that suppresses symptoms of chicken pox, shingles, and herpes simplex of the oral and genital areas.

Many viral infections can be prevented by the use of vaccines. Examples include polio, influenza, measles, mumps, rubella, and hepatitis A and B. (See also IMMUNITY, ACTIVE.)

Vistaril   See HYDROXYZINE.

visualization [guided imagery]   A technique in which a patient, while in a deep state of relaxation, is "guided" through individualized mental images of eliminating pain, tumors, infections, and other stressors. For example, one may imagine one's immune system's antibodies and white blood cells gobbling or zapping the enemy cells. Dr. Carl Simonton, of the Simonton Cancer Center in Pacific Palisades, California, said, "The idea is to use any or all of the senses to quiet the mind."

vital capacity   The volume of air that can be exhaled following a full inspiration. The timed vital capacity is the volume of air that can be forcibly exhaled in a given time. In asthma patients this important value is often expressed as the forced expiratory volume in one second, or FEV_1. The FEV_1 is considered by most physicians to be the most important guide to the severity of an asthma attack. (See also SPIROMETRY.)

vital signs Body temperature, pulse, and number of respirations per minute. (See PULSUS PARADOXUS.)

vitamins Chemical compounds, produced by the body (vitamins A from its precursor carotene, vitamin D from the action of sunlight—ultraviolet light—on the skin, and vitamin K from natural bacteria of the intestines), preformed in animals or plants used as foods, or synthesized. Vitamins are necessary in small quantities for normal body functioning. The use of large amounts of vitamins has not been scientifically proven to prevent or improve the symptoms of allergy or respiratory infections. Excessive doses of certain vitamins can be toxic: High doses of vitamin A can cause severe headaches and vomiting from increased intracranial pressure and may result in death. Other vitamins known to cause adverse effects are vitamins D and K in excessive doses. Vitamin deficiencies, on the other hand, are responsible for gastrointestinal, endocrine, nervous system, thyroid, reproductive, and sensory disturbances, anorexia, scurvy, pellagra, beriberi, amemia, pyorrhea, hemorrhage, rickets, bone diseases, and others.

vocal cords See LARYNX.

Voll testing See ELECTROACUPUNCTURE.

Volmax Brand of sustained-release albuterol. (See ALBUTEROL.)

von Behring, Emil Prussian surgeon (1854–1917) who coined the term hypersensitivity after experimenting with animals who reacted to repeated doses of toxin. Appointed professor and director of the Institute of Hygiene at Philips University in Marbur in 1895, he founded the laboratory Behring-Werke, which produced diphtheria and tetanus antiserums. The laboratory eventually became an international pharmaceutical company, and in 1901, von Behring won the first Nobel Prize in physiology or medicine for his discovery of antiserum.

W

walnut   The nut borne by the tree of the genus *Juglans*; it can be a cause of anaphylaxis (life-threatening allergic shock). A toxic reaction can occur if the nuts are contaminated by aflaxtoxins, poisons produced by molds.

warehouseman's itch   Eczema appearing on the hands from contact with any irritating agent or allergen. (See CONTACT DERMATITIS.)

washerwoman's itch   Eczema appearing on the hands of those who work in laundries or who are in frequent contact with detergents and other cleaning chemicals. (See CONTACT DERMATITIS.)

wasp   Insect of the order Hymenoptera and the superfamilies Scolioidea, Vespoidea, and Specoidea. Female wasps have a stinger, and the injection of wasp venom into skin may result in an allergic reaction in sensitized individuals. Wasps feed on the larvae of other insects, which they kill by stinging them repeatedly. They also feed on sap and nector. Odors of fruit juices, soft drinks, and spoiling foods, bright colors, water, and leather attract wasps. (See HYMENOPTERA STING ALLERGY.)

watercress   A green, leafy plant that grows in fresh running water whose leaves are used in salad. Large amounts of this vegetable can cause goiters (enlarged thyroid glands) because of its ability to produce goitrogenic compounds in individuals who lack dietary iodine.

water itch   A common name for schistosome dermatitis. (See SCHISTOSOME DERMATITIS.)

weather   Changes in temperature, especially cold weather, which may trigger asthma. Symptoms of some mold allergies are more apparent during damp weather, whereas others, such as Alternaria, depend on dry, warm, windy air for transportation. Heavy rainfall will lower ragweed pollen counts because the pollen will settle to the ground. (See also TRIGGERS OF ALLERGIES AND ASTHMA.)

weed pollen allergy   Hay fever caused by exposure to the windblown, or anemophilous, pollen of plants that grow wild. Weeds often grow in areas despite minimal nutrition and water and tend to choke out more attractive plants. Most weeds are considered of little or no value and a nuisance. However, notable exceptions include the crops alfalfa, beets, castor bean, hemp, hops, sunflower, and ornamental plants such as roses and tulips. Various species of ragweed are the most important producers of allergy causing weed pollen. (See ANEMOPHILOUS PLANTS, RAGWEED.)

weeping eczema   Blisters of dermatitis that have burst and exuded fluid. (See ATOPIC DERMATITIS, CONTACT DERMATITIS.)

Wegener's granulomatosis [Wegener's syndrome]   A rare, multisystem disease characterized by the formation of granulomas (collections of abnormals cells in nodules) or vasculitis (inflammation of blood vessels) or both. The granulomas form most commonly in the nasal passages, especially the sinuses, lungs, and kidneys, but can affect any organ system. Although the exact cause is unknown, Wegener's is thought to be an autoimmune disorder (i.e., the body attacks its own tissues).

Symptoms include blood-streaked mucus drainage from the nose, coughing up bloody sputum, chest pain, and blood in the urine. Fever, weakness, joint pains, and weight loss occur when the sinuses become infected. The sinusitis that accompanies this disorder may be easily confused with allergic rhinitis. Renal failure may result. Diagnosis is confirmed by biopsy of involved tissue.

WEEDS THAT ARE A CAUSE OF HAY FEVER IN THE UNITED STATES AND CANADA

Common Name	Technical Name	Plant Family	Distribution	Pollination Season
Alfalfa	*Medicago sativa*	Leguminosae	Cultivated crop	May–Oct.
Allscale[1]	*Atriplex polycarps*	Chenopodiaceae	Colorado and Mohave Desert, alkali flats of C. CA, So. NV, UT and AZ	July–Oct.
Aster	*Aster species*	Compositae	Cultivated ornamentals and native weeds	
Balsamroot	*Balsamorrhiza sagittata*	Compositae	So. B.C. to So. CA, E. to MT, SD, CO	Apr.–July
Bassia	*Bassia hyssopifolia*	Chenopodiaceae	B.C. to CA, E. to MT, ID, NV, spreading elsewhere	July–Oct.
Beachbur	*Franseria bipinnatifidia*	Compositae	Coastal beaches and dunes B.C. to So. CA	Mar.–Sept.
Beachbur, San Francisco	*F. chamissonis*	Compositae	Coastal beaches and dunes B.C. to So. CA	July–Sept.
Beet	*Beta vulgaris*	Chenopodiaceae	Cultivated crop (sugar and red) established locally in So. U.S.	July–Oct.
Bractscale[1]	*Atriplex bracteosa*	Chenopodiaceae	C. and So. CA, E. to NM, TX	July–Nov.
Brewers scale[1]	*A. breweri*	Chenopodiaceae	C. and So. CA	July–Oct.
Brittle bush (incienso)	*Encelia farinosa*	Compositae	C. and So. CA, to S.W. UT, AZ	Mar.–May
Broom, Scotch	*Cystisus scoparius*	Leguminosae	Naturalized, CA, No. to WA, B.C.	Apr.–June
Broomweed	*Gutierrezia dracunculoides*	Compositae	C. TX and OK	July–Oct.
Bulrush	*Scirpus microcorpus*	Cyperaceae	So. CA, No. to AK, Rocky Mts., NM	May–Aug.

WEEDS THAT ARE A CAUSE OF HAY FEVER IN THE UNITED STATES AND CANADA (continued)

Common Name	Technical Name	Plant Family	Distribution	Pollination Season
Burrobrush[1]	Hymenoclea monogyra	Compositae	So. CO E. to TX	Aug.–Nov.
Burrobrush[1]	H. salsola	Compositae	So. CA, NV, S. UT, AZ	Mar.–June
Canaigre (wild rhubarb)	Rumex hymenosepalus	Polygonaceae	C. and So. CA, WY, W. TX	Jan.–May
Carelessweed[1]	Amaranthus palmeri	Amaranthraceae	So. CA, E. to C. U.S.	Aug.–Nov.
Castor bean[1]	Ricinus communis	Euphorbiaceae	Cultivated ornamental, established in So. U.S.	Jan.–Dec.
Cattail, broad-leaf	Typha latifolia	Typhaceae	Widespread weed	June–Aug.
Cattail, narrow-leaf	T. angtistifolia	Typhaceae	Widespread weed	June–Aug.
Chamise (greasewood)	Adenostoma fasciculatum	Rosaceae	Common component of California chaparral	May–June
Clover, red	Trifoliutm pratense	Leguminosae	Cultivated hay crop	June–Aug.
Clover, sweet	Melilotus species	Leguminosae	Cultivated hay crop, widespread weed	May–Nov.
Clover, white	Trifolium repens	Leguminosae	Cultivated lawn plant	Apr.–Sept.
Cocklebur, common[1]	Xanthium strumarium	Compositae	Widespread weed	Aug.–Oct.
Cocklebur, spiny	X. spinosum	Compositae	Widespread weed i n warm and temperate regions	July–Oct.
Daisy, ox-eye	Chrysanthemum leucantheum	Compositae	Widespread weed, cultivated as Shasta daisy	June–Aug.
Dandelion officinale	Taraxacum	Compositae	Widespread weed	Jan.–Dec.
Dock, bitter[1]	Rijmex obtrusifolis	Polygonaceae	Widespread weed	June–Dec.

WEEDS THAT ARE A CAUSE OF HAY FEVER IN THE
UNITED STATES AND CANADA (continued)

Common Name	Technical Name	Plant Family	Distribution	Pollination Season
Dock, green[1]	*R. conglomeratus*	Polygonaceae	Widespread weed	Apr.–Oct.
Dock, white[1]	*R. mexicanus*	Polygonaceae	Widespread weed	June–Sept.
Dock, yellow (curly dock)[1]	*R. crisptis*	Polygonaceae	Widespread weed	May–Oct.
Dog fennel (mayweed)	*Anthemis cotula*	Compositae	Widespread weed	June–Oct.
Fern, bracken	*Pterdium aquilinum*	Dennstaedtiaceae	Widespread weed	June–Aug.
Fern, royal	*Osmunda regalis*	Osmundaceae	Widespread weed	Summer
Fern, sword Christmas fern	*Polystichum munitum*	Polypodiaceae	AK to So. CA, to ID and MT	Summer
Firebush, Mex. (smr. cypress)[1]	*Kochia scoparia*	Chenopodiaceae	Widespread weed	Aug.–Oct.
Fireweed	*Epilobrium angustifolium*	Onagraceae	Widespread weed	July–Sept.
Goldenrod	*Solidago* species	Compositae	Widespread weed	May–Oct.
Goosefoot, Lamb's-quarter[1]	*Chenopodium album*	Chenopodiaceae	Widespread weed	June–Oct.
Goosefoot, nettle-leaf	*Chenopodium murale*	Chenopodiaceae	Widespread weed	Most of year, esp. spring
Greasewood	*Sarcobatus vermiculatus*	Chenopodiaceae	So. CO to E. WA, Alta., ND, TX	May–Aug.
Hemp	*Cannabis sativa*	Cannabidaceae	Cultivated crop and widespread weed, diminishing	July–Sept.
Hops, cultivated	*Humulus lupulus*	Cannabidaceae	Cultivated crop	Summer

WEEDS THAT ARE A CAUSE OF HAY FEVER IN THE UNITED STATES AND CANADA (continued)

Common Name	Technical Name	Plant Family	Distribution	Pollination Season
Hop-sage	*Grayia spinosa*	Chenopodiaceae	CA to E. WA, WY, AZ	Mar.–June
Iodine bush	*Allenrolfea occidentalis*	Chenopodiaceae	CA to OR, UT	June–Aug.
Jerusalem oak	*Chenopodium botrys*	Chenopodiaceae	Widespread weed	June–Oct.
Lenscale[1]	*Atriplex lentiformis*	Chenopodiaceae	So. and C. CA, to UT	Aug.–Oct.
Marshelder, August	*Iva augustifolia*	Compositae	AR, OK, TX, LA	Late summer–fall
Marshelder, rough (poverty weed)[1]	*I. ciliata*	Compositae	IL to LA, W. to N.B., NM	Late spring–summer
Mugwort[1]	*Artemisia douglasiana*	Compositae	CA E. to W. NV, to WA, ID	June–Oct.
Mugwort[1]	*A. heterophylla*	Compositae	CA. E. to W. NV, to WA, ID	June–Oct.
Mustard (Black)	*Brassica nigra*	Cruciferae	Widespread weed	Apr.–July
Mustard	*B. campestris*	Cruciferae	Widespread weed, esp. in CA	Jan.–May
Nettle	*Urtica dioica*	Urticaceae	Widespread weed	July–Sept.
Pea, sweet	*Lathyrus odoratus*	Leguminosae	Cultivated ornamental	Jan.–Dec.
Phlox	*Phlox species*	Polemoniaceae	Cultivated ornamental	Spring–summer
Pickleweed (glasswort)	*Salicornia ambigua*	Chenopodiaceae	Atlantic and Pacific coastal, salt marshes and adjacent salt flats	Aug.–Nov.
Pigweed, green	*Amaranthus hybridus*	Amarathaceae	Widespread weed	June–Nov.
Pigweed, redroot[1]	*A. retroflex*	Amarathaceae	Widespread weed	June–Nov.
Pigweed, spiny	*A. spinosus*	Amarathaceae	Advancing weed	June–Sept.

WEEDS THAT ARE A CAUSE OF HAY FEVER IN THE
UNITED STATES AND CANADA (continued)

Common Name	Technical Name	Plant Family	Distribution	Pollination Season
Pigweed, spreading	*A. blitoides*	Amarathaceae	Widespread weed	July–Nov.
Plantain, common	*Plantago major*	Plantaginaceae	Widespread weed	Jan.–Dec.
Plantain, English (buck-horn)[1]	*P. lanceolata*	Plantaginaceae	Widespread weed	June–Sept.
Poppy, California	*Escholzia californica*	Papaveraceae	CA, cultivated ornamental elsewhere	Feb.–Sept.
Povertyweed, giant	*Iva xanthifolia*	Compositae	P.Q. to Alta., So. to DC, OH, MD, TX, NM, AZ	July–Sept.
Povertyweed, small	*I. axilaris*	Compositae	CA to No.B., Canada	May–Sept.
Rabbitbrush	*Chrysothamnus nauseosus*	Compositae	E. CA, No. to B.C., E. to Sask., TX	July–Oct.
Rabbitbrush[1]	*Franseria deltoides*	Compositae	So. AZ and Mexico	Spring
Ragweed, canyon[1]	*F. ambrosiodes*	Compositae	So. CA, So. AZ	Mar.–June
Ragweed, desert (burroweed)[1]	*F. dumosa*	Compositae	So. CA, S.W. UT, AZ	Mar.–May
Ragweed, false (Sandbur)[1]	*F. acanthicarpa*	Compositae	C. and So. CA to WA, Sask., TX, advancing eastward	Aug.–Nov.
Ragweed, giant (crownweed)[1]	*Ambrosia trifida*	Compositae	So. Canada and U.S. to Rocky Mts.	July–Sept.
Ragweed, short[1]	*A. artemisifolia*	Compositae	So. Canada and U.S., except W. and S.W. U.S.	Aug.–Oct.
Ragweed, silver[1]	*Dicoria canescens*	Compositae	So. CA, S.W. AZ, NV, S.W. UT	Sept.–Jan.
Ragweed, slender[1]	*Franseria tenuifolia*	Compositae	C. and So. CA, to KS, TX	May–Nov.
Ragweed, southern[1]	*Ambrosia bidentata*	Compositae	So. IL, to LA, W. to N.B. and TX	Aug.–Sept.

WEEDS THAT ARE A CAUSE OF HAY FEVER IN THE UNITED STATES AND CANADA (continued)

Common Name	Technical Name	Plant Family	Distribution	Pollination Season
Ragweed, western[1]	A. psilostachya	Compositae	CA to WA, Sask., IL	July–Nov.
Redscale	Atriplex rosea	Chenopodiaceae	CA to WA, Atlantic coast	July–Oct.
Rose	Rosa species	Rosaceae	Cultivated ornamentals and native shrubs	Jan.–Dec.
Sagebrush, annual	Artemisia annua	Compositae	Widespread weed	July–Sept.
Sagebrush, biennial	A. biennis	Compositae	Widespread weed	Aug.–Sept.
Sagebrush, California[1]	A. californica	Compositae	Coastal C., and So. CA	Aug.–Dec.
Sagebrush, carpet (pasture)[1]	A. frigida	Compositae	Some forms cultivated annuals	July–Sept.
Sagebrush, common (giant)[1]	A. tridentata	Compositae	So. CA to B.C., Rocky Mts.	Aug.–Oct.
Sagebrush, prairie[1]	A. ludoviciana	Compositae	CA to WA, Alta., Ont., AR, NM	July–Sept.
Sagebrush, sand dune	A. ludoviciana	Compositae	Coastal C. CA, and OR	June–Aug.
Sagebrush, Sukasdorf	A. pycnocephala	Compositae	Coastal N. CA to Vancouver Island	May–Aug.
Saltbush, annual	A. suksdorfii	Chenopodiaceae	So. AZ and So. NM	July–Sept.
Sea blite (seepweed)	Suaeda moquini	Chenopodiaceae	So. CA to Alta.	July–Oct.
Sea blite (seepweed)	S. californica	Chenopodiaceae	Coastal salt marsh, San Francisco Bay to So. CA	July–Oct.
Sea blite (seepweed)	S. suffrutescens	Chenopodiaceae	C. CA to WA, Rocky Mts.	July–Sept.
Sedge	Carex species	Cyperaceae	Widespread, largest genus of flowering plants in North America	Spring–summer
Shadscale (sheep fat)	Atriplex conifertifolia	Chenopodiaceae	So. CA to E. OR, ND	Apr.–July

WEEDS THAT ARE A CAUSE OF HAY FEVER IN THE
UNITED STATES AND CANADA (continued)

Common Name	Technical Name	Plant Family	Distribution	Pollination Season
Sheep sorrel[1]	Romex acetosella	Polygonaceae	Widespread weed	Mar.–Aug.
Silverscale	Atriplex argentea	Chenopodiaceae	So. CA to B.C., ND, NM	June–Sept.
Snapdragon	Antirrhinum majus	Scrophulariaceae	Cultivated crop	Jan.–Dec.
Spearscale	Atriplex patula	Chenopodiaceae	Widespread weed	June–Nov.
Sunflower	Helianthus species	Compositae	Cultivated crop, ornamental, native So. Canada to Mexican border	Feb.–Oct.
Tansy	Tanacetum vulgare	Compositae	Cultivated ornamental, naturalized weed	July–Sept.
Tarragon (green sagebrush)	Artemisia dracunculus	Compositae	C. and So. CA, N. to B.C., WI, TX, cultivated form sterile	Aug.–Oct.
Tarweed	Hemizonia species	Compositae	30 species, all in CA	Apr.–Nov.
Tea, Mexican (wormseed)	Chenopdium ambrosiodes	Chenopodiaceae	Widespread weed	June–Dec.
Thistle, Russian[1]	Salsola kali	Chenopodiaceae	Widespread weed	July–Oct.
Tulip	Tulipa species	Liliaceae	Cultivated ornamentals	Spring
Water hemp[1]	Acnida tamariscina	Amaranthaceae	E. TX, No. to So.OK, E. to IN	Aug.–Sept.
Wingscale, (shadescale)[1]	Atriplex canescens	Chenopodiaceae	C. and So. CA to E. WA, SD, KS, TX	June–Aug.
Winter fat	Eurotia lanata	Chenopodiaceae	C. and So. CO, WA, Rocky Mts., TX	Mar.–June
Wormwood	Artemisia absinthium	Compositae	Cultivated ornamental, naturalized weed	July–Sept.

[1]Pollen is a major source of hay fever.
Adapted from *Pollen Guide for Allergy*, Hollister-Stier.

Immunosuppressant drugs, such as azathioprine or cyclophosphamide, are combined with corticosteroids to threat Wegener's, a disease that may go into remission or prove fatal. Wegener's Foundation is a support group for patients with this disorder. Patients may contact:

Wegener's Foundation, Inc.
National Institutes of Health
Building 31, Room B1W30
Bethesda, Maryland 20892
Phone (301) 496–8331

Wegener's syndrome   See WEGENER'S GRANULOMATOSIS.

welt   A raised, unbroken area of skin produced by allergic stimulus or trauma. Welts are commonly found in cases of urticaria, or hives, and dermatographia. (See URTICARIA, DERMATOGRAPHIA.)

West, Geoffrey B.   See RILEY, JAMES F., AND WEST, GEOFFREY B.

wheal   A round, itchy skin elevation, typically white in the middle with a red or pink delineation, often seen accompanying insect bites, anaphylaxis, and urticaria, or hives. A wheal may also emerge as a result of an intradermal injection of allergens during skin testing. (See SKIN TESTS, TRIPLE RESPONSE OF LEWIS, URTICARIA.)

wheal and flare reaction   See SKIN TESTS, TRIPLE RESPONSE OF LEWIS, URTICARIA, WHEAL.

wheat   A grain from one of the many cereal grasses, genus *Triticum*, used in the making of flour; it is the world's most important grain crop. The husk or outer coat is removed before grinding. A mineral containing bran coat is removed in making white flour. The gluten portion contains fat and protein. Gluten makes dough rise in the presence of yeast. The center of the kernal is starch.

Wheat can cause anaphylaxis and allergic vasculitis (see HENOCH-SCHONLEIN PURPURA).

Baker's asthma is an occupational lung disease caused by prolonged inhalation of flour dust, usually wheat flour (see BAKER'S ASTHMA). This exposure can also cause allergic rhinitis and rashes (see BAKER'S ECZEMA, BAKER'S RHINITIS). Individuals exhibit positive skin tests to wheat flour extracts, but they do not exhibit any symptoms from eating wheat products.

If an infant shows food intolerance, breast-feeding mothers should avoid wheat products in addition to other foods known to be highly allergenic for newborns (milk, eggs, nuts, citrus, shellfish, and fish).

Gluten-sensitive enteropathy (celiac disease) is an intolerance to gluten resulting in severe damage to the small bowel (see GLUTEN-SENSITIVE ENTEROPATHY). Individuals inflicted with this disorder must avoid wheat and other gluten-containing foods, rye, and barley their entire lives. Some breads are labeled "no wheat" but do contain gluten. Wheat- and gluten-free diets are available from the American Dietetic Association (see AMERICAN DIETETIC ASSOCIATION). (See also BREAST-FEEDING AND PREVENTION OF ALLERGIES, FOOD ALLERGY.)

wheezing   A breathing difficulty characterized by a high-pitched whistling or moaning sound. Caused by constriction of the airways of the upper respiratory tract, wheezing may be offensively loud or only audible through a stethoscope in the case of asthma, bronchitis, pulmonary edema, a foreign object inhaled into an airway, and other respiratory disorders.

whelk   An alternate term for wheal. (See WHEAL.)

whey   A liquid milk by-product, created after rennet has been added to the milk in order to coagulate it. (See MILK.)

whiskey   An alcoholic beverage made from fermented grain. Whiskeys contain complex mixes of ingredients, and individuals may have allergic or other adverse effects from some but not other blends. (See ALCOHOL.)

white blood cells   See LEUKOCYTES.

whooping cough   See PERTUSSUS.

Widal, G. Fernand I.   Algerian physician and scientist (1862–1929) who originated the Widal test for typhoid fever, described (the Hayem-Widal type) hemolytic anemia and hemolytic shock, and reported on nasal polyps, asthma, aspirin intolerance with eosinophilia and leukopenia related to anaphylaxis, and other topics. Widal received the Grand Cross Legion of Honor, France's highest civilian decoration.

Willis, Thomas E.   British physician, "natural philosopher," and writer (1621–75) acclaimed for his descriptions and illustrations of arterial channels at the base of the brain, known today as the "circle of Willis," and for his writings on diseases of the central nervous system. Willis also studied and discussed the nerve supply to the bronchial tubes, which he believed corresponds to asthmatic spasms. His views are considered a gateway to modern understanding of bronchial asthma.

windpipe   See TRACHEA.

wine   An alcoholic beverage made from the fermented juice of fruit, especially grapes, containing about 10 to 14% alcohol. Any wine or brandy product exceeding 14% alcohol content, approximately the limit of alcohol by natural fermentation, contains additional alcohol distilled from other sources, such as corn. There may be histamine-releasing substances in wine, particularly red varieties, which can cause urticaria (hives) or headaches in sensitive individuals. Many wines contain the preservatives sodium metabisulfite and related products (see SULFITING AGENTS) that can trigger an asthma attack. This phenomenon is often referred to as "restaurant asthma." (See also ALCOHOL.)

winter itch   Itching associated with cold weather and dryness of the skin.

Witebsky, Ernest   German physician (1901–69) who researched and published papers on autoimmune phenomena, the Rh factor, blood groups and transfusion, cancer, and tolerance to self-antigens, among other topics involving immunologic problems. Highly regarded by his colleagues, Witebsky was elected dean of the School of Medicine at the State University of New York at Buffalo in 1959.

wood- and coal-burning stoves   Home heating alternatives that may be excellent sources of inexpensive fuel. More than 11 million wood-burning stoves are in use in the United States since the energy crisis of the early 1970s caused a significant increase in home heating costs. Wood stoves should have a catalytic converter to burn off smoke produced by burning wood. Do not store wood in the home. Always keep the doors to stoves or fireplaces closed. Once the fire has been started, use only hard wood. Soft pine, poplars, twigs, or unseasoned wood should be avoided. Coal stoves may be safe but only if they are airtight. Poorly ventilated coal stoves may result in unsafe levels of carbon monoxide, nitrogen and sulfur dioxides, formaldehyde, and benzopyrene in the home. Kerosene heaters produce unpleasant fumes that can trigger asthma.

wool   The heavy coat of various hairy mammals including sheep, which is commercially valuable as fibers for clothing and blankets. Although some persons suffer skin irritations from contact with woolen garments, these rashes are nonallergenic.

wool fat   See LANOLIN.

woolsorter's disease   A form of the bacterial infection anthrax of the lungs caused by exposure to natural wool contaminated by *Bacillus anthracis*.

wool wax   See LANOLIN.

Wyman, Morrill   American physician (1812–1903), born in Chelmsford, Massachusetts and educated at Harvard University, who wrote a treatise on ventilation that influenced the subsequent construction of public buildings, including hospitals. Wyman's later invention of a small, hollow needle represented a major improvement in the treatment of pleurisy. In 1872, he published *Hay Fever*, which identified pollen as the cause of this allergic disease. It seemed to Wyman that some families had predisposi-tions to an "Autumnal Catarrh," the title of another of his writings, while others would suffer regularly from what was then called "June Cold." He spoke of a peculiar sensitivity of the respiratory system that predisposed individuals to developing severe attacks of difficult breathing, sneezing, eye irritation, and coughing.

In Wyman's own family, his father, two brothers, his sister, and his son and daughter all suffered from allergies.

X

xanthelasmoidea Another term for urticaria pigmentosum. (See URTICARIA PIGMENTOSUM.)

xeroderma Rough, dry skin, a mild form of ichthyosis. (See ICHTHYOSIS VULGARIS.)

xeromycteria Dryness of the mucous membranes of the nose.

X ray [roentgen ray] A diagnostic method in which invisible electromagnetic energy of short wavelength is produced when high-speed electrons strike a heavy metal. Discovered by Wilhelm Conrad Roentgen in 1896, X rays have been widely used to diagnose various allergic diseases such as chronic lung disorders and sinusitis, as well as pneumonia, fractured bones, and many other conditions. An X ray resembles a photographic negative, but it allows physicians to detect anomalies in numerous ways.

X-ray dermatitis A superficial skin inflammation caused by exposure to X rays.

X-ray dye reactions See RADIOCONTRAST MEDIA REACTIONS.

Xylocaine See LIDOCAINE.

xylometazoline A nasal decongestant drug.

Y

yarrow A wild herb (*Achillea millefolium*), family Compositae, native to Europe and Asia, used for its strong scent and spicy taste in astringents, shampoos, beverages, liquors, and tonics. It may cause photosensitive skin rashes with sun or artificial light exposure.

yeast A fungus that reproduces by budding. Foods contaminated by molds and made with brewer's or baker's yeasts and the yeast *Candida albcans* have been implicated as the cause of a multitude of physical complaints, including urticaria (hives). (See CANDIDIASIS, CANDIDIASIS ALLERGY.)

Yellow Dye No. 5 See TARTRAZINE.

yellow jackets Various small, yellow-marked, stinging insects of the family Vespidae, order Hymenoptera, related to wasps. These venomous insects resemble hornets except for a lack of a dark band under their eyes. They live in nests in the ground, frequently stinging those walking barefoot, and in walls. They are aggressive. (See also HYMENOPTERA STING ALLERGY.)

yoga The Hindu philosophy that embraces various methods of mental and physical exercise that render one capable of lowering blood pressure and heart rate and suppressing other bodily functions in order to achieve a state of total relaxation. Yoga techniques, including meditation, stretching, and breathing, may have a positive outcome for asthmatics, according to P. K. Vedanthan, M.D., a Fort Collins, Colorado allergist. Vedanthan conducted a 12-week study of patients with mild asthma whose lung function, exercise tolerance, relaxation levels, and attitude improved significantly with the practice of yoga three times a week. The patients also required less asthma medication, especially adrenergic inhalers, whereas other similar patients who did not practice yoga required the same or increased medication.

yogurt A form of curdled milk eaten for its therapeutic value to the bowels in the treatment of diarrhea and for maintaining correct acidity in the urinary bladder. Yogurt owes its effectiveness to acidophilus, a fermenting culture known as lactobacillus, used in the curdling process.

Z

Zafirlukast (Accolate) Leukotriene receptor antagonist or drug that blocks the effects of leukotriene D4, a substance produced in certain cells of the immune system. Leukotrienes contribute to inflammation and obstruction in the airways of asthma patients. See also LEUKOTRIENES.

Zantac   See RANITIDINE.

Zileuton (Zyflo) Leukotriene inhibitor—a drug that prevents the action of 5-lipoxygenase, an enzyme that causes inflammation in the airways in asthmatic patients. Although Zyflo is not effective for acute attacks of asthma, it may add to the beneficial effects of inhaled corticosteroids in the prevention of asthma symptoms. (See also LEUKOTRIENES.)

zinc salts   Derivatives of the metal zinc, including zinc pyrithionine, zinc salicylate, and zinc sulfate, which are used in cosmetic products and may be skin sensitizers.

Zithromax   Brand of azithromycin. (See AZITHROMYCIN.)

zygomycosis [mucormycosis] A serious, potentially fatal fungal infection. It is usually found in debilitated patients, especially diabetics. Zygomycosis is caused by a water-borne mold; its initial symptoms include a watery nasal discharge, which may be confused with allergic conditions, and fever. It may spread to the lungs and other vital organs.

Zyrtec   Brand name for the antihistamine cetirizine. (See CETIRIZINE.)

APPENDIX I: POLLENS: MAJOR BOTANICAL AREAS OF THE UNITED STATES AND CANADA

The United States and Canada are divided into 23 botanical regions. The regions are generally composed of contiguous areas having similar climatic and geographic features. State and province boundaries may be used for easy identification whenever possible, but other boundaries may be identified by counties within states or by major geographic features.

In addition, a plant should not be considered allergenically significant unless it fulfills the five postulates of Thommen:

1. The plant must be seed bearing (spermatophyte); only seed-bearing plants produce pollen.
2. The plant must have wide distribution, or the plant must be close to the human environment.
3. The plant must produce large quantities of pollen.
4. The pollen must be light enough to be airborne, between 15 and 50 microns (1 micron = .001 millimeter) in diameter.
5. The pollen must be allergenic.

Species fulfilling all five postulates are considered a *primary*, or *index, species*. If a plant lacks one or more of the postulates, the species may still provoke allergy in some people, but its significance as an allergen is reduced.

Region I

North Atlantic states, U.S.: Connecticut, Maine, Massachusetts, New Hampshire, New Jersey, New York, Pennsylvania, Rhode Island, and Vermont.

Index trees: Appalachian oak forest and northern hardwood forest (beech, birch, hemlock, and maple); pollinating season is late winter through spring.

BOX ELDER/MAPLE (*Acer* species)
BIRCH (*Betula* species)
OAK (*Quercus* species)
HICKORY (*Carya ovata*)
ASH (*Fraxinus americana*)
PINE (*Pinus strobus*)
SYCAMORE (*Platanus occidentalis*)
COTTONWOOD/POPLAR (*Populus deltoides*)
ELM (*Ulmus americana*)

Index grasses: Several genera, naturalized and/or cultivated for hay and lawns, although inconspicuous, are abundant and significant in hay fever; pollinating season is spring through summer.

REDTOP (*Agrostis alba*)
ORCHARD (*Dactylis glomerata*)
FESCUE (*Festuca elatior*)
TIMOTHY (*Phleum pretense*)
BLUEGRASS/JUNE GRASS (*Poa* species)

Index weeds: Although relatively few species of weeds are important, their widespread abundance and heavy pollination over a long season make them important hay fever plants; pollinating season is summer through early fall.

LAMB'S QUARTERS (*Chenopodium album*)
RAGWEED, GIANT and SHORT (*Ambrosia* species)
COCKLEBUR (*Xanthium strumarium*)
PLANTAIN (*Plantago lanceolata*)
DOCK/SORREL (*Rumex* species)

Region II

Mid-Atlantic states, U.S.: Delaware, District of Columbia, Maryland, North Carolina, and Virginia.

Index trees: Appalachian oak forest and northern hardwood forest (beech, birch, hemlock, and maple); pollinating season is late winter through spring.

BOX ELDER/MAPLE (*Acer* species)
BIRCH (*Betula nigra*)
CEDAR/JUNIPER (*Juniperus virginiana*)
OAK (*Quercus* species)
HICKORY/PECAN (*Carya* species)
WALNUT (*Juglans nigra*)
MULBERRY (*Morus* species)
ASH (*Fraxinus americana*)
COTTONWOOD/POPLAR (*Populus deltoides*)
HACKBERRY (*Celtis occidentalis*)
ELM (*Ulmus americana*)

Index grasses: Same as Region I.

REDTOP (*Agrostis alba*)
VERNAL GRASS (*Anthoxanthum* species)
BERMUDA GRASS (*Cynodon dactylon*)
ORCHARD GRASS (*Dactylis glomerata*)
RYEGRASS (*Elymus* and *Lolium* species)
TIMOTHY (*Phleum pretense*)
BLUEGRASS/JUNE GRASS (*Poa* species)
JOHNSON GRASS (*Sorghum halepense*)

Index weeds: Same as Region I.

PIGWEED (*Amaranthus retroflexus*)
LAMB'S QUARTERS (*Chenopodium album*)
MEXICAN FIREBUSH (*Kochia scoparia*)
RAGWEED, GIANT and SHORT (*Ambrosia* species)
COCKLEBUR (*Xanthium strumarium*)
PLANTAIN (*Plantago lanceolata*)
DOCK/SORREL (*Rumex* species)

Region III

South Atlantic states, U.S.: Northern Florida (north of Orlando), Georgia, and South Carolina.

Index trees: Oak-hickory-pine forest and southern mixed forest (beech, oak, pine); pollinating season is late winter through spring.

BOX ELDER/MAPLE (*Acer* species)
BIRCH (*Betula nigra*)
CEDAR/JUNIPER (*Juniperus virginiana*)
OAK (*Quercus* species)
HICKORY/PECAN (*Carya* species)
WALNUT (*Juglans nigra*)
MESQUITE (*Prosopis juliflora*)
MULBERRY (*Morus* species)
ASH (*Fraxinus americana*)
COTTONWOOD/POPLAR (*Populus deftoides*)
HACKBERRY (*Ceftis occidentalis*)
ELM (*Ulmus americana*)

Index grasses: Several genera, naturalized and/or cultivated for hay and lawns, although inconspicuous, are abundant and significant in hay fever; pollinating season is spring through early summer.

REDTOP (*Agrostis alba*)
VERNAL GRASS (*Anthoxanthum* species)
BERMUDA GRASS (*Cynodon dactylon*)
ORCHARD GRASS (*Dactylis glomerata*)
RYEGRASS (*Elymus* and *Lolium* species)
FESCUE (*Festuca elatior*)
TIMOTHY (*Phleum pretense*)
BLUEGRASS/JUNE GRASS (*Poa* species)
JOHNSON GRASS (*Sorghum halepense*)

Index weeds: Although relatively few species of weeds are important, their widespread abundance and heavy pollination over a long season make them important hay fever plants; pollinating season is summer through early fall.

LAMB'S QUARTERS (*Chenopodium album*)
RAGWEED, GIANT and SHORT (*Ambrosia* species)

SAGEBRUSH (*Artemisia* species)
COCKLEBUR (*Xanthium strumarium*)
PLANTAIN (*Plantago lanceolata*)
DOCK/SORREL (*Rumex* species)

Region IV

Subtropical Florida (below Orlando).

Index trees: Southern mixed forest, palmetto prairie, and everglades; pollinating season is winter through spring.

BOX ELDER (*Acer negundo*)
CEDAR/JUNIPER (*Juniperus virginiana*)
OAK (*Quercus* species)
PECAN (*Carya pecan*)
PRIVET (*Ligustrum lucidum*)
PALM (*Cocos plumosa*)
AUSTRALIAN PINE (beefwood) (*Casuarina equisetifolia*)
SYCAMORE (*Platanus occidentalis*)
COTTONWOOD/POPLAR (*Populus deftoides*)
ELM (*Ulmus americana*)
BRAZILIAN PEPPERTREE (Florida holly) (*Schinus terebinthifolius*)
BAYBERRY (wax myrtle) (*Myrica* species)
MELALEUCA (*Melaleuca* species)

Index Grasses: Several genera, naturalized and/or cultivated for hay and lawns, although inconspicuous, are very abundant and significant in hay fever; pollinating season is spring through early summer.

REDTOP (*Agrostis alba*)
BERMUDA GRASS (*Cynodon dactylon*)
SALT GRASS (*Distichlis* species)
BAHIA GRASS (*Paspalum notatum*)
CANARY GRASS (*Phalaris minor*)
BLUEGRASS/JUNE GRASS (*Poa* species)
JOHNSON GRASS (*Sorghum halepense*)

Index weeds: Although relatively few species of weeds are important, their widespread abundance and heavy pollination over a long season make them important hay fever plants;

pollinating season is summer through early fall.

PIGWEED (*Amaranthus spinosus*)
LAMB'S QUARTERS (*Chenopodium album*)
RAGWEED, GIANT and SHORT (*Ambrosia* species)
SAGEBRUSH (*Artemisia* species)
MARSH ELDER/POVERTY WEED (*Iva* species)
DOCK/SORREL (*Rumex* species)
PLANTAIN (*Plantago lanceolata*)

Region V

Greater Ohio Valley states, U.S.: Indiana, Kentucky, Ohio, Tennessee, and West Virginia.

Index trees: Mixed forest (beech, maple, oak), beech-maple forest, and oak-hickory forest; pollinating season is late winter through spring.

BOX ELDER/MAPLE (*Acer* species)
BIRCH (*Betula nigra*)
OAK (*Quercus rubra*)
HICKORY (*Carya ovata*)
WALNUT (*Juglans nigra*)
ASH (*Fraxinus americana*)
SYCAMORE (*Platanus occidentalis*)
COTTONWOOD/POPLAR (*Populus deltoides*)
ELM (*Ulmus americana*)

Index grasses: Several genera, naturalized and/or cultivated for hay and lawns, although inconspicuous, are very abundant and significant in hay fever; pollinating season is spring through early summer.

REDTOP (*Agrostis alba*)
BERMUDA GRASS (*Cynodon dactylon*)
ORCHARD GRASS (*Dactylis glomerata*)
FESCUE (*Festuca elatior*)
RYEGRASS (*Lolium* species)
TIMOTHY (*Phleum pretense*)
BLUEGRASS/JUNE GRASS (*Poa* species)
JOHNSON GRASS (*Sorghum halepense*)

Index weeds: Although relatively few species of weeds are important, their widespread abundance and heavy pollination over a long season make them important hay fever plants; pollinating season is summer through early fall.

WATER HEMP (*Acnida tamariscina*)
PIGWEED (*Amaranthus retroflexus*)
LAMB'S QUARTERS (*Chenopodium album*)
RAGWEED, GIANT and SHORT (*Ambrosia* species)
SAGEBRUSH (*Artemisia* species)
COCKLEBUR (*Xanthium strumarium*)
DOCK/SORREL (*Rumex* species)
PLANTAIN (*Plantago lanceolata*)

Region VI

South central states, U.S.: Alabama, Arkansas, Louisiana, and Mississippi.

Index trees: Southern floodplain forest, surrounded by oak, hickory, and pine forest and oak and hickory forest; pollinating season is late winter through spring.

BOX ELDER/MAPLE (*Acer* species)
CEDAR/JUNIPER (*Juniperus virginiana*)
OAK (*Quercus* species)
HICKORY/PECAN (*Carya* species)
WALNUT (*Juglans nigra*)
ASH (*Fraxinus americana*)
SYCAMORE (*Platanus occidentalis*)
COTTONWOOD/POPLAR (*Populus deltoides*)
HACKBERRY (*Celtis occidentalis*)
ELM (*Ulmus americana*)

Index grasses: Several genera, naturalized and/or cultivated for hay and lawns, although inconspicuous, are very abundant and significant for hay fever; pollinating season is spring through early summer.

REDTOP (*Agrostis alba*)
BERMUDA GRASS (*Cynodon dactylon*)
ORCHARD GRASS (*Dactylis glomerata*)

RYEGRASS (*Lolium* species)
TIMOTHY (*Phleum pretense*)
BLUEGRASS/JUNE GRASS (*Poa* species)
JOHNSON GRASS (*Sorghum halepense*)

Index weeds: Although relatively few species of weeds are important, their widespread abundance and heavy pollination over a long season make them important hay fever plants; pollinating season is summer through early fall.

CARELESSWEED/PIGWEED (*Amaranthus* species)
LAMB'S QUARTERS (*Chenopodium album*)
RAGWEED, GIANT and SHORT (*Ambrosia* species)
SAGEBRUSH (*Artemisia* species)
MARSH ELDER/POVERTY WEED (*Iva* species)
COCKLEBUR (*Xanthium strumarium*)
PLANTAIN (*Plantago lanceolata*)
DOCK/SORREL (*Rumex* species)

Region VII

Northern midwestern states, U.S.: Michigan, Minnesota, and Wisconsin.

Index trees: Northern hardwood and Great Lakes pine forests, bluestem prairie and oak savannahs; pollinating season is late winter through spring.

BOX ELDER/MAPLE (*Acer* species)
ALDER (*Alnus incana*)
BIRCH (*Betula* species)
OAK (*Quercus rubra*)
HICKORY (*Carya ovata*)
WALNUT (*Juglans nigra*)
ASH (*Fraxinus americana*)
SYCAMORE (*Platanus occidentalis*)
COTTONWOOD/POPLAR (*Populus deltoides*)
ELM (*Ulmus americana*)

Index grasses: Several genera, naturalized and/or cultivated for hay and lawns, although inconspicuous, are very abundant and significant in hay fever; pollinating season is spring through early summer.

REDTOP (*Agrostis alba*)
BROME (*Bromus inermis*)
ORCHARD GRASS (*Dactylis glomerata*)
FESCUE (*Festuca elatior*)
RYEGRASS (*Lolium* species)
CANARY GRASS (*Phalaris arundinacea*)
TIMOTHY (*Phleum pretense*)
BLUEGRASS/JUNE GRASS (*Poa* species)

Index weeds: Although relatively few species of weeds are important, their widespread abundance and heavy pollination over a long season make them important hay fever plants; pollinating season is summer through early fall.

WATER HEMP (*Acnida tamariscina*)
LAMB'S QUARTERS (*Chenopodium album*)
RUSSIAN THISTLE (*Salsola kale*)
RAGWEED, GIANT and SHORT (*Ambrosia* species)
MARSH ELDER/POVERTY WEED (*Iva* species)
COCKLEBUR (*Xanthium strumarium*)
DOCK/SORREL (*Rumex* species)
PIGWEED (*Amaranthus retroflexus*)
PLANTAIN (*Plantago lanceolata*)

Region VIII

Central midwestern states, U.S.: Illinois, Iowa, and Missouri.

Index trees: Mixed bluestem prairie and oak and hickory forest, and relatively large mixed areas; pollinating season is late winter through spring.

BOX ELDER/MAPLE (*Acer* species)
BIRCH (*Betula nigra*)
OAK (*Quercus* species)
HICKORY (*Carya ovata*)
WALNUT (*Juglans nigra*)
MULBERRY (*Morus* species)

ASH (*Fraxinus americana*)
SYCAMORE (*Platanus occidentalis*)
COTTONWOOD/POPLAR (*Populus deltoides*)
ELM (*Ulmus americana*)

Index grasses: Several genera, naturalized and/or cultivated for hay and lawns, although inconspicuous, are very abundant and significant in hay fever; pollinating season is spring through early summer.

REDTOP (*Agrostis alba*)
BERMUDA GRASS (*Cynodon dactylon*)
ORCHARD GRASS (*Dactylis glomerata*)
RYEGRASS (*Lolium* species)
TIMOTHY (*Phleum pretense*)
BLUEGRASS/JUNE GRASS (*Poa* species)
JOHNSON GRASS (*Sorghum halepense*)
CORN (*Zea mays*)

Index weeds: Although relatively few species of weeds are important, their widespread abundance and heavy pollination over a long season make them important hay fever plants; pollinating season is summer through early fall.

PIGWEED (*Amaranthus retroflexus*)
LAMB'S QUARTERS (*Chenopodium album*)
MEXICAN FIREBUSH (*Kochia scoparia*)
RUSSIAN THISTLE (*Salsola kall*)
RAGWEED, GIANT, SHORT, and WESTERN (*Ambrosia* species)
MARSH ELDER/POVERTY WEED (*Iva* species)
PLANTAIN (*Plantago lanceolata*)
DOCK/SORREL (*Rumex* species)
WATER HEMP (*Acnida tamariscina*)

Region IX

Great Plains states, U.S.: Kansas, Nebraska, North Dakota, and South Dakota.

Index trees: Mixed prairies; predominant trees cultivated. Pollinating season is late winter through spring.

BOX ELDER/MAPLE (*Acer* species)
ALDER (*Alnus incana*)
BIRCH (*Bethla* species)
HAZELNUT (*Corylus americana*)
OAK (*Quercus macrocarpa*)
HICKORY (*Carya ovata*)
WALNUT (*Juglans nigra*)
ASH (*Fraxinus americana*)
COTTONWOOD/POPLAR (*Populus deltoides*)
ELM (*Ulmus americana*)

Index grasses: This region is predominantly grassland, but the more important hay fever grasses are cultivated for hay or lawns or are naturalized pests; pollinating season is spring through early summer.

QUACK GRASS/WHEATGRASS (*Agropyron* species)
REDTOP (*Agrostis alba*)
BROME (*Bromus inermis*)
ORCHARD GRASS (*Dactylis glomerata*)
RYEGRASS (*Elymus* and *Lolium* species)
FESCUE (*Festuca elatior*)
TIMOTHY (*Phleum pretense*)
BLUEGRASS/JUNE GRASS (*Poa* species)

Index weeds: Although relatively few species of weeds are important, their widespread abundance and heavy pollination over a long season make them significant hay fever plants; pollinating season is summer through early fall.

WATER HEMP (*Acnida tamariscina*)
PIGWEED (*Amaranthus retroflexus*)
LAMB'S QUARTERS (*Chenopodium album*)
MEXICAN FIREBUSH (*Kochia scoparia*)
RUSSIAN THISTLE (*Salsola kale*)
RAGWEED, FALSE, GIANT, SHORT, and WESTERN (*Ambrosia* species)
SAGEBRUSH (*Artemisia* species)
MARSH ELDER/POVERTY WEED (*Iva* species)
COCKLEBUR (*Xanthium strumarium*)
PLANTAIN (*Plantago lanceolata*)
DOCK/SORREL (*Rumex* species)

Region X

Southwestern grasslands states, U.S.: Oklahoma and Texas.

Index trees: Shrub savannah in the west and south, central and northern mixed prairies, and eastern oak, hickory, and pine forests; pollinating season is late winter through spring.

BOX ELDER (*Acer negundo*)
CEDAR/JUNIPER (*Juniperus virginiana*)
OAK (*Quercus virginiana*)
MESQUITE (*Prosopis juliflora*)
MULBERRY (*Morus* species)
ASH (*Fraxinus americana*)
COTTONWOOD/POPLAR (*Populus deftoides*)
ELM (*Ulmus americana*)

Index grasses: This region is predominantly grassland, but the more important hay fever grasses are cultivated for hay or lawns or are naturalized pests; pollinating season is spring through early summer.

QUACK GRASS/WHEATGRASS (*Agropyron* species)
REDTOP (*Agrostis alba*)
BERMUDA GRASS (*Cynodon dactylon*)
ORCHARD GRASS (*Dactylis glomerata*)
FESCUE (*Festuca elatior*)
RYEGRASS (*Lolium* species)
TIMOTHY (*Phleum pretense*)
BLUEGRASS/JUNE GRASS (*Poa* species)
JOHNSON GRASS (*Sorghum halepense*)

Index weeds: Although relatively few species of weeds are important, their widespread abundance and heavy pollination over a long season make them important hay fever plants; pollinating season is summer through early fall.

WATER HEMP (*Acnida tamariscina*)
CARELESSWEED/PIGWEED (*Amaranthus* species)
SALTBUSH/SCALE (*Atriplex* species)
LAMB'S QUARTERS (*Chenopodium album*)

MEXICAN FIREBUSH (*Kochia scoparia*)
RUSSIAN THISTLE (*Salsola kale*)
RAGWEED, FALSE, GIANT, SHORT, and
  WESTERN (*Ambrosia* species)
SAGEBRUSH (*Artemisia* species)
MARSH ELDER/POVERTY WEED (*Iva*
  species)
COCKELBUR (*Xanthium strumarium*)
DOCK/SORREL (*Rumex* species)
PLANTAIN (*Plantago lanceolata*)

Region XI

Rocky Mountain empire states, U.S.: Arizona (mountainous), Colorado, Idaho (mountainous), Montana, New Mexico, Utah, and Wyoming.

Index trees: Mixed prairies and steppes to pinyon and juniper woodlands and mixed conifer forests, from lower elevation and latitude to higher; pollinating season is late winter through spring.

BOX ELDER (*Acer negundo*)
ALDER (*Alnus incana*)
BIRCH (*Betula fontinalis*)
CEDAR/JUNIPER (*Juniperus scopulorum*)
OAK (*Quercus gambelii*)
ASH (*Fraxinus americana*)
PINE (*Pinus* species)
COTTONWOOD/POPLAR (*Populus
  deltoides*) (*P. sargentii*)
ELM (*Ulmus* species)

Index grasses: Several genera, naturalized and/or cultivated for hay and lawns, although inconspicuous, are very abundant and significant in hay fever; pollinating season is spring through early summer.

QUACK GRASS/WHEATGRASS (*Agropyron*
  species)
REDTOP (*Agrostis alba*)
BROME (*Bromus inermis*)
BERMUDA GRASS (*Cynodon dactylon*)
ORCHARD GRASS (*Dactylis glomerata*)

RYEGRASS (*Elymus* and *Lolium* species)
FESCUE (*Festuca elatior*)
TIMOTHY (*Phleum pretense*)
BLUEGRASS/JUNE GRASS (*Poa* species)

Index weeds: Although relatively few species of weeds are important, their widespread abundance and heavy pollination over a long season make them important hay fever plants; pollinating season is summer through early fall.

WATER HEMP (*Acnida tamariscina*)
PIGWEED (*Amaranthus retroflexus*)
SALTBUSH/SCALE (*Atriplex* species)
SUGAR BEET (*Beta vulgaris*)
LAMB'S QUARTERS (*Chenopodium album*)
MEXICAN FIREBUSH (*Kochia scoparia*)
RUSSIAN THISTLE (*Salsola kale*)
RAGWEED, FALSE, GIANT, SHORT, and
  WESTERN (*Ambrosia* species)
SAGEBRUSH (*Artemisia* species)
MARSH ELDER/POVERTY WEED (*Iva*
  species)
COCKLEBUR (*Xanthium strumarium*)
PLANTAIN (*Plantago lanceolata*)
DOCK/SORREL (*Rumex* species)

Region XII

Arid southwestern states, U.S.: Arizona and southern California (S.E. desert).

Index trees: Creosote bush shrub and paloverde and cactus shrub; predominant trees cultivated. Pollinating season is winter through spring.

CYPRESS (*Cupressus arizonica*)
CEDAR/JUNIPER (*Juniperus californica*)
MESQUITE (*Prosopis juliflora*)
ASH (*Fraxinus velutina*)
OLIVE (*Olea europaea*)
COTTONWOOD/POPLAR (*Populus
  fremontii*)
ELM (*Ulmus parvifolia*)

Index grasses: Several genera, naturalized and/or cultivated for hay and lawns wherever possible, although inconspicuous, are significant in hay fever; pollinating season is spring through early summer.

BROME (*Bromus* species)
BERMUDA GRASS (*Cynodon dactylon*)
SALT GRASS (*Distichlis* species)
RYEGRASS (*Elymus* and *Lolium* species)
CANARY GRASS (*Phalaris minor*)
BLUEGRASS/JUNE GRASS (*Poa* species)

Index weeds: Although relatively few species of weeds are important, their widespread abundance and heavy pollination over a long season make them important hay fever plants. Many of these are shrubby relatives of weeds common in regions with more precipitation. Pollinating season is summer through early fall.

CARELESSWEED (*Amaranthus palmeri*)
IODINE BUSH (*Allenrolfea occidentalis*)
SALTBUSH/SCALE (*Atriplex* species)
LAMB'S QUARTERS (*Chenopodium album*)
RUSSIAN THISTLE (*Salsola kale*)
ALKALI BLITE (*Suaeda* species)
RAGWEED, FALSE, SLENDER, and
 WESTERN (*Ambrosia* species)
SAGEBRUSH (*Artemisia* species)
SILVER RAGWEED (*Dicoria canescens*)
BURROBRUSH (*Hymenoclea salsola*)

Region XIII

Southern coastal California.

Index trees: Chaparral and coastal sagebrush shrub to California steppe; many species of ornamental trees cultivated. Pollinating season is late winter through spring.

BOX ELDER (*Acer negundo*)
CYPRESS (*Cupressus arizonica*)
OAK (*Quercus agrifolia*)
WALNUT (*Juglans* species)

ACACIA (*Acacia* species)
MULBERRY (*Morus* species)
EUCALYPTUS (*Eucalyptus* species)
ASH (*Fraxinus velutina*)
OLIVE (*Olea europaea*)
SYCAMORE (*Platanus racemosa*)
COTTONWOOD/POPLAR (*Populus trichocarpa*)
ELM (*Ulmus* species)

Index grasses: Several genera, naturalized and/or cultivated for hay and lawns, although inconspicuous, are very abundant and significant in hay fever; pollinating season is spring through early summer.

OATS (*Avena* species)
BROME (*Bromus* species)
BERMUDA GRASS (*Cynodon dactylon*)
ORCHARD GRASS (*Dactylis glomerata*)
SALT GRASS (*Distichlis* species)
RYEGRASS (*Elymus* and *Lolium* species)
FESCUE (*Festuca elatior*)
BLUEGRASS/JUNE GRASS (*Poa* species)
JOHNSON GRASS (*Sorghum halepense*)

Index weeds: Although relatively few species of weeds are important, their widespread abundance and heavy pollination over a long season make them important hay fever plants; pollinating season is summer through early fall.

CARELESSWEED/PIGWEED (*Amaranthus* species)
SALTBUSH/SCALE (*Atriplex* species)
LAMB'S QUARTERS (*Chenopodium album*)
RUSSIAN THISTLE (*Salsola kali*)
RAGWEED, FALSE, SLENDER, and
 WESTERN (*Ambrosia* species)
SAGEBRUSH (*Artemisia* species)
COCKLEBUR (*Xanthium strumarium*)
PLANTAIN (*Plantago lanceolata*)
DOCK/SORREL (*Rumex* species)

Region XIV

Central California valley regions: Sacramento and San Joaquin valleys.

Index trees: California steppe bordered by California oakwoods; many species of ornamental, nut, and fruit trees cultivated. Pollinating season is late winter through spring.

BOX ELDER (*Acer negundo*)
ALDER (*Alnus rhombifolia*)
BIRCH (*Betula fontinalis*)
CYPRESS (*Cupressus arizonica*)
OAK (*Quercus lobata*)
PECAN (*Carya pecan*)
WALNUT (*Juglans* species)
ASH (*Fraxinus velutina*)
OLIVE (*Olea europaea*)
SYCAMORE (*Platanus acerifolia*)
COTTONWOOD/POPLAR (*Populus fremontii*)

Index grasses: Several genera, naturalized and/or cultivated for hay and lawns, although inconspicuous, are very abundant and significant in hay fever; pollinating season is spring through early summer.

REDTOP (*Agrostis alba*)
OATS (*Avena* species)
BROME (*Bromus* species)
BERMUDA GRASS (*Cynodon dactylon*)
ORCHARD GRASS (*Dactylis glomerata*)
SALT GRASS (*Distichlis* species)
RYEGRASS (*Elymus* and *Lolium* species)
FESCUE (*Festuca elatior*)
CANARY GRASS (*Phalaris minor*)
TIMOTHY (*Phleum pratense*)
BLUEGRASS/JUNE GRASS (*Poa* species)
JOHNSON GRASS (*Sorghum halespense*)

Index weeds: Although relatively few species of weeds are important, their widespread abundance and heavy pollination over a long season make them important hay fever plants; pollinating season is summer through early fall.

PIGWEED (*Amaranthus retroflexus*)
SALTBUSH/SCALE (*Atriplex* species)
SUGAR BEET (*Beta vulgaris*)
LAMB'S QUARTERS (*Chenopodium album*)
RUSSIAN THISTLE (*Salsola kali*)
RAGWEED, FALSE (*Franseria, acanthicarpa*)
RAGWEED, SLENDER (*Franseria tenuifolia*)

Region XV

Intermountain western states, U.S.: Idaho (southern) and Nevada.

Index trees: Sagebrush steppe, saltbush-greasewood and Great Basin sagebrush shrub; predominant trees cultivated. Pollinating season is late winter through spring.

BOX ELDER (*Acer negundo*)
ALDER (*Alnus rhombifolia*)
BIRCH (*Betula fontinalis*)
CEDAR/JUNIPER (*Juniperus utahensis*)
ASH (*Fraxinus velutina*)
SYCAMORE (*Platanus occidentalis*)
COTTONWOOD/POPLAR (*Populus trichocarpa*)
ELM (*Ulmus* species)

Index grasses: Several genera, naturalized and/or cultivated for hay and lawns wherever possible, although inconspicuous, are significant in hay fever; pollinating season is spring through early summer.

QUACK GRASS/WHEATGRASS (*Agropyron* species)
REDTOP (*Agrostis alba*)
BROME (*Bromus inermis*)
BERMUDA GRASS (*Cynodon dactylon*)
ORCHARD GRASS (*Dactylis glomerata*)
SALT GRASS (*Distichlis* species)
RYEGRASS (*Elymus* and *Lolium* species)
FESCUE (*Festuca elatior*)
TIMOTHY (*Phleum pratense*)
BLUEGRASS/JUNE GRASS (*Poa* species)

Index weeds: Although relatively few species of weeds are important, their widespread abundance and heavy pollination over a long season make them important hay fever plants. Many of these are shrubby relatives of weeds common in regions with more precipitation. Pollinating season is summer through early fall.

PIGWEED (*Amaranthus retroflexus*)
IODINE BUSH (*Allenrolfea occidentalis*)
SALTBUSH/SCALE (*Atriplex* species)
LAMB'S QUARTERS (*Chenopodium album*)
MEXICAN FIREBUSH (*Kochia scoparia*)
RUSSIAN THISTLE (*Salsola kali*)
RAGWEED, FALSE, SLENDER, and
    WESTERN (*Ambrosia* species)
SAGEBRUSH (*Artemisia* species)
MARSH ELDER/POVERTY WEED (*Iva*
    species)
COCKLEBUR (*Xanthium strumarium*)
PLAINTAIN (*Plantago lanceolata*)
DOCK/SORREL (*Rumex* species)

Region XVI

Inland empire states, U.S.: Oregon (central and eastern). and Washington (central and eastern).

Index trees: Bluegrass-fescue-wheat grass grasslands and sagebrush steppe bordered by coniferous forests; predominant trees cultivated. Pollinating season is late winter through spring.

BOX ELDER (*Acer negrundo*)
ALDER (*Alnus incana*)
BIRCH (*Betula fontinalis*)
OAK (*Quercuis garryana*)
WALNUT (*Juglans nigra*)
PINE (*Pinus* species)
COTTONWOOD/POPLA (*Populus
    trichocarpas*)
WILLOW (*Salix lasiandra*)

Index grasses: This region is predominantly grassland, but the more important hay fever grasses are cultivated for seed, hay, or

lawns or are naturalized pests; pollinating season is spring through early summer.

QUACK GRASS/WHEATGRASS (*Agropyron*
    species)
REDTOP (*Agrostis alba*)
VERNAL GRASS (*Anthoxanthum* species)
BROME (*Bromus inermis*)
ORCHARD GRASS (*Dactylis glomerata*)
RYEGRASS (*Elymus* and *Lolium* species)
VELVETGRASS (*Elymus* and *Lolium* species)
TIMOTHY (*Phleum pretense*)
BLUEGRASS/JUNE GRASS (*Poa* species)

Index weeds: Although relatively few species of weeds are important, their widespread abundance and heavy pollination over a long season make them important hay fever plants; pollinating season is summer through early fall.

PIGWEED (*Amaranthus retroflexus*)
SALTBUSH/SCALE (*Atriplex* species)
LAMB'S QUARTERS (*Chenopodium album*)
MEXICAN FIREBUSH (*Kochia scoparia*)
RUSSIAN THISTLE (*Salsola kali*)
RAGWEED, FALSE, GIANT, SHORT, and
    WESTERN (*Ambrosia* species)
SAGEBRUSH (*Artemisia* species)
MARSH ELDER/POVERTY WEED (*Iva*
    species)
PLAINTAIN (*Plantago lanceolata*)
DOCK/SORREL (*Rumex* species)

Region XVII

Cascade Pacific Northwest states, U.S.: California (northwestern), Oregon (western), and Washington (western).

Index trees: Mixed coniferous forests; hardwoods primarily cultivated. Pollinating season is late winter through spring.

BOX ELDER (*Acer negrundo*)
ALDER (*Alnus incana*)
BIRCH (*Betula fontinalis*)

HAZELNUT (*Corylus cornuta*)
OAK (*Quercuis garryana*)
WALNUT (*Juglans nigra*)
ASH (*Fraxinus oregona*)
COTTONWOOD/POPLAR (*Populus trichocarpas*)
WILLOW (*Salix lasiandra*)
ELM (*Ulmus* species)

Index grasses: Several genera, naturalized and/or cultivated for hay and lawns, although inconspicuous, are very abundant and significant in hayfever. Grass seed is produced extensively in parts of this region. Pollinating season is spring through early summer.

BENT GRASS (*Agrostis maritima*)
VERNAL GRASS (*Anthoxanthum* species)
OATS (*Avena* species)
BROME (*Bromus inermis*)
BERMUDA GRASS (*Cynodon dactylon*)
ORCHARD GRASS (*Dactylis glomerata*)
SALT GRASS (*Distichlis* species)
RYEGRASS (*Elymus and Lolium* species)
FESCUE (*Festuca elatior*)
CANARY GRASS (*Phalaris arundinacea*)
VELVETGRASS (*Elymus* and *Lolium* species)
TIMOTHY (*Phleum pretense*)
BLUEGRASS/JUNE GRASS (*Poa* species)

Index weeds: Although relatively few species of weeds are important, their widespread abundance and heavy pollination over a long season make them significant hay fever plants; pollinating season is summer through early fall.

PIGWEED (*Amaranthus retroflexus*)
SALTBUSH/SCALE (*Atriplex* species)
LAMB'S QUARTERS (*Chenopodium album*)
RUSSIAN THISTLE (*Salsola Kali*)
RAGWEED, FALSE, GIANT, SHORT, and WESTERN (*Ambrosia* species)
SAGEBRUSH (*Artemisia* species)
COCKELBUR (*Xanthium strumasrium*)
PLAINTAIN (*Plantago lanceolata*)
DOCK/SORREL (*Rumex* species)

Region: Alaska

Typical hay fever species of the three plant forms, trees, grasses, and weeds, are found in the southern coastal region that forms an arc from the southernmost point of the state northward, westward, and then southward to the Alaska peninsula. As a whole the state has three principal vegetation types:

1. Dense Sitka spruce and western hemlock forests. These trees are generally considered of very minor significance in allergy, if significant at all. However, alder, aspen, birch, and willow may be found in clearings and near watercourses and may be associated with grasses and some weeds in the early stages of plant succession.
2. Less dense forests of birches and white spruce. The birches may be the most significant pollinating trees because they form such extensive forests.
3. Tundra and tundralike, characterized by low vegetation, in the Aleutian Islands and on the Bering Sea coast and the Arctic slope. Very cold winters and very cool, moist summers are detrimental to tree growth. Grasses are predominant, but (as in tropical regions) the humidity and precipitation are so great that whatever airborne pollen is shed is not likely to remain airborne very long.

Index grasses and weeds are most common in the temperate agricultural and urban regions. The whole hay fever season is short, from three to six months according to latitude, elevation, and proximity to the seacoasts.

Index trees: Pollinating season is spring.

ALDER (*Alnus incana*)
ASPEN (*Populus tremuloides*)
BIRCH (*Betula papyrifera*)
CEDAR (*Thuja plicata*)
HEMLOCK (*Tsuga hetrophylla*)
PINE (*Pinus contorta*)
POPLAR (*Populus balsamifera*)
SPRUCE (*Picea sitchensis*)

WILLOW (*Salix* species)

Index grasses: Pollinating season is late spring and summer.

BROME (*Bromus inermis*)
ORCHARD GRASS (*Dactylis glomerata*)
RYEGRASS (*Elymus* and *Lolium* species)
FESCUE (*Festuca elatior*)
CANARY GRASS (*Phalaris arundinacea*)
TIMOTHY (*Phleum pretense*)
BLUEGRASS/JUNE GRASS (*Poa* species)
QUACK GRASSS (couch) (*Agropyron repens*)
REDTOP (*Agrostis alba*)

Index weeds: Pollinating season is summer.

BULRUSH (*Scirpus* species)
LAMB'S QUARTERS (*Chenopodium album*)
SAGEBRUSH/WORMWOOD (*Artemisia* species)
ENGLISH PLAINTAIN (*Plantago lanceolata*)
DOCK/SORREL (*Rumex* species)
NETTLE (*Urtica dioica*)
SEDGE (*Carex* species)
SPEARSCALE (*Atriplex patula*)

Region: Hawaiian Islands

Although Hawaii is small in total land surface, it has a wide range of habitats that vary from dense tropical forests to virtually barren mountaintops, from wet windward parts of islands to dry scrubland in the rain shadows. Consequently, the vegetation is extremely varied and complex, changing abruptly within short distances.

The seasonality of hay fever is less defined because the major agricultural and urban centers enjoy virtually a continuous growing season. Grasses and annual weeds may be flowering all year with one or few peak periods.

The long growing season and diversity of habitats create optimum situations for the establishment of newly introduced species, both deliberately and accidentally. (Humans have introduced some 500 species of grasses alone.) Entomophilous (insect vector) flowers abound; although they produce relatively little pollen per individual flower, their sheer abundance and widespread use may make them more important than would be expected according to Thommen's postulates. The enormous task of identifying, collecting, and purifying these pollens for clinical testing and assessing is still in developmental stages.

The pollinating season is more well defined than in continental regions.

Index trees:

ACACIA (*Acacia* species)
AUSTRALIAN PINE (beefwood) (*Casuarina equisetfolia*)
MONTEREY CYPRESS (*Cupressus macrocarpa*)
CEDAR/JUNIPER (*Juniperus* species)
DATE PALM (*Phoenix dactylifera*)
EUCALYPTUS (gum) (*Eucalyptus globulus*)
MESQUITE (*Prosopis juliflora*)
PAPER MULBERRY (*Broussonetia paspyrifera*)
OLIVE (*Olea europaea*)
PRIVET (*Ligustrum* species)

Index grasses:

BERMUDA GRASS (*Cynodon dactylon*)
CORN (*Zea mays*)
FINGER GRASS (*Chloris* species)
JOHNSON GRASS (*Sorghum halepense*)
LOVE GRASS (*Eragrotis* species)
BLUEGRASS/JUNE GRASS (*Poa* species)
REDTOP (*Agrostis alba*)
SORGHUM (*Sorghum vulgare*)

Index weeds:

COCKLEBUR (*Xanthium strumarium*)
SALTBUSH/SCALE (*Atriplex* species)
RAGWEED, SLENDER (*Ambrosia* species)
SAGEBRUSH (*Artemisia* species)
PIGWEED (*Amaranthus retroflexus*)
ENGLISH PLAINTAIN (*Plantago lanceolata*)
KOCHIAS (*Kochia scoparia*)

Canada: Region I

Atlantic provinces and Quebec: Prince Edward Island, Nova Scotia, New Brunswick, Newfoundland, and Quebec.

Index trees: From south to north, mixed wood forests and boreal forests open into woodlands and tundras through Quebec and Newfoundland, Acadian forests in the other provinces; pollinating season is late winter through spring.

BOX ELDER (*Acer negrundo*)
HARD MAPLE (sugar) (*Acer saccharum*)
TAG ALDER (speckled) (*Alnus incana*)
PAPER BIRCH (white) (*Betula papyrifera*)
BEECH (*Fagus grandifolia*)
WHITE ASH (*Fraxinus americana*)
GREEN ASH (*Fraxinus pennsylvanica*)
BUTTERNUT (*Juglans cinerea*)
SYCAMORE (*Platanus occidentalis*)
BALSAM/POPLAR (*Populus balsamifera*)
TREMBLING ASPEN (*Populus tremuloides*)
BUR OAK (*Quercuis macrocarpa*)
BLACK WILLOW (*Salix nigra*)
AMERICAN ELM (*Ulmus americana*)

Index grasses: Several genera, naturalized and/or cultivated for hay and lawns, are very abundant and more significant than the native grasses in hay fever; pollinating season is spring through early summer.

QUACK GRASS (couch) (*Agropyron repens*)
REDTOP (*Agrostis alba*)
BROME (*Bromus* species)
ORCHARD GRASS (*Dactylis glomerata*)
RYEGRASS (*Elymus* and *Lolium* species)
TIMOTHY (*Phleum pretense*)
BLUEGRASS/JUNE GRASS (*Poa* species)

Index Weeds: Although relatively few species of weeds are important, their abundance in agricultural and urban areas make them important hay fever plants. Pollinating season is summer through early fall.
REDROOT PIGWEED (*Amaranthus retroflexus*)

LAMB'S QUARTERS (*Chenopodium album*)
RUSSIAN THISTLE (*Salsola kali*)
RAGWEED (*Ambrosia* species)
ENGLISH PLAINTAIN (*Plantago lanceolata*)
DOCK/SORREL (*Rumex* species)

Canada: Region II

Ontario

Index trees: From south to north, mixed wood forests and boreal forests open into woodlands and tundras; pollinating season is late winter through spring.

BOX ELDER (Manitoba maple) (*Acer negrundo*)
HARD MAPLE (sugar) (*Acer saccharum*)
TAG ALDER (speckled)(*Alnus incana*)
PAPER BIRCH (white) (*Betula papyrifera*)
BEECH (*Fagus grandifolia*)
WHITE ASH (*Fraxinus americana*)
GREEN ASH (*Fraxinus pennsylvanica*)
BUTTERNUT (*Juglans cinerea*)
SYCAMORE (*Platanus occidentalis*)
BALSAM/POPLAR (*Populus balsamifera*)
TREMBLING ASPEN (*Populus tremuloides*)
BUR OAK (*Quercuis macrocarpa*)
BLACK WILLOW (*Salix nigra*)
AMERICAN ELM (*Ulmus americana*)
CHINESE ELM (Siberian) (*Ulmus pumila*)

Index grasses: Several genera, naturalized and/or cultivated for hay and lawns, are very abundant and more significant than the native grasses in hay fever; pollinating season is spring through early summer.

QUACK GRASSS (couch) (*Agropyron repens*)
REDTOP (*Agrostis alba*)
BROME (*Bromus* species)
ORCHARD GRASS (*Dactylis glomerata*)
RYEGRASS (*Elymus* and *Lolium* species)
TIMOTHY (*Phleum pretense*)
BLUEGRASS/JUNE GRASS (*Poa* species)

Index weeds: Although relatively few species of weeds are important, their abundance is agricultural and urban areas make them significant hay fever plants; pollinating season is summer through early fall.

REDROOT PIGWEED (*Amaranthus retroflexus*)
LAMB'S QUARTERS (*Chenopodium album*)
RUSSIAN THISTLE (*Salsola kali*)
RAGWEED (*Ambrosia* species)
ENGLISH PLAINTAIN (*Plantago lanceolata*)
DOCK/SORREL (*Rumex* species)

Canada: Region III

Prairie provinces and eastern British Columbia: Alberta, eastern British Columbia, Manitoba, and Saskatchewan.

Index trees: The southern third of the region is grassland and parkland, where the predominant trees are found only along watercourses or are cultivated. Cordilleran forests are in the west, mixed wood forests in the north, and boreal forests in the northern most parts. Pollinating season is late winter through spring.

BOX ELDER (Manitoba maple) (*Acer negrundo*)
TAG ALDER (speckled) (*Alnus incana*)
PAPER BIRCH (white) (*Betula papyrifera*)
GREEN ASH (*Fraxinus pennsylvanica*)
BALSAM/POPLAR (*Populus balsamifera*)
TREMBLING ASPEN (*Populus tremuloides*)
BUR OAK (*Quercus macrocarpa*)
YELLOW WILLOW (*Salix* species)
CHINESE ELM (Siberian) (*Ulmus pumila*)

Index grasses: The most populous part of this region is predominantly grassland, but the more important hay fever grasses are cultivated for hay or lawns or are naturalized pests; pollinating season is spring through early summer.

QUACK GRASS or WHEATGRASS (couch) (*Agropyron* species)
REDTOP (*Agrostis alba*)
COMMON WILD OATS (*Avena fatua*)
BROME (*Bromus* species)

ORCHARD GRASS (*Dactylis glomerata*)
RYEGRASS (*Elymus* and *Lolium* species)
TIMOTHY (*Phleum pretense*)
BLUEGRASS/JUNE GRASS (*Poa* species)

Index weeds: Although relatively few species of weeds are important in Canada, there are several more species in this region; their abundance in agricultural and urban areas make them important hay fever plants. Pollinating season is summer through early fall.

REDROOT PIGWEED (*Amaranthus retroflexus*)
LAMB'S QUARTERS (*Chenopodium album*)
RUSSIAN THISTLE (*Salsola kali*)
RAGWEED (*Ambrosia* species)
PLAINTAIN (*Plantago lanceolata*)
DOCK/SORREL (*Rumex* species)
SAGEBRUSH (*Artemisia* species)
MARSH ELDER/POVERTY WEED (*Iva* species)

Canada: Region IV

Western British Columbia and Vancouver Island.

Index trees: Except for the steppe, where the predominant trees are found only along watercourses or are cultivated, this region is cordilleran forest; pollinating season is late winter through spring.

BOX ELDER (Manitoba maple) (*Acer negrundo*)
RED ALDER (*Alnus rubra*)
SITKA ALDER (*Alnus sinuata*)
PAPER BIRCH (white) (*Betula papyrifera*)
SYCAMORE (*Platanus occidentalis*)
BLACK COTTONWOOD (*Populus trichocarpa*)
TREMBLING ASPEN (*Populus tremuloides*)
DOUGLAS FIR (*Pseudotsuga mwenziesii*)
GARRY'S BUR OAK (*Quercus garryana*)
YELLOW WILLOW (Pacific) (*Salix lasiandra*)
CHINESE ELM (Siberian) (*Ulmus pumila*)

Index grasses: Several genera, naturalized and/or cultivated for hay and lawns, are very abundant and more significant than the native grasses in hay fever; pollinating season is spring through early summer.

QUACKGRASS or WHEATGRASS (couch) (*Agropyron* species)
REDTOP (*Agrostis alba*)
TALL OAT GRASS (*Arrhenatherum elatius*)
COMMON WILD OATS (*Avena fatua*)
BROME (*Bromus* species)
ORCHARD GRASS (*Dactylis glomerata*)
RYEGRASS (*Elymus* and *Lolium* species)
TIMOTHY (*Phleum pretense*)
BLUEGRASS/JUNE GRASS (*Poa* species)

Index weeds: Although relatively few species of weeds are important, their abundance in agricultural and urban areas make them important hay fever plants; pollinating season is summer through early fall.

REDROOT PIGWEED (*Amaranthus retroflexus*)
LAMB'S QUARTERS (*Chenopodium album*)
RUSSIAN THISTLE (*Salsola kali*)
RAGWEED (*Ambrosia* species)
ENGLISH PLAINTAIN (*Plantago lanceolata*)
DOCK/SORREL (*Rumex* species)
MARSH ELDER/POVERTY WEED (*Iva* species)

Adapted from the *Pollen Guide for Allergy*, Hollister-Stier.

APPENDIX II: AVAILABLE RADIO-ALLERGOSORBENT (RAST) ALLERGY TESTS

(Some may not be available from all reference laboratories; the authors make no claims for significance of these substances as allergens, and they are listed only for purposes of completeness.)

OCCUPATIONAL ALLERGENS

Castor bean
Cottonseed
Ethylene oxide
Formaldehyde
Green coffee bean
Isocyanate, HDI
Isocyanate, MDI
Isocyanate, TDI
Ispaghula
Latex
Phtalic anhydride
Silk
Sunflower seed
Trimellitic anhydride
Wild silk

EPIDERMALS

Australian parrot droppings
Australian parrot feathers
Australian parrot serum protein
Budgerigar (parakeet) droppings
Budgerigar (parakeet) feathers
Budgerigar (parakeet) serum
Cat dander
Cat epithelium
Chicken feathers
Cow dander
Cow epithelium
Dog dander
Dog epithelium
Duck feathers
Gerbil hair
Goat epithelium
Goose feathers
Guinea pig epithelium
Hamster epithelium
Horse dander
Horse epithelium
Mouse epithelium
Mouse serum proteins
Mouse urine proteins
Parakeet (see Budgerigar)
Pigeon droppings
Rabbit epithelium
Rat epithelium
Rat serum proteins
Rat urine proteins
Sheep epithelium
Sheep wool
Swine epithelium

HOUSE DUST MITES

Dermatophagoides farinae
Dermatophagoides pteronyssinus

HOUSE DUST

House dust (Greer)
House dust (Hollister-Stier)

STORAGE MITES

Storage mite (*Acarus siro*)
Storage mite (*Glycytinagus domesticus*)
Storage mite (*Lepidoglypus destructor*)
Storage mite (*Tyrophagus putreus*)

INSECTS—Whole body

Cockroach

Fire ant (*Invicta*)
Fire ant (*Richteri*)
Flea
Mosquito

INSECTS—Venom
Bumble bee
Fire ant
Honeybee
Hornet, white face
Hornet, yellow face
Wasp, polistes
Yellow jacket

PARASITES
Ascaris
Echinococcus
Schistosoma

MISCELLANEOUS
Seminal fluid

GRASSES
Bahia grass
Bermuda grass
Brome grass
Canada bluegrass
Canary grass, reed
Corn, cultivated
Fescue, meadow
Gramma grass
Johnson grass
Kentucky bluegrass (June grass)
Koeler's grass
Meadow foxtail
Oat, cultivated
Oatgrass, tall
Orchard grass
Perennial rye
Quack grass
Redtop (Bent grass)
Reed grass, common
Ryegrass, cultivated
Ryegrass, Italian
Rye, wild
Salt grass

Sorghum grass
Sudan vernal
Sweet vernal
Timothy
Velvetgrass
Wheat, cultivated
Wheat, western

WEEDS
Alfalfa
Baccharis
Bassia
Burrobush
Burweed
Clover
Cocklebur
Daisy
Dandelion
Dog fennel
Eastern lily
English plantain
Firebush (Kochia)
Goldenrod
Honeysuckle
Iodine bush
Jerusalem oak
Lamb's quarters
Marsh elder, rough
Mexican tea
Mugwort (sagebrush)
Nettle
Ox-eye daisy
Pigweed, rough
Poverty weed
Rabbitbrush
Ragweed, common (short)
Ragweed, false
Ragweed, giant (tall)
Ragweed, southern
Ragweed, western
Russian thistle
Saltbush
Scale
Sheep sorrel
Sunflower
Water hemp

Wingscale
Wormwood (sagebrush)
Yellow dock

TREES
Acacia
Alder, tag
Alder, white
Almond
Apple
Ash, Arizona
Ash, white
Aspen
Bayberry
Beech
Birch, white
Box elder (maple)
Cedar, mountain
Cedar, red
Cedar, Rocky Mountain
Ceder, salt
Cottonwood, common eastern
Cottonwood, Fremont
Cottonwood, western
Cypress, Arizona
Cypress, bald
Cypress, Italian
Elm, American
Eucalyptus
Fir, Douglas
Gum, sweet
Hackberry
Hazelnut, American
Hemlock, eastern
Hickory, shellbark
Hickory, white
Juniper, western
Lilac
Locust, black
Maple (see box elder)
Maple, coastal
Maple, red
Maple, silver
Maple, sugar
Melaleuca
Mesquite

Mulberry, red
Mulberry, white
Oak, California black
Oak, coastal live
Oak, interior live
Oak, red
Oak, valley
Oak, Virginia live
Oak, white
Olive
Palm, queen
Pecan
Pine, Australian
Pine, loblolly
Pine, long-leaf
Pine, Monterey
Pine, short-leaf
Pine, slash
Pine, Virginia scrub
Pine, white
Poplar, Lombardy
Privet
Spruce
Sycamore, American
Walnut, black
Walnut, English
Willow, black
Willow, pussy

MOLDS
Alternaria tenuis
Aspergillus fumigatus
Aspergillus niger
Aureobasidium pullulans
Botrytis cinerea
Candida albicans
Cephlosporium acremonium
Chaetomium globosum
Cladosporium hebarum
Crytococcus terrus
Curvularia lunata
Curvularia specifera
Epicoccum purpurascens
Epidermophypton floccosum
Fusarium moniliforme
Fusarium solani

Helminthosporium holades
Helminthosporium sativum
Johnson grass smut
Monilia Sitophilia
Mucor racemosus
Nigrospora sphaerica
Oidiodendrum
Penicillium notatum
Phoma betae
Pullularia pullulans
Rhizopus nigricans
Rhodotorula
Spondylocladium citrovirens
Stemphylium botryosum
Stemphylium solani
Trichoderma viride
Trichophyton
Wheat stem rust

DRUGS
Insulin Specific IgE—Beef
Insulin Specific IgE—Human
Insulin Specific IgE—Pork
Insulin Specific IgG—Beef
Insulin Specific IgG—Human
Insulin Specific IgG—Pork
Protamine (insulin) Specific IgE
Protamine (insulin) Specific IgG
Penicilloyl Specific IgE (Pencillin)
Penicilloyl Specific IgG (Pencillin)

FOODS
Almond
Alpha lactalbumin
Apple
Baker's yeast
Barley
Beef
Beta lactoglobulin
Blue mussel
Brazil nut
Buckwheat

Carrot
Casein
Celery
Cheese, cheddar
Cheese, mold type
Chicken meat
Chocolate
Coconut
Codfish
Corn
Crab
Egg white
Egg yolk
Garlic
Gluten
Hazelnut
Kiwi fruit
Lamb
Lobster
Malt
Mango
Melons
Milk
Mustard
Oat
Orange
Parsley
Pea
Peanut
Pork
Potato
Rice
Rye
Salmon
Sesame seed
Shrimp
Soybean
Strawberry
Tomato
Tuna
Wheat
White bean

APPENDIX III: PROFESSIONAL ALLERGY ORGANIZATIONS

American Academy of Allergy and
Immunology (AAAI)
   611 E. Wells Street
   Milwaukee, WI 53202-3889
   800-822-2762 or 800-822-ASMA

American College of Allergy and
Immunology (ACAI)
   800 E. Northwest Highway
   Suite 1080
   Palatine, IL 60067
   800-842-7777 or 708-359-2800

American Dietetic Association
   216 West Jackson Blvd.
   Chicago, IL 60606-6995
   312-899-0040

American Lung Association
   (Call local Lung Association)

National Allergy and Asthma Network/
Mothers of Asthmatics
   3554 Chain Bridge Road
   Suite 200
   Fairfax, VA 22030
   800-878-4403

National Asthma Education Program
   National Heart, Lung, and Blood Institute
   Information Center
   P.O. Box 3015
   Bethesda, MD 20824
   301-251-1222

National Institute of Allergy and Infectious
Diseases
   National Institutes of Health
   Building 31
   9000 Rockville Pike
   Bethesda, MD 20892
   301-496-5717

National Jewish Center for Immunology and
Respiratory Medicine (formerly National
Jewish Hospital)
   1400 Jackson Street
   Denver, CO 80206
   800-222-LUNG

APPENDIX IV: LAY ALLERGY, ASTHMA, AND LUNG ORGANIZATIONS

The Asthma & Allergy Foundation of America
(AAFA)
1125 15th Street, NW, Suite 502
Washington, DC 20005
1-800-7-ASTHMA

U.S. Chapters

CALIFORNIA
AAFA Los Angeles Chapter
5225 Wilshire Blvd., Suite 705
Los Angeles, CA 90036
213-937-7859

FLORIDA
AAFA Florida State Chapter
c/o University Community Hospital
3100 E. Fletcher Ave.
Tampa, FL 33613
813-972-7872

ILLINOIS
AAFA Greater Chicago Chapter
111 North Wabash, Suite 909
Chicago, IL 60602
312-346-0745

MARYLAND
AAFA Maryland Chapter
5601 Loch Raven Blvd.
Baltimore, MD 21239
301-532-4135

Immune Deficiency Foundation
P.O. Box 586
Columbia, MD 21045
410-461-3127

MICHIGAN
AAFA Michigan State Chapter
6900 Orchard Lake Road, Suite 207
West Bloomfield, MI 48322
313-427-2202

MISSOURI
AAFA Greater Kansas City Chapter
7905 E. 134th Terrace
Grandview, MO 64030
816-966-8164

AAFA St. Louis Area Chapter
222 South Central, Suite 600
St. Louis, MO 63105
314-726-6866

NEW ENGLAND
AAFA New England Chapter
220 Boylston St., Suite 305A
Chestnut Hill, MA 02167
617-965-7771

NEW YORK
American Lung Association
1740 Broadway
New York, NY 10019
212-315-8700

NEBRASKA
Asthma and Allergy Foundation
Community Health Place, Suite 209-D
7101 Newport Avenue
Omaha, NE 69152
402-572-3073

PENNSYLVANIA
AAFA S.E. Pennsylvania Chapter
P.O. Box 249
Plymouth Meeting, PA 19402
215-825-0583

VIRGINIA
The Food Allergy Network
4744 Holly Avenue
Fairfax, VA 22030-5647
703-691-3179

Mothers of Asthmatics
5316 Summit Drive
Fairfax, VA 22030
703-385-4403

Canada Chapter

ONTARIO
Allergy/Asthma Information Association
65 Tromley Drive
Suite 10
Etobicoke, ON M9B 5Y7

APPENDIX V: PARAMETERS FOR THE OPERATION OF CAMPS FOR CHILDREN WITH ASTHMA

The Consortium on Children's Asthma Camps was established in 1988 to coordinate the camp activities of national organizations involved in the care of children with asthma. The consortium is a separate entity composed of representatives from the American Academy of Allergy and Immunology, the American College of Allergy and Immunology, the American Lung Association (ALA), the American Thoracic Society, the American Academy of Pediatrics, and the Asthma and Allergy Foundation of America (AAFA). Administrative staffing is currently provided by a representative of the American Lung Association.

The purpose of the consortium is to promote and foster asthma camps. The following individuals participated in the project: Allen Sosin, M.D., consortium chairman 1990–92, Farmington, MI; Joann Blessing-Moore, M.D., Palo Alto, CA; Rose Cardinal, AAFA, Washington, DC; Linda Ford, M.D., Papillion, NE; Paul Giroux, Fisons Corporation, Rochester, NY; Penny Goitier Fena, ALA of Hennepin County, Minneapolis, MN; Mark Holbrelch, M.D., Indianapolis, IN; Robert Lemanske, M.D., Madison, WI; Shane McDermott, ALA, New York, NY; Richard Nicklas, M.D., Rockville, MD; Sharon Reynolds, AAFA, Washington, DC; Diane Schuller, M.D., Danville, PA; David Seaman, M.D., Canton, MI; William Silvers, M.D., Englewood, CO; Robert Strunk, M.D., St. Louis, MO; Dick Sveum, M.D., Minneapolis, MN; Stephen Weisberg, M.D., consortium chairman-elect 1992–95, Minneapolis, MN; Michael Welch, M.D., San Diego, CA; Mary Worstell, AAFA, Washington, DC.

For information concerning the activities of the consortium contact: Penny Gettier Fena, Executive Administrator, Consortium on Children's Asthma Camps, c/o American Lung Association of Hennepin County, 1829 Portland Avenue, Minneapolis, MN 55404; 612-871-7332.

Disclaimer The purpose of these parameters is to educate staff and volunteers regarding practices and procedures to be followed in the operation of camps for children with asthma.

It should be recognized that each part of every parameter may not be applicable to all asthma camps. Further, it is not the intention of the Consortium on Children's Asthma Camps and its members to attempt to include every practice or procedure that might be desirable for or implemented by an asthma camp since conditions, facilities and the goals or objectives of all asthma camps are not identical or uniform.

In developing these parameters, the Consortium on Children's Asthma Camps and its members do not warrant, guarantee or insure that compliance with these parameters will prevent any or all problems related to the operation of camps for children with asthma; nor does the Consortium on Children's Asthma Camps assume any responsibility or liability concerning these problems.

Further, the Consortium on Children's Asthma Camps and its members hereby expressly disclaim any responsibility or duty to asthma camps directors, medical personnel, camp personnel and to campers and their families, for any such liability arising out of illness, injury or loss to any persons by the failure of such asthma camps, directors, medical personnel and camp personnel to adhere to these parameters.

Introduction Many organizations are involved in the area of health promotion for children with asthma. Over the past 20 years, asthma camps have been one of the vehicles which have been used to improve the quality of life for children with asthma. Asthma camps provide an enjoyable summer experience for children who may otherwise be unable to attend camps. The parameters that follow are derived in large part from the position statement of the American Lung Association published in March 1984 and the guidelines developed by the Pediatrics Committee of the American College of Allergy and Immunology.

The parameters that follow are the result of a collaborative effort of the American Lung Association, the American Thoracic Society, the American Academy of Allergy and Immunology, the American College of Allergy and Immunology, the Asthma and Allergy Foundation of America, and the American Academy of Pediatrics. The goals of this effort are to:

1. Promote the quality of medical care delivered at existing camps;
2. Provide parameters for educational goals; and
3. Promote the development of new asthma camps.

There are a number of formats that are in existence for asthma camps. The first is a day camp experience. In these camps, children spend their evenings at home but attend an organized camping program during the day. An overnight camping experience is the most common type of camp. These vary in format. At many camps for children with asthma the children participate in their own camping program. They either occupy a campsite for one or two weeks or they employ a portion of a larger campsite but do not integrate into the daily routine of the campers without asthma. A final format integrates children with asthma into a routine camping experience. The children with asthma are integrated into groups of regular campers. They do have spe-

cial times set aside for medical evaluation and asthma education. However, their recreational activities are taken along with the campers without asthma.

Regardless of the format, the goals and recommendations for medical care remain the same.

Goals and Objectives
A. *Goal:* The goal of any asthma-camp experience should be to decrease asthma morbidity and improve the quality of life of children with asthma.

B. *Objectives:*
1. Provide an enjoyable camping experience for children with asthma;
2. Provide education for children, adults, parents and medical personnel;
3. Promote improved self-care, self-image and independence for children with asthma, and
4. Graduate to regular camping experience.

Organization
A. *Support Organization:* Camps generally require a parent or support organization. This could be a local affiliate of the American Lung Association, a local medical society, a chapter of the Asthma and Allergy Foundation of America or a local children's hospital. Before beginning a new camp, such an organization would need to establish whether or not there is a need for a camp for children with asthma and what type of camping experience this should be. They should be fully aware of the potential costs of such an experience and the risks and benefits of a camp in their area.

B. *Medical Director:* The medical director should be a licensed physician with special training in asthma and allergy or pulmonary medicine.

C. *Planning Committee:* To ensure an enjoyable and educational camping experience, the work of many individuals is needed. Policy planning and direction for a camp should result from the combined efforts of a group of people. It is encouraged this group include a medical director, a head nurse and a camp staff member. The medical staff should have expertise in pulmonary problems in children. The planning committee may also include a head counselor, a psychologist, a pharmacist, a respiratory therapist and a social worker.

D. *Asthma Camp Policy:* Asthma camp policies including organization, chain of responsibility, physician responsibilities, nursing responsibilities, respiratory therapist responsibilities and standards of care should all be in writing. The camp should be accredited and/or its campsite should hold Site Approval from the American Camping Association.

Medical Policies

A. *Infirmary*: There should exist an infirmary or equivalent area where children may receive medical care. Dispensing of medications may take place in a variety of locations. However, a central infirmary should be provided to allow for medical assessment of acute or increasing asthma episodes. Recommended equipment includes:

1. A sufficient supply of a broad range of routine asthma medications. This will be the responsibility of the medical doctor and/or pharmacist.
2. Appropriate medications and equipment to manage increasing episodes of asthma. This should include oxygen, intravenous fluids and medications as well as equipment for resuscitation.
3. Routine medical supplies to deal with non asthma related problems such as infections, wounds and gastrointestinal problems.

B. *Medical Management:* A written protocol for the management of increasing asthma and non-asthma conditions should be developed by the medical director and head nurse and distributed to all personnel. These procedures should be followed by all physicians rotating through the camp in order to provide continuity.

C. *Staffing:*
1. There should be, at least, one physician on site and available 24 hours per day.
2. Allied health care personnel, including nurses and respiratory therapists, should be provided in an adequate number to assure good supervision of the campers.
3. All medical personnel should be trained and certified in cardiopulmonary resuscitation (CPR). Life support training is encouraged.
4. At least one nurse, skilled in first aid and asthma management, should be on site in the infirmary at all times. Nurses can otherwise participate in camp activities, educational programs and monitoring of camper status away from the infirmary. Nurse/camper ratio should be determined by each camp's planning committee.
5. All personnel should be fully oriented prior to the camping experience.

D. *Emergency Care:* Planning for transport of critically ill children to a specialized center must be arranged prior to the camp. This should include air transport where indicated. Local arrangements should also be made at the nearest emergency room for the treatment of non-asthma problems which cannot be handled in the infirmary.

E. Trips off campsite and special activities should be cleared with the medical director or day chief. Off-site guidelines for medical management and equipment should be established.

F. *Administrative Policy for Emergencies:* The administration of a camp should have a written policy in place to deal with any potential crisis at camp. This should include telephone numbers of all responsible individuals as well as an organized plan to be put into place at the time of any particular emergency. Such factors as counseling children, notifying parents and medicolegal aspects should all be kept in mind.

G. *Measurement of Pulmonary Functions:* Adequate equipment should be available for the objective measure of pulmonary functions.

H. *Camp Check-in and Check-out:* There should be an organized check-in and check-out time. Check-in for campers includes recent medication changes, increasing symptoms, questions and review of routine medications. Check-out should provide parents with information on medication changes.

I. Immunotherapy at camp is not recommended.

J. An infectious disease policy should be developed.

Suggested Medicines and Supplies
Medications:
1. Infeasible, inhaled and oral bronchodilators

2. Corticosteroids: oral, intravenous and topical
3. Antihistamines
4. Oxygen
5. Intravenous fluids
6. Antibiotics (oral and topical)
7. Acetaminophen
8. EpiPen or equivalent\

Supplies and Equipment:
1. Nebulizers
2. Adequate tubing and mouth pieces
3. Intravenous equipment
4. Peak flow meters
5. Sphygmomanometer
6. Theophylline level kits
7. Oxygen equipment
8. Resuscitation equipment
9. Equipment for minor trauma including antiseptics and dressings
10. Stethoscope
11. Otoscope
12. Communication system
13. Flashlight and tongue blades

Medical Questionnaire A complete medical questionnaire should be developed and provided to all potential campers. This should include a portion to be filled out by the family and a portion to be filled out by the physician. The information to be filled out by the parents should include:

1. History and severity of the child's asthma including recent hospitalizations, ICU care, hypoxic seizures, drug allergies and respiratory arrest, unconsciousness during severe episodes or extremely labile asthma.
2. Corticosteroid usage including type, dosage and dates of recent use, in the last year.
3. Personal data including parents' address and emergency telephone numbers. Additional telephone numbers if the parents are not available should be requested as well as insurance information.
4. A parental consent form for the administration of routine medical care in the event that the parent cannot be reached. Include consent for photographs and trips off campsite.
5. A recent photograph of child.
6. Dates of emergency visits and average school absenteeism in the last year.

Minimal Information Supplied by the Physician Should Include:

1. Current medications including dose.
2. Drug, food, animal, and stinging insect allergies.
3. Other health conditions.
4. Recent data base from a physical examination including height, weight, blood pressure, pulse rate, respiratory rate, pulmonary functions and theophylline level.
5. Physician telephone and beeper number.
6. Date of most recent tetanus booster, measles vaccine and history of varicella.
7. A physician's assessment of the potential benefits for the particular child.
8. Assessment of school absenteeism and emergency visits.

9. Indication if problems with depression, use of asthma to manipulate or disregard of increasing symptoms.

Record Keeping It is important to maintain adequate records on all children at camp. The following information should be routinely kept:

1. All medications including routine and emergency medications, their date and time of administration.
2. All physician orders should be in legible writing and signed.
3. The child's medical application, including a parent consent form, should be kept in a central location.
4. Pulmonary functions should be recorded.
5. A post-camp report should be prepared on each child and supplied to the physician and the parent in a timely fashion.
6. Documentation of all visits to the infirmary.
7. Charting of all medical problems.

Criteria for Camper Selection Camper selection should be established by the support organization and the medical staff. Criteria to assess need should include:

1. Severity of asthma;
2. Previous camping experience;
3. Parent and physician assessment of potential benefits of a camping experience; and
4. Appropriate age limits met.

In camps that are over subscribed, a policy should be developed concerning the prioritization of applications.

Administration

A. *Insurance:*
1. The camp should make arrangements for liability coverage in an amount appropriate to the size and scope of the camp.
2. All medical and allied health care personnel should be required to carry malpractice insurance.
3. Accident insurance should be provided for all children.
4. Director liability.

B. *Contracts:* Detailed contracts should be obtained from the camping facility and this should be the responsibility of the administrative director of the supporting organization.

Program of Activities

A. *Education—Children:* Most camps will develop their own education program based on their facilities, personnel and previous experience with an asthma education program. These should be integrated into the camping day. A written program with goals should be prepared prior to camp. The education program should be age appropriate.

The following objectives should be considered:

1. Identify and react to early warning signs of asthma;
2. Identify and avoid triggers;
3. Proper relaxation technique and breathing technique;
4. Understanding of medication therapy;
5. Appropriate inhaler use;
6 Improvement in self-care skills;
7. Appropriate use of a peak flow meter;
8. Education of others who don't have asthma;
9. Treatment of exercise induced asthma; and
10. Dealing with peer groups in areas of medications and possible decreased exercise tolerance, smoking, etc.

B. *Education—Parents:* An optional program for parents should be considered. It should cover the topics noted above.

C. *Education—Medical Personnel:* Fellows, residents, medical, nursing, pharmacy and respiratory therapy students can get valuable experience as observers of camp participants.

D. *Camp Activities:* Camp activities should be designed with enjoyment for the children in mind. Certain restrictions may need to be taken into account. However, in general, they should be encouraged to participate in all activities. Children can often be integrated into the usual program developed by the camp. If the camp has its own staff of counselors, then these individuals should be made aware of any limitations that the children might have. When children are taken off the campsite for activities, a nurse, respiratory therapist or other trained personnel must accompany them. The medical staff need to be made aware of special activities and off-site trips.

Appendix I.

Suggested Recreational Facilities:
1. Swimming pool or lake
2. Class area
3. Area for educational activities
4. Nature activities
5. Sports activities

Appendix II.

Responsibilities of the Medical Director:
1. Responsibility for recruiting appropriate physician coverage for camp.
2. Development of protocols for the therapy of increasing asthma and other medical problems.
3. General supervision of the entire medical staff and designating a daily chief.
4. Responsible for assuring all appropriate medications and emergency equipment is obtained and readily available.

5. Developing liaisons with local emergency rooms and arrangement for transportation and admission of critically ill children.
6. Reviewing plans for dealing with medical emergencies.
7. Reviewing the medical records of all campers.
8. Communicate in a timely manner with physicians referring children to camp.
9. Communicate in a timely manner with family members.

Appendix III

Responsibilities of the Head Nurse:
1. Recruit appropriate nursing personnel for camp.
2. Determine appropriate camper/nurse ratios.
3. Coordinate administration of medications with respiratory therapy.
4. Take responsibility for appropriate charting of medications.
5. Coordinate protocols for treatment of asthma and non-asthma related medical problems.
6. Institute treatment protocol for increasing asthma episodes.

Slightly revised from the *American Academy of Allergy & Immunology News & Notes*, Issue 3, 1991, pages 28-31.

BIBLIOGRAPHY

Adams, R. M. "Recent Advances in Contact Dermatitits." *Annals of Allergy* 67 (1991):552–67.

Allergy Control Products, Inc. *Allergy Control Solution.* Ridgefield, Conn., 1990.

Allergy Products Directory. 2d ed. American Allergy Association, 1987.

Alexander, A. G.; Barnes, N. C.; and Kay, B. K. "Trial of Cyclosporin in Corticosteroid-dependent Chronic Severe Asthma." *Lancet* 339 (1992):324–28.

American Academy of Allergy and Immunology. *Allergy Relief Guide.* Milwaukee, Wis., 1990.

American Academy of Allergy and Immunology. "Position Statements from the American Academy of Allergy and Immunology." *Journal of Allergy and Clinical Immunology* 78 (1986):269–77.

American College of Allergy and Immunology. *Position Statement: Beta-2 Agonists.* Palentine, Ill., 1991.

American College of Allergy and Immunology. *Position Statement: Monosodium Glutamate (MSG).* Palatine, Ill., 1991.

American Thoracic Society. "Guidelines for the Approach to the Patient with Severe Hereditary Alpha-1-Antitrypsin Deficiency." *American Review of Respiratory Disease* 140 (1989):1494–97.

Anderson, J. A., and Adkinson, N. F. "Allergic Reactions to Drugs and Biologic Agents." *Journal of the American Medical Association* (hereafter, *JAMA*) 258 (1987):2891-99

Anderson, J. A., and Sogn, D. D., eds. *Adverse Reactions to Foods.* American Academy of Allergy and Immunology Committee on Adverse Reactions to Foods and National Institute of Allergy and Infectious Diseases. U.S. Department of Health and Human Services, Public Health Service, National Institutes of Health, Bethesda, Md., Publication No. 84-2442, 1984.

"Asthma Linked to Tot Stress." *Asbury Park Press,* May 6, 1992.

Bachman, J. L. *Ensuring Clean Air.* Delmar, Calif.: Health Services Consultants, 1989.

Bahna, S. L., ed. *Adverse Reactions to Foods and Additives.* VI International Food Allergy Symposium, Boston, Nov. 13–14, 1987.

Bahna, S. L.; Berman, B. A.; and Bernstein, I. L., eds. "Allergy and Headache: Current Concepts." *Allergy Observer* 7 (1990):1–2.

Bahna, S. L.; Berman, B. A.; and Bernstein, I. L., eds. "Cat Antigen, Lurking 'Everywhere' Appears to Be Dispersed Casually from Clothing." *Allergy Observer* 7 (1990):6.

Bahna, S. L.; Berman, B. A.; and Bernstein, I. L., eds. "Permanent Anonychia Tied to Nail Preparation Use." *Allergy Observer* 7 (1990):6.

Bahna, S. L.; Berman, B. A.; and Bernstein, I. L., eds. "Prolonging Venom Rx in High-Risk Cases Held 'Benign' Option." *Allergy Observer* 7 (1990):3.

Bahna, S. L.; Berman, B. A.; and Bernstein, I. L., eds. "Viral URIs and Asthma: Case for Prolonged Attacks Bolstered." *Allergy Observer* 7 (1990):1–2.

Barkman, W. B.; Merchant, J. A.; and Yeung, M. "When Asthma Is Work Related." *Patient Care,* Oct. 15, 1991.

Bellanti, J. A., ed. *Immunology III.* Philadelphia: W. B. Saunders, 1985.

Bennett, D. R. ed. in chief. *Drug Evaluations Subscription.* Chicago: American Medical Association, 1992.

Berkow, R., and Fletcher, A. J., eds. *Merck Manual, General Medicine.* 15th ed. Rahway, N.J.: Merck, Sharp, & Dohme Research Labs, 1987.

Bernstein, D. I., ed. "Guidelines for the Diagnosis and Evaluation of Occupational Lung

Disease." *Journal of Allergy and Clinical Immunology* (supplement), 84 (1989):791–844.

Bierman, C. W., and Pearlman, D. S. *Allergic Diseases of Infancy, Childhood, and Adolescence.* Philadelphia: W. B. Saunders, 1980.

Borish, L. "Cytokines and Allergy." *Allergy Principles and Practice,* 3d ed., edited by E. Middleton, et. al. St. Louis: C. V. Mosby, 1991.

Braunwald, E.; Isselbacher, K. J.; Petersdorf, R. G.; et al., eds. *Harrison's Principles of Internal Medicine.* 11th ed. New York: McGraw-Hill; 1987.

Butcher, B. T., and Salvaggio, J. E. "Occupational Asthma." *Journal of Allergy and Clinical Immunology* 78 (1986):547–59.

Casale, T. B.; Sampson, H. A.; Hanifin, J.; et al. "Guide to Physical Urticarias." *Journal of Clinical Immunology* 82 (1988):758–63.

Centers for Disease Control. "HIV/AIDS Knowledge and Awareness of Testing and Treatment—Behavioral Risk Factor Surveillance." *JAMA* 267 (1992):27.

Centofanti, M. "Immunotherapy by Mouth." *Johns Hopkins Asthma and Allergy Center Update* 1 (1992):1–3.

Chandra, et. al. *Clinical Allergy* 15 (1985):45–48.

Chan-Yeung, M. "A Clinician's Approach to Determine the Diagnosis, Prognosis, and Therapy of Occupational Asthma." *Medical Clinics of North America* 74 (1990): 811–22.

Chapman, M. D. "Purification of Allergens." *Current Opinion in Immunology* 1 (1989):647–53.

Condemi, J. J. "The Autoimmune Diseases." *JAMA* 287 (1981):2920–29.

Council on Scientific Affairs of the American Medical Association. "In Vitro Testing for Allergy; Report II of the Allergy Panel." *JAMA* 258 (1987):1639–43.

"A Daily Pill to prevent IDDM?" *Modern Medicine* 60 (1992):37.

Denny, F. W. "Defined Diets and Childhood Hyperactivity." *National Institutes of Health Consensus Development Conference Summary,* Vol. 4, 1982.

Dwyer, J. M. "Immunological Disturbances in Patients with the Chronic Fatigue Syndrome." *Immunology Updates* 3 (1991):1–6.

Fearson, D. "Complement, C Receptors, and Immune Complex Disease." *Hospital Practice,* Aug. 15, 1988, 63–72.

Fisons Corporation. *The Environmental Answer.* Rochester N.Y., 1990.

Food and Drug Administration. *Backgrounder: Monosodium Glutamate (MSG).* Washington, D.C., 1991.

Food and Drug Administration. "New Warnings for Seldane, Hismanal." *FDA Medical Bulletin,* Sept. 1992.

Food Sensitivity. Ross Laboratories General Information Series (pamphlet), Columbus Ohio,1989.

Gardner, R. M. "American Thoracic Society: Standardization of Spirometry—1987 Update." *American Review of Respiratory Disease* 136 (1987):1285–98.

Gerrard, J. W. *Food Allergy—New Perspectives.* Springfield, Ill.: Charles C. Thomas, 1980.

Gershwin, M. E., and Nagy, S. M. *Evaluation and Management of Allergic and Asthmatic Diseases.* New York: Grune & Stratton, 1979.

Geurkink, N. "Nasal Anatomy, Physiology, and Function." *Journal of Allergy and Clinical Immunology* 72 (1983):123–28.

Glanze, W. D.; Anderson, K. N.; and Anderson, L. E. *The Signet/Mosby Medical Encyclopedia.* New York, C. V. Mosby, 1987.

Glovsky, M. M. "Applications of Complement Determinations in Human Disease." Pasadena: Nichols Institute, 1992.

Graft, D.; Aaronson, D., Chervinsky, P., et al. A placebo- and active-controlled randomized trial of prophylactic treatment of seasonal allergic rhinitis with mometasone furoate aqueous nasal spray. *Journal of Allergy and Clinical Immunology* 98 (1996) 724–731).

Grekin, R. C., and Auletta, M. J. "Local Anesthesia in Dermatologic Surgery." *Journal of the American Academy of Dermatology* 19 (1988):599–614.

Hanifin, J. M. "Management Strategies for Atopic Dermatitis and Urticaria." *Journal of Respiratory Disease* 13 (1992):S14–23.

Healy, M. "Passive Smoke Linked to Kids' Ear Infections." *USA Today*, Aug. 5, 1992.

How to Avoid Stinging Insects. West Haven, Conn.: Hollister-Stier, 1988.

Jaret, P. "Our Immune System, the Wars Within." *National Geographic* 6 (1986):708.

Kaplan, A.; Buckley, R. H.; and Mathews, K. P. "Allergic Skin Disorders." *JAMA* 2588 (1987):2900–09

Keahey, T. M. "Urticaria and Angioedema: Differential Diagnosis." Workshop No. F301, American Academy of Allergy and Immunology 46th Annual Meeting, 1990.

Knapp, P. H. "Behavioral Help for Asthmatics." *Practical Psychology for Physicians*, Apr. 1975, 49–55.

Kordash, T. R., ed. *Allergy Forum* 3 (1991):1–8.

Lanzkowsky, S.; Lanzkowsky, L.; and Lanzkowsky, P. "Henoch-Schöenlein Purpura." *Pediatrics in Review* 13 (1992):130–37.

Lawlor, G. J., and Fischer, T. J., eds. *Manual of Allergy and Immunology.* 1st ed. Boston: Little, Brown, 1981.

Lawlor, G. J., and Fischer, T. J., eds. *Manual of Allergy and Immunology.* 2d ed. Boston: Little, Brown, 1982.

Letz, G. A. "Sick Building Syndrome: Acute Illness among Office Workers—The Role of Building Ventilation, Airborne Contaminants, and Work Stress." *Allergy Proceedings* 11 (1990):109–16.

Lichtenstein, L. M., and Simons, F. E. R. "Advancement in Antiallergy Therapy: Beyond Conventional Antihistamines." *Journal of Allergy and Clinical Immunology* 86 (1990): 995–1046.

Lindgren, S.; Lokshin, B.; Stromquist, A.; et al. "Does Asthma or Treatment with Theophylline Limit Children's Academic Performance?" *New England Journal of Medicine* 327 (1992):926–30.

Lockey, R. F., and Bukantz, S. C., eds. "Primer on Allergic and Immunologic Diseases." *JAMA* 258 (1987):2832–3038.

Mabry, R. L. "Uses and Misuses of Intranasal Corticosteroids and Cromolyn." *American Journal of Rhinology* 15 (1991):121–24.

McGrew, R. E. *Encyclopedia of Medical History.* New York: McGraw-Hill, 1985.

Mackay, I. S. ed. *Rhinitis Mechanisms and Management.* London: Royal Society of Medicine Services Limited, 1989.

Margileth, A. M. "What to Use for Cat-Scratch Fever." *Medical Tribune,* Mar. 1992.

Mathison, D. A.; Stevenson, D. D.; and Simon, R. A. "Precipitating Factors in Asthma—Aspirin, Sulfites, and Other Drugs and Chemicals." *Advances in Diagnosis and Treatment of Asthma,* Supplement to Chest (1985):50–54S.

Mead Johnson Nutritionals. *Pediatric Products Handbook.* Evansville, Ind., 1990.

Middleton, E.; Reed, C. E.; Ellis, E. S.; et al. eds. *Allergy Principles and Practice.* 3d ed. St. Louis: C. V. Mosby, 1988.

Mizel, S. B. "The Interleukins." *FASEB Journal* 3 (1989):2379–88.

Munro, C. S., et al. "Cyclosporin A in Atopic Dermatitis: Therapeutic Response Is Dissociated from Effects on Allergic Reactions." *British Journal of Dermatology* 124 (1991):43–48.

Nardi, G. L., and Zuidema, G. D. *Surgery.* 3d ed. Boston: Little, Brown, 1972.

National Asthma Education Program. Working Group on Asthma and Pregnancy. *Management of Asthma during Pregnancy.* U.S. Department of Health and Human Services, Public Health Service, National Institutes of Health, Bethesda, Md., Publication No. 93-3279A, Oct. 1992.

National Asthma Education Program Expert Panel Report. *Guidelines for the Diagnosis and Management of Asthma.* U.S. Department of

Health and Human Services, Public Health Service, National Institutes of Health, Bethesda, Md., Publication No. 91-3042, 1991.

National Heart, Lung, and Blood Institute. *Asthma*. Bethesda, Md., 1990.

National Heart, Lung, and Blood Institute. *Data Fact Sheet: Asthma Statistics*. Bethesda, Md., 1989.

National Heart, Lung, and Blood Institute. *Mastocytosis: Backgrounder*. Bethesda, Md., 1993.

Navarra, T. "A Guide to Alternative Treatments." *Asbury Park Press*, Apr. 7, 1992.

Navarra, T. *Your Body: Highlights of Human Anatomy*. Asbury Park, N.J.: Asbury Park Press, 1991.

Nelson, H. S.; Hirsch, S. R.; Ohman, J. L.; Platts-Mills, T. A. E., et al. "Recommendations for the Use of Residential Air-cleaning Devices in the Treatment of Allergic Respiratory Diseases." *Journal of Allergy and Clinical Immunology* 82 (1988):661–69.

Nelson, R. *Pollen Guide for Allergy*. Hollister-Stier Laboratories, 1975.

Nelson, R. P., and Lockey, R. F. "How You Can Control Asthma Triggers." *Journal of Respiratory Disease* 13 (1992):1175–76.

Nolte, H. "Clinical Aspects of Basophil Histamine Release." *Immunology and Allergy Practice* 14 (1992):255.

Ownby, O. R.; Johnson, C. C.; and Peterson, E. L. "Maternal Smoking Does Not Influence Cord Serum IgE or IgD Concentrations." *Journal of Allergy and Clinical Immunology* 88 (1991):555.

Parks, D. "Exercise-induced Asthma." *Update—National Jewish Center for Immunology and Respiratory Medicine* 10 (1992):1–5.

Parks, P. "The Role of Cockroach Sensitivity in Chronic Asthma." *Allergy Forum* 3 (1991):2–7.

Paterson R. "Diagnosis and Treatment of Drug Allergy." *Journal of Allergy and Clinical Immunology* 267 (1988):27.

Patient Information on Allergic Reactions to Insect Stings. American Academy of Allergy and Immunology.

Peter, J. B., and Reyes, H. *Use and Interpretation of Tests in Allergy and Immunology*. Santa Monica: American Academy of Allergy and Immunology, 1992.

Pierson, W. E., and Bierman, C. W. "Exercise-induced Asthma and How to Manage It." *Current Issues in Allergy and Immunology* 2 (1991):1–11.

Platts-Mills, T. A. E. "Allergens and Asthma." *Allergy Proceedings* 11 (1990):269.

Platts-Mills, T. A. E., and de Weck, A. L. "Report of the International Workshop on Dust Mite Allergens and Asthma." *Journal of Allergy and Clinical Immunology* 83 (1989):416–17.

Pollart, S. M., and Platts-Mills, T. A. E. "Mite and Mite Allergy as Risk Factors for Asthma." *Annals of Allergy* 63 (1989):364–65.

Rubenstein, E., and Federman, D. D., eds. *Scientific American Medicine*. New York: Scientific American, 1987.

Salvaggio, J. E. "Hypersensitivity Pneumonitis." *Journal of Allergy and Clinical Immunology* 79 (1987):559–71.

Sampson, H. A. "Food Allergy and the Role of Immunotherapy." *Journal of Allergy and Clinical Immunology* 90 (1992):151–52.

Sampson, H. A. "Late-Phase Response to Food in Atopic Dermatitis." *Hospital Practice* (1987):111–28.

Sampson, H. A., and McCaskill, C. C. "Food Hypersensitivity and Atopic Dermatitis." *Journal of Pediatrics* 107 (1985):69975.

Sampson, H. A.; Mendelson, L.; and Rosen, J. P. "Fatal and Near-Fatal Anaphylactic Reactions to Food in Children and Adolescents." *New England Journal of Medicine* 327 (1992):380–84.

Sanders, N. *A Parent's Guide to Asthma*. New York: Doubleday, 1989.

Schatz, M. "Can Menstruation Worsen Allergy Symptoms?" *Journal of Respiratory Diseases* 9 (1988):13.

Scherr, M. S. *Broncho Junction*. Red House, W. Va., n.d.

Schindler, L. W. *Understanding the Immune System.* U.S. Department of Health and Human Services, Public Health Service, National Institutes of Health, Bethesda, Md., Publication No. 88-529, 1980.

Seligmann, M., Chairman, IUIS/WHO Working Group. "Use and Abuse of Laboratory tests in Clinical Immunology: Critical Considerations of Eight Widely Used Diagnostic Procedures." *Clinical and Experimental Immunology* 46 (1981):662–74.

Sheffer, A. L. "Anaphylaxis." *Journal of Allergy and Clinical Immunology* 75 (1985):227.

Simon, R. A. "Adverse Reactions to Food and Drug Additives." *Immunology and Allergy Practice* 9 (1989):12–16.

Slater, J. E. "Latex Allergy—What Do We Know?" *Journal of Allergy and Clinical Immunology* 90 (1992):279–81.

Slavin, R. G., and Norback, C. T., eds. *The Allergy Encyclopedia.* St. Louis: C. V. Mosby, 1981.

Smith, L. G., and Sensakovic, J. W. "The Quinolones: Antibiotics for the 1990s." *Clinician* 9 (1991):2–4.

Solomon, W. R. "Fungi as Factors in Allergy." *Asthma and Allergy Advance* 10 (1992):1–2.

Sorkness, C. A. "Clinical Pharmacology of New Agents in the Airways and Other Organs." Syllabus, American College of Allergy, Asthma and Immunology Annual Meeting, Boston, 1996, pp. 1–5.

Sosin, A. Chairman, Consortium on Children's Asthma Camps, "Parameters for the Operation of Camps for Children with Asthma." *American Academy of Allergy and Immunology News and Notes* 3 (1991):28–31.

Spector, S., and Sandor, S. *Understanding Asthma.* Palatine, Ill.: American College of Allergy and Immunology, 1990.

Stafford, C. T. "Fire Ant Allergy." *Allergy Proceedings* 13 (1992):11–16.

Stoy, P. J.; Roitman-Johnson, B.; Walsh, G.; et al. "Aging and Serum Immunoglobulin E Levels, Immediate Skin Tests, and RAST." *Journal of Allergy and Clinical Immunology* 68 (1989):421–26.

Strunk, R. C.; Mascia, A.V.; Lipkowitz, M.A.; Wolf, S.I. "Rehabilitation of a patient with asthma in the outpatient setting." *Journal of Allergy and Clinical Immunology* 87 (1991):608

U.S. Department of Health and Human Services. *Diptheria, Tetanus, and Pertussis—What You Need to Know.* Atlanta: Centers for Disease Control, 1992.

U.S. Department of Health and Human Services. *Measles, Mumps, and Rubella—What You Need to Know.* Atlanta: Centers for Disease Control, 1992.

Use of Hydrolysate Feedings in Infants. Columbus: Ross Laboratories, 1989.

Wall, M. A. "Update of the Effects of Passive Smoking in Children." *Journal of Respiratory Disease* 9 (1987):31–36.

Wallis, C. "Why New Age Medicine Is Catching On." *Time,* Apr. 4, 1991.

Weis, B. ed. in chief. "Interaction between the Allergest and the Occupational Physician." *Symposium Digest* 4 (1992):1–6.

Williams, P. V., and Shapiro, G. G. "Avoiding the Abuses of Allergy Skin Testing." *Journal of Respiratory Disease* 11 (1990):891–904.

Winter, R. *A Consumer's Dictionary of Cosmetic Ingredients.* New York: Crown, 1989.

Winter, R. *A Consumer's Dictionary of Food Additives.* New York: Crown, 1989.

Wynbrandt, J., and Ludman, M. D. *The Encyclopedia of Genetic Disorders and Birth Defects.* New York: Facts On File, 1991.

Young, S. H.; Shulman, S. A.; and Shulman, M. D. *The Asthma Handbook.* Toronto: Bantam Books, 1985.

Yunginger, J. W. "Lethal Food Allergy in Children—An Editorial." *New England Journal of Medicine* 327 (1992):421–22.

INDEX

Boldface page numbers indicate extensive treatment of a topic.
Page numbers followed by t indicate tables.

A

AAAI *see* American Academy of Allergy and Immunology
AAFA *see* Asthma and Allergy Foundation of America
AAT deficiency *see* alpha-1-antitrypsin deficiency
ABAI *see* American Board of Allergy and Immunology
abdominal cramps
  amines, vasoactive 18
ABGs *see* arterial blood gases
abietic acid (sylvic acid) **1**
abirukana 187t
ABPA *see* allergic bronchopulmonary aspergillosis
acacia (gum acacia, gum Arabic, catechu) **1**, 187t, 257t
  hay fever 257t
  occupational asthma 187t
  pollen distribution (U.S.)
    Hawaiian Islands 305
    southern coastal California (Region XIII) 301
    radioallergosorbent (RAST) tests 311t
ACAI *see* American College of Allergy and Immunology
acaracides **1** *see also* benzyl benzoate; tannic acid solution
acetaldehyde (acetic aldehyde, ethanal) **1**
acetanilid **1**
acetarsone (acetarsol) **1**
acetic acid *see* vinegar
acetic aldehyde *see* acetaldehyde
acetic anhydride (acetic oxide, acetyl oxide) **1–2**
acetone (dimethyl ketone) **2**
acetophenone **2**
acetyl cysteine (Mucomist) **2**
acetyl oxide *see* acetic anhydride
acid anhydrides
  chemical sensitivity 66
acid-base balance *see* pH
acne medications
  calcium sulfide 59
acquired cold urticaria *see* cold urticaria, essential
acquired immunodeficiency syndrome *see* AIDS (acquired immunodeficiency syndrome)
acrivastine (Prolert, Semprex-D) **4**
  antihistamines 30t
acrylates and acrylics **4**
  contact dermatitis 79

ACTH *see* corticotropin
ACTH (adrenocorticotropic) 94t
Actidil *see* triprolidine
Actifed *see* triprolidine
actinomycetes **4**
  air-conditioning 7
  farmer's lung 108
active immunity *see* immunity, active
Acular *see* ketorolac tromethamine
acupressure **4**
acupuncture **4–5**
additives *see* food additives
adenoids **5**
adhesives
  latex allergy 162
  metals and metallic salts 172
adipic acid 187t
adolescents
  asthma in 35
adrenal glands
  corticosteroids 81–82
  epinephrine 103
Adrenalin *see* epinephrine
adrenergic drugs **5** *see also* alpha-adrenergic agonists; beta-adrenergic agonists
adverse reaction to food *see* food allergy
Advil *see* ibuprofen
aeroallergens **5–6** *see also* fungi; inhalant allergies; pollen
Aerobid *see* flunisolide
aerosol gas
  huffing 134
aerosols **6**, 6t *see also* Autohaler; nebulizer; Rotocaps; Spinhaler
African-Americans
  asthma
    deaths 38
    prevalence 40
    statistics 41
  lupus erythematosus, systemic 167
Afrin
  oxymetazoline 196
Afrinol
  pseudoephedrine 218
after-shave lotions
  benzalkonium chloride 50
  benzocaine 50
agammaglobulinemia xv
agar **6**
aging **6–7**
  asthma deaths 38
agonists **7** *see also* adrenergic drugs
agranulocytes
  leukocytes 164
agricultural workers 186t
  actinomycetes 4
  animal allergy 24

AIDS (acquired immunodeficiency syndrome) **2–4**, 3t
AIDS-related complex (ARC) 3
airborne antigens *see* aeroallergens
air compressor *see* nebulizer
air-conditioning **7**
  fiberglass 108
  fungi and molds 116
air curtain **7**
air ducts, cleaning **7**
air-filtration systems **7–8**
airflow obstruction *see* airways; asthma
airplane glue
  huffing 134
air sampling **8** *see also* pollen collectors; pollen count
air travel **8**
airways **8**
AK-Con-A
  pheniramine 203
Alabama 109t, 261–266t, 297
Alaska 304–305
Alberta (Canadian province) 122t, 260t, 283–284t, 286t
albumen, egg **8**, 99
albuterol (Proventil, Ventolin) **8–9**
  aerosols 6t
  beta-adrenergic agonists 51t, 52
  pregnancy complicated by asthma 214t
  Rotocaps 229
alcohol (ethanol) **9**
alcoholic beverages *see* beer; liquor; wine
Alconefrin *see* phenylephrine hydrochloride
alder
  hay fever 257t
  pollen distribution (Canada)
    Atlantic provinces and Quebec (Region I) 306
    Ontario (Region II) 306
    prairie provinces and eastern British Columbia (Region III) 307
    western British Columbia and Vancouver Island (Region IV) 307
  pollen distribution (U.S.)
    Alaska 304
    midwestern and central states
      Great Plains states (Region IX) 299
      northern midwestern states (Region VII) 297

    western and Pacific states
      Cascade Pacific Northwest states (Region XVII) 304
      central California valley regions (Region XIV) 302
      inland empire states (Region XVI) 303
      intermountain western states (Region XV) 302
      Rocky Mountain empire states (Region XI) 300
    radioallergosorbent (RAST) tests 311t
aldol **9**
alfalfa 281t, 310t
algae
  agar 6
alizarin (Turkey red) **9**
alkali blite
  arid southwestern states (Region XII) 301
alkyl sodium sulfates and alkyl sulfates **9**
allergen-free diet *see* diet, elemental
allergenic extracts **9–10**, 94t
allergen nomenclature **10**
allergens **10–11**, 78t, 186–190t, 309t *see also* aeroallergens; *specific allergens (e.g., pollen)*
allergic angiitis *see* Churg-Strauss syndrome
allergic bronchopulmonary aspergillosis (ABPA) **11**
  fungi and molds 115t, 116
  immunoglobulin E (Ige) 148t
allergic conjunctivitis *see* conjunctivitis, allergic
allergic contact dermatitis *see* contact dermatitis
allergic crease
  allergic rhinitis 12
  physical appearance 204
allergic dermatitis *see* atopic dermatitis
allergic drug reactions *see* drug allergy and reactions
allergic otitis media *see* otitis media, secretory
allergic purpura *see* Henoch-Schonlein Purpura; vasculitis
allergic reactions *see* allergy; anaphylaxis; hypersensitivity
allergic rhinitis (pollinosis, hay fever) **12–13**, 127, 209–210 *see also* pollen; tree pollen allergy; weed pollen allergy
allergic salute
  allergic rhinitis 12
allergic shiners
  allergic rhinitis 12
  physical appearance 204